Headlines 3

Halachic Debates of Current Events

Dovid Lichtenstein

Shikey Press

Design by Marzel A.S. — Jerusalem
Layout by Rivkah Wolfson
Cover design by Rachel First

Second edition produced by:
Shikey Press
Cambridge, MA
www.ShikeyPress.com
info@ShikeyPress.com

בס"ד

ישיבת בית יוסף ברוקלין, בידידות כבוד והערכה

מרדכי זאב יפה'ן

מיסודם של
מרן הגאון רבי אברהם יפה'ן זצוק"ל
ומרן הגאון רבי יעקב חיים יפה'ן זצוק"ל
ראשי ישיבות בית יוסף נובהרדוק
1502 Ave. N
Brooklyn, New York 11230

Rabbi Mordechai Jofen
Rosh Hayeshiva

מרדכי זאב יפהן
ראש הישיבה

עש"ק פ' בשלח ט' שבט תשע"ד

הנה ידיד נפשי הרה"ג ר' דוד ליכטנשטיין שליט"א שלח לי חבור שעומד
להוציא על שאלות ובעיות חדשות העומדות על הפרק, דברים שהרב המחבר
השמיע ברבים לפני שומעי לקחו מדי שבת בשבתו. ואין כוונת המחבר לקבוע
הלכה בשאלות חמורות אלו, אלא להעמיד אותן בקרן אורה ולהאיר עליהם
מאור תורתו והבנתו הישרה והבהירה כיד ה' הטובה עליו בתקוה שבעקבותיו
יבאו מורי הוראה מובהקים להתעסק בשאלות אלו.

ודבר גדול עשה ידידי שליט"א ואני מברכו שיזכה לישב באהלו של תורה שידוע
לי שזה מגמת נפשו ללמוד וללמד לפלפל ולחדש מתוך הרחבת הדעת.

בידידות כבוד והערכה,

מרדכי זאב יפה'ן

Mailing address:
Yeshiva Beth Joseph
P.O.Box 191001
Brooklyn, NY 11219

ביהמ״ד נבוק יעבץ   דוד קאהן

ברוקלין, נוא יארק

ב״ה

To whom it may concern:

At the insistance of my good friend Reb Dovid Lichtenstein; I am stating that this is not a haskomo, but a michtav brocho; thusly I remove from my shoulders any responsibility if one wants to rely on the "rulings" of Reb Dovid.

The sefer which he sent me to peruse has, as yet, no name but it highly original and a delightful study of various halachic questions.

My blessings that כ״א אשר יסד יפעל ישכיל

כה דברי קאהן

דוד

הרב נתן שערמאן

Rabbi Nosson Scherman
1181 East Ninth Street
Brooklyn, New York 11230

ב"ה

‏ו' תמוז ה' תשנ"ג

כב' ידידי גאמ"ר, הרה"ג אלן רבן

הרה"ג ר' דוד כהן

Thank you for sharing with me your manuscript on complex modern halachic issues. These are questions that engage thinking people, but rarely do the disputants delve into halachic sources. As you show in your brilliant and far-reaching discourses, Chazal and poskim through the centuries have shown how halachic principles relate to all sorts of "new" situations, although it is easy to think that because the questions occur in a modern setting, eternal Halachah has nothing to say about them.

The range of your sources and your skill in showing how they apply to the questions you discuss are extremely enlightening and stimulating, especially to those of us whose learning concentrates on Shas and poskim without attempting to apply our learning to what might be called "practical Halachah." It is important and constructive to show, as you do in this work, that the Torah speaks authoritatively to every age and every question.

I appreciate, as you stress in your Introduction, that your intention is not to issue final rulings, but to show the range and depth of פסקי תורה and their teachings and how there is no modern situation that cannot be resolved through Torah.

[Hebrew lines]

נאסאן שערמאן

Rabbi Hershel Schachter
24 Bennett Avenue
New York, New York 10033
(212) 795-0630

הרב צבי שכטר

ראש ישיבה ורב כולל
ישיבת רבינו יצחק אלחנן

מכתב ברכה

כבוד ידידנו הרה"ג לוי ריסקין שליט"א

עוסק בבזר הלכות להוצאת היו"ל

שהרבה הרה' ... שמה להאיר ... ושום

... העומדים על הפרק, אשר לא

נכתבה של תורה, ואהבת ציונה

של תורה וגדולות להפיץ את התורה

אשר יקר לאת הרומיה לחבר ... יותר

ויותר הלכות שרת וכתב להוציא ספרי הכולל

מקרב מרגיורות, ... ומתכונו ... ...

רבות לתורה

הירושה והחכמה לכבוד של תורה

... בקרוב, ...

ידידו של תורה

הסכמות מרנן ורבנן גדולי התורה והפוסקים שליט"א

מכתב מרן שר התורה הגר"ח קניבסקי שליט"א

[כתב יד]

בס"ד, שלהי אדר א' תשע"ט.

ראיתי קצת החיבור הנפלא משנה אחרונה על מ"ב ח"א וח"ג מהר"ר דוד ליכטנשטיין שליט"א
ועמו חבר תלמידי חכמים שנכתב מתוך יגיעה ועמל רב. והוא ליקוט נפלא מאד, וגם אני נהניתי מזה.
ואף שאין האחריות עלי, מ"מ הנני לחזק ידיו מאד ויזכה להגדיל תורה ולהאדירה.

(-)

רפאל שמואלביץ
ראש ישיבה מיר ירושלים

ב"ה ט"ז אדר א' תשע"א

שמחתי מאד לראות גליונות נדפסים מתוך ספרך
הגדול "משנה אחרונה", ובו איסוף התשובות מתוך גדולי
הדורות הללו, שנתחברו לאחר המשנה ברורה, והן עוסקות
בשאלות אשר לא שייך שתהא להן התייחסות במשנה
ברורה, כיון שהן שאלות שנתחדשו לפי תנאי החיים
בדורות הללו, וענין גדול מאד להביא לפני לומדי תורה
את המקורות לתשובות לשאלות הללו, כדי שתהא להם
האפשרות לברר את כל פרטי הדינים, ללמוד מהתשובות
במקורותיהן, את הדרך ילכו בה ואת המעשה אשר יעשון
בענינים הללו, ומצוה רבה בידך להביא לאור עולם ספר
גדול זה. ותועלת גדולה מזה לכל אלו המסוגלים לרדת
לעומקם של דברי הפוסקים. שמחה כפולה ומכופלת יש
לי באופן אישי לראות את ספרך הגדול, וזאת לאור הטעם
המתוק שנשאר בפי משנות הלימוד בחברותא בשנים
בו למדנו בישיבתנו, ישיבת מיר הק'. והנני לברך אותך,
שספרך הגדול יתקבל ברעוא אצל קהל מבקשי תורת
השם, ועוד תוסיף אומץ ותגביר חיל לפתוח הרבה שערי
תורה, ולהנות את עולם התורה גם בספריך הבאים, אשר
רבים ישוטטו בהם לבקש דעת ולהוסיף חכמה.

השמח בשמחתך ומברכך שברכת ה'
יתברך תהא שרויה בביתך תמיד

[חתימה]

משה שטרנבוך
ראב"ד לכל מקהלות האשכנזים
ראש הישיבה ברמות א'
מח"ס מועדים וזמנים ושו"ת תשובות והנהגות ועוד
עיה"ק ירושלים ת"ו

ר"ח אייר התשע"ו

בימים אלו הגיע לידי ביאור "משנה אחרונה"
שמדפיסים עם המ"ב מאת הרה"ג המהולל לתהלה ה"ה
הרב דוד ליכטנשטיין שליט"א. ויש בו אוצר שלם שליקט
ואסף בחכמה ומלאכה לזכות הרבים. ובלשון צח וקל מביא
גם דברי אחרוני זמנינו וראוי לתהלה. לכן אני אומר לו חזק
ואמץ לכתוב ולהפיץ עוד על כל הש"ע או"ח, ורבים יהנו
מאורו ואף שטרוד בעסקים תורתו עיקר, ואשריו שזכה
לכך. ואסיים בברכה שמתוך נחת וברכה ימשיך במלאכת
הקודש, ונזכה לראות ישועת ה' נחמת ציון וביאת הגואל.

יעקב מאיר שטרן
דומ"ץ בב"י דמרן הגר"ש ואזנר זצ"ל
דומ"ץ דקהילת וזניץ מח"ס משנת הסופר ואמרי יעקב
רב אב"ד קהילות יעקב - בני ברק

ב"ה, כ"ח מרחשון תשע"ט לפ"ק

הן ראיתי ספר משנה אחרונה שנתחבר ע"י הרה"ג
המהולל מוה"ר דוד ליכטנשטיין שליט"א ועמו חבר ת"ח
שעמדו לימינו, והנה החיבור כולל בתוכו ביאורים עיונים
ופסקי הלכות על סדר המ"ב ח"ג ומהבטה קלה ניכר בו
היטב גודל מלאכת הקודש שיש בה חכמה ותבונה, ונעשה בהשכל ודעת וברוב כשרון באופן נפלא מאד לבאר מקצוע גדול
זה בטוב טעם ובעיון הנצרך, ולאסוף בעמיר גורנה שיטות כל הפוסקים ולסדר אותם על כל סעיף וסעיף באופן שכל הלומד
והמעיין ירוץ בו, ויש בו תועלת עצומה לאין ערוך ושיעור, והוא בגדר זיכוי הרבים להגדיל תורה ולהאדירה, ומד' ישאו ברכה
על פועלם המבורך.

וע"ז בעה"ח מצפה לרחמי ד'

[חתימה]

הסכמות מרנן ורבנן גדולי התורה והפוסקים שליט"א

הרב שמאי קהת הכהן גרוס

מו"ץ דקהל מחזיקי הדת דחסידי בעלזא בא"י
רח' דברי חיים 7 קרית בעלזא ירושלים תובב"א

בס"ד, ר"ח טבת תשע"ט יהיו ניסים רבים אמן ירושלים עיה"ק תובב"א

הובא לפני ספר נפלא הנקרא משנה אחרונה שהוא חיבור על המשנה ברורה ח"ג הל' שבת שחברו הרה"ג גברא רבא ויקירא כמה"ר דוד ליכטנשטיין שליט"א עם צוות אברכים ת"ח מופלגים בתורה. הספר מיוסד לבאר ולפרש ביאורים ועיונים ופסקי הלכות של גדולי הפוסקים, והוא חכמה גדולה ומלאכה קשה לברר אוכל מתוך אוכל ובלישנא קלילא, והולך ומדפיס המ"ב כמתכונתו הראשונה בצורת הדף בדפוס משובח ומפואר, ובעמוד הצמוד הפירוש הצמוד הביאור והעיון. וכבר הדפיס לפני כמה שנים משנה אחרונה על מ"ב חלק ו' ומאוד נהנו מזה התח"ח וגם אני הק' השתמשתי הרבה בזה ודברים נחוצים שחפשתי מצאתי בספר, ובמיוחד הנני שמח שמו"ר עכשיו על כל הלכות שבת הלכות חמורות, ומאוד נהנתי מכל סימן בפנ"ע וספרו יש לו חן מיוחד, והספר אינו ליקוט גרידא אלא עבודה יסודית הדק היטב, ועשה ג"כ מפתחות נפלאים שכל אחד ימצא מבוקשו בנקל. ומובטחני שרבינו החפץ חיים זצ"ל זי"ע יכיר לו טובה על שעשה אזנים לתורתו של המ"ב שמקובל ומרוצה לתוך כלל ישראל. השי"ת יעזור שימשיך לבאר ולפרש על כל חלקי מ"ב, דהמתחיל במצוה אומרים לו גמור.

בעה"ח לכבוד המחבר שליט"א

מנחם מנדל פוקס

רב ור"מ קרית שומרי החומות, רמות
ומו"צ בהעדה החרדית עיה"ק ירושלים תובב"א

בס"ד, ג' טבת תשע"ט לפ"ק

זכה רבינו הק' הכהן הגדול רשכבה"ג מרן החפץ חיים זצוק"ל ונתקבלו ספריו הקדושים בכל תפוצות ישראל, ובכל התקופות והזמנים דולים מן הבאר מים חיים ומרים צמאונם ומשקים לאחרים להגדיל תורה ולהאדירה.

ובפרט ספריו הק' משנה ברורה על שו"ע או"ח אשר כידוע נתקבלו באהבה אצל כל שבטי ישראל כספר יסוד בהלכה, וכל שכבות הציבור עוסקים בדבריו, כאו"א לפום דרגא דיליה, אם בעיון ובעמקות והיקף הסוגיות, ואם בפשטות העניינים לדעת את המעשה אשר יעשון. ולא רק זה, אלא נתקים בו הברכה שדברי תורתו פרים ורבים, והרבה ספרים מתחברים בקרב ישראל לברר וללבן את משנתו הטהורה בפלפולא דאורייתא ולאסוקי שמעתתא, ובהיות שתורתו והוראתו הי' תמיד לשם שמים כדבעי, לכן חלה עליו המציאות שבתב קדוש ישראל המקובל בעל מגלה עמוקות זצוק"ל בספרו על התורה סוף פרשת נצבים וז"ל: מצוה ראשונה של תורה ממנין תרי"ג, מצות פרו ורבו, ומצוה אחרונה ממנין תרי"ג, מצות ועתה כתבו לכם השירה הזאת, לכתוב כל אחד ספר תורה לעצמו. נעץ סופו בתחילתו, שכל אחד מישראל יכתוב ספר תורה ולרבות בתורה [כלומר שדברי תורתו יפרו וירבו]. זה שאמר רבא (שבת לא.) [בשעה שמכניסין אדם לדין אומרים לו] נשאת ונתת באמונה, [קבעת עתים לתורה] עסקת בפריה ורביה, הכל על התורה קאמר וכו' עכ"ל [בתוספת המעמתיק בסוגריים]. ושפתיו ברור מללו, שדנים אותו אם זכה שמספר תורה שלו פרה ורבה, עיי"ש. [ובעקבותיו דרכו הרבה ספריו דרוש לחבר שתי מצוות אלו].

לזאת הבה נחזיק טובה מרובה להאי גברא רבה וחשיבא ה"ה הרה"ג המופלג רבי דוד ליכטנשטיין שליט"א, אשר הגה ויום להאיר עיני ישראל לאסוף כעמיר גורנה מכל ספרי האחרונים אשר דנו בדברי המשנה ברורה או בנושאים אשר עסק בהם המשנה ברורה, לסדרם ולערוך אותם לשבצם ולקובעם לפי סדר המשנ"ב לתועלת רבים. לצורך זה גם מינה צוות אברכים חשובים מופלגי תורה בראשות ידידי הרה"ג המופלג רבי דוד כהנוביץ שליט"א, אשר עבדו ועמלו וערכו הדברים בגיעה גדולה לצלול במים אדירים ולהעלות פנינים יקרים, ביאורים ובירורים הן בהבנת עמקות העניינים, והן בבירורי הלכות ותוספות פסקי הלכות מגדולי פוסקי הדורות, וסידו הדברים דבר דיבור על אופניו באופן נעלה למען ירוץ הקורא בכל העניינים.

בודאי יתקבל ספר זה בס"ד באהבה אצל התלמידי חכמים וחכמי הדור, ויעלה על שלחן מלכים, מאן מלכי רבנן, להגדיל תורה ולהאדירה, לתועלת כלל ישראל.

זכות מרן החפץ חיים זצוק"ל תעמוד להמחבר החשוב הגר"ד ליכטנשטיין שליט"א, ואתו עמו צוות האברכים שליט"א, להתברך בכל מילי דמיטב, ויפוצו מעיינותיהם חוצה פאר ברור פאר והדר, מתוך השפעות טובות וכט"ס.

כד"ח הכו"ח לכבוד התורה ולומדיה

משה שאול קליין

דומ"ץ בביד"צ דמרן הגר"ש ואזנר זצלל"ה
ורב שכונת "אור החיים" בני ברק

ב"ד, יום ד' בכסלו תשע"ט לפ"ק

זכה מרן בעל החפץ חיים זי"ע שספרו ה"משנה ברורה" נתקבל בכל תפוצות ישראל ללמוד ולהגות בו ולנהוג על פי דבריו הלכה למעשה, אולם הרבה דברים נתחדשו ע"י גדולי ופוסקי הדור שאחר המשנ"ב, וגם יש דברים שנשתנתה המציאות בזמנינו ע"י השימוש בכלים השונים מהמציאות של פעם, ועל כ"ב יפה עשה כבוד הרה"ג מוה"ר דוד ליכטנשטיין שליט"א אשר הנה לחבר אל ספר המשנ"ב ביאורים וחידושים מגדולי הדורות, ולקח חבר ת"ח חשובים שיעברו ע"י שלא תצא תקלה תחת ידו ח"י, וקראו בשם 'משנה אחרונה'.

והנה אף שאין בכוחנו ליתן הסכמה על ספר הלכה בלא לעבור עליו בדיוק רב מרישא לסיפא, מ"מ מאחר שציין מקור כל דבר, ולא בא לפסוק אלא להרבות הדעת בישראל, ע"כ אמינא לפעלא טבא יישר, יה"ר שיזכה להוציא הספרים הנ"ל לאור, וחפץ ד' בידו יצלח להרבות ידיעת ההלכה בבתי ישראל, ויזכה להמשיך להוציא לאור חיבורים טובים ומועילים כיד ד' הטובה עליו מתוך בריות גופא ונהורא מעליא.

וע"ז באתי עה"ח

הרב זלמן נחמיה גולדברג

אב"ד בד"ץ ובית הוראה
לדיני ממונות "הישר והטוב"
חבר בית הדין הרבני הגדול

ב"ה, יום ח' טבת תשע"ב

הראוני ספר חשוב מאד ותועלתו מרובה למען ישמרו בני ישראל את השבת את הדין, בשם משנה אחרונה, שהוא בירור בשאלות חדשות שנתחברו בדור שאחר המשנה ברורה על פי גדולי עולם, והמחבר ברוב חכמה הצליח להביא כל הדעות ברב כמות ורב איכות.

וכל זה חיבר הרב המאור הגדול ר' דוד ליכטנשטיין ועוד ידו נטויה להמשיך ולהוציא שאר חלקי המשנה ברורה.

ובודאי מצוה גדולה לסייעו בכל מה שניתן שיתאפשר לו להמשיך בפעלו הטוב.

הכותב לכבוד התורה ושמירת המצוות

ז"נ גולדברג

דוד קאהן

ביהמ"ד גבול יעבץ - ברוקלין, נוא יארק

בס"ד, ערב ראש חודש תמוז תשע"ב

ידידי הרב ר' דוד ליכטנשטיין שליט"א בן ידידי הגאון רב שמואל צבי זצ"ל הראה לפני עבודה כבירה שליקט כעמיר גורנה דברים השייכים למשנה ברורה במה שפוסקים שבאו אחריו העירו על דבריו וגם חולקים עליו, והלא נחוץ לו לבעל הוראה לדון ולברר ולהכריע עד כמה שידו מגעת. מלאכה גדולה ויפה עשה, ידוע שאין כל עבודות ליקוט שוות ומי שיש לו עין חדה וחוש הביקורת מלקט באופן אחר ממי שחסרות לו הכוחות הנ"ל. בעסק זה קיים הרב דוד הכתוב "בן יכבד אב" ואין ספק שגרם רב נחת לנשמתו של אביו הגאון זצ"ל, והנני תפילה שהרב דוד ימשיך עבודתו בקודש עד כי יבא שילה.

החותם ברגשי כבוד ויקר

דוד קאהן

שלו' ראובן פיינשטיין

ראש ישיבה
ישיבה ד'סטעטן אוילענד

ב"ה, י' כסלו תשע"א

לכבוד ר' דוד ליכטנשטיין נ"י

שמחתי מאד לקבל גליונות מספרך משנה אחרונה שאתה עומד להוציא לאור על חלק שלישי של המשנה ברורה. ומהמעט שעיינתי בו נהניתי לראות שהוא ראוי לעלות על שלחן מלכים, והוא ליקוט מספרים וסופרים נאמנים ובתוכם מספרי אאמו"ר זצו"ל כדי להראות בקל להמעיין בו השאלות הנוגעים למעשה בזמן זה הנובעים מהלכות הנחוצות והחמורות האלו, ובודאי שיהיה לנחת רוח לכל מי שילמוד ממנו, להעשיר לימודו בהלכות שבת ולהיות לסיוע לאסוקי שמעתתא אליבא דהלכתא.

ויש עוד ענין גדול בהוצאת הספר הזה להראות שייך לקיים ואספת דגנך בלי לעזוב כותלי הבית המדרש לגמרי וכמו שביאר אותך אאמו"ר זצ"ל להיות שקוע בתלמוד תורה בכל זמן ובכל מצב. ואשריך שזכית לקיים דבריו ולברך על המוגמר להוציא ספר חשוב כזה.

ויה"ר שתתקבל עובדתך ברצון לפני הקב"ה ועמו, ושתזכה להמשיך עבודתך ולהוציא לאור ספרים על כל חלקי שו"ע ולהיות תמיד מהלומדי תורה ומהתומכי תורה מתוך הרחבה במנוחת הנפש ובריאות הגוף ולהתברך בכל טוב עד ביאת הגואל.

ראובן פיינשטיין

שמואל אליעזר שטרן

חבר בד"צ דמרן הגר"ש ואזנר זצ"ל
ראש ישיבת חוג חתם סופר, רב מערב בני ברק

ב"ה, כ"ב מרחשון תשע"ט

באו ונחזיק טובה וברכה מרובה להאי גברא רבא ויקירא
כבוד הרה"ג רבי דוד ליכטנשטיין שליט"א אשר הגה לבו
הטהור לערוך ספר חשוב ונכבד אשר יקבו בשם "משנה
אחרונה" והוא יכיל בקרבו ביאורים עיונים ותוספת פסקי
הלכות של גדולי הפוסקים לדעת את המעשה אשר יעשון.
ספר חשוב זה נערך על ידי צוות אברכים מופלגי תורה, אשר
ידם רב להם בעריכת ספרים וחפץ ה' בידם הצליח להוציא
מתחת ידם דבר נאה ומתקבל, אשר בודאי יהיה לתועלת
מרובה לדורשי ומבקשי ה' - זו הלכה ברורה, להאיר עיני
העוסקים בהלכות שבת החמורות, שהיו ההלכות והפסקים
מחוורים ופרוסים כשמלה וישמחו במלאכתך שומרי שבת
וקוראי עונג.

ביקרא דאורייתא

הרב אביגדר יחזקאל נבנצל

רב בירושלים העתיקה תובב"א
מח"ס ביצחק יקרא, מצוין מכלל יופי
שיחות לחמשה חומשי תורה ומועדים

בס"ד, תאריך ג' פרשת שבע גדול תשע"ח, ב' דחנוכה
ירושלים עיה"ק תובב"א.

לכל אחינו בית ישראל שליט"א. ראו הביא לנו איש עברי
מתנה גדולה, ספר משנה אחרונה על המשנה ברורה והוא
לקט נפלא מדברי הפוסקים, למען נוכל להבין ולקיים את כל
ההלכות והמנהגים, ושם האיש הגאון ר' דוד ליכטנשטיין
שליט"א ידיו רב לו שריבץ פעלים לתורה. יזכהו הקב"ה
להוסיף עוד כהנה וכהנה, כי מן הבאר ההיא ישקון העדים
הצמאים לדעת מה יעשה ישראל ויפוצו מעינותיו חוצה עדי
מלאה הארץ דעה בב"א.

צעיר הלוים

הרב עזריאל אוירבאך

רב בית הכנסת "חניכי הישיבות", בית וגן

כ"א למבנ"י תשע"ב

שמחתי מאוד מאוד כאשר ראיתי את הספר הנכבד משנה
אחרונה שהוא איסוף וליקוט של הרבה תשובות בשאלות
שנשאלו מאת גדולי הלכה וביניהם מדברי אאמו"ר ז"ל
בהלכות שבת המצווים ובדברי המשנה ברורה בהלכות

שבת, והדברים מפורטים בספר עם ציון המקורות שע"ז יהי'
לתועלת המעיינים. וכל זה ליקט ואסף הרב החשוב רבי דוד
ליכטנשטיין שליט"א ברב עמל ויגיעה וזכה להוציא מתחת
ידו דבר נאה ומתוקן בכלי מפואר. והנני בברכה נאמנה
להרב המחבר שליט"א שיזכה לישב תמיד באהלה של
תורה בבריות גופא ונהורא מעליא, ולזכות הרבים בספרים
מועילים שרבים יהנו לאורם, וירבה כבוד שמים על ידו.

בברכה להמשיך זיכוי הרבים מתוך הרחבת הדעת.

הרב יהושע י. נויבירט

רח' ברגמן 10, בית וגן

בס"ד, ניסן תשע"ב

הנה ראיתי את עבודתו הנכבדה של הרה"ג ר' דוד
ליכטנשטיין שליט"א אשר בשם "משנה אחרונה" יקרא,
והוא איסוף דברי פוסקי דורינו על דברי "המשנה ברורה".
דבר גדול עשה הרב הנ"ל אמנם לא עלה בידי לעבור על כל
הדברים, אבל מוכח מעבודתו שעמל הרבה להוציא דבר
מתוקן מתחת ידו. יתן ה' יתברך שימשיך בעבודת הקודש
ויזכה להרבות כבוד שמים ויצליח ה' דרכו.

החותם לכבודה של תורה ולכבוד שבת קודש

שריאל רוזנברג

ראב"ד בית דין צדק - בני ברק
רב שכונת רמת דוד (פרדס ברמן) בני ברק

בס"ד, אור לי"ט כסלו תשע"ח

ראיתי את הספר משנה ברורה עם משנה אחרונה
על המ"ב ח"ו, ובו מובאים דברי המ"ב כצורתם על הדף,
ובדף שבצידו מבאר הרבה דברים מדברי המ"ב, וגם מדברי
הפוסקים שהביא המ"ב, ועוד מוסיף והולך פסקים והוראות
מגדולי זמנינו, ומה שנו"נ בדברי המ"ב. ויש בחיבור זה הרבה
ידיעות נכבדות ללומד המ"ב על אתר, ולומדי
המ"ב בודאי יהנו ויפיקו תועלת מחיבור זה. וכ"ז מעשה ידי
הרה"ג ר' דוד ליכטנשטיין שליט"א, אשר אסף וערך הדברים
בטו"ט ודעת. וכבר הסכימו על ידו כו"כ רבנים מפורסמים
ות"ח, ואף אני אצרף ברכתי, שיזכה להמשיך מפעל
גדול זה, להגדיל תורה ולהאדירה, ולישב באהלה של תורה
מתוך בריית גופא ונהורא מעליא ומנוחת הנפש.

וע"ז באעה"ח

Contents

KASHRUS

Social Distancing in the Rabbinic Tradition

March 16, 2020
By Jeremy Brown

As many synagogues are closed for Shabbat, and others limit the numbers who may attend, the time seems right to see what our rabbinic tradition has to say about a new phrase that has entered our lexicon: social distancing.

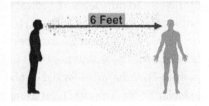

There is a long history of isolating those with disease, beginning with our own Bible:

As long as they have the disease they remain unclean. They must live alone; they must live outside the camp. (Lev. 13:46)

Command the people of Israel to remove from the camp anyone who has a skin disease or a discharge, or who has become ceremonially unclean by touching a dead person. (Num. 5:2)

These are examples of social isolation, that is, individual and community measures that reduce the frequency of human contact during an epidemic. Here, for example, are some of the ways that social distancing was enforced during the Spanish flu epidemic of 1918-1920, an outbreak that killed about 40 million people worldwide:

… isolation of the ill; quarantine of suspect cases and families of the ill; closing schools; protective sequestration measures; closing worship services; closing entertainment venues and other public areas; staggered work schedules; face-mask recommendations or laws; reducing or shutting down public transportation services; restrictions on funerals, parties, and weddings; restrictions on door-to-door sales; curfews and business closures; social-distancing strategies for those encountering others during the crisis; public-health education measures; and declarations of public health emergencies. The motive, of course, was to help mitigate community transmission of influenza.[1]

The Talmud emphasizes not the isolation or removal of those who are sick, but rather the reverse – the isolation of those who are well:

Our Rabbis taught: When there is an epidemic in the town keep your feet inside your house. (Bava Kama 60b)

Of course the effect is the same: there is no contact between those who are ill and those who are well, but since there are usually many more well than there are sick, the effort and social disruption of isolation of the healthy will be much greater.

It is not hard to see a relationship between expelling those who are ill and denying entry to those whose health is in doubt. In the 14th century, when Europe was ravaged by several waves of bubonic plague that killed one-third of the population, many towns enacted measures to control the disease. Around 1347 the Jewish physician Jacob of Padua advised the city to establish a treatment area outside of the city walls for those who were sick.[2] "The impetus for these recommendations," wrote Paul Sehdev from the University of Maryland School of Medicine, "was an early contagion theory, which promoted separation of healthy persons from those who were sick. Unfortunately, these measures proved to be only modestly effective and prompted the Great Council of the City to pursue more radical steps to prevent spread of the epidemic." And so the notion of quarantine was born. Here is Sehdev's version of the story:

In 1377, the Great Council passed a law establishing a trentino, or thirty-day isolation period. The 4 tenets of this law were as follows: (1) that citizens or visitors from plague-endemic areas would not be admitted into Ragusa until they had first remained in isolation for 1 month; (2) that no person from Ragusa was permitted go to the isolation area, under penalty of remaining there for 30 days; (3) that persons not assigned by the Great Council to care for those being quarantined were not permitted to bring food to isolated persons, under penalty of remaining with them for 1 month; and (4) that whoever did not observe these regulations would be fined and subjected to isolation for 1 month. During the next 80 years, similar laws were introduced in Marseilles, Venice, Pisa, and Genoa. Moreover, during this time the isolation period was extended from 30 days to 40 days, thus changing the name trentino to quarantino, a term derived from the Italian word quaranta, which means "forty."

The precise rationale for changing the isolation period from 30 days to 40 days is not known. Some authors suggest that it was changed because the shorter period was insufficient to prevent disease spread. Others believe that the change was related to the Christian observance of Lent, a 40-day period of spiritual purification. Still others believe that the 40-day period was adopted to reflect the duration of other biblical events, such as the great flood, Moses' stay on Mt. Sinai, or Jesus' stay in the wilderness. Perhaps the imposition of 40 days of isolation was derived from the ancient Greek doctrine of "critical days," which held that contagious disease will develop within 40 days after exposure. Although the underlying rationale for changing the duration of isolation may never be known, the fundamental concept embodied in the quarantino has survived and is the basis for the modern practice of quarantine.[3]

In addition to staying indoors, the Talmud recommends two other interventions during a plague:

Our Rabbis taught: When there is an epidemic in the town, a person should not walk in the middle of the road, for the Angel of Death walks in the middle of the road…

Our Rabbis taught: When there is an epidemic in the town, a person should not enter the synagogue alone, because the Angel of Death deposits his tools there… (Bava Kama, ibid.)

It probably won't surprise you to learn that neither of these two measures is discussed in the medical literature, and in fact if there's an epidemic in town, you probably shouldn't go to shul at all. Jewish behavior during an epidemic is even regulated in the Shulhan Arukh (Yoreh De'ah 116:5):

In addition, it has been written that one should flee from a city in which there is an epidemic. You should leave the city as soon at the start of the outbreak, rather than at the end. All these issues are a matter of life and death. To save yourself you should stay far away. It is forbidden to rely on miraculous help or to endanger yourself…

The suggestion made by the rabbis – to isolate yourself from others during an epidemic – is a basic part of public infection control. We'd be wise to listen. And as we sit in relative isolation, perhaps now is the opportunity to recite this long-forgotten Talmudic prayer, originally composed by Yehudah bar Nahmani, the secretary of Reish Lakish:

Master of the worlds, redeem and save, deliver and help your nation Israel from pestilence, and from the sword, and from plundering, from the plagues of wind blast and mildew [that destroy the crops], and from all types of misfortunes that may break out and come into the world. Before we call, you answer. Blessed are You, who ends the plague. (Ketuvot 8b)

---

[1] Institute of Medicine (IOM), Ethical and Legal Considerations in Mitigating Pandemic Disease, Workshop Summary (Washington, DC: The National Academies Press, 2007).

[2] Susan Mosher Stuard, A State of Deference. Ragusa/Dubrovnik in the Medieval Centuries (University of Pennsylvania Press, 1992), 46.

[3] Paul Sehdev, "The Origin of Quarantine," Clinical Infectious Diseases 35 (2002):1071–2.

Infectious Diseases in Torah Literature

The notion of an infectious disease — an illness spread by germs which migrate from one person to another — became widely recognized relatively recently. Even into the late 19th century, the prevailing belief was the "miasma theory," which stated that illnesses are caused by polluted air. This belief resulted in mass migrations from regions struck by plague, as populations assumed that geography, not germs, was responsible for the epidemic.

This belief likely underlies Rava's practice to close the windows to his home בעידן רתחא — "in times of anger," referring, presumably, to epidemics (*Bava Kama* 60b). The Maharshal[1] explains that Rava closed his windows in order to prevent the אויר המעופש — "rotten air" — from entering his home. This reflects the belief in the miasma theory, that plagues were caused by polluted air, not by pathogens passed from one person to another.

A number of sources, however, indicate that our tradition was aware of the spread of infection. In *Maseches Kesubos* (77b), the Gemara speaks of a dreadful illness called ראתן, which caused secretions from the eyes and nose, and uncontrollable drooling from the mouth, and also attracted flies to the patient's body. The Gemara tells that the *Amoraim* advised undertaking certain distancing measures to avoid contracting this disease. Rabbi Yochanan issued a directive to stay away from the flies that had landed on the patient's body, and Rabbi Zeira would stay far enough away from these patients that the air around them would not reach him via wind. Rabbi Elazar would not enter the tent of a ראתן patient, and Rabbi Ami and Rabbi Assi would not eat eggs which had been in the vicinity of a patient.

Interestingly enough, these four measures reflect the four different methods of disease transmission: vector born transmission (through insects), airborne transmission, direct contact, and oral transmission (through shared food items).

Biblical Contagions

A number of commentators attributed the Biblical requirement to quarantine the *metzora* — individual stricken with a *tzara'as* infection[2] — to the concern to avoid the

---

1. *Yam Shel Shlomo, Bava Kama*, 6:26.
2. בדד ישב מחוץ למחנה מושבו, *Vayikra* (13:46).

disease's spread. This claim was advanced already by the Ramban[3] in his explanation for why Lot and his family were instructed not to look upon the city of Sedom as it was overturned. The Ramban asserts that even looking upon אוויר הדבר ובכל החליים הנדבקים — "the pestilence air and all contagious illnesses" — makes one susceptible to contracting the condition, and for this reason, the Ramban explains, the Torah commands a *metzora* to live in quarantine — in order to protect the public. It seems that according to the Ramban, certain diseases are caused by changes in the air, whereas others pass from one person to another.

Later,[4] the Ramban writes that menstrual women in ancient times would be isolated, because it was believed that the blood polluted the air and thus had the potential to make people around the woman sick. The Ramban returns to this theory in his commentary to *Sefer Vayikra* (12:4), adding that this explains the unique severity associated with the *tum'a* (ritual impurity) resulting from menstruation, to the point where materials and furniture upon which a menstrual woman sits or lies become *tamei*.[5]

The *Beis Yosef*[6] speaks of the contagious nature of *tzara'as* in reference to the case of a groom who seeks to annul his marriage upon discovering after the wedding that his wife has *tzara'as*. As *tzara'as* is both unattractive and contagious, the *Beis Yosef* writes, such a condition is certainly grounds for annulling the marriage if it had been concealed from the groom. Similarly, the Maharit[7] writes that as doctors have established the risk of infection through contact with a leper, a man who suffers leprosy is compelled to divorce his wife.

Rav Meir Simcha Ha-Kohen of Dvinsk, in his *Meshech Chochma*,[8] suggests that it is because *tzara'as* is so contagious that the Torah charged specifically *kohanim* with the task of inspecting discolorations to determine their status. The *kohanim* were graced with special protection, Rav Meir Simcha writes, and so they were the only ones who could safely inspect suspected *tzara'as* infections.

The notion of *tzara'as* as a contagious condition can be traced back to the Midrash,[9] which brings Rabbi Yochanan and Reish Lakish's instruction to keep a distance of four *amos* from a *metzora*, and 100 *amos* when wind is blowing.

Another possible Biblical reference to an infectious disease is noted by Rabbeinu Bechayei, in his comments to the story of Korach.[10] God instructed Moshe and Aharon,

---

3.   *Bereishis* 19:17.
4.   *Bereishis* 31:35.
5.   *Vayikra* 15:22-23.
6.   E.H. 39.
7.   Vol. 2, E.H. 14.
8.   *Vayikra* 13:2.
9.   *Vayikra Rabba*, 16:3.
10. *Bamidbar* 16:21.

הבדלו מתוך העדה הזאת ואכלה אותם כרגע — "Separate yourselves from this congregation, and I will annihilate them in an instant," and Rabbeinu Bechayei understands this to mean that they were to stand apart from Korach and his followers.[11] According to Rabbeinu Bechayei, God had planned to bring a plague upon Korach and his cohorts, and so He ordered Moshe and Aharon to keep their distance, so they would not be affected by the pestilence that God had planned to bring upon the rebellious group. (Following the Ramban, Rabbeinu Bechayei here adds that the angels' warning to Lot and his family was intended to keep them away from the harmful air which had descended upon Sedom.)

Another possible Biblical source for the concept of infectious diseases is a verse in *Sefer Devarim* (28:21) which, amidst the description of the calamities which Moshe threatens would befall the nation if they disobey God's laws, warns, ידבק ה' בך הדבר — "God shall make pestilence adhere to you." Rav Yitzchak Karo (uncle of Rav Yosef Karo, author of the *Shulchan Aruch*), in his *Toldos Yitzchak* Torah commentary, explains that the word ידבק is used in the context of pestilence to refer to its contagious properties:

> אמר לשון ידבק לפי שהדבר נדבק מאד יותר מחלאים אחרים המדבקים שאף
> מבגדי החולים הדבר נדבק.

> It uses the expression "adhere" because pestilence is very contagious, more so than other contagious illnesses, for pestilence is contracted even through the patients' garments.

Indeed, the Talmud Yerushalmi[12] comments on this verse that a plague is comparable לאשה הזאת שהיא מדבקת שלשה ככרים זה אחר זה — to a woman who attaches three loaves of bread to one another as she bakes.[13] Rav Baruch Epstein, in his *Torah Temima*, explains this analogy as intended to illustrate the spread of a disease from one person to another.

This reading of the verse is also suggested by Rav Moshe Ha-Kohen in his *Penei Moshe*,[14] where he addresses the situation of a boy who was born during a period of plague, when the people quarantined themselves. Rav Moshe ruled that the parents were not required to summon a *mohel* to circumcise the infant, due to the danger

---

11. Rabbeinu Bechayei writes that Moshe and Aharon misunderstood God's command, thinking that He intended to destroy the entire nation, and so they responded, האיש אחד יחטא ועל כל העדה תקצוף — "Shall one person sin, and You are incensed with the entire congregation?!"

12. *Ta'anis* 3:5.

13. The Yerushalmi makes this comment in reference to the Mishna's ruling that a plague requires public fasting and prayer if at least three people die — one person a day over the course of three consecutive days.

14. Y.D. 263:1.

involved in allowing into the home somebody who had been outdoors. To substantiate the fear that the infection could spread in this manner, Rav Moshe cites the verse ידבק הי את בך הדבר, which refers to a contagious disease that spreads through interpersonal contact.

Rav Eliyahu Ha-Kohen of Izmir, in his *Chut Shel Chesed* Torah commentary,[15] likewise points to this verse as an example of the spread of an infectious disease. He adds that Rav Yitzchak Apomado explained on this basis God's instruction to Moshe and Aharon to distance themselves from *Bnei Yisrael* before He unleashed a plague against them.[16] As the plague was contagious, Moshe and Aharon had to move away to protect themselves.

The Rama's Denial of Infectious Disease

Interestingly enough, the Rama, in one of his responsa,[17] outright denies the entire notion of an infectious disease which is spread through interpersonal contact. The responsum addresses the situation of a rental agreement, whereby a homeowner leased part of his home to a couple. After the deal was finalized, the wife fell ill with חולי הקדחת — likely referring to yellow fever — and the homeowner refused to allow the couple to move in, fearful of contracting the woman's illness. The homeowner contended that he was freed from his contractual obligations to the couple, to which he had committed before knowing of the woman's condition.

The Rama emphatically denies the homeowner's claim, ridiculing the notion that her condition was contagious: מה שאומר שהוא חולי מתדבק כולו הבל — "That which he says, that this is a contagious illness, is nonsense." In the Rama's view, illness is not transmitted through person-to-person contact, but rather השם יעלה הוא המוחץ והרופא — it is God who brings illness and cures illness. The Rama argues that as *Chazal* specified only ראתן as a contagious malady, urging people to keep a distance from patients suffering from this condition, we may conclude that this is not the case regarding other ailments. If disease did spread through transmittable pathogens, the Rama argues, then בטל כל דיני ביקור חולים — there could be no *mitzva* of visiting the sick, given the risk of infection.

The Rama suggests drawing proof from the Gemara's remark in *Maseches Kesubos* (77a) singling out a condition called נכפה as grounds for annulling a marriage, when a groom discovers after his wedding that the bride suffers from this illness. Whereas Rashi identifies נכפה as epilepsy, the Rama claims that this is a form of the contagious ראתן disease, and for this reason the groom can annul the marriage. All other illnesses, however, are not presumed contagious, and thus do not justify annulment. The Rama

---

15. *Bamidbar* 31:16.
16. הרמו מתוך העדה הזאת ואכלה אותם כרגע, *Bamidbar* 17:10.
17. 20.

insists that the condition suffered by the woman in the case under discussion is the result of עיפוש האויר — contaminated air — which is a common phenomenon that impacts all homes in an affected region. As such, there are no legitimate grounds for voiding the agreement.

Rav Chaim Palagi, in his *Nishmas Kol Chai*,[18] and Rav Moshe Nachum Yerusalimsky, in his *Be'er Moshe*,[19] question the Rama's assumption, based on the aforementioned comments of the Ramban clearly expressing the notion of a contagious disease. Indeed, the Rama's ruling is disputed by the *Nesivos*,[20] among others.

Rav Eliezer Waldenberg, in *Tzitz Eliezer* (9:17:5), suggests defending the Rama's comments. He explains that in the Rama's view, since *Chazal* urged distancing only from patients stricken with ראתן, we are not absolved of our halachic interpersonal obligations — such as visiting the sick, or honoring financial commitments — due to the concern of the possibility of contagion when it comes to other illnesses. As *Chazal* did not issue such a warning with regard to other illnesses, we must fulfill our obligations to patients even if we suspect that the condition is contagious, and trust that the merit of the *mitzva* will protect us. According to this reading of the Rama's responsum, the Rama acknowledged the possibility that other illnesses might be contagious, only in his opinion, we are to disregard this risk for the sake of fulfilling *mitzvos*, except in the case of ראתן.

However, the simple reading of the Rama's comments would certainly indicate that he negated entirely the notion of infectious diseases, considering such a concept הבל — "nonsense."[21]

Many have noted that the Rama himself fled from a plague that befell Cracow in the year 5316 (1556), as he describes in the introduction to his *Mechir Yayin* commentary to *Megillas Esther*. He writes that he resided during this time in a place called Shidlov where there was little food or water. Unable to properly celebrate Purim that year, the Rama decided to instead compose this commentary to *Megillas Esther*. And, in his glosses to *Yoreh Dei'a*,[22] the Rama cites the ruling of the Maharil[23] that it is proper to flee from one's city when it is struck by an epidemic.

While some found the Rama's personal practice, and his citation of the Maharil's responsum, to contradict his own comments denying the reality of infectious diseases,

---

18.   49.

19.   P. 132.

20.   312:2.

21.   Regardless, Rav Waldenberg himself writes that if there is a clear danger of infection, then it is forbidden to risk oneself to visit a patient: כל שהסכנה ודאית דאזי לא רק שאינו מחוייב ליכנס בזה אלא גם אסור לו הדבר לסכן את עצמו בכך.

22.   116:5.

23.   41.

in truth, there is no contradiction. Both in his responsum regarding the rental agreement, and in his testimony about his escape from the epidemic in Cracow, the Rama attributes these phenomena to אויר המעופש, in accordance with the miasma theory. He therefore supported fleeing from plague, believing that plagues resulted from a change in the air of a specific geographic location, and that they could thus be avoided by relocating. Hence, the homeowner had no grounds for voiding his rental agreement, because if he feared catching the woman's disease, then he would leave the area, as in the Rama's opinion, it was the air, not the woman's germs, that caused her illness.

Visiting a Contagious Patient

The Rama's responsum is cited and discussed by later *poskim* in reference to the question as to whether the *mitzva* of ביקור חולים — visiting ill patients — applies if a patient is contagious and could infect the visitor.

As mentioned, the Rama sought to prove his view — that no contagious illnesses exist besides ראתן — by arguing that the risk of transmittable infection would undermine the entire institution of ביקור חולים, as nobody would ever visit ill patients. It is clear that in the Rama's view, one must visit ill patients even if there is a perceived risk of infection, the only exception being ראתן, which the Gemara singled out as an infectious disease from which one must protect himself through distancing measures.

Some have suggested that the Rama's view is sourced in the famous story told in *Maseches Nedarim* (40a) of Rabbi Akiva who visited an ill student whom nobody else visited. Rabbi Akiva cleaned the patient's room and tended to his needs, and the patient afterward credited Rabbi Akiva with saving his life. It is unclear why the other Sages did not want to visit this patient, but one possibility is that they feared the risk of infection, and so they kept their distance to protect themselves. Rabbi Akiva, however, was not concerned. The Gemara's emphasis on the fact that Rabbi Akiva's visit saved the student's life might thus serve as a source to the Rama's contention that we need not be concerned about person-to-person infection.[24]

The Rama's ruling was accepted by the *Kenesses Ha-Gedola*,[25] whereas others strongly disagreed. The *Shulchan Gavoah*[26] writes, מי שומע לו להכנס בסכנת נפשות — "who will listen to him [the Rama], and put himself in mortal danger?" Rav Chaim Palagi, in the aforementioned responsum, also disputes the Rama's position. Likewise, Rav Shmuel Wosner[27] wondered why the Rama assumed that we entirely do away with ביקור חולים if we acknowledge the phenomenon of person-to-person disease transmis-

---

24.   See Rav Yehoshua Weisinger's discussion in *Asya*, Marcheshvan 5777.
25.   Y.D. 335.
26.   Y.D. 335.
27.   *Shevet Ha-Levi*, 8:251:5.

sion. Nobody suggests that all maladies are contagious, and it is only in cases of certain illnesses, which are known to be transmittable, that we would forbid visiting patients to protect against infection. Moreover, Rav Wosner adds, the *Shulchan Aruch*[28] writes that certain illnesses are exacerbated by the presence of visitors, and in such cases the *mitzva* of ביקור חולים is fulfilled by going to an adjacent room to inquire about the patient's condition and offer practical assistance. This can also be done in cases of a contagious illness, where visiting the patient is unsafe, and thus acknowledging the notion of infectious disease does not undermine the *mitzva* of ביקור חולים.

In any event, it seems clear that the Rama's conclusion was predicated on the faulty scientific assumptions of his time. Once epidemiological research has conclusively determined that certain diseases are transmitted through person-to-person contact, it is clear that we must take precautions and avoid contact with known carriers of a dangerous illness in order to avoid infection.

A Patient's Responsibility

A number of sources note that a patient suffering from a contagious illness, for his part, must take precautions to ensure not to infect other people.

The Midrash[29] relates that when Reish Lakish would see a *metzora* walking about in town, he would angrily scold the patient, and demand, פוק לאתרך, לא תזהום ברייתא — "Go to your place [of quarantine], do not infect people!"

The *Sefer Chassidim*[30] writes that a person stricken with boils must not bathe together with another person unless he first notifies the other bather of his condition. This is required by virtue of several Biblical commands, the *Sefer Chassidim* writes, including ואהבת לרעך כמוך ("You shall love your fellow as yourself"[31]), לפני עור לא תתן מכשול ("You shall not place a stumbling block before a blind man"[32]), and לא תעמוד על דם רעך ("Do not stand idly by your fellow's blood"[33]).[34]

Rav Moshe Dov Wolner[35] references these comments of the *Sefer Chassidim*, and notes

---

28. Y.D. 335:8.
29. *Vayikra Rabba*, 16:3.
30. 673.
31. *Vayikra* 19:18.
32. *Vayikra* 19:14.
33. *Vayikra* 19:16.
34. Rav Yaakov Epstein, in *Chevel Nachalaso* (21:64), boldly asserts that even the Rama — who, as cited above, appears to deny the concept of infectious diseases — would agree that a patient who has a presumably contagious condition must avoid coming in contact with people so as not to infect them.
35. *Chemdas Tzvi*, 3:43.

also the requirement established by the Gemara in *Maseches Moed Katan* (5a) to inform the public of one's status of *tum'a* so people know to keep a distance and avoid becoming *tamei* themselves. This requirement is codified by the Rambam, in *Hilchos Tum'as Tzara'as*,[36] where he cites the Torah's instruction, וטמא טמא יקרא — that the *metzora* must announce his status to the public.[37] Rav Wolner reasons that if the Torah required an individual to warn the people in his vicinity of his status of impurity to protect them from contracting his halachic condition, then *a fortiori* it requires patients with a contagious illness to warn the public to protect them from contracting his medical condition.

Similarly, Rav Chaim Palagi[38] addresses the case of a congregation that sought to bar entry to a physician who was treating patients during an epidemic, given the likelihood that he is a carrier of the illness and could then infect the congregants. Rav Palagi rules that the congregation was entitled to ban the doctor, in light of the real danger which his presence in the synagogue would pose. And the doctor himself, Rav Palagi explains, was bound by the aforementioned command of לא תעמוד על דם רעך to avoid contact with people in order not to infect them.[39]

More recently, in a letter dated 27 Nissan, 5780 (April 21, 2020), Rav Moshe Sternbuch presented guidelines for responding to those who disregarded health ministry directives to stop the spread of the coronavirus. While strongly emphasizing the need for discretion and halachic consultation before reporting a fellow Jew to the authorities, Rav Sternbuch ruled that somebody who is confirmed to have been infected, or is likely infected, and refuses to self-quarantine, should be reported:

> מי שיש לו סימני המחלה (וכ״ש אם ידוע בבירור שחלה במחלה) ויוצא להסתובב בין אנשים, מצווה להתרות בו מיד, ואם אינו מקבל ההתראה או שאי אפשר להתרות בו, דינו כרודף שחייבים למוסרו לשלטונות כדי למנוע היזק הרבים.

> One who has signs of illness (and certainly if it is confirmed that he has the illness) and goes about among people — there is a *mitzva* to immediately warn him. If he does not heed the warning, or if it is impossible to warn him, then his status is that of a "pursuer" who must be reported to the authorities in order to prevent public danger.

---

36.   10:8.

37.   *Vayikra* 13:45.

38.   Referenced above, note 18. ⁷

39.   As for the question of whether a physician may endanger his health to treat patients suffering from a highly contagious disease, see *Headlines 2*, chapter 13.

NewScientist

How a Jewish ghetto beat a typhus epidemic during the second world war

July 24, 2020
By Alice Klein

Jewish people confined inside a Nazi ghetto during the second world war were able to curb a massive typhus outbreak by introducing similar infection control measures to those being used to fight covid-19 today.

Typhus, an often-fatal bacterial disease that is spread by body lice, swept through Europe during the second world war. Nazi propaganda portrayed Jews as major spreaders of the disease as a way of garnering public support for imprisoning them in ghettos.

Jewish civilians were forcibly removed from the Warsaw ghetto by German SS soldiers during an uprising in May 1943 (US National Archives / Alamy)

In November 1940, the Nazis walled more than 400,000 Jewish people inside a 3.4-square-kilometre ghetto in Warsaw, Poland. The overcrowded conditions, lack of sewage maintenance and inadequate food and hospital resources meant that typhus rapidly infected about 100,000 people and caused 25,000 deaths.

However, by October 1941, just before the following winter, new infections suddenly ground to a halt. This was unexpected, because typhus normally accelerates at the start of winter, and ghettos in other places like Ukraine were still being ravaged by the disease. "Many thought it was a miracle," says Lewi Stone at RMIT University in Australia.

To find out how the Warsaw ghetto stamped out typhus, Stone and his colleagues trawled through historical documents from libraries around the world, including some kept by doctors who lived in the Warsaw ghetto. They discovered that doctors imprisoned there – including eminent microbiologist and Nobel prize nominee Ludwik Hirszfeld who helped discover blood types – helped lead community efforts to stop the disease from spreading.

Hundreds of lectures were held to educate the public about the importance of personal hygiene, social distancing and self-isolating when sick. A secret university was also set up to train medical students in infection control, and community leaders helped to organise elaborate sanitation programmes and soup kitchens.

Mathematical modelling by Stone and his colleagues suggests that these measures prevented more than 100,000 typhus infections in the ghetto and tens of thousands of deaths.

Tragically, almost all the ghetto residents were later sent to die in extermination camps, which the Nazis tried to justify as a means to prevent future typhus outbreaks.

The Warsaw example shows how pandemics have been exploited to foster hatred of minority groups, which is something to be wary of in the covid-19 era, says Stone. "But one positive is that it also shows how communities can use simple public health measures to beat infectious diseases, and that these can make a big difference," he says.

Journal reference: Science Advances, DOI: 10.1126/sciadv.abc0927

Escaping an Epidemic

The coronavirus epidemic of 2020 was responded to with widespread lockdown and quarantine, as millions upon millions of people across the globe were either urged or required by law to stay in their homes and venture outside only for essential purposes. Historically, epidemics were often handled in the precise opposite manner — through mass migration. As mentioned in the previous chapter, it was widely believed that epidemics were caused not by transmittable viruses or bacteria, but rather by changes in the air over a specific geographic location. People thus sought to protect themselves by fleeing to a different region.

This practice gave rise to a fascinating body of halachic literature, as *poskim* were called upon to address the question of whether this is a legitimate response to an epidemic. It was less than obvious that fleeing was the appropriate thing to do, both because of a seemingly clear-cut directive in the Gemara to the contrary, and because of the theological question of whether one has the ability to avert a divine decree by escaping.

I. Remaining versus Fleeing

The Gemara in *Maseches Bava Kama* (60b) teaches, דבר בעיר כנס רגליך — "When there is pestilence in the city, keep your feet inside,"[1] citing as a source Moshe's strict instruction to *Bnei Yisrael* in preparation for the plague of the firstborn in Egypt: ואתם לא תצאו איש מפתח ביתו עד בוקר — "and as for you, no man shall leave the door to his home until morning" (*Shemos* 12:22). The command to *Bnei Yisrael* to remain in their homes throughout the plague is seen not as a specific directive for that miraculous night, but rather as a prescription for all situations of plague, that we should remain in our homes and not venture out. This would seem to mean that people should stay put during epidemics, and not leave their city.

Individual Escape versus Mass Migration

The earliest post-Talmudic source addressing the proper conduct during an epidemic is Rabbeinu Yehuda Ha-Chasid, in *Sefer Chassidim* (372). Without citing any Talmudic

---

1. This directive is presented as contrasting the instruction, רעב בעיר פזר רגליך — "If there is a famine in the city, scatter your feet," urging people to leave the poverty-stricken city and search for sources of livelihood.

basis — or, for that matter, offering an explanation — he distinguishes between organized, mass evacuations, and individuals fleeing. He writes that when שיירות ("caravans") leave an afflicted city to find refuge elsewhere, the "Angel of Death" has the power to reach them in their new location. "But if individuals go and their intention is not for commerce," the *Sefer Chassidim* writes, "it will not harm [them], and anyone who wishes to spare his soul would act wisely to leave for a different land until the plague ends."

Apparently, the *Sefer Chassidim* felt that once a decree of pestilence has been issued against a population, the population cannot hope to escape the decree through mass migration, though individuals can save themselves by fleeing.

The likely source for this distinction is the Gemara's brief discussion in *Maseches Ta'anis* (21b) of a time when the sage Shmuel was informed of a plague that raged in a distant community. Despite the large distance between his town and the affected region, Shmuel nevertheless decreed a fast day in his own town, because איכא שיירתא דלווי — caravans would occasionally travel from the affected region to his area, thus spreading the illness. Accordingly, the *Shulchan Aruch*[2] rules:

> היה דבר במדינה ושיירות הולכות ובאות ממנה למדינה אחרת שתיהן מתענות אף
> על פי שהן רחוקות זו מזו.

> If there was a plague in a region, and caravans travel back and forth from it to a different region, they both fast, even though they are distant from one another.

The *Sefer Chassidim* seems to have understood that when large numbers of people travel from a city afflicted by an epidemic, it can spread to the new location, whereas if small numbers of people flee, the epidemic does not spread.[3] As for the Gemara's instruction, דבר בעיר כנס רגלך, the *Sefer Chassidim* likely felt that this is intended to discourage mass migration, but does not mean that lone individuals should not flee.

Fleeing as the Preferred Response

A more elaborate discussion appears in a responsum of the Maharil,[4] who observed

---

2.   O.C. 576:2.

3.   Moshe David Chechik, writing in the journal *Ha-Ma'ayan* (Nissan 5780), postulates that the *Sefer Chassidim*'s view may have resulted from empirical evidence, his having seen or heard of mass migrations of people trying to escape a plague who ended up bringing the epidemic with them. Without the knowledge of microbiology, people at that time did not realize that germs could be carried and transmitted, and thus resorted to speculative theories to explain the spread of illness. They did not realize that mass migration spread the illness because of contagions.

4.   41.

that even גדולים — great people — had the practice of fleeing from epidemics. Noting the proverb, דבר בעיר כנס רגלך, the Maharil cites his mentor, Rav Shalom of Neustadt, as distinguishing between the incipient stages of an epidemic, and the later stages, לאחר שהתחיל ונתחזק — once it has established itself in the region. He explains that once an epidemic rages with full force, one should remain in place, whereas fleeing is acceptable and even advisable in the earlier stages. The Maharil notes the Gemara's aforementioned discussion concerning the epidemic in Shmuel's time, which indicates that a plague — once it has established itself — can travel, such that attempting to flee is unwise at that point.

The Maharil's ruling is cited — though without attribution — by the Maharshal, in his *Yam Shel Shlomo*.[5]

It is brought also by the Rama, both in his *Darchei Moshe*[6] and in his glosses to the *Shulchan Aruch*.[7] Surprisingly, however, although the Rama rules in accordance with the Maharil's distinction between different stages of an epidemic, he offers (in *Darchei Moshe*) a different explanation for the Gemara's directive, דבר בעיר כנס רגלך. Apparently uncomfortable with Rav Shalom of Neustadt's theory that this refers only to the latter stages of an epidemic, the Rama explains that the Gemara here allows staying in place if one is able to quarantine himself without ever leaving his home. It goes without saying, the Rama writes, that the best way to protect oneself during an epidemic is to relocate. The instruction כנס רגלך is for those who choose to remain, demanding that they quarantine themselves. But if they cannot remain in isolation during the plague, then they must flee.

This explanation is offered also by the Maharsha, in his *Chiddushei Aggados* (in *Bava Kama*), where he writes:

ודאי בדבר בעיר נמי טוב לפזר רגליו ולהימלט על נפשו ; אלא דהכי פירושו, כל זמן שאינו מפזר רגליו מן העיר יכנס רגליו לביתו ולא יצא ברחובות.

> Certainly, when there is a plague in the city, too [like when there is a famine], it is beneficial to "scatter one's legs" and run for one's life. Rather, this is the meaning [of the Gemara]: as long as one does not "scatter his legs" from the city, he should "gather his legs" into his home and not go out into the streets.

Although the Rama understood the Gemara differently than the Maharil, it seems that he nevertheless felt obliged to follow the Maharil's ruling that fleeing is appropriate only in the earlier stages of an epidemic. Interestingly, the Rama himself, in the introduction to his *Mechir Yayin* commentary to *Megillas Esther*, tells of the time when he

---

5.   *Bava Kama* 6:26.

6.   Y.D. 116.

7.   Y.D. 116:5.

fled from a plague that ravaged Cracow (as it was during this period that he composed *Mechir Yayin*).

Following the Rama's ruling, Rav Yeshaya Horowitz — the *Shela*[8] — strongly condemns those parents who did not bring their children away from cities during periods of smallpox outbreaks. He writes that these parents would be held accountable for their children's death if the children died from this illness. The *Shela*'s comments are referenced by the *Magen Avraham*[9] and *Mishna Berura*.[10]

Along generally similar lines, Rav Yechiel Michel of Arptchik writes in his *Mincha Chadasha* commentary to *Avos*[11] that the directive of כנס רגלך was stated not to forbid fleeing, but rather to warn against flagrant indifference to the plague. During a plague, he urges, "One should not dare stand before his King at the time He is angry at him." An epidemic signifies divine anger, to which we are to respond with shame. Showing one's face outside during a plague would be an outrageous expression of apathy to God's anger, and the Gemara therefore instructs remaining indoors. However, Rav Yechiel Michel writes, this directive does not negate the option of fleeing, which, like self-isolating, expresses shame and fear of God's wrath. And so the custom developed to flee, he explains, so that the discomfort and hardship of exile would provide atonement in the merit of which one would be worthy of protection.

Avoiding Anxiety

The *Ben Ish Chai*, in his *Ben Yehoyada*,[12] adds a different factor — the emotional impact of living in an area ravaged by an epidemic. He writes that during a cholera outbreak, the aforementioned *poskim* would require fleeing at any stage of the epidemic, because living in an affected area causes fear and anxiety, which makes one especially susceptible to this illness. Therefore, he writes, even in the later stages of a cholera outbreak, one should flee to avoid the anxiety resulting from the constant news and sounds of suffering or dying patients.

Already earlier sources noted the dangers of anxiety during an epidemic. For example, the Maharil, in his responsum, mentions ביעתותא (fear) as a reason to flee from an epidemic, noting the custom in some communities (specifically, in Lombardy, Italy) not to mourn for lost family members during an epidemic, to avoid anxiety.[13]

---

8. *Shnei Luchos Ha-Bris, Sha'ar Ha-Osiyos*, 4.
9. 576:3.
10. 576:14.
11. P. 59b.
12. *Bava Kama* 60b.
13. This custom is mentioned by the *Shulchan Aruch*, Y.D. 374:11.

   Interestingly, although the Maharil acknowledges the importance of fleeing to avoid

The Rashbash (Rav Shlomo ben Shimon Duran), in discussing proper conduct during an epidemic,[14] writes that one should ensure to rest, relax, and ירחיק האנחה וירבה השמחה — "distance aggravation and increase joy."

Rabbi Akiva Eiger penned a number of famous letters during the deadly cholera epidemic that raged in Poland in the late summer and autumn of 1831,[15] presenting instructions to Jewish communities for how to conduct themselves during that time. In one such letter, he urges, שלא לדאוג ולהרחיק כל מיני עצבות — "not to feel anxious, and to send far away all types of sorrow."

His son-in-law, the *Chasam Sofer*, in a fascinating responsum written to Rav Shaul Landau of Cracow,[16] addresses the time when, during a cholera outbreak, the moon was not visible for the recitation of *kiddush levana* during the first two weeks of the month, when this *beracha* is to be recited over the sight of the new moon. The community in Cracow saw this as an inauspicious omen, which caused them a great deal of anxiety. Given the danger that the widespread anxiety could increase the people's susceptibility to the disease, Rav Landau made the controversial decision to permit reciting *kiddush levana* on the night of the 16th of the month, on the basis of the *Shiyurei Kenesses Ha-Gedola*,[17] who writes that he found an opinion in the *Rishonim* permitting the recitation of *kiddush levana* even on the night of the 16th. Sure enough, the skies were clear on the night of the 16th, and hundreds of people enthusiastically recited *kiddush levana*, overjoyed and relieved to have been given the opportunity to fulfill this *mitzva*. Rav Landau then turned to the *Chasam Sofer* to ask whether his ruling was correct, and the *Chasam Sofer*, after a lengthy discussion, concluded that under the circumstances, he did the right thing to permit reciting *kiddush levana* on the night of the 16th.

Rav Chaim Palagi, in his *Sefer Ha-Chayim*,[18] writes that he decreed a ban on gambling, adding:

זולת אם יהיה ח"ו חולה או אם יהיה חולי בעיר ח"ו כמגפה וקוליר"ה ב"מ וכיוצא
והוא מתפחד הרבה ולבו דואג עליו, וע"י שישחוק ימצא קורת רוח לאסוחי דעתיה
בבא דואג בזה דוקא הותר לו לשחוק...

Except if, Heaven forbid, one is ill, or if there is illness in the town,

---

anxiety, he permits fleeing only in the early stages of the epidemic, whereas the *Ben Ish Chai* felt that during a cholera outbreak, one should flee at any time.

14. Responsa, 195.

15. These letters can be found in *Iggros Sofrim*, a collection of letters compiled by Rabbi Akiva Eiger's great-grandson Rav Shlomo Sofer, #29, #30.

16. O.C. 102.

17. O.C. 426.

18. Chapter 27.

Heaven forbid, such as a plague or cholera, may it stay away from us, and the like, and one is frightened and his heart worries, and by playing he will experience composure by distracting his mind when this anxiety comes — then it is actually permitted for him to play...

For the purpose of alleviating anxiety during an epidemic, Rav Chaim Palagi permitted gambling. He references the Chida's comment in *Birkei Yosef*[19] that although there were great Torah sages who were said to have sometimes played games, this was likely done when they experienced anxiety, in order to divert their attention from their worries so they could properly focus on their studies.

Self-Isolation in Rabbinic Sources

Alongside the well-documented practice to flee from epidemics, there are also numerous references in rabbinic literature — mostly from relatively more recent times — to self-isolation as a means of protecting oneself during times of plague, following the straightforward meaning of the rabbinic dictum דבר בעיר כנס רגלך.

Rav Chaim ben Betzalel, the brother of the Maharal of Prague, and a contemporary of the Rama, describes in the introduction to his *Sefer Ha-Chayim* the time when a plague struck his town, killing his housekeeper and causing two of his children to fall ill, though they survived. He writes that because of the crisis, דלתי ביתי סגרו בעדי, כמעט שני חודשים מאין יוצא ובא — "the doors of my house are closed to me; for nearly two months, I have not gone out or come."

Rav Chaim proceeds to explain that as he needed to remain quarantined in his home, he decided to spend this time immersed בשעשוע ההוויות אביי ורבא — "in the delights of the discussions of Abayei and Rava," meaning, the in-depth study of intricate halachic passages in the Talmud. But then a voice inside his mind urged him to instead study and compose a work on *Aggada* — religious ethics and thought. Troubled times, this voice said, are better suited for the study of *Aggada* than for the study of complex halachic material. And so Rav Chaim went ahead and composed his *Sefer Ha-Chayim*, a text of *mussar* and religious thought.

Rav Menachem Mendel of Vitebsk, one of the primary disciples of the Maggid of Mezritch, emigrated to *Eretz Yisrael* in 1777, and settled in Tiberias in 1783. Three years later, in 1786, he wrote a letter[20] describing a plague in Tiberias which lasted from Purim until early Iyar. This plague "raged like a raging fire" (יקד יקוד כיקוד אש), and in response, סגרנו עצמנו בחצר החדשה אשר לנו — "we locked ourselves in the new courtyard which we had," and virtually nobody was in the streets. Although the plague ended in early Iyar, Rav Menachem Mendel says, היינו סגורים ומסוגרים מפורים עד

---

19. O.C. 338:1.

20. Published in *Peri Ha-Aretz*, #17.

שבועות — they remained quarantined for an additional month, through Shavuos. He writes that the vast majority of those who followed his example were spared, whereas most of those who tried to flee were afflicted by the plague and died.[21]

The Chida, in *Birkei Yosef*,[22] addresses the question that was posed to him by a certain Torah scholar who described שאנו סגורים מחמת המציק מדבר באופל — that he and his people remained indoors because of a plague. This scholar wondered whether he could recite *kiddush levana* inside his home, seeing the moon from his window, being that he could not go outdoors. The Chida ruled leniently, noting, among other sources, the *Bach's* position that if one is afraid, for whatever reason, to go outdoors, then he may recite *kiddush levana* upon seeing the moon from the window of his home.

Rav Efrayim Laniado, who served as the Chief Rabbi of Aleppo in the late 18th century, writes[23] about a man whose son was born during a time when הוא סגור בהסגר מדבר בעיר יהלוך — he was quarantined out of fear of a plague which raged through the city. The father refused to invite a *mohel* to circumcise the child, and Rav Laniado writes that this was acceptable, דבההוא פחדא יתיב שלא יפתח פתח הבית מפני הסכנה — the father was afraid to open the door to his home because of the danger that lurked outside. A similar ruling was issued by Rav Moshe Ha-Kohen of Djerba, Tunisia, in his *Penei Moshe*,[24] where he speaks of an epidemic called סיר"ו as a result of which the community remained in their homes. Rav Moshe Ha-Kohen ruled that it was permissible to delay the *bris mila* for the boys born during this period, given the danger entailed. He writes that just as *Bnei Yisrael* did not perform circumcisions throughout the forty years of desert travel, due to the harsh conditions which made the procedure dangerous, it is similarly legitimate to delay circumcision during the time of an epidemic when people quarantine themselves out of fear of infection.

Likewise, Rav Chaim Nissim Modai of Izmir, Turkey[25] relates that during the cholera epidemic in the summer of 5614 (1854), a firstborn boy was born and the father was in a different town. The epidemic prevented him from going to where his child was to perform the *pidyon ha-ben*.

Rav Avraham Antebi, the Chief Rabbi of Aleppo during the 19th century, addressed a question concerning the permissibility of grinding wheat with a mill that had been used with *chametz*. He describes how עושים הסגר פה ארם צובה מיום ערב פסח עד כלות ימי הדבר — the people were quarantined in their homes from Erev Pesach until after the plague.

---

21. כל אשר ממנו ראו וכן עשו להסתיר מפני חרון אף בחצרותיהם ובטירותם, ועל הרוב עלתה בידם, ואשר נסו נמלטו על הרוב בעו"ה רדפו אחריהם והשיגום, כי המכה המהלכת היא הייתה כמאכולת אש, נפשות רבות חסרונם בימים אחדים אלו מן הספרדים והאשכנזים.

22. O.C. 426:4.

23. *Degel Machaneh Efrayim*, Y.D. 2.

24. Y.D. 263.

25. *Meimar Chayim*, Y.D. 24.

Rabbi Akiva Eiger, in his letters instructing people during the cholera epidemic, recommended neither complete self-isolation nor fleeing (though as the epidemic had spread throughout much of Europe, fleeing was not an option). Based on the prevalent medical science of the time, he urged Jews to assemble in small *minyanim* in large spaces, to maintain strict standards of hygiene, and to walk in the fields in the afternoon.

II. The Theological Dilemma of Self-Protection

The practice of fleeing to protect oneself from an epidemic generated some discussion of the broader topic of self-protection, whether such measures reflected a lack of belief in God's judgment, His determining every person's fate at the beginning of each year, on Rosh Hashanah.

This question was formulated by the Rashbash, in the aforementioned responsum, as follows:

> הניסה בימי דבר ממקום למקום אם תועיל לאדם או לא, שאם נכתב בראש השנה
> למיתה מה תועילנו הניסה, ואם נכתב לחיים לא תזיקנו העמידה.

> Should one flee from one place to another during times of pestilence? Is this beneficial for a person, or not? For if he was inscribed on Rosh Hashanah for death, then how will fleeing help him? And if he was inscribed for life, then staying in place will not harm him.

The question posed to the Rashbash related specifically to attempts to escape a plague, but it of course touches upon the general issue regarding the value of our efforts to care for ourselves. What purpose is served by such efforts, if in any event our fate is decided and sealed by the Almighty?

The Decree of Neither Life nor Death

The Rashbash begins his response by establishing that כל אדם יש לו קץ קצוב מספר ימי חייו — every person is brought into the world with a predetermined lifespan. And thus, as the Rashbash cites, God promises in the Torah[26] that if we observe His commands, את מספר ימיך אמלא — "I will fill the number of your days" — referring to our completing our predetermined lifespans. Likewise, the prophet Yeshayahu[27] informed King Chizkiyahu in God's Name that in response to his heartfelt prayers, הנני יוסף על ימיך חמש עשרה שנה — "I am hereby adding fifteen years to your days," implying that he was

---

26. *Shemos* 23:26.
27. 38:5.

destined to live until a certain point, but he then earned an additional fifteen years. These verses show that each person has a specific amount of time he is destined to live. However, one can extend his life beyond his preordained number of years through his merits, as in the case of Chizkiyahu, or shorten his life through his misdeeds.

On Rosh Hashanah, the Rashbash explains, every person whose predetermined lifespan does not end during the coming year is judged as to whether his sins warrant his premature death. And those whose preordained lifespans are scheduled to end during the coming year are judged as to whether they deserve to have their lives extended further. If a person is meant to die, either because his preordained lifespan ends, or because he was sentenced to death on Rosh Hashanah, then that individual will die regardless of anything he does to protect himself, because God executes His judgments with His unlimited power, and nothing a human being does can possibly prevent the Almighty from carrying out His decrees.

However, according to the Rashbash, most people are not sentenced to either life or death on Rosh Hashanah, because their preordained lifespan does not end during the coming year, and they are not deemed deserving of premature death. Such people, the Rashbash writes, are subject to what he calls חק האפשר, referring to the laws of nature. They have not been sentenced to death, but they must nevertheless take care of themselves and avoid danger in order to continue living. It is to these people, the Rashbash writes, that the Gemara refers in its numerous comments about the importance of self-protection. For example, the Gemara teaches in *Maseches Shabbos* (32a), לעולם אל יעמוד אדם במקום סכנה — "A person must never stand in a dangerous place." And in *Maseches Kesubos* (30a), the Gemara teaches, הכל בידי שמים חוץ מצינים ופחים — "everything is determined by God except for illnesses caused by overexposure to the cold or to the sun." Even if no decree of illness or death has been issued against a person, he could still suffer such a fate if he fails to take reasonable measures to protect himself. This includes doing what one must to avoid infection during an epidemic, and thus it was customary to flee.

This general approach is taken also by the Mabit, in his *Beis Elokim*.[28] He emphasizes that one who is sentenced to die will die regardless of whether he flees from a plague, and that one who is sentenced to live will survive even if he remains and exposes himself to the illness. However, the Mabit writes, there are those who are not definitively sentenced to live or to die, but rather have their fate left to the forces of nature. As none of us know what was sentenced, we bear the obligation to take precautions to protect ourselves from harm that could be caused through natural forces, and such precautions in no way reflect a lack of belief in God's having determined our fate at the beginning of the year. It is very likely that our sentence was that our fate would depend on the degree to which we conduct ourselves responsibly.

---

28. *Sha'ar Ha-Tefilla*, 16.

The Withdrawal of Providence

In a somewhat similar vein, a number of sources indicate that God sometimes decrees upon an individual that His השגחה פרטית — the personal providence and protection which He would otherwise bestow upon that person — would be withdrawn, such that his fate is now subject to the natural order.

Rav Yehonasan Eibushitz, for example, writes in his *Yearos Devash* (1:11) that on some occasions, when a person sins and is worthy of punishment, ה׳ מסלק השגחתו ומניחו למנהגו של עולם — "God withdraws His providence, and places him under the natural course of the world."

Rav Simcha Zissel Ziv of Kelm (the Saba of Kelm) formulated this concept similarly, in his work *Chochma U-Mussar*[29]:

אי אפשר לומר חס ושלום כי המקרה הוא בלי רצונו יתברך... אין בעולם שום מציאות מעצמה בלי רצון ממציא המציאות בכלל ובפרט מהחל ועד כלה. אמנם ברא הוא יתברך שתי הנהגות בעולם, מהלך הטבעי ומהלך הנסי... ומי שאינו מקיים התורה כהלכתה יעזבנו בדרך הטבע כפי שיעור עונשו הן רב הן מעט.

It is impossible to say that, Heaven forbid, an incident occurred without His will, may He be blessed. There is no existence in the world on its own, without the will of He who created this existence, neither in general nor in specifics, from beginning to end. However, He, may He be blessed, created two systems of governance in the world — a natural process, and a miraculous process. And one who does not properly fulfill the Torah — He leaves him to the natural course, to an extent warranted by his punishment, whether a lot or a little.

Rav Chaim Friedlander, in *Sifsei Chayim*,[30] explains on this basis the Gemara's famous comment in *Maseches Bava Kama* (60a), כיון שניתן רשות למשחית אינו מבחין בין צדיקים לרשעים — "Once permission has been granted to the 'destroyer' to destroy, he does not distinguish between the righteous and the wicked." The Gemara makes this remark in reference to the verse in which Moshe instructed *Bnei Yisrael* to remain indoors throughout the night of the plague of the firstborn.[31] Although the decree of death was, quite obviously, issued only against the Egyptian firstborn, nevertheless, *Bnei Yisrael* needed to protect themselves by remaining indoors, because once the "destroyer" was authorized by God to perpetrate the deadly plague, it had the license to kill anyone in its path, including those who did not deserve to die. Rav Friedlander explains:

---

29. Vol. 2, p. 195.
30. אמונה והשגחה, pp. 112–113.
31. *Shemos* 12:22.

אל לו לאדם לחשוב אני אינני רע במידה כזו שנתחייבתי על חטאי מיתה בידי
שמיים, ולכן איני צריך להזהר מהסכנה, כי בוודאי לא יאונה לי רע. מחשבה כזו
היא מחשבה פסולה, כי אם אמנם אינך חייב מיתה, אבל גם אינך במדרגה גבוהה
כזו שאתה משוגב מכל המקרים ותנצל בנס. ולכן אתה צריך להשמר מהסכנה
ואם אינך נשמר אתה מתחייב בנפשך.

A person should not think, "I am not evil such that I deserve death
at the hands of God for my sins, and therefore, I do not need to avoid
danger, because certainly no harm will befall me." Such a thought is an
illegitimate thought. For even if you are not deserving of death, you are
also not on such a high level that you are protected from all incidents
and will be saved through a miracle. Therefore, you must avoid danger,
and if you are not careful, you owe your life.

The rule of כיון שניתן רשות למשחית אינו מבחין בין צדיקים לרשעים, according to Rav
Friedlander, means that the natural order affects all people, whether or not they deserve
to die. Exceptionally righteous people earn God's providence that shields them from
harm that would otherwise be caused by the natural forces, but we cannot assume that
we have reached such a level. We must conduct ourselves on the assumption that we
are not worthy of such special protection, and we are thus exposed to natural dangers,
from which we must therefore do everything we can to protect ourselves.

Similar to the Rashbash and Mabit, these sources maintain that we can never know
whether or not God assures our continued survival and wellbeing, or if He has made
our fate subject to the forces of nature. As such, we must assume the latter possibility,
and take protective measures to ensure our safety.

Public Decrees

Others, however, took a different approach, maintaining that plagues — and perhaps other
widespread calamities — can indeed affect even those who are undeserving of death.

This is indicated already by the Maharil, in the responsum mentioned earlier. In
justifying the practice to flee, the Maharil references the startling story told in *Maseches Chagiga* (4b) of a time when the Angel of Death sent its messenger to take the life
of a certain woman whose time had come, and the messenger mistakenly took the
life of a different woman with the same name. The Gemara pointed to this unfortunate incident as an example of King Shlomo's teaching in *Sefer Mishlei*,[32] יש נספה בלא
משפט — there are those who die unjustly, without deserving death. Without explaining
the relevance of this story to the question of fleeing from plagues, the Maharil writes
that it shows that it is proper to flee. Apparently, he drew proof from the Gemara that

---

32.   13:23.

under certain circumstances, even one who does not deserve to die can fall victim, and thus it is advisable to do everything one can to protect himself, because even if he was sentenced to live, he might still perish if he fails to care for himself.

The Maharil further cites the rule of כיון שניתן רשות למשחית אינו מבחין בין צדיקים לרשעים, which also, apparently, indicated to him that one should take precautions to protect himself from a plague because it has the potential to kill anyone, even those who have been sentenced to life and do not deserve to die.

A number of writers explained this concept by establishing the notion of a public decree, one which is issued against an entire population, and thus includes even those who, as individuals, do not deserve the tragic fate destined to befall that group.

Rav Elchanan Wasserman, in *Kovetz Ma'amarim*,[33] cites this idea from the Vilna Gaon's *Even Shleima*, where the Gaon addresses the חוזרי מעורכי מלחמה — the soldiers who are sent home before battle because they had just built a home, planted a vineyard, or betrothed a woman. The Torah[34] instructs that these soldiers do not participate in battle so that they do not die before completing the process which they had begun — meaning, before living in the home, enjoying the grapes, or marrying the bride. The Gaon raised the question of why this concern would require exempting the soldiers from battle, given that their fate in any event depended on God's decree. If these soldiers had been sentenced to life, then they would assuredly survive the battle, and if they had been sentenced to die, then they would die even if they are sent home. The Gaon answers by establishing that if a decree was issued against a nation or a city, then all its members are included in that decree. Therefore, when an entire group — such as an army — faces grave danger, one can indeed rescue himself by fleeing, because if the group had been sentenced to death, but he as an individual has not, then he might die if he remains but survive if he escapes. Like the Maharil, the Gaon references in this context both the verse יש נספה בלא משפט, and the Talmudic teaching of כיון שניתן רשות למשחית אינו מבחין בין צדיקים לרשעים. He understood these sources to mean that when a public decree is issued, even those who individually deserve to live are at risk.

This idea is formulated also by Rav Eliyahu Ha-Kohen of Izmir, in his *Chut Shel Chesed* Torah commentary.[35] He writes:

נראה לי...שטעם המנהג שיוצאים לעיר אחרת בשעת הדבר משום שבראש השנה גוזר הקב״ה על המדינות איזו לחרב איזו לרעב איזו לדבר, וכיון שגזרת הדבר בעיר הזאת ולא באחרת טוב לברוח לעיר אחרת אשר שם אין שליטה למלאך המות כי שם לא נגזר דבר.

It seems to me that the reason for the practice to leave to a different city

---

33.   P. 38.
34.   *Devarim* 20:5–7.
35.   *Bamidbar* 31:16.

during a time of pestilence is because on Rosh Hashanah, the Almighty decrees about countries "which to the sword, which to famine, which to pestilence,"[36] and once pestilence is decreed upon a certain city, and not upon another, it is beneficial to escape to the other city where the Angel of Death has no authority, because the pestilence was not decreed there.

According to this view, it is possible that a person who has been sentenced to life would die if he remains in an area, or among a population, upon which a decree has been issued, and for this reason relocation is an effective means of protecting oneself from an epidemic.

Conclusion

We find in rabbinic writings regarding proper conduct during epidemics a great deal of material that is valuable as a matter of historical intrigue, as well as discussions on the fundamental question of how to square the obligation of self-protection with our belief in providence and divine judgment.

Specifically, *poskim* were called upon to address the question of whether and under what circumstances it is appropriate to flee from an area affected by an epidemic, a practice which was historically quite common, at least through the time of the Rama in the 16th century. The Rama, who himself testifies to having fled from an epidemic that struck Cracow, followed the Maharil's position that fleeing is appropriate only at the earlier stages of an epidemic.

Later, it seems that it became accepted to quarantine to protect oneself from plagues, and numerous interesting halachic questions arose in times of self-quarantine, including the question of reciting *kiddush levana* indoors, and delaying a *bris mila* rather than invite a *mohel* to one's home.

As for the theological question of why cautionary measures do not amount to an implicit denial of God's judgment on Rosh Hashanah, several different approaches have been taken:

1. The Rashbash and Mabit explained that many people are not definitively sentenced to either life or death on Rosh Hashanah, and their fate will therefore be subject to the course of nature. Such people could die if they do not take responsible precautions to protect themselves, and since nobody can know whether or not he belongs to this group, we must all take precautions.

2. Somewhat similarly, some writers explain that many people are undeserving of God's special providence, which guarantees safety under all circumstances, and are rather subject to the course of nature. We can never assume that we

---

36. This phrase is borrowed from the זכרונות section of the Rosh Hashanah *musaf* prayer: ועל
     המדינות בו יאמר איזו לחרב ואיזו לשלום איזו לרעב ואיזו לשובע.

deserve God's special providence, and we are therefore obliged to take reasonable precautions to care for ourselves.

3. The Vilna Gaon, among others, maintained that God will occasionally issue a decree against an entire population, which will affect even the righteous among that population, and they must therefore try to protect themselves if they can to avoid harm.

The New York Times

What If We Have to Decide Who Gets a Ventilator?

April 2, 2020
By Daniela J. Lamas, critical care doctor

BOSTON — I was not sure what to say.

We were midway through one of the family update phone calls that have become our new reality in the visitor-free intensive-care unit when he paused. He had a question. Anything, I said. He spoke hesitantly. His wife had been on the ventilator for a few days now and he understood that these machines might be in short supply. He just wanted to make sure: Were we planning to take her ventilator away?

I found myself suddenly aware of the cacophony of the unit. The rhythmic beep of heart-rate monitors. The singsong alerts of the ventilators. On the other end of the phone line, I heard him breathing. I realized that I did not know what he looked like. We had never met.

You don't know her, he went on. Yes, her cancer is advanced. But before this pneumonia she was taking conference calls from her hospital room. She's smart as a whip. Funny too. We have plans together, he told me. Places we want to see.

It was then that I realized what my patient's husband was doing. He was trying to prove to me that his person was worth saving. And even though I could reassure him that here in my hospital we have enough ventilators, that we are doing everything we can for his wife and will not stop unless he makes that decision, I was shaken. Because there will be more conversations like this one. And one day, the answer might be different.

There is much we don't yet know about Covid-19. But we know this: People get sick quickly. Their lungs fill with fluid and fail. Oxygen levels plummet. Ventilators are often necessary for these patients to survive, and yet, if our estimates are accurate and our supply is not augmented, we won't have enough of them.

One of the recently acquired ventilators at the New York City Emergency Management warehouse last week. (Stephanie Keith for The New York Times)

As I consider this future, I remember afternoons spent working in my hospital's pre-transplant clinic. I served as a sort of gatekeeper there, examining patients and reviewing their records to see whether they could move forward with the evaluation for lung transplant. Our criteria were clear. And sometimes I had to say no.

The names are long gone but I remember their faces. A woman in her 60s fiddles nervously with her oxygen tubing as she acknowledges to me that she is entirely alone. I must tell her that no social support means no transplant. A grandfather admits to a recent cigarette, which means he will need to wait another six months. I make him a follow-up appointment and hope that he will be alive for it.

In a way, then, I am not unfamiliar with what it means to allocate a scarce resource. But transplant is different. We are all sadly accustomed to the scarcity of transplantable organs and aware that we can't help every patient who needs one. Besides, the trans-plant surgery itself poses tremendous risk, and there are many clear examples where such an intervention would do more harm than good.

Maybe what we are facing now is more similar to another moment seared into memory: an overnight in the intensive-care unit. Two patients with progressive lung failure, a man and a woman, both teetering despite maximal support from the venti-lator, both potentially candidates for a lung bypass machine, called ECMO, that could offer them more time for their lungs to heal. Most hospitals have only a few of such machines and on that night, only one is free. Who gets it?

We convene a team of doctors whose role it is to decide. They weigh the risks and benefits for each patient. As with transplant, we have clear rules for who gets started on ECMO. You must be sick enough to benefit, but not so sick — with other comorbidities like metastatic cancer or multi-organ failure — that you will most likely die regardless. That night, the man's lungs are more fragile and the calculus is that he is the one who gets the machine.

I grasp at these memories because I am stuck trying to understand what it might feel like for doctors like me to come face-to-face with the reality of a limited supply of ventilators. But the truth is, nothing in my experience could possibly ready me for this. I turn to the literature.

In the wake of Hurricane Katrina, clinicians and ethicists began to have these tough discussions, and several states advanced frameworks for how to allocate scarce resourc-es during disasters. These guidelines prioritize the likelihood of a patient's surviving to hospital discharge and beyond, and in some cases factor in age — meaning that a younger patient would get a ventilator rather than an older one.

They also suggest that we consider withdrawing the ventilator from a patient who has had a trial of critical care but is not improving, to make it available for someone else. These concepts all make sense to me in the abstract. And I suppose I should be reassured that if this moment comes to pass, there will be protocols.

But I think of explaining this to a patient or over the phone to a loved one I will never meet, and my heart breaks. As a critical-care doctor, I am comfortable with end-of-life conversations and I am familiar with death. But I have learned to initiate these conversations based on a patient's goals and medical realities — not because of a shortage of machines that can be manufactured in a warehouse. Recently, a colleague told me about a patient who said he was willing to give up his ventilator to someone younger and healthier, who might benefit more. This is the world we live in now. The story gutted me.

But in Boston, we are not there. I hang up the phone and return to the buzz of the unit, to check on my patient. Sepsis from her pneumonia, coupled with the immune compromise of chemotherapy, threatens to overwhelm her. Though the ventilator is helping to buy her time, she still might not make it.

But I know that if she dies, I will be able to tell her husband that we did everything we could. I will be able to tell myself that too.

Halachic Triage

The rapid spread of coronavirus in the early weeks of the 2020 pandemic put the staff in some hospitals in the dreadful position of having to play the role of God, making the decision that only He is supposed to make, the decision of, to borrow from the ונתנה תוקף High Holiday prayer, מי יחיה ומי ימות — "Who shall live and who shall die?"

At the peak of the outbreak, there were fears that hospitals would not have enough ventilators for all COVID-19 patients with respiratory troubles, and some hospitals did not have enough beds, staff or equipment to handle the influx of patients. This raised the gut-wrenching issue of triage — deciding who takes precedence when several people suffer life-threatening conditions, and only one of them can be saved. According to *halacha*, how does a doctor, medic or other health professional decide whom to prioritize when several patients need urgent, life-saving treatment, and there is not enough staff or equipment for all of them? By what criteria should professionals determine to whom to grant precedence?[1]

It should be emphasized from the outset that this question is relevant only for those legally authorized to make such decisions. If a physician is hired by a hospital and is bound by the terms of his contract to follow the hospital's procedures and protocols, which include triage guidelines, then he is certainly required to abide by those guidelines. The question regarding *halacha*'s stance vis-à-vis triage applies to administrators who establish protocol, or to doctors whom the hospital administration authorizes to decide on their own which patients to prioritize.

I. The Patient with the Greater Chance of Recovery

Rav Moshe Feinstein[2] addresses the case of two gravely ill patients who require urgent care, one of whom is not expected to live for more than several days, even with treatment, whereas the other, in the doctors' estimation, has a greater chance of a full recovery. In such a case, Rav Moshe writes, precedence is given to the second patient.

---

1. We deal here only with the case of two seriously ill patients, both in life-threatening condition, who arrive at a hospital at the same time for care and treatment. A separate question arises regarding proper protocol when several patients in need of care are waiting for the doctor to arrive. See *Tzitz Eliezer* 18:69, and Rav Yitzchak Zilberstein's discussion in *Halacha U-Refua*, vol. 3, pp. 91–101.

2. *Iggeros Moshe*, C.M. 2:73.

However, Rav Moshe adds, once the hospital has admitted a patient with little chance of fully recovering, the staff may not then stop treating him in order to treat a newly arrived patient with a higher likelihood of recovery. Rav Moshe writes that although the hospital staff has a requirement to give priority to the patient who is most likely to recover, the other patient, for his part, bears no obligation to sacrifice his life, or further endanger his life, for the sake of a patient with greater chances of a full recovery. Therefore, once he is given a bed in the hospital, or attached to a machine, in Rav Moshe's words, כבר זכה במקום — he acquires the right to his place in the hospital, and is under no obligation to relinquish this right in favor of another patient.[3] In fact, Rav Moshe writes, it might even be forbidden for this patient to waive his rights to treatment for the sake of enabling the staff to tend to a patient with higher chances of recovery.

This position was also advanced by Rav Shlomo Zalman Auerbach,[4] who noted the *Peri Megadim*'s ruling[5] that priority is given to a patient whose life has been definitively determined to be at risk, over a patient whose condition cannot be conclusively established. If medication is available for only one of these two patients, the *Peri Megadim* writes, it should be given to the patient whom the doctors have definitively determined to be in danger. Rav Shlomo Zalman notes that this policy would, presumably, apply also in the case of two patients in certain danger, but only one of whom has a good chance of survival with treatment. Like Rav Moshe, Rav Shlomo Zalman makes an exception in the case where the patient with little chance of recovery was admitted first, positing that once this patient has begun to receive treatment, the hospital staff may not then leave him to tend to a patient with greater chances of recovery.[6]

An earlier source for this final ruling — that once admitted, the patient with a slim chance of recovery does not relinquish his right to treatment even when a patient with greater chances of recovery arrives — is Rav Naftali Hertz Landau's *Cheiker Halacha*.[7] Addressing the *Peri Megadim*'s discussion, Rav Landau asserts that if the patient whose condition is uncertain owns the medication, he is not required, and not permitted, to give the medication to the patient whose life-threatening condition has been ascer-

---

3. Rav Moshe emphasizes that this applies even if the patient with a slim chance of recovery cannot afford healthcare and is being treated by the hospital free of charge. Even so, the hospital is not allowed to discontinue treatment to make room for another patient who is likely to recover, and who is paying in full for healthcare, once the first patient has been admitted.

4. *Minchas Shlomo, Tinyana* 86:1.

5. *Mishbetzos Zahav* 328:1.

6. Importantly, Rav Shlomo Zalman concludes by humbly acknowledging that he did not feel qualified to reach a definitive conclusion on this weighty matter: אגיד לו נאמנה שאין אני קובע מסמרים בכל מה שכתבתי כי השאלות הן חמורות מאד, ואינני יודע ראיות ברורות.

7. חולה, 2.

tained. Rav Landau notes Rabbi Akiva's famous ruling in *Maseches Bava Metzia* (62a) that a desert traveler suffering life-threatening dehydration may drink his water to save his life, even if his travel companion faces similar risk and has no water. Rabbi Akiva established the principle of חייך קודמין לחיי חברך — that protecting one's own life takes precedence over protecting another individual's life, thus allowing, and requiring, the desert traveler to save his own life even if this means that his fellow traveler will perish. By the same token, Rav Landau rules, a patient who can save himself from potential danger by taking his medication may do so, even if this means denying the medication to his fellow patient, whose life is certainly at risk.[8]

Likewise, it stands to reason that once a patient has been admitted to a hospital and begun treatment, he does not forfeit his right to treatment if another patient with a higher chance of survival then arrives.

This was also the ruling of Rav Asher Weiss, in a responsum[9] written during the coronavirus pandemic. Rav Weiss adds, however, that if a hospital receives a patient with little chance of surviving for more than several days, and, due to the rapid spread of the pandemic, the hospital expects the arrival of many other patients, with a higher chance of long-term recovery, then the hospital should save their respirators for future patients. Such a case, Rav Weiss asserts, is akin to the case of a hospital which receives a patient with a small chance of long-term recovery, and at the same time an ambulance calls to inform the hospital that a different patient is being brought, one with a higher chance of survival. Clearly, Rav Weiss writes, if the hospital must choose between these two patients, it should choose the patient who has yet to arrive. The situation of a rapidly spreading epidemic, where large numbers of seriously ill patients are overwhelming medical facilities, is no different. Since the hospital staff knows with certainty that many more patients will be arriving, and resources are in short supply, they may withhold treatment from a patient with little chance of survival in order to be able to treat patients with higher chances of survival who are expected to soon arrive. This position was also articulated by Rav Hershel Schachter, in a letter[10] circulated during the coronavirus pandemic.[11]

---

8.   Rav Eliezer Waldenberg (*Tzitz Eliezer*, 9:28) cites Rav Landau's discussion in reference to the case of a patient in a potentially life-threatening condition who managed with great difficulty to obtain a rare medication that would cure his condition. This patient, Rav Waldenberg ruled, is not required, or even permitted, to give the medication to another patient, even to a patient whose life-threatening condition has been definitively established.

9.   *Minchas Asher – Corona, Mahadura Tinyana* (available at https://rabbinicalalliance.org/wp-content/uploads/2020/04/Minchas-Asher-Corona-2nd-edition.pdf), p. 18.

10.   Dated 11 Nissan, 5780 (April 5, 2020), available online at http://torahweb.org/torah/docs/rsch/RavSchachter-Corona-12-April-06-2020.pdf.

11.   Rav Weiss, in his responsum, references an article by Rav Zalman Nechemia Goldberg

Rav Schachter added that if after a patient with little chance of survival was attached to a respirator the physicians see that the patient is not improving, and new patients have arrived in the meantime who have a greater chance of survival, then the physicians should sign a DNR ("Do Not Resuscitate") order for the first patient. When the ventilation is to be renewed, at that point, we consider this patient as having arrived together with the new patients, who have a greater chance of survival, and so they are given priority.

Does Age Matter?

If two patients in equally serious condition require treatment, should precedence be given to the younger patient? If, for example, one COVID-19 patient is 30 years old, and another is 80, should the hospital grant priority to the 30-year-old, as he is likely to live longer after recovery than the 80-year-old would? Do we take into account the number of remaining years expected in each patient's life when determining priority?

Rav Yaakov Emden,[12] in establishing a list of precedence when it comes to rescuing lives, indeed writes that a בחור (young man) takes precedence over a זקן (elderly man). A possible basis for this claim[13] is the comment in the *Sefer Chassidim*[14] that murder-

---

(in *Halacha U-Refua*, vol. 2, pp. 191–195), in which Rav Goldberg takes a different view, requiring doctors to discontinue treating a patient with little chance of survival if they are needed for a new patient with a high chance of survival. In contrast to the *poskim* mentioned here, Rav Goldberg maintained that even if physicians had begun treating a patient who is not likely to survive, they must discontinue their treatment if another patient arrives with a higher likelihood of recovering. Rav Goldberg argued that while we generally follow the rule of עוסק במצוה פטור מן המצוה — a person involved in one *mitzva* is exempt from other *mitzvos* that arise — this does not apply if the *mitzva* which arises entails a לא תעשה, meaning, if refraining from the *mitzva* violates a Biblical prohibition. Saving a life, according to Rav Goldberg, not only constitutes a *mitzva*, but is also required to avoid transgressing the prohibition of לא תעמוד על דם רעך ("Do not stand idly by the blood of your fellow," *Vayikra* 19:16). Therefore, if the newly arrived patient has a good chance of survival, the physicians must discontinue their care of the first patient, who is not likely to survive, in order to rescue the second patient.

The other *poskim* likely disagreed because they felt that the prohibition of לא תעמוד על דם רעך requires endeavoring to save a life even if one's efforts will result in just several additional days of life. Therefore, the physicians in this instance are no less duty-bound to prolong the life of the first patient than they are to prolong the life of the second patient.

12. *Migdal Oz* (*Even Bochein*, 1:86–88).
13. This point is made by Rav Shlomo Dichovsky, *Lev Shomei'a Le-Shlomo*, 2:39.
14. 671.

ing a young, fertile individual constitutes a more grievous crime than murdering a person who is no longer capable of begetting children, because in the former case, the murderer not only takes a life, but prevents the birth of countless potential children and descendants. Rav Reuven Margoliyos, in his notes to *Sefer Chassidim* (*Mekor Chesed*), points to the Gemara's comment in *Maseches Sota* (46a) that emphasizes the unique gravity of the murder of a person capable of reproduction. The Gemara discusses the law of *egla arufa*, requiring performing a special atonement ceremony when a murder victim was discovered near a town, and the killer has not been identified. The Torah[15] requires conducting this ceremony in an uncultivated area, signifying the fact that the murderer denied the victim the opportunity to produce "fruit." The Gemara explains that in the case of a victim who was young enough to procreate, this refers to both children and *mitzvos*, whereas in the case of an older victim who could no longer reproduce, this refers only to *mitzvos*. The Gemara's implication is that the death of somebody capable of reproducing is a greater tragedy than the death of an older person, as in the former case, the person's death means the loss of an incalculable number of lives. This likely forms the basis of Rav Yaakov Emden's claim that if the decision must be made whether to rescue an elderly person or a young person, the younger person is saved.

Other *poskim*, however, disagreed. Rav Moshe Feinstein,[16] after establishing that the obligation to treat the ill applies equally to the young and to the elderly, adds, אף לעניין קדימה להרופא למי ילך מסתבר שאין להתחשב בזה — "Also with regard to precedence, to whom the physician should go, it stands to reason that this [age] should be no consideration." Rav Shlomo Zalman Auerbach, in the aforementioned responsum, similarly writes, התחשבות בגיל לא באה כלל בחשבון — "The factor of age does not come into consideration at all."

Likewise, Rav Asher Weiss (in the aforementioned responsum) wrote:

> גילו של האדם אין לו משמעות ומשקל הלכתי. רק הקוצב חיים לכל חי יודע וקובע
> "מי בקיצו ומי לא בקיצו", ועוד דבאמת משקל החיים הסגולי לא בהכרח תלוי
> במספר ימיו, תהיה הסברא אשר תהיה לא מצינו בהלכה משקל לגילו של אדם.

> A person's age has no halachic significance or weight [with respect to triage]. Only He who allots life to every being knows and determines "who is at his end, and who is not at his end." Moreover, in truth, the essential weight of life does not necessarily depend on the number of one's days. Whatever the reasoning, we have not found in *halacha* weight being assigned to a person's age.

According to these *poskim*, it seems, a distinction is drawn between the severity of

---

15. *Devarim* 21:3.
16. *Iggeros Moshe*, C.M. 2:75:7.

murder and the obligation to save a life. After a murder has been perpetrated, we can look back at the lost potential of life, which makes the crime even more severe. But when people's lives are in danger, we regard both lives as equally precious, and equally worthy of being rescued.

II. Patients in Identical Conditions

Having established the protocol when one patient is likely to recover and the other is not, let us now turn our attention to the case of two patients in similar conditions, when the doctors find no reason to believe that one has a greater chance of responding to treatment to the other. Is there any sequence of priority in such a case, or are the healthcare workers allowed to choose which patient to prioritize?

An "Ignored" Mishna?

At first glance, the answer is provided explicitly and unequivocally by the Mishna in *Maseches Horiyos* (13a). The Mishna there establishes that להחיות ולהשב אבידה — when it comes to "sustaining" a person and returning lost objects, האיש קודם לאשה — men take precedence over women. The exceptions, as the Mishna proceeds to clarify, are with regard to clothing and freedom from captivity. If both a man and a woman require clothing, and funds are available to help one but not the other, then the woman is clothed, because a woman's shame when unclothed exceeds that of a man. Similarly, if both a man and a woman fall captive, then since the woman is likely to be raped and abused, she takes precedence if the amount of money raised for ransom suffices for only one. The Mishna notes that if the captors are known to perpetrate homosexual rape, then the man is ransomed first. The reason, it would seem, is because in such a case both the man and the woman are at equal risk of sexual exploitation, and so we revert to the basic principle that האיש קודם לאשה.

Later, the Mishna establishes additional principles, granting priority to a *kohen* over a *Levi*, a *Levi* over a *Yisrael*, and a regular *Yisrael* over a *mamzer* (the product of an adulterous or incestuous relationship), except that a Torah scholar takes precedence over a layman, regardless of their pedigree.

The Rambam and Rav Ovadya of Bartenura, in their respective commentaries to the Mishna, explain that a man takes precedence over a woman because men are obligated in a greater number of *mitzvos*.

Seemingly, we need to look no further for *halacha*'s view on triage. The Mishna appears quite definitive in establishing the sequence of priority when several different individuals need assistance. Indeed, several *poskim* maintained that the sequence presented in the Mishna must be followed when several lives are at risk and one cannot rescue them all.[17]

---

17. This view was taken by Rav Yaakov Emden (referenced above, note 12), the *Chazon Ish*

However, a number of recent *poskim* dismissed the practical relevance of the sequence established by the Mishna. Rav Moshe Feinstein[18] writes about this sequence, קשה לעשות מעשה בלא עיון גדול — "it is difficult to put this into practice without extensive study." Without elaborating, Rav Moshe clearly expresses the view that this sequence does not represent the final word when it comes to triage. Similarly, Rav Shlomo Zalman Auerbach writes, חושבני שבזמננו קשה מאד להתנהג על פי זה — "I feel that in our times, it is very difficult to follow this."

Neither of these two *poskim*, however, explain why this is the case. Why should a clear-cut ruling of the Mishna be ignored?

Rav Hershel Schachter, in the letter referenced earlier, suggests the following explanation:

בזמננו יש הרבה נשים שעוסקות בתורה ובמצוות יותר מאשר הגברים...וכללי המשנה מיוסדים על ההנחה שלפי סדר קדימות זה נרויח יותר בעבור הקהילה. וד"ז קשה מאוד לקבוע מי נצרך לקהילה יותר ממי... ומטעם זה המקובל אצל הפוסקים שלא לנהוג על פי המשנה.

> In our time, there are many women who are more involved in Torah and *mitzvos* than men, and the rules of the Mishna are predicated on the assumption that with this sequence of priorities, we will gain more on behalf of the community. But this is very difficult to determine — who is needed more for the community than others... And for this reason, it is accepted among *poskim* not to follow this Mishna.

Rav Schachter reasons that the Mishna arrived at this sequence based on the realities of that time, when women generally stayed at home and were not active in community affairs. Hence, although, quite obviously, every human life is precious and valuable, in the tragic situation where only one of two endangered lives can be saved, *Chazal* determined that we save the life of the person on whom the public is more dependent. It therefore outlined a priority scale that listed men before women, and Torah scholars before others. Nowadays, however, such an assessment is impossible, because all groups of people are involved in various ways in communal affairs, and we cannot point to one group of people as contributing more than others.[19]

(C.M., *Bava Metzia, Likutim*, 20), and Rav Shmuel Wosner, in *Shevet Ha-Levi* (10:167). Rav Wosner emphasizes, however, that the obligation to rescue lives applies to everybody, and the question here relates only to sequence, and, that once a medic or doctor has begun treating a patient, he should not leave the patient if he then receives another patient to whom the Mishna grants precedence.

18. *Iggeros Moshe*, C.M. 2:74.

19. Rav Eliezer Waldenberg, in the responsum discussed below, raises a similar possibility (after first explaining why *halacha* likely does not follow the rule of איש קודם לאשה, as we will discuss). He writes:

Conflicting Talmudic Sources?

Rav Eliezer Waldenberg, however, in his responsum on the topic,[20] advances the theory that at least according to some *poskim*, the Mishna here does not address at all the question of precedence when multiple individuals face a life-threatening situation.

The basis for his claim is the fact that the Rambam,[21] the *Tur* and the *Shulchan Aruch*[22] cite the Mishna's list of priorities in the context of the laws of charity, but state explicitly that women take precedence over men. In direct contradistinction to the Mishna, the Rambam — and, later, the *Tur* and *Shulchan Aruch* — writes that a woman who needs charity money takes precedence over a man in need of charity. This ruling is based on a *beraysa* in *Maseches Kesubos* (67a) which establishes that if a community has two orphans to care for, one male and one female, and funds are limited, the female takes precedence, because males are more accustomed to begging and asking for assistance. Of course, this *beraysa* appears to contradict the Mishna's ruling in *Maseches Horiyos* that men in danger take precedence over women in danger.

The *Beis Yosef* reconciles these two Talmudic sources by drawing a simple distinction between life-threatening situations, and conditions of moderate poverty. The Mishna in *Maseches Horiyos*, which requires granting priority to males over females, refers to situations of danger, such as if a man and woman are both drowning, and one is able to rescue only one of them. The *beraysa* in *Maseches Kesubos*, by contrast, deals with

---

זה לא מוגדר כדבר הקבוע, אלא הדבר תלוי לפי מידת הקיום של המצוות שהאיש והאשה מקיימים, ולפי הניתונים והשיקולים שיהא בזה למצילים באותה שעה. ולכן מצאו לנכון לא לקבוע בזה מסמרות נטועים והשאירו את הדבר להכרעת המתעסקים.

This theory is presented also by Rav Abraham-Sofer Avraham, *Nishmas Avraham*, vol. 4, Y.D. 251:1.

Professor Avraham Steinberg (פעילות בחזית העורף — היבטים הלכתיים קדימויות, סיכון) עצמי ופיקוח נפש, *Asya*, vol. 16, 5779) adds also the factor of מוטב שיהיו שוגגים ואל יהיו מזידים — that when a *halachic* directive will assuredly be met with neglect, it is preferable not to publicize it. Even if we were to assume that certain genders or other groups should be granted precedence over others in regard to triage, such directives will be ignored in modern times, which abhors drawing any distinctions between genders or other groups of people. Under such circumstances, it is far preferable to leave these decisions to the discretion of the health professionals.

Rav Shlomo Dichovsky (referenced above, note 13) writes that in modern-day realities, selecting patients on the basis of gender or lineage might create a חילול השם, and when a חילול השם is at stake, we deny groups the privileges to which they are, in principle, entitled.

20.   *Tzitz Eliezer*, 18:1.

21.   *Hilchos Matanos Aniyim* 8:15–18.

22.   Y.D. 251:8–9.

orphans whose state of deprivation is not life-threatening, and it therefore requires granting precedence to the female, and having the male beg for charity. The *Beis Yosef* explains that the *Tur* (based on the Rambam) requires feeding a needy woman before a needy man in situations of poverty that does not pose a threat to life, but when such a threat indeed exists, then a man's life takes precedence.

This explanation is cited approvingly by the *Shach*.[23] This also appears to be the view of the *Taz*,[24] in explaining the Rama's ruling later[25] regarding the rescue of a man and woman from drowning. The *Shulchan Aruch* there codifies the Mishna's ruling that a female captive takes precedence over a male captive, unless the male captive is at risk of homosexual rape, and the Rama then adds, אם שניהם רוצים לטבוע בנהר הצלת האיש קודם — "If they both [a man and a woman] wanted to drown in a river, rescuing the man takes precedence [over rescuing the woman]." The phrase אם שניהם רוצים לטבוע ("If they both **wanted** to drown") seems difficult to understand, but the *Taz* explained this ruling as referring simply to a case where both a man and a woman are drowning, and one must choose whom to rescue. The Rama — according to the *Taz's* understanding — rules that the man takes precedence, following the view of the *Beis Yosef.*

Redefining "להחיות"

Rav Waldenberg, however, advances an entirely different approach to explaining these sources.

First, he cites the *Levush*[26] — a close disciple of the Rama — as presenting a much more compelling explanation of the Rama's otherwise unusual remark. The *Levush* addresses the situation mentioned by the *Shulchan Aruch*, where a man and woman are held captive and both face the risk of being raped by their captors. As mentioned, the man is given precedence over the woman in this case. The *Levush* explains that the reason the man is granted priority is because האיש אין דרכו בכך — men are not accustomed to such an act. Whereas both captives are equally exposed to the horror of rape, the man's situation is considered slightly more dire because besides being violated, he is also forced into an act into which he is not accustomed. This is in contrast to the woman, who, although enduring a traumatic experience, is being forced into a familiar sexual act. This difference makes the man's plight ever so slightly more severe, and so he is ransomed first. The *Levush* then writes, "Therefore, if they both seek to drown in a river in order that they not be violated, rescuing the man takes precedence, because he is doing this due to greater distress than the woman, and so he is worthier of being saved."[27]

23. Y.D. 251:11.

24. Y.D. 252:6.

25. Y.D. 252:8.

26. 252:8.

27. The background to the *Levush's* understanding of the Rama's ruling is the tragic story

Although the *Levush* does not cite the Rama, he clearly works off the Rama's comment about a man and woman who "wanted to drown in a river." He appears to have understood the Rama's ruling to mean not that in general, rescuing a man takes precedence over rescuing a woman, but rather that specifically in this particular case, when both a man and a woman are captured and enduring rape, precedence is granted to rescuing the man. The implication, then, is that in a different circumstance where both a man and a woman are in danger, neither necessarily takes precedence over the other.

If, indeed, this is the Rama's intent, then how did the Rama understand the Mishna's explicit ruling that a man is granted precedence over a woman להחיות?

Rav Waldenberg explains that evidently, the Rama understood the word להחיות as referring not to rescuing from a life-threatening situation, but rather to sustenance, providing for the poor. The Mishna in *Horiyos* disputes the ruling of the *beraysa* in *Kesubos*, and grants precedence to men over women even when it comes to the distribution of charity, just as it grants precedence to men with regard to השבת אבידה, returning his lost object. Rav Waldenberg posits that the Rambam — and, following his lead, the *Tur* and *Shulchan Aruch* — sided with the *beraysa* against the Mishna, and for this reason, he ruled that a woman is granted precedence over a man in receiving charity funds.

Alternatively, Rav Waldenberg adds, one might suggest that the Mishna in *Horiyos* deals with the case of a man who, for whatever reason, is incapable of begging. As we saw, the *beraysa* in *Kesubos* grants precedence to women with regard to charitable assistance because men are more accustomed to begging. Quite possibly, then, when the Mishna grants precedence to a man over a woman, it refers to a man who cannot go around to beg, such that he has no practical advantage over women, and so he is given precedence, just as he is given precedence with regard to lost objects.

It turns out, then, that the Mishna in *Horiyos* does not address at all the question of precedence when it comes to rescuing from danger. The word להחיות refers to charitable assistance when there is no danger to life. When it comes to rescuing people from danger, the Mishna does not grant precedence to any gender or group over any other. Although the *Beis Yosef, Shach* and *Taz* all understood the Mishna as establishing a sequence of priority in rescuing from danger, the *Levush* appeared to have understood the Mishna differently.

---

related by the Gemara in *Maseches Gittin* (57b) of a group of 400 Jewish youngsters — both boys and girls — who were captured, and then discovered that their captors intended to sexually violate them. The girls all committed suicide by jumping into the sea, to protect themselves from defilement. The boys then figured that if the young women, who were threatened with a familiar sexual act, jumped into the sea to save themselves, then certainly they, the boys, who were going to be forced into an unfamiliar sexual act, should do the same, and so they, too, jumped into the sea.

Rav Waldenberg draws proof to this understanding from the Talmud Yerushalmi (*Horiyos* 3:4), which, commenting on the Mishna, states, כסות אשת חבר וחיי עם הארץ כסות אשת חבר קודמת — clothing for a Torah scholar's wife takes priority over "the life" (חיי) of an ordinary layman. At first glance, this appears to mean that if a charity fund can afford to either rescue a layman's life or purchase clothing for an impoverished scholar's wife, it should buy clothing for the woman, out of respect for the Torah scholar. It seems inconceivable, however, that the Yerushalmi would grant precedence to a woman's clothing over the life of another person. Undoubtedly, Rav Waldenberg explains, the word חיי in this passage refers to alleviating a state of poverty that is not life-threatening, and although food provisions would normally take precedence over clothing, in the unique case of a Torah scholar's wife who cannot afford proper clothing, her clothing needs take precedence over a pauper's need for food. But if the pauper's life is in danger, then certainly, his needs take precedence. The Yerushalmi made this remark in reference to the Mishna's discussion of priorities להחיות, clearly indicating that the Mishna, too, speaks of sustaining those enduring poverty which does not threaten their lives. When it comes to saving lives, however, no group necessarily deserves priority over others.

Rav Waldenberg draws further proof from the Meiri's commentary to the Mishna in *Horiyos*, where the Meiri interprets the word להחיות as להאכיל — "to feed" — and notes the seeming contradiction between this Mishna and the *beraysa* in *Kesubos*. The Meiri reconciles these sources by distinguishing — precisely as Rav Waldenberg suggested — between the case of a man who has the ability to beg, and the case of a man who does not have this ability. This is in contrast to the *Beis Yosef*, who claimed that the Mishna in *Horiyos* deals with life-threatening situations and the *beraysa* in *Kesubos* addresses a case of mild poverty. The Meiri thus clearly understood that the Mishna in *Horiyos* does not address at all the question of priority when several people's lives are at risk.

This easily explains why many *poskim* generally ignored the Mishna's sequence of priority when addressing situations where triage decisions need to be made. Quite simply, this Mishna does not speak of such situations at all, as the word להחיות refers to charity distribution when life is not at risk. When two people's lives are at risk, neither is given precedence over the other, and so the rescuer has the right to choose whom to save first (unless one is more likely to survive than the other, as discussed at length earlier).

Conclusion

1. If a physician or other medical professional needs to choose to treat one of two patients in a similar condition, and who both have the same chances of survival, then the professional may choose whichever patient to whom he or she wishes to grant precedence. According to a minority position among the *poskim*, a younger patient takes precedence over an older patient if their conditions and

chances of survival are equal, though the consensus view is that age plays no role in determining precedence.

2. If physicians must choose between a patient who has little chance of recovering, and a patient with a good chance of recovering, then they should give precedence to the patient whom they assess is more likely to recover. If large numbers of patients are certain to require treatment, and the influx could overwhelm the hospital, then the hospital should refuse treatment to a patient with little chance of survival so they will have the manpower and equipment available for treating the patients with a greater of chance of recovery. If, however, the staff had already admitted and begun treating a patient with little chance of recovery, they should not discontinue treatment in order to treat a new patient with a better chance of recovery.

INTERVIEWS

Rabbi Dr. Daniel Roth

Interviewed on *Headlines with Dovid Lichtenstein*, 25 Adar 5778 (March 21, 2020)

Unfortunately, this is a real question which they're dealing with in Italy, and which we will probably have to deal with in the United States, even if the ICU has a ventilator, and even if they start building more of them, and even if they get some companies to start building them — there will be a shortage.

We have guidance from the *poskim* about this. When two patients come in at the same time, we give the ventilator to the sicker patient, who needs it the most. If one patient can wait, and the other will die sooner, we give it to the one who is likely to die without it. If they both have the same level of illness, and one is חיי שעה (in any case will not live much longer, even with treatment), or less likely to survive, and the other has a higher chance of full recovery, this is a terrible decision to have to make, but the *halacha* dictates that you give it to the one who has the better chance of a full recovery. This is based mostly on Rav Moshe Feinstein's *teshuvos* on this topic, as well as some *teshuvos* from the *Tzitz Eliezer* and Rav Zilberstein. Rav Moshe says that if someone is already hooked up, already given an emergency room bed, or ICU bed, then even if he has only חיי שעה, it's forbidden to take him out, because he's קונה מקום ("acquires his place"). This applies even if he is poor, and even if he did not pay a penny for it. You cannot remove him to make room for a patient with a chance of חיי עולם (full recovery) or with a higher likelihood for recovery.

There is a דין קדימה (order of precedence) in the Mishna in *Horiyos*, but these criteria are typically not so practical, unless they have the exact same level of illness, because if one is sicker, then you give precedence to the sicker person. Furthermore, there is a concept of איבה (the need to avoid arousing gentiles' hostility), which can be used in two ways, and it's important to know this distinction. There's a type of איבה that is a limited *heter*, which overrides איסורים דרבנן if it would create animosity and tension among the non-Jews. But then there's a kind of איבה that could potentially cause Jews to die. If we follow the rule that a *kohen* takes precedence to a *Levi* and things like that, this would create tremendous איבה. People are always trying to look at *Yidden* as the scapegoat.

Fortunately, this is not so relevant, because it's not up to the Jewish doctors to make these kinds of decisions. There are protocols, hospital guidelines, and Rav Zilberstein writes that if you're an employee in the hospital, which is basically the case all the time — you're not in private practice while working in the ICU or emergency room — then there's no דין קדימה, and you are beholden to the hospital's triage principles. That being the case, we follow the system we mentioned before, that you give the ventilator to the sicker patient.

It's a terrible decision to have to make, but technically, if two patients come at the exact same time, then the ventilator would have to be given to the patient with the higher likelihood of survival. And if they're both likely to survive, and the younger patient can wait a while, then the obligation would be to give it to the one who is more likely to die now. If they're both critically ill, and they both need the ventilator to live, you give it to the younger patient who is more likely to make a full recovery.

This is an awful decision, and I hope it will not have to be made.

According to what I understand from Rav Moshe, if both patients have years of survival ahead of them, and their likelihood of survival is more than just a חיי שעה, then age does not matter. It makes no difference that one is 15 and one 40.

THE CANADIAN JEWISH NEWS

Walker: Minyanim in the Time of the Coronavirus

March 24, 2020
By Robert Walker

If I could have peered two weeks into the future back on March 10, I probably would not have believed it. On Purim, the vast majority of synagogues across Canada were holding megillah readings and parties for the festive holiday. COVID-19 was definitely in the headlines, but with fewer than 100 cases in Canada, it was hiding just below the surface.

(Pixabay photo)

Within a few days, nearly all synagogues and Jewish day schools across the country were closed, joined by other schools and places of worship coast to coast, in an attempt to slow the rapid growth of COVID-19.

Virtually all synagogues, but not quite all.

As of this writing, there are still a small number of groups which continue to hold minyanim (prayer quorums of 10 men) – contrary to the overwhelming evidence of wide transmission of the virus, and public health pleas to severely limit social gatherings.

Clearly, ceasing communal prayers is not something to be taken lightly. Prayers are a lifeblood of our faith – indeed, according to our sages, the daily Amidah prayer replaces the Holy Temple in Jerusalem until it is rebuilt – and yet, pikuach nefesh, the saving of a human life, takes precedence over nearly all other circumstances, including praying in a minyan.

And while the overwhelming majority of Orthodox rabbis in Canada have shuttered their synagogues, a tiny minority of minyanim are continuing to flout public health regulations, putting at risk both those who come to pray, and anyone who may come into contact with them.

Despite an apparent attempt at discretion on the part of these small number of minyanim, it seems that their continued activity has nonetheless sparked considerable attention online.

As an Orthodox Jew active in the Jewish community, I have been approached countless times over the last 10 days, and have been asked to explain this incongruent response. How can Jews who believe that our role in the world is to bring God's morals and ethics to the world simultaneously be so irresponsible and cavalier when it comes to halting the spread of a rapidly growing and deadly virus?

While I don't have the answer, I remember a story I was told during my own journey to religious observance more than a decade ago that helps give clarity.

One of the obstacles to my own religious observance was seeing some ostensibly religious Jews engaging in behaviour that I saw as unbecoming of God-fearing people.

A rabbi I was learning with challenged me: "Once," he said, "I saw a religious Jew eating pork on Yom Kippur." I replied incredulously that this person couldn't possibly have been a religious Jew. "Exactly!" he responded.

His point was made; eating pork on Yom Kippur is as "religious" as cheating on taxes. Using this example, this rabbi forced me to reconsider how I define "religious." Clearly, being a "religious" Jew meant following Jewish law as much as possible, and not selectively choosing what was comfortable, and what wasn't. Being a "religious" Jew meant going out of one's comfort zone and doing what may look weird and feel weird, but ultimately is in line with one's values and search for truth. In short, we can never guess what is driving someone's actions, and we can only evaluate our own.

There is more at stake here, of course, than any individual's personal religious observance. Safety from infectious disease in our neighbourhoods and beyond are critical, and is absolutely a matter of life and death. As such, authorities across the Canadian Orthodox community have spoken out vociferously against attending minyanim and organized study groups in person until it is safe to do so. And while tragically there is a tiny fringe of Jews who flout both rabbinic leadership and public health regulations, it is absolutely worth remembering with pride that the overwhelmingly vast majority of synagogues and Jewish organizations across Canada are now operating virtually.

And this is where perspective is critical. While the world is disgusted with thousands of teenagers partying on Florida beaches in contravention of public health guidelines, the Jewish community is appalled by a few dozen fringe individuals. And we should be; because if the Jewish people has a holy mission to perfect the world, then we must start at home, and hold ourselves to the highest standard that we can.

The Renegade Coronavirus Minyan

The social distancing requirements that were enacted in the wake of the coronavirus epidemic of 2020 disrupted virtually every aspect of people's lives. In the effort to curb the spread of this extraordinarily contagious virus — which in many people is asymptomatic, thus making it impossible to track — governments across the world forbade public gatherings of any kind, thus denying many people the opportunity to work, and eliminating all social functions. For observant Jews this also meant the elimination of one of the most important elements of religious life — public prayer.

This was, understandably, a very difficult pill for many to swallow. תפילה בצבור (public prayer) essentially structures a Jew's day, forming the center point around which his daily schedule revolves. It is also, for many, a social and spiritual lifeline. More importantly, many essential portions of the prayer service — *kaddish, barchu, kedusha* and Torah reading — require a *minyan*, and must be omitted when one prays privately. This is an especially vexing and disheartening problem for mourners who wish to recite *kaddish* for the soul of their beloved family member. And, in general, תפילה בצבור is one of the most important *mitzvos* we observe. The Gemara teaches in *Maseches Berachos* (8a), אין הקב״ה מואס בתפילתן של רבים — "The Almighty does not reject the public's prayer," adding that God tells us, כל העוסק בתורה ובגמילות חסדים ומתפלל עם הציבור מעלה אני עליו כאילו פדאני לי ולבני מבין אומות העולם — "Whoever involves himself in Torah and kindness, and prays with the congregation, I consider him to have redeemed Me and My children from among the nations of the world." The *Shulchan Aruch*[1] clearly states, ישתדל אדם להתפלל בבית הכנסת עם הציבור — "A person should endeavor to pray in a synagogue with the congregation." The *Mishna Berura,*[2] citing the *Chayei Adam*, writes, חוב על האדם למהר לבא לבית הכנסת כדי שיגיע להתפלל י״ח בצבור — "It is obligatory for a person to quickly come to the synagogue so he arrives [in time] to pray the *Shemoneh Esrei* with the congregation."[3] This

---

1. O.C. 90:9.

2. 90:28.

3. The *Chayei Adam* here seeks to dispel the misconception that a *minyan* is important only to allow for the recitation of *kaddish* and *kedusha*, and for the Torah reading. He emphasizes the importance of personally arriving in the synagogue and praying with the congregation, as opposed to merely ascertaining the presence of ten men to facilitate these portions of the service.

formulation suggests that תפילה בצבור constitutes an outright halachic obligation. Similarly, the *Shulchan Aruch Ha-Rav*[4] (the first Rebbe of Lubavitch) writes that praying with a *minyan* constitutes a מצות עשה מדבריהם — an obligation enacted by the Sages — but its importance exceeds even Biblical obligations, because it brings glory to God (הואיל ומקדשין בה ה׳ ברבים). Indeed, Rav Moshe Feinstein, in one of his responsa,[5] establishes that praying with a *minyan* is a strict halachic requirement. Others,[6] however, ruled that praying with a *minyan* is not strictly required, though they certainly do not deny its importance in, or centrality to, religious life.

The vast majority of observant Jews throughout the world, understanding the gravity of the COVID-19 crisis, heeded the call of health officials and leading rabbis to pray privately in order to help prevent the spread of the illness. Others, however, formed "porch *minyanim*" (מנייני מרפסות), whereby neighbors prayed together while standing on their porches or in their yards. And, especially in the early days of the epidemic, there were those who simply ignored social distancing rules and assembled together for prayers.

This essay will survey the relevant rabbinic literature on this topic, exploring our tradition's attitude towards health precautions generally, and to situations where religious observance poses a potential medical risk, and how the relevant sources should inform our outlook on the phenomenon of the "renegade" *minyanim* held during the coronavirus pandemic.

Heeding the Advice of Medical Experts

The importance of maintaining good health and refraining from practices which compromise one's physical wellbeing is famously discussed by the Rambam in the fourth chapter of *Hilchos Dei'os*. The Rambam writes that since a person is incapable of properly focusing his mind when he suffers illness, צריך להרחיק אדם עצמו מדברים המאבדין את הגוף ולהנהיג עצמו בדברים המברין והמחלימים — one is required to avoid that which could harm his body, and follow practices which are beneficial to the body.

Similarly, Rav Moshe Rivkes, in his *Be'er Ha-Gola* notes to the *Shulchan Aruch*,[7] writes:

הטעם שהתורה הזהירה על שמירת הנפש הוא מטעם שברא הקב״ה את העולם

---

4. O.C. 90:17.

5. *Iggeros Moshe*, O.C. 2:27.

6. Rav Yair Bachrach (*Chavos Yair*, 115), citing the Maharil, writes that praying with a *minyan* אינו מצוה כולי האי. Rabbi Aryeh Pomrantzik (*Eimek Beracha*, 1 ,קי״ש ברכות) asserts that one should pray with a *minyan* because public prayer is more readily accepted by God, but there is no technical requirement to do so.

7. C.M. 426:90.

בחסדו להטיב להנבראים שיכירו גדולתו ולעבוד עבודתו בקיום מצוותיו ותורתו...
והמסכן את עצמו כאילו מואס ברצון בוראו ואינו רוצה לא בעבודתו ולא במתן
שכרו, ואין לך זלזול ואפיקורסתא יותר מזו.

The reason why the Torah commanded guarding one's life is because the Almighty created the world in His kindness in order to benefit His creatures, so they recognize His goodness and serve Him through fulfilling His commands and His Torah… One who endangers himself is as though he rejects his Creator's will and wants neither His service nor His reward. And there is no greater disdain or heresy than this.[8]

The Rashbash (Rav Shlomo ben Shimon Duran), in one of his responsa,[9] emphasizes the particular importance of living a healthy lifestyle during an epidemic. He notes the Gemara's instruction in *Maseches Bava Kama* (60b), דבר בעיר, אל יהלך אדם באמצע הדרך, מפני שמלאך המות מהלך באמצע הדרכים — "If there is pestilence in the city, a person should not walk in the middle of the road, because the Angel of Death walks in the middle." The Rashbash explains this to mean that normally, we are encouraged to care for our health in a reasonable, moderate fashion, without veering to either extreme — neither to extreme recklessness, nor to excessive caution which can cause unnecessary anxiety and deprive a person of the joys of life. During a time of plague, however, extreme caution is warranted. When a dangerous epidemic rages, the "Angel Death" threatens those in the "middle" — meaning, those who carry on as usual, without taking special precautionary measures to protect themselves.

The halachic imperative to care for one's physical wellbeing includes strict adherence to the guidance of medical experts, as expressed in the requirement to feed a patient on Yom Kippur if a physician determines that the patient would otherwise put his life at risk. The *Shulchan Aruch*,[10] based on the Gemara, writes explicitly that if a medical expert warns of a potential danger to a patient's life if he fasts, then the patient must be fed even if he says he does not require food. And if two experts determine that the patient must be fed, then no matter how many experts disagree, and feel that fasting does not pose any danger, the patient must be fed. *Halacha* requires us to follow the medical expertise of health professionals even at the expense of a severe Torah prohibition such as eating on Yom Kippur.

Rabbi Akiva Eiger, in one of his famous letters instructing Jewish communities how to conduct themselves during the deadly cholera epidemic in Poland,[11] urged the people to abide by all the medical experts' guidelines:

---

8. See *Headlines 2*, chapter 12, "Maintaining Good Health as a Halachic Imperative."
9. Responsa, 195.
10. O.C. 618.
11. *Iggeros Rabbi Akiva Eiger*, 73.

גם הזהרתי פעמים הרבה באזהרה אחר אזהרה שיהיו הנהגתם באכילה ושתיה
כפי אשר סדרו ואשר שפטו הרופאים, להזהר מזה ויִרחקו כמטחוי קשת כאילו
הם מאכלות אסורות, ולא יעברו על דבריהם אף כמלא נימא... והעובר על ציווי
הרופאים בסדר ההנהגה חוטא לה׳ במאוד מאוד כי גדול סכנתא מאיסורא ובפרט
במקום סכנה לו ולאחרים שגורם ח״ו התפשטות החולי בעיר וגדול עונו מנשוא.

I have also repeatedly warned, time and time again, that their eating and
drinking habits must be as the doctors specified and determined. Care
must be taken in this regard, and they must distance themselves [from
foods deemed dangerous by the doctors] the distance of an arrow's flight,
as though they were forbidden foods, and they should not violate their
[the doctors'] words, even a hairsbreadth… One who violates the doctors'
instructions in the way he conducts himself sins grievously against God,
for danger is more important than prohibition, especially in a place of
danger for oneself and for others, where he causes the spread of the illness,
Heaven forbid, in the city. His sin is then too great to bear.

Rav Yisrael Salanter[12] similarly urged during the cholera outbreak in his region, לשמור
את ההנהגה אשר יורונו חכמי הרופאים, אשר לאור דבריהם נלך גם עפ״י הדת — "follow the
practice instructed by the expert physicians, to the light of whose words we tread, even
according to our religion." Guidelines issued by medical experts, in the eyes of Rav Yisrael Salanter, essentially become binding Torah law, given the obligation to protect one's
physical wellbeing and avoid danger. Rav Yisrael added his empirical observation that
"everyone whose shoulder bore the burden of the physicians' conduct in terms of eating,
and so on, like a wise man, instead of a fool, did not show any affliction or illness."

Rav Menachem Mendel Lefin, in his *Cheshbon Ha-Nefesh*,[13] emphasizes the importance of trusting only trained, professional physicians for medical guidance. The
Gemara in *Maseches Bava Kama* (85a) famously states that from the Torah's requirement to pay the medical expenses incurred by a person whom one has harmed,[14] we
may infer that the Torah authorizes physicians to administer medical treatment. Rav
Lefin understood this to mean that the Torah requires consulting with medical experts
and following their guidance, as opposed to relying on one's own intuition or on people
with no medical training. Therefore, if the consensus among health professionals warns
that certain conduct could threaten one's physical wellbeing, he is bound by Torah law
to avoid that behavior.

---

12.   *Or Yisrael*, 22.

13.   #591. Although Rabbi Lefin was identified with the *Haskala* movement, his work *Cheshbon Ha-Nefesh* was hailed as a valuable source of religious and ethical teachings by Rav
Yisrael Salanter, who encouraged the publication of this book in Vilna, in 1845.

14.   ורפא ירפא, *Shemos* 21:19.

Thus, given the broad consensus across the spectrum of medical experts urging social distancing as a necessary means of lowering the rate of coronavirus infection, it seems unquestionably clear that social distancing guidelines at that time became halachically binding.

Danger to the Public

Additionally, the medical establishment deemed social distancing necessary not merely for one's own individual safety, but also as a matter of public policy in the interest of protecting the entire population. The rapid rate of infection at the outset of the outbreak gave rise to the real fear that the pandemic would overwhelm hospitals, such that patients in serious condition — whether from coronavirus or any other illness — would not have access to the lifesaving care they required. Government officials took the drastic steps that they did, demanding and enforcing social distancing, in order to lower the rate of infection so that the hospitals would be able to competently tend to every patient in need of urgent medical attention.

Halacha accords great importance to public health and safety, drastically lowering the level of risk warranting the suspension of Torah law in situations of threats to the public. The Ran[15] establishes the rule that נזקא דרבים כסכנת נפשות חשיב לן — potential harm to the public is treated by *halacha* as a threat to life. Even if the danger is not inherently life-threatening, it is treated as such if the danger is posed to the public.

Rav Shaul Yisraeli, in *Amud Ha-Yemini,*[16] introduces this factor as a reason to permit Jewish policemen in Israel to patrol the streets on Shabbos. Even though they are not responding to a potentially life-threatening emergency, the goal of ensuring the public's safety by having a police presence qualifies as פקוח נפש, and thus overrides the Shabbos prohibitions.[17]

Another example of this principle is a fascinating response[18] given by Rav Shlomo Zalman Auerbach to a soldier serving in the intelligence corps of the Israeli Defense Forces, whose job was to intercept and decode messages from the enemy's communications network, via computer. The soldier asked his superiors for permission to skip on Shabbos messages which he felt were unlikely to involve Israeli security, such as messages to African countries. As such messages were, in all probability, entirely unre-

---

15. *Shabbos*, 19b in the Rif.
16. 17.
17. Rav Yisraeli emphasizes, however, that he would not allow patrols on Shabbos on the basis of this argument alone, if there weren't additional halachic considerations for permitting them.
18. This response is reported by Rav Moshe Mordechai Farbstein in an article published in *Asya*, vol. 33–4, p. 99.

lated to the hostile country's plans against Israel, the soldier felt there was no justification for decoding these messages on Shabbos, and so he asked if the decoding of these messages could be delayed until after Shabbos. His superiors insisted that he decode all messages on Shabbos, though they did grant him the discretion to choose which decoded messages needed to be urgently passed on during Shabbos, and which could wait until after Shabbos ended.

The soldier presented his question to Rav Shlomo Zalman, who ruled that the soldier must decode each and every intercepted message on Shabbos. He explained that when it comes to national security, even a very small chance of risk is treated by *halacha* as a significant risk and thus overrides the Shabbos prohibitions.

Hence, a crucial distinction exists between assessments of potential risk to an individual, and assessments of potential danger to the public. In the case of the coronavirus, an exceptionally contagious virus which can be carried asymptomatically, decisions must be made in consideration of not only one's personal safety, but also the public safety. Even if a given situation poses a very low risk of infection, that very low risk suffices to override Torah law, because every infected patient is very likely to infect many other people. Moreover, every individual belongs to a community and a society, all of whose members must work collectively to prevent public hazards. This means adhering to policies deemed vital for maintaining the public's wellbeing, even if those policies require avoiding an activity which poses little risk to the individual.

Suspending Torah to Publicize the Law of פקוח נפש

In fact, we find a number of sources indicating that the Torah is violated even when there is no immediate danger, when this is necessary for the sake of educating others, dispelling dangerous misconceptions, and preventing people from making life-threatening mistakes.

One of the famous examples of this kind of suspension of Torah law is the story told of Rav Yisrael Salnter's public recitation of *kiddush* on Yom Kippur during the cholera epidemic. As related by Rav Baruch Epstein in his *Mekor Baruch*,[19] Rav Yisrael walked up to the *bima*, together with two prominent *poskim*, and announced that everyone needed to eat in order to avoid contracting the illness. He proceeded to recite *kiddush* and partake of some food, in order to make it very clear that this was permitted — and, in fact, required.[20]

---

19.   P. 1012. Other versions of the story appear in *Tenuas Ha-Mussar* (vol. 1, p. 184), and other sources.

20.   Rav Moshe Feinstein (*Iggeros Moshe*, O.C. 3:91) points to this episode as a precedent for allowing violating Shabbos for the sake of immunization. He addresses the case of somebody treating a patient suffering from a contagious illness, and the means of protecting

Rav Moshe Sternbuch[21] understood that Rav Yisrael himself was healthy, and thus not in any sort of danger. Nevertheless, he broke his fast for the sake of impressing upon the community the importance of protecting their health during that dangerous time.[22] Rav Sternbuch noted in this context a comment of Maharil Diskin in reference to the Talmud Yerushalmi's discussion[23] of the special permission granted to till the land during the *shemita* year if the government imposes a crippling agricultural tax. Such a tax, combined with the Torah's demands of *shemita*, could lead to widespread starvation, and so the *shemita* restrictions were waived to allow producing food. Maharil Diskin noted that this applied even to the wealthy landowners who were not threatened by the tax. They, too, were to cultivate their fields, as otherwise, the less privileged landowners would be hesitant to work their fields, thus putting themselves in danger. These precedents demonstrate that Torah law may be suspended even by those whose lives are not threatened, in order to ensure that those whose lives are threatened do not hesitate to do everything needed to protect themselves, including Torah violations.

This concept finds expression in the Rambam's ruling in *Hilchos Shabbos*[24] that when the need arises to violate Shabbos to protect a life, אין עושין אותן לא ע"יי גוים ולא ע"יי קטנים...אלא על ידי גדולי ישראל וחכמיהם — the forbidden act should be performed not by gentiles, or by children, but rather by גדולי ישראל and scholars. This ruling is cited by the *Shulchan Aruch*,[25] though the Rama cites an opinion (that of the *Or Zarua*) that if a gentile is available and willing to perform the act no less quickly than a Jew, then he should be asked to perform the necessary act of Shabbos desecration. The *Taz* sharply challenges this opinion, noting that such a practice — asking a gentile to perform a life-saving mission — could pose a risk in the future:

יש חשש שמא אתה מכשילם לעתיד באם יראו עכשיו שאין עושין רק על ידי עכו"ים
יסברו שיש איסור ע"יי ישראל ולפעמים לא יהיה עכו"ים מצוי ועי"יז יסתכן החולה
במה שימתינו על עכו"ים.

---

against infection require violating the Shabbos prohibitions. Rav Moshe rules that this is allowed, just as Rav Yisrael Salanter required eating on Yom Kippur to help prevent against cholera infection.

21. *Teshuvos Ve-Hanhagos*, 4:152.

22. Rav Sternbuch applied this principle to the case of an ill patient who stubbornly refused to eat on Yom Kippur despite the physician's warning that fasting could risk his life, and the only way to have him eat is to convince him that it is not Yom Kippur and eating in his presence to prove it. In such a case, Rav Sternbuch writes, it would be permissible to eat in the patient's presence in order to ensure he eats and does not endanger his health.

23. *Shevi'is* 4:2

24. 2:3.

25. O.C. 328:21.

There is a concern that you might be causing them to stumble in the future, for if they see now that this is done only by a gentile, they will think it is forbidden by a Jew, and sometimes there will not be a gentile available, and as a result, the patient will be endangered as they wait for a gentile.

The *Taz* proceeds to assert that when the Rambam requires desecrating Shabbos in life-saving situations על ידי גדולי ישראל וחכמיהם, he refers to leading sages. Specifically the pious, righteous scholars are chosen for this purpose in order to impress upon the masses the importance of violating Shabbos to protect against life-threatening danger. This is in contrast to the *Beis Yosef*, who understood גדולי ישראל וחכמיהם as referring to intellectually mature adults, as opposed to children or ignoramuses. According to the *Taz*'s understanding, the Rambam considered it a מצוה מן המובחר — an especially high standard of *mitzva* performance — to have Shabbos violated when necessary to protect human life by great spiritual figures, as this helps reinforce the requirement to desecrate Shabbos in life-threatening situations, a requirement which some might be reluctant to accept.

In any event, according to the *Shulchan Aruch* and the *Taz*, even if the life-saving act of Shabbos desecration can be performed by a gentile with absolutely no additional risk to the endangered individual or individuals, the act must be performed by a Jewish adult, to dispel the possible misconception that Shabbos may not be desecrated in life-threatening circumstances.[26]

This underscores the role of public perception in determining whether a situation of danger warrants overriding *halacha*. Even if one is certain that his *mitzva* observance would not directly put himself or anybody else in danger, he still must consider the long-term consequences of his conduct, whether it might cause others to act with irresponsible laxity that could endanger their or other people's lives.

When Suspending Torah Law Is a "*Chumra*"

Underlying this principle is a basic psychological truth: devout Jews are reluctant to commit an act that is normally forbidden by Torah law, even in rare situations when it isn't. Halachic observance is so deeply ingrained within our essence that we will

---

26. The *Mishna Berura* (328:37) cites the *Taz*'s position, and appears to accept this opinion.

   The *Taz* adds that if one prefers having the act performed by a gentile, in accordance with the view cited by the Rama, he must ensure to announce to everyone present that this act would be permitted under these circumstances even by a Jew.

   Rav Shlomo Kluger, in one of his responsa (*Eitz Chayim*, 317), tells that Rav Alexander Sender Shor once needed to eat on Yom Kippur, and he requested that the food be brought to him in the yard outside the *beis midrash* so everyone would see him eat and learn that protecting one's health overrides the Yom Kippur fast.

naturally hesitate before violating *halacha* even for the sake of preserving life. We want to wait and hold out until we feel assured that the danger is real and the risk level high enough to warrant the suspension of Torah law. This is why the *Taz* urged specifically the righteous leaders to perform acts of Shabbos violation that are necessary to save a life — to counter people's instinctive reluctance to desecrate the Shabbos even in situations of פקוח נפש.

The proper perspective with which we are to approach such situations, where *mitzva* observance clashes with the imperative to maintain health, is expressed by Rav Shlomo Yosef Zevin, in his *Moadim Be-Halacha*,[27] where he relates what has become a well-known story about Rav Chaim Soloveitchik. When he became the rabbi of the city of Brisk, and ill patients in the community consulted with him before Yom Kippur to determine if and how much they should eat on Yom Kippur, he demanded that they eat as much as they felt they needed. He did not instruct them to limit their intake of food or water at all.

Rav Chaim faced criticism for this lenient policy, and he responded by explaining, "I am not being lenient with regard to the fast; to the contrary, I am being stringent with regard to פקוח נפש."

And, when Rav Chaim instructed a patient to eat on Yom Kippur, and he saw that the patient felt troubled, he would say, "Have you ever been to a *bris* on Shabbos? Was the *mohel* upset that he needed to commit an act of Shabbos desecration? Of course not. He rejoices over the opportunity to fulfill the will of Hashem. The One who forbade performing *melacha* on Shabbos required performing a *bris mila* on Shabbos for an eight-day old child. The same applies to eating on Yom Kippur to maintain one's health."

It is similarly told[28] that when Rav Chaim's grandson, Rav Yosef Dov Soloveitchik, was a young child, he was ill, and a doctor came to examine him on Shabbos. Rav Chaim asked a family member to tend to the fire so the doctor would have more light and could perform a proper, thorough, and precise examination. The family member refused, and Rav Chaim reacted very angrily. When a medical concern demands performing an action that is normally forbidden by Torah law, that action becomes a *mitzva*, and thus refusing to perform the action is akin to refusing to perform a *mitzva*.

This outlook was expressed also by the *Chazon Ish*.[29] He noted the Gemara's famous remark in *Maseches Rosh Hashanah* (9a) that whoever eats and drinks heartily on Erev Yom Kippur is considered to have fasted for two days. The *Chazon Ish* explains that since

---

27. P. 82.

28. This story was told by Rav Mayer Twersky, Rav Chaim's great-great-grandson, in an address to his students during the coronavirus pandemic, available online at http://torah-web.org/torah/special/2020/rtwe_chaybohem_eng.html.

29. See *Pe'er Ha-Dor*, vol. 3, p. 215.

halacha requires festive eating on Erev Yom Kippur, just as it requires fasting on Yom Kippur, there is no difference between feasting on Erev Yom Kippur and fasting on Yom Kippur; both are fulfillments of the Almighty's will. The *Chazon Ish* shared this thought with a patient who was distraught over having to eat on Yom Kippur, assuring him that he would be fulfilling God's will by eating to care for his health on Yom Kippur, no less than he would be fulfilling God's will by fasting if he were healthy. He said, "We are just simple soldiers who follow the orders issued to us — if it's to fast, we fast, and if it's to eat, we eat."

The *Chazon Ish* related to this patient that he himself went through periods when he could not wear *tzitzis* or *tefillin* due to a severe digestive illness. During those times, he would pray to God to cure him, and would say, "Master of the world, You commanded me to wear *tzitzis* and to lay *tefillin*, and I did so, but now You command me not to…"[30]

An earlier source for this concept is a fascinating passage in Rav Chaim Ben-Attar's *Or Ha-Chayim* Torah commentary.[31] He explains the Torah's command אך את שבתותי תשמרו ("Only, you shall observe My Sabbaths") to mean that at times we observe Shabbos through its desecration. When a potential risk to life is at stake, we must enable the endangered individual to continue living and observing Shabbos in the future by desecrating Shabbos in the present. As the Gemara (*Yoma* 85b) famously teaches, אמרה תורה חלל עליו שבת אחת כדי שישמור שבתות הרבה — "The Torah said: Desecrate one Shabbos for him, in order that he observe many Shabbosos [in the future]." The *Or Ha-Chayim* writes that when one desecrates Shabbos for the sake of preserving life, אין זה קרוי חילול, אדרבה, זה קרוי שמירת שבת — "this is not called 'desecrating'; to the contrary, this is called 'observing.'" He later adds, הנמנע מהדבר אין זה אלא מזלזל במצוות הקל ח"ו — "one who refrains from this is only belittling the commands of the Almighty, Heaven forbid."

Violating Torah law to protect against life-threatening danger is not a sin, but a *mitzva*. There is nothing virtuous whatsoever about taking risks for the sake of Torah observance. To the contrary, those who do so do not observe the Torah, but violate it, because the same Torah which commanded us to perform *mitzvos* when it is safe to do so, commanded us not to perform *mitzvos* when it is unsafe to do so.

Returning to the coronavirus pandemic, once the medical establishment determined that praying with a *minyan* posed a health risk, whether to oneself or to others, or both, or simply as a matter of public policy to curb the virus' spread, private prayer became a halachic imperative. The רצון ה׳ — divine will — at that time was to pray privately in one's home, no less than the רצון ה׳ under ordinary circumstances is to pray with a *minyan*.

---

30. Similarly, it is told that the rabbis in the Bergen-Belsen concentration camp composed a special prayer for the inmates to recite on the night of the *seder* in 1944 before eating bread, proclaiming that they were eating bread on Pesach in fulfillment of the *mitzva* to preserve their lives.

31. *Shemos* 31:13.

Provoking Hostility

Beyond violating the halachic imperative to heed the advice of medical experts, the *minyanim* conducted during the coronavirus pandemic also had the effect of inviting the hostility of the gentiles among whom we live.

In a situation of שמד — religious persecution — the Torah requires one to fulfill every precept, including the minutest halachic details, in violation of the gentile authorities' edicts, even at the threat of death. This obligation is established explicitly by the Gemara in *Maseches Sanhedrin* (74a), and codified by the Rambam, in *Hilchos Yesodei Ha-Torah*.[32] However, this does not apply when the government issues an edict in a time of an actual national emergency, in an effort to protect its population. Even if these provisions affect religious observance, this situation does not fall under the rule of שעת השמד, and we instead apply the halachic concept of איבה, which permits committing normally forbidden actions in order not to evoke the hostility of our gentile neighbors.

Thus, for example, Rav Moshe Feinstein ruled[33] that a doctor is permitted to treat gentile patients on Shabbos if necessary, even if this entails acts that are forbidden on Shabbos by force of Torah law, out of the concern of איבה. Rav Moshe emphasizes that even if the physician himself will not endanger himself in any way by refusing, nevertheless, arousing the hostility of non-Jews could pose a long-term risk to the Jewish community. Moreover, Rav Moshe adds, the news of a Jewish doctor refusing to treat a gentile patient would be widely reported throughout the world, putting the lives of Jews everywhere in danger, and this must therefore be avoided even if this requires suspending Torah law.

This concern, of course, is magnified exponentially in our technological age, when news and video clips are disseminated throughout the world within a matter of minutes. Sadly, videos of Orthodox Jews violating social distancing orders surfaced during the coronavirus pandemic, and evoked not a small amount of hostility, to the point where there were calls to deny medical treatment to Orthodox Jewish patients suffering from the virus, because they held the Jews partly responsible for the spread of COVID-19.[34] This is a clear and frightening example of how the איבה evoked by neglecting the government's rules posed a real threat to Jewish lives.

Interestingly enough, Rav Yitzchak Lipkin, a son of Rav Yisrael Salanter, wrote in

---

32. 5:3.
33. *Iggeros Moshe*, O.C. 4:79.
34. The Anti-Defamation League published a post on April 29, 2020 entitled, "On Social Media, Haredi and Orthodox Jewish Communities are Scapegoated and Blamed for COVID-19," available online at https://www.adl.org/blog/on-social-media-haredi-and-orthodox-jewish-communities-are-scapegoated-and-blamed-for-covid-19.

his memoirs[35] that one of the factors which Rav Yisrael took into account in deciding to require eating on Yom Kippur during the cholera epidemic was the fear of the gentiles blaming the epidemic on the Jews' religious practices. This serves as a clear and compelling precedent for the need to refrain from performing *mitzvos* during a medical emergency in order to avoid arousing the gentiles' resentment and their blaming the Jews for the epidemic.

The Torah famously commands us bring glory to God's Name, and to avoid dishonoring His Name: ולא תחללו את שם קדשי ונקדשתי בתוך בני ישראל — "You shall not desecrate My Name, and I shall be glorified amongst the Children of Israel."[36] Rav Yoel Teitelbaum of Satmar[37] explains this to mean that we may not defile God's Name as we attempt to glorify Him. The Torah here warns ולא תחללו את שם קדשי — that we not defame the Almighty — in the course of pursuing the goal of ונקדשתי בתוך בני ישראל, of bringing Him glory. Even if our intentions are sincere, and we truly seek to serve God and bring Him honor, we must ensure that in the process, we do not create a חילול ה'. Those who arranged *minyanim* in defiance of social distancing requirements during the coronavirus epidemic were guilty of this precise violation — creating a חילול ה', bringing great dishonor to Orthodox Jewry, in their sincere but grievously misguided attempt to achieve a קידוש ה'.[38]

The Status of a Prayer Recited in a Forbidden Manner

Having established that public prayer in defiance of the authorities' social distancing orders is strictly forbidden, it follows that those who participate in such *minyanim* do not fulfill their prayer obligation.

The basis for this conclusion is Rav Moshe Feinstein's responsum[39] in which he expresses his view that praying with a *minyan* constitutes an outright halachic obligation. Amidst his discussion, Rav Moshe postulates the theory that the obligation of prayer is rooted in the possibility of its being accepted. He writes that when there is no possibility that God would accept a prayer, then by definition, such a prayer cannot be a halachic תפילה. The essence of תפילה is a petition to God which is eligible for His acceptance and favorable response.[40]

---

35. *Kedosh Yisrael*, *Sifsei Chachamim* edition, vol. 1, p. 99.
36. *Vayikra* 22:32.
37. *Divrei Yoel*, Simchas Torah.
38. It goes without saying that outdoor *minyanim* which disturbed the non-Jewish neighbors clearly caused a grave חילול ה', and unnecessarily invited hostility against Jews.
39. Referenced above, note 5.
40. Rav Moshe postulates on this basis that since public prayer is always accepted, as the Gemara teaches in *Maseches Berachos* (8a), whereas private prayer might not be accepted,

Rav Moshe proves this theory from the disqualification of prayers recited under circumstances when they were not to have been recited. The *Shulchan Aruch*, in discussing the laws of the *Shema* recitation,[41] addresses the case of one who recited the *Shema* in a place where there was reason to suspect the presence of excrement, thus requiring him to carefully examine the area, yet he neglected to make such an examination. If he then discovered that excrement had been present while he recited *Shema*, then he has not fulfilled his obligation, and he must repeat *Shema*. The *Mishna Berura*[42] writes that this applies also to תפילה. Later,[43] the *Shulchan Aruch* rules that one who prayed when he needed to relieve himself has not fulfilled his obligation, and his prayer is deemed "abominable." Rav Moshe proceeds to demonstrate that in both these instances, the prayer is invalid because of one's wrongdoing, and not because of the presence of excrement or the experience of needing to perform bodily functions. If one had prayed in an area where there was no reason to suspect the presence of excrement, and later discovered that excrement had been present, his prayer is valid, and he does not need to repeat it. Likewise, if one began experiencing the need to relieve himself in the middle of his prayer, he should complete his prayer,[44] and it is considered valid. This proves that in both cases, the determining factor is the person's impropriety, his having prayed under circumstances when he should not have prayed.

Rav Moshe explains that when a person prays under halachically improper circumstances, then, by definition, his prayer cannot earn acceptance, because God certainly does not accept prayers recited in a manner of which He disapproves. Hence, the prayer cannot, by definition, be considered a halachic תפילה, which means a prayer that has the possibility of earning God's acceptance.

It would seem clear that this would apply also to "renegade" *minyanim* formed during the coronavirus pandemic, when *halacha* quite clearly required praying privately, both to avoid the virus' spread, and to avoid inviting hostility and creating a חילול ה'. These public prayers were recited in defiance of *halacha* and Torah values, and thus most certainly stood no chance of being accepted by God. By definition, then, these prayers were halachically invalid, and the participants did not fulfill their prayer obligations and were guilty of reciting numerous ברכות לבטלה (*berachos* in vain).[45]

---

halacha requires one to pray with a *minyan* when possible, because the essential definition of the prayer obligation is to recite a prayer which has the greatest possibility of earning God's acceptance.

41. O.C. 76:8, 81:2.

42. 81:7.

43. 92:1.

44. *Shulchan Aruch*, O.C. 92:2.

45. We do not address here the question of whether ten men situated in different yards and/or porches can combine to form a halachic *minyan*. The *Mishna Berura* (55:57) cites different

In fact, we might apply to such *minyanim* God's sharp condemnation of the people of the First Commonwealth in a famous prophecy to Yeshayahu (1:15): ובפרשכם כפיכם אעלים עיני מכם גם כי תרבו תפילה אינני שומע ידיכם דמים מלאו — "And when you outstretch your hands [in prayer], I shall turn My eyes away from you; even when you pray in abundance, I do not listen to you; [for] your hands are filled with blood." If people pray in a manner which endangers themselves and others, their prayers are worthless and cannot possibly be accepted.

This conclusion also has implications for those who prayed privately during the pandemic. The *Shulchan Aruch*[46] rules that one who is unable to pray with the congregation in the synagogue, and must pray privately at home (such as if he is ill), should endeavor to pray at the same time as the congregation. At first glance, then, we might have assumed that if a person obeyed social distancing regulations and prayed privately at home, but knew of a *minyan* being formed against the rules in his neighborhood, he should have tried to pray at the same time as that service. In light of what we have seen, however, that *minyan*'s prayers do not qualify as תפילה at all, and there is thus no value whatsoever in praying at the same time as that group.

Reporting Violators to the Authorities

If one had information about a group of fellow Jews violating social distancing orders, and conducting a *minyan* against the rules, would it be permissible, or appropriate, for him to report them to the authorities?[47]

Generally, of course, מסירה — reporting a fellow Jew, or information about him and his finances, to the gentile government authorities — is regarded as one of the most grievous of all sins. However, the *Shulchan Aruch*[48] rules explicitly that a person who causes harm to the public (מיצר הצבור ומצערן) may be reported to the authorities. The Rama gives the example of counterfeiters, who could potentially cause considerable harm to the public, and may therefore be reported to the authorities,

---

opinions, and concludes that under extenuating circumstances, the group can be considered a *minyan* as long as they see one another. One wonders, however, why people would rely on this lenient position in their zeal to pray with a *minyan*, given that according to the stringent view, the *berachos* of חזרת הש״ץ and over the Torah reading are considered ברכות לבטלה. Even leaving aside health concerns and the risk of arousing hostility, it would seem halachically preferable to pray privately than to conduct a public prayer in a manner that does not, according to a number of *poskim*, qualify as a *minyan*.

46. O.C. 90:9.
47. See also *Headlines*, volume 1, chapter 4, "Reporting Child Molesters: מסירה or Obligation?"
48. C.M. 388:12.

though the Rama adds that the violators must first be warned before the authorities are notified.

Rav Moshe Sternbuch[49] applies the Rama's ruling to the case of a reckless driver, who endangers the public. Such a person, Rav Sternbuch writes, must be warned, and if he ignores the warnings and continues driving irresponsibly, he should be reported to the authorities.[50]

It stands to reason that this should apply as well to violators of social distancing regulations during the COVID-19 pandemic. Indeed, Rav Chaim Kanievsky, in a series of halachic rulings issued during the pandemic,[51] ruled that institutions ignoring guidelines may be reported, even if they will be handed heavy fines.

Conclusion

1. Caring for one's health and following the guidance of health experts constitutes an outright halachic imperative.
2. Refraining from praying with a *minyan* when health experts ordered social distancing to prevent the spread of COVID-19 was required for the sake of protecting one's own health, of protecting the public welfare, and of avoiding hostility towards the Jewish community.
3. When praying with a *minyan* is forbidden due to these concerns, one must recognize that just as God normally wishes that we pray together with a *minyan*, under such circumstances it is His will that we pray privately.
4. Those who pray with a *minyan* under circumstances when this is forbidden — such as during the coronavirus pandemic — do not fulfill the *mitzva* of prayer, and the *berachos* they recite are all considered to have been recited in vain.
5. Those who conduct *minyanim* in violation of health guidelines should be reported to the authorities, just as other people who endanger the public — such as reckless drivers — should be reported, in the interest of public safety.

---

49. *Teshuvos Ve-Hanhagos*, 1:850.
50. See also *Minchas Yitzchak*, 8:148.

   Rav Sternbuch notes incidentally in this context that the Steipler Gaon would speak angrily about drivers who violate traffic safety laws. He tells that a person once came to the Steipler Gaon asking for a *beracha* because he feared he would be handed a severe punishment for violating traffic laws, and the Gaon berated him and told him he deserved to be severely punished.

51. These rulings were published in media outlets on March 29, 2020. See, for example, https://www.bhol.co.il/news/1090634.

Rabbi Dr. Daniel Roth

Interviewed on *Headlines with Dovid Lichtenstein*, 25 Adar 5778 (March 21, 2020)

Clearly, throughout the ages, the *rabbanim* never claimed to be medical experts unless they happened to be. On Yom Kippur, *rabbanim* consult with medical professionals to understand what the level of *sakana* is, and they take that information and they *pasken*. In this situation [COVID-19], I think the *rabbanim* do that, and I'm sure this is the appropriate method and the way it should be done. It's not a matter of listening to rabbis versus listening to the doctors. The discussion about the medical information and what should be done to prevent *sakana* is really up to the doctors who have the knowledge and information to transmit, and then it's for the *rabbanim* to make the *psak* on how we conduct ourselves knowing what the level of *sakana* is.

Let's day a doctor says that, for whatever reason, he feels that a one-in-a-million risk of *sakana* should make people do A, B or C. In *halacha*, we do not recognize a need to uproot life for this level of danger. Now let's say a doctor forbids his patient from going into a certain profession because there's some level of risk. *Halacha* might say you're allowed to, because for *parnasa* we allow certain levels of risk. So then we won't listen to the doctor.

We trust the guidance of our *rabbanim* about how to live life, but the *rabbanim* cannot ignore the medical data.

Rav Hershel Schachter

Interviewed on *Headlines with Dovid Lichtenstein*, 10 Nissan 5778 (April 4, 2020)

If people conduct a *minyan* in violation of health officials' warnings, could it be that they have not fulfilled the obligation to *daven*?

It's a serious question. I seem to remember that there's a *teshuva* of the Maharam Shick, that a fellow was the *ba'al tokei'a* for years and years, and then he developed, I think, a heart condition. The doctors said he absolutely must not blow the *shofar*, it's dangerous, he could get a heart attack, but he did not listen. He blew the *shofar*, and he survived. The Maharam Shick raises the possibility that the *tzibur* was not *yotzei*, because he acted against the *halacha*.

Somebody who makes a *minyan*, does he have the status of מיצר הרבים, who the *Shulchan Aruch* says has the status of a רודף?

Yes. The *rabbanim* asked me if they are permitted to call up the authorities to report these people, and I said yes.

Rav Menachem Genack

Interviewed on *Headlines With Dovid Lichtenstein*, 22 Iyyar 5780 (May 16, 2020)

Rav Soloveitchik said that when his father, Rav Moshe, got his first *rabbanus*, Rav Chaim told him several things about the job. The Rav said that some he could share, some he can't. One of the things he shared was the job of a *rav* is to do *chesed*, to care for the indigent, for the most vulnerable members of society, the widows and orphans. Another thing he told him is that when it comes to a dangerously ill patient on Yom Kippur, don't feed him פחות פחות מכשיעור. You should feed him a full amount, because he's a חולה שיש בו סכנה. The Brisker Rav quotes this *psak* from Rav Chaim. It seems to be against an explicit *psak* of the *Shulchan Aruch*, and against מנהג העולם. Rav Velvele explains that Rav Chaim held that in the case of a dangerously ill patient, עושים לו כל צרכו — he eats normally. You feed him פחות פחות if he could [otherwise] reach a situation of danger. But if he's already in danger, like a cancer patient, then you don't give him פחות פחות, you give him a full amount. Rav Chaim thought that this is fundamental to the job of a *rav*. All these issues of פקוח נפש have to take precedence over everything else.

As for why we shouldn't be *moser nefesh* for *mitzvos* during the pandemic, like Rabbi Akiva was — Rabbi Akiva's situation was a שעת השמד, and so he needed to defy the Romans to learn Torah. This was necessary to preserve the Torah. This is different than simply being careful about פקוח נפש, to ensure not to be infected. Rabbi Akiva was unique in what he represented in terms of Torah.

PART OF THE USA TODAY NETWORK

Coronavirus in NJ: Yeshiva BMG to close Lakewood campus, accommodate students with nowhere to go

March 16, 2020
By Mike Davis

LAKEWOOD — Beth Medrash Govoha, the largest yeshiva in the world outside of Israel, is temporarily closing due to the spread of COVID-19, the novel coronavirus that has infected nearly 3,500 people across the United States.

Rabbi Aaron Kotler, the yeshiva's president, said the campus would be closed by Wednesday in accordance with Gov. Phil Murphy's executive order, which mandated the closure of all schools — public, private and religious institutions of all age groups — as part of strict social distancing guidelines.

RELATED:Inside BMG, the Orthodox Jewish school behind Lakewood's boom

"Like any institution of higher education, we have a large campus and a large staff that requires a lot of coordination," Kotler said. "These are great professionals, highly-qualified people and we've anticipated the possibility that we'd be closing for a while."

Each course curriculum was already set, and students have "ample time" to complete remaining requirements, he said.

The college had a planned break for Passover — which begins April 8. Kotler is "exploring all angles" with the state higher education office for next semester.

The closure of New Jersey schools comes as the number of positive coronavirus cases nears 200, with two fatalities linked to the disease. More than 70 people have been killed by coronavirus across the United States.

But unlike other colleges, students at BMG won't be able to take classes online while the campus is closed, Kotler said. Students at BMG study the Torah and other rabbinical works in text form.

Study halls are completely devoid of computers and students leave their cell phones outside.

While most students will leave the campus, the yeshiva is making accommodations for some who don't have housing or food beyond that which is provided by BMG, Kotler said.

All accommodations would still go "above and beyond" the state-mandated 50-person gathering limit, he said.

"We have some students who would not have anywhere to go. We're making accommodations," Kotler said. "We don't want anyone to go hungry, so we're going to continue offering limited food service and keep praying for the best."

Over the last few weeks, BMG has shared guidance on the importance of hand-washing, social distancing and what to do if a student or staff member had been possibly exposed to coronavirus, Kotler said.

"We're as ready as we could be," he said.

In addition to mandating the shutdown of educational institutions, Murphy on Monday — along with New York Gov. Andrew Cuomo and Connecticut Gov. Ned Lamont — ordered that all casinos, bars, movie theaters, nightclubs, performing arts centers and gyms must shut down at 8 p.m. and remain closed until further notice. Restaurants can't provide dine-in service but can still provide takeout or delivery.

Rabbi Aaron Kotler speaks during the "Ask the Editor" that was webcast from the Asbury Park Press on Thursday, June, 8, 2017. (Thomas P. Costello)

The New Jersey National Guard is mobilizing to assist the state in enforcing the new social distancing regulations in order to halt the spread of coronavirus.

Torah Learning and the Coronavirus

With a small handful of unfortunate exceptions, yeshivos around the world closed their doors in the wake of the coronavirus outbreak in March 2020. Once it became clear just how contagious this life-threatening virus is, the yeshiva community, like the rest of society, recognized the importance of social distancing in preventing the spread of the deadly illness, and shut down.

While it is all but universally agreed that the concern to prevent infection overrides the precious *mitzva* of Torah study, the Gemara in *Maseches Kesubos* (77b) tells of one rabbi who seems, at least at first glance, to have disagreed.

The Gemara there speaks of an illness called ראתן, whose symptoms included incessant teary eyes, runny nose and drooling from the mouth. This condition was quite contagious, and the Gemara tells of several *Amoraim* who advised keeping a distance from patients afflicted with ראתן in order to avoid becoming infected. One *Amora*, however, felt otherwise. Rabbi Yehoshua ben Levi, the Gemara tells, מיכרך בהו ועסיק בתורה — would sit together with these patients and learn Torah with them,[1] confident that the merit of Torah study would protect him from harm. Rabbi Yehoshua ben Levi defended his practice by citing the verse in *Sefer Mishlei* (5:19) which describes Torah as אילת אהבים ויעלת חן — "A loving doe, a graceful goat." He said, "If it brings grace upon those who study it, then does it not protect?"

Later, the Gemara tells of an exchange between Rabbi Yehoshua ben Levi's colleague, Rabbi Chanina bar Papa, and the Angel of Death, during which the latter remarked that Rabbi Chanina was not as pious as Rabbi Yehoshua ben Levi, who would risk his life sitting among ראתן patients and studying Torah with them. This clearly indicates that Rabbi Yehoshua ben Levi's practice was looked upon with approval, and even regarded as a display of great piety.

The obvious question arises as to why Rabbi Yehoshua was permitted to endanger himself in this fashion, even for the sake of teaching Torah. The Gemara in *Maseches Kiddushin* (39b) states explicitly that despite the principle of שלוחי מצווה אינן נזוקין —

---

1. We follow here Rashi's understanding, that Rabbi Yehoshua ben Levi learned together with the ראתן patients. The Ritva understood the Gemara differently, to mean that Rabbi Yehoshua ben Levi sat with these patients even when he was not learning, confident that the merit of his Torah study would protect him even when he did not study.

people on their way to perform a *mitzva* are protected from harm through the merit of the *mitzva* — this does not apply in a situation of high risk, where one is likely to be harmed. The Gemara reaches this conclusion on the basis of the story of the prophet Shmuel, who, after being commanded to anoint David as king, expressed to God his fear of being killed by King Shaul, whom David would replace.[2] This proves that one should not expose himself to a clear and present danger for the sake of fulfilling a *mitzva*. Thus, the Gemara states, one who climbs a rickety ladder to send away a mother bird in fulfillment of the *mitzva* of שילוח הקן is unlawfully putting his life in danger, as the merit of this *mitzva* does not safeguard against the high risk of falling. Another example appears in *Maseches Pesachim* (8b), where the Gemara establishes that when searching for *chametz* on the night of Erev Pesach, one should not place his hands inside holes and crevices in walls where scorpions are likely to hide, as he would then be putting himself at risk.

Similarly, the Gemara teaches in *Maseches Bava Kama* (61a) that King David received a tradition from the prophet Shmuel that כל המוסר עצמו למות על דברי תורה אין אומרים דבר הלכה משמו — credit should not be given for Torah information obtained through dangerous methods. If a person risked his life in the effort to acquire knowledge, the information he shares should not be cited in his name, so that he would not be honored for his dangerous conduct.[3]

Accordingly, the *Sefer Chassidim*[4] sharply condemns those who travel along dangerous roads in order to learn Torah, applying to them the verse in *Koheles* (7:15), יש צדיק אובד בצדקו — "There is a righteous person who is destroyed by his righteousness." Risking one's life for the sake of Torah, the *Sefer Chassidim* writes, is misguided piety. He acknowledges the famous stories of Rabbi Akiva and Rabbi Chanina ben Tradyon, who defied the Romans' edicts banning Torah study, and were martyred. However, the *Sefer Chassidim* explains, an exception is made during שעת השמד — a period of religious persecution, when a foreign government seeks to obliterate Torah, thus necessitating courageous defiance in order to preserve Torah scholarship. Ordinarily, however, risking one's life for Torah learning is foolish and grievously sinful.[5]

---

2.   *Shmuel I* 16:2.

3.   The Gemara in *Maseches Pesachim* (8b) tells that Rav permitted students who lived in outlying villages to travel early in the morning, before dawn, to the yeshiva, despite the risk involved, because the merit of the *mitzva* of Torah learning would protect them. However, as noted by the *Avnei Nezer* (O.C. 454:2), the level of risk in that area was low enough to apply the rule of שלוחי מצווה אינן ניזוקים, whereas in situations of clear and present danger, one may not expose himself to risk even for the sake of Torah learning.

4.   955.

5.   See Rav Pinchas Zevichi's lengthy discussion in *Ateres Paz*, vol. 3, Y.D. 7.

How, then, did Rabbi Yehoshua ben Levi risk his life by learning together with patients suffering from the highly contagious ראתן disease?

Permitting High-Risk Danger for *Mitzvos*

Rav Elchanan Wasserman,[6] surprisingly, explained that Rabbi Yehoshua ben Levi learned with these patients because although the merit of a *mitzva* generally does not protect from harm in high-risk situations, the *mitzva* of Torah study marks the exception to this rule. Rabbi Yehoshua ben Levi cited the verse אילת אהבים ויעלת חן precisely to emphasize the unique stature of Torah study, which, unlike other *mitzvos*, offers protection even in situations of considerable risk.

Rav Elchanan's contention appears to directly contradict the Gemara's remark in *Maseches Bava Kama* condemning those who risk their lives for the sake of Torah study. Quite possibly, Rav Elchanan intended that Rabbi Yehoshua ben Levi deviated from the practice of his colleagues, who kept a distance from ראתן patients, because he held a unique opinion, recognizing the power of the merit of Torah study to protect from even clear and present danger. Rabbi Yehoshua ben Levi's colleagues avoided the company of these patients precisely because they disagreed with his view concerning the merit of Torah study. If so, then Rav Elchanan presented his theory simply to explain Rabbi Yehoshua ben Levi's position, which does not represent the normative, accepted view, which forbids putting oneself at risk for Torah study.

Alternatively, we might explain that these sages disputed the broader question as to whether the principle of שלוחי מצוה אינן ניזוקין applies in situations of high risk. Rav Yaakov Ettlinger, in his *Aruch La-Ner*,[7] asserts that a minority view among the *Tannaim* maintained that the merit of *mitzvos* protects even from clear and present danger. Rav Ettlinger notes the debate recorded in the Mishna in *Maseches Nazir* (66a) regarding Chana's pledge as she prayed for a child that if God blessed her with a boy, מורה לא יעלה על ראשו (*Shmuel I* 1:11). Rabbi Yossi understood the word מורה to mean מורא ("fear"), such that Chana promised that her child would always fear only the Almighty, and never feel intimidated by powerful human beings. Rabbi Nehorai, however, disputed this reading, noting that Shmuel indeed feared being killed by King Shaul after God commanded him to anoint David as king in Shaul's place. As Chana's son did, in fact, experience fear of a human being, the word מורה cannot refer to fear of human beings, and must mean something else. Rabbi Nehorai therefore maintained that מורה means "razor," and he concludes that Shmuel was a lifelong *nazir*, who never cut his hair. Rav Ettlinger observes that according Rabbi Nehorai, Shmuel's fear of King Shaul was unwarranted, despite the clear and present danger he faced by anointing a

---

6. *Kovetz Shiurim, Kesubos.*

7. *Yevamos* 65b.

king to take Shaul's place. Apparently, Rav Ettlinger writes, Rabbi Nehorai disagreed with the view taken by the Gemara in *Maseches Kiddushin*, cited earlier, that Shmuel's fear demonstrates that the merit of *mitzvos* does not provide protection in situations of clear and present danger. In Rabbi Nehorai's view, Shmuel should not have been afraid of Shaul, because the merit of obeying God's command guarantees protection even in situations of high risk.[8]

If so, then Rabbi Yehoshua ben Levi perhaps followed Rabbi Nehorai's opinion, and therefore felt confident relying on the merit of Torah learning to protect him from infection as he studied together with the ראתן patients. The other *Amoraim* followed the majority view, that one may not expose himself to a high level of risk for the sake of performing a *mitzva*.

A Non-Deadly Health Risk

A different theory is proposed by Rav Yosef Aryeh Lorintz, in his *Mishnas Pikuach Nefesh*,[9] suggesting, quite simply, that ראתן was not a deadly condition. The Gemara tells of the extreme discomfort this illness caused, but did not say that it was life-threatening. Perhaps, then, Rabbi Yehoshua ben Levi felt that although the merit of Torah learning does not protect one from mortal danger, it does protect against the risk of a painful but non-lethal condition.

The other *Amoraim*, according to this possibility, did not trust the merit of their Torah study to protect them even from an illness that was not life-threatening. Therefore, since *halacha* does not require one to subject himself to pain for the sake of fulfilling a *mitzva*,[10] they chose to keep a distance from the ראתן patients and not learn Torah with them.

The Merits of the Exceptionally Pious

Another possibility is that uniquely pious individuals are permitted to rely on the merit of their piety and expose themselves to danger when necessary. The Rashba, in one of his responsa,[11] establishes the prohibition against placing oneself in danger with

---

8.   One might question Rav Ettlinger's theory in light of the fact that the Rambam (*Hilchos Nezirus* 3:16) follows Rabbi Nehorai's opinion, that Shmuel was a *nazir* (and thus one who vows, "I shall be like Shmuel the Ramatite" becomes a *nazir* for life), even though the Rambam clearly rules that the principle of שלוחי מצוה אינן ניזוקין does not apply in situations of high risk (*Hilchos Chametz U-Matza* 2:5).

9.   P. 227.

10.   Rav Lorintz discusses this point at length in chapter 68.

11.   Vol. 1, 413.

the trust that God will protect him, and then writes that an exception is made for
האנשים השלמים ושזכויותיהם מרובות — "people who are complete and whose merits are
numerous." He references the famous story told in the Gemara[12] of Rabbi Chanina ben
Dosa, who killed a dangerous snake by placing his foot on the hole in the ground that
led to the den. The snake bit Rabbi Chanina's foot and then immediately died. Several
other stories, too, are told of Rabbi Chanina ben Dosa's relying on God's supernatural
assistance, something that only people of exceptional spiritual stature are allowed to
do.[13] Conceivably, this could have been true also of Rabbi Yehoshua ben Levi, whose
unique level of piety perhaps entitled him to trust in God's miraculous protection as he
studied with patients with a contagious disease.

This point is made by Rav Meir Simcha Ha-Kohen of Dvinsk, in his *Meshech
Chochma*.[14] He writes:

רבי יהושע בן לוי היה מובטח בדביקותו תמיד להשי״ת ולתורתו, כי חומרו זך
ונעלה מגדרי הטבע.

Rabbi Yehoshua ben Levi trusted in his constant attachment to God,
may He be blessed, and His Torah, because his physical being was pristine and transcended the limits of nature.

Rabbi Yehoshua attained a pristine level of spirituality which granted him supernatural
protection on which other people are not permitted to rely.[15]

Rav Meir Simcha writes that Rabbi Yehoshua ben Levi reached the level described
by Rabbi Shimon bar Yochai, who said that people who attain an especially exalted
spiritual standard do not need to work for a livelihood, and may instead devote themselves entirely to Torah, and trust that their needs will be supplied miraculously.[16] And
for this reason, Rav Meir Simcha writes, the Gemara[17] tells that Rabbi Yehoshua ben
Levi's place in the next world was alongside Rabbi Shimon bar Yochai — as he reached

---

12. *Berachos* 33a.

13. For example, the Rashba mentions the story told in *Maseches Chullin* (7b) of how Rabbi
    Chanina ben Dosa felt confident in his protection from a spell which a certain witch tried
    to cast on him. His unique stature of piety lent him special protection such that he was
    allowed to expose himself to danger.

14. *Vayikra* 26:6.

15. This explanation is offered also by the *Haflaa* in *Maseches Kesubos*, and by Rav Yosef
    Shalom Elyashiv (*Hearos* to *Maseches Kesubos*). See also the Netziv's comments in *Haamek
    Davar* to *Vayikra* 13:44.

    Rav Moshe Sternbuch, in *Teshuvos Ve-Hanhagos* (vol. 5, p. 596), suggests that even Rav
    Elchanan Wasserman, in stating that one should risk his life for Torah learning, referred
    only to somebody on the unique level of Rabbi Yehoshua ben Levi.

16. *Berachos* 35b.

17. *Kesubos* 77b.

Rabbi Shimon's unique level of piety whereby he succeeded in transcending the restrictions of nature by which ordinary people are bound.

תלמוד תורה דרבים

Elsewhere in his *Meshech Chochma*,[18] in an entirely different context, and without mentioning Rabbi Yehoshua ben Levi, Rav Meir Simcha boldly asserts, על תלמוד תורה דרבים צריך למסור עצמו למיתה ולסכן עבור זה — one must be prepared to risk his life for the sake of public Torah learning. Even if one's personal studies do not justify endangering himself, one may — and should — risk his life when necessary in order to teach Torah to the masses. Rav Meir Simcha explains on this basis the Gemara's comment in *Maseches Megilla* (3a) that Yehoshua was criticized for not teaching the people Torah on the night before the battle against the city of Jericho. Although this was a time of war, Yehoshua should nevertheless have maintained the nation's Torah study schedule, because תלמוד תורה דרבים must not be suspended even out of concern of danger.

Citing this novel theory advanced by the *Meshech Chochma*, Rav Yitzchak Zilberstein[19] permitted a Torah lecturer to travel to the yeshiva in northern Israel where he taught during the Second Lebanon war, when the region came under rocket attack. Since the lecturer taught a large group of students, his work fell under the category of תלמוד תורה דרבים, and warranted endangering himself by traveling to areas which were under bombardment.

Conceivably, this theory could explain Rabbi Yehoshua ben Levi's practice. The Gemara might mean that there was a group of quarantined patients who would otherwise be unable to learn Torah — as the other rabbis urged everyone to keep a distance from them — and so Rabbi Yehoshua ben Levi risked his life to teach them.

However, Rav Moshe Sternbuch[20] writes that even according to the *Meshech Chochma*'s theory, one is permitted to endanger himself for the sake of תלמוד תורה דרבים only if הסכנה אינה קרובה — the danger is not clear and present. In Yehoshua's case, although the nation was mobilizing for battle and thus there was some element of danger involved, there was no immediate risk, and so Yehoshua was expected to teach the people Torah. This does not necessarily mean, however, that one should put himself in immediate danger for the sake of public Torah study. If so, then the *Meshech Chochma*'s rule cannot be applied to Rabbi Yehoshua ben Levi who put himself in real danger by learning with patients suffering from a highly contagious disease.

Moreover, it is unclear whether Rav Meir Simcha applied this rule to all public Torah gatherings, or only to nationwide Torah assemblies, which is what was expected

---

18. *Shemos* 27:11.
19. *Chashukei Chemed, Kesubos* 77b.
20. Referenced earlier, note 15.

of Yehoshua. The fact that Rav Meir Simcha required endangering oneself to teach Torah to the entire nation does not necessarily mean that he would require, or even allow, endangering oneself to teach Torah to a group.

ראתן as a Spiritual Malady

Finally, the Chida, in his *Pesach Einayim*,[21] offers a creative, allegorical reading of this Talmudic passage, according to which Rabbi Yehoshua ben Levi was not risking his life at all.

The Chida explains that the Gemara's depiction of ראתן patients actually refers to spiritually "ill" individuals, who live without restraint, wantonly indulging in worldly delights. Their condition is called ראתן, the Chida explains, because אין להם אלא ראות עיניהם לפי שעה — they see only what is currently in front of them, the opportunities for fleeting physical enjoyment, without considering the long-term consequences of their behavior or setting for themselves loftier, more meaningful goals.

The majority of the *Amoraim*, the Chida writes, felt that people should stay away from these "patients," because their condition is "contagious" and can easily spread. Those who spend time in these individuals' company can easily be lured by their permissive, unrestrained way of life. Rabbi Yehoshua ben Levi, however, disagreed. He spent time with these people, teaching them in an effort to inspire them to change. He was not afraid of falling under their negative influence, because he fully trusted in the power of the sanctity of the Torah which he taught them to protect him from any potential spiritual harm.

According to the Chida, then, the Gemara's account has nothing at all to do with the question of whether one may risk his life for the sake of learning Torah with contagious patients. Rather, interestingly enough, this discussion relates to the oft-debated question surrounding outreach, whether it is appropriate to befriend and spend time with non-observant or insufficiently observant Jews in an effort to inspire positive change, or if the spiritual dangers of falling under their influence outweigh the potential benefits of reaching out to them.

Conclusion

The Gemara in several contexts states clearly that one should not put himself in a situation of considerable danger for the sake of a *mitzva*, and even for Torah study. It is told, however, that Rabbi Yehoshua ben Levi would learn with patients suffering from a serious, contagious illness. Different explanations have been offered for Rabbi Yehoshua ben Levi's conduct in this regard, but as a practical matter, it is clear that the concern to

---

21. *Kesubos* 77b.

protect human life — such as containing the spread of a dangerous virus — overrides even the precious *mitzva* of Torah study, and thus yeshivos acted correctly by shutting their doors in response to the coronavirus outbreak in 2020.

Yale Medicine

The Country Is Reopening—Now What?

May 20, 2020
By Joseph Piccirillo

Summer is here. Usually, the season comes with thoughts of beach days, ice cream, baseball, and day camp. But for many, the prospect of summer during the COVID-19 pandemic is met with an overall sense of anxiety and confusion—and questions.

Is the beach safe? The ice cream shop is open, but should I really go? And more importantly, how are we any better off, in terms of infection prevention and treatment, than we were in mid-March, when stay-at-home orders were first put into place?

In other words, why are we reopening now, and how do we make sense of it all?

"I think it is hard for all of us to wrap our heads around reopening," says Jaimie Meyer, MD, MS, a Yale Medicine infectious disease specialist. "There is nothing magically 'safe' about May 20, and very little difference in epidemiologic risk between May 19 and May 21. Only a public health approach that is data-driven will dictate a slow and measured reopening."

Reopening criteria confusion

Part of the confusion may lie in the number and scope of documents detailing the suggested criteria required for reopening the country. The White House has a protocol called "Opening Up America Again," the Centers for Disease Control and Prevention (CDC) has its own version, in addition to six one-page infographics, and some states, including Connecticut, have their own plans, some of which are more or less stringent than the White House's protocol.

The idea, in theory, is that once the state-specific version of the reopening criteria has been met, it will be safe to begin what's called a "phased reopening"—in other words, a gradual relaxing of some restrictions, as well as the opening of some businesses. With a phased reopening, state officials (working with county and local officials) are presumably able to monitor the number of COVID-19 cases, and can move forward with—or stop—further reopenings, or phases, based on changes in those case numbers.

But many states have opted to overlook federal criteria—or create their own smaller-scale benchmarks—and move forward with a phased reopening anyway, leaving it up to individuals to make their own decisions about when and how to venture outside safely.

Most Americans are worried about this. According to a recent Reuters national poll, 72% of adults in the United States said people should stay at home "until the doctors and public health officials say it is safe."

With that in mind, we spoke with Dr. Meyer, who provided answers to frequently asked questions about COVID-19, especially as it relates to the reopening of the country.

The interview has been edited for length and clarity.

Q. Why is it important to have a consensus on the criteria for reopening?
A. The purpose of having standards for a phased reopening is to ensure that the response is data-driven. I strongly believe that if criteria are not met, we risk an uptick in new cases and a setback in terms of progress with this disease.

Q. What does a data-driven public health approach to reopening look like?
A. Five things, really. **1) The presence of protective immunity.** There are a number of people (depending on where you live) who have now been infected with SARS-CoV-2, recovered, and have potentially developed antibodies against the virus. Although it's not clear yet whether these antibodies will completely protect them from reinfection, at what level and for how long, there is likely some protective immunity; **2) The ability for hospitals to care for patients.** As hospitals reduce their overload, they will have expanded capacity to care for people who become sick; **3) Adequate testing.** Testing is expanding (or should be) in most states, increasing the potential to identify people who are sick and isolate them; **4) Contact tracing.** This is also scaling up (or should be) in most states, increasing the potential to identify even more people who are infected and isolate them; and **5) Careful restrictions on social distancing, cleaning and disinfecting, and PPE [personal protective equipment] in public spaces**, all of which reduce the spread of disease. We need all of these components together to keep the curve going down and to prevent a second wave.

Q. Before a safe and effective vaccine is developed, is the goal to make the virus disappear or to let people get infected, but at slower rates that hospitals can keep pace with?
A. The goal of the combined public health measures I just mentioned is to reduce the number of new cases which, in turn, reduces the number of hospitalizations and the number of COVID-related deaths. No one can expect that these measures will "disappear" the virus, or that everyone will eventually become infected. The truth will likely lie somewhere in between, but only the data will tell us exactly where.

Q. How can we be sure that testing is accurate across all states?
A. It's hard to know. There are a wide variety of types of tests being used across health

systems, and they have varying degrees of sensitivity—meaning the ability to pick up 'true positives' for people who actually have the disease—and specificity, which is the ability to tease out 'true negatives' for those who do not have the disease.

Tests generally fall into three major categories: tests that look for the genetic material [RNA] of the virus; "antigen" tests that look for a particular part of the virus; and "antibody" tests that look for the human body's response to the virus.

Some of these tests have been fully vetted and validated before they were approved by the FDA [Food and Drug Administration], and others were authorized under an emergency use authorization [EUA] but have not yet been fully vetted and validated. We are really learning on the fly.

Q. Why is there still a delay in the number of tests being made available?
A. This relates to the capacity to collect the samples, availability of materials to run the tests (nasal swabs or liquid reagents to process the samples, for example), and certified labs to analyze the tests.

Q. The FDA issued two EUAs for at-home tests, one for a nasal swab sample and, more recently, one for a saliva sample. Does that mean we will be able to pick these up at a drug store for routine testing
A. Yes, home collection kits are likely headed our way. This is exciting because it will not only make the tests more widely available, but also reduce risks of exposure to health care workers that can happen during the collection process. But, I believe home collection kits will still need to be ordered by a health care provider instead of being available over the counter.

Q. What is contact tracing? If I am contacted, does that mean I have the virus?
A. Contact tracing is a way to identify those who have been exposed to people with confirmed cases of COVID so they can get tested—it's a key component of disease containment strategies. Departments of Public Health everywhere, including in Connecticut, are ramping up their ability to conduct contact tracing. They already have systems in place for other highly communicable diseases, such as syphilis, so I imagine it will operate in a similar way. If you are contacted, it means you had a potentially high-risk exposure to someone who was infected with COVID. This is not a reason to panic, but rather a reason to self-isolate and get tested.

Q. For how long will we have to wear masks?
A. We may have to have some sort of barrier protection for our faces, like cloth face coverings, until we have highly effective vaccines available.

Q. So, it could be for a while—years, even.
A. Yes.

Q. How does wearing a surgical mask or a cloth mask protect others if small particles carrying the virus can still get through?

A. I like to think of facial coverings as putting your thumb over a hose—some water may escape, but the major flow is blocked. Facial coverings like cloth masks prevent many particles from being disseminated into the environment, but not all. That is why we need social distancing and other prevention strategies, like hand washing and cleaning or disinfection, in addition to cloth masks.

Q. The six-foot physical distance is based on previous coronaviruses, correct? Is it enough? If I am around runners or people who are coughing a lot, should I move farther away?

A. Yes, that's true. If people are coughing, sneezing, or breathing heavily they may aerosolize more droplets, which may be propelled further. That is why we ask people who are sick to stay home, wear facial coverings, and remain socially distant.

Q. If you're running for a long distance behind someone, though, wouldn't that increase your risk? Is it better to move across the street?

A. There is no data on whether it is better to run behind, in front of, or to the side of someone while running. The best bet is to run at least six feet apart, regardless of the direction.

Q. There was a study in The New England Journal of Medicine (NEJM) about SARS-CoV-2 being in aerosols and remaining in the air for three hours. Is that the same as airborne transmission?

A. This means that once virus-coated droplets are sprayed into the air, they can remain there and survive for up to three hours. This facilitates airborne transmission of the virus from person to person, because that live virus can infect someone else if it enters their respiratory tract.

Q. Wouldn't that mean that we are all susceptible to potential infection in any enclosed space, even if we all wear cloth face coverings?

A. We have to be careful when we translate lab experiments into real-life scenarios. The experiment discussed above found that live virus could be recovered from aerosol for up to three hours, but it's not known whether the quantity is enough to actually cause infection in someone else.

As the state/country reopens, however, we know that better-ventilated spaces result in less distribution of the virus-laden droplets. This is the reason for states recommending reopening of outdoor spaces first, where transmission is less likely, especially with social distancing.

Q. That means that two families who are on separate blankets six feet apart

at the beach would be relatively safe, even if they stayed on their blankets for 8 hours or so, breathing in the same air.
A. Yes.

Q. Some people think they've already had COVID-19 in December or January. Is there a way for people to know if they had it? And if they did, do they have some immunity?
A. People who have COVID-19 (whether or not they were ever officially diagnosed) and recover often develop antibodies against the virus. Antibody tests have been developed but are problematic because of high rates of false negatives and false positives. So, right now it's not recommended that they be used to make individual decisions about personal health or safety. We suspect that antibodies will offer some protection from reinfection, but it's not known what level of antibodies is sufficient and how long that protection will last. So, we don't want people going out to get tested for antibodies and then feeling falsely assured that they are protected.

Q. When returning from the grocery store, is it really a smart strategy to wipe down packaged food with bleach wipes, or is it overkill? If a delivery driver with COVID sneezed on or near my cardboard Amazon package and then dropped it off on my doorstep and I picked it up immediately and opened the box, could I get sick?
A. I think we need to balance anxiety with practicality and safety. I suggest that people practice reasonable precautions. This means unpacking groceries/deliveries from their containers or boxes, washing hands, and wiping down countertops with bleach. Even though the virus can be found on cardboard for up to 72 hours, the NEJM article suggests viable [live] virus is probably on cardboard for closer to 8 hours. Your best bet is to wash your hands after handling potentially contaminated surfaces.

Q. Do we know how long someone is contagious when they're asymptomatic?
A. People can shed virus (and potentially infect others) for three to five days prior to developing symptoms. Those who don't develop symptoms at all can shed virus for approximately 14 days at high enough levels that they may be contagious to others. People can shed virus for weeks following recovery, but we think that this is either dead virus or virus at low enough levels that they are not contagious to others.

Q. In Connecticut, gatherings of 5 or fewer are OK, and most people have been sheltering-in-place for about two months. So, is it safe for one person to have an indoor visit with someone else if both have sheltered-in-placed

for two months and have not had any symptoms for 14 days?

A. Data from over 1,000 people hospitalized in a single week in New York showed that the majority of people infected and newly admitted were people who identified as "mostly staying home." The likely reason for this discrepancy was that there were gaps in home isolation behaviors—social visits with others, being in public spaces without face coverings or appropriate hand hygiene, interacting with others without taking precautions, etc. I know many people who would say they are fully isolated, but are still spending time in public spaces. So, if both people were truly isolated, it would be reasonable to have a visit without any additional risk. Ideally, people could get tested before they gather together.

Q. Some have missed a mammogram or a colonoscopy or a dental procedure, and they're afraid to go to the doctor. Is there a safe way to get these things done?

A. Over the next few months at Yale New Haven Hospital, we are looking towards reopening ambulatory services and elective procedures, as are places elsewhere that are on the downside of their COVID curve. I think telehealth will be with us for the foreseeable future at least to some extent. In the earliest phases of reopening, in-person care will likely be prioritized for urgent health concerns. But please don't miss your routine vaccines and health screenings as we move forward in reopening. General preventive healthcare remains important for long-term and overall health.

Q. What do you think needs to happen before you're confident that we can get this under control?

A. Expanded testing and contact tracing. Safe and effective vaccines. Effective treatment. All are on the horizon and scientists globally are working at a breakneck pace to make these a reality.

Q. Anything you want people to know as we start to reopen around the country?

A. People who have underlying health conditions that place them at higher risk of severe COVID-19 will need to practice precautions for the foreseeable future. I know everyone has COVID fatigue. We have message burnout, are tired of being home, and mourn our "regular" lives. But reopening must be paced and careful and responsive to data so that we don't backtrack.

Leaving Quarantine:
Going to Shul and Going to Work after "Reopening"

In late spring, 2020, after several months of government-ordered lockdown, restrictions gradually began to ease as the rate of COVID-19 infections slowed, hospitals were no longer overwhelmed by patients, and, more generally, it became clear that a complete lockdown could not continue until a vaccine or cure is ready.

For halachically observant Jews, the lifting of government restrictions does not necessarily represent the final word on the permissibility of resuming activities out of the house that expose one to other people, and thus, by extension, to the risk of infection. The Torah clearly requires us to avoid endangering our physical wellbeing,[1] and thus our willingness to expose ourselves to a degree of risk must be grounded in halachic sources. Even after health officials allowed "reopening," the question arose as to whether "reopening" was sanctioned by *halacha*, as well.

Rav Yehoshua Neuwirth, in his *Shemiras Shabbos Ke-Hilchasah*,[2] cites the Chafetz Chayim, in *Bei'ur Halacha*,[3] as warning that in consulting with a doctor to determine whether a patient should be permitted to eat on Yom Kippur, one must ensure that the doctor properly understands the gravity of the Yom Kippur fast. A doctor who is not an observant Jew, the Chafetz Chayim writes, might not properly appreciate the importance of fasting, and might therefore be too quick to determine that the patient should eat and drink on Yom Kippur. However, Rav Neuwirth writes, the opposite is also true. A doctor without a halachic awareness might not appreciate the extent to which *halacha* requires avoiding risk to one's physical wellbeing and demands the suspension of Torah law for the sake of maintaining good health. The commitment to protecting our health requires an especially strict standard, one that even medical professionals might not necessarily insist upon.

How, then, should we respond to the calls of health officials to relax restrictions during a pandemic? Can we follow their guidelines and allow ourselves to venture into

---

1. See, for example, Rambam, *Hilchos Rotzei'ach* 11:4. See also our discussion in *Headlines 2*, chapter 12, "Maintaining Good Health as a Halachic Imperative."
2. Chapter 39, note 15.
3. 618.

the public sphere despite the ongoing risk of infection, or are we halachically bidden to adhere to even stricter safety guidelines to protect ourselves?

I. Defining Halachic Danger[4]

The first question we will address is how *halacha* defines a "danger" that we are halachically mandated to avoid. What level of risk is too high to willingly expose ourselves to, and what level is considered acceptable, as part of normal living?

One in a Thousand

In a number of sources, we find a risk level of 1/1000th mentioned as an example of a far-fetched possibility of danger for which we need not be concerned.

One such source is a comment made by Rabbi Akiva Eiger, in one of his responsa,[5] regarding the case discussed by the Tosefta (*Mikvaos* 8:4) of a metal arrow lodged in person's leg. The *Tannaim* debate the question of whether the arrow would constitute a halachic חציצה (obstruction) that would disqualify the individual's immersion in a *mikveh* for the sake of attaining purity. The Rash Mi-Shantz, in his commentary to *Maseches Mikvaos,*[6] writes that Rabbi Yehuda Ha-Nasi, who does not regard the arrow as a חציצה, maintains that since removing the arrow poses a סכנה, the individual has no plans to remove it. As such, it has the status of אינו מקפיד — something that a person does not care to remove from his body, and which therefore does not have the status of חציצה. If, indeed, this is Rabbi Yehuda's view, Rabbi Akiva Eiger reasons, then we might be forced to conclude that the majority view, which does not permit the individual to immerse in this fashion, maintains that even something which is dangerous to remove constitutes a חציצה and disqualifies immersion. Rabbi Akiva Eiger dismisses this conclusion, asserting that the Rash Mi-Shantz uses the word סכנה to refer not to actual danger, but rather to a situation דאיכא כאב וצער טובא ואפשר על צד הריחוק אחת מני אלף דיצמח מזה סכנה — "where there is a great deal of pain and discomfort, and it is remotely possible, one in a thousand, that this could cause danger." If an object is truly dangerous to remove, Rabbi Akiva Eiger posits, then all agree that it does not constitute a חציצה, and the situation addressed here is one of a very remote "danger," like "one in a thousand."

According to Rabbi Akiva Eiger, then, a 1/1000th risk does not qualify as halachic danger.

---

4. Some of the information presented here appears also in *Headlines 2*, chapter 13: "Ebola: May a Doctor Endanger Himself by Treating Patients?"
5. *Mahadura Kama*, 60.
6. 10:8.

Similarly, the *Magen Avraham*[7] criticizes those who on Shabbos kill a certain insect called שממית which they consider dangerous and thus permissible to be killed on Shabbos, despite the prohibition against killing living creatures on Shabbos. The *Magen Avraham* writes that the chances of this insect posing a risk is one in a thousand, and this level of risk does not justify violating the Shabbos prohibitions.

The *Magen Avraham* makes a similar comment later,[8] in reference to the *Shulchan Aruch*'s ruling that although one may perform actions forbidden on Shabbos for the sake of helping a woman in labor, these must be done in an unusual manner. On the level of Torah law, one is considered in violation of Shabbos only if he performs forbidden actions in the usual manner; performing them in an unusual fashion is forbidden only on the level of rabbinic enactment. When tending to the needs of a woman in labor, the *Shulchan Aruch* writes, one should try as much as possible to avoid Biblical violations of Shabbos, by performing necessary activities in an unusual fashion. The *Magen Avraham* explains that אין אחת מאלף מתה מחמת לידה — not even one in one thousand women die as a result of childbirth, and so every effort must be made to lower the level of Shabbos desecration to that of rabbinic violations, given that the situation does not qualify as an actual סכנה.

Like Rabbi Akiva Eiger, the *Magen Avraham* uses the figure of 1/1000 as an example of a risk which does not meet the criteria of halachic danger.

How, then, does *halacha* define "danger"? By what standard do we determine when something is dangerous enough that it must be avoided for the sake of protecting our wellbeing, or serious enough to warrant violating Shabbos?

שומר פתאים ה׳

A surprising view on this subject is advanced by Rav Yaakov Ettlinger, in his *Binyan Tziyon*,[9] addressing the Gemara's discussion of certain kinds of women for whom pregnancy could be dangerous, either to the woman herself or to her nursing infant. According to the majority view among the *Tannaim*, these women are allowed to engage in intercourse, and are not allowed to use forbidden contraceptive devices. Despite the danger involved, this view permits ordinary intercourse, because, in the Gemara's words, "from the heavens they will receive compassion, as it says, שומר פתאים ה׳ ['God guards the fool-hearted'[10]]." This passage marks one of several contexts where the Gemara introduces the consideration of שומר פתאים ה׳ as a basis for permitting dangerous behavior and relying on God's protection.[11]

---

7.   316:23.

8.   330:3.

9.   137.

10.   *Tehillim* 116:6.

11.   See *Avoda Zara* 30b, *Shabbos* 129b, *Nidda* 31a.

Rav Ettlinger explains by drawing a fine distinction between situations where there is already a clear and present threat to life, and situations where a risk could potentially arise. For example, if an avalanche fell on Shabbos and we know somebody was present in the area, rescue work may be done on Shabbos even if it is questionable whether the individual is under the rubble, and it is questionable whether he is still alive if he is under the rubble.[12] Likewise, if a patient is seriously ill, then we violate Shabbos to protect against even a small risk to life, since this risk is already present. However, Rav Ettlinger writes, this does not mean that one must avoid situations which may expose him to a degree of risk. After all, *halacha* requires reciting ברכת הגומל to thank God after a trip through a desert or ocean,[13] clearly presuming that such journeys expose a person to danger, and yet nowhere do we find *Chazal* forbidding or even discouraging them. Since most desert or sea travelers arrive safely at their destination, such journeys are not considered dangerous situations, even though they could pose danger. By the same token, Rav Ettlinger explains, the Gemara permits intercourse for women who could be endangered by pregnancy, since this is not inherently a dangerous situation, even though it could result in a dangerous situation.

According to Rav Ettlinger, then, *halacha* draws a fine line between placing oneself in a situation of danger, which is forbidden, and placing oneself in a situation which could be dangerous, which is permitted, and it is regarding this second category that the Gemara establishes the principle of שומר פתאים ה'.

Rav Chaim Ozer Grodzinsky[14] remarked about Rav Ettlinger's theory, קשה לשקול במשקל סברות מחודשות במקום סכנה — it is hard to accord too much weight to novel ideas such as these when a risk to human life is at stake. Fine, abstract distinctions are legitimate, and could be compelling, in theoretical study and analysis, but in determining guidelines for avoiding danger, we cannot rely on such theories. Indeed, the consensus among the *poskim* does not appear to follow Rav Ettlinger's view, and it is commonly assumed that one must, indeed, avoid situations where the risk of danger lurks.

How, then, do we respond to Rav Ettlinger's proof from ברכת הגומל? Why is it not forbidden to go on trips which pose danger, if we are bidden to avoid risks to our physical wellbeing? And how do we explain the concept of שומר פתאים ה', which, as we saw, the Gemara enlists in several contexts as a basis for permitting potentially risky behavior?

This question was posed — without an answer — by Rav Malkiel Tzvi Tanenbaum of Lomza, in *Divrei Malkiel:*[15]

---

12.   *Shulchan Aruch*, O.C. 329:3.

13.   *Shulchan Aruch*, O.C. 219:1.

14.   *Achiezer*, 23:2.

15.   5:35.

הרי מצינו שיורדי הים צריכים להודות...משום דשכיחא סכנתא, ומ״מ ודאי מותר
לירד בים ולא מיקרי מאבד עצמו לדעת. ואם צריך לירד לים כדי לקיים איזה
מצוה בודאי מחוייב לירד ואסור לו למנוע משום חשש סכנה. הרי חזינן שמותר
להכניס א״ע בחשש סכנה היכא שאינו רק חשש בעלמא. ויש להאריך בזה ולבאר
הגבול לזה, אך אין העת מסכמת.

We find, after all, that sea travelers are required to thank [God upon
the safe completion of their voyage]…because danger is common [when
traveling by sea], yet it is certainly permissible to sail at sea, and this
is not considered knowingly killing oneself. And if one must travel by
sea to fulfill a certain *mitzva*, he is certainly obligated to travel, and it is
forbidden for him to refrain because of the possible danger. We thus see
that it is permissible to place oneself in a situation of possible danger, as
long as there is only a remote risk. Elaboration is needed to explain the
limits in this regard, but time does not allow.

מנהגו של עולם

The answer to this question is expressed by Rav Aryeh Leibush Lifshitz, in a responsum published in his *Sheim Aryeh*:[16]

ודע דאף בדברים שיש בהם סכנה, מ״מ בדבר שהוא מנהגו של עולם ודרך הכרח
אין לחוש, דהרי ארבעה צריכים להודות, וב׳ מהם הולכי מדברות והולכי ימים.
הרי דאיכא בהם סכנה, ומ״מ מותר לפרוש בספינה ולילך במדבר... ולמה לא
נאסור משום סכנה... אלא ודאי דבדברים כאלו אשר הם לצורך העולם אין איסור
כלל.

You should know that when it comes to things that entail danger —
nevertheless, if it is something which is the way of the world and a
necessity, there is no concern. After all, "four people are required to give
thanks," and two of them are desert travelers and travelers at sea. Thus,
they entail danger, and yet it is permissible to voyage out to sea and
to travel in the desert... Why do we not forbid [this] due to danger...
Rather, it is clear that when it comes to things such as these, which are
necessary for the world, there is no prohibition whatsoever.

Although traveling overseas and through deserts is considered dangerous, it is nevertheless permissible because it falls under the category of מנהגו של עולם — common
and conventional human activity. Societies establish which behaviors and activities
are acceptable despite their posing certain risks, and *halacha* does not forbid such

---

16. Y.D. 28.

activities. In modern times, for example, people travel by vehicles, trains and airplanes, despite the risks entailed, because these modes of transportation have been accepted by society as an essential part of day-to-day living.

This theory is also advanced by Rav Elchanan Wasserman, in *Kovetz Shiurim*,[17] where he explains that this is precisely the meaning of the halachic concept of שומר פתאים ה':

> צ"ל דאין האדם חייב להמנע ממנהג דרך ארץ, וממילא הוי כאילו אין בידו לשמור
> את עצמו, ואז נשמר מן השמיים. אבל היכא שבידו להזהר אינו בכלל פתאים,
> ואם לא ישמור את עצמו הוא מתחייב בנפשו ולא יהא משומר מן השמיים.

> We must explain that a person is not required to refrain from ordi-
> nary conduct, and hence one is considered unable to protect himself
> [with respect to ordinary activities], and he is then protected by God.
> But where one is able to be careful, he is not in the category of the
> "fool-hearted," and if he does not protect himself, he puts his life at risk
> and will not be protected by God.

Rav Elchanan establishes that dangerous activities which have become part of ordinary life are considered non-voluntary risks. Although one can, theoretically, avoid them, nevertheless, the very fact that such behaviors are societally accepted as necessities makes them unavoidable from a halachic perspective. The rule of שומר פתאים ה' means that in order for society to function, we have no choice but to engage in certain activities that pose a low level of risk, and *halacha* allows us to expose ourselves to such risks.

This concept was similarly formulated by Rav Shlomo Zalman Auerbach[18]:

> לעניין עיקר הדבר מה נקרא פיקוח נפש ומה לא, ועד איפה הוא הגבול, גם אנכי
> בעניי הסתפקתי טובא בזה. אלא שמצד הסברא נלענ"ד דכל שדרך רוב בני אדם
> לברוח מזה כבורח מפני הסכנה, הרי זה חשיב כספק פיקוח נפש... אבל אם אין
> רוב בני אדם נבהלים ומפחדים מזה, אין זה חשיב סכנה.

> As for the issue itself, what is considered "risk to life" and what isn't, and
> where the boundary lies, I, too, in my humility, have had many doubts about
> this. But logically, it would seem, in my humble opinion, that anything
> which most people normally run away from for the sake of escaping danger
> is considered a possible risk to life... But if most people are not frightened
> and afraid of something, then it is not considered danger.

If so, then we might conclude that indeed, the guidelines established by a country's

---

17.   *Kesubos*, 136.

18.   *Minchas Shlomo, Tinyana*, 37, ד"ה ולעניין.

health officials in an attempt to balance the need to avoid the risk of widespread infection against the need for a functioning economy, *ipso facto* become the halachically acceptable standard. To the extent to which these guidelines reflect society's accepted protocol for running an economy in the shadow of the COVID-19 pandemic, they determine the halachic definitions of danger in this regard. As such, going out into the public in accordance with health officials' safety requirements would be permissible under the rule of שומר פתאים ה׳.

II. Are Businesses More Important Than Shuls?

As the restrictions began to ease after a number of months of quarantine, many observant Jews reasoned, understandably, that if the government was allowing people to return to their offices, then certainly they must return to the synagogues. After all, if work is considered important enough to justify the risk of exposure to the coronavirus, then certainly תפילה בצבור, with the numerous *mitzvos* that we perform in the synagogue, justifies this risk.

In truth, however, there is a strong halachic basis to claim that to the contrary, we must adhere to stricter safety standards in the performance of *mitzvos* than in our pursuit of a livelihood.

אליו הוא נושא את נפשו

First, the Gemara in *Maseches Bava Metzia*[19] speaks explicitly of employees risking their lives to perform their work. The Torah[20] requires paying a worker on time, explaining, כי עני הוא ואליו הוא נושא את נפשו — literally, "for he is poor, and he makes his life dependent on it [his salary]." The Gemara explains the phrase אליו הוא נושא את נפשו to mean that employees put themselves in danger, such as by climbing trees to harvest fruits. Rav Eliezer Waldenberg[21] cites this Gemara as a basis for permitting physicians to put their health at risk by treating patients with contagious infections. Since doctors practice medicine for their livelihood, and, very often, their license requires treating contagious patients, such that their sustenance depends on their exposure to risk, this is allowed.

Rav Moshe Feinstein[22] similarly permits pursuing an athletic career for a living, even if the sport poses some degree of danger, citing the Gemara's aforementioned explanation of the verse ואליו הוא נושא את נפשו. As part of his discussion, Rav Moshe

---

19.   112a.

20.   *Devarim* 24:15.

21.   *Tzitz Eliezer*, 9:17 (*Kuntras Refu'a Be-Shabbos*, 5:9).

22.   *Iggeros Moshe*, C.M. 1:104.

references a famous responsum of the *Noda Be-Yehuda*[23] in which he forbids hunting for sport, due to both moral and safety concerns, but permits hunting for a livelihood, despite the dangers entailed. The *Noda Be-Yehuda* writes:

מי שהוא עני ועושה זו למחייתו, לזה התורה התירה כמו כל סוחרי ימים מעבר לים שכל מה שהוא לצורך מחייתו ופרנסתו אין ברירה, והתורה אמרה ואליו הוא נושא את נפשו.

Someone who is poor and does this for his sustenance — this the Torah allowed, as is the case regarding all merchants who sail overseas, since for all that is required for one's sustenance and livelihood, there is no alternative, and the Torah said, ואליו הוא נושא את נפשו.

Although the Torah forbids placing ourselves in situations in danger, it also recognizes that the necessities of human life require performing certain jobs that entail a degree of risk. Thus, similar to the principle of שומר פתאים ה', which, as we have seen, permits potentially risky activities that have become integral to day-to-day life, *halacha* permits working in jobs which expose the employee to some level of danger. When it comes to earning a livelihood, then, we may adhere to somewhat looser safety standards than we would allow in other realms of life.

גנאי למצוה

At the same time, we find sources stating explicitly that, counterintuitively, *mitzvos* require a stricter standard of safety than other areas.

The Gemara in *Maseches Pesachim* (116a) brings an opinion that the reason we eat *charoses* with *marror* at the *seder* is to avoid the risk of קפא — a toxic substance that, apparently, was present in herbs in ancient times. It was believed that the sweet *charoses* negated the harmful effects of this substance, and according to one view, this is the reason for eating *charoses* at the *seder*. Rabbeinu Yona[24] explains that although we eat *marror* throughout the year alone, without fear of the risk of קפא, nevertheless, when it comes to the performance of *mitzvos*, we must adhere to higher standards of safety.[25]

The *Leket Yosher*[26] (a disciple of the *Terumas Ha-Deshen*) explains similarly, and infers from this principle that one who lodges in a gentile's home during Chanukah should kindle just the minimum required one candle (as well as the *shamash*). He writes: שמא אחת למאה פעמים שיבוא סכנה ממנה והיה גנאי למצוה — "Perhaps, once in

---

23. *Mahadura Tinyana*, Y.D. 10.
24. Cited by the Rosh, *Pesachim* 10:25.
25. Rabbeinu Yona's words are: אבל טיבול שני שהוא של מצוה הזהירו חכמים שלא יהא בו חשש סכנה.
26. Chanukah, pp. 152–3.

a hundred times, danger will result from this, and **this would be a disgrace to the mitzva.**" Lighting multiple candles in a gentile's home might, on very rare occasions, arouse hostility, and thus the *Leket Yosher* rules that as a precaution, one should mini-mize the risk by lighting just one candle, satisfying the basic obligation and foregoing on the additional candles, which we light to enhance the *mitzva*.

Remarkably, these two *Rishonim* maintain that stricter safety standards are required while performing *mitzvos* than while conducting our regular affairs — to the point where, according to the *Leket Yosher*, we sacrifice the usual number of Chanukah candles in the interest of avoiding even a slight risk.

Many have raised the question of how to reconcile this view with the famous rule of שלוחי מצווה אינן נזוקין — performing a *mitzva* will not bring one harm. The Gemara in *Maseches Kiddushin* (39b) makes an exception in cases of high risk,[27] but when it comes to small risks, one need not fear harm when performing a *mitzva*. One application of this rule appears in *Maseches Pesachim* (8a), in regard to the search for *chametz* on the night before Erev Pesach. In principle, the Gemara states, one would be required to search even in crevices of walls where *chametz* might be present, despite the risk of being bitten by a deadly scorpion,[28] because of the rule of שלוחי מצווה אינן נזוקין. In practice, one does not search in crevices, due to the concern that he might spend extra time looking for small items which he had lost, and as this search does not fulfill a *mitzva*, the individual will not receive special protection. This clearly indicates that we receive greater protection, not less, while performing a *mitzva*, thus calling into question the claim of Rabbeinu Yona and the *Leket Yosher* that we must adhere to stricter standards of safety in the performance of *mitzvos*.

The simplest answer, as some have noted, is that a distinction exists between refraining from a *mitzva* due to potential risk, and ensuring to avoid even slight risks during the performance of a *mitzva*. The principle of שלוחי מצווה אינן נזוקין requires performing a *mitzva* even if it poses a small risk. However, in the performance of a *mitzva*, one must take precautions that are not necessarily required in other contexts, out of respect for the *mitzva*. And, according to the *Leket Yosher*, this means foregoing on enhancements to a *mitzva* if they pose even a small risk of danger.[29]

---

27. The Gemara gives the example of climbing an unsteady ladder to send a bird away from its nest in fulfillment of the *mitzva* of שילוח הקן.

28. The Gemara clarifies that it refers to the case of a wall with safe crevices where one may have stored bread, but the wall had since collapsed. Going through the rubble to search for the bread may expose one to the risk of a scorpion bite.

29. It should be noted that the *Chasam Sofer* appears to disagree with the *Leket Yosher* in this regard. In his commentary to *Maseches Pesachim*, the *Chasam Sofer* posits that שלוחי מצוה אינן ניזוקין applies to searching in crevices even if one has the option of hiring a profes-sional to search the crevices with special protective gear to guard against scorpions. The

One could argue, then, that during a pandemic, it is appropriate to apply stricter guidelines with regard to prayer than with regard to businesses. Performing *mitzvos* in a manner that exposes us to even a small degree of risk brings dishonor to *mitzvos*. Therefore, although we would certainly not refrain from a *mitzva* entirely to avoid a small risk of harm, we should be prepared to compromise our standards of *mitzva* performance, and settle for the bare minimum requirements — similar to a single Chanukah candle each night of Chanukah — to avoid a slight possibility of danger. Conceivably, this might mean praying privately in one's home, fulfilling the *mitzva* of daily prayer at the minimum standard, rather than expose oneself to a small risk of infection for the sake of fulfilling the higher standard of תפילה בציבור (public prayer).

Another factor to consider is the Gemara's ruling that despite the rule of שלוחי מצווה אינן נזוקין, one does not search the crevices for *chametz* in such a case, given the likelihood that he might afterward search for lost objects, thus exposing himself to danger. Applying this conclusion to prayers during the COVID-19 pandemic, attending the synagogue clearly lends itself to socialization before and after the service, when no *mitzva* is being performed. If we compare the risk of COVID-19 infection to the risk of a scorpion bite in the situation described by the Gemara,[30] then this consideration could suffice to forbid public prayer.

Food but Not *Sefarim*

This counterintuitive perspective, regarding one's livelihood as a matter of greater urgency than *mitzvos*, is reflected in a responsum by Rav Moshe Feinstein[31] addressing the situation of Israeli soldiers assigned to patrol a border on Shabbos to guard against enemy attack. While patrolling in a vehicle is undoubtedly allowed on Shabbos due to the obvious security needs, the question arose as to which provisions the soldiers may bring with them into the jeep.[32]

---

rule of מצוה בו יותר מבשלוחו, which the Gemara discusses in *Maseches Kiddushin* (41a), establishes that although certain *mitzvos* can be fulfilled through an agent, one fulfills the *mitzva* at a higher standard by performing the act himself. The *Chasam Sofer* writes that the added value of personal performance assures one protection from danger to which he exposes himself by choosing to perform the *mitzva* himself, rather than hire a professional. In direct contradistinction to the *Leket Yosher*, the *Chasam Sofer* maintains that one should not compromise the standards of *mitzva* performance for the sake of safety concerns (assuming, of course, that the risk is low).

30. One could, however, counter that if one follows the health officials' guidelines — wearing a mask, maintaining a distance, and ensuring ventilation in the synagogue — the risk of infection becomes much lower than the risk described by the Gemara.

31. *Iggeros Moshe*, O.C. 5:26.

32. As Rav Moshe notes in his responsum, bringing provisions into the jeep poses two poten-

Rav Moshe references the Mishna's discussion in *Maseches Rosh Hashanah* (22a) regarding witnesses who come to Jerusalem to testify about the sighting of the new moon.[33] The Mishna cites a verse[34] indicating that witnesses are permitted to violate Shabbos, if necessary, to travel to Jerusalem for this purpose, and the Mishna adds that if they must travel a long distance, they may bring with them a day's worth of food, despite the Torah prohibition against carrying through a public domain on Shabbos. Rav Moshe explains that although most people do not endanger their lives by abstaining from food for one day, nevertheless, the witnesses are permitted to violate Shabbos by bringing food with them given the small risk involved in embarking on a long journey without food provisions.

By the same token, Rav Moshe writes, soldiers who spend long shifts patrolling the border on Shabbos may take with them a normal day's worth of food. However, he adds, they are not allowed to take with them anything else — not even *siddurim* for *davening*, not to mention Torah learning materials. They may bring into the jeep only normal food provisions — despite the fact that, in all likelihood, they would not suffer any harm by refraining from food during this period — but they may not take *siddurim* with which to *daven*.

Returning to the "reopening" after the COVID-19 quarantine, while it is understandable why people felt uncomfortable applying tighter restrictions to synagogues than to businesses, there is a valid basis for doing so. Earning a livelihood to obtain one's basic needs is considered a more urgent necessity than praying with a *minyan*, and thus, at least in principle, we would not in any way be disrespecting our synagogues, or the institution of תפילה בצבור, by praying at home out of safety concerns despite going to work.

Conclusion

According to numerous *poskim*, the kind of danger which *halacha* requires avoiding is one which is considered irresponsibly risky by accepted societal norms. It thus stands to reason that guidelines issued by the health officials appointed by a democratically elected government, which reflect the general consensus regarding appropriate safety precautions, determine the parameters of permissible and forbidden activity even with respect to *halacha*. During a pandemic, then, restrictions issued by health officials

---

tial halachic problems: weighty objects cause the engine to burn more fuel, in violation of the prohibition of הבערה (burning on Shabbos); and bringing them beyond 2000 *amos* (3,000–4,000 feet) in an unpopulated area violates the restrictions of תחום שבת (the restrictions on where one may travel and bring objects on Shabbos).

33. In ancient times, new months were declared by the High Court in Jerusalem after hearing testimony from two witnesses who saw the new moon. The night of the sighting was then declared as the onset of the new month.

34. אלה מועדי ה׳ אשר תקראו אותם במועדם (*Vayikra* 23:37).

should be treated as halachically binding, and activities permitted by health officials are halachically permissible.

Such guidelines are perfectly acceptable even if they call for tighter restrictions regarding synagogue prayer than they do for professional and commercial activities, as there is ample halachic basis for demanding stricter safety standards in the performance of *mitzvos* than in the pursuit of a livelihood.

INTERVIEWS

Rav Aharon Sorscher

Interviewed on *Headlines with Dovid Lichtenstein*, 22 Iyyar 5780 (May 16, 2020)

There are a lot of other areas where if we would do something which would be considered a great toll on society, it would definitely save lives. If we would decide that any houses with wood would be outlawed, and houses have to be made with just concrete and metal, this would probably save lives, because houses wouldn't catch fire. But this would be a tremendous inconvenience. If we lower the speed limit to 25 miles per hour, we would probably save lives.

If you're doing something which *halacha* considers dangerous, this is an איסור חמור [grave prohibition]. But in the normal course of regular living, the chances of something happening to each person individually is low, though the cumulative effect costs lives. This would not necessarily be halachically considered a סכנה (forbidden danger). In the case of driving, when you drive 65 miles per hour on the highway, the chances of anything happening at this particular time are very small. It's more the cumulative effect. And the same is true of houses.

When you have an active pandemic, this is something which is an extraordinary event, and it is halachically considered a סכנה. You have to take unusual measures in order to contain the pandemic. But once the *halacha* considers it a normal thing, then it wouldn't be within the boundaries of normal השתדלות [effort to care for ourselves] to do unusual things — like having every man, woman and child stay home, and having all businesses remain closed.

For the most part, people got the coronavirus when it was undetected and uncontrolled — when they were going to weddings, Purim parties, large gatherings, and so on. Of course, as long as the virus is still around, we have to tone down large gatherings, conventions, weddings, ball games, whatever it is. This is going to take a long time. On the other hand, there comes a point where we need to get back to the business of living. Children need to go to school, *bochrim* need to go to yeshiva, people need to *daven*, people need to go to *shiurim*, and people need to work. We need to make a number of modifications in all these things to make it as safe as possible. The question becomes, where is the point where we say there is an active pandemic and we need to take extreme measures, and when do we say that although we can't go totally back to normal, we do appropriate השתדלות with some mitigation and this is good enough. This is the very weighty decision to be made by *gedolei Torah*.

פקוח נפש [risk to life] is not defined statistically. There are going to be inconsistencies with regard to statistics in *halacha*'s definition of *pikuach nefesh*. This is because part of what *halacha* deals with is what is considered normal, and what is considered abnormal. Some acts are considered a necessary part of living, and some acts are considered an aberration, which we would be more inclined to forbid. The *Noda Be-Yehuda* has a *teshuva* about hunting, and he discourages it, saying it's dangerous, but if there's a poor person who needs to hunt for *parnasa*, we allow him more leeway, as opposed to somebody who is doing it just for sport, for whom we are not going to allow even smaller amounts of danger.

Halacha says that you may not go on a sea voyage by ship within three days of Shabbos, because this close to Shabbos you need to be thinking about Shabbos, and you might have to be מחלל שבת on the ship. The *Magen Avraham* writes that people do not observe this *halacha*, and they go on ships within three days of Shabbos, and he explains that they prepare themselves [mentally] such that they will not be מחלל שבת when things come up on the ship. This is a very difficult *Magen Avraham*. It sounds like he makes the problem even worse — not only are they going on a ship within three days of Shabbos, but then, when some danger arises, they aren't מחלל שבת to protect themselves, as they should. Rav Moshe Feinstein discussed this *Magen Avraham*, and he did not like the answer that if one brought the danger upon himself then he cannot be מחלל שבת. He said it makes no difference. He explained that whether a situation is called a סכנה such that you can be מחלל שבת really depends on the subjective interpretation of each person. It's not an objective thing. When you have grey areas, a person thinks it's a סכנה, then we allow him to be מחלל שבת. But if he does not see it as a סכנה, then he is not מחלל שבת. The *Magen Avraham* is saying that people who might have considered it a סכנה, since it would then be forbidden for them to go on the ship within three days of Shabbos, kind of strengthen themselves in their minds so they do not consider it a סכנה. The *Chazon Ish* said something similar — that when you have something which is pretty hard to decide [whether or not to consider it a סכנה], it really depends on the person. If he is a cautious person, a nervous type, and he feels uncomfortable, then for him it is not considered מנהגו של עולם ["the way of the world"], and so he is allowed to be מחלל שבת. But if somebody else considers this part of daily living, then for him it is not a סכנה. Of course, this is only in grey areas. Some things are a סכנה no matter what, and if somebody doesn't think so, then בטלה דעתו אצל כל אדם [his perspective is outweighed by the perspective of the vast majority of people]. And, there are things which are certainly not dangerous, and if one is nervous about it, then בטלה דעתו אצל כל אדם. But in grey areas, it depends on each individual's perception.

However, society's perception is also a factor. In ancient times, sailing on a rickety boat was normal, so it wasn't a סכנה. For us, in our society, going on such a ship would be a סכנה, because we have better boats. The same is true about houses. We should not be living in the kinds of houses they had long ago, because in our society, such houses are considered dangerous. We must ensure to take safeguards which are deemed appropriate in our society.

So, when we are looking at the pandemic as an aberration, as something extraordinary, it requires extreme measures which everyone is required to follow. But when it reaches the point where you say, "Look, this is life," then we have to do some mitigation, or a lot of mitigation, but it is impractical in the long-term to keep people home. The economy needs to run — this isn't just about becoming rich and prosperous; you need food and healthcare to survive, you need money and you need an economy, so at a certain point it becomes the "new normal." I cannot give a *psak* as to what that point is. For this you need the שיקול הדעת [careful consideration] of leading *poskim*.

People going out and not keeping social distancing rules — I would think this is wrong. But to me it seems that the time has come to allow *Klal Yisrael* to start again — not to have hundreds of people, or even tens of people, together without mitigation, but with appropriate mitigation, it would seem that the time is right, but it's up to the *gedolei ha-poskim* to give their *psak*.

Rav Avraham Cohen

Interviewed on *Headlines with Dovid Lichtenstein*, 22 Iyyar 5780 (May 16, 2020)

I would say that in regard to reopening, the government must make a decision which way more lives can be saved, and which way more lives would be lost. This is the question of how we keep 30 million people out of work. These are 30 million people who might not be able to pay their bills, who might be suffering. This decision is much different than the decision of whether we should go to shul. When it comes to whether to go back to having *minyanim* and opening yeshivos — our standard is much higher. The criteria used for opening up the country are not the same for opening up yeshivos. Our standard is: why would we take a chance of losing נפש אחת בישראל [a single Jewish life]?

We are much stricter than anybody else when it comes to פקוח נפש. The *Chazon Ish* would tell people to visit patients in the hospital even if this required some חילול שבת because patients with visitors get better medical attention. Why compare our decision to what society is pushing to do? *Halacha* says to be very stringent when it comes to פקוח נפש. There is nothing more important today than to save נפש אחת מישראל. I don't know why we're comparing to what the rest of society is doing. We're talking about possibly saving people's lives.

Are we really going to be able to enforce social distancing in shul? We're going to open up a shul, and we're going to take the first 20 people who sign up. And what happens when 24 people show up? What are we going to do? We're going to tell them to leave? And then somebody refuses to leave — then what? We're asking for issues that we really won't be able to control.

My suggestion is to follow the best medical advice of the day and err on the side of caution. The government has their issues they need to deal with. But our situation is one of פקוח נפש, and we need to be very careful.

Is Reopening an Economy Worth the Lives of Its Workers?

May 7, 2020
By Jabari Simama

Public officials often must make life and death decisions, and rarely has that been more true than now that the coronavirus has disrupted our financial, physical and emotional lives. But in moving to rev and open up state and local economies, they should not be guided by economics alone. They must also be guided by moral values and a belief that all of human life is precious.

On the state level, governors, presumably after consulting with professional staff, will make the call on what and when businesses can reopen and when to end social distancing. In their deliberations and public statements, I have been deeply disturbed by some casually equating the life of our economy with the lives of human beings. I am uncomfortable with the notion that it is acceptable to endanger the health of workers, so many of whom are low-wage employees who have to interface directly with the public. If these workers were to become infected with COVID-19, they would run a serious risk of, in turn, infecting their families and communities. The painful cycle of closing down communities would start over again, but how many more would have died unnecessarily?

In my home state of Georgia, Gov. Brian Kemp was slow to order residents to stay home and non-essential businesses to close, although Atlanta and some other cities mandated those steps much earlier. And last week Georgia became the first state to begin moving to reopen its economy despite lacking capacity for widespread coronavirus testing or a plan to address the social determinants of health. No one would suggest that COVID-19 has been defeated in Georgia: Over the first two days after the governor partially lifted the lockdown, the state reported about 1,000 new confirmed coronavirus cases per day and two dozen deaths.

Kemp allowed restaurants to resume dine-in service and certain other businesses, including hair and nail salons, gyms, bowling alleys, and massage and tattoo parlors, to reopen under conditions that seem impossible to enforce and unlikely to effectively keep the virus from spreading. Recently I read about a reopened restaurant in the exurbs of Atlanta that requires staff to wear faceguards along with gloves and masks.

The optics of this are of customers dining in a hazardous bio lab with servers wearing hazmat suits. It would be comical were it not sadly necessary. This picture, alone, suggests that these businesses probably should not be open at this point.

It's not that the public is demanding that their communities' economies be restarted now. In a recent University of Georgia poll, 62 percent of Georgians said Kemp was moving too fast to reopen the state, while only 10 percent opposed the statewide lockdown. And nationally, a recent Axios-Ipsos poll found that 88 percent of Democrats and 56 percent of Republicans were concerned about their communities opening too soon.

Since Georgia began its partial reopening, at least a dozen other states have moved to follow suit and others plan to do so soon. With all the unknowns, why are states willing to risk undermining the progress they've made over the past two months in flattening the curve of the virus? The answer seems to be driven by several factors. One is strong influences from business leaders who don't want to see the economy shut down for too long and profits to continue to plummet. And, sadly, some of the groups most negatively impacted by the virus are minorities, low-wage earners, sick elderly people, and those with underlying health conditions, groups that have always been considered by some to be superfluous to the American economy. Finally, the political fallout of entering a national election in November with high unemployment and low GDP is nothing any party in power would want.

The future will reveal much about the true soul of America. It will tell us who we really are at heart. Will more public officials prematurely reopen their economies, sending desperate, helpless workers onto the frontlines of the virus, risking spreading it to their families and communities? Or will they follow the advice of scientists, doctors and other professionals who have been dealing with the pandemic up close and personal?

As public officials answer these questions, they must prioritize people over profits. They must make sure that when they decide how to proceed in this crisis they do so with an understanding that life is precious and that at the end of their days of public service they will have only their good names to take with them.

Governing's opinion columns reflect the views of their authors and not necessarily those of Governing's editors or management.

The Economy as a Matter of Life-and-Death:
Reopening Businesses During a Pandemic

As the COVID-19 pandemic of 2020 lingered beyond the one or two-month period to which people had hoped it would be confined, governments around the world that had imposed a lockdown began recognizing that the time had come to reopen their nations' economies. The dire need to contain the rate of coronavirus infection needed to be balanced against the dire need for society to function, and thus the decision was made to "reopen," each nation and each state at its own pace and with its own guidelines.

Painful as it is to say, this decision effectively ensured that more people would get sick and more people would die. Indeed, the numbers of infections and deaths in most countries and states spiked at some point after reopening. Government officials were undoubtedly aware of this eventuality, but they viewed the inevitable, tragic consequences of reopening as a price that needed to be paid for the sake of resuming economic activity.

How would the Torah approach this question? If the government would set out to reach a decision about reopening based on *halacha*, which decision would it reach?

It goes without saying that *halacha* regards human life as sacred, and protecting even a single life takes precedence over virtually all Torah laws, with very few exceptions. Instinctively, then, we might assume that a government may not enact any policy that will result in increasing the spread of a fatal illness.

However, many proponents of reopening have argued that the economy is also a matter of life death. Widespread joblessness and poverty are no less dangerous a condition than widespread illness, and could be just as deadly, leading to suicide and violence.

Interestingly enough, a number of sources in Torah literature quite clearly concur with this viewpoint, and point to a nation or community's overall economic health as a "life-and-death" matter.

דוחקא דצבורא

One such source is the Gemara's discussion in *Maseches Gittin* (45a) regarding the case of captors who demand an exorbitantly high amount as ransom. The Mishna states: אין פודין את השבויין יתר על כדי דמיהן מפני תיקון העולם — "Captives are not ransomed for more than their value,[1] for the betterment of the world." The Gemara proposes two possible explanations for the phrase מפני תיקון העולם in this Mishna, for why refusing to pay an unreasonable ransom achieves "the betterment of the world." According to one view, this refers to דוחקא דצבורא — financially crippling the community. As important as it is to release the captive, even this urgent matter does not justify subjecting the community to economic ruin. The second view understands the Mishna to mean that overpaying to ransom a captive incentivizes additional kidnappings, and is therefore not allowed.

The Gemara adds that the practical difference between these two explanations of the Mishna involves a situation where a certain wealthy family has the means to pay the exorbitant ransom demanded by the captors. If the prohibition stems from the concern of crippling the community, then we would allow the family to pay the ransom, as this will have no effect on the community's overall economic condition. But if the reason is to avoid incentivizing kidnapping, then we would not permit this family to free the captive. The Rambam[2] and the *Shulchan Aruch*[3] accept the second reason, that overpaying is forbidden so as not to encourage the kidnappers to continue this evil enterprise.[4]

The *Chasam Sofer*, in one of his responsa,[5] raises the question of why the concern of דוחקא דצבורא would justify refraining from ransoming a captive. The *Shulchan Aruch*[6] lists four Torah prohibitions that one transgresses by ignoring the plight of a captive, most notably, the famous prohibition of לא תעמוד על דם רעך — failing to save an endangered person's life when in a position to do so.[7] And the Rama[8] rules that although *halacha* does not require a person to pay more than one-fifth of his assets

---

1.   *Pischei Teshuva* (Y.D. 252:5) cites two different opinions as to the definition of כדי דמיהם ("their worth"). One opinion explains this to mean the sum for which the captive would be sold on the slave market, even after slavery has been abolished, whereas others maintain that this refers to the sum for which gentile captives would normally be ransomed.

2.   *Hilchos Matanos Aniyim* 8:12.

3.   Y.D. 252:4.

4.   We elaborated on this *halacha* in the first volume of *Headlines*, chapter 23: "Many Terrorists for One Israeli? The Gilad Shalit Deal Through the Prism of Halacha."

5.   C.M. 177.

6.   Y.D. 252:2.

7.   *Vayikra* 19:16. The other three prohibitions listed by the *Shulchan Aruch* are: לא תאמץ את לבבך (Devarim 15:7); ולא תקפוץ את ידך (ibid.); and לא ירדנו בפרך לעיניך (Vayikra 25:53).

    The *Shulchan Aruch* writes that ignoring a captive also constitutes the neglect of four affirmative commands: פתוח תפתח את ידך לו (Devarim 15:8); וחי אחיך עמך (Vayikra 25:36); ואהבת לרעך כמוך (Vayikra 19:18); and הצל לקוחים למות (Mishlei 24:11).

8.   O.C. 656.

for the sake of performing a *mitzva*, one must be prepared to sacrifice all his property when necessary to avoid transgressing a Torah prohibition. Seemingly, then, as the Torah forbids refraining from freeing a captive, a community must be prepared to bear any financial burden necessary to bring about a captive's freedom. Why, then, does one opinion explain the prohibition against paying an exorbitant ransom as predicated on the concern of דוחקא דצבורא?[9]

The *Chasam Sofer* answers by referencing a brief comment of the Rosh[10] stating that maintaining general economic welfare is a matter of הצלת נפשות — saving lives. The context of the Rosh's discussion is the question of whether a charity fund may redirect resources which had been donated for Torah education, for the sake of paying the heavy taxes imposed by the government. The Rosh ruled that since many community members would be unable to meet the tax requirements, this qualifies as הצלת נפשות, thus allowing the diversion of charity money to this cause. If so, the *Chasam Sofer* writes, then we can understand why the Sages forbade communities to pay outrageous ransoms — because crippling an entire economy is treated by *halacha* as a threat to life. And when we face an unfortunate situation that forces us to make a choice between communal "life" and an individual life, the former takes precedence.[11] As such, we do not force — or even allow — a community to impoverish itself for the sake of ransoming a captive.

These responsa of the Rosh and *Chasam Sofer* provide a strong halachic basis for the notion that closing an economy qualifies as a threat to life.

Still, one might distinguish between the case of an outrageous ransom and the government's decision to open the economy. When it comes to rescuing a captive, the choice is whether or not to impoverish the public to rescue one person, and in such a

---

9.   The *Chasam Sofer* himself, in his notes to the *Shulchan Aruch* (O.C. 656), disputes the Rama's ruling, and contends that the distinction lies not between affirmative commands (מצוות עשה) and prohibitions (מצוות לא תעשה), but rather between forbidden actions (קום ועשה) and forbidden inaction (שב ואל תעשה). A forbidden action — whether it is forbidden by force of a מצוות עשה or a מצוות לא תעשה — must be avoided even at the expense of all one's assets, whereas an obligatory action — whether it is required to fulfill a מצוות עשה or to avoid violating a מצוות לא תעשה — must be performed only if it does not necessitate spending more than one-third of one's assets. According to this view, of course, it is clear that the prohibition against ignoring the plight of a captive does not require paying crippling costs. In his responsum, the *Chasam Sofer* clarifies that he poses this question under the assumption of the Rama's position, that one must sacrifice all his property to fulfill an action required by a מצוות לא תעשה.

10. Responsa, 6:2. (The *Chasam Sofer* identifies as his source the Rosh's work on *Maseches Bava Basra*, but annotated editions indicate that the correct source is the Rosh's responsa.)

11. In the essay referenced above, note 4, we elaborated on the issue of whether we should sacrifice a captive's life for the sake of protecting many lives.

case, *halacha* forbids causing widespread financial harm for the sake of the captive. In the case under discussion, however, the economy had been shut down to prevent the infection's spread, and the decision is whether to restart economic activity in a manner that will, undoubtedly, result in deaths. Reopening the economy during a pandemic actively causes death, and one might therefore argue that although we do not sacrifice general economic stability to save a life, we should not endanger lives for the sake of resuming economic stability.

Waging War for *Parnasa*

In truth, however, we find sources that justify even proactively endangering lives for the sake of public economic welfare.

The Gemara in *Maseches Berachos* (3b) tells of King David's advisors informing him of the kingdom's economic troubles: אדוננו המלך, עמך ישראל צריכין פרנסה — "Our lord, the king, your nation Israel needs sustenance." King David responded that the army should wage war in order to seize the resources which the population needs.

This account clearly indicates that waging war — which, by definition, endangers lives — is justified when necessary for the sake of economic stability. If war is the only answer to a shortage of resources, then it is allowed, despite the sacrifice of life entailed. As leader of the nation, the king has the authority to weigh the costs and benefits of different possibilities and determine the course of action that best serves the population's overall interests. If sacrificing lives through warfare is needed for the sake of maintaining a viable economy, then the king has the authority to order the army to wage war.[12]

During the coronavirus pandemic, too, it would seem that the government is indeed authorized to make the decision that restarting the economy is worth the unfortunate loss of life that would likely result. *Halacha* regards a nation's financial health as a matter of life-and-death, as discussed above, and, moreover, the government is charged with the responsibility to weigh the cost of an ongoing state of economic crisis against the cost of life incurred by the renewed spread of the deadly virus after reopening. Just as David determined that the kingdom's economic needs were worth the tragic costs of warfare, similarly, a government can decide that the country's economic needs are worth the tragic cost of a spike in coronavirus infections.[13]

---

12.   Significantly, however, the Gemara adds that after David gave the order, permission to wage battle was obtained from both the *Sanhedrin* and the *Urim Ve-Tumim* on the *Kohen Gadol*'s breastplate, because the decision to wage war requires authorization from these two institutions. A thorough exploration of the conditions that must be met to allow initiating military conflict lies beyond the scope of our discussion.

13.   It must be emphasized that this discussion relates entirely to the government's decision of

Conclusion

A number of halachic sources indicate that a nation or community's general economic stability is to be treated as a "life-and-death" matter, such that, conceivably, the government is authorized to enact a policy that will result in the loss of life for the sake of maintaining overall economic health. It would thus appear that governments were permitted to reopen their economies during the COVID-19 pandemic, despite the spike of infections this would inevitably cause, in order to protect their constituencies from economic ruin.

---

whether or not to reopen. The question of how each individual should conduct himself after reopening is discussed in this volume in a separate chapter, "Leaving Quarantine: Going to Shul and Work After 'Reopening.'"

THE CANADIAN JEWISH NEWS

CJN

The Kiddush Clubs Are All Right (Wait, are they?)

September 7, 2017
By Ron Csillag

It's precisely 10 a.m. on Shabbat at Toronto's Beth David B'nai Israel Beth Am synagogue, and it's time to take out the Torah scrolls. As the Ark is opened, about 30 worshippers – mostly men, but some women – rise, leave the sanctuary and make their way to a boardroom in the basement. Awaiting them is a long table covered with paper plates full of gefilte fish, three kinds of herring, sponge cake and cookies.

But attention is focused on several bottles at the end of the table. There's Havana Club white rum, Crown Royal Canadian whisky, Sabra liqueur and a single malt scotch from Islay. These are soon joined by a frosted bottle of vodka from the freezer.

In a scene repeated at other Canadian synagogues that have kiddush clubs (as opposed to a Kiddush for the whole congregation at the end of services), alcohol is poured into one-ounce plastic cups, a blessing is recited and the drinks are downed. Some members have another. An announcement or two is made and small talk ensues, until everyone makes his or her way back to the sanctuary within 30 minutes.

Proponents of kiddush clubs like this one say it is a harmless activity that breaks up the service with a little l'chaim and some camaraderie. They also point out that the clubs raise a lot of money for charities and the synagogues themselves.

But detractors note a dark side: that worshippers leaving mid-service for a belt is profoundly disrespectful to the synagogue and the sanctity of the proceedings (not to mention the clergy); that the clubs promote, and even glorify, the consumption of alcohol; and that they set a poor example for children, who may notice that some adults have booze on their breath and may act a bit loopy.

Some rabbis have dubbed congregants who come to synagogue solely for the drinks and food "JFKs" – Just For the Kiddush.

There's no question this is a sensitive subject. One Toronto rabbi queried for this article said his synagogue has a kiddush club, "but I'd rather not comment. It would be politically toxic for me."

Another rabbi who tried, unsuccessfully, to rid his synagogue of its several kiddush clubs agreed to be interviewed, but later changed his mind, saying this is "not a topic I'm comfortable discussing."

"There have been kiddush clubs in shuls for as long as there have been shuls," states the website of the International Kiddush Club (IKC), formed in North America in the early 2000s, as part of the International Federation of Jewish Men's Clubs.

Kiddush clubs meet "any time after Shacharit, after the Torah reading, before the Haftorah, after the Haftorah, before the sermon, after the sermon," the IKC explains. "There is no fixed time, just custom in each shul. A quick l'chaim, a little schmaltz herring on a (cracker), maybe some smoked fish or more. Then back to the service and Musaf, refreshed, well-fed and ready."

That rosy description was not shared by Toronto's Vaad Harabanim, which represents Orthodox rabbis. In a sharply worded statement issued last spring, the Vaad said kiddush clubs "should be a cause for concern throughout the entire Jewish community."

Beyond the halachic considerations of showing "blatant" disrespect to the synagogue and a bad example for kids, the clubs contribute "in a very real way to the growing crisis of alcoholism in the Jewish community," the Vaad said. They should take place after prayers, in a public area and be open to all, the rabbis stated.

The Vaad's statement came in response to the steps one large Toronto synagogue took to address the situation with its kiddush club. The shul's rabbi published an article decrying alcohol abuse in the community and the difficulties rabbis face countering "the contemporary sense of entitlement that underpins the kiddush club mentality."

At Montreal's Beth Zion Congregation, there are three kiddush clubs, noted synagogue president Shlomo Benarroch.

The one he's in provides a chance "for the guys to schmooze a bit and get a little break in the middle of davening."

Congregants, he said, tend to get antsy during a long service. "People can't sit in davening for three hours any more. People need a break. Davening needs to be broken up a bit." Besides, the kiddush club "adds a certain camaraderie," and raises money for the synagogue.

As for the alcohol, "when you have a mature group of people and they're acting like responsible adults, it doesn't get out of hand. I can't remember the last time we had an issue with somebody who had too much. It doesn't happen," Benarroch said.

Allen Richman, head of the kiddush club at Beth David synagogue, points out that the club has raised money for a variety of projects at the shul.

"We don't drink a lot," he said. "We're older people. Some people just come down for a minute, have a shot, or half a shot, and go back up."

Much of the criticism of kiddush clubs has come from the Orthodox community in the United States. It has been harsh and much more open than in Canada.

In 2005, the New York-based Orthodox Union (OU) called for an end to kiddush clubs, in response, it said, to a request from 65 pulpit rabbis and yeshiva principals.

It claims that missing the Haftorah reading leaves a void in the service for kiddush club participants. "The Haftorah," said the OU's then-executive vice president, Rabbi Tzvi Hersh Weinreb, "is the one opportunity during the Sabbath prayers to encounter the message of the prophets."

Besides "denigrating" the Sabbath prayer service, the clubs idealize alcohol consumption, Rabbi Weinreb went on. "This is particularly disturbing because it is emblematic of the larger dangers of alcohol consumption and substance abuse in our community."

He conceded that kiddush clubs are in a minority of Orthodox synagogues and their members are a minority of congregants. Still, in an article in OU's magazine, Jewish Action, titled, "Why Kiddish Clubs Must Go," Rabbi Weinreb warned that "we are at war against substance abuse and we are fighting for the koved beit haknesset (the honour of our shuls)."

The OU didn't keep track of the impact of its directive, "but it definitely raised people's awareness of the problem and there were quite a few rabbis and shul presidents who thanked us for our effort," Rabbi Weinreb told The CJN.

In a 2009 article in the New York Jewish Week entitled, "Choose Life, not Kiddush Clubs," three professors of pediatrics at Yeshiva University's Albert Einstein College of Medicine blasted kiddush clubs for providing "an implicit sanction for a form of covert drinking" and "a veneer of respectability and exclusivity, suggesting a 'coolness' about those individuals who are part of this private, select drinking group. These adults become the enablers of youth drinking."

And in 2011, Rabbi Shmuly Yanklowitz, an influential leader in the Open Orthodox movement, called kiddush clubs "destructive," "disrespectful" and "a terrible influence on children."

The Toronto Board of Rabbis has no position on kiddush clubs, said TBR president Rabbi Adam Cutler.

Kiddush clubs are "not the type of thing the Montreal Board of Rabbis would have a policy on," said MBR co-president Rabbi Mark Fishman. "Each shul decides its own, some in favour, some against, and grey in the middle."

Synagogue services are "more inviting when there's a bit of a recess at half-time," said Stan Greenspan, the Toronto-based president of the International Kiddush Club.

But the IKC's "real purpose," Greenspan stressed, is to raise money for the group's Tefillin Fund, which provides tefillin and mezuzot to those outside Canada and the United States who cannot afford them. To date, more than $70,000 has been raised for the Tefillin Fund.

The group recently sponsored a mission to Cuba, in which mezuzot were delivered to more

Stan Greenspan of Toronto, far left, with fellow members of the International Kiddush Club.

than 200 Jewish families. The IKC has also sent tefillin to Argentina, France, Spain and Hungary, Greenspan noted.

The IKC's annual convention in Washington, D.C., in July drew 600 people and fund-raising topped US$80,000 ($99,950), he said.

"The smart rabbis found out long ago that (kiddush clubs are) the prime location for any special fundraising drives for special projects or regular synagogue events," said Greenspan.

But one rabbi interviewed for this story called the money raised by kiddush clubs "debased."

Greenspan said the IKC treats alcohol consumption "seriously," but "in all my years of kiddush club attendance, I have rarely, if ever, seen someone become intoxicated, and any instances took place long ago, before societal changes in how we understand alcohol."

While it's hard to say kiddush clubs cause addiction, "to say they contribute to the problem is clearly a possibility," said David Kaufman, director of outreach and education at Toronto's Jewish Addiction Community Services (JACS).

"We have lots of young people who started out at kiddush clubs drinking more than their fair share and got hooked that way," Kaufman said. "To say that was the cause … it's complicated. The cause of addiction is complicated. But it certainly didn't help."

Kaufman said "numerous" rabbis have called him to discuss the issue over the years. "We do see it as a problem," he said.

Jewish values are "not supposed to be celebrating the whisky, but life," said Kaufman. "By saying a l'chaim, you don't reduce the risk of addiction. A l'chaim doesn't make it holy."

Alcohol Consumption — a Torah Perspective

The disgraceful phenomenon of the *"kiddush* club" — groups of men not-so-clandestinely leaving the sanctuary at a predetermined point in the Shabbos morning service to enjoy snacks with hard liquor — is not only horribly disrespectful to the shul, to the prayer service, and to the congregation, but also highlights a growing alcohol problem in the Orthodox Jewish world. Jews are increasingly indulging in drinking — and, most alarmingly of all, our drinkers' ages are getting lower.

Zvi Gluck, Director of the Amudim organization, which provides expert, comprehensive crisis management for Jewish families, and seeks to spread awareness in the Orthodox community about problems such as addiction and abuse, penned an op-ed for the *Baltimore Jewish Life* in 2018[1] lamenting some of the scenes that he observed while spending Sukkos in Jerusalem:

> While it was a truly remarkable and uplifting experience in so many ways, it was sadly tarnished by certain behaviors that I witnessed over Yom Tov.
>
> As I walked with my wife and children to and from meals…I could not believe the amount of drinking that was going on by the many students, both boys and girls, who are spending a year (or two or three) in *Eretz Yisrael*. They were being liberally supplied with drinks at meals and *kiddeishim*, and I cannot even begin to tell you how many of them I heard speaking openly about the amount of alcohol they had enjoyed, identifying the various bottles by brand, year and price. Some of the kids I saw had had so much to drink that they were literally stumbling over their own two feet trying to make their way home.
>
> …Things were exponentially worse on the last days of Yom Tov, particularly when it came to those who don't live in *Eretz Yisrael* who found themselves facing a 48-hour drinking bonanza. First they got plastered on Shemini Atzeres, joining Israeli shuls and families who were also

---

1.   "Taking a Stand Against Out of Control Drinking in Our Community…Because the Alcohol Keeps on Flowing," *Baltimore Jewish News*, October 16, 2018.

celebrating Simchas Torah on the same day. Then they enjoyed an encore alcohol binge on the next day, joining foreigners for their Simchas Torah celebrations and, once again, getting completely and totally bombed.

But wait, it gets worse. There was one location where well-meaning individuals set up second day *minyanim* for the *chutznikim*, but there was no supervision whatsoever. From that site alone there were over 25 students who were so drunk that they were rolling around on the floor. Six more kids from that location ended up hospitalized, two of whom had to have their stomachs pumped because they had alcohol poisoning.

It goes without saying that not every young adult who goes to study in Eretz Yisrael engages in this kind of destructive behavior. I witnessed beautiful Yom Tov celebrations...there was zero alcohol present, just true *simcha* that emanated from the hearts of everyone present as they experienced the pure joy of Yom Tov. I have no doubt that there were many other sober events throughout Eretz Yisrael and I applaud everyone who participated in those as well. But there is no question that there were way too many events where the alcohol flowed freely and multiple friends who spent Sukkos in different neighborhoods in Eretz Yisrael told me that they had seen exactly the same type of drinking that my family and I witnessed.

It is impossible for adults to protect children from irresponsible alcohol consumption without modeling responsibility and a generally healthy approach to the subject of alcohol. Let us, then, briefly examine the Torah's complex perspective on the enjoyment of drinking.

Pouring Wine like Water

On the one hand, as we all know, drinking wine on certain occasions is a strict halachic obligation. Wine is required for the *kiddush* recitation every Shabbos and Yom Tov;[2] we must drink four cups of wine at the *seder*; and a cup of wine is used at every *chupa*, *sheva berachos* and *bris*. *Chazal* required drinking ten cups of wine in a house of mourning after the funeral (*Kesubos* 8b), though this practice is no longer observed.[3] And, of course, the Gemara famously and startlingly rules in *Maseches Megilla* (7b)

---

2.   The generally accepted view is that while the *kiddush* recitation is required on the level of Torah obligation, the requirement of wine was enacted by *Chazal*. See *Tosfos, Pesachim* 106a, ד״ה זוכרהו; and *Tosfos, Nazir* 4a, ד״ה מאי היא. Some *Rishonim*, however, maintained that wine is required as a Torah obligation. See *Aruch Ha-Shulchan*, O.C. 271:1-4.

3.   See *Tur*, Y.D. 378.

that one is obligated to drink to the point of inebriation on Purim, an obligation codi-fied in the *Shulchan Aruch*.[4]

Beyond the halachic requirement to drink wine on certain occasions, we find sever-al passages extolling the value of wine in bringing happiness. Already King Shlomo taught in *Mishlei* (31:6), תנו שכר לאובד ויין למרי נפש — "Give a strong drink to one who is lost, and wine to those with embittered souls" — advising using alcohol as a means of soothing pain and grief. The Gemara in *Maseches Eiruvin* (65a) teaches that המתפתה ביינו — one who can be cajoled through drinking wine — resembles God, who was moved by the "scent" of Noach's sacrifice after the flood to promise to never again destroy the earth, essentially celebrating the value of wine in making people relaxed and more flexible. In another passage there in *Maseches Eiruvin*, the Gemara actually expresses criticism towards those who do not drink wine: כל שאין יין נשפך בתוך ביתו כמים אינו בכלל ברכה — "Anyone in whose home wine is not poured like water, is not included in the [Torah's] blessing…"

Wine and Calamity

By contrast, many sources in Torah literature sternly warn of the dangers of wine, and sharply condemn intoxication.

Already in the Chumash, we find intoxication associated with inappropriate behav-ior — Noach's inebriation resulted in his being shamed by his son (*Bereishis* 9:21–22), and Lot committed incest with his daughters on two successive nights as a result of drinking wine (*Bereishis* 19:33–35). And according to one opinion,[5] Nadav and Avihu were punished with death because they entered the *Mishkan* to offer incense in a state of inebriation. Indeed, the story of their tragic death is followed by the command forbidding *kohanim* from performing the service in the *Beis Ha-Mikdash* after drink-ing wine,[6] which itself seems to reflect a disapproving attitude towards drinking.

The Tosafists, in *Da'as Zekeinim*,[7] comment on this prohibition, and elaborate at great length on the evils of indulgence in alcohol. They write, על ידי שתיות יותר מדאי בושות וחרפות באות עליו — excessive drinking leads to embarrassing behavior. The Tosaf-ists proceed to cite King Shlomo's warning in *Mishlei*, אל תרא יין כי יתאדם[8] — which

---

4. O.C. 695:2. However, the Rama famously qualifies this ruling, citing the *Kolbo*'s position that one is required only to drink more than he is normally accustomed to. Later we will cite additional sources relevant to this *halacha*.

5. Rabbi Yishmael, cited by Rashi to *Vayikra* 10:2.

6. *Vayikra* 10:9.

7. *Vayikra* 10:9.

8. 23:31.

the Gemara[9] explains to mean, "Do not desire wine, for it leads to blood," referring to destructive conduct. The verse continues, כי יתן בכוס עינו יתהלך במישרים (literally, "it lends its color to the cup, and flows freely") — meaning, when one lusts after cups of wine, he will end up "walking straight" (יתהלך במישרים) in his home, because he will be forced to sell all his possessions to pay for his addiction, such that he will have nothing in his house.[10] *Da'as Zekeinim* later asserts that Adam's sin in *Gan Eden* was the result of drinking wine:

על ידי יין ששתה אדם הראשון בברכת נישואין שלו...נשתכר ועבר על צווי של מקום.

As a result of the wine which Adam drank over the *beracha* at his wedding…he became inebriated and violated the Almighty's command.

For this reason, *Da'as Zekeinim* suggests, some have the custom to announce, "*le-chaim*" before reciting a *beracha* over wine — because death was decreed upon mankind as a result of Adam's sin, which he committed because he drank wine. Before one drinks wine, we wish "*le-chaim*," praying that this drinking should lead to more life, and not the opposite.

The Gemara contains several stern warnings about the potential harm of wine. In *Maseches Berachos* (29b), we read that the prophet Eliyahu spoke to one of the Sages and urged him, לא תרתח ולא תחטי, לא תרוי ולא תחטי — "Do not be angry, and you will not sin; do not drink, and you will not sin." And in *Maseches Yoma* (76b), the Gemara interprets the word יין ("wine") as a reference to calamity,[11] and it interprets the alternate word for wine — תירוש — as a derivative of the term רש — impoverishment. The Hebrew words for wine, then, point to its potential to bring catastrophe and destitution. More famously, the Gemara in *Maseches Sota* (2a) comments that the laws of the *nazir* — one who vows to abstain from wine — are presented in the Torah following the laws of the *sota* (suspected infidel woman), to teach that הרואה סוטה בקלקולה יזיר עצמו מן היין — one who beholds the fate of an adulteress is advised to vow abstinence from wine. The Gemara here clearly links alcohol consumption with promiscuity. Rabbeinu Bechayei[12] explains that a *nazir* is commended for refraining from wine כי כל הנמשך אחריו נמשך אחר התאוות והוא מביא לידי חטאים ומכשולים רבים — "anyone drawn after

---

9. *Yoma* 76b.

10. *Da'as Zekeinim* also points out that the word כוס ("cup") in this verse is written כיס — "pocket." This alludes to the fact that while a customer "places his eye" (יתן עינו) upon wine, desiring to purchase more, the seller "places his eye" upon his כיס, his pocket, eager to make money on another sale.

11. Rashi explains that the Gemara here links the word יין with the phrase תאניה ואניה (*Eicha* 2:5) — wailing and mourning.

12. *Bamidbar* 6:2

it is drawn after desires, and it leads to many sins and stumbling blocks." Elsewhere,[13] Rabbeinu Bechayei writes, היין בטבעו מוליד שלשה דברים: שינה וגסות הרוח ובלבול השכל — "Wine naturally engenders three things: sleep, incivility and confusion of the mind."

Of course, there is no contradiction between these sources and the sources cited earlier extolling the virtues of wine. When consumed in appropriate, measured quantities, wine offers great benefits; but when one indulges excessively, wine is destructive.

The Gemara makes this point very clearly in *Maseches Sanhedrin* (70a), commenting on the verse in *Tehillim* (104:15), ויין ישמח לבב אנוש — "and wine that gladdens the heart of man." The word ישמח ("gladdens"), the Gemara observes, resembles the word ישמה — referring to causing madness and insanity (as in the word שממה — desolation). The Gemara thus teaches, זכה, משמחו, לא זכה, משממהו — if one uses wine properly, it brings him great joy, and if not, then it causes him mental dysfunction. Similarly, the Gemara notes that the word תירוש is sometimes spelled תירש, implying that זכה, נעשה ראש, לא זכה, נעשה רש — if one drinks wine appropriately, he emerges as a "leader," but if he drinks inappropriately, he falls into destitution.

The anonymous *Sefer Ha-Chinuch*,[14] in discussing the prohibition of כלאי הכרם (planting vines together with other species), writes that the Torah permitted the consumption of wine בשביל קצת תועלת שנמצא במיעוטו אל הגופים — because of the slight benefit it offers some people in limited quantities — but it also warns against excessive consumption, which can yield disastrous consequences. Similarly, the Rashba, in his *Ma'amar al Yishmael*,[15] writes that the Torah did not want to forbid the consumption of wine, and it could not give a precise quantity beyond which one should not drink, because each person has a different level of alcohol tolerance. Therefore, instead of introducing an outright prohibition against excessive drinking, the Torah instead told the story of Lot and his daughters as a warning of how severely excessive drinking can impair one's judgment.

It emerges, then, that *Chazal* were keenly aware of the great benefits of wine, and strongly encouraged us to enjoy these benefits — while just as strongly warning of the grave dangers of excessive wine consumption.

Intoxication as a חילול ה'

However, whereas our tradition's attitude to wine consumption generally is complex and nuanced, its attitude towards intoxication is clear-cut, simple and straightforward.

The Rambam, in a number of places, condemns in the harshest terms drinking to intoxication. In *Hilchos Dei'os*,[16] he writes:

---

13. *Vayikra* 10:9.

14. 549.

15. Betzalel Naor edition, p. 72.

16. 5:3.

כשהחכם שותה יין אינו שותה אלא כדי לשרות אכילה שבמעיו. וכל המשתכר הרי
זה חוטא ומגונה ומפסיד חכמתו. ואם נשתכר בפני עמי הארץ הרי זה חילל את השם.

> When a scholar drinks wine, he drinks only to settle the food in his
> digestive track. And any [scholar] who becomes drunk — he is a sinner,
> he is contemptible, and he loses his knowledge. And if he becomes
> drunk in the presence of simple people, he defiles the Name of God.

The Rambam considers drunkenness a sin for a Torah scholar under any circumstances, and in the presence of other Jews, this constitutes a חילול ה' — a defamation of God, the most grievous of all sins, for which one cannot achieve atonement until death.[17]

It should be emphasized that although the Rambam speaks here only of scholars, nowadays, there is little doubt that his comments are applicable to every visibly devout Torah Jew. Each and every one of us is a representative of Torah, and of Torah Jewry. And so when a Torah Jew is seen drunk, this is a disgraceful חילול ה'.

The Rambam warns against intoxication also in a famous passage in *Hilchos Yom Tov*,[18] where he clarifies that the obligation of festivity on Yom Tov does not mean inebriation and frivolity, but rather an experience of meaningful, substantive and spiritual joy. He concludes this passage by stating that this obligation requires the joy of serving the Almighty, ואי אפשר לעבוד את השם לא מתוך שחוק ולא מתוך קלות ראש ולא מתוך שכרות — "and it is impossible to serve God through laughter, through frivolity, or through drunkenness."

In his concluding passage to *Hilchos Issurei Bi'a*,[19] the Rambam lists inebriation among the behaviors which lead to sexual misconduct, and must therefore be avoided.

But the Rambam's most strident remarks about the ills of intoxication appear in his *Guide for the Perplexed*,[20] where he writes, "…to form parties for the purpose of drinking wine together must be considered more disgraceful than the unrestrained conduct of persons who in daylight meet in the same house undressed and naked." Willfully shutting off one's mental faculties through intoxication, the Rambam explains, is more reprehensible than exposing oneself in the presence of other people.

The *poskim*'s attitude towards intoxication is expressed in their discussions concerning the requirement to drink on Purim. The *Beis Yosef* (O.C. 695) cites Rav Aharon of Lunel, in *Orchos Chayim*, as insisting that the obligation לבסומי בפוריא — to drink on Purim — cannot possibly require actual inebriation, because ואין השיכרות איסור גמור, לך עבירה גדולה מזו, שהוא גורם לגילוי עריות ושפיכות דמים וכמה עבירות זולתן — "**inebriation is an outright prohibition, and there is no greater sin than this**, as it leads to sexual misconduct, bloodshed, and several other transgressions."

---

17. Rambam, *Hilchos Teshuva* 1:4, based on *Yoma* 85b.
18. 6:20.
19. 22:21.
20. 3:8.

Similarly, the Meiri, cited by the Chafetz Chayim in *Bi'ur Halacha* (695), writes in regard to the obligation to drink on Purim, אין אנו מצווין להשתכר ולהפחית עצמינו מתוך השמחה — "we are not commanded to become inebriated and to degrade ourselves as a result of the celebration."

The *Bi'ur Halacha* also cites the *Chayei Adam*, who acknowledges a requirement to drink to the point of inebriation on Purim, but qualifies this ruling by stating that if one has reason to suspect that inebriation will lead him to disregard even a single *mitzva* — such as the recitation of a *beracha*, *birkas ha-mazon* or one of the prayer services — or to act inappropriately, then it is preferable not to drink at all on Purim. Furthermore, the *Elya Rabba*, also cited by the *Bi'ur Halacha*, raises the question of how *Chazal* could require on Purim something which is a מכשול גדול — "great stumbling block" — and he answers that this was enacted to commemorate the feasts in Shushan through which the Purim miracle unfolded. It is clear, then, that even those *poskim* who require drinking to the point of intoxication on Purim either qualify this obligation, or emphasize that it marks an exception to the general rule that the Torah strongly and adamantly discourages such drinking.

Habitual Drinking

Rav Moshe Feinstein, in 1973, was asked about the permissibility of smoking marijuana, and his response was published in his *Iggeros Moshe* (Y.D. 3:35). He ruled unequivocally that marijuana use is forbidden by *halacha*, for several reasons — some of which are relevant also to habitually drinking in significant quantities, even without reaching the point of inebriation.

He begins by noting the health risks involved — הוא מקלקל ומכלה את הגוף ("it ruins and destroys the body"), and adds that even if there are some for whom marijuana causes no physical harm, it compromises their mental faculties (מקלקל את הדעת ואינם יכולים להבין דבר לאישורו). This hinders their ability to properly pray, learn, and perform the other *mitzvos*, all of which require concentration and attentiveness.

Rav Moshe then adds another consideration: the fact that taking drugs has the effect of introducing a new תאווה גדולה — "strong desire." He notes that even when it comes to the natural craving for food, the Torah forbids excessive indulgence — referring to the Gemara's comment in *Maseches Sanhedrin* (63a) interpreting the command לא תאכלו על הדם (*Vayikra* 19:26) as forbidding gluttonous indulgence in food.[21] If the Torah forbids overindulgence in food — for which one is born with a natural craving — then certainly, Rav Moshe reasons, it forbids knowingly causing oneself an additional, unnatural craving. Rav Moshe also points to the obligation to respect one's parents — who, undoubtedly, would be distressed by their child's drug use — as well as the command of קדושים תהיו

---

21. We discuss this prohibition at length in the chapter, "Is the $1000 Sandwich Kosher?"

("You shall be sacred," *Vayikra* 19:2), which the Ramban famously explains as requiring moderation in our indulgence in physical pleasures. He concludes:

סוף דבר הוא פשוט וברור שהוא מאיסורים חמורים וצריך להשתדל בכל היכולת
להעביר טומאה זו מכל בני ישראל ובפרט מאלו שלומדין בישיבות.

> In sum, it is obvious and clear that this is among the grave prohibitions, and every effort must be made to eliminate this impurity from the entire Jewish Nation, particularly from those who study in yeshivos.

It seems clear that frequent consumption of large amounts of alcohol, too, causes both physical and mental harm, and transgresses the command of קדושים תהיו which demands maintaining our dignity and sanctity by avoiding overindulgence (and, assuming the parents disapprove, it violates the *mitzva* of respecting parents). Additionally, while alcohol — unlike drugs — is a beverage, and thus something which people naturally crave, knowingly engendering in oneself a desire for alcohol through habitual consumption might very likely fall under the prohibition of לא תאכלו על הדם as understood by Rav Moshe. We are not born with an urge to consume alcohol; people create this urge within themselves by habitually drinking large quantities. Seemingly, then, according to Rav Moshe, this would be forbidden, even if one avoids intoxication.[22]

Rav Moshe mentions this point also in a different responsum, on the subject of cigarette smoking.[23] He writes that irrespective of the health risks of tobacco, it is forbidden to accustom oneself to smoking, because אין להמשיך עצמו לריבוי תאוות והנאות — one must avoid increasing his desires for physical gratification.

While Rav Moshe's extension of the prohibition of gluttony to include causing oneself cravings seems novel, and does not appear in other halachic sources, never-

---

22.   There is room to consider, however, whether this would apply to marijuana, which has been shown to be far less harmful than large quantities of alcohol, and thus from a strictly medical standpoint, there seems to be no more reason to forbid moderate use of marijuana than to forbid moderate consumption of alcohol. On the other hand, if, as Rav Moshe ruled, it is forbidden to knowingly develop within oneself a new craving, this might apply to any addictive drug, even one which does not pose considerable harm. (Interestingly, the Radbaz, in *Hilchos Kil'ayim* (5:19), speaks of עלי הקנבוס — "cannabis leaves" — which were eaten in Egypt, and had intoxicating properties. He notes, אומרים שהוא משמח — "They say it brings joy." However, the Radbaz gives no indication as to whether or not he approved of the consumption of these leaves.)

　　If we determine that marijuana is allowed, we must also examine whether or not it would be considered *kitniyos* and thus forbidden on Pesach. Rav Yitzchak Zilberstein penned a widely circulated letter in the spring of 5776 (2016) affirming that medicinal cannabis is permissible for Pesach, though he was referring to smoking, not eating.

23.   *Iggeros Moshe*, C.M. 2:76.

theless, his perspective is an important one to consider, at least in regard to the spirit of *halacha*, if not in regard to the letter of *halacha*. It is difficult enough to restrain our natural impulses; there is certainly no need to create additional urges and desires for us to have to struggle with. Therefore, while it is certainly permissible and acceptable to enjoy an occasional drink, caution must be exercised to ensure that one does not develop a craving for, or dependency upon, alcohol — for both medical and spiritual reasons.

Alcoholics Anonymous in a Church

If a person suffers from a drug or alcohol addiction, and he has made the courageous decision to seek help, would it be permissible to join a support group that meets in a church? These meetings are generally held not in the sanctuary, but in the church's social hall or another room in the building, and the question thus becomes whether entering the building is allowed for the purpose of participating in a therapeutic support group.[24]

The Rama[25] cites two views among the *Rishonim* as to whether one may enter the yard of a house of pagan worship at a time when no worship is taking place. Rav Eliezer Waldenberg, in his *Tzitz Eliezer*,[26] writes that *halacha* follows the stringent opinion. If so, then *a fortiori*, it would be forbidden to enter the building of a church, even to go to a different room, and even when services are not taking place. Indeed, Rav Moshe Feinstein[27] rules that children may not be permitted to play in a room in the building of a church. He cites the Gemara's statement in *Maseches Avoda Zara* (17a) that when King Shlomo admonishes in *Sefer Mishlei*,[28] הרחק מעליה דרכך ("Distance your path from her"), this refers to a requirement to physically distance oneself from idolatry. And thus the *Shulchan Aruch*[29] writes, מצוה להתרחק מדרך אלילים ד' אמות — one should keep at least a four-cubit distance from an idol. Rav Moshe writes that this warning forbids entering a church even if one remains outside the sanctuary.

A similar position was taken by Rav Menashe Klein, in his *Mishneh Halachos*,[30] regarding voting stations set up in churches. Rav Klein writes that entering a church to vote is forbidden by force of the requirement to keep a distance from idols, as well the

---

24. We addressed the question regarding entering the building of a church as part of our discussion of the permissibility of touring the Vatican, in *Headlines*, vol. 1, pp. 161–165.

25. Y.D. 149:2.

26. Vol. 14, 91:2.

27. *Iggeros Moshe*, O.C. 4:40.

28. 5:8.

29. Y.D. 150:1.

30. 6:139.

Shulchan Aruch's ruling[31] that one may not lean down in front of an idol to pick up something from the ground, or to remove a thorn from his foot, as this gives the appearance of prostrating before the idol. Entering the building of a church, Rav Klein contends, likewise gives the appearance of respecting the institution, and is thus forbidden.

However, Rav Moshe Sternbuch, in his *Teshuvos Ve-Hanhagos*,[32] ruled that although fundamentally, it is forbidden to enter a church even if one remains in a room outside the sanctuary, this is allowed when necessary, if the room is often used for non-religious functions, as in the case of a social hall. Although optimally one should not enter even such a room — and thus, for example, one should not hold an affair or other event in a church's social hall — under extenuating circumstances, this is permitted. Rav Sternbuch therefore permitted voting in the social hall of a church, if the hall is used for non-religious functions, and the door to the building is not used only for entering the sanctuary.

Given the grave dangers of alcohol addiction for both the addict and his family, it would certainly appear that if an addict believes he could be helped by an Alcoholics Anonymous group which meets in the social hall of a church, he may rely on Rav Sternbuch's lenient ruling and attend the meeting so he receives the help he desperately needs.[33]

Conclusion

In light of all we have seen, the fact that frequent consumption of alcohol — and inebriation — has become accepted in some circles in the Orthodox Jewish world is nothing short of outrageous. Drunkenness stands in direct opposition to virtually everything the Torah requires of us — such as attentiveness, scholarship, dignity, discipline, respect for ourselves and respect for other people. Those who see some sort of value in getting drunk on Shabbos or Yom Tov, or at social functions, or even who deem such conduct acceptable, must realize that this is a grave breach of some of our most cherished and fundamental values. There is simply no way of reconciling this acceptance of intoxication with Torah tradition.

This issue demands greater vigilance in our generation than it did in the past. The *Sefas Emes*[34] advances the theory that Noach became inebriated after the Flood

---

31. Y.D. 150:2.

32. 2:410.

33. It should be noted that unlike idol-worship itself, the prohibition against entering a house of pagan worship does not override the concern for human life. Thus, for example, the *Shulchan Aruch* (Y.D. 157:3) rules that one may enter a house of pagan worship to hide from those seeking to kill him.

34. *Likutim, Parshas Noach.*

because נשתנו הדורות והטבע — the Flood wrought certain physical changes, which lowered people's tolerance level for alcohol. Quantities of wine which Noach had been accustomed to drinking before the Flood were too large for his body to handle after the Flood, thus resulting in his inebriation. The *Sefas Emes* here warns that every generation must set limits that are appropriate and necessary in light of its particular conditions. In our time, although our alcohol tolerance level is no lower than in previous generations, our risk of alcoholism is, without question, infinitely greater than ever before. The availability of large quantities of wine and hard liquor, as well as the sharp decline in self-control and self-discipline — not to mention a culture that views the consumption of large amounts of alcohol as impressive and a sign of social status — have combined to pose grave danger, especially to our youth. Now more than ever, it is imperative that we limit our consumption of alcoholic beverages, and heed the stern warnings of the sages of yesteryear about the severity of intoxication and its destructive effects on our pursuit of spirituality and holiness.

Additionally, while there are many different reasons why people turn to alcohol and drugs for enjoyment, likely the most common reason is to fill an emotional void. When people feel dissatisfied and empty, lacking a sense of fulfillment, they are prone to seek illicit pleasures in a misguided, dangerous attempt to experience contentment. In order to combat the scourge of alcoholism and addiction in our communities, we must not only emphasize the grave dangers of alcohol and substance abuse, but also encourage and help both youngsters and adults find appropriate sources of gratification. Healthy, constructive hobbies, pastimes and social activities must be made available and strongly encouraged, as should career options that draw a person's interest. Denying people the opportunity to do what they enjoy is a prescription for discontentment and frustration, which raise the chances of their turning to harmful habits in the search of the excitement and happiness which they crave. And, of course, we must find ways to make Torah study and *mitzva* observance gratifying and enjoyable. People need to know that they can experience satisfaction and enjoyment by learning and participating in *chesed* projects or worthwhile community undertakings. The corpus of Torah is so vast, and the range of *mitzvos* is so wide, that everyone can find an area to enjoy and in which to excel. The more we encourage a variety of constructive, worthwhile outlets within the framework of Torah and *mitzvos*, the likelier people are to find fulfillment and contentment within that framework, thus lowering their chances of falling into the devastating downward spiral of addiction.

INTERVIEWS

Rabbi Dr. Abraham Twerski

Interviewed on *Headlines with Dovid Lichtenstein*, 16 Adar Sheni, 5776 (March 26, 2016)

When I grew up, I believed, like everybody else, that a שיכור (drunkard) is a goy, and alcoholism isn't a problem among Jews. Then I gradually discovered that it's a problem among Jews. Still, I thought it's not a problem among *frum* Jews. I then discovered that it's a problem among *frum* Jews. There's no immunity, no discrimination. It's a problem, it's a serious problem, and it's a particularly serious problem when we speak about young people.

We don't know what causes alcoholism and addiction. Certainly, there are factors in a person's life — such as if he's under a great deal of stress, he'll look to alcohol or drugs as a tranquilizer. That's understandable. But this doesn't explain the disease. With alcoholism, there's a genetic factor. Children who are born to an alcoholic parent have four times the likelihood of turning out having alcoholism than children who don't. And that's true even though they weren't raised by that parent. Excellent studies have shown that children given over to adoption at birth, who had an alcoholic parent, have the same ratio. So we know there is a genetic factor. This doesn't mean they will become alcoholics, but it means they have a greater predilection to become alcoholics. So, if there's been an alcoholic in your family, such as an uncle or grandfather, be especially careful, because your children may be more vulnerable.

Parents must look out for signs of early onset drinking. If you go to a *kiddush* on Shabbos morning, you'll see some kids, maybe aged eleven or twelve, or so, hanging around after the *kiddush* drinking whatever is left over in the little cups. This is a clear sign of an alcohol problem.

Even before addiction, there is alcohol abuse — when a person doesn't handle alcohol normally. He — and it could just as well be a "she"; a *frum* Jewish woman can also become an alcoholic — drinks excessively, maybe not regularly. He goes to a *shalom zachor*, a *farbrengen*, or whatever, and drinks more than is appropriate, enough to effect a change in his behavior — this is alcohol abuse. If the person becomes more aggressive, if the drinking changes his personality — he needs to be on the lookout.

Children with an alcohol problem will never admit it. We know yeshiva boys in some places get together Friday night to get drunk. They will never admit it to their parents. And parents might choose not to recognize the problem. And so there's the issue of denial — we don't recognize that our kids have a problem. We're ashamed to admit it, and we're afraid that if we do anything about it, then the kids will not find a *shidduch*. This denial is a serious problem.

Lying about drinking is a sign that there's a problem. If parents ask a kid if he had any beer, and he denies it, but then they found out that he did — this is an indication.

Children before the age of 21 should not be given any alcohol to drink for any reason, besides the minimum *shiur* for *kiddush*. I know this is extreme, but this is like cancer, and it requires extreme measures. The young brain is not mature enough to make the decision to know when to stop. The reason why I compare it to cancer is because cancer does not begin with severe symptoms. It's usually silent, and then when the first symptoms appear, it's already a problem.

People who drink in order to socialize, or for another reason — like to sleep — this is dangerous. This is alcohol dependency. You can't live without sleeping, and you can't live without socializing, and if you need a drink to sleep or socialize, you can be certain that after a period of time, the amount you're having won't be effective, and you'll need more.

I treated a fellow who could not sleep, so he drank a beer to help him sleep. After a few weeks, one beer didn't do it anymore, so he took two. To make a long story short, he ended up after a couple of years drinking one-fifth of a pint of alcohol in order to sleep. Incidentally, he is a doctor.

If you're dependent on alcohol, then you should know that the amount is going to increase, so you need to avoid it. I know this is not pleasant for people to hear, because people like to drink, and I hate to deny it to them, but if you're allergic to penicillin, you can't use it.

When ingested excessively, alcohol kills brain cells. Now you can knock off some brain cells and act normally, and there are some functioning alcoholics, but with time, it takes its toll.

Alcoholism is not curable. It's like a diabetes — it can be controlled, but it cannot be cured. By "cured" I mean that a person no longer has a problem and can now drink safely. There is no such thing. Either a person has a problem or doesn't have a problem. If he has a problem, then his system is geared towards reacting badly to alcohol. It can be controlled. I've had people who were sober without a drink for 45 years, and they would still talk about themselves as "recovering alcoholics." They can never be "recovered," in the sense that they no longer have a problem. As one person put it, once a cucumber becomes a pickle, it never goes back to being a cucumber again.

If someone in your family has an alcohol problem, don't use your own judgment about what to do. Get expert advice. Don't listen to a neighbor. Go to somebody who is an expert on alcoholism, or, better yet, go to meetings of Al-Anon Family groups — these are husbands, wives or parents who have lived with the problem. They know what works and what doesn't. And don't say it's just one incident and it won't happen again. These are excuses which pave the way to disaster. So get expert help. A good way to start is to get Al-Anon literature and becoming educated. There's also an excellent video available called "Lechaim," made by the Yehuda Mond Foundation. The parents made this in memory of their son, who died in a DUI accident. Everybody should see this film.

The Torah tells us that Noach was an איש צדיק תמים — a perfect *tzadik*. But then he goes and plants a vineyard, gets drunk, and acts shamefully. How does that happen to a perfect *tzadik*? The *Sefas Emes* says something so true — Noach used to use wine safely, and he knew how much he could drink without it having a bad effect. But after the *mabul*, he came out of the *teiva*, planted a vineyard and drank the amount he knew would not have a bad effect. But he didn't realize that it wasn't the same world anymore. There was a flood that destroyed the world, and once it's no longer the same world, you can't go by the previous rules. You have to follow new rules.

The world today is not the same world I grew up in. It's not even the same world of twenty years ago. This is a new world, run by the slogan that became popular in 1960 — "if it feels good, do it." That's what's operating the world now. People have no concept that there's something higher in life than having a good time. Youngsters believe that they're entitled to a good time, and if they're not having a good time, then they need to go have a good time. So they go for alcohol or drugs.

Technology has been so wonderful that it's eliminated so many of the hardships that existed in the 1930s when I grew up, such that now even adults believe that the world is an amusement park, and so there is no reason to avoid having a good time. I'm not against having a good time or enjoying things, but you have to have a better goal in life than "if it feels good, do it."

The world today is different. Not too long ago, marijuana was an illegal drug, yet now, almost all states are moving toward legalization, saying it's no different than alcohol. But it's much worse than alcohol — alcohol leaves the system within a few hours, whereas marijuana stays in the brain for three weeks. This is a sign of the times.

The *Midrash Tanchuma* says that when Noach planted his vineyard, the Satan came to him and offered to help. The Satan went ahead and slaughtered a lamb. It took its blood and used it to fertilize the vineyard. He then slaughtered a monkey and used its blood as fertilizer. It then slaughtered a lion, and then, finally, a pig. The Midrash is telling us that if a person has one drink, he becomes meek like a lamb. After a second drink, he acts foolishly like a monkey. Then, after the third, he acts bold like a lion, and then, eventually, he becomes like a *chazir*.

Rav Shmuel Kamenetsky made it very clear that these days, drinking to excess on Purim is not a *mitzva*, and is absolutely forbidden. I think we need to make that clear to our kids. Parents need to know that when kids come to their house, they must not give them any alcohol. If you give a youngster alcohol — then you are responsible for any damage that happens to him or to others as a result. We have to realize, like Noach, that we're living in a different world.

To the best of my knowledge, there is no reputable *frum* rehab center. Some have chaplains, and will provide kosher food, and they will understand that the Orthodox patient cannot do certain things on Shabbos, but there is no *frum* rehab center — and the reason is because we are still in denial. Some people say that they can't go to Alcoholics Anonymous meetings because they're held in churches. But there are very few not held in churches, and hardly any meet in shuls. Why is this? Because we don't recognize that the problem is ours. When we recognize that the problem is ours, we'll get together and have our own rehab center.

Rav Moshe Hauer

Interviewed on *Headlines with Dovid Lichtenstein*, 4 Elul, 5777 (August 26, 2017)

It's such a disaster, and so fundamentally contrary to every value of the Torah. קדושים תהיו is also a *mitzva*, whether it's counted among the 613 *mitzvos* or not. It requires living a proper, clean life. This is so fundamental. Drinking is so destructive.

I don't know how widespread this phenomenon is. But I can tell you that a caterer came over to me during the *chasan's tisch* at a wedding around three years ago, picked up a shot glass, and said, "Rabbi Hauer, this is an endangered species. We don't use these anymore. A shot glass holds too little. People want to pour their drinks in larger glasses."

This is a shift that has taken place, and every person, in his realm, has to stand up against it.

In our shul, we don't allow it. It's not that we don't allow any schnapps in the building, like prohibition. If a person wants to have a modest "*le-chaim*," that's fine. But not four "*le-chaims*." This is not our way. When we're dealing with the kinds of crises we're dealing with, with children and teens — we cannot allow it.

We have a lot of empty spaces in our lives. The Rambam at the end of *Hilchos Issurei Bi'a* writes about a different struggle which people sometimes have, and he writes that different things fill a לב פנוי — empty heart. We need to focus on bringing people a תורת חיים, a life that is satisfying. People need to develop relationships with friends, with family members, with Torah, and then life becomes satisfying.

We have an annual banquet for our shul, like shuls do, and we usually have a musical program as our central focus — we get up and dance. One year, a group came from *Eretz Yisrael* to play at the banquet, and it was a beautiful event. People were dancing, and the guys who played had an amazing time. They came over to me afterward and said, "Rabbi Hauer, we want to tell you — we never experienced a situation where people were so joyous in a dry room. You didn't serve any alcohol, yet people were really into it, excited and happy."

Evidently, it can be done.

We've somehow lost the ability to internally generate the joy. You can't have an *oneg Shabbos* anymore without cases of beer. This shouldn't be. People should be able to dance at a *simcha*, and *bochrim* at a friend's wedding, without getting tanked. We've created a void that is being filled by all kinds of things. Communally, there needs to be an emphasis in *chinuch*, in shuls and yeshivos, on making people excited over what they're doing so they don't need external stimuli.

I don't know exactly when this started, but something basic has changed. When we were growing up — and, to a greater degree, when people a little older than us were growing up — learning and living a *frum* life was itself a little bit of a *chiddush*. To some extent, it was courageous, it was pioneering, and therefore it required some decision, some energy, some excitement about what you were doing. But we've become so strong that doing these things is natural. It's become the "path of least resistance." It doesn't require any energy or excitement. It doesn't generate any adrenaline doing what everybody is expecting you to do. And so you need to get your rush from something else. But it doesn't need to be that way. We need to give people opportunities to find some specific purpose that's theirs, so they're not just going through the motions. And then the heart is filled in a much better way.

Additionally, we have glorified drinking… Someone told me about a *gemach* in a certain large Jewish city, where a person gives people designated bottles of scotch when they're making a *kiddush*. They refill the bottle with regular scotch, because nobody knows the difference, and this way the person can meet the standards and expectations. This is in an עיר התורה. When you glorify drinking, when the bottle of scotch has to come with its own "pillow and blanket," what do you expect kids to do? People see what we admire, what we give importance to. We need to take some of this out. We're not in a position to make a communal decree, but we need to promote the right values, the value of living a clean, healthy life, the joy of a father sitting around the table with his wife and kids instead of, Heaven forbid, lying in bed in a state of שכרותו של לוט.

We must enhance the sense of the individual worth of each and every person. As a child grows and develops, he must come to understand his specific talents, just as Rabban Yochanan ben Zakai listed the special qualities of all his students, what distinguished each one. We need to nurture within each person a sense of ambition. Children need to be ambitious, so they will accomplish something at every stage of life. If they're just going through the motions, punching the clock, then where is the excitement supposed to come from? They need to set for themselves a goal, something which gives them satisfaction, an area where they really flourish, something which they enjoy and which they do well — these are the critical pieces, identifying within themselves their uniqueness. This is the most valuable gift.

Some institutions are overburdened. They are very large, such as yeshivos with large numbers of *talmidim*, and so it's obvious that students are not going to receive individual attention from the *rebbe*. The parents then need to make sure that the child's individual strengths are being nurtured so the child develops ambition, which in turn breeds passion and excitement.

Chaya — a Victim of Alcohol Addiction

Interviewed on *Headlines with Dovid Lichtenstein*, 4 Elul, 5777 (August 26, 2017)

When I first got married, my husband was not into drinking. It came about after a couple of years, starting with my son's *shalom zachor*. At first, I didn't pay any attention. He'd have some at the table on Shabbos. But then he started investing in more things. He started using the word "connoisseur" a lot at the beginning. I didn't recognize it for what it was. I said, "Ok, he's into it, it's a hobby, he does it for fun, he prides himself over knowing the fancy names." But things progressed, and little by little, it got worse. It started at the Shabbos table, but eventually crossed over into other times during Shabbos, and then weeknights.

It's pretty horrifying watching a grown man out of control, just having no control over himself. A grown man is strong, and when he can't control his movement, it's terrifying. You don't know his next move. *Baruch Hashem*, this didn't happen that often, but he would yell at the kids. He wouldn't hit them, but he would throw things. This happened maybe ten times. He would throw whatever was around — a plate, a table, a glass, a picture frame. My first priority was getting the kids out of that room.

Usually, though, he would drink at the Shabbos table, then move to the couch, and then to the bed, and he would pretty much sleep through the rest of Shabbos. Often, I would make *havdala* myself, though sometimes he would wake up in time for *havdala*, especially during the summer, when there was more time for him to sleep.

When it reached its worst point, he would be drinking all night and then sleep all day. He had his own business, but he ran it into the ground. He wouldn't go to any clients because he wasn't able to. This was the worst point of my marriage. He wasn't able to move. He would sleep until 2 or 3 p.m., and then get up and start the whole process all over again.

When we would go away for Shabbos, he would go to shul just for the *kiddush*. And if there was a *shalom zachor*, he would go. When we stayed home for Shabbos, too, he made it a priority to go wherever there were drinks — a *shalom zachor*, a *kiddush*. But mostly he was happy drinking by himself. He would just closet himself away and be in his office drinking. Whenever he was out on Shabbos and Yom Tov, he was definitely drinking.

I think it just started out as a hobby, an interest. He felt it was "cool." When he went to a *kiddush*, it was a talking point, or something like that. But then he couldn't stop. It completely overtook his life. It took priority over everything else — over his family responsibilities and over his business responsibilities.

…Growing up, my family didn't use alcohol, and I didn't know anyone who was an alcoholic. I had no baseline, no experience. This was something completely new for me…

I had to pretend that everything was fine, while my husband was sleeping all day and not making any money. I had a part-time job which helped pay for a couple of grocery orders a month, but was not enough to live off of. I had to pretend that this was normal. But it was completely exhausting.

There was absolutely no sign of this when we were dating. Even during the first year or two of marriage, there was no clue. His father is an alcoholic, but he had absolutely no substance abuse when we got married, or during the first two years of our marriage. He was not drinking at all. We made *kiddush* on grape juice, maybe once in a while on wine.

He had a horrible childhood and was very scarred from it. His parents got divorced, and he was very hurt by it. He never really got over it. I don't know if he used alcohol as a way to cope with his past. It could be. But once he got into it, it didn't matter.

The difference between him and a recovering alcoholic is that a recovering alcoholic recognizes that he has a problem. My ex didn't acknowledge that there was a problem. He didn't think there was anything wrong with what he was doing.

My story is kind of extreme, but I guess it helps illustrate the point about the dangers of alcohol. Because of my husband's addiction, I wasn't able to pay a lot of the bills. My car was repossessed. The guy came on a bright, sunny, summer day, when all the kids and families were out in the street, and they all watched. It was so humiliating. I had my utilities shut off several times. Once, our water was shut off on Erev Yom Tov. It was so awful, so humiliating.

On one occasion — I think it was Yom Tov — my husband was pretty drunk and he started yelling at me outside. We were standing outside, and he was upset about something, so he started yelling at me. This was in the middle of the street, and there were other couples and families around. I begged him to stop, but he was completely unhinged and kept screaming. I'll never forget that.

Alcohol is a drug. It might seem fun at first, especially for *bochrim*, but there is no excuse to give any alcohol whatsoever to anyone underaged. People might laugh at me for saying this, but I saw what could happen. Alcohol is an extremely addictive substance, and it's so easily available. It's not illegal, and it doesn't take much to get one's hands on it and give it out, especially in yeshivos. Somebody told me that her son was in a yeshiva camp and they were drinking pretty heavily — this was in a pretty serious yeshiva camp. It might seem "cool" to get into it, that there are so many different types, fancy wines and expensive whiskeys, and there's nothing wrong with a little bit at a *seuda* or during a *simcha* or dinner, but abusing it can completely ruin someone's life. Once a person goes down that path, they let alcohol consume their life, and it completely takes over. And it's easy for that to happen. They're always thinking about their next drink, and this becomes their primary goal. When a person gets to that point, it can tear a family apart.

A recovering alcoholic can never have another drink. It's that serious.

If people educate themselves and really become aware of the dangers of alcohol, it will be much easier for them to get a handle on this, and they won't be running to a *kiddush* or *simcha* to get drunk.

This is the message I want to leave people with. Alcohol helped destroy my marriage, and it almost destroyed my life. Having a healthy attitude toward alcohol is essential, so it does not reach the point where it ruins your life.

Tom Gagliano

Interviewed on *Headlines with Dovid Lichtenstein*, 4 Elul, 5777 (August 26, 2017)

If we drink a little bit, that's ok. But when we start drinking to numb a pain, to medicate a pain, to fill a void inside ourselves — that's what addiction is. The person thinks he's in control of the addiction, but in reality, the addiction is in control of him, and it gets worse.

I see a lot of people who think that the problem is the drinking, or the pornography. But that's not the problem. The problem is going on underneath, inside them. Drinking becomes a coping mechanism to medicate the problems. We would like children to use religion as their coping mechanism, as the solution to life. But what happens, many times, is that the child stops trusting people, and needs something else to make him whole, to fill that void.

Many men are addicted to working. They put work ahead of other things. I did that. I'm a recovering addict. One of my addictions was work. Work became too important in my life. It was a way of medicating a pain, of distracting myself from how I felt inside. Another common addiction is eating. A lot of people eat because they're addicted, not because they're hungry. They're eating to fill a void inside. All addictions have the same problem underneath — something inside needs to be filled.

I wrote in my book that the real problem is the childhood messages. The messages we receive during childhood dictate the intimacy we have or don't have, and the roles we play. This is why most addicts start their addiction by the time they're eighteen. All children are egocentric, they all want their parents' attention, they want to know that they're number one to their parents. This is the mindset in all children. So whatever you put in front of the child, whether it's religion or anything else, they are going to rebel against it, and then not use it as the solution to medicate their pain and their problems. Then, when they get older, they'll find something to fill that void. That's the ultimate reason why people become addicts, whether it's drinking, pornography, or anything else. I have many Orthodox Jewish clients, and I tell parents to give the child the message that they come first, and then the child is more likely to walk towards religion on their own, as opposed to believing that they must first be religious and only then they can be loved by the parents. When a child feels they're important, that they come first, then they won't need something else to fill the void, because there is no void. Healthy children grow up believing that their parents' love is unconditional. This means that they are able to express their feelings, and those feelings will be validated, that they won't be told that their feelings are wrong, or silly, or that they don't make sense. And when a child feels they're important, that their feelings are important, they won't look to alcohol, pornography, drugs, or anything else to fill a void — because they won't have a void. They'll feel enough inside.

I'm not knocking parents, by any means. We all do the best we can. But even for the most diligent parents, it is hard to give all the children the time they need to feel that they're important. It's not their fault; it's reality. So some kids become lost in their families. They lose a sense of self. And if they lose a sense of self, they try to find it in different areas.

The addict doesn't feel good about himself. He feels he's letting down the people around him, that he's not there for them. I tell recovering addicts — and I work with many — that besides sobriety, the biggest piece in recovery is self-forgiveness. I say, "Can you forgive yourself?" The addict needs to know that he's not a bad person.

Addiction leads us to make bad choices, but that doesn't make us bad people. There's a huge difference between the two. Do I identify myself as a defective human being, or do I realize that my choices were bad?

Another important point to realize is that addiction is always progressive. It gets worse, not better. Eventually, the alcoholic is picked up for a DUI violation and could spend time in jail. Or he can't hold down a job, because he can't get up for work. Or the family decides it's time to tell him to leave. These are the three areas that get somebody to realize he has a problem that he cannot handle on his own — employment, the law, and family…

I say to parents — all parents do the best they can, but sometimes, I think, they don't fully understand how the child feels growing up, or what's going through their minds. So create a safe place where your child can share their feelings, where feelings are neither right nor wrong. Don't tell your child how to feel. Acknowledge their feelings even when you disagree. Make them feel that their feelings matter, and then they will feel that they matter. Be curious with your kids — know how they feel, ask them what the best and worst parts of their day were. Make them feel they're important to you. And if there is any kind of addiction or a mental illness — seek professional help. As much as we love our kids, sometimes we need to seek people who know about this stuff, who can nurse the child back to health.

Rabbi Yehoshua Kaganoff

Interviewed on *Headlines with Dovid Lichtenstein*, 4 Elul, 5777 (August 26, 2017)

There is a letter in my *sefer* written by a pornography addict in recovery. He was a *talmid* of mine, whom I helped get through recovery, and for whom I *paskened shaylos*. He wanted to write a letter to his *menahel* about how the *menahel* got this all wrong, and I offered to be the go-between. In this letter, he basically outlines that this is not just a *ta'ayva* (desire) — it's a disease. And so it needs to be treated like a disease. He explains that he could have written a whole *sefer* quoting the Maharal, Rav Tzadok, and all the ספרים הקדושים about השחתת זרע and שמירת עיניים, but it didn't matter, because when he returned to his dorm room, the pornography drew him. It took the 12-step program for him to realize that this was a disease that requires a certain treatment.

The Chazon Ish writes that if a person has שפלות הנפש — a feeling of lowliness — then learning *mussar* makes things worse for him. Instead of it helping him, the person will take the *mussar* and throw it at other people. It won't help him. It's like water off a duck's back.

I say — don't learn *mussar*.

We're always telling people what's wrong with them, from the moment they're born. In Elul, for example, there are a lot of *shmuessen* about all the *aveiros* we've done. If a businessman has an accountant who makes a spreadsheet calculating only the debit side, without bothering to calculate the income, the businessman will fire the accountant. This is an inaccurate calculation. Accounting must include both profits and losses. When we always tell people how bad they are, this hurts their self-esteem — and I use the term "self-esteem" the way Rav Twerski does, as referring to a feeling of self-worth, a feeling of importance. Rav Twerski discusses this in his book *Let Us Make Man*, where he explains the difference between kosher self-esteem and arrogance. If a person grows up thinking, "I'm terrible," then giving him *mussar* makes him feel worse, or will just bounce right off him, because he already feels terrible about himself.

In the world of addiction recovery, we call this the "hole in the soul." There's a void. The person feels like a piece of trash. And if a person feels like a piece of trash, he will look for anything he can find that will make him feel better. The *Ribono Shel Olam* put into human beings something called endorphins — chemicals which get released when a person does things that bring pleasure. Things like drugs, alcohol, shopping and sexual stimulation cause chemicals to be released that make a person feel good. So people utilize these methods of medicating themselves. They feel terrible about themselves because of the message that the educational system and our society is pumping into them, so when they find something that makes them feel good, of course they go there. The only reason not to go there is if they realize that this won't make them feel better, that they need to take a different direction to feel better.

And that different direction is the realization that you are worth something, that you are important in the eyes of the *Ribono Shel Olam*. You're not a piece of junk! Let's talk about all the *mitzvos* you've done. Tell a *bochur* that every time he rode the New York subway in the summer and did not look at something inappropriate, he will be rewarded infinitely for that. This is a much different message than saying that he's a *sheigitz* because of the times when he did look. Knowing that he is important, that he is earning reward, is a far better motivator.

We're not emphasizing enough the importance of every person, or doing enough to develop each child on his own, in the spirit of חנוך לנער על פי דרכו.

Another piece is what Rav Reuven Feinstein teaches his *talmidim* all the time: educate, don't legislate. If people feel responsible, that what they do is important, then they have self-esteem, and then we don't have to legislate to them what they shouldn't be doing. The best *shemira* is one's own *shemira*, when he wants to grow, he wants to be a better person, and not because there's a stick hanging over him.

Addiction is a מחלת מדינה — a widespread disease. I believe that about 70 percent of the Jewish population is addicted in one way or another. There are pornography addicts, internet addicts, alcoholics, shopaholics, and "religaholics" — people who use religion as a means of escaping, rather than dealing with the "hole in the soul." I've seen this in my experience.

Addiction is a disease. Science has proven that it's a disease, a change in the brain's chemicals, and it needs to be treated as such. Once you know that, you treat it like a heart condition, diabetes or cancer.

I had a whole conversation with one of the *rabbanim* about addicts in recovery who need to attend 12-step meetings, which are usually held in the basement of a church. Why are they held only in church basements? Because the shuls won't invite them. The shuls don't want to recognize that we have a problem, so they don't want the meetings held there. I have a *teshuva* in my *sefer* explaining why this is allowed. One rav came to me and said that this is forbidden. I explained that the 12 steps are a matter of פקוח נפש for an addict, and even if not, he's an ill patient, so for certain this is allowed for him.

Rav Mendel Kaplan

Interviewed on *Headlines with Dovid Lichtenstein*, 11 Marcheshvan, 5779 (October 20, 2018)

I think that there is a very clear Torah perspective with regard to the use of marijuana, and I want to draw a distinction between medicinal marijuana and recreational marijuana. I think the real issue is not with medicine. If a person is in pain, and this is the way to alleviate the pain, then there is no *mitzva* for the person to be in *tza'ar* (discomfort). *Tza'ar*, as a rule, is not a good thing, and makes a person unable to serve Hashem properly… A Yid has to be *gezunt* (healthy), and we should want to feel good and feel a sense of equilibrium and balance. The Torah does not advocate, *chas ve-shalom*, pain in any way, shape or form. We don't wish it on anybody, and we don't look for it. As we say daily in our morning *berachos*, אל תביאנו...לידי נסיון.

When it comes to recreational marijuana — this is a huge subject of discussion, and something which people are talking about. People claim, why is it different from alcohol? After all, alcohol, too, is a substance which alters one's state of consciousness. And the Torah encourages the consumption of alcohol on a weekly basis. *Chazal* said that the *mitzvas asei* of זכרהו should be על היין, with wine. And on Pesach night, they instituted the four cups of wine. We have stories in the Gemara of *chachamim* who suffered terribly yet partook of alcohol on Pesach night. The Gemara talks about it in great detail in *Maseches Pesachim*, and discusses the alcohol content. *Chasidim* have a *minhag* going back to the days of the Ba'al Shem Tov to say "le-chaim." It was usually on Vodka in the old country. It's no secret that in Lubavitch, at *farbrengens*, alcohol is consumed. Around the world, people drink seriously on Simchas Torah. And everyone knows that on Purim חייב איניש לבסומי בפוריא.

So this is the question. People ask, "Hey, rabbi, you say not to use marijuana, but you yourself say 'le-chaim'! What could be wrong with marijuana? Why don't you want us to be happy, to enjoy Shabbos?"

There is a distinction between alcohol and narcotics. Never once does the Torah encourage the use of a mind-altering substance. Alcohol, essentially, lowers inhibitions. It is not as much about "getting high" as about feeling free and open. When people lose their inhibition, this brings social cohesion, togetherness. The essence of a *farbrengen* is the actualization of the *mitzva* of אהבת ישראל, of people being able to connect with each other, to relate to each other. Sometimes there is even תוכחה (criticism), but it all has to be done in the spirit of אהבת ישראל, without any kind of negativity. The reality is that the consumption of alcohol brings people together. The use of narcotics, especially marijuana, does exactly the opposite. It puts people in their own world, it removes them from others. It's the opposite of cohesion, and it puts them in a state of complacency. People don't smoke "socially," in order to get together. They get high on their own.

I've spoken with many, many people who have used marijuana and alcohol, and just about everyone said the same thing.

I think this is a very critical point. There is a world of difference between alcohol and marijuana.

Of course, the abuse of alcohol is not ok. It's the opposite of what the Torah wants. I was told as a very young *bochur* that *chasidim* never drink alone. It was always about לגימה שמקרבת, and never, *chas ve-shalom*, about using it on your own. I saw *chasidim* say "le-chaim" at *farbrengens*, always with other people, always with the goal of being able to connect with others. And really, this is what the *seder* on Pesach is about. It's about people drinking four cups and feeling free to speak, to convey the messages of *cheirus*, of the eternity of *Am Yisrael*, and God's having chosen us. The four cups of wine make it a more memorable moment, and bring the family together.

When it comes to unusual behavior, we always have a rule, אין לך בו אלא חידושו — we can't extend it any further than what is explicitly stated. You can't say that since the Torah talks about alcohol, it must necessarily include other things. No. The Torah talks about alcohol, and אין לך בו אלא חידושו. If you're coming to push forward and add other mind-altering things — nowhere in the Torah or *Chazal* is there any kind of discussion about it, and this is very telling. Mind-altering substances are not something new. They've been around for millennia, and the fact that we have absolutely no record anywhere in *Chazal* or Midrashim of any kind of hallucinogens, drugs or narcotics being used speaks volumes as to whether these are appropriate for a Torah Yid. Hallucinogens are never mentioned in any kind of positive context anywhere. There is no mention of narcotics, and I think there is a very significant distinction here.

They had mind-altering narcotics in the ancient world. Eastern spirituality is based on many of these psychedelic and hallucinogenic experiences. There is no question that marijuana and drugs are not a novelty, that they've been used for millennia. This is well-documented in other civilizations and cultures, and the fact is that it's not found anywhere in תורה שבכתב or תורה שבעל פה. This is very telling, and this cannot be glossed over. And the only time alcohol is mentioned in a negative way is when somebody drank on his own. So even alcohol is consumed only בחבורה, in a group, in a manner of לגימה שמקרבת. With regard to narcotics, there is not a single example anywhere in the Torah where this is mentioned.

There was a *kiddush* club for a short while in my shul, and *baruch Hashem*, I was successful in quashing it. This came with a great deal of עגמת נפש, but I do not allow anything like that here.

I've heard people say things which are really a חילול הקודש, that great chassidic figures used to get high, רחמנא ליצלן. It is very, very important for us to understand that all of *avodas Hashem* is based on effort and toil. Any spirituality which is induced in a counterfeit way, which does not come with יגיעה and hard work, is worthless. It's absolutely worthless. Rav Yosef Engel, in *Gilyonei Ha-Shas*, says that there is תשובה ומעשים טובים even in the next world, but the fulfillment of *mitzvos* over there doesn't have the value it has in our world, because in our world, there's a *yetzer hara*. It comes with toil; it's not a given. In the other world, it comes without any kind of toil, without any effort. The notion that Yidden should experience any kind of spirituality without effort, by simply "lighting up" or eating a "marijuana brownie," is totally alien to Yiddishkeit.

Marijuana is not just an "enhancer" [which can be used to help one's *avodas Hashem*]. It takes over. It creates a state of mind, a consciousness that did not come through hard work.

The truth is that this is an old idea. According to one opinion in the Gemara, Nadav and Avihu were killed because שתויי יין נכנסו להיכל — they entered the *Mishkan* in a state of intoxication. They were trying to obtain a higher level of spiritual consciousness. The way Chassidus explains the story of Nadav and Avihu is that they were rushing forward in a spiritual yearning and craving, but one which wasn't grounded. They wanted to go to a very lofty level without doing the work.

The purpose of alcohol at a *farbrengen* is to be able to speak one's mind, and to be able to accept what somebody says. It's not about connecting to Hashem per se. We don't drink, *chas ve-shalom*, before *davening*. The whole idea of saying "*le-chaim*" at a *farbrengen* is so that people will be open with one another. It is never done to experience spirituality, because this has to be experienced only through toil and effort.

The Midrash says that when Avraham Avinu began his journey of לך לך, he saw היו שותין ופוחזין — people were drinking and acting frivolously, and he said that he hoped his descendants would not act that way. He was very unimpressed. Then he came to a place and saw people working very hard tilling the ground, and he said that he hoped his descendants would be among those people. The Rebbe explained that this is the essence of Yiddishkeit — toil and effort in *avodas Hashem*.

Recreational marijuana is anathema to a Torah Yid. Feeling happy by using a foreign substance is totally antithetical to the message that the Torah has for each and every one of us.

JEWISH TELEGRAPHIC AGENCY

Why some American Jews pay more than $20,000 to get buried in Israel

June 7, 2019
By Josefin Dolsten

NEW YORK (JTA) — Within hours of his mother's funeral, Rabbi Abba Cohen was driving from Baltimore to New York's John F. Kennedy Airport. That night Cohen, together with his brother and sister, sat on a plane to Israel. The following day he would watch his mother being buried next to his father on the Mount of Olives, in Jerusalem. Only

The Jewish cemetary of the Mount of Olives overlooks Jerusalem's Old City. (Thomas Coex/AFP/Getty Images)

hours later he was once again on a flight, this time back to the United States, where he would sit shiva with the rest of the family.

"I was going to Israel, which I don't do every day and I always associate with joy and excitement, and here I was going to bury a loved one, so that was a very surreal experience," Cohen, who works as vice president for federal affairs at Agudath Israel of America, recalled of the burial four years ago.

Like many Jews, Cohen's parents wanted to be buried in Israel. The practice can be traced back to the Bible, where Jacob asks his son Joseph not to bury him in Egypt, but rather among his ancestors in Hebron.

In addition, Jewish tradition says that the dead will be resurrected when the Messiah arrives, starting with those buried in Israel. The process is prophesied to begin at the Mount of Olives, just beyond the eastern wall of Jerusalem's Old City.

But organizing a Jewish burial in Israel can be both complicated and costly.

Israel's national insurance system covers "burial expenses for anyone (even a foreign tourist) who dies in Israel and is buried near his place of death, or for an Israeli buried near his home here," according to Itim, the religious rights organization. However, those living abroad have to pay their own way and there are no rules limiting how much cemeteries can charge.

Cohen's parents bought their plots in the 1970s, but since then costs have risen dramatically. Today a plot on the Mount of Olives could cost as much as $30,000, according to Rabbi Shaul Ginsberg, who arranges burials in Israel for the New York-based Plaza Jewish Community Chapel.

Traditionally people have favored being buried in Jerusalem at either the Mount of Olives cemetery, the most ancient one in the city, or the Givat Shaul cemetery, the largest one, in the city's west. But with rising costs, people are looking elsewhere.

One cemetery popular among Americans Jews is Eretz HaChaim, which is located near the city of Beit Shemesh, about a 40 minute drive from Jerusalem. The majority of people buried there are foreigners, and out of those Americans make up the largest group, said Jonathan Konig, who assists the cemetery's burial society and sells headstones. The cemetery is Orthodox, as were "the overwhelming majority" of the approximately 5,000-6,000 people buried there, but Jews of all denominations are welcome, according to Konig.

Plots at Eretz HaChaim go for $9,500, in addition to a $1,500 one-time maintenance fee. The cemetery organizes transportation and other services necessary from arrival at Israel's Ben Gurion Airport for $2,200.

People can also expect to pay an additional $10,000-$15,000 for a range of necessary permits, transporting the body and services performed in the U.S., including ritual cleansing of the body. Ginsberg said El Al charges about $2,300 and United about $2,900 to transport a casket and body. That does not include flights for family members to attend the funeral in Israel.

Haaretz cited the Foreign Ministry as saying that 1,590 people died abroad and were buried in the Jewish state in 2016, an increase from 850 in 2007. That number includes Israelis who died while on vacation. Israel's Foreign and Interior Ministry did not respond or referred the Jewish Telegraphic Agency to people who did not respond to multiple requests for more current numbers.

Many Jewish organizations — including the National Council of Young Israel, Yeshiva University and the Rabbinical Council of America — have reserved plots at Eretz HaChaim for its members.

The National Council of Young Israel has held reserved plots at Eretz HaChaim since the late 1960s. Rabbi Binyamin Hammer, the organization's director of rabbinic services, says he has seen an increase in interest among Young Israel members in being buried in Israel in the last 20 years and that many are motivated by Zionism.

"The success of the day school movement has caused a tremendous amount of aliyah from America as well as people saying 'if I can't live there, at least let me be buried there,'" Hammer said, using the Hebrew word for immigration to Israel.

Rabbi Yehudah Prero, who coordinates burial in Israel for Young Israel, also attributes an increase to the fact that people today are less likely to stay in the same town or city for generations.

"They feel that if they pass away in a certain city, they don't know if their kids are going to be there," Prero said. "And even if they are, who knows where the grandkids are going to end up? But if they're buried in Israel, they know someone is going to come and be able to visit graveside."

For those who aren't members of an organization with reserved plot, there is Achu-zat Kever, an Israel-based organization founded by Rabbi Micheol Fletcher in 2004.

Fletcher helps people from abroad secure plots at cemeteries across Israel and helps coordinate transportation and a range of other services. The rabbi works directly with a number of cemeteries who offer him commissions when he sells plots. In cases where he does not receive a commission, he charges clients a fee of about $500.

Itim also offers guidance on holding funerals in Israel.

Rabbi Seth Farber, the organization's founder and director, says that cemeteries and funeral homes in the U.S. often cater to the needs and wishes of the family. But in Israel, the focus is on providing a funeral that the cemetery sees as adhering to their interpretation of Jewish law.

"It's not as user friendly for the family as America would be," he said.

For example, a family may bring with them their hometown rabbi thinking he or she will be able to lead the ceremony, but few Israeli cemeteries allow that. Some cemeteries do not allow women to give a eulogy and each one has certain traditions they follow without exception. Sometimes, the person who leads the funeral at the cemetery does not speak English.

Since 1996, says Itim, Israelis, Jewish or not, can choose to be buried in a civil cere-mony at cemeteries that allow them.

Burial in Israel also has geographic challenges.

Surella Baer, 64, has visited her father's grave three times since he passed away in 1991. But health problems currently prevent her from traveling there from her home in Queens, N.Y.

"My husband's parents are buried here out on Long Island and he gets to see them every year twice a year," she said. "I really wouldn't mind doing that, but the truth is it's what my father wanted, so we did it."

Still, the practice holds deep meaning for many.

"It's not just going to a cemetery to visit your loved one," said Cohen of visiting his parents' graves on the Mount of Olives. "It is that, but the entire experience of the setting and the meaning and the place all of that is extremely, extremely powerful and whenever I've gone, I've felt it."

This article is sponsored by UJA-Federation of NY, to raise awareness and facilitate conversations about end of life care in a Jewish context. The story was produced inde-pendently and at the sole discretion of JTA's editorial team.

Burial in Eretz Yisrael — Is It Worth the Cost?

One of the growing trends in the Orthodox Jewish world which has been made possible by modern-day affluence and transportation is קבורה בארץ — transporting the dead from abroad for burial in Israel. This is an expensive operation, with plots on the Mount of Olives costing as much as $30,000 apiece. A cheaper alternative is the Eretz Hachaim Cemetery outside Beit Shemesh — a popular resting place for Americans who seek the privilege and benefits of קבורה בארץ — which offers plots for approximately $10,000. Of course, these prices do not include transportation costs, which are considerable when transporting a body, as well as additional costs for the *chevra kadisha*. Neither do they take into account the physical and emotional toll on family members who, in a state of bereavement, must make the necessary complicated arrangements and endure the long flight to Israel for burial.

The question of "Is it worth it?" is one which Torah-committed Jews are not accustomed to asking when faced with the costs and efforts entailed in fulfilling *mitzvos*. We understand that the value of fulfilling God's will, and the immense privilege we have of being His special nation to whom He assigned unique obligations through which we lead an elevated, meaningful life, far outweigh the expense and inconvenience that these obligations impose. And so we joyfully bear the burden of yeshiva tuition, Shabbos and Yom Tov observance, *kashrus*, and the countless other responsibilities that we are so fortunate to have been given.

However, given the high costs of Orthodox Jewish living, there is little question that we need to carefully prioritize in choosing how to spend our limited resources. We must determine which religious causes should take precedence over others, and ensure that less important causes are not funded at the expense of more basic and vital needs.

We must ask, then, whether $10,000–$20,000 is a worthwhile expenditure for burial in *Eretz Yisrael*. There is no question or debate that the basic obligation to bury the remains of a deceased individual can be fulfilled anywhere in the world, and so the question arises as to whether the additional value of burial in Israel justifies the expense entailed.

Yaakov and Yosef's Request

The Gemara discusses the value of burial in *Eretz Yisrael* in *Maseches Kesubos* (111a), where it notes the request made by Yaakov before his passing that his remains be brought from Egypt for burial in his homeland,[1] and the similar request made by Yosef before his death.[2] The reason they made this request, the Gemara explains, is because at the time of the future resurrection, those who are buried outside *Eretz Yisrael* will not be revived unless they had been righteous, in which case God will provide special underground "tunnels" (מחילות) through which to reach the Land of Israel. Yaakov and Yosef, the Gemara explains, were not confident that they would earn this special miracle, and so they wished to be buried in *Eretz Yisrael* to guarantee their future resurrection.

The Midrash (*Bereishis Rabba* 96:5) also cites a slightly different reason for why Yaakov and Yosef requested burial in *Eretz Yisrael*, explaining: מתי ארץ ישראל חיים תחילה בימות המשיח ואוכלין שנות המשיח — "the deceased of the Land of Israel are revived first during the times of *Mashiach*, and 'consume' the years of *Mashiach*." This seems to mean that although all will be resurrected, those who were buried in *Eretz Yisrael* will rise at an earlier stage than those buried elsewhere, and will enjoy several years in the redeemed world before being joined by those buried abroad. This concept is taught also by the Talmud Yerushalmi, in *Maseches Kil'ayim* (9:3), where Reish Lakish is cited as commenting that *Eretz Yisrael* is called ארצות החיים ("the lands of the living"[3]) because it is the land שמתיה חיין תחילה לימות המשיח — "whose dead are revived first in the Messianic Era."

The Gemara (there in *Kesubos*) also cites an additional benefit of burial in *Eretz Yisrael*, in the name of Rav Anan: כל הקבור בארץ ישראל כאילו קבור תחת המזבח — "Whoever is buried in the Land of Israel is considered as though he is buried beneath the altar." The Torah states, וכפר אדמתו עמו — the ground of *Eretz Yisrael* brings atonement,[4] and, as Rav Anan notes, the word אדמה is associated with the altar (מזבח אדמה תעשה לי, *Shemos* 20:21), thus implying that the sacred ground of the Land of Israel brings atonement to the deceased just like the altar brings atonement to the living.

It seems clear, then, that there is immense value in being buried in *Eretz Yisrael*, both for the future resurrection, as well as for achieving atonement.

However, Rav Yekusiel Yehuda Halberstam of Klausenberg, in a responsum[5] on the subject of קבורה בארץ, asserts that this premise is not universally accepted. Just prior to the citation from Rav Anan regarding the atonement earned through קבורה בארץ, the Gemara brings an argument among the *Amoraim* surrounding the interpretation of a certain verse in the Prophets.[6] One view interprets the verse as indicating that one

---

1. *Bereishis* 47:29–30.
2. *Bereishis* 50:25.
3. *Tehillim* 116:9.
4. *Devarim* 32:43.
5. *Divrei Yatziv*, Y.D. 224.
6. *Yeshayahu* 33:24: ובל יאמר שכן חליתי העם היושב בה נשוא עוון.

who resides in *Eretz Yisrael* שרוי בלא עוון — "lives without sin," because his sins are all forgiven in the merit of his residence in the Holy Land. A second opinion, however, reads this verse differently, as stating that those stricken with illness earn atonement through their suffering. Rav Yaakov Reisher, in his *Iyun Yaakov* commentary, asserts that Rav Anan's statement, assuring atonement for those who are buried in *Eretz Yisrael*, is dependent on these two interpretations of the verse. Rav Anan's teaching follows the view interpreting the verse to mean that living in *Eretz Yisrael* earns a person atonement, whereas according to the other view, there is no source for the notion of earning atonement through living in *Eretz Yisrael*, and so there is likewise no basis to claim that one earns atonement by being buried in *Eretz Yisrael*. It thus emerges, the Klausenberger Rebbe notes, that different views exist as to whether there is value to being buried in *Eretz Yisrael*.

The Rebbe further observes that the *Sifrei*[7] brings other interpretations of the verse וכפר אדמתו עמו. For example, it suggests that this verse refers to the atonement earned by those Jews who are killed by gentiles, or to the atonement achieved by the wicked after their suffering in the afterlife.[8] This might suggest that the notion of earning atonement through קבורה בארץ is subject to dispute.

We should also add that Rashi, in his Torah commentary,[9] cites from the Midrash different views as to why Yaakov asked his son to bring his remains to *Eretz Yisrael* for burial — namely, Yaakov's fear that his grave in Egypt would become a site of pagan worship, and the concern that his remains would be affected by the plague of lice which God would visit upon Egypt, and which originated from the ground. These different opinions might point to the fact that not all *Tanna'im* accepted the premise that there is special value to burial in *Eretz Yisrael*.

ותבואו ותטמאו את ארצי

Additionally, we find some controversy regarding the propriety of bringing to *Eretz Yisrael* for burial the remains of those who lived outside the land.

Amidst the Gemara's discussion in *Kesubos*, it relates that Ula, a Babylonian scholar who frequently visited *Eretz Yisrael*, passed away outside *Eretz Yisrael*. Rabbi Elazar,

---

7.   *Ha'azinu*, 333.

8.   The Rebbe noted that the *Sifrei* cites Rabbi Meir as explaining וכפר אדמתו עמו as referring to the atonement earned through burial in *Eretz Yisrael* — a view that perhaps sheds light on the story told by the Yerushalmi (*Kil'ayim*) of how Rabbi Meir sensed during a trip abroad that he would soon die, and requested that his remains be sent to *Eretz Yisrael* for burial. As Rabbi Meir understood וכפר אדמתו עמו to mean that one's sins are atoned through קבורה בארץ, he specifically asked to be buried in his homeland.

9.   *Bereishis* 47:29.

upon hearing the news, lamented, "You, Ula, should die upon impure land?!" His disciples tried consoling him with the information that Ula's remains were being brought to the Land of Israel for burial. He responded, אינו דומה קולטתו מחיים לקולטתו לאחר מיתה — "His absorption [by the land] in his lifetime is not the same as his absorption after death." In other words, while there is certainly value in bringing one's remains to *Eretz Yisrael* for burial, this value cannot be compared to the value of a person living and then being buried in *Eretz Yisrael*.

This story clearly indicates that while the benefit of קבורה בארץ for one who died outside *Eretz Yisrael* is less than that for one who died in *Eretz Yisrael*, it is nevertheless valuable.

A different position, however, seems to emerge from a story told in the Yerushalmi (in *Kil'ayim*, as cited earlier) of two Sages — Rebbi bar Kiriya and Rabbi Elazar — who once observed coffins being transported to *Eretz Yisrael*. Rebbi bar Kiriya commented, "What benefit is there for them?" He proceeded to cite the verse in the *Book of Yirmiyahu* (2:7) where the prophet harshly condemned the people in God's Name, crying, ותבואו ותטמאו את ארצי ונחלתי שמתם לתועבה — "You have come and defiled My land, and you have made My portion abominable." The first phrase in this verse — "You have come and defiled my land" — is understood by Rebbi bar Kiriya as referring to those who live outside *Eretz Yisrael* and are brought only after death, when they are a source of *tum'a* (impurity). Rebbi bar Kiriya sharply decried the practice of bringing bodies for burial in *Eretz Yisrael*, regarding it as a "defilement" of the sacred land.

Rabbi Elazar responded to this criticism by defending those transporting the bodies, explaining, כיון שהן מגיעין לארץ ישראל הן נוטלין גוש עפר ומניחין על ארונן — "once they reach the Land of Israel, they take a block of earth and place it on their coffins." Just before the bodies crossed the border into *Eretz Yisrael*, earth from the Holy Land was placed on the coffin, such that the deceased would be included in the aforementioned promise, וכפר אדמתו עמו — that burial in the earth of *Eretz Yisrael* brings atonement — even before they entered the land. According to Rabbi Elazar, this suffices to then permit bringing the coffin across the border and interring it in the sacred ground of the Land of Israel, as the individual has already achieved atonement and thus does not compromise the sanctity of *Eretz Yisrael*. It is unclear whether Rebbi bar Kiriya accepted this defense, or felt that even if earth is placed on the coffins at the border, their arrival in *Eretz Yisrael* for burial constitutes a sinful "defilement" of the land.

The *Zohar*, in several contexts, elaborates at great length on the sinfulness of "defiling" *Eretz Yisrael* by bringing corpses to the land for burial. In *Parshas Vayechi*,[10] the *Zohar* questions why Yaakov asked that his remains be brought to *Eretz Yisrael* for burial, and it answers, שאני יעקב דשכינתא הות אחידת ביה ואתדבקת ביה — "Yaakov is different, because the divine presence clung to him and was attached to him." The

---

10.   225b.

Zohar cites God's promise to Yaakov before he settled in Egypt, אנכי ארד עמך מצרימה — "I shall descend with you to Egypt,"[11] and explains that Yaakov earned special spiritual protection in exile such that the impurities of foreign lands had no effect on him. For this reason — and for this reason only — Yaakov was allowed to have his remains transported to *Eretz Yisrael* for burial. Yaakov's case, according to the *Zohar*, was exceptional, and for all other people, bringing a body after death to the Land of Israel for burial constitutes a defilement of the land.

The *Zohar* returns to this concept later, in *Parshas Teruma* (141b), where it explains that a dead body brought for burial brings the impurity of foreign lands to the sacred land of *Eretz Yisrael*, requiring God to "cure" the land by bringing a special wind to cleanse it of its impurities. And in *Parshas Acharei-Mos* (72b), the *Zohar* says about a person whose soul departed abroad but his body was buried in *Eretz Yisrael*, כביכול עביד קדש חול וחול קדש — "it is as though he makes the sacred profane, and makes the profane sacred." Such an individual, according to the *Zohar*, gives his soul, the sacred component of his being, to the "profane" domain of foreign lands, and gives his body, the lower component of his being, to the sacred domain of *Eretz Yisrael*.

Thus, whereas numerous sources speak of the great value of קבורה בארץ, the *Zohar* — and, seemingly, Rebbi bar Kiriya — strongly discourage the practice of bringing the dead to the Holy Land for burial.

Rav Levi Ibn Chabiv, in one of his published responsa,[12] asserts that this issue, as to the propriety of bringing the deceased to *Eretz Yisrael* for burial, is subject to dispute, and the clear majority among the sages permits and sees value in this practice.

Rav Shmuel Wosner, in his *Shevet Ha-Levi*,[13] dismisses this conclusion, arguing that it is inconceivable that Rebbi bar Kiriya would dispute the numerous, emphatic statements in the Talmud emphasizing the immense value of קבורה בארץ. In Rav Wosner's view, the seemingly contradictory sources can easily be reconciled by distinguishing between those who resided abroad because they were unable to live in *Eretz Yisrael*, and those who had the ability to live in *Eretz Yisrael* but willingly chose not to. Rav Wosner writes:

באלו ארונות של מתי עשירי חו"ל וכדומה שהיה להם האפשרות לעלות גם בחייהם ומאסו לעלות בחיים כי חמדו להם ישיבת ארץ טמאה, ובאים לאחר מותם, באלה סבר רבי בר קיריא כיוון דנחלתי שמתם לתועבה בחייכם א"כ סניגור יעשה קטיגור במיתתכם שתבואו ותטמאו אותה.

It is regarding these coffins of wealthy residents of the Diaspora and the like, who had the possibility of emigrating [to *Eretz Yisrael*] even in their

---

11. *Bereishis* 46:4.
12. 63.
13. 2:207.

lifetimes, but they rejected [the option of] emigrating in their lifetime, because they desired for themselves residence in the impure land, and they then come after death — regarding these Rebbi bar Kiriya felt that since "you made My portion abominable" in your lifetime, that which would advocate [for you] becomes a prosecutor [against you] when you die, if you come and defile it [the land].

According to Rav Wosner, there is no disagreement among the sages, and all agree that קבורה בארץ is beneficial even if one died outside *Eretz Yisrael* — unless one had the opportunity to move to *Eretz Yisrael* during his lifetime and willfully chose not to. For such an individual, the sanctity of *Eretz Yisrael* which he disregarded when he was alive cannot now serve as a means of atonement for him after his passing.

This theory is advanced also by Rav Moshe Sternbuch, in his *Teshuvos Ve-Hanha-gos*,[14] where he writes:

> ונראה שזה תלוי אם באמת ובתמים השתוקק בחייו לנסוע לארץ ישראל ונאנס,
> וכי"ש אם הוא תושב ארץ ישראל שנפטר פתאום בחו"ל מצוה להוליכו לארץ
> ישראל... אבל כשנשאר בחו"ל בחייו, מפני חיי רווחה וכדומה, ולאחר מיתה דוקא
> רוצה שגופו המת ינוח בארץ ישראל יש מקום לקטרג ע"ז.

> It would seem that this depends on whether he truly and sincerely longed during his lifetime to journey to the Land of Israel, but was unable to — and certainly if he was a resident of the Land of Israel who suddenly died outside the land, [in which case] there is certainly a *mitzva* to bring him to the Land of Israel... But if he remained outside the land during his lifetime because of the comfortable living conditions and the like, and he wants specifically that after his passing his body would rest in the Land of Israel, there is room to protest against this.[15]

---

14. 1:689.

15. This distinction is made also by Don Isaac Abarbanel, in his Torah commentary (*Bereishis* 49), where he elaborates at length on the folly of living outside *Eretz Yisrael* but requesting burial in *Eretz Yisrael*:

> יש רבים מבני אדם שיבלו ימיהם בטוב בתורה ובמצוות ותמיד ילכו לפני ה' בארצות
> החיים ומפני דבקותם ושלמותם בחייהם הם ראויים להוליכם במותם לא"י ולקברם שמה
> והאנשים ההמה אינם מטמאים את הארץ כי היו גופותיהם תשמישי קדושה טהורים
> ונקיים והם המעותדים לתחיית המתים ולזה ראוי שיקברו בארץ החיים ויקומו מבלי
> גלגול ומבלי צער. ויש אנשים אחרים רבים מאד שיבלו בהבל ימיהם ורצים אחר התאוות
> הגשמיות והם אשר בחייהם קרויים מתים וכאשר ימותו יצוו את בניהם לעשות צדקה
> ומתנות לאביונים מה שלא עשו בימיהם ומהם יצוו ויקברו אותם מעוטפים בציצית
> ותפילין בהיותם לובשים בחייהם צמר ופשתים יחדו. וכן יש מהם שיצוו שיוליכו את

The *Shulchan Aruch*'s Ruling

Regardless, it seems quite clear that the accepted *halacha* is to consider קבורה בארץ valuable for all people.

The Rambam, in his discussion of the great importance and value of living in *Eretz Yisrael*, writes:[16]

> אמרו חכמים כל השוכן בארץ ישראל עונותיו מחולין... אפילו הלך בה ארבע אמות זוכה לחיי העולם הבא וכן הקבור בה נתכפר לו וכאילו המקום שהוא בו מזבח כפרה...ואינו דומה קולטתו מחיים לקולטתו אחר מותו, ואעפ״כ גדולי החכמים היו מוליכים מתיהם לשם. צא ולמד מיעקב אבינו ויוסף הצדיק.

> The Sages said, "Whoever resides in the Land of Israel — his sins are forgiven…" Even if one walks just four cubits there, he earns life in the next world. Likewise, whoever is buried there achieves atonement, and it is as though his place is an altar that brings atonement…. And one's absorption [by the land] in his lifetime is not the same as his absorption after death, but the greatest Sages nevertheless would bring their deceased [family members] there. Go learn from our patriarch Yaakov, and Yosef the pious one.

The Rambam explicitly cites the Gemara's teaching that burial in *Eretz Yisrael* brings atonement, and emphasizes that although the benefits are fewer when one's remains are brought from abroad for burial than when one lives and then dies in *Eretz Yisrael*, even these benefits are valuable, as evidenced by Yaakov and Yosef's desire to have their remains brought to *Eretz Yisrael*.[17]

עצמותיהם להקבר בא״י בהיותם בחייהם מרחיקים ומואסים אותה כאלו בחייהם היו רשעים ובמותם נעשו צדיקים ומקימי המצוות. וידוע שזה דעת נפסד והוא לפי שהמצוות יעשו אותם החיים לא המתים וכארז״ל מאי דכתיב כי אי עבד חפשי מאדוניו כיון שמת אדם נעשה חפשי מהמצוות ועל כיוצא בזה א״ר אלעזר בחייכם לא עליתם במיתתכם ותבאו ותטמאו את ארצי כי הנה על רשעי דורו אמר הנביא אותו פסוק שהיו מתחסדים במיתתם ולא בחייהם. וכבר ארז״ל שלא יוכל אדם לעשות משעטנז מרדעת לחמורו אבל יוכל לעשות ממנו תכריכין למת. שהורו בזה שהמת הוא פטור מן המצות והחמור החי הוא יותר ראוי אליהם מהאיש המת ולכן לא יועיל לאדם הטוב אשר יעשה במותו אם בחייו לא היה נזהר בזה הנה התבאר שהאבות הקדושים להיותם בחייהם טהורים וקדושים דבקים באל היה משתוקקים להקבר בארץ הקדושה היה נכון אליהם לצות שאחרי מותם יוליכום להקבר שמה ושלא נאמר עליהם בחייכם לא עליתם במיתתכם ותבאו ותטמאו את ארצי כי הם בחייהם במחשבתם ותשוקתם היו עולים שמה תמיד ולכן במיתתם גופיהם שהיו תשמישי קדושה לא היו מטמאים את הארץ.

16. *Hilchos Melachim* 5:11.
17. The Klausenberger Rebbe, in the responsum referenced earlier, understands the Rambam's

Likewise, the *Shulchan Aruch* (Y.D. 363:1) writes:

אין מפנין המת והעצמות, לא מקבר מכובד לקבר מכובד, ולא מקבר בזוי לקבר
בזוי, ולא מבזוי למכובד, ואין צריך לומר ממכובד לבזוי — אפילו
ממכובד לבזוי מותר, שערב לאדם שיהא נח אצל אבותיו. **וכן כדי לקוברו בארץ
ישראל מותר**.

The deceased or his bones shall not be exhumed — not from a respectful grave to another respectful grave, not from a disrespectful grave
to another disrespectful grave, not from a disrespectful [grave] to a
respectful [grave], and, it goes without saying, not from a respectful
[grave] to a disrespectful [grave]. But within his own [family plot], then
it is permissible [to transfer the remains] even from a respectful [grave]
to a disrespectful [grave], for a person wishes to rest near his forefathers.
Likewise, it is permissible [to exhume one's remains] in order to bury
him in the Land of Israel.

The prohibition against exhuming and reinterring human remains is suspended for the
sake of reburial in *Eretz Yisrael*, without any conditions or qualifications. This ruling is
based on the comments of the Ramban, in his *Toras Ha-Adam* (*Sha'ar Ha-Kevura*). The
Shach, commenting on this ruling, explains that reburial is permitted in this instance
because it is done for the benefit of the deceased, who will earn atonement in the merit
of קבורה בארץ. We should add that Rav Levi Ibn Chabiv, in the responsum cited above,
ruled that even if the deceased left specific instructions asking that his remains not be
brought to *Eretz Yisrael* for burial, the family may ignore his instructions, due to the
benefits of קבורה בארץ.[18]

---

comments differently. In his view, the fact that "one's absorption in one's lifetime is not
the same as his absorption after death" negates altogether the value of burial in *Eretz
Yisrael*, except for uniquely righteous individuals such as Yaakov and Yosef, for the reason
explained by the *Zohar* (as discussed earlier). And thus the Rambam writes that although
bringing a body from abroad for burial in *Eretz Yisrael* generally offers no benefit, "the
greatest sages" would have their remains brought to *Eretz Yisrael*, following the example
set by Yaakov and Yosef, because for the exceptionally righteous, this is beneficial.

However, the straightforward reading of the Rambam's comments, and certainly the
overall tenor of this passage, suggest that the Rambam here unconditionally extols the
virtue of קבורה בארץ, albeit with the qualification that the benefits are less for those whose
remains are brought from abroad. And, in any event, the *Shulchan Aruch*'s ruling cited
below clearly points to the value of קבורה בארץ without any distinction between the
exceptionally righteous and others.

18. Rav Moshe Feinstein, in *Iggeros Moshe* (Y.D. 3:153), asserts that the *Shulchan Aruch*'s

Therefore, notwithstanding the indications of disagreement on this matter among the Sages of the Talmud, the *Shulchan Aruch* issued a clear, unequivocal ruling permitting bringing a body to *Eretz Yisrael* for reburial, because of the benefits this offers the deceased. There is no indication in the *Shulchan Aruch* or its commentaries that this does not apply to those who had the opportunity to live in *Eretz Yisrael* but willfully chose not to, as Rav Wosner and Rav Sternbuch proposed. It thus appears that it is permissible, and valuable, for any deceased person to be brought to *Eretz Yisrael* for burial.

Indeed, Rav Ovadia Yosef, in his responsum concerning the permissibility of bringing the remains of Sir Moses Montefiore from England to Israel,[19] ruled that as the *Shulchan Aruch* does not follow the *Zohar*'s position, it is permissible to bury in *Eretz Yisrael* somebody who had lived in the Diaspora.

It must be emphasized, however, that although the Rambam extols the value of קבורה בארץ, and the *Shulchan Aruch* rules that the value of קבורה בארץ is sufficient reason to exhume a body for reburial, neither refers to קבורה בארץ with the term מצוה. Burial in *Eretz Yisrael* is valuable as a source of atonement and in preparation for the time of the resurrection, but it is not spoken of as a מצווה מן המובחר — a higher standard of *mitzva* observance — not to mention that it is certainly not obligatory in any way.[20]

---

ruling applies only to the deceased's children, who wish to bring a parent's remains for burial in *Eretz Yisrael*. Others, however, are not permitted to move a deceased's remains for reburial in *Eretz Yisrael*. Rav Moshe thus opposed the idea to bring Sir Moses Montefiore's remains to Israel for burial. This ruling was disputed by Rav Ovadia Yosef, in the responsum referenced below, who permitted reinterring Montefiore's remains in *Eretz Yisrael*, and dismissed Rav Moshe's claim that only the children are authorized to make this decision. Rav Ovadia pointed to the reinterring of the remains of the Chida, which were transferred from Livorno to Jerusalem in 1960, an undertaking initiated by the Sephardic Chief Rabbi at the time, Rav Yitzchak Nissim, with full support from leading Torah sages. Similarly, Rav Tzvi Pesach Frank (*Har Tzvi*, Y.D. 274), among others, permitted bringing the remains of Rav Aharon of Karlin to Israel for reburial.

19. *Yabia Omer*, vol. 7, Y.D. 39.

20. This point is made by the Klausenberger Rebbe, in the aforementioned responsum, where he questions why Rav Levi Ibn Chabiv used the word מצוה in reference to burial in *Eretz Yisrael*.

    Notably, the Rambam, in one of his published responsa (Freiman edition, 372), writes about somebody who brought his parents' remains to *Eretz Yisrael*, מה שעשה הוא טוב מאד — "That which he did is very good." The Rambam clearly felt that קבורה בארץ is valuable, but he stopped short of referring to it as a מצוה.

Financial Priorities

This final point becomes critically important as we seek to determine whether it is worthwhile, or even appropriate, to accept an immense financial burden for the sake of קבורה בארץ. Even for an outright Torah obligation, the Rama[21] writes explicitly that one is not required to spend more than 20 percent of his assets if this is necessary to fulfill the requirement. Unlike the Torah's prohibitions, which one must avoid even at the expense of all his possessions, the *mitzvos asei* (affirmative commands) are waived when an overbearing financial burden is at stake.[22] Certainly, then, when it comes to קבורה בארץ, which, as we have seen, is most definitely not obligatory, and is not even referred to as a מצוה מן המובחר, there is no need whatsoever to subject oneself to financial strain for this purpose.[23]

The *poskim*'s concern to prevent people from overspending on non-obligatory religious practices is expressed in a remark of the *Magen Avraham*[24] regarding Shabbos expenses. The *Magen Avraham* cites the *Tikunei Shabbos* as stating that it is proper to include fish in all three Shabbos meals, but then immediately writes that if the price of fish is too high, "it is proper to enact that fish should not be purchased." In his view, not only is excessive spending for non-obligatory religious practices unnecessary, but rabbis bear the responsibility of discouraging such profligacy through formal enactments.

A Talmudic source for such an enactment, interestingly enough, relates to the

---

21. O.C. 656.

22. A different view appears to emerge from the comments of the Ritva, cited by *Shita Mekubetzes* (*Beitza* 16a), in reference to the Gemara's comment that God repays a person the money he spends for Shabbos and Yom Tov observance, and for his children's Torah education. The Ritva asserts that this is true of all *mitzva* expenses, and not only those mentioned by the Gemara. According to this view, it seems, one should spend any amount of money necessary to fulfill a Torah obligation, and trust that God will return the money to him.

    Clearly, however, the Rama did not accept this position, and, in any event, even the Ritva likely refers only to money paid for clear-cut *mitzvos*, as opposed to expenses which have religious value but do not formally qualify as *mitzvos*. And, as mentioned below, even when it comes to Shabbos expenses, the *poskim* warn against overspending.

23. Rav Moshe Feinstein (*Iggeros Moshe*, O.C. 4:2) was asked whether one may go to work without a *yarmulke* if he fears that wearing it might jeopardize his career, and he ruled unequivocally that this is allowed. He explained that according to the vast majority of *poskim*, wearing a *yarmulke* is required only on the level of מידת חסידות (a measure of piety), and not as a strict halachic requirement, and, as such, there is certainly no obligation to risk one's financial stability for the sake of this practice. This would apply *a fortiori* to קבורה בארץ, which, unlike wearing a *yarmulke*, is not required at all, on any level.

24. O.C. 242:1.

particular phenomenon of unnecessary, crippling expenses for funerals. The Gemara relates in *Maseches Kesubos* (8b) that there was a time when הייתה הוצאת המת קשה לקרוביו יותר ממיתתו — funerals caused the surviving family members more grief than the loss of their loved one, due to the cost of the customary lavish shrouds. Rabban Gamliel set out to solve this problem by instructing that the deceased should be buried in simple linen shrouds, setting an example that others then followed, thereby lowering funeral costs.

Rabban Gamliel's edict was referenced by Rav Yosef Eliyahu Henkin[25] in lamenting the high sums that people were paying for funerals and tombstones, and for קבורה בארץ. He writes that this practice directly violates Rabban Gamliel's edict, and imposes an unnecessary financial burden on the family of the deceased.

Rav Henkin cites also the story told in the Talmud Yerushalmi[26] of two rabbis who observed an ornate synagogue in Lod, and one praised those who donated such large sums for the sake of building beautiful houses of prayer, marveling, כמה ממון שיקעו אבותי כאן — "Look how much money my ancestors invested here!" The other replied, כמה נפשות שקעו אבותיך כאן — "How many lives did your ancestors invest here!" He noted that this money should have been used to support impoverished Torah scholars instead of being wasted on extravagant synagogues. In the case of burial, too, Rav Henkin comments, the value and wisdom of spending large sums of money for an especially respectful funeral, or for קבורה בארץ, must be considered in light of the numerous pressing needs that are not being met because of insufficient funding.

Rav Henkin thus writes: "The rule is — if one's father left him money, or he has a lot of money of his own, and he does not want to lose it, he should not swim with the current and spend it on wood and marble stone, or on traveling, but rather to support the study of Torah and charity in general."

In a separate letter,[27] Rav Henkin elaborates further, citing the timeless, poignant teaching of Rabbenu Bachya Ibn Pekuda in *Chovos Ha-Levavos*,[28] אין התוספת ניתנת אלא כשהחובה נפרעה — there is no value in voluntary, non-obligatory measures unless one has fully met all his strict requirements.[29] Rav Henkin writes that requesting burial in *Eretz Yisrael* would likely constitute יוהרא (arrogance), as it implicitly reflects confidence in one's having satisfied all his strict obligations, such that he imposes an exorbitant financial burden upon his inheritors for the sake of the non-obligatory practice of קבורה בארץ.

---

25. *Kisvei Ha-Rav Henkin*, vol. 2, 66.

26. *Pei'a* 8:8.

27. 68:3.

28. *Sha'ar Yichud Ha-Ma'aseh*, 5.

29. In Rav Yosef Kapach's translation of *Chovos Ha-Levavos*, this passage reads, אין הנדבה מתקבלת אלא לאחר מלוי החובה.

Certainly, Rav Henkin adds, creating any sort of pressure upon the deceased's family members to accept the cost of קבורה בארץ is wrong, and it likely constitutes גזל אלמנה ויתומים — stealing from widows and orphans.

Similarly, it is told[30] that Rav Aharon Kotler was once asked by a family in Kletzk whether they should bring their deceased loved one's remains to *Eretz Yisrael* for burial, or bury him in Kletzk and donate to a yeshiva the money they would have paid for קבורה בארץ. Rav Kotler replied that the deceased's soul would receive more benefit from a donation to support Torah study. The family then asked Rav Shach to bring the question to the Chafetz Chayim, who gave the same answer. The Chafetz Chayim added that it is customary to visit the grave on the *yahrtzeit* and to give charity in the deceased's merit, and the needy in the deceased's community should be given precedence over the needy in *Eretz Yisrael*. For this reason, too, the Chafetz Chayim said, it would be preferable to bury the deceased in his hometown rather than to bring his remains to *Eretz Yisrael*.[31]

Rav Yosef Shalom Elyashiv likewise reportedly determined[32] that charity, an explicit Biblical command, takes precedence over קבורה בארץ, the religious value of which is not explicated in the Torah.[33]

Rav Yaakov Kamenetsky is said[34] to have discouraged transporting bodies from the United States to Israel for other reasons, noting that this often results in הלנת המת — delaying the burial — which may not be done unnecessarily. Moreover, some countries require first removing the blood from the body before allowing its transportation abroad, which constitutes ניוול המת — a desecration of the body.[35] And, Rav Kamenetsky noted, if the deceased is buried far from the surviving family members, they are unable to pay frequent visits to the grave, which would inspire them to repent.[36]

---

30. *Aleinu Leshabeïach, Shemos*, p. 538; *Meir Einei Yisrael*, vol. 2, p. 173.

31. A slightly different version of this story appears in *Path to Greatness: The Life of Maran Harav Elazar Menachem Man Shach* (p. 240). There it is told that the Chafetz Chayim refused to write a letter expressing his opinion on this matter, certain that the family would in any event not heed his guidance. Rav Shach then brought the question to Rav Chaim Ozer Grodzinsky, who likewise felt that supporting Torah learning was preferable to קבורה בארץ, and wrote a letter to this effect. Nevertheless, as the Chafetz Chayim suspected, the family ignored the letter and brought their loved one to *Eretz Yisrael* for burial.

32. *Shu"t Divrei Chachamim*, p. 223.

33. Rav Elyashiv conceded, however, that if the deceased had expressly requested to be buried in *Eretz Yisrael*, then the family must obey his wishes.

34. *Be-Mechitzas Rabbeinu*, p. 188.

35. This concern is expressed also by Rav Sternbuch, in the responsum noted above.

36. Visits to the gravesite by family members also brings great benefit to the soul of the

Rabbi Doniel Neustadt[37] stated that as קבורה בארץ does not constitute a *mitzva*, financially assisting a family to bring their loved one to *Eretz Yisrael* for burial does not qualify as *tzedaka*, and it is improper to launch fundraising campaigns for this purpose.

Conclusion

1. Burial in *Eretz Yisrael* certainly has religious value, and while some *poskim* discouraged bringing to *Eretz Yisrael* the remains of a person who had the ability to live in *Eretz Yisrael* but chose not to, the *Shulchan Aruch* seems to permit this practice. However, according to Rav Henkin, it is improper to specifically request burial in *Eretz Yisrael*, as such a request implicitly reflects the person's arrogant belief that he has satisfied all his strict religious obligations and is thus worthy of insisting on the non-obligatory measure of קבורה בארץ.

2. The value of קבורה בארץ must be carefully weighed against other considerations, including the delay this causes before burial, and the great value of family members frequenting the gravesite of their loved one on a regular basis, which will not be possible if the body is interred in a different country.

3. As a community, we must ensure not to create a trend that would cause people to feel pressured to undertake the expense of קבורה בארץ, in accordance with Rabban Gamliel's effort to keep funeral costs at bay.

4. On both an individual and a communal level, we must carefully prioritize our limited resources. Supporting the poor and providing funding for Torah education should, without question, be given a much higher position on our priority scale than paying to transport the dead to *Eretz Yisrael* for burial.

5. Lending financial assistance to a family for קבורה בארץ does not qualify as *tzedaka*, and it is improper to fundraise for this purposes.

---

deceased. See *Sefer Chassidim*, 710.

37. In an interview on *Headlines with Dovid Lichtenstein*, 19 Teves, 5778 (January 6, 2018), transcribed below.

Rabbi Doniel Neustadt

Interviewed on *Headlines with Dovid Lichtenstein*, 19 Teves 5778 (January 6, 2018)

Paying tuition is an obligation and a *mitzva*; bringing a body for burial in *Eretz Yisrael* is neither. At most, it's an *inyan* (worthwhile religious practice). According to some, it should not be done. If someone has the money to do it, he can do it. If someone left the money to do it, then there's a מצוה לקיים דברי המת (obligation to fulfill the requests made by the deceased before his death), but there's no *mitzva* per se. It would be forbidden to raise money for it. It's not *tzedaka*. My grandfather, Reb Yaakov Kamenetsky, was not in support of being buried in *Eretz Yisrael*. He said the most important thing is that the children should be able to visit the grave on the *yahrtzeit* and other occasions. For him to be buried in *Eretz Yisrael* when his kids are living in America — he felt this was completely not *mentschlech*. Reb Moshe [Feinstein] was opposed to it. I know people whom he counseled against it. The Satmar Rav was opposed. And Rav Henkin writes strongly against it.

Rabbi Avrohom Cohen

Interviewed on *Headlines with Dovid* Lichtenstein, 19 Teves 5778 (January 6, 2018)

There's a dispute about קבורה בארץ, but although there are those who are against it, I would differentiate. Someone who wished their whole life to move to *Eretz Yisrael* but couldn't — there's no opposition to bringing him to *Eretz Yisrael*. However, if someone could have gone [to live in *Eretz Yisrael*] during his lifetime, and he didn't, then the Yerushalmi and *Zohar* oppose burying him in *Eretz Yisrael*, because he despised the land during his lifetime, and he now makes the land impure by coming after his death.

THE JERUSALEM POST

For Orthodox Jews, George Floyd protests stir complicated feelings

June 6, 2020
By Shira Hanau/JTA

On Sunday night, Rabbi Richard Altabe marched arm in arm with two black politicians protesting police brutality at a demonstration in Far Rockaway.

The next morning, Orthodox Jews in the same New York neighborhood showed up at the local police precinct to drop off pastries for the officers – 101 danishes for the 101st Precinct.

The principal of the Hebrew Academy of Long Beach's lower school, Altabe sees no contradiction between Orthodox Jews participating in a march against police misconduct and their sugary goodwill gesture the next morning.

Members of the Orthodox Jewish community watch as protesters walk through the Brooklyn borough on June 3, 2020. (Angela Weiss/AFP via Getty Images/JTA)

"We wanted them to know that even though we support the protests, we also supported the police and we're grateful to the police and the work they do," Altabe said.

The two gestures – opposing police misconduct while supporting the police more generally – are emblematic of the fine line Orthodox Jews have navigated in responding to sweeping protests sparked by the killing of George Floyd at the hands of white Minneapolis police officers.

"Many Orthodox Jews have had negative interactions personally with the police and have seen others who have and certainly understand and are sympathetic to the idea around police accountability and reform," said David Greenfield, a former New York city councilman who now leads the Met Council, a Jewish nonprofit serving needy New Yorkers. "At the same time, however, they are generally supportive of the NYPD because they're generally concerned about public safety and the looting."

Orthodox Jewish communities are both more politically conservative and more inward-focused than non-Orthodox Jewish communities in America. That dynamic was on display this week in the flood of statements from Jewish organizations weighing in on the protests and the societal conditions they aim to upset. While some organizations were quick to respond with detailed descriptions of proposed policy changes and pledges to work toward them, Orthodox organizations were slower to weigh in, vaguer in their visions and made a point of condemning the violence that unfolded at some of the protests.

In a statement yesterday, the National Council of Young Israel, an umbrella group of Orthodox synagogues, said Floyd's killing showed that "racism is regrettably still alive and well in our country" and that it is critical that "the grave danger posed by systemic racism is duly addressed once and for all." But the statement also noted that most law enforcement officers are "heroes" who risk their lives to protect ordinary citizens, regardless of skin color.

"These honorable officers should not be attacked or tarnished by the misconduct of others; however, it is essential that an effort be undertaken to remove any police officer that does in fact exhibit a degree of racial and ethnic bigotry," the group said.

The Orthodox Union and the Rabbinical Council of America, the two principal national organizations representing Modern Orthodoxy, both condemned Floyd's killing and expressed support for peaceful protests against racism while condemning the violence and looting. Agudath Israel, which represents haredi Orthodox communities, did much the same, though the Agudath statement did not use the word "racism."

"Like all decent Americans, we are horrified by the senseless and ruthless killing of George Floyd, and we join in solidarity with the outpouring of hurt, anger and frustration expressed by responsible citizens protesting peacefully," the group said. "We are also greatly saddened by the frightening scenes of innocent bystanders and store owners under siege, threatened by violence and mayhem, and facing the prospect of lost livelihoods and uncertain futures."

The differing responses of Orthodox groups from their Reform and Conservative counterparts may be explained at least in part by politics. Unlike most American Jews, who tend to vote for Democrats, Orthodox Jews have leaned increasingly Republican in recent years. According to the most recent Pew Center study of American Jews, 57% of Orthodox Jews are Republican or lean Republican compared to just 22% of American Jews as a whole.

Several Orthodox politicians in New York put out statements to similar effect, supporting peaceful protests and condemning the death of George Floyd without directly criticizing the police. But some also spent several days questioning why protesters were allowed to gather en masse while religious gatherings are still restricted because of the coronavirus pandemic.

On Tuesday, Simcha Eichenstein, a state assemblyman representing two heavily Orthodox neighborhoods in Brooklyn, and Kalman Yeger, a New York City councilman, sent a letter to Governor Andrew Cuomo saying that the protests are evidence that the time for lockdown had passed.

"Protesters are gathering, perhaps well-meaning, but surely with little regard for social-distancing standards. It has also unfortunately brought out rioters who are destroying what is left of our economy, eviscerating the life's work of our fellow New Yorkers," they wrote. "The lockdown may not have formally ended, but the calls for mass peaceful marching without any regard for social-distancing have rendered a continual lockdown at this point ludicrous."

Eichenstein also tweeted in frustration over the different rules regarding protests and religious gatherings.

"Sure, protesters have the right under the first amendment to march against racism, which needs to be confronted head on in this country, but the same first amendment guarantees religious people the right to practice their faith," he wrote in response to a statement by the mayor at a press conference.

By Thursday, Eichenstein's focus had shifted. He placed a sign in the window of his Borough Park office with the words George Floyd repeated before his death, "I can't breathe," in large print. He also expressed mourning and solidarity with the black community in a video Thursday. "As a Hasidic Orthodox Jew, my message is we, the Orthodox Jewish people, stand with you in solidarity, we must eliminate hate wherever it exists," Eichenstein said.

The city council's Jewish caucus, chaired by Orthodox city councilman Chaim Deutsch, put out a statement Monday expressing solidarity with the black community but without mentioning the police. And in a letter to constituents Thursday, State Senator Simcha Felder called George Floyd's death an "act of pure evil," saying that to ignore the message being sent by the black community about continued discrimination would be "unconscionable."

But Felder also condemned the looting and violence against police officers.

"So let's protest what we see is wrong and let's inspire change without vilifying every member of the NYPD- they are people, too. Let's not trade one evil for another," he wrote.

Devorah Halberstam, an activist on anti-Semitism in Crown Heights who frequently speaks to new police recruits as part of their training, said the statements this week reflect the Orthodox community's priorities.

"I think most people feel that people have a right to protest," Halberstam said. "However, people are just concerned about safety and everyone wants to feel that they're safe and that their stores are safe, their communities are safe."

Protests — a Torah Perspective

Public protest is one of the cherished freedoms of modern democracies. Western Civilization recognizes the right of all people to publicly and openly denounce perceived injustices. Observant Jews have taken full advantage of this precious right. A large group of American rabbis conducted the so-called "Rabbis' March" in Washington, D.C. in 1943 to urge the United States and its Allies to intervene to save European Jewry from the Nazis. Orthodox Jews were at the forefront of the campaign to free Soviet Jewy during the 1970s and 1980s. And in Israel, religious groups frequently organize rallies to protest government policies or actions deemed hostile to Torah Jewry.

More recently, in the wake of the murder in Minneapolis of George Floyd, an African American suspected of a crime, by a white police officer, protests were held throughout the United States, many of which became destructive. Protestors set fire to a number of business, and many shops were looted.

What do our Torah sources have to say about protesting injustice? Are we encouraged to take to the streets and hold rallies to decry evil? And, if so, is there any justification for destructive activity as part of this outcry?

Yehuda ben Shamua's Rally

A possible ancient rabbinic precedent for staging protest rallies is the story told in *Maseches Rosh Hashanah* (19a) of a time when the Roman authorities enacted a ban against Torah learning, *bris mila* and Shabbos observance. Yehuda ben Shamua and his colleagues approached a certain Roman noblewoman, who is described as having been very influential among the Roman leaders, to consult with her. She advised them, בואו והפגינו בלילה — to hold a nighttime demonstration to protest the harsh legislation against the Jews. This noblewoman even recommended the "slogans" that the Jews should use — "Are we not your brothers?" "Are we not the children of one father?" "Are we not the children of one mother?" "Why are we singled out from among every nation and tongue that you enact harsh decrees against us?!"

The Jews followed her advice, and the protest was successful — the decree was rescinded. That day, the 28th of Adar, was observed each year as a quasi-festival to celebrate the annulment of the ban, as recorded in *Megillas Taanis*.

At first glance, this story forms a strong basis for the validity, and value, of protest demonstrations, at least when it comes to injustices against the Jewish Nation.

However, the opposite conclusion might be reached in light of the Ben Ish Chai's understanding of this incident in his *Ben Yehoyada* commentary. He raises the question of why the noblewoman would advise the Jews to stage a demonstration instead of appealing directly to the authorities.[1] The Ben Ish Chai therefore advances a novel reading of this story, suggesting that the Roman authorities frequently consulted with this noblewoman on matters of public policy, and such a meeting was scheduled for that night. She therefore urged the Jews to stage a protest near her home[2] so that the officials who would be assembling at her residence would hear the cries and then ask for her input. The Ben Ish Chai explains that the woman could not bring up the topic in her meeting with the government officials, because she would then be viewed as a traitor, siding with the Jews. And so she devised a strategy whereby the topic would naturally come up, and she would then convince the authorities to rescind the ban.

It appears from the Ben Ish Chai's comments that to the contrary, public demonstrations are not the appropriate response to injustice. In his view, the correct strategy is direct dialogue with the relevant officials, not public gatherings, and he therefore needed to arrive at a creative reading of this story to explain why such a gathering was held in the times of Yehuda ben Shamua.

However, the straightforward reading of the story would certainly suggest that a public demonstration was held as an appropriate and effective response to unjust government actions.

The פילגש בגבעה and the Boundaries of Valid Protest

Turning our attention to the question of whether normally forbidden activity is allowed for the sake of decrying injustice, an intriguing precedent that must be explored is the tragic story of the פילגש בגבעה ("the concubine in Giva"), which is told in *Sefer Shoftim* (chapter 19). The story involves a man who was traveling with his concubine and lodged for the night in the town of Giva, and the townspeople seized the concubine and violently raped her, to the point where she died. The bereaved husband, determined to arouse the ire of the entire nation against the people of Giva, undertook the shocking measure of cutting his concubine's remains into twelve pieces, and sending one to each tribe, to graphically show them the gravity of the crime that had been committed. The people were outraged, and they demanded that the leaders of the tribe of Binyamin — the tribe to which Giva belonged — hand over the perpetrators for execution. The leaders of Binyamin refused, and the other tribes launched a catastrophic war against Binyamin that resulted in hundreds of thousands of deaths, and nearly erased the tribe of Binyamin.

---

1.   צריך טעם למה יעצה אותם שיפגינו מרחוק ולא יעצתם שילכו אצל גדולי רומי לביתם ויתחננו לה ויבכו לפניהם.

2.   Significantly, the noblewoman told the Jews, **בואו** והפגינו בלילה, suggesting that she urged the Jews to "come" protest near her residence.

Dismembering a body clearly violates the halachic prohibition of ניוול המת —
desecrating the body of a deceased person, which the Gemara explicitly mentions in
Maseches Bava Basra.[3] And yet, the man in this story determined that it was appropriate to perform such an act for the "shock effect," to rattle the people by showing them
the horrific crime that was perpetrated.

Interestingly enough, the question of whether this gruesome act serves as a legitimate halachic precedent arose at the time when the religious community in Israel
protested against autopsies in hospitals, in 1967. Rav Moshe Feinstein was asked
whether it would be appropriate to bring dissected body parts to the protests in order
to impress upon the public the grave desecration that was being perpetrated. In his
response,[4] Rav Moshe pointed to the story of פילגש בגבעה as proof to the fact that
disrespecting a corpse is permissible for the sake of arousing a public outcry against
evil. Rav Moshe notes the Gemara's discussion in *Maseches Gittin* (6b) concerning the
verse in *Sefer Shoftim* (19:2) which appears to say that the concubine in this story had
previously been unfaithful to her husband. Although this is the straightforward reading of the text, the Gemara cites those who explain that she committed a far less serious offense. *Tosfos* comment that the Gemara did not consider the simple reading of
the text because the man, after initially sending the concubine away, later brought her
back, which would be forbidden if she had committed adultery. This discussion clearly
presumes that the man was religiously devout, and Rav Moshe thus proves that his
drastic action after the crime committed against his concubine was halachically valid.
He thus concludes that although it would normally be forbidden to publicly display a
piece of a human corpse,[5] this would be permitted for the sake of arousing warranted
public outrage, just as the remains of the פילגש בגבעה were displayed to protest the
crime committed against her.

A different view was taken many years earlier by Rav Yedidya Weil, who addressed
the question of whether an autopsy may be performed on a murder victim so that the
killer would be brought to justice. The country's laws required examining the body of a
murder victim before prosecuting the killer, in order to ascertain that he had not previously suffered from a deadly condition. In one instance, an elderly Jew was murdered,
and the family members refused to allow an autopsy to be performed so that the killer
could be prosecuted, figuring that this did not justify desecrating the body. In Rav Weil's
discussion of this topic,[6] he establishes that the story of פילגש בגבעה does not serve as

---

3. 154a. For sources regarding the particular severity of this prohibition, see Rav Eliezer
   Waldenberg's discussion in *Tzitz Eliezer*, 5:20:4.

4. *Iggeros Moshe*, Y.D. 2:150.

5. Rav Moshe cites Rashi's comment in *Maseches Sanhedrin* (46b ד"ה משום בזיונא הוא) that
   leaving a decomposing corpse publicly exposed is disrespectful to the deceased (שלא
   יתבזה לעין כל שיראוהו מת וירקב ונבקע).

6. In his responsa, 100.

a valid precedent for desecrating a victim's body for the sake of justice. First, he argues, it is entirely possible that the husband acted improperly, in direct contradistinction to Rav Moshe Feinstein's inference from *Tosfos* in *Maseches Gittin* that the husband was a religiously committed Jew whose conduct can be presumed to model halachically acceptable conduct. Secondly, the case of פילגש בגבעה might be exceptional, in that it was deemed necessary to undertake this drastic measure to ensure that such a heinous crime would never again be perpetrated. Rav Weil writes, נדחה ניוול דיחיד בשביל מכשול דרבים — it was deemed appropriate to defile one individual for the sake of preventing a public disgrace like the one perpetrated by the townspeople of Giva.[7]

This second reason opens the door for allowing such drastic measures when public interests are at stake, such as in the situation addressed by Rav Moshe Feinstein, when it became necessary to protest the desecration of bodies.

Others, including Rav Eliyahu Klatzkin[8] and Rav Malkiel Tanenbaum,[9] permitted autopsies that are necessary for bringing the killer to justice because under such circumstances, the autopsy serves the deceased's interests. Tampering with a body is forbidden because of the disgrace this brings to the deceased, and therefore, when an autopsy is required for the deceased's honor, so his murderer would be prosecuted and

---

7.   We might add that the Ramban, in discussing the story of פילגש בגבעה (*Bereishis* 19:8), writes that the people of Giva were שטופי זמה — steeped in promiscuity. This was, apparently, not an isolated incident, but rather part of a broader trend that needed to be loudly and forcefully protested, perhaps supporting Rav Weil's point regarding the exceptional nature of the incident of פילגש בגבעה.

Rav Weil suggests drawing proof to the contrary, that defiling a body is forbidden even for the sake of the deceased's honor, from the Gemara's discussion in *Maseches Chullin* (11b) regarding the Biblical source for the concept of *rov*, whereby *halacha* relies on a statistical majority. The Gemara notes that this rule can be inferred from the Torah's requirement to execute a murderer, despite the small possibility that the victim already suffered from a fatal condition that would absolve the killer of capital punishment. In discussing this proof, the Gemara acknowledges that in principle, it would be possible to inspect the body to establish that he had not suffered from such a condition. Although desecrating a dead body is forbidden, the Gemara states, this would be allowed for the sake of possibly saving the murderer from wrongful execution. The Gemara says this is not an option because the victim might have suffered a fatal injury in the place where the incision was made for the autopsy, and thus went unnoticed. Rav Weil observes that the Gemara considered allowing the body's defilement only for the sake of saving a life, indicating that this would not be allowed for any other purpose.

8.   Responsa, 71.

9.   *Divrei Malkiel*, 5:60.

punished, it may be performed.[10] And thus the husband's drastic measure in the story of פילגש בגבעה was permissible, as this was done to evoke outrage and motivate the people to avenge this crime.

According to this line of reasoning, the story of פילגש בגבעה does not provide a precedent for suspending halachic prohibitions for the sake of igniting outrage over injustice. Dismembering the body was permitted only because this served the interests of the deceased, as it aroused the nation's fury and drove them to avenge her death. This does not mean that other drastic measures that would normally be forbidden become permissible for the sake of evoking outrage.

Rav Tanenbaum adds also a different factor, namely, that failure to bring the killer to justice encourages hostile anti-Semites to kill Jews with impunity, as they know they will not be prosecuted due to the Jews' refusal to permit inspecting the victim. This is comparable, Rav Tanenbaum writes, to the *halacha* forbidding paying an exorbitant sum to ransom a Jewish captive.[11] According to one view in the Gemara, this is forbidden so as not to encourage further kidnapping by making it lucrative. This *halacha* shows that we are prepared to forego on a Jewish captive to prevent the public danger of widespread kidnappings. By the same token, Rav Tanenbaum writes, we should be prepared to permit defiling the body of a murder victim if this is necessary for the sake of deterring prospective killers.[12]

In principle, this might allow for undertaking drastic measures, including denying an individual his basic rights, in response to a ghastly crime if this is deemed necessary to prevent it from recurring. Just as we will deny the victim his normally due honor in order to prosecute the killer and thereby deter prospective criminals, we might, conceivably, permit other violations for the sake of establishing deterrence. Needless

---

10. See also Rav Yosef Shaul Nathanson's *Sho'eil U-Meishiv — Mahadura Kama* (1:231), where he writes that tampering with a body is forbidden only when this is done for no legitimate purpose.

    Ironically, these *poskim* draw proof to their position from the Gemara's discussion in *Maseches Chullin* from which, as mentioned above (note 7), Rav Weil proved his stringent ruling. These *poskim* cite the novel reading of the Gemara advanced by the *Noda Be-Yehuda* (*Mahadura Tinyana*, Y.D. 210) according to which the Gemara allows, in principle, inspecting the body of a murder victim for the sake of ascertaining the murderer's guilt so justice could be served.

11. *Gittin* 45a. For a thorough discussion of this topic, see the first volume of *Headlines*, chapter 23, "Many Terrorists for One Israeli? The Gilad Shalit Deal Through the Prism of Halacha."

12. Rav Tanenbaum acknowledges that this proof is not ironclad, as one could easily distinguish between שב ואל תעשה — passively allowing the captive to remain in confinement, and קום ועשה — actively performing an autopsy.

to say, this would apply only if it is certain that the drastic measure will indeed achieve the desired result of deterrence, as in the case addressed by Rav Tanenbaum where an autopsy is necessary for the sake of prosecuting a murderer.

Punishing Apathy

While the defilement of the פילגש's remains might not provide us with a precedent for suspending Torah violations for the sake of arousing outrage against a crime, it might serve as a precedent for punishing an entire society for its tacit acceptance of, and indifference towards, evil.

As mentioned, the nation's leaders demanded that the tribe of Binyamin hand over the people of Giva who perpetrated this crime, and when the Binyaminites refused, the other tribes went to war against Binyamin. This might demonstrate that when a society reacts tolerantly to outrageous crimes, it is appropriate to respond even with violence and military force to protest the tacit acceptance of evil.

However, the relevance of this precedent might depend on the discussion among the commentators as to the propriety of the other tribes' extreme response to Binyamin's failure to prosecute the offenders. The other tribes suffered tens of thousands of casualties during this war, which might suggest to us that God looked unfavorably upon their decision to respond with such force. The Ramban, in his lengthy analysis of the story of פילגש בגבעה and its aftermath,[13] indeed writes that the other tribes acted wrongly in launching this war against Binyamin. He writes that it was Binyamin's responsibility to respond to the crime, not the other tribes', and thus the other tribes were wrong for initiating a military conflict. The Ramban adds that the tribes did not consult God (by posing a query to the *Urim Ve-Tumim* oracle on the *Kohen Gadol*'s breastplate) before attacking Binyamin, as is generally required before going out to war. According to the Ramban, then, military conflict is not an appropriate response to a society's failure to properly address evil in its midst.

Of course, this does not mean that the Ramban felt the other tribes should have done nothing in response to the appalling incident. He says only that a military response requires authorization from God, which the other tribes did not receive.

Regardless, other sources indicate that the war was, in itself, justified, and the tribes were liable to punishment for other reasons. The Gemara[14] comments that the people were punished because of the contrast between their drastic response to the incident of פילגש בגבעה and their indifference to פסל מיכה — the statue and temple erected by Micha in the Efrayim region, of which the Torah tells in the chapters preceding the story of פילגש בגבעה. When the tribes set out to wage war against Binyamin, the

---

13. Commentary to *Bereishis* 19:8.
14. *Sanhedrin* 103b.

Gemara teaches, God announced, בכבודי לא מחיתם, על כבודו של בשר ודם מחיתם? —
"For My honor you did not protest, yet for the honor of a human being you protest?"[15]
According to the Gemara, then, it is not the war itself of which God disapproved, but
rather the people's inconsistency, reacting with military force to one grievous incident
while ignoring another.[16]

Pirkei De'Rabbi Eliezer[17] similarly states:

> אמר להם הקב״ה : קנאתם על הזנות של שבט של בנימין ולא קנאתם על פסל מיכה?!
> לפיכך הרגו בהם בני בנימין.

> The Almighty said to them: You were zealous over the promiscuity of
> the tribe of Binyamin, but you were not zealous over Micha's statue?!
> This is why the Binymanites killed many of them.

According to these sources, it is appropriate — and even obligatory — to respond with
military force against a population that fails to address its grave moral and spiritual ills.

Another possible precedent for violent protest in response to a heinous crime is the
story of Shechem (*Bereishis* 34), where Shimon and Levi launched a vicious attack on
the city, killing all the men, after the city's prince — named Shechem — abducted and
defiled their sister Dina. Much has been written in an attempt to explain why Shimon
and Levi undertook this drastic, violent measure to avenge their sister's honor, and why
Yaakov strongly condemned them, as we read at the conclusion of the story (34:30). The
Rambam, in *Hilchos Melachim,*[18] famously explains that the people of Shechem were in
violation of one of the seven Noachide laws — the requirement of דינין, to establish and
maintain an effective justice system to punish and deter criminals. Shechem faced no
consequences for his horrific crime, reflecting the failure of the population of Shechem
to set up a proper system to try criminals. As the Rambam cites from the Gemara,[19] a
gentile who transgresses any of the Noachide laws is liable to capital punishment, and
for this reason, the entire population of Shechem deserved to be killed.

In a somewhat similar vein, the Radak[20] notes that the Torah says of the people

---

15. The Gemara's comments are referenced by both Rashi and the Radak in their respective
    commentaries to *Sefer Shoftim* (20:21).
16. The Ramban cites the Gemara's comment, but he insists that the Gemara meant that the
    military response was itself improper. (In the Ramban's words: לומר, בכבודי לא מחיתם
    במחוייבי מיתה ופושטים ידיהם בעיקר, בכבוד בשר ודם מחיתם יותר משורת הדין.) Abarbanel,
    in his commentary to *Sefer Shoftim,* sharply rejects the Ramban's analysis and insists that
    the tribes acted correctly in waging war in response to פילגש בגבעה, and were punished for
    failing to do the same in response to פסל מיכה.
17. 38.
18. 9:14.
19. *Sanhedrin* 58b.
20. *Bereishis* 34:27.

of Shechem, אשר טמאו אחותם — **they** defiled Shimon and Levi's sister, implying that all the townspeople played a role in this evil crime. The Radak explains that many townspeople witnessed Shechem's abduction of Dina and failed to protest, such that they all bore some degree of guilt for this wicked act.[21] This premise, that those with the authority to protest who fail to do so share in the culpability for wrongdoing, is expressed by the Gemara in *Maseches Shabbos* (54b):

כל מי שאפשר למחות לאנשי ביתו ולא מיחה נתפס על אנשי ביתו, באנשי עירו — נתפס על אנשי עירו, בכל העולם כולו — נתפס על כל העולם כולו.

> Everyone who is able to protest against his family members and did not protest is held accountable for his family; against his townspeople — is held accountable for his townspeople; against the entire world — is held accountable for the entire world.

Accordingly, the Radak understood that the general population of Shechem was to have expressed outrage over the unspeakable crime perpetrated by their leader, and their failure to protest rendered them partially culpable for this evil act. This collective guilt warranted the extraordinary, violent response of Shimon and Levi.[22]

If so, then this incident perhaps provides us with a precedent for a society's collective guilt when it fails to effectively respond to criminal activity. According to the Rambam, the story of Shechem shows that when a society fails to fulfill its duty to maintain law and order by prosecuting criminals, there is an obligation to resort even to violence for the sake of protesting the injustice.

Importantly, however, the Ramban[23] famously objects to the Rambam's explanation, arguing that Yaakov would not have berated his sons for their violent response if it were halachically mandated. In the Ramban's view, gentiles are punished only for violating Noachide prohibitions, but not for failing to perform the affirmative command of דינין, and thus Shimon and Levi's assault on Shechem was unjustified and worthy of condemnation. This challenge against the Rambam's view was posed also by the Ran[24] and the Radbaz (in his commentary to *Hilchos Melachim*).

Shimshon's Violence

At first glance, another precedent for allowing wanton violence in protest of evil is the

---

21. A similar comment is made by Rav Yaakov Mecklenberg, in his *Ha-Kesav Ve-Ha'kabbala* commentary to an earlier verse (34:7).
22. The topic of collective punishment in *halacha* is addressed at length in *Headlines 2*, pp. 146–153.
23. Commentary to *Bereishis* 34:13.
24. *Sanhedrin* 56b.

story of Shimshon, who committed numerous violent acts against the Philistines who were oppressing *Bnei Yisrael* at that time, as we read in the Book of *Shoftim*. On one occasion, he killed thirty random Philistines in Ashkelon.[25] On another, he set fire to Philistines' agricultural fields.[26] Perhaps, we might infer from these incidents that haphazard acts of murder and destruction are warranted for the sake of protesting evil.

In truth, however, no proof may be drawn from the story of Shimshon, which occurred during a period of military conflict. During wartime, many measures which are ordinarily prohibited are allowed as part of the military effort.[27] The Radak[28] applies this rule to Shimshon, in his discussion as to why Shimshon was allowed to kill, given that this resulted in direct contact with a human corpse, which was, seemingly, forbidden for him by force of the nazirite vow to which he was bound from birth. After citing *Chazal's* understanding, that Shimshon's nazirite status did not include a requirement to avoid contact with a human corpse,[29] the Radak proceeds to explain that even if Shimshon was bound by such a prohibition, this was allowed for the purpose of waging war against the Philistines, who oppressed *Bnei Yisrael* at this time.[30] A situation of a מלחמת מצוה, a war which must be fought for the sake of defending the Jewish Nation, marks an exceptional circumstance which does not provide a halachic precedent which we may apply under other conditions.

The Purpose of Protest

In the year 5742 (1982), religious Jews in the city of Petach-Tikva staged demonstrations each week on Shabbos, for thirty-three weeks, to protest the opening of movie theaters in the city on Shabbos. The city's Chief Rabbi, Rav Moshe Malka, strongly opposed these protests, and penned a lengthy responsum on the subject which he published in his work *Ve-Heishiv Moshe.*[31] He explained that the obligation of *tocheicha* — to reprove sinners[32] — had already been fulfilled, such that additional

---

25. 14:19.

26. 15:4–5.

27. This point is discussed at length in *Headlines 2*, chapter 17, "Killing a Neutralized Terrorist," pp. 354–360.

28. *Shoftim* 14:19.

29. *Mishna, Nazir* 4a.

30. In the Radak's words: נוכל לומר כי היה נזהר מלהטמא למת אלא במקום מצוה, והמלחמה בפלשתים מצוה היתה, להלחם בהם ולהושיע את ישראל מידם. The Radak also suggests that Shimshon may have killed the Philistines without touching their bodies afterward, thereby avoiding the status of impurity which was forbidden for him.

31. *Kuntras Lema'an Ha-Shabbos*, printed in the beginning of the volume.

32. הוכיח תוכיח את עמיתך, *Vayikra* 19:17. See Rambam, *Sefer Ha-Mitzvos, asei* 205; *Sefer*

rallies on Shabbos were unnecessary and hence unjustified. Moreover, this obligation does not apply when there is no reasonable likelihood of the violator accepting the criticism, in which case continuing the criticism only evokes anger and resentment.[33] And, staging protests on Shabbos actually has the effect of increasing Shabbos desecration, as it is all but certain that the police, journalists and others will violate Shabbos to tend to these events.

Rav Yosef Shalom Elyashiv wrote a response to Rav Malka,[34] vehemently dismissing his arguments. He explained that the purpose of protest rallies is not to fulfill the *mitzva* of *tocheicha*, but rather לעצור את מגיפת התפשטות הריסת השבת — "to stop the epidemic of the destruction of Shabbos." The objective is not to try to elicit a change in the behavior of the violators themselves, but rather to defend the honor and sanctity of Shabbos by opposing the policy of permitting flagrant Shabbos desecration in the public square.[35]

This point is made also by Rav Moshe Sternbuch,[36] who writes that the demonstrations are held not for the purpose of reprimanding the violators themselves, but rather to emphasize the gravity of public Shabbos desecration:

> אין תפקיד המחאות למנוע את חבירו מחילול שבת... רק שורש המחאה היא לנו לעצמנו ולבננו אחרינו שנדע שאין שבת הפקר וחמור הדבר מאד עד שיוצאים אפילו למחות... שאין המחאה רק למנוע את המחלל שבת, אלא גם למנוע חילול שבת מאחרים, וכן להדגיש חומר השבת...

> The purpose of the protests is not to prevent one's fellow from desecrating Shabbos... Rather, the root of the protest is for us, for ourselves, and for our children after us, so that we know that Shabbos is not "*hefker*" [meaning, worthless], and this matter is very serious to the point where we even go to protest... For the protest is not just to prevent the Shabbos

---

Ha-Chinuch 218.

33. I recall many years ago being on Jerusalem's Bar-Ilan St. one Shabbos during a protest against those who were driving on Shabbos. The protesters shouted, "Shabbos! Shabbos!" at the drivers. My children, who were little at the time and did not understand what was happening, began shouting, "Good Shabbos! Good Shabbos!" It occurred to me that if instead of staging protests and shouting, "Shabbos!" we would warmly wish our fellow Jews, "Good Shabbos" and offer them some cholent and kugel, the results might be different...

34. Printed in *Koveitz Teshuvos*, 4:35.

35. As for the argument that demonstrations cause additional Shabbos desecration on the part of law enforcement and journalists, Rav Elyashiv references a responsum of Maharil Diskin (*Kuntras Acharon*, 145) as a basis for disregarding this concern.

36. *Teshuvos Ve-Hanhagos*, 1:842.

desecrator, but also to prevent other people's Shabbos desecration, and also to emphasize the severity of Shabbos.

Rav Sternbuch addresses this topic also in a later responsum,[37] in reference to the rallies staged in protest of the Pride Parade in Jerusalem. He writes that this parade was intended "to announce opposition to God and His Torah, and to proclaim, 'We are not subservient to the Torah of Moshe,' Heaven forbid." As such, Rav Sternbuch explained, this situation differs from one of a lone violator, who is to be reprimanded subject to the specific guidelines of the *mitzva* of *tocheicha*. When a large group of people gather to publicly declare their rejection of the Torah's principles, a public protest must be held to defend the Torah's honor.[38]

The obligation of protest, then, differs from the obligation of *tocheicha*, which requires reprimanding with the objective of effecting a change in the sinner's conduct, and thus does not apply when reprimanding is not likely to have such an effect. Protesting outrageous conduct is required both for ourselves and for the world at large, to make a statement that such conduct should not be considered acceptable.[39]

בואו ונחשב חשבונו של עולם — Weighing the Benefits Against the Losses

Earlier, we noted the controversial view taken by the Rambam explaining the halachic rationale behind Shimon and Levi's violent assault on the city of Shechem. As mentioned, the Ramban — among others — objected to the Rambam's theory, questioning why, according to the Rambam, Yaakov so vehemently condemned his sons' violent act.

The Meiri[40] defends the Rambam's view by suggesting that Yaakov condemned his sons' actions because he had made a pact with the leadership of Shechem which he felt should be honored, notwithstanding the city's collective culpability for the crime committed against Dina. Fundamentally, Yaakov agreed that killing the townspeople was warranted, but under the circumstances, this should not have been done.

---

37. 5:399.

38. Rav Sternbuch cites a number of sources (e.g. *Shabbos* 55a) indicating that those who fail to express condemnation of sinful behavior are held partially responsible for the misconduct.

39. In a generally similar vein, Rav Binyamin Zilber (*Az Nidberu*, 14:4) writes that protest is needed to counter the effects of other people's misdeeds upon our own beings. When we see or hear of people acting wrongly, their misconduct can erode our intuitive rejection of such behavior, and we must therefore rebuild our instinctive disdain for sin through protesting. However, Rav Zilber takes the view that a non-observant Jew's Shabbos desecration does not have this kind of effect, and there is thus no need for protest. Later, we present Rav Zilber's other arguments for opposing rallies in protest of Shabbos desecration.

40. *Sanhedrin* 56b.

We might perhaps add that in condemning his sons' action, Yaakov expressed fear that Shimon and Levi put the family in grave danger, as they would now be seen as a threat to the local populations, who might launch a preemptive strike against them.[41] Even if, as the Rambam established, the townspeople deserved capital punishment, this was unwise under the circumstances.

This analysis underscores the importance of considering all the various angles of a situation before deciding whether and how to respond to evil. Even if extreme measures appear appropriate in protesting against injustice, careful thought must be invested to examine all consequences of those measures. Even when, in principle, a society deserves a violent response to their apathy towards evil, such a response might not necessarily serve our overall, long-term best interests, as was the case in the story of Shechem. Yaakov might have agreed with his sons' decision in principle, but in practice, he determined that this response was unwise and posed grave danger. Similarly, even when we feel legitimately outraged by injustice, and our instincts lead us to react with extreme measures, we must carefully assess the long-term repercussions of our reaction and determine whether a drastic response might yield the precise opposite result of that which we seek.

This need to weigh the benefits of protest against its potential harm is discussed by the Netziv, in a remarkable passage in his Torah commentary.[42] The Torah in *Sefer Bamidbar* tells of the poem composed by the מושלים (literally, "poets," or "speakers of fables") depicting the conquest of the city of Cheshbon: יאמרו המושלים בואו חשבון. The Gemara[43] comments that these words may be understood as referring to המושלים ביצרם — those who "govern" their sinful impulses, who have the strength to restrain and control their negative tendencies. The words בואו חשבון, the Gemara explains, mean, בואו ונחשב חשבונו של עולם הפסד מצוה נגד שכרה, שכר עבירה נגד הפסדה — "Let us make the 'calculation of the world': the loss caused by a *mitzva* against its reward, the benefit of a sin against its loss." The righteous succeed in restraining their sinful impulses by making this "calculation" — recognizing that the benefits of a *mitzva* far outweigh that which one forfeits to fulfill it, and that the damage caused by a sin far outweighs the benefits one enjoys by committing the act. The Netziv creatively explains that the Gemara speaks here of those who instigate strife and conflict for the sake of a *mitzva*. He writes:

יש עושים מחלוקת בשביל שרוצה לעשות מצוה שגורם בזה לידי מחלוקת, ויש מחשב לרדוף את הרשע או את הצבור בשביל איזה עול, ואף על גב שהוא עבירה לרדוף, מכל מקום מחשב שיקבל שכר על עבירה לשמה... והנה אם אינו מושל

41. ...ויאמר יעקב אל שמעון ואל לוי עכרתם אותי להבאישני ביושב הארץ...ונאספו עלי והכוני (*Bereishis* 34:30).

42. *Harchev Davar*, Bamidbar 21:30.

43. *Bava Basra* 78b.

ביצרו ואינו מכוין לשם שמים, אלא יש בזה איזה הנאת עצמו, פשיטא שישא
עונש, אפילו חשבונו ברור שכדאי שתבוא העבירה נגד המצוה שבזה, מכל מקום
ישא עונש ככל הנאה מעבירה... אך אפילו הוא מושל ביצרו ומכוין אך לשם שמים
עדיין עליו לבא בחשבונו של עולם, אם כדאי הפסד מצוה שיגיע על ידי שיעשה נגד
שכרה, כי יכול להיות שההפסד שיגיע על ידי המחלוקת רבה על השכר ממנה...

There are those who instigate a fight because one wishes to perform a
mitzva which causes an ensuing fight, and one might think to pursue a
wicked person or the public because of some evil, [and] even though it is
a sin to pursue, nevertheless, he thinks he will receive reward for committing a sin altruistically... Now if he does not control his inclination, and
his intentions are not for the sake of Heaven, but rather it involves some
personal benefit, then obviously he will be liable to punishment, even if his
calculation is accurate, that it is worth causing the sin in consideration of
the *mitzva* involved, nevertheless, he will be liable to punishment like all
enjoyment from sin... But even if he controls his inclination, and intends
solely for the sake of Heaven, still he must consider "the calculation of the
world," whether the loss which will result from performing the *mitzva* is
worth it for its reward, because it could be that the loss which will result
from the fight exceeds its reward...[44]

The Netziv here establishes that before instigating a fight even sincerely for truly noble
causes, one must carefully weigh the benefits of the fight against the damage it will
cause, and honestly determine whether the harm outweighs the benefit.

For this reason, Rav Binyamin Zilber[45] — in contradistinction to the *poskim* cited above
— opposed holding demonstrations to protest public Shabbos desecration. He writes:

מהנסיון אנו רואים שאין זה מועיל ובפרט ההפגנות התמידיות אשר מתרגלים
בזה, והשלילה יותר מהחיוב, ויש לנצל כל העצות של דרכי השכנוע...

We see from experience that this is ineffective, especially the regular
demonstrations, to which they are accustomed, and the negative exceeds
the positive, and so every strategy of persuasion must be exploited...

Earlier in his discussion, Rav Zilber writes:

בשנים האחרונות הם רואים בזה מלחמת תרבות וכפיה דתית ומגיבים בחריפות
לכן יש בזה בודאי חשש של פקו"נ וגם התוצאות הן ללא תועלת.

In recent years, they [secular Israelis] see this as a culture war and reli-

---

44. See also the Netziv's comments in his *Meishiv Davar*, 2:9.
45. In the responsum referenced above, note 39.

gious coercion, and they react sharply. Therefore, this certainly involves
the possibility of a danger to life, and also the results are fruitless.

Notwithstanding the value of defending the honor of Torah observance, this inherently
noble cause must be carefully weighed against the negative repercussions of protesting.
In many instances, particularly when inflammatory rhetoric is employed, and when
protests become a public nuisance — such as when roads are closed or property is
damaged — these gatherings can end up causing far greater long-term harm to the
cause of Torah observance than any policy enacted by the Israeli government or public
Shabbos desecration.

Another example is a letter signed by Rav Moshe Feinstein, Rav Aharon Kotler and
other leading American rabbis in 1987 objecting to protests staged by American Jews
when Mikhail Gorbachev, Premier of the Soviet Union, visited the United States.[46] The
signatories felt very strongly that these protests gravely endangered Russian Jews, and
thus even if the Russian government was truly deserving of criticism, public protests
were, in their estimation, unwise.

A Question of Sincerity

The Netziv, in his discussion, points also to another factor which could undermine the
validity of an otherwise noble protest — insincerity. He writes that if a person instigates
conflict allegedly for the sake of protesting religious infractions, but he is not among
the מושלים ביצרם — those who restrain their dark impulses — and instead relishes
the opportunity to malign and express disdain towards others, then, in the Netziv's
words, פשיטא שישא עונש — such a person is unquestionably deserving of punishment.
Publicly protesting another person's behavior cannot be justified unless the protestors'
motives are pristinely pure, and not driven by personal grievance, animosity, or the
vain thrill of controversy. It goes without saying that looting cannot ever be justified as
a legitimate expression of protest, as one then personally benefits from this so-called
"protest," which *ipso facto* undermines its validity.

This point is emphasized by Rav Shlomo Zalman, great-nephew of the Vilna Gaon,
in his *Beis Avos* commentary to *Pirkei Avos*.[47] He writes that although it is imperative
to protest against evildoers, עם כל זה בקרבו יצטער ויתמרמר לבו על שנתגלגל דבר זה —
"nevertheless, inside, one should regret and his heart should feel embittered over the
fact that such a situation unfolded." Rav Shlomo Zalman adds that if the violator is a
personal adversary, then one should refrain from protesting, because his protest would
be at least partially fueled by insincere motives. In fact, Rav Shlomo Zalman concludes,
it is told that the Vilna Gaon said about an incident that occurred during his lifetime,

---

46.   See *Hapardeis*, Kislev 5748, p. 24.
47.   2:24.

אם לא עשו עבור כבוד ה' לבד רק ששיתפו גם עבור עצמם הרי הם שופכי דמים — "If they had not acted only for the sake of God's honor, but rather combined also their own interests, then they would have been murderers."

Another expression of this concept is the comments of the Sema[48] regarding the *Shulchan Aruch*'s ruling permitting one to rescue somebody from physical assault by striking the attacker. The Sema writes that if the bystander does not normally intervene in such situations by striking the assailant, he may not intervene now, as we must presume that he acts out of personal animus towards the assailant, and not out of a sincere desire to rescue the victim. Protesting evil and injustice loses its legitimacy if it is accompanied by vested personal interests, and is less then perfectly altruistic and sincere.

We might also point to the command of עיר הנידחת, which requires killing a Jewish city's entire population if its inhabitants embrace idol-worship.[49] The Torah strictly forbids keeping any of the city's possessions,[50] explaining, "so that God shall rescind His anger and grant you compassion…" The Netziv, in his *Ha'amek Davar* commentary, explains that only if the mass execution is done with perfectly pristine intentions, without any selfish motives, would God protect the people from the natural catastrophic consequences of the murder of an entire city. The Torah insisted that nothing be taken from the city to ensure the absence of any vested interests in killing the city's population, and only then will the action be accepted as a legitimate fulfillment of God's command.

If so, then we might perhaps return to the story of Shechem, and suggest an explanation for why Yaakov harshly reprimanded Shimon and Levi. As mentioned earlier, some questioned the Rambam's theory, that the people Shechem deserved execution, by noting that Yaakov strongly disapproved of his sons' assault on the city. The answer, perhaps, is found in the Torah's emphasis on Shimon and Levi's having looted the city after killing all the men: ויבזו העיר...את צאנם ואת בקרם ואת חמוריהם ואת אשר בעיר ואת אשר בשדה לקחו — "They looted the city… Their sheep, their cattle, their donkeys, and everything in the city and everything in the fields, they took."[51] The looting may have completely undermined the validity of Shimon and Levi's drastic response to their sister's abduction. Even if, in principle, as the Rambam contends, the people of Shechem deserved their fate, the fact that Shimon and Levi helped themselves to the city's riches rendered their action illegitimate.[52]

---

48. C.M. 421:28.

49. The Gemara (*Sanhedrin* 71a) famously comments that a situation meeting all the conditions for applying this command never occurred and will never occur (עיר הנידחת לא היתה ולא עתיד להיות), and it was written as an instructive hypothetical law.

50. ולא ידבק בידך מאומה מן החרם, *Devarim* 13:18.

51. *Bereishis* 34:27–28.

52. The Maggid of Dubno (*Ohel Yaakov, Parshas Vayechi*), though without mentioning the looting of Shechem, writes that Yaakov condemned Shimon and Levi's violent attack on the city because he recognized that their motives were less than purely sincere. Addi-

Protesting One's Own Misconduct

Earlier, we noted the Gemara's comment that the other tribes who waged war against Binyamin after the incident of פילגש בגבעה suffered tens of thousands of calamities because they did not react with such vehemence to פסל מיכה — Micha's institution of a site of idol-worship. This inconsistency, showing greater concern for the פילגש בגבעה than for God Himself, rendered them worthy of punishment.

Abarbanel, in his commentary to *Sefer Shoftim*,[53] discusses the Gemara's remark, and he writes, שהיה להם לישראל לקשט עצמם ואחר כך יקשטו את אחרים — "Israel should have 'adorned' themselves and only then 'adorn' others."[54] Rav Yitzchak Arama similarly writes in his *Akeidas Yitzchak* commentary:[55]

> היה להם להתקדש ולמלאת את ידם בטהר עצמם מכל פשעיהם לכל חטאתם
> קודם שיבואו למלחמה עם אחיהם...

> They were to have sanctified themselves and prepared by purifying themselves from all their iniquities and sins before they came to wage war against their brethren...

Protesting wrongful conduct does not earn legitimacy unless a person also "protests" against himself, unless he seeks to correct his own flaws and shortcomings with no less vigilance and passion with which he seeks to protest other people's misconduct. We have no right to react with stern opposition to other people's failings if we complacently accept our own failings. It is only if we are exacting with ourselves and our own conduct that we may then go out to protest against the conduct of others.[56]

---

tionally, Rav Cham Kanievsky (*Ta'ama Di'kra, Parshas Vayishlach*) cites a tradition that Shimon married one of the women taken captive from Shechem, and he suggests that since Shimon derived benefit from his assault on the city, he was punished by having a descendant — Zimri — who committed a public sinful act for which he was killed. Enjoying personal benefit from an act of zealotry undermines its validity, thus rendering the zealot worthy of punishment.

We should note, however, that some commentators assert that Shimon and Levi did not, in fact, loot the city, as the Torah speaks of בני יעקב taking the city's possessions, perhaps indicating that this was done specifically by Yaakov's other sons, and not Shimon and Levi. See *Tzeror Ha-Mor* and *Chasam Sofer* to *Bereishis* 34:27.

53. Chapter 20.

54. This formulation is based on the famous rabbinic adage introduced by Reish Lakish, קשט עצמך ואחר כך קשט אחרים (*Sanhedrin* 18a) — that one must fix himself before proceeding to criticize others in an attempt to fix them.

55. *Parshas Vayeira, Sha'ar* 20.

56. See also Rabbeinu Yona's comments in *Sha'arei Teshuva* (3:219) warning against criticizing

Indeed, very often, people are driven to protest other people's misconduct because this enables them to feel morally or religiously superior without having to address their own faults. Part of the appeal of angry protest is the feeling of condescension that it engenders, the satisfaction of seeing oneself as superior. Rather than going through the difficult and uncomfortable process of self-growth, many prefer to focus on what others do wrong so they could ignore their own faults. Before we even consider protesting the misconduct of other people, we must acknowledge and seek to rectify our own wrongs, and be at least as troubled — if not much more troubled — by our own failings than by those of others.

Conclusion

There is ample basis in Torah sources for the need to loudly protest injustice and sinful conduct, and even to resort to violent means if this is absolutely necessary for the sake of drawing attention to the cause. However, several conditions must be met for protesting to be valid:
1. All angles of the situation have been carefully examined to determine that protest is the most effective response, and that protesting will not yield detrimental effects that outweigh the benefits.
2. One's motives are pristinely sincere, without even a tinge of self-interest. Protesting for the thrill, out of personal animus, or for the sake of condescension, is wholly illegitimate, and it goes without saying that looting or other financial gain from protesting undermines its validity at its very core.
3. One must be at least as vigilant in scrutinizing and seeking to improve himself before he is allowed to go out and protest what other people do wrong.

INTERVIEWS

Rabbi Yitzchok Grossman

Interviewed on Headlines with Dovid Lichtenstein, 14 Sivan, 5780 (June 6, 2020)

There's a big difference between protests and riots. Protests go back to the Gemara — צא והפגינו בלילה. This is about applying pressure on authorities to behave in a way that's more responsible and more decent. Riots, the destruction of property and injury, is much less justifiable.

Poskim discuss destroying property to prevent someone from doing an *issur*... [But] those examples are limited to destroying the actual things that are being used

---

and protesting wrongful behavior of which one is himself guilty.

to commit the wrongdoing. In general, to loot random businesses in the hope that it'll put pressure on the authorities is hard to justify. If you wanted to burn down a police station, the place of the evildoers where they do their terrible things, this is perhaps justifiable. But to just attack the economy and random private citizens is very hard to justify.

In the story of פילגש בגבעה, the husband cut up her limbs and sent them around even though it was defiling the body. The son of the Korban Nesanel, Reb Yedidya Weil, discusses this in a *teshuva*. He's talking about a case where a Jew was murdered, and they want to file a criminal complaint against the murderer. According to the law, the government would have to do an autopsy. The question was whether we allow the autopsy in order to catch the murderer. He brings a proof from פילגש בגבעה that we can defile a body in order to get justice, but he then gives two reasons as to why he thinks the proof is not compelling. Number one, who says the person was right to do it, to cut up the פילגש? Number two, he says it wasn't a private murder; it was an endemic problem and it was important for all of *Klal Yisrael*. There are a number of *poskim*, like Reb Eliyahu Klatskin and the *Divrei Malkiel*, who allow ניוול for the benefit of the מת, to bring the murderer to justice. Many feel that that's for the benefit of the מת to bring his murderer to justice. It's hard to stretch that to permit damaging innocent third parties to get a point across.

Shimon and Levi killed the whole city of Shechem, according to the Rambam, because they sat by and didn't do anything. They didn't protest, and so they were also guilty. However, some *Rishonim* disagree and say it's unreasonable to expect that they would have been able to judge their king. In our case, too, you have to make a reasonable assessment how much society as a whole should be held accountable for. Obviously, in a morally bankrupt society, where there is a complete lack of justice, it would justify violent action. It's hard to say that in America today that's where we are. There is a justice system. I agree that there's definitely some egregious behavior going on, but that doesn't hold society as a whole guilty of a capital violation.

Regarding *hafganos* in *Eretz Yisrael*, there's an issue of *chillul Hashem* and *bittul Torah*. *Chillul Hashem* is tricky. Many of the *gedolei Yisrael* in *Eretz Yisrael* who condoned or even encouraged these *hafganos* felt that unchecked *chillul Shabbos* is a tremendous *chillul Hashem*. The question is whether you are making a *chillul Hashem*, and whether you are relieving any of the existing *chillul Hashem*. You have to judge one against the other. There's also a question of *tocheicha*. Rav Eliyashiv held that *hafganos* should be held not because of *tocheicha*, but rather to effect a policy change. In terms of the *chillul Hashem*, there are two considerations, one that's inherent with any protest, and secondly, that there will be foolish people that will do actions not condoned by *gedolei Yisrael*. It seems that the *gedolei Yisrael* in *Eretz Yisrael* mostly were in favor of such protests. The balance between the *kiddush Hashem* and *chillul Hashem* has to be carefully balanced and taken into consideration.

If the *hafganos* can cause *chillul Shabbos* (such as by causing the police to come out and drive on Shabbos, etc.), that has to definitely be taken into account. There's a big issue of לפני עור. Even if you say that לפני עור doesn't apply to a מומר, we still don't want to promote *chillul Shabbos*, as Rav Eliyashiv notes in his *teshuva*. However, as he writes over there, the whole point of the protests is to stop the furtherance of *chillul Shabbos* — לעצור את מגיפת התפשטות הריסת השבת. We would have to weigh one against the other. If it can prevent a long-term *chillul Shabbos*, but will cause a short-term *chillul Shabbos*, then that's what has to be weighed. We don't believe in Judaism that the end automatically justifies the means. The *poskim* discuss the question that comes up in outreach, of inviting someone who's not religious for Shabbos. It will cause short-term *chillul Shabbos*, but in the long term, it can facilitate the observance of many *Shabbosos*. In general, there is a disagreement among the *poskim* if לפני עור applies in our scenario because we're causing the police to show up on Shabbos. Some hold that this does not violate לפני עור, because we didn't ask them to come and we would rather if they don't show up.

As for whether or not the protests are effective, this is a question of *metzius* that must be brought to experts. Sometimes they do, sometimes they don't. Reb Moshe was sometimes against and he was sometimes pro. In 1975 Reb Moshe wrote a letter opposing the protests to free Soviet Jewry. However, in 1968, he wrote a letter in support of the protests. I believe in Reb Yosef Dov Soloveitchik's approach, that we should ask the professionals. Just as we ask the doctors when we have a medical question, we should always ask the professionals in that field to see it they think it's effective to protest or not, just like the Gemara says that the Jews asked the מטרוניתא for advice. We see historically that some protests worked — like the Vietnam protests and the civil rights protests — and some didn't, like the Tiananmen Square protests. It's hard to give a general rule as to whether or not they help. Some do, some don't. And even when they do, it's hard to know if the protests are just a symptom of changing public opinion, or they actually caused the change in public opinion.

Rav Chaim Tzvi Senter

Interviewed on *Headlines with Dovid Lichtenstein*, 14 Sivan, 5780 (June 6, 2020)

There's a difference between a protest, and a riot where there's damage and destruction of property. In my opinion, they're definitely effective. They get people to stand up and listen. They're not getting sympathy or understanding, but they're definitely getting a reaction. I can't say it's beneficial, but it's definitely effective.

I don't let the *bochrim* [in my yeshiva] go [to protests]. Many times, *bochrim* go not because they want to go to a *hafgana*, but because they like the "action." I try to explain to them that a protest rally is *Yidden* pitted against *Yidden*. How can you go to such a place? It's a tragedy. If a person goes to a *hafgana* because Shabbos really bothers him, this is one thing. But if he's just going because he wants "action," that's another thing. Even if sometimes we have to make a *hafgana*, it's still a terrible thing. It's a tragedy.

I was at two protests in my life. They were peaceful protests. We said *Tehillim* and heard דברי התעוררות. There was no fighting or destruction of property. A peaceful protest is probably more effective because you outclass your opponent. But when it comes to a protest that borders on a riot, we end up with *Yidden* fighting with *Yidden*. That's terribly painful. Reb Aryeh Levine, who left such a rich legacy, was able to change so many people through love, understanding and appreciation.

Most times, the police are just doing their job. They're trying to help.

I don't think *yeshiva bochrim* belong even at peaceful protests unless it's something that's risking the very fabric of our community. *Yeshiva bochrim* belong in the *beis midrash*.

There's a major difference between the riots that are happening now in America [in response to George Floyd's murder] and the ones in *Eretz Yisrael*. Even when there were destructive protests in *Eretz Yisrael*, I have never heard of one riot where people took anything for themselves. In addition, they never hurt innocent people or stole from them. They may have damaged public property, but not private property. When you take something for yourself, it changes the entire agenda of what you are doing. Are you really protesting the injustice, or are you trying to take things for yourself? It doesn't change what you are trying to do if you burn something. It has the same effect. When you take it for yourself, it really has nothing to do with the gentleman who was killed. It's an opportunity to steal.

I think Martin Luther King brought about change. He outclassed his opponents. He did it because he didn't fight, he was bigger than them and more in control than them. I don't think the rioters are gaining anyone's respect. They are getting attention, but if you want change, this is not going to get it. Studies show there's usually more police brutality after protests, not less. In the long term, you're not going to get anywhere this way. I understand where they are coming from, and their frustration, but this approach [of violent rioting] is not going to help. In the story of פילגש בגבעה, even though what the husband did was hair-raising and startling, he didn't harm any people or damage any property. The only time I've seen change is when someone stood up with nobility, class and direction. These protests don't have any direction, they don't have a goal. They don't have leadership. The civil rights movement had all of the above, but they have nothing. It's just pandemonium.

When Reb Elya Baruch Finkel was sitting *shiva* for his mother, he told us a story about his mother's father, Rav Dovid Levin, who wrote the *sefer Darchei Dovid*. In the early years of the State [of Israel], there was a struggle with regard to *kedushas Shabbos*. He was walking along the street in Yerushalayim on Friday night when he saw someone who was clearly Jewish driving. He fainted. A few weeks later, the same thing happened. This time, he didn't faint, but just started trembling. He said, "If seeing *chillul Shabbos* has this kind of an effect on me, causing me to be desensitized, then I never want to walk out on Shabbos again!" From then on, he never walked through the streets of Yerushalayim on Shabbos. I think that part of the reason people make *hafganos* in *Eretz Yisrael* is for themselves — so that the desecration does not affect their own sensitivity towards Shabbos.

My great-grandfather, Reb Moshe Aharon Poleyeff, grew up in the house of Rav Isser Zalman Meltzer when he attended his yeshiva in Slutsk. Once, the *bochrim* complained that the *mashgiach* wasn't treating them properly, and they decided to make a protest. One day, they all didn't show up in the *beis midrash*, and when the *mashgiach* entered the *beis midrash*, the *bochrim* suddenly stormed in and picked him up on his chair and removed him from the *beis midrash*. Rav Isser Zalman called the *bochrim* in, and they explained to him the situation.

He told them, "I hear what you are saying, perhaps it's a problem, but this is not the way to deal with it."

He had the *mashgiach* stay away from the yeshiva for a while until the situation calmed down, and then slowly brought him back in. The Rebbetzin, though, felt that the *bochrim* were right, and eventually, the *mashgiach* was asked to leave the yeshiva. Still, Rav Isser Zalman felt that this is not proper behavior for *bnei Torah*. We have to hold ourselves to a certain standard, and there's a way to protest.

Orthodox Rabbi Group Condemns Racism At 'Highest Levels Of Government'

July 22, 2019
By Ron Kampeas

WASHINGTON (JTA) — The Orthodox Rabbinical Council of America said it "condemns the most recent outburst of racist rhetoric in the highest levels of government," an apparent reference to President Trump's call on four Democratic congresswomen to "go back" to unspecified countries.

President Donald Trump speaks about the resignation of Labor Secretary Alex Acosta while talking to the media at the White House on July 12, 2019. (Mark Wilson/Getty Images)

The statement Thursday also alluded to statements by two of the congresswoman Trump has named, Rashida Tlaib of Michigan and Ilhan Omar of Minnesota, that have insinuated dual loyalties by advocates for Israel. Omar has apologized for some, but not all, of her controversial statements.

The other two targets of Trump's ire are Reps. Alexandria Ocasio-Cortez of New York and Ayanna Pressley of Massachusetts.

"Whether statements that question the loyalty of American Jews when the safety and security of Israel is at stake or rallies that call upon descendants of immigrants to return to countries they never knew, we see these pronouncements as dangerous to the core values of our faith and the foundations of American society," the statement said.

The statement's tough tone was unusual for a body representing a segment of the community that has embraced Trump for aligning his policies with those of the Israeli government led by Benjamin Netanyahu, particularly in moving the U.S. embassy to Jerusalem. Centrist and leftist Jewish groups have also slammed Trump for his attacks on the congresswomen.

"The lack of civil discourse, the racist and xenophobic chants at political rallies, and rise of fringe hate groups all demand that we take a stand for goodness and respect," RCA Vice President Rabbi Binyamin Blau said in the statement.

Trump in a tweet this week said the four congresswomen should "go back and help fix the totally broken and crime-infested places from which they came." Omar was born in Somalia; the other four are born in the United States, and what "places" Trump was referring to is not clear.

At a rally Wednesday night in North Carolina, Trump supporters chanted "send her back" repeatedly when Trump attacked Omar.

Racism — a Torah Perspective

One of the most important and pronounced societal changes that unfolded in the latter part of the 20th century, and carrying over into the 21st, is a heightened sensitivity towards the evils of racism, of the belief that certain ethnicities are inherently inferior and should be treated as such. A strong consensus has emerged in the modern world that such a belief must be resoundingly and unequivocally rejected, and that all races and ethnicities must be granted equal rights and privileges. Actions and words expressing racial prejudices, or which are interpreted as such, are instantly met with strong condemnation. This is a welcome change to the notion which was accepted as axiomatic even among much of the civilized world for many centuries, that certain ethnic groups do not, because of their ethnicity, deserve the same rights and privileges are other groups. Here in the United States, of course, our society has, to its credit, evolved from one which assumed the right of white people to enslave people of color to one in which people of color are treated equally and invited to fully participate in all levels of society.

What does the Torah say about racism? Is the revulsion to racism in the modern Western world something which the Torah teaches, as well? Or do our sources reflect a different belief, that indeed, some ethnicities are inherently superior to others?

כמה מכוער כלי זה שעשית

We begin our discussion with the specific question surrounding people of color, whether our tradition accepts as valid the notion that some people are to be regarded differently than others by virtue of their skin color.

The Gemara in *Maseches Ta'anis* (20a) tells the story of Rabbi Elazar ben Rabbi Shimon, who was on his way home from yeshiva, when he encountered a man with an unsightly appearance. The man greeted Rabbi Elazar, who ignored him, saying to himself, "What an ugly man that is!" Rabbi Elazar then turned to the man and asked whether all his fellow townspeople were as unattractive as him.

"I don't know," the man replied. "But go tell the Artisan who made me: כמה מכוער כלי זה שעשית [What an ugly utensil this is that You made]!"

Rabbi Elazar accepted the criticism and acknowledged that he had sinned. He begged the man for forgiveness.

The Maharsha explains that Rabbi Elazar mocked the man's appearance because he had colored skin.[1] The man, in his response, was telling Rabbi Elazar, in the Maharsha's words, אתה נותן חסרון ביצירה — he was pointing to some deficiency in God's creation. If we deride a person because of his skin color — or, for that matter, because of any other physical property — then we are, in effect, deriding God Himself who created that person with all his physical characteristics.

It must be emphasized that the Gemara speaks of Rabbi Elazar's remark as an outright sin, as opposed to merely his falling short of the highest standards of refinement, stating, כיון שידע בעצמו שחטא — "Once he recognized that he had **sinned...**" And, it is clear from the Gemara that Rabbi Elazar needed to ask forgiveness not only from the man himself, but also from his Creator, indicating that he sinned not only by offending the man, but also by expressing disdain for one of God's creatures. It would follow, then, that there is no justification for using a derogatory term in reference to people of color, as is, unfortunately, still very common in some Orthodox Jewish circles. Even if no person of color is present, the use of such a term shows contempt for God's creations, and is akin to turning to the Almighty and saying, כמה מכוער כלי זה שעשית.

Rav Moshe Feinstein, in a responsum concerning the status of Ethiopian Jews,[2] decried the discrimination which, as was reported to him, Ethiopian Jews suffered upon arriving in Israel. He wrote:

> מאוד נצטערתי על מה ששמעתי שיש כאלו בא"י שמונעים מלקרבם בענייני
> רוחניות, וגורמים ח"ו שיהיו אובדים מדת יהודי. ונראה לי שכך נוהגים רק משום
> שצבע עורם הוא שחור. דפשוט שיש לקרבם, לא רק מצד שאינם גרועים משאר
> יהודים, ואין לדינא חילוק במה שהם שחורים, אלא גם מצד שיש בהם הטענה
> שאולי הם גרים, ונכללים במצות ואהבתם את הגר. ואסיים בתקוה שישופר
> המצב...

> I was very distressed over that which I heard, that there are those in Israel who refrain from drawing them [Ethiopian immigrants] close in regard to spiritual matters, causing them to be lost, Heaven forbid, from the Jewish

---

1. We should note that in the version of this story which appears in *Maseches Derech Eretz* (2:1), Rabbi Elazar insulted the person he encountered by exclaiming, כמה מכוערין בניו של אברהם אבינו — "How ugly are the children of our patriarch, Avraham!" According to this version, the man was a Jew (or otherwise a descendant of Avraham), and not a person of color, in contradistinction to the Maharsha's understanding. Nevertheless, the fact that the Maharsha understood the story as involving a person of color shows the impropriety of insulting people because of their skin color.

2. *Iggeros Moshe*, E.H. 5:1. Rav Moshe ruled that it is questionable whether Ethiopian Jews can be presumed to be halachically Jewish, and so, in his view, they must be rescued and helped, but should undergo conversion if they wish to immigrate to Israel. This question, however, is irrelevant as far as the issue of racial discrimination is concerned.

religion. It seems to me that they act this way only because the color of their skin is black. But it is obvious that they should be drawn close, not only because they are not inferior to other Jews, and that they are black is of no practical consequence, but also because of the claim that they might be converts, and are thus included in the command "You shall love the convert."[3] I conclude with the hope that the situation improves...

Rav Moshe dismissed out of hand the notion that Ethiopian Jews' skin color makes them inferior in any way. It was obvious to him that they are to be treated like all other Jews, and, if they are considered converts,[4] then they must be shown special love and affection in accordance with the Biblical command of ואהבתם את הגר.

In fact, the Mishna in *Maseches Sanhedrin*[5] appears to explicitly admonish against harboring any sort of theories of racial superiority, stating: ?מפני מה נברא האדם יחידי שלא יאמר אדם לחבירו אבא גדול מאביך — "Why was man created alone? So that a person should not say to his fellow, 'My father was greater than your father.'" At the time of the world's creation, God brought many of each species of animal into existence, whereas the human race began with just one creature, Adam, who then reproduced. This was done, the Mishna teaches, to preclude the possibility of any person feeling superior to another by virtue of his pedigree.

Rav Yaakov Kamenetsky[6] explains that God singled out the human being in this fashion precisely כדי שלא יבואו בני האדם לידי מדה מגונה זו — to prevent people from adopting racial theories, to make it impossible for any ethnicity to feel genetically superior to another, as we all descend from Adam and Chava. The Mishna's point is precisely that no human being should ever feel entitled due to his racial background. God specifically arranged that all humans for all eternity would descend from a single person so that we will all regard each other as racially equal, such that no ethnic group can ever claim a status of superiority over others.

The Potential of Every Human Being

Numerous sources in our tradition unmistakably express the basic tenet of humanism, that every human being is precious because he is a human being, irrespective of any other factor. Our designation as the "chosen people," which we emphasize repeatedly in our liturgy,[7] does

---

3.   *Devarim* 10:19.

4.   See note 2.

5.   37a.

6.   *Emes Le-Yaakov, Bereishis* 9:25.

7.   We recite each morning in the second blessing over Torah study, אשר בחר בנו מכל העמים ונתן לנו את תורתו ("...who has chosen us from all the nations and given us His Torah"), and we pronounce each week at *kiddush*, כי בנו בחרת ואותנו קדשת מכל העמים — "...for You

not in any way point to a belief in our ethnic superiority, but rather to a special mission we have been assigned.

The most obvious proof that the Torah does not regard the Jewish People as racially superior is the institution of *geirus* (conversion), which allows any human being from any nation to become full-fledged members of the Jewish People, who enjoy all rights and privileges as other Jews, and bear the same obligations. Needless to say, a gentile does not undergo any genetic transformation over the course of conversion, a process which entails a number of rituals (circumcision, immersion, and, in the times of the *Beis Ha-Mikdash*, a sacrifice) and a commitment to observe *halacha*. The fact that a gentile who takes these steps assumes the status of a full-fledged Jew suffices as iron-clad proof that the Torah does not believe in the Jews' racial superiority.

In fact, already in God's first prophecy to Avraham, informing him of the special bond that He would forge with him and his offspring, He announced to the patriarch, ונברכו בך כל משפחות האדמה — commonly translated as, "all families of the land shall be blessed through you."[8] The Rashbam,[9] however, interprets the word ונברכו in this verse to mean "grafted," referring to the possibility of other peoples joining Avraham's descendants and becoming part of God's treasured nation. At the very moment when God announced the designation of *Am Yisrael* as a special people, He emphasized the opportunity allowed for all others to join.[10]

Additionally, the Mishna famously teaches in *Pirkei Avos*,[11] חביב אדם שנברא בצלם — "Man is beloved, in that he is created in the image [of God]." The Mishna cites the verse, שופך דם האדם...דמו ישפך כי בצלם אלוקים עשה את האדם — "He who spills a man's blood, his blood shall be spilt, for it was in the image of God that He created man."[12] The

---

have chosen us and sanctified us from all the nations." The Biblical source of this concept is God's declaration at Mount Sinai, והייתם לי סגולה מכל העמים — "You shall be for Me special from all the nations," (*Shemos* 19:5), and the verse in *Devarim* (10:15), ויבחר בזרעם אחריהם בכם מכל העמים — "and He chose in their [the patriarchs'] descendants after them, you, from all the nations."

8. *Bereishis* 12:3.
9. *Bereishis* 28:14.
10. The Ramchal, in *Derech Hashem* (2:4), elaborates at great length on the notion of the Jewish People's designation. He explains that only Avraham displayed the capability to rise to the lofty state that God had initially intended human beings to attain, and for this reason He established a special covenant with Avraham and his descendants. However, members of other nations can join our nation and attain this unique potential, just as the branch of a tree can be grafted onto another and thereby attain the properties of the host tree.
11. 3:14.
12. *Bereishis* 9:10.

Tosfos Yom Tov, commenting on this Mishna, proves that the Mishna speaks here of all human beings. He explains that the Mishna cited specifically this verse, as opposed to others that also speak of man's creation in the divine image, because it is here where the divine image is the source of responsibility and accountability. This verse appears as part of God's instructions to all mankind following the flood, as Noach and his family prepared to rebuild the world anew, and it thus demonstrates that, in the *Tosfos Yom Tov*'s words, הואיל שחבבו לבראו בצלמו, לכן מוטל עליו לעשות רצון קונו — "since He has cherished him [man] such that He created him in His image, therefore, it behooves him to fulfill his Creator's will." Man's having been created in the divine image imposes upon him demands and expectations, a responsibility to fulfill God's commands. For gentiles, this means obeying the seven Noachide laws, whereas for Jews, this means observing all the Torah's commands, due to the special covenant which God forged with the Jewish Nation. But every human being, regardless of race or physical properties, is endowed with the divine image such that he is able and expected to live a life of devotion to God. This is the Mishna's intent, the *Tosfos Yom Tov* writes, in teaching, חביב אדם שנברא בצלם.

Indeed, Seforno, in the introduction to his Torah commentary, explains that God's initial intention was for all of humanity to achieve greatness, without any distinction between one nation and the other. It was only after mankind's repeated failures to reach the anticipated level that God forged a special covenant with Avraham, due to his unique piety, so that his descendants would commit to living at an exceptionally high spiritual standard and thereby uplift the rest of the world. The Jewish People's "chosen" status does not signify any sort of genetic preeminence, but rather assigns a special mission to fulfill for the benefit of all other nations, to guide and elevate them.

Elsewhere,[13] Seforno comments that the Jewish People's "treasured" status means that we bear the obligation to represent God to the world, to teach them to serve only Him, and not other deities. The Torah designates the Jewish Nation as ממלכת כהנים — "a kingdom of priests," which Seforno explains to mean that we are charged with the role of religious leaders of the world, just as the *kohanim* serve as the religious leaders within our nation.[14]

Our "chosen" status means not that we are inherently greater than other peoples, but that we are charged with the mission of helping all humanity reach its potential.

---

13. *Shemos* 19:6.
14. Seforno adds, כמו שיהיה ענין ישראל לעתיד לבא — that we will fulfill this role in the future, after the final redemption, indicating that in our current state of exile, we are incapable of serving as religious guides to the other nations. This question — of whether we are to seek to teach and guide other peoples under current conditions — was explored in *Headlines 2*, chapter 6: "Light Unto the Nations, or None of Our Business? Influencing Gentiles to Observe the Noachide Laws."

Judaism believes in the great potential latent within each and every person, and this is precisely why *Am Yisrael* was set apart — to help all mankind achieve the greatness of which it is capable.

This perspective also underlies the Rambam's unequivocal statement[15] that any gentile who commits to and obeys the Noachide laws is considered מחסידי אומות עולם — a righteous gentile — and earns a share in the next world. We bear a greater burden of responsibility by virtue of our having accepted the Torah and forged a special covenant with God, but this does not reflect any kind of disdain on our part towards other peoples. In fact, Seforno comments in a different context,[16] וחסידי אומות העולם יקרים אצלי בלי ספק — the righteous gentiles are undoubtedly precious to God. People are judged based on their conduct, not on their racial background.

An earlier source of this concept is *Toras Kohanim,*[17] which states: אפילו גוי ועושה את התורה הרי הוא ככהן גדול — a gentile who observes the Torah earns a stature as lofty as that of the *Kohen Gadol.*[18] And *Tanna De-Bei Eliyahu*[19] establishes:

> בין גוי ובין ישראל, בין איש ובין אשה, בין עבד בין שפחה — הכל לפי מעשה
> שעושה כך רוח הקודש שורה עליו.

> Whether a gentile or Jew, man or woman, servant or maidservant — everything depends on the actions one performs: to this extent, the sacred spirit rests upon him.

Even a gentile, *Tanna De-Bei Eliyahu* teaches, can become worthy of prophecy.

Likewise, the Midrash,[20] commenting on the verse in *Tehillim*[21] ה' אוהב צדיקים ("God loves the righteous"), writes that God loves every righteous person regardless of his or her background, including gentiles.[22]

---

15. *Hilchos Melachim* 8:11.
16. *Shemos* 19:5.
17. *Parshas Acharei-Mos*, 8:13.
18. The Gemara in *Maseches Sanhedrin* (59a) clarifies that this refers to a gentile who studies the seven Noachide laws, as it is forbidden for non-Jews to study the rest of the Torah.
19. Chapter 9.
20. *Bamidbar Rabba*, 8:2.
21. 146:8.
22. The Meiri, in numerous places in his Talmud commentary, emphasizes that whenever the Gemara mentions laws which treat gentiles differently than Jews (such as the exemption of liability when a Jew's animal kills a gentile's animal), it refers only to nations שאינם גדורים בדרכי דתות ונימוסים — "who are not bound by ways of civility and etiquette." Meaning, these distinctions were intended to exclude barbaric nations who did not follow reasonable norms of ethical conduct. Gentiles who are part of a generally moral, civilized society, according to the Meiri, are to be treated no differently from Jews with regard to

Extending Kindness to Gentiles

Many sources emphasize that while we bear a special responsibility towards our fellow Jews, we are expected to treat all human beings with courtesy, respect and kindness.

The Talmud Yerushalmi[23] cites Rabbi Akiva's famous pronouncement that the command ואהבת לרעך כמוך ("You shall love your fellow as yourself"[24]) constitutes כלל גדול בתורה — "the great principle of the Torah." However, the Yerushalmi then proceeds to cite Ben Azai as disagreeing, and pointing to a different verse as expressing an even more fundamental principle — the verse in the Book of Bereishis,[25] זה ספר תולדות אדם ("This is the account of man's history"). As the *Penei Moshe* commentary explains, Ben Azai clearly refers to the latter part of the verse — "on the day God created man, He made him in the form of God." Ben Azai considers this verse "the great principle of the Torah," the *Penei Moshe* explains, because כשיתבונן אדם בזה יזהר מאד בכבוד חבירו — "when a person contemplates this, he will exercise great care with regard to his fellow's honor."

The *Penei Moshe* notes that this debate appears also in the Midrash,[26] which comments in reference to this verse:

שלא תאמר הואיל ונתבזיתי, יתבזה חברי עמי...אם עשית כן, דע למי אתה מבזה — בדמות אלוקים עשה אותו.

---

civil law. The Meiri expresses this view in many different contexts, including: *Berachos* 58a (ד"ה ראה אכלסי), *Shabbos* 156a (ד"ה מפנות הדת), *Yoma* 84b (ד"ה פיקוח נפש), *Beitza* 21b (ד"ה ממה שכתבנו), *Yevamos* 98a (ד"ה זה שבארנו), *Kesubos* 3b (ד"ה אשת ישראל), *Gittin* 59a (ד"ה אין ממחין) and 62a (ד"ה עובדי הגלילים), *Kiddushin* 17b (ד"ה הגוי), *Bava Kama* 113a (ד"ה כל שגדור) and 59a (ד"ה כבר בארנו), *Bava Metzia* 27a (ד"ה היה המוכס), and in numerous other places.

Although the general consensus does not follow the Meiri's position, Rav Avraham Yitzchak Kook wrote in one of his letters (*Iggeros Ha-Re'iya*, 1:89):

העיקר הוא כדעת המאירי שכל העמים שהם גדורים בנימוסים הגונים בין אדם לחבירו הם כבר נחשבים לגרים תושבים בכל חיובי האדם.

The accepted view is that of the Meiri, that all nations who are bound by proper behaviors between man and his fellow are already considered like "resident aliens" regarding all of a person's obligations.

Rav Yosef Eliyahu Henkin also seems to have accepted the Meiri's view (see below, note 61).

23. *Nedarim* 9:4.
24. *Vayikra* 19:14.
25. 5:1.
26. *Bereishis Rabba* 24:7.

You shall not say, "Since I have been disgraced, my fellow shall be disgraced along with me." …If you did so, you shall know whom you are disgracing — "He made him in the form of God."

The "great principle" taught by this verse is that if we belittle or humiliate any human being, then we are, in effect, belittling or humiliating the Almighty Himself. This verse thus serves as an effective warning to exercise care with regard to the respect of dignity of all people.

This passage in the Yerushalmi appears also in *Toras Kohanim*,[27] and the *Korban Aharon* commentary explains:

כולם תולדות אב אחד הם, וכולם אחים, ולזה אין להתגדל על זה ולא לשנוא את זה.

They are all the descendants of a single father, and they are all brothers, and thus one may not feel superior to another or despise another.

Likewise, Rav Yisrael Lifschitz, in his *Tiferes Yisrael* commentary to the Mishna, explains the intent of the aforementioned Mishna in *Pirkei Avos* which states that all people are created in the divine image:

משום כך יראה האדם להיטיב לכל, אפילו למי שאינו בן ברית, וכ״ש שלא יגרום לו נזק לגופו ממונו וכבודו, ולא יבזהו להלבין צלם אלוקים המציץ מפניו.

Because of this, a person will ensure to extend goodness to all, even those who are not part of the covenant, and certainly not to cause harm to his body, money or honor, and will not humiliate him, shaming the divine image which shines forth from his face.

The *Sefer Chassidim*[28] writes about a gentile who observes the Noachide laws, אל תזלזלהו, אלא תכבדהו יותר מישראל שאינו עוסק בתורה — "Do not denigrate him; rather, respect him more than a Jew who does not involve himself in Torah."

Particularly striking is the position taken by Rav Pinchas Horowitz (the *Ba'al Hafla'a*), in his *Sefer Ha-Bris*,[29] asserting that the command of ואהבת לרעך כמוך applies to our dealings with all people, Jew and non-Jew alike. Rav Horowitz acknowledges that the word רעך in a different context is taken as referring specifically to Jews. The Torah uses the word רעהו in establishing the laws of damages caused by one's animals,[30] and the Gemara[31] understands this term as limiting the laws to cases where a Jew's property was damaged. However, Rav Horowitz establishes that this limited meaning

---

27.　*Parshas Kedoshim* 4:12.

28.　358.

29.　2:13:5.

30.　וכי יגף שור איש את שור רעהו, *Shemos* 21:35.

31.　*Bava Kama* 37b–38a. See also the *Mechilta's* comments to this verse.

of the word רע is intended only in that context, where the Sages specifically established this definition. But in other contexts, unless noted otherwise, the term רע must be taken to mean רעך שהוא אדם כמוך ועוסק בישובו של עולם כמוך — "your fellow who is a person like you, and is involved in the settlement of the world like you." The command ואהבת לרעך כמוך, then, requires us to show love and consideration to all generally good, upstanding people, and not only to our fellow Jews.

Rav Horowitz draws proof to his theory from the fact that Chushai Ha-Arki, a close confidant of King David, is called רעה דוד ("David's peer"), even though he belonged to a different nation.[32] Furthermore, Rav Horowitz adds, *Tanna De-Bei Eliyahu*[33] tells that the prophet Eliyahu interpreted the command לא תעשוק את רעך ("You shall not defraud your fellow"[34]) as forbidding deceiving even gentiles. The *Zikukin De'nura* commentary to *Tanna De-Bei Eliyahu* explains that the word רעך in this verse implies אפילו עכו"ם המטיב לו — even gentiles who act kindly. Accordingly, the famous command of ואהבת לרעך כמוך requires us to deal benevolently with any generally decent individual, regardless of his ethnicity. Rav Horowitz also cites Rav Chaim Vital's admonition in his *Sha'arei Kedusha*,[35] יאהב כל הבריות אפילו גוי — "One must love all people, even a gentile."

Rav Shimshon Raphael Hirsch, in his Torah commentary,[36] explains that this is the message conveyed by the story of Avraham's welcoming three angels — whom he thought were idolatrous wayfarers — immediately after undergoing circumcision. As the Midrash[37] teaches, Avraham feared that after having undergone circumcision, which is intended to set our nation apart from all others, people would no longer come to visit him. For precisely this reason, Rav Hirsch explains, Avraham sat outside in the blazing sun looking for people to invite — to allay his fears that his *bris mila*, the symbol of his exclusive designation, would isolate him from other people, and to assure that he would continue extending kindness to all people even after being set apart via circumcision. Rav Hirsch writes:

> The Abrahamites flourishing in the circumcision-isolation are to be the
> most humane mortals. They form the most definite contrast to the world
> in general but nevertheless they are always to be found ready for all gener-
> al humane purposes. For fostering such humaneness they are set apart...

---

32. However, Rav Uri Shachar, in his *Ori Ve-Yish'i* (*Sefer Shmuel*, p. 245), notes that there is no indication that Chushai Ha-Arki was not Jewish.

33. 15.

34. *Vayikra* 19:13.

35. 1:5.

36. *Bereishis* 18:1.

37. *Bereishis Rabba* 48:9.

If his sons, the defamed Jews, have inherited anything from him, this spirit of general benevolence and universal charity they certainly have had as their heritage from him… Where open hearts, open houses, open hands are sought for, where readiness for sacrifice of time, energy and money for general humane purposes is required…even today, even the disparagers of Judaism turn in the first place to Jews.

This obligation — to deal kindly with gentiles — has sources in the Talmud, as well. In *Maseches Berachos* (17a), the Gemara cites Abayei as teaching that one should conduct himself in a peaceful manner עם אחיו ועם קרוביו ועם כל אדם, ואפילו עם נכרי בשוק — "with his brethren, with his kin, and with all people, even a gentile in the marketplace." The Gemara tells that Rabban Yochanan ben Zakai greeted all people, without waiting for them to greet him first, emphasizing אפילו נכרי בשוק — even non-Jews whom he encountered in the marketplace. And in *Maseches Kiddushin* (33a), the Gemara tells that Rabbi Yochanan would stand in the presence of the elderly, even gentiles, as an expression of respect.

The Gemara in *Maseches Gittin* (61a) states explicitly:

מפרנסים עניי נכרים עם עניי ישראל, ומבקרין חולי נכרים עם חולי ישראל, וקוברין מתי נכרים עם מתי ישראל, מפני דרכי שלום.

We support non-Jewish paupers just like Jewish paupers; we visit non-Jewish ill patients just like Jewish ill patients; we bury the non-Jewish dead like the Jewish dead — in the interest of peaceful relations.

The conclusion of this passage — מפני דרכי שלום — might give the impression that we are to deal kindly with non-Jews and assist gentiles in need for purely pragmatic reasons, to avoid the hostility and resentment that we would trigger by extending kindness only to our fellow Jews and not to gentiles. Fundamentally, one may think, we owe favors and generosity only to fellow Jews, and it is only the fear of animosity that necessitates acting kindly to others. The Rambam, however, clearly understood otherwise. He writes[38]:

אפילו העכו"ם צוו חכמים לבקר חוליהם, ולקבור מתיהם עם מתי ישראל, ולפרנס ענייהם בכלל עניי ישראל, מפני דרכי שלום, הרי נאמר טוב ה' לכל ורחמיו על כל מעשיו, ונאמר דרכיה דרכי נועם וכל נתיבותיה שלום.

Even the gentiles, the Sages instructed to visit their ill patients, to bury their dead like the Jewish dead, and to support their poor together with the Jewish poor, because of [the value of] peaceful relations. After all, it says, "God is good to all, and His compassion is upon all His creations."[39]

---

38. *Hilchos Melachim* 10:12.
39. *Tehillim* 145:9.

And it says, "Its ways are ways of pleasantness, and all its paths are peace."[40]

The Rambam cites two verses as Biblical sources for the importance of דרכי שלום — one which extols God's compassion and kindness to all His creations, and another which establishes that "the ways of Torah" are peaceful. This would seem to indicate that for the Rambam, the concept of דרכי שלום involves not simply the pragmatic interest to avoid hostility, but rather our obligation to follow God's example of kindness to all people,[41] and it also reflects the inherent importance of peaceful relations with people as a defining characteristic of the Torah way of life.

This perspective finds expression also in the *Sefer Chassidim*,[42] which teaches that one must grant precedence when walking along a narrow road to somebody carrying a heavy load, regardless of whether or not he is Jewish. The *Sefer Chassidim* cites the verse in *Mishlei* (3:4), ומצא חן ושכל טוב בעיני אלוקים ואדם — "Find favor and goodwill in the eyes of God and man," which implies that we must act kindly to all human beings.

It emerges, then, that there are three possible Biblical sources for the obligation to extend kindness to gentiles:

1. The command of ואהבת לרעך כמוך, which, according to Rav Pinchas Horowitz, refers to our relationships with all upstanding people;
2. The fact that God Himself extends kindness to all His creatures, and that Torah life is to be characterized by "ways of pleasantness" and peaceful relations among people;
3. King Shlomo's exhortation in *Mishlei*, ומצא חן ושכל טוב בעיני אלוקים ואדם.

Despise the Sin, Not the Sinner

Furthermore, even when it comes to evildoers, whose conduct legitimately should invite contempt, we are taught that our feelings of hostility must be directed towards their actions, and not towards the people themselves.

The Gemara in *Maseches Berachos* (7a) tells of an apostate who frequently badgered Rabbi Yehoshua ben Levi. Rabbi Yehoshua considered placing a curse on this man so he would die and no longer disturb him. But he later realized that this was improper, citing the aforementioned verse, ורחמיו על כל מעשיו, which teaches that we must have compassion upon all people, including sinners.

The Gemara later (10a) tells the far more famous story of Rabbi Meir, who suffered

---

40. *Mishlei* 3:17.
41. It is worth noting that the Rambam considers it a Biblical command to follow God's example of compassion and graciousness. See *Sefer Ha-Mitzvos*, asei 8; *Hilchos Dei'os* 1:5–6.
42. 551.

harassment at the hands of a group of "bullies,"[43] and considered praying for their deaths. His wife, Bruria, reprimanded him, noting King David's plea in *Tehillim*,[44] יתמו חטאים מן הארץ — "Sins shall cease from the earth." Bruria observed that King David pleads not for the demise of the sinners, but rather for the end of sin. Rabbi Meir accepted his wife's guidance, and prayed instead that his harassers should repent, which they did.

As much as we must despise wrongdoing, we must also respect the divine image within even evil people.

Rabbi Meir himself expresses a similar idea elsewhere, as cited by the Tosefta,[45] in explaining the prohibition against leaving the body of an executed offender hanging on a tree beyond the day of his execution. According to Rabbi Meir, this is forbidden because of the resemblance between the human being and God. Rabbi Meir draws an analogy to a king's twin brother who is caught committing a capital offense. Hanging the criminal on a tree disgraces the king, by giving the appearance that he was convicted and executed. By the same token, leaving the remains of an executed offender hanging in public brings dishonor to God, in whose image every human being is created, and thus the body must be hung for only a very brief period. Rabbi Meir here expresses the notion that even those guilty of capital offenses have the divine image which must be respected.[46]

Accordingly, Rav Yaakov Emden writes in his *Migdal Oz*,[47] אפילו עובדי אלילים יאהב בבחינה שהם יצורי ה', ולא ישנא אלא מעשיהם — "One should love even idol-worshippers in the sense of their being God's creatures, and he should despise only their actions." We should feel contempt for the misconduct of evil people, but still respect them as God's creatures.

This concept is indicated already by the Rambam, in *Hilchos Avel*,[48] where he emphasizes the great value and importance of hospitality, pointing to Avraham as the paradigm of this religious ideal:

---

43. בריוני.

44. 104:35.

45. *Sanhedrin* 9:7.

46. *Targum Sheini* to *Megillas Esther* (9:24) tells that Queen Esther was asked why she allowed the bodies of Haman and his ten sons to remain hung on a tree for an extended period, in violation of the command requiring that the body of an executed offender be removed from the gallows the same day. Esther explained that this case was exceptional — proving that fundamentally, the law requiring removing the body the same day it was hung applies even to an evil figure such as Haman. We may thus conclude that the divine image of even the worst villains must be respected.

47. *Aliyas Ahava*, chapter 12.

48. 14:2.

הוא החק שחקקו אברהם אבינו ודרך החסד שנהג בה, מאכיל עוברי דרכים ומשקה אותן ומלוה אותן, וגדולה הכנסת אורחים מהקבלת פני שכינה.

This is the rule instituted by our patriarch Avraham, and the path of kindness which he followed — feeding wayfarers, giving them water and escorting them. And hospitality is greater than greeting the divine presence.

The paradigmatic example of hospitality is the story of Avraham's welcoming three strangers, who turned out to be angels, but whom, according to tradition, Avraham mistook for idolaters.[49] The Rambam clearly speaks here not of the pragmatic value of welcoming and caring for guests, but rather of its inherent importance — and his example is the kindness extended by Avraham to three strangers whom he thought worshipped idols.

In fact, the Netziv, in the introduction to his *Ha'amek Davar* Torah commentary, writes that Avraham was given the name אברהם, which expresses his stature as אב המון גויים ("the father of a multitude of peoples"),[50] precisely because of his love and compassion for all people, even those who acted wrongly. Just as a father loves and cares for his child despite the child's misconduct, Avraham loved and cared for all people despite their improper behavior, and thus he is called אב המון גויים — the father of all people. The Netziv adds that the stories of our saintly patriarchs are included in the Book of *Bereishis*, which tells of the world's creation, because their example of benevolence and respect for all people, including sinners, is necessary for קיום הבריאה — preserving creation.[51] And this book is called ספר הישר ("Book of the Upright"), the Netziv explains, precisely because of this outstanding quality of the patriarchs, who showed kindness and consideration to all people. As strongly as we must condemn wrongful behavior, we must respect and love people who engage in such behavior, and hope and pray that they change their conduct.[52]

---

49. Rashi, *Bereishis* 18:4, based on *Bereishis Rabba* 50:4 and *Bava Metzia* 86b.

50. *Bereishis* 17:5.

51. The Netziv shows how Yitzchak and Yaakov, too, like Avraham, showed kindness and concern even for wicked people such as Avimelech and Lavan.

52. Rav Meir Simcha Ha-Kohen, in his *Meshech Chochma* (*Shemos* 12:16), observes that the Torah always refers to the festival of Pesach as the occasion celebrating our nation's departure from Egypt, and not the occasion of the Egyptians' downfall. We celebrate our victory; not our enemies' defeat. For the same reason, Rav Meir Simcha writes, our celebration of Chanukah focuses not on the miraculous military triumph over the Greeks, but rather on the miracle of the oil which sustained the candles in the *Beis Ha-Mikdash* for eight nights when it was rededicated following the ousting of the Greeks. Our primary celebration is not the defeat of the enemy, but rather the opportunity we were miraculously granted

לא תחנם

Some have proved that Torah Judaism accepts racism from the prohibition of לא
תחנם — literally, "Do not show them favor," which the Torah introduces in the Book
of *Devarim*.[53] The simple reading of the text indicates that the Torah speaks here of the
seven Canaanite nations whom *Bnei Yisrael* were commanded to vanquish, warning
Bnei Yisrael not to make any concessions to these peoples. The Gemara,[54] however,
explains that this command governs our relationships to all gentiles,[55] and establishes
three prohibitions: 1) not to grant them possession of property in the Land of Israel; 2)
not to give them gifts; 3) not to speak in praise of them.[56] This law might, at first glance,
be taken as a reflection of disdain towards other nations, the belief that our nation is
innately superior to others.

However, both the Rambam and *Sefer Ha-Chinuch* state very clearly that the
purpose of these prohibitions is to help protect against cultural assimilation. The
Rambam[57] writes that the actions and words proscribed by לא תחנם can cause us
להדבק עמו וללמוד ממעשיו הרעים — to bond with gentiles and learn from their conduct.
Similarly, the *Sefer Ha-Chinuch*[58] writes that the command of לא תחנם is intended to
prevent us מלהתחבר עמהם ומלרדוף אחר אהבתם ומללמוד דבר מכל מעשיהם הרעים — "from
joining them, pursuing their affection, and learning something from their evil deeds."
The laws, beliefs and lifestyle mandated by the Torah set us apart, making us a small
minority that will constantly be swimming against the powerful cultural current of
popular beliefs and values. The prohibitions included under the command of לא תחנם
are intended to safeguard our resolve to live as a counterculture. It most certainly does
not demand that we look with disdain upon other nations. Rather, it helps prevent us
from feeling excessive admiration and affection for other cultures so that we will not be
attracted to the beliefs and lifestyles of the gentile nations.

This brings us to the crucial difference between racism, on the one hand, and, on

---

to resume the service of God in the Temple. Rav Meir Simcha adds that Purim, too, is
celebrated not on the day when the Jews defeated their enemies who sought to kill them,
but rather the day following the battles. We do not revel in the downfall of evil people, as
we would much prefer that they mend their ways and continue living.

53. 7:2.

54. *Avoda Zara* 20a.

55. Although, according to the Meiri (*Avoda Zara* 20a), as mentioned earlier (note 22), this
prohibition does not apply with regard to gentiles who conduct themselves in a generally
civilized, upright manner.

56. These prohibitions are subject to many different conditions, a comprehensive discussion
of which lies beyond the scope of our discussion here.

57. *Hilchos Avodas Kochavim* 10:4.

58. 426.

the other, firm, unwavering commitment to, and enthusiastic pride in, one's principles and values. We must never consider ourselves genetically advantaged, but we most certainly can and must consider ourselves fortunate and blessed to have been chosen by God to lead the lifestyle mandated by the Torah. The command of לא תחנם seeks to preserve our unflinching devotion to the Torah's values and laws, to help us maintain our distinctive lifestyle amid the cultural pressures exerted by the world's other nations and religions. This has nothing at all to do with racism, the belief that one group of people is genetically superior to others.

Unfortunately, the clear line between racism and pride in our Torah lifestyle often becomes blurred, in both directions. On one side, some Jews find it "racist" to resist acculturation and stubbornly adhere to our unique traditions, practices and values. In the name of opposing racism, they demand greater assimilation into general society, instead of standing firm in our defiance of societal trends which conflict with our values. On the other end, many committed religious Jews mistake our special status as racial superiority, and they fail to appreciate and respect the innate value and worth of every human being. The *mitzva* of לא תחנם requires us to always recognize Torah lifestyle as the best way for us to live, but this does not entitle us to regard ourselves as racially superior. We must compromise neither our fealty to our unique way of life, nor our respect for all human beings by virtue of their humanity, regardless of their ethnicity or national identity.

עשו שונא ליעקב

Some have contended that even if we do not regard our nation as racially superior, nevertheless, we are entitled to resent and feel hostility towards all gentiles, because, as Rashi[59] writes, citing from the *Sifrei*,[60] הלכה היא בידוע שעשו שונא ליעקב — "It is a known rule that Esav despises Yaakov." The *Sifrei* makes this remark in reference to the story of Yaakov's reunion with his brother, Esav, who had sought to kill him. Yaakov dreaded this encounter, sensing that Esav sought to wage war against him, but in the end, Esav embraced and kissed him. The *Sifrei* cites Rabbi Shimon bar Yochai as teaching that Esav certainly despised Yaakov, and had, indeed, planned on killing him, but at that moment, he was suddenly overcome by love and affection for his brother. Some have understood this remark to mean that Jew-hatred is endemic among gentiles, and thus we must naturally look with disdain upon members of other nations, who, we have to assume, despise us.

However, nowhere in the Talmud or Midrash do we find any indication that all gentiles must be presumed to hate Jews. Rabbi Shimon made this comment about Esav, and we have no reason to extend this principle to all non-Jews.

---

59. *Bereishis* 33:4.
60. *Beha'aloscha*, 69.

This point is developed at length by Rav Yosef Eliyahu Henkin,[61] who noted the explicit Biblical commands[62] לא תתעב מצרי and לא תתעב אדומי, which forbid deriding people from the nations of Edom and Egypt. Rav Henkin explains:

> אף שלכאורה נראה כשונא אפשר להפכו לאוהב, והנסיון הורה זה וכמעשה עשו
> נגד יעקב שהכנעה גרמה אהבה תחת שנאה.

> Although he at first seems like an enemy, it is possible to turn him into one who loves, and experience shows this, like the incident of Esav's confrontation with Yaakov, when [Yaakov's] submission caused love instead of hatred.

According to Rav Henkin, the story of Esav proves that to the contrary — although it might appear that עשו שונא ליעקב, this hostility can, at least sometimes, be reversed through respect and affability, just as Yaakov succeeded in transforming his brother's enmity into love and affection. In Rav Henkin's view, this is the principle underlying the commands of לא תתעב מצרי and לא תתעב אדומי — that we must treat other nations respectfully, because their hostility can, in many instances, be transformed into kindness.

Rav Henkin sharply condemns those who cite the phrase עשו שונא ליעקב as indicating that gentiles always despise Jews:

> ועון פלילי מצד אותם המטיפים הפטפטנים שדורשים תמיד הלכה הוא שעשו
> שונא ליעקב והשנאה עולמית זה נגד האמת ונגד חז"ל והמקרא, שעשו גופא לא
> היה רשע תמיד ושנאתו פסקה ע"י הנהגה מתאמת, וכמו עשו הראשון כן הם ג"כ
> דורותיו שהכנעה מביאה לשלום.

> Those driveling lecturers who always teach הלכה הוא שעשו שונא ליעקב, and the hatred is forever, commit a criminal sin. This is against the truth, and against our Sages and the Biblical text. For Esav himself was not always evil, and his hatred stopped through appropriate behavior. And just as it was with the first Esav, so was it in later generations — submission brought peace.

Rav Henkin explained on this basis Ben-Zoma's teaching in *Pirkei Avos*[63], איזהו מכובד? המכבד את הבריות — "Who is respected? He who respects people." This refers not only to our relationships with our fellow Jews, Rav Henkin writes, but also to our relationships with gentiles, calling upon us to earn their respect by treating them with respect.

Rav Henkin proceeds to reference numerous sources that emphasize the importance of courteous, kind and considerate behavior in our dealings with non-Jews. For exam-

---

61. *Kisvei Rabbi Yosef Eliyahu Henkin*, vol. 2, *Teshuvos Ibra*, p. 233.

62. *Devarim* 23:8.

63. 4:1.

ple, Rav Moshe Rivkes, in his *Be'er Ha-Gola* notes to the *Shulchan Aruch*,[64] discusses the law which allows, technically speaking, keeping money which one received due to a gentile's miscalculation, but emphasizes that one should nevertheless return the money. He then writes:

אני כותב זאת לדורות שראיתי רבים גדלו והעשירו מן הטעות שהטעו הגוי, ולא
הצליחו וירדו נכסיהם לטמיון ולא הניחו אחריהם ברכה...ורבים אשר קדשו
ה' והחזירו טעויות הגוים בדבר חשוב, גדלו והעשירו והצליחו והניחו יתרם
לעולליהם.

I am writing this for the generations, for I have seen many who gained and became wealthy because of their having deceived a gentile, and they did not succeed; all their possessions fell into oblivion and they did not leave any blessing after them... And many glorified God and returned the [money received due to] mistakes of gentiles concerning substantial amounts, and they gained, became wealthy, succeeded and left over their surplus for their children.

Rav Henkin notes as well Rav Yechezkel Landau's introduction to his *Noda Be-Yehuda*, where he strongly emphasizes that stealing is forbidden from both Jews and gentiles, and he adds:

וקל חומר האומות של זמננו שאנחנו יושבים בתוכם שהמה מאמינים בעיקרי
הדת, שמאמינים בבריאת העולם ומאמינים בנבואת הנביאים ובכל הנסים
והנפלאות הכתובים בתורה ובספרי הנביאים. אם כן פשיטא ופשיטא שאנחנו
מחויבים לכבדם ולנשאם.

[This applies] all the more so to the nations in our times, in whose midst we reside, who believe in the main principles of our religion, who believe in the world's creation and believe in the prophecies of the prophets and all the miracles and wonders written in the Torah and books of the prophets. Therefore, it is plainly obvious that we are obligated to respect them and hold them in esteem.[65]

Rav Henkin adds:

רבים מהאומות היטיבו לישראל וקרבום בזרועות אהבה, ואסור לספר בגנותם...
וכ"ש לא לעוות דיני האומות הגדורים בדרכי הדתות...וטעות רע בפי התולים
עצמם בלשון חז"ל "הלכה שעשו שונא ליעקב" לומר כן על הכלל, כי זה נאמר
על עשו עצמו שכתוב עליו מפורש "וישטום עשו" ולא אפילו על זרעו...ורעה

---

64. C.M. 348:5.

65. Rav Henkin references as well the view of Meiri (discussed above, note 22), and the comments of Rav Yaakov Emden cited earlier.

רבה עושים אלה הדוברים רעה על כל האומות או אומה שעי״ז נעשים שונאים
גמורים...

Many of the nations acted kindly towards Jews and embraced them
with loving arms. It is forbidden to speak about them derogatorily, and
certainly to deviate from the laws of the nations who are bound by civilized conduct[66]... A bad mistake is made by those who base themselves
on the Sages' formulation, "It is a rule that Esav despises Yaakov" to say
this about them all — for this was said about Esav himself, about whom
it is stated explicitly, "Esav despised [Yaakov],"[67] and not even about his
offspring...[68] A grave evil is committed by those who drivel in negative talk about all the nations, or a single nation, for this results in their
becoming full-fledged enemies.

ואתם ידעתם את נפש הגר

The Torah on numerous occasions forbids taking advantage of foreigners, and even
requires according a foreigner special affection — ואהבתם את הגר.[69] In one context,[70] the
Torah instructs, וגר לא תלחץ ואתם ידעתם את נפש הגר כי גרים הייתם בארץ מצרים — "Do
not oppress a foreigner, and you understand the foreigner's emotional condition, for
you were foreigners in the land of Egypt."

The *Sefer Ha-Chinuch*[71] explains that this *mitzva* forbids causing foreigners distress
and disrespecting them because of their being foreigners. It also requires us to do what
we can to alleviate their plight. In fact, the *Sefer Ha-Chinuch* writes that מתרשל בהצלתם
או בהצלת ממונם — if one lazily refrains from doing what he can to save a foreigner
or his property from those seeking to take advantage of him, then he has violated a
Biblical command. New immigrants, who are generally vulnerable and disadvantaged
in some way, must be welcomed and assisted, not ignored, and certainly not taunted
or abused.

The *Sefer Ha-Chinuch* adds:

הזכיר לנו שכבר נכוינו בצער הגדול ההוא שיש לכל איש הרואה את עצמו בתוך

אנשים זרים ובארץ נכריה, ובזכרנו גודל דאגת הלב שיש בדבר וכי כבר עבר עלינו
והשם בחסדיו הוציאנו משם, יכמרו רחמינו על כל אדם שהוא כן.

[The Torah] mentioned to us that we already suffered the great distress experienced by anyone who finds himself among foreign people and in a foreign land. When we remember the magnitude of the heart's anxiety in this condition, and that we have already gone through this and God, in His kindness, took us from there, our compassion will be aroused upon every person in such a situation.

After leaving Egypt, where they suffered inhumane, brutal oppression and torment, *Bnei Yisrael* might have reserved for themselves the right to use their newfound freedom to inflict this kind of suffering on other nations. God therefore commanded that to the contrary, their unfortunate history of oppression while living in a foreign land must make them especially sensitive to the plight of foreigners. Our ancestors' experience in Egypt casts upon us a unique responsibility to care for foreigners, to help them and show them compassion.

The same can be said about racism in our generation. We suffered millions of deaths at the hands of the Nazis and their allies because of their perverse racial theories. This tragic experience should make us especially sensitive to the evils of racism, and imposes upon us a unique obligation to champion the belief in the equality of all ethnicities.

It is told[72] that Rav Binyamin Diskin was invited to attend and to deliver an address at a celebration held in honor of Napoleon after he liberated Poland from the Russians. Rav Diskin began by raising the question of why Yosef, a righteous man, needed to endure such hardship and suffering before rising to his position of fame and prestige in Egypt. He was cruelly sold into slavery by his own brothers, and brought to a foreign country. And there, after refusing to consent to the advances of his master's wife, he was falsely accused of a heinous crime and imprisoned in a dungeon. Why would such a righteous person have to endure such torment?

Rav Diskin answered that if a person is destined to leadership and fame, to rise to a position which invests him with great power, Providence arranges that he first experiences suffering and humiliation so he feels the effects of evil and the abuse of power. When he then assumes power and authority over people, he will still feel the pain and trauma of the suffering he endured by others in positions of power and authority. And so Yosef first endured suffering and imprisonment before he was raised to the highest level of power in Egypt.

Rav Diskin proceeded to apply this message to the nation of Poland, which had suffered a great deal of hardship and persecution under foreign rule. He suggested that Providence subjected Poland to these tribulations to prepare the nation for the

---

72. In *Amud Esh*, a biography of the Maharil Diskin by Rav Yosef Scheinberger, p. 7.

glorious days which awaited them. The painful memories of oppression, he hoped, would serve them well and help ensure that they would not oppress those who come under their rule.

No nation has suffered the consequences of racism more painfully than the Jewish people. We, more than any other nation on earth, recognize the evils of racial theory, the notion that some people are genetically inferior and thus undeserving of the rights and privileges which others enjoy. Just as the Torah expects the memory of our suffering in Egypt to make us especially sympathetic to the plight of foreigners, so should the memory of our suffering at the hands of the Nazis make us especially sympathetic to the plight of those subjected to racial discrimination.

INTERVIEWS

Rabbi Yoel Asher Labin

Interviewed on *Headlines with Dovid Lichtenstein*, 7 Elul, 5778 (August 18, 2018)

Our parents looked at the outside world based on their horrible experience, how the world stood by silently when they were being killed in the Holocaust. That's understandable, but now, years later, it's time to revisit our approach.

There's a discussion if the uniqueness of *Klal Yisrael* is that they're a different creation than the rest of the world and they have a special *neshama*, or if all of the world has a *tzelem Elokim*, and the uniqueness of *Am Yisrael* is because of what they do, because they keep the Torah. According to this second perspective, the rest of the world also has a *tzelem Elokim*, and if they do what they're supposed to, like the חסידי אומות העולם (righteous gentiles), then they also have a portion in the world to come. That's the simple explanation of the *pasuk*, בצלם אלוקים ברא אותו written about Adam Ha-Rishon, that it refers to all humanity. And the simple explanation of חביב אדם שנברא בצלם is that it refers to all the nations, as the end of the Mishna implies, חביבים ישראל שנקראו בנים למקום, indicating that the beginning is not talking about Yisrael.

Chazal, in many places, teach that we have to respect non-Jews, and that they are included in ואהבת לרעך כמוך, and so on. We see in the *pesukim* that in the end of times, the non-Jews will get the correct *emuna* and join us. There's also an obligation to give charity to non-Jews because "the ways of the Torah are peace," as the Rambam explains in *Hilchos Melachim*. Rav Yochanan ben Zakai used to initiate greetings to *goyim*. And he said elderly *goyim* should be respected for having a rich life experience. It's clear in the Rambam in numerous places that *goyim* who keep the seven *mitzvos* can reach big levels.

As for the expression עם הדומה לחמור (*Kiddushin* 68a and elsewhere), a lot of *sefar-*

im say that all the references are to the gentiles of yesteryear, that it depends on their behavior. Regarding עשו שונא ליעקב, it doesn't say anywhere that it's a *mitzva* to hate non-Jews because of that. Of course, you shouldn't become the *goy's* best friend. Stick to your people. But that's not our discussion. As you said, people's response is based on our experience during the Holocaust. When the Germans said, "You're the lowest of the low," the response was, "No, we're the best." That helped us survive — to look on ourselves as great and on the other people as nothing. That was then. But now, in 2018, you have to treat everyone equal. The whole lesson of the Holocaust should be to see what racism can cause. How can we be racist when we know what it feels like to be at the persecuted end of racism?

Every person should be judged by his own merits — מעשיך יקרבוך ומעשיך ירחקוך.

Rabbi Mayer Schiller

Interview on *Headlines with Dovid Lichtenstein*, 7 Elul, 5778 (August 18, 2018)

To look at any ethnic or religious group with disdain goes against what we say in ועל כן נקוה לך [expressing our hopes that the entire world will come to recognize and serve God]. In addition, it's against כי ביתי בית תפילה יקרא לכל העמים. The non-Jew figures in very heavily. There are the Seven Noachide Laws. The Rambam says that a non-Jew who keeps the Seven Noachide Laws has a place in the world to come.

Whatever the nuance of the denigration is, it's very negative. There are different people on the face of the earth, and each one has his own purpose in the world. I seem to recall that one of the *Rishonim* says that the sin of the דור הפלגה was that Hashem wanted different nations and communities in the world. It wasn't just a punishment. So by honoring different communities, we are honoring Hashem. Eventually, all of them will come to see moral and religious truth. Some of them already have, to a large extent.

I think our whole *chinuch* system needs to address the question of the denigration of the non-Jew. If you denigrate someone face-to-face, it's needless cruelty. If it's not face-to-face, it's taking very real social problems and trivializing them in a disdainful fashion. These jokes do nothing. They just make you feel good for a second. Even if there's truth that a big percentage of the population of one of these races is crime riddled and the like, this doesn't justify denigration. On the contrary, it should arouse sympathy and concern that there's a grave problem here which needs to be solved. A lot of them were put into an education system that was severely lacking. There are a lot of social problems here other than inherent ones.

I would refer everyone to the Seforno, who explains that being the סגולה מכל העמים is a responsibility. It means that we have to minister to the physical and spiritual needs of all men. Obviously, we have obligations in Torah and *mitzvos*, as well. אתה בחרתנו means to me that we are chosen to be an example, chosen to help, chosen to serve. We are here to be examples of kindness and justice. Look at the *davening* on Rosh Hashanah, where we pray that the whole of mankind should recognize Hashem. To say that all the billions of non-Jews were created for no reason at all depicts a very cruel god.

Our education about this is frightfully inadequate. Most people don't spend any time pondering the reason of the creation of the non-Jews.

...Someone who treats the Guatemalan janitor in yeshiva with cruelty will do the same to others. It's going to pollute his *neshama*.

The New York Times

Yes, Even George Washington

July 28, 2020
By Charles M. Blow

On the issue of American slavery, I am an absolutist: enslavers were amoral monsters.

The very idea that one group of people believed that they had the right to own another human being is abhorrent and depraved. The fact that their control was enforced by violence was barbaric.

People often try to explain this away by saying that the people who enslaved Africans in this country were simply men and women of their age, abiding by the mores of the time.

A statue of George Washington near the New York Stock Exchange in New York. (Brendan Mcdermid/Reuters)

But, that explanation falters. There were also men and women of the time who found slavery morally reprehensible. The enslavers ignored all this and used anti-black dehumanization to justify the holding of slaves and the profiting from slave labor.

People say that some slave owners were kinder than others.

That explanation too is problematic. The withholding of another person's freedom is itself violent. And the enslaved people who were shipped to America via the Middle Passage had already endured unspeakably horrific treatment.

One of the few written accounts of the atrocious conditions on these ships comes from a man named the Rev. Robert Walsh. The British government outlawed the international slave trade in 1807, followed by the United States in 1808. The two nations patrolled the seas to prevent people from continuing to kidnap Africans and bringing them to those countries illegally. In 1829, one of the patrols spotted such a ship, and what Walsh saw when he boarded the ship is beyond belief.

The ship had been at sea for 17 days. There were over 500 kidnapped Africans onboard. Fifty-five had already been thrown overboard.

The Africans were crowded below the main deck. Each deck was only 3 feet 3 inches high. They were packed so tight that they were sitting up between one another's legs, everyone completely nude. As Walsh recounted, "there was no possibility of their lying down or at all changing their position by night or day."

Each had been branded, "burnt with the red-hot iron," on their breast or arm. Many were children, little girls and little boys.

Not only could light not reach down into the bowels of those ships, neither could fresh air. As Walsh recounted, "The heat of these horrid places was so great and the odor so offensive that it was quite impossible to enter them, even had there been room."

These people, these human beings, sat in their own vomit, urine and feces, and that of others. If another person sat between your legs, their bowels emptied out on you.

These voyages regularly lasted over a month, meaning many women onboard experienced menstruation in these conditions.

Many of the enslaved, sick or driven mad, were thrown overboard. Others simply jumped. In fact, there was so much human flesh going over the side of those ships that sharks learned to trail them.

This voyage was so horrific that I can only surmise that the men, women and children who survived it were superhuman, the toughest and the most resilient our species has to offer.

But of the people who showed up to greet these reeking vessels of human torture, to bid on its cargo, or to in any way benefit from the trade and industry that provided the demand for such a supply, I have absolute contempt.

Some people who are opposed to taking down monuments ask, "If we start, where will we stop?" It might begin with Confederate generals, but all slave owners could easily become targets. Even George Washington himself.

To that I say, "abso-fricking-lutely!"

George Washington enslaved more than 100 human beings, and he signed the Fugitive Slave Act of 1793, authorizing slavers to stalk runaways even in free states and criminalizing the helping of escaped slaves. When one of the African people he himself had enslaved escaped, a woman named Ona Maria Judge, he pursued her relentlessly, sometimes illegally.

Washington would free his slaves in his will, when he no longer had use for them.

Let me be clear: Those black people enslaved by George Washington and others, including other founders, were just as much human as I am today. They love, laugh, cry and hurt just like I do.

When I hear people excuse their enslavement and torture as an artifact of the times, I'm forced to consider that if slavery were the prevailing normalcy of this time, my own enslavement would also be a shrug of the shoulders.

I say that we need to reconsider public monuments in public spaces. No person's honorifics can erase the horror he or she has inflicted on others.

Slave owners should not be honored with monuments in public spaces. We have museums for that, which also provide better context. This is not an erasure of history, but rather a better appreciation of the horrible truth of it.

The Torah's Perspective on Slavery

*W*e hold these truths to be self-evident, that all men are created equal, that they are endowed by their Creator with certain unalienable Rights, that among these are Life, Liberty and the pursuit of Happiness...

This timeless proclamation introduces the United States' Declaration of Independence, which was signed by fifty-six leaders of the struggle for independent statehood. Ironically, the majority of these signatories did not, in practice, respect the liberty of all men, and owned slaves kidnapped from Africa.[1] This glaring contradiction between the foundational principle upon which the United States was founded and the abominable practice of slavery which was rampant at that time, continues to be a stain on America's history. The southern states seceded from the United States in order to continue this practice that President Lincoln had sought to abolish, sparking the catastrophic American Civil War.

Recently, some have called for revisiting the respect and reverence commonly accorded to the country's Founding Fathers — including iconic figures such as George Washington and Thomas Jefferson — given that they owned slaves even while officially championing the belief in every human being's inalienable right to liberty.

Living and participating in a society that, for good reason, regards the institution of slavery as intrinsically and enormously evil, the Torah-observant community must formulate an approach to explain the Torah's explicit endorsement of such an institution. The Torah speaks of the ownership of slaves as a legitimate practice, and the Talmud and halachic codes contain entire sections devoted to the detailed laws concerning the process of purchasing, selling and releasing slaves, as well as their personal status during their period of slavery. In fact, the Torah not only speaks of slave ownership as an accepted reality, but openly permits purchasing slaves — מהם תקנו עבד ואמה.[2]

---

1. See Colman Andrews, "These are the 56 People Who Signed the Declaration of Independence," *USA Today*, July 3, 2019.

2. *Vayikra* 25:44. It should be clarified that *halacha* recognizes two separate institutions of slavery — the עבד עברי (indentured Hebrew servant) and עבד כנעני (gentile servant). The former refers to the status of a Jew who sells himself into the service of a fellow Jew, and serves either for six years, or, if he wishes, until the jubilee year. The Gemara (*Kiddu-*

This Torah's endorsement of slavery, at first glance, conflicts not only with our society's instinctive revulsion towards such an institution, but also with the Torah's own values. The Gemara[3] teaches that the Jewish People's defining characteristics are being רחמנים, ביישנים וגומלי חסדים — "merciful, bashful, and performers of kindness." The Rambam[4] codifies the obligation to deal kindly with all people, including gentiles, citing the verse in *Tehillim*,[5] טוב ה׳ לכל ורחמיו על כל מעשיו ("God is good to all, and His compassion is upon all His creations"), and the verse in *Mishlei*,[6] דרכיה דרכי נעם וכל נתיבותיה שלום ("Its ways are ways of pleasantness, and all its paths are peace"). In fact, the Gemara in *Maseches Berachos* (7a) tells that Rabbi Yehoshua ben Levi decided not to wish harm upon a certain heretic in his neighborhood who used to badger him, citing the verse, ורחמיו על כל מעשיו — showing that we are to show compassion even to agitators.

What's more, we are expected to deal kindly and compassionately even with animals. The Gemara[7] tells that Rabbi Yehuda Ha-Nasi was punished with a painful illness because a young calf once ran from the slaughterer and sought refuge inside Rabbi Yehuda's coat, and Rabbi Yehuda failed to show compassion, ordering the calf to return to the slaughterer. His illness was cured, the Gemara relates, when Rabbi Yehuda instructed his housekeeper not to kill the rodents in the home, citing the verse השמר מלצער בע״ח הן בהמה ורחמיו על כל מעשיו.[8] Rabbeinu Yona writes in *Sefer Ha-Yir'a*,

---

shin 20a) establishes that an עבד עברי must be treated as an equal, given the same food and accommodations that the master enjoys, and the Torah explicitly forbids forcing the servant to perform arduous or demeaning labor (לא תרדה בו בפרך, *Vayikra* 25:43). In fact, the Gemara (*Kiddushin* 20a) writes that one who acquires an עבד עברי is כקונה אדון לעצמו — "like he acquired a master," due to the responsibilities which he must assume in properly caring for the servant. (See *Tosfos*, as well as Rambam, *Sefer Ha-Mitzvos*, lo ta'aseh 259; *Hilchos Avadim* 1:6.) The institution of עבד עברי, then, is more of an employment arrangement than "slavery." Our discussion here thus focuses on the status of עבד כנעני.

3.   *Yevamos* 79a.

4.   *Hilchos Melachim* 10:12.

5.   145:9.

6.   3:17.

7.   *Bava Metzia* 85a.

8.   The *Chasam Sofer* (*Bava Metzia* 32b) points to this verse as the source for the prohibition of צער בעלי חיים — causing pain to animals. The question as to the source of this prohibition, and whether it is forbidden by Torah law or by force of rabbinic enactment, lies beyond the scope of our discussion. Regardless, it is clear from the story of Rabbi Yehuda Ha-Nasi, who cited a verse from *Tehillim*, that the general principle of showing compassion even to animals is taught already in the *Tanach*. Moreover, the Midrash (*Devarim Rabba* 6:1) explains the command of שילוח הקן, which requires sending away a mother

הן עוף, וכ״ש שלא לצער אדם שהוא עשוי בצלם המקום — "Ensure not to cause distress to a living creature, be it an animal or a bird, and, all the more so, not to cause distress to a person, who is made in the Almighty's image." If the Torah demands that we show sensitivity to animals, then *a fortiori* it demands that we show compassion to all human beings.

The centrality of this ethos of kindness and compassion to Torah life is expressed in the famous story told[9] of the gentile who approached Hillel and agreed to convert to Judaism if he could be taught the Torah "while I stand on one foot." Hillel replied, שעלך סני לחברך לא תעביד, זו היא כל התורה כולה, ואידך פירושה הוא, זיל גמור — "That which you despise, do not do to your fellow; this is the entire Torah; the rest is commentary, go study it."[10] The "entire Torah" revolves around the basic principle that we are to treat other people with decency and consideration.

In fact, the *Tur*[11] famously cites the Yerushalmi as explaining the custom to cover the bread on the table during *kiddush* on Shabbos as intended to protect the bread from "embarrassment." Normally, bread is eaten first at a meal, but on Shabbos, *kiddush* is recited before the bread is eaten. In order to spare the bread the "humiliation" of seeing the wine take precedence, we cover it. Quite obviously, bread does not experience shame. This simple, though cherished and time-honored, custom serves to underscore just how far we must go in ensuring to preserve all people's dignity and avoiding causing anyone any sort of embarrassment.

How does the institution of slavery square with the Torah's vision of a pleasant, peaceful society, in which we follow God's example of respecting and bestowing grace and kindness upon all people? If the Torah is grounded in the principle of sensitivity and consideration to all people, then how could it allow the inhumane practice of slavery?

---

bird before taking her eggs or chicks, as a display of compassion for the mother bird: כשם שנתן הקב״יה רחמים על הבהמה כך נתמלא רחמים על העופות. This point is developed by the Rambam, in his *Guide for the Perplexed* (3:48), where he explains in this vein also the prohibition of אותו ואת בנו, which forbids slaughtering an animal and its young on the same day.

9. *Shabbos* 31a.

10. Rashi offers two explanations of Hillel's response, the first of which is that "your fellow" refers to God, and Hillel was speaking of the commitment to avoid that which God abhors. The conventional understanding, however, is that Hillel speaks of sensitivity in one's interpersonal conduct.

11. O.C. 271.

The Nature of Halachic Slavery

For one thing, it must be clarified that the institution of halachic slavery bears virtually no resemblance to the notoriously horrific slave trade. Firstly, *halacha* does not permit under any circumstances capturing a person and forcing him to work as a slave. The Torah allows people in financial straits to sell themselves as slaves as a means of sustaining themselves, voluntarily surrendering their personal liberty in exchange for a secure sustenance. Slaves may be bought and sold, but free men may not be kidnapped and enslaved against their will.

Moreover, unlike the condition of slaves in the American South, the slaves spoken of by the Torah enjoy basic rights. Inflicting certain forms of physical injury on one's slave sets him free,[12] and killing one's slave constitutes a capital offense no different than ordinary murder, the only exception being that the master is absolved of capital punishment if his blow does not immediately kill the slave.[13] And even when it comes to the slaves' duties to his master, the Rambam[14] writes that masters are to treat their slaves with compassion and graciousness:

מותר לעבוד בעבד כנעני בפרך, ואע"פ שהדין כך מדת חסידות ודרכי חכמה שיהיה אדם רחמן ורודף צדק ולא יכביד עולו על עבדו ולא יצר לו, ויאכילהו וישקהו מכל מאכל ומכל משתה. חכמים הראשונים היו נותנין לעבד מכל תבשיל ותבשיל שהיו אוכלין, ומקדימין מזון הבהמות והעבדים לסעודת עצמן, הרי הוא אומר: כעיני עבדים אל יד אדוניהם כעיני שפחה אל יד גבירתה. וכן לא יבזהו ביד ולא בדברים, לעבדות מסרן הכתוב לא לבושה. ולא ירבה עליו צעקה וכעס, אלא ידבר עמו בנחת וישמע טענותיו. וכן מפורש בדרכי איוב הטובים שהשתבח בהן: אם אמאס משפט עבדי ואמתי בריבם עמדי, הלא בבטן עושני עשהו ויכוננו ברחם אחד. ואין האכזריות והעזות מצויה אלא בגוי עובדי ע"ז, אבל זרעו של אברהם אבינו והם ישראל שהשפיע להם הקדוש ברוך הוא טובת התורה וצוה אותם בחקים ומשפטים צדיקים, רחמנים הם על הכל. וכן במדותיו של הקב"ה שצונו להדמות בהם הוא אומר: ורחמיו על כל מעשיו. וכל המרחם מרחמין עליו, שנאמר: ונתן לך רחמים ורחמך והרבך.

---

12. *Shemos* 21:26–27.

13. *Shemos* 21:20–21. The Torah formulates the death penalty imposed for killing one's slave with the unusual expression, נקום ינקם ("he shall surely be avenged"). Rav Shimshon Raphael Hirsch explains the particular meaning and significance of this expression being used in reference to the crime of murdering one's slave:

> …So that murdering anybody, is an attack on the godly nature of the whole of the human race, and in particular, that of the circle to which the victim belonged. Hence, in any ordinary case, the nearest relative takes the matter up… A slave has no relative to take up his cause… It — the Community — has to come forward as the avenger of the godly dignity of the human being which has been dragged in the dust in his case.

14. *Hilchos Avadim* 9:8.

It is permissible to impose arduous labor upon a gentile slave, but although this is the law, it is a measure of piety and the ways of wisdom for a person to be merciful and pursue righteousness. One should not make his yoke heavy upon his slave or cause him pain, and he should feed him and give him drink from every food and from every beverage. The early sages would give the slave some of each and every dish they ate, and would feed their animals and slaves before their own meal. After all, it says, "Like the eyes of slaves to the hand of their masters; like the eyes of a maidservant to the hand of her mistress."[15] Likewise, he shall not denigrate him, neither with his hand nor with words.[16] The Scripture handed them over for service, not for humiliation. He should not treat him with a lot of shouting and anger, but should rather speak to him pleasantly and listen to his complaints. This is clear from Iyov's good deeds, in which he took pride: "I did not reject the judgment of my slave and maidservant in their contention against me... Did He not make him in the same belly in which He made me, and they were formed in the same womb?"[17] Cruelty and harshness are found only among idolatrous gentiles, whereas the offspring of our patriarch, Avraham — namely, Israel, upon whom the Almighty bestowed the goodness of the Torah and commanded them righteous statutes and laws — are compassionate to all. Likewise, of the qualities of the Almighty, regarding which He commanded us to resemble Him, it says, "His compassion is upon all His creatures."[18] Whoever has compassion is treated with compassion, as it says, "He shall grant you compassion, have compassion on you, and make you increase."[19]

Elsewhere,[20] the Rambam writes, ישראל מצווין להחיות העבדים שביניהם — that the obligation to give charity to the poor includes slaves who, for whatever reason, do not have sufficient food.

While Torah law clearly allows for the institution of slavery, Torah values most certainly demand showing compassion and kindness to all people, including one's slaves. There is no question that the inhumane cruelty shown to the slaves in the American South violates the basic traditional Jewish values of kindness and compassion.

---

15. *Tehillim* 123:2.
16. It is worth noting the remark of the *Minchas Chinuch* (338) that it is "obvious" that the prohibition of אונאת דברים — verbally inflicting pain upon a person — applies also to the way a master speaks to his slave.
17. *Iyov* 31:13, 15.
18. *Tehillim* 145:9.
19. *Devarim* 13:18.
20. *Hilchos Avadim* 9:7.

It must also be emphasized that *halacha* does not designate any particular race or nationality as a slave class which others are entitled to exploit.[21] It is strictly forbidden to force any gentile into slavery, and it is permissible to buy and sell any gentile who wishes to become a slave. The Torah institution of slavery thus does not reflect the belief in racial inferiority that formed the justification of the American slave trade.[22]

לא דברה תורה אלא כנגד יצר הרע

Additionally, it is quite possible that even the limited form of slavery allowed by the Torah was never intended as an ideal arrangement, but merely reflects the social and economic realities of the ancient world.

The Gemara in *Maseches Kiddushin* (21b) makes the following famous remark about the law of אשת יפת תואר, which outlines a procedure whereby a soldier is allowed to bring home a female captive whom he desires:

לא דברה תורה אלא כנגד יצר הרע, מוטב שיאכלו ישראל בשר תמותות שחוטות
ואל יאכלו בשר תמותות נבילות.

> The Torah spoke only in response to the evil inclination — it is prefera-
> ble that Jews eat the meat of slaughtered dying animals, so that they do
> not eat carcasses of dying animals.

This means that the Torah's ideal is that soldiers would not have a relationship with captive women. It permits such a relationship (after following the procedure outlined in *Sefer Devarim*[23]) only because soldiers would otherwise likely act illicitly. The Torah understands the difficulty of exercising self-restraint under the conditions of warfare, and so it compromised its ideal standard, prescribing a procedure whereby a relation-ship with a captive woman becomes permissible, to prevent wanton sexual misconduct

---

21. Although Noach pronounced a curse upon his son Cham, that his descendants would be slaves (עבד עבדים יהיה לאחיו, *Bereishis* 9:25), this is not a prescriptive pronouncement, authorizing the forceful enslavement of Cham's heirs.

22. While it is true that the Torah forbids owning a fellow Jew as a slave (the institution of עבד עברי is actually a form of employment, as discussed above, note 2), the Torah clearly explains, כי עבדי הם...לא ימכרו ממכרת עבד (*Vayikra* 25:42) — the Jewish People have been designated as servants of God, and therefore, just as one cannot enslave somebody who is already bound to a different master, we cannot enslave a fellow Jew, who is already subservient to God. Additionally, the Torah emphasizes in this context that all Jews are considered members of the same family — ובאחיכם בני ישראל איש באחיו לא תרדה בו בפרך (*Vayikra* 25:46). We are not to enslave a fellow Jew because we are to see one another as brothers and sisters, and family members would never treat one another like slaves.

23. 21:10–14.

and abuse. The Midrash[24] draws an analogy to a prince who craved a certain harmful food, and although his father, the king, tried convincing him to abstain, the son made up his mind that he would eat it. The king instructed his son what he should do to avoid the food's harmful effects. Similarly, God realizes that some soldiers would likely not succeed in resisting the temptations presented by the presence of female captives of war, and so the Torah made a concession through the institution of אשת יפת תואר.

Chazal's perspective on this law provides an instructive precedent for a Torah law allowing something which ideally should be avoided, out of consideration for human nature. Not every situation or arrangement permitted by the Torah represents the Torah's ideal condition. As the Gemara in *Maseches Avoda Zara*[25] teaches, אין הקב״ה בא בטרוניא עם בריותיו — God does not make unreasonable demands of people. He understands human nature and the challenges of subduing natural impulses for a higher spiritual purpose. And so the Torah permits things which ideally should be avoided if a blanket prohibition would pose too difficult a challenge.

Another example of such an institution of that of גואל הדם — the "blood avenger," the family member of the victim of an accidental murder. The killer must immediately flee to a city of refuge for protection, and the Torah[26] states that if, before the killer reaches the city of refuge, he is killed by a גואל הדם, then the גואל הדם is not liable for murder.[27] The Torah adds, לו אין משפט מות כי לא שונא הוא לו מתמול שלשום — "he does not have a death sentence, because he does not despise him since one or two days prior." The Netziv, in his *Ha'amek Davar* commentary, explains[28] this to mean that the גואל הדם never harbored any feelings of animosity towards the killer, and his desire to kill him is purely the result of his overpowering grief and rage. These emotions, the Netziv writes, bring the relative to the point where, in the Netziv's words, הרי זה כמו שלבו אונסו — he is practically compelled against his will to avenge his loved one's death.[29]

---

24. *Midrash Tannaim* to *Devarim* 21:11.

25. 3a.

26. *Devarim* 19:6.

27. The Gemara (*Makkos* 10b) cites a view which understands this verse differently, but the accepted view is that although a גואל הדם is not permitted to kill the murderer before he reaches a city of refuge, if he did, he is not liable to punishment. (And if the killer reaches the city of refuge and then leaves, the גואל הדם is permitted to kill him.) See Rambam, *Hilchos Rotzei'ach* 5:10.

28. As the Netziv writes, his interpretation of this verse follows the approach taken by the Ritva in his commentary to *Maseches Makkos*, in contrast to Rashi's understanding.

29. This point is developed by Rav Yechezkel Berstein, in *Divrei Yechezkel* (23:8), where he distinguishes between the גואל הדם's exemption from capital punishment in this case, and the permission granted to the גואל הדם to kill the killer if the killer willfully leaves the

This perspective on the exemption granted to the גואל הדם is formulated also by Rav Meir Simcha of Divnsk, in his *Or Sameïach*,[30] in explaining the Mishna's ruling[31] that an accidental murderer must relocate in a city of refuge even if he is a crucially important public official, such as the general of the nation's military.[32] Rav Meir Simcha raises the question of why, in such a case, the government does not simply issue an edict that anyone who takes the general's life would be liable to execution. After all, as Rav Meir Simcha shows, the government is authorized to administer capital punishment even to criminals against whom Torah law does not assign a death sentence, when this is deemed a great necessity. Seemingly, then, in the case of a vitally important national asset who accidentally killed, the government could announce a death sentence upon those who kill him, thus assuring his protection so he would not need to be confined to a city of refuge. Rav Meir Simcha answers, very simply, that the government cannot issue an edict in opposition to basic human nature. The Torah recognized the emotional response that could lead a גואל הדם to avenge his kin's blood, and this cannot be overridden by a special governmental decree.[33]

Clearly, the Torah does not want the גואל הדם to murder the accidental killer. The ideal response to this tragedy is restraint.[34] However, the Torah is given to frail, flawed

---

city of refuge. In the latter case, the killer has defied the obligation to remain in the city, and so the Torah penalizes him by authorizing the גואל הדם to take his life. Before the killer reaches the city of refuge, however, the גואל הדם is not permitted to kill him, but he is exempt from capital punishment if he does, in consideration of his overpowering emotions.

30.   *Hilchos Rotzeïach* 2:4.

31.   *Makkos* 11b.

32.   The Mishna gives the example of Yoav, the general who served under King David and led the Israelite army to victory over the surrounding nations, and upon whom *Bnei Yisrael's* national security depended.

33.   Rav Meir Simcha returns to this idea later, *Hilchos Rotzeïach* 7:8. Consistent with this general theme, Rav Meir Simcha posits elsewhere in his writings (*Meshech Chochma, Bereishis* 9:7) that the reason the Biblical command of procreation is given to men, and not women (according to the accepted view, *Yevamos* 65b), is because of the pain and life-threatening danger posed by pregnancy and childbirth. Since the Torah does not impose unreasonably difficult demands upon people, it cannot demand that a woman put herself through his ordeal. (God did, however, implant within women a natural desire to produce children.) Rav Meir Simcha elaborates further on this premise, that the Torah does not require that which opposes human nature, later in *Meshech Chochma* (*Vayikra* 18:2).

34.   According to one opinion among the *Tannaim* (*Makkos* 12a), the גואל הדם fulfills a *mitzva* by killing the killer if the killer willfully leaves the city of refuge. However, as Rav Shmuel

human beings, who are plagued by a variety of powerful emotions and passions, and while it expects and demands that we live with discipline and self-restraint, it also recognizes the limits on what can be expected. And so there are things which the Torah permits despite their being undesirable, and despite the hope that we succeed in overcoming the ingrained negative impulse that leads us to such behavior. The Torah's ideal is that soldiers restrain their desire for captive women, and that a גואל הדם suppress his rage towards the killer, but it nevertheless allows ways for these feelings to be acted upon, within the framework of specific guidelines.[35]

Another example is the institution of halachic divorce. The Gemara teaches at the end of *Maseches Gittin* (90b) that when a couple divorces, "even the altar sheds tears." Ideally, a married couple should find a way to make their marriage successful, but the Torah recognizes that this cannot always be reasonably demanded, and so it allows for the institution of divorce.

Likewise, the Torah allows, and perhaps even commands, appointing a king — שום תשים עליך מלך (*Devarim* 17:15),[36] and yet, according to one view, that of Rabbi Nehorai, cited in the *Sifrei*,[37] appointing a king is דבר גנאי לישראל, a mark of shame for the Jewish Nation, which ought not to occur (as we are to regard God as the one and only Ruler). In Rabbi Nehorai's view, the Torah strongly discourages appointing a king, but nevertheless allows it, recognizing that the people would likely wish to establish a monarchy like other nations.

The Rambam's View of Sacrifices

This concept also underlies the Rambam's famous and controversial approach to the nature of sacrifices, presented in his *Guide for the Perplexed*.[38] There the Rambam boldly asserts that God commanded *Bnei Yisrael* to offer sacrifices only because they had grown so accustomed to this mode of worship, that it would have been unreal-

---

Rozovsky explains (*Shiurim Rabbi Shmuel — Makkos*, 11b), this *mitzva* serves as a punishment for the killer whose flagrant defiance reflects a degree of apathy towards his accidental murder. Thus, the *mitzva* is intended not to encourage the גואל הדם to act upon his feelings of vengeance, but rather as a punishment for the killer.

35. In a similar vein, the Rama (C.M. 421:13) writes that if a person is beaten or falsely accused of a crime by his fellow, and he angrily responds by publicly calling him an offensive name, he is not liable to pay בושת (compensation for humiliating someone), because he acted out of understandable rage and frustration.

36. The Rambam lists the appointment of a king as one of the Torah's 248 affirmative commands (*Sefer Ha-Mitzvos, asei* 173).

37. *Parshas Shoftim*, 156.

38. 3:32.

istic to expect them to embrace a religious lifestyle without it. The Rambam writes:

> It is, namely, impossible to go suddenly from one extreme to the other: it is therefore according to the nature of man impossible for him suddenly to discontinue everything to which he has been accustomed... But the custom which was in those days general among all men, and the general mode of worship in which the Israelites were brought up, consisted in sacrificing animals in those temples which contained certain images, to bow down to those images, and to burn incense before them; religious and ascetic persons were in those days the persons that were devoted to the service in the temples erected to the stars... It was in accordance with the wisdom and plan of God, as displayed in the whole Creation, that He did not command us to give up and to discontinue all these manners of service; for to obey such a commandment it would have been contrary to the nature of man, who generally cleaves to that to which he is used; it would in those days have made the same impression as a prophet would make at present if he called us to the service of God and told us in His name, that we should not pray to Him, not fast, not seek His help in time of trouble; that we should serve Him in thought, and not by any action. For this reason God allowed these kinds of service to continue; He transferred to His service that which had formerly served as a worship of created beings, and of things imaginary and unreal, and commanded us to serve Him in the same manner...to build unto Him a temple...to have the altar erected to His name...to offer the sacrifices to Him...to bow down to Him and to burn incense before Him... By this Divine plan it was effected that the traces of idolatry were blotted out, and the truly great principle of our faith, the Existence and Unity of God, was firmly established; this result was thus obtained without deterring or confusing the minds of the people by the abolition of the service to which they were accustomed and which alone was familiar to them.

The Rambam proceeds to draw an analogy to God's leading *Bnei Yisrael* along a circuitous route from Egypt to the Land of Israel, due to the concern that the people might otherwise wish to return to Egypt:[39]

> Here God led the people about, away from the direct road which He originally intended, because He feared they might meet on that way with hardships too great for their ordinary strength; He took them by another road in order to obtain thereby His original object. In the same manner

---

39. ויהי בשלח פרעה את העם ולא נחם אלוקים דרך ארץ פלשתים כי קרוב הוא, כי אמר אלוקים: פן ינחם העם בראותם מלחמה ושבו מצרימה (*Shemos* 13:17).

God refrained from prescribing what the people by their natural disposition would be incapable of obeying, and gave the above-mentioned commandments as a means of securing His chief object, viz., to spread a knowledge of Him [among the people], and to cause them to reject idolatry. It is contrary to man's nature that he should suddenly abandon all the different kinds of Divine service and the different customs in which he has been brought up, and which have been so general, that they were considered as a matter of course; it would be just as if a person trained to work as a slave with mortar and bricks, or similar things, should interrupt his work, clean his hands, and at once fight with real giants.

Later in his discussion of this subject, the Rambam writes:

Although in every one of the signs [related in Scripture] the natural property of some individual being is changed, the nature of man is never changed by God by way of miracle... I do not say this because I believe that it is difficult for God to change the nature of every individual person; on the contrary, it is possible, and it is in His power, according to the principles taught in Scripture; but it has never been His will to do it, and it never will be. If it were part of His will to change [at His desire] the nature of any person, the mission of prophets and the giving of the Law would have been altogether superfluous.

Just as God does not impose upon us commands which require a degree of self-restraint which cannot be reasonably expected of all people, so did He not command our nation in its incipient stages to accept doctrines and precepts which it was not prepared to embrace.[40]

We might apply the Rambam's theory to explain the halachic institution of slavery. The Torah did not envision slavery as an ideal condition, where some people acquire

---

40. Many later writers — most notably, the Ramban (*Vayikra* 1:9) — sharply rejected the Rambam's theory regarding the nature of sacrifices, insisting that the sacrifices required by the Torah have profound intrinsic value, and are not merely a concession to the realities of religious life in the ancient world. Nevertheless, the underlying assumption that the Torah would sanction that which ideally should be avoided, remains valid even if one disputes its application to the particular context of sacrifices.

It is noteworthy that Rav Meir Simcha of Dvinsk (*Meshech Chochma*, introduction to *Vayikra*) suggests a compromise stance. He proposes that the rituals required in the *Beis Ha-Mikdash* are inherently valuable, whereas the permission granted at certain periods in Jewish history to offer sacrifices on private altars (see Mishna, *Zevachim* 112b) was a concession to the people's having grown accustomed to sacrificial worship.

ownership over other people. Clearly, the Torah values of compassion and respect for the divine image within each human being should lead us to frown upon the notion of a slave class. However, the Torah permitted a limited form of slavery because, just as the Rambam writes in regard to the sacrifices, it would have unreasonable to demand the complete elimination of slavery.

Indeed, we find two indications in the Talmud that already in the time of the *Tannaim*, there was a trend among Jewish society to favor the release of slaves. While on the one hand, the Gemara[41] establishes that it is forbidden to free a gentile slave[42] unless this is necessary for a *mitzva* purpose,[43] there seems to have been a tendency to encourage the release of slaves. It is told[44] that Rabban Gamliel once caused his slave, Tavi, to lose his vision in one eye,[45] and he rejoiced — not because he caused his slave physical harm, but because by Torah law, Tavi could now go free.[46] In the parallel version presented by the Talmud Yerushalmi,[47] Rabban Gamliel exclaimed, מצאתי עילה לשחררו — "I found an opportunity to set him free." This would certainly suggest that Rabban Gamliel eagerly anticipated the time when he would have a legitimate reason to release his servant.

Even more tellingly, the Gemara in *Maseches Avoda Zara*[48] tells that Rabbi Chanina ben Tradyon was arrested by the Roman authorities and charged with a number of violations of edicts they had enacted against the Jews, including releasing his slave. Rashi explains that the Romans had prohibited the releasing of slaves לפי שהוא דת יהודית — because releasing slaves was a Jewish religious practice. A number of writers raised the question of how to reconcile Rashi's remark with the prohibition against freeing slaves.[49] Regardless, it seems clear that already during the period of the Roman

---

41.   *Gittin* 38a–38b.

42.   In the next section, we suggest an explanation for this seemingly peculiar prohibition.

43.   The Gemara addresses the case of a female slave who was luring men to sin, and a situation where a tenth man was needed for a *minyan*, and so a slave was freed, thereby becoming a full-fledged Jew who could then count towards a *minyan*. Later (*Gittin* 41a–b), the Gemara addresses the case of a "half slave" who cannot marry either a regular Jewish woman or a maidservant, and is thus freed so he can marry and procreate.

44.   *Bava Kama* 74b.

45.   In the version of this story which appears in the Talmud Yerushalmi (*Kesubos* 3:10), Rabban Gamliel caused Tavi to lose a tooth.

46.   Rabban Gamliel was later told that Tavi did not, in fact, earn his freedom, as there were no witnesses to the incident, and penalties are not imposed based on the guilty party's confession.

47.   Referenced above, note 45.

48.   17b.

49.   See Rabbi Yaakov Emden's notes, and Rav Yaakov Kamenetsky's *Emes Le-Yaakov*, to *Maseches Avoda Zara*.

occupation of Judea, releasing slaves was encouraged among Jewish society, so much so that the Romans outlawed it as part of their assault on Jewish observance.

Why Does the Torah Forbid Freeing Slaves?

The question, however, remains as to how to explain the halachic prohibition against freeing slaves. As we have seen, *halacha* permits freeing a gentile slave under certain circumstances,[50] but as a rule, the Gemara in *Maseches Gittin*[51] establishes המשחרר עבדו עובר בעשה — one who releases a slave is in violation of the Torah's command, לעולם בהם תעבודו — "you shall always enslave them."[52] This issue is actually subject to a debate among the *Tannaim*,[53] but the Gemara presumes that freeing a slave is, indeed, forbidden, and the Rambam lists this law as one of the Torah's affirmative commands.[54] Why would the Torah forbid releasing a slave? If the institution of slavery does not represent the Jewish ideal, but was rather allowed in a limited form due to its prevalence in the ancient world, then should we not have expected the Torah to encourage, rather than prohibit, the release of slaves?

The answer might be that releasing a slave requires him to begin assuming responsibility to support himself, and as a foreigner, with no assets or property with which to begin his new life, this would, very often, mean living in abject poverty. The Torah therefore forbids masters from releasing their slaves and leaving them without food, shelter or savings. This prohibition might be understood as actually protecting the slave's interests by preventing the master from choosing to relieve himself of the responsibility of caring for the slave by releasing him and sending him away, thereby condemning him to poverty.

Proof may perhaps be drawn from the Gemara's discussion in *Maseches Gittin* (12a) regarding a situation where the master decided to allow his slave to work for others in exchange for his assuming responsibility for his own sustenance. If such an arrangement was in place during a period of financial hardship, when the slave is unable to

---

50. See note 43.

51. 38a–b.

52. *Vayikra* 25:46. It must be emphasized that nowhere does the Gemara intimate that purchasing a gentile slave fulfills a *mitzva*. The command לעולם בהם תעבודו is understood as requiring maintaining one's hold on a slave that has come under his possession, not actively looking to purchase a slave.

53. Sota 3a.

54. *Asei* 235. See also *Hilchos Avadim* 9:6, and *Shulchan Aruch* Y.D. 267:79. It should be noted that the Ritva, in his commentary to *Maseches Megilla* (25a), writes that the Gemara does actually mean that freeing a slave constitutes a Biblical prohibition, as this rather falls under the category of מידת חסידות (a measure of piety).

earn enough for his livelihood, then, according to one view, the slave can force the master to either free him or support him. The rationale, according to this opinion, is that the slave will be more likely to receive charitable assistance after earning his freedom than he would be as a slave. This would seem to demonstrate that freeing a slave is permitted when this serves his financial best interests — thus proving that the command of לעולם בהם תעבודו is intended to protect the slave from being abandoned, and does not reflect the belief that slavery represents the ideal condition.

It must be noted, though, that *halacha* technically permits a master to deny his slave food, and force him to go around begging — יכול הרב לומר לעבדו עשה עמי ואיני זנך.[55] Seemingly, then, releasing a slave does not appear to condemn him to any more financial insecurity than he currently faces, since even as a slave, he can end up having to rely on charity. However, the Rambam[56] explains this law as based on the reality that *beis din* cannot control the way a person handles his own property;

> שאין בית דין נזקקין לגדולים לשמור ממונם, ואם לא יאכיל לעבדיו וישקם כראוי
> הם יברחו או ימותו, ואדם חס על ממון עצמו יתר מכל אדם.

> For the court does not force adults to protect their property, and if one does not adequately feed and give water to his slaves, they will escape or die, and a person cares for his own property more than all other people.

In other words, the expectation, clearly, is that a master will want to properly care for his slaves, as otherwise, they would either run away or fall ill and perish. The court cannot legally compel the master to adequately feed his slaves, but it was naturally assumed that this was in his best interest. The rule of עשה עמי ואיני זנך thus reflects a technical limitation on *beis din*'s jurisdiction, as opposed to a license granted to the master to starve his slaves.

In conclusion, it is worth noting the comments of the *Sefer Ha-Chinuch*[57] and the Rashba, in his *Ma'amar al Yishmael*,[58] regarding the consumption of wine. These writers assert that the Torah permits drinking wine, despite the grave dangers that it poses, because wine also brings great benefit if it is consumed responsibly.[59] The Torah allows us to enjoy these benefits with the expectation that we will set appropriate limits on our consumption to avoid the harmful effects of alcoholism. We might apply this general outlook to the institution of slavery, as well. In ancient times, this institution provided

---

55.   *Shulchan Aruch*, Y.D. 267:20. The Rama adds, citing the Rosh (based on the Gemara's discussion in *Gittin* 12a), that during periods of widespread financial crisis, when charity funds are scarce, a master is obligated to feed his slave.

56.   *Hilchos Avadim* 9:7.

57.   549.

58.   Betzalel Naor edition, p. 72.

59.   See the chapter about alcohol consumption in this volume.

great benefit for both the masters and slaves. Without the conveniences of modern inventions, slave labor was all but a necessity for many people, such as landowners and ranchers, who needed help tending to their crops and their herds, but also for ordinary people who needed help to run their households smoothly. The institution benefited also those who lacked the ability to support themselves, by providing a way to have their basic needs cared for in exchange for their loyal service. The Torah therefore allowed for such an arrangement, with the expectation that it would not be misused in the form of cruel, heartless treatment of the slaves. *Am Yisrael* was assigned the challenge of showing the world a model of a kind of "slave class" that would be cared for and treated properly as long as such an institution was deemed necessary.

Summary

1. The Torah allows only voluntary slavery. Under no circumstances is one permitted to seize another person against his will and force him into slavery.
2. The Torah does not view slavery as an ideal arrangement. It was widespread in the ancient world, and so the Torah accepted a limited form of slavery, which benefitted not only the slave owners, but also the slaves themselves, whose financial needs were cared for by their master.
3. The Torah strictly forbids mistreating or abusing a slave. And, as the Rambam emphasizes, we are bidden to conduct ourselves with graciousness, mercy and compassion, and even when slavery was practiced, masters were expected to treat their slaves with dignity, sensitivity and consideration.

RCA Condemns Presumptuous Theological Justifications of Pittsburgh Massacre

November 7, 2018

By The Rabbinical Council of America - RCA (Facebook page)

The Rabbinical Council of America, the leading membership organization of orthodox rabbis in North America, notes that in the aftermath of the Pittsburgh tragedy there were some rabbis who promoted a hateful message claiming that the kedoshim (holy Jews) murdered in the Tree of Life synagogue died as punishment for sinful behavior.

We condemn this assertion in the strongest of terms as a gross distortion of our holy Torah's values as well as being presumptuous and insensitive. The kedoshim of Pittsburgh were murdered Al Kiddush Hashem (sanctifying God's Name) in that they were targeted because they were Jews (See Responsa Mi-Ma'amakim 2:4).

We call upon everyone to refrain from offering theological pronouncements that are based on false assumptions and distortions. To claim to understand God's intent when tragedy strikes is itself the ultimate Chillul Hashem (desecration of God's Name).

May God grant our leaders the wisdom to comport ourselves with dignity and wisdom.

The Pittsburgh Massacre

On 18 Cheshvan, 5779 (October 27, 2018), American Jewry was shaken to its core by the news of a deadly attack on the Tree of Life Congregation, a Conservative synagogue in Pittsburgh, Pennsylvania, during the Shabbos morning service. The gunman, later identified as forty-six-year-old Robert Gregory Bowers, reportedly announced, "All Jews must die" as he perpetrated his attack, which left eleven people dead and six wounded — making this the deadliest anti-Semitic attack to date on American soil. It was widely reported after the tragedy that Bowers was a passionate white supremacist who frequently posted anti-Semitic conspiracy theories on social media.

In the days following the tragedy, as American Jews were struggling to come to terms with the reality of deadly anti-Semitism in the country that has always been a welcoming, safe haven, the Orthodox Jewish world found itself embroiled in some internal controversy regarding the proper outlook with which to view this event. A widely circulated video featured a rabbi in the New York area instructing his followers not to mourn the deaths of the victims, who were not halachically observant and belonged to a non-Orthodox congregation. He further alleged that the circumcision of a boy adopted by a gay couple was being held that Shabbos morning (which was later determined to be untrue), and indicated that the tragedy was God's angry response to this act of sacrilege. These remarks were roundly criticized and condemned by mainstream Orthodoxy. They contrasted sharply with the statement issued by Agudath Israel of America in the wake of the shooting, stating: "We are devastated and heartbroken over the savage murders of eleven of our precious Jewish brethren who were killed only because they were Jews. We share in the deep pain of the survivors and friends of the Pittsburgh *kedoshim*."

Let us, then, explore the Torah's outlook on this painful subject, to determine what the proper attitude should be towards fellow Jews who are not halachically observant and fall victim to deadly anti-Semitic attacks. Does the fact that they died because of their Jewish ethnicity and/or identity require us to honor and cherish their memory?

God's Pain

We begin by addressing the most extreme and most offensive version of the argument against mourning for the victims — the claim that their deaths naturally resulted from their disregard for Torah law, and are thus not a cause for mourning.

The Torah prohibition of לא תלין נבלתו forbids leaving overnight the remains of a convicted offender after execution[1] — a prohibition which must be viewed off the backdrop of the exceptionally high standard of evidence required by the Torah for *beis din* to sentence a defendant to execution. If, in the times when courts were authorized to execute offenders, such a sentence was issued, this was only because the court heard the testimony of two witnesses who met strict standards of credibility and who attested that the defendant committed a capital offense in their presence after being explicitly warned of the consequences. And, the court would reach the decision to execute only after considering every possible basis for an acquittal.[2] Indeed, the Mishna (*Makkos* 7a) famously states that a court which executed one defendant every seven years was considered inappropriately harsh, and Rabbi Elazar ben Azarya countered that this is true even of a court that administered an execution once in seventy years. Clearly, then, a defendant who was executed was thoroughly and undeniably a flagrant evildoer. And yet, the Torah strictly forbids leaving an executed offender's remains exposed overnight, which would compromise his dignity, and, by extension, the respect of the Creator in whose image the offender was created.

The Mishna in *Maseches Sanhedrin* (46a), in discussing this prohibition, cites Rabbi Meir's remark, בשעה שאדם מצטער, שכינה מה לשון אומרת? קלני מראשי, קלני מזרועי — "At the time a person feels pain, what does the *Shechina* say? 'Oh, my head! Oh, my arm!'" Even when a convicted offender is being punished, the Almighty shares his pain, as it were. The Mishna concludes, אם כן המקום מצטער על דמן של רשעים שנשפך קל וחומר על דמן של צדיקים — "If this is how the Almighty is pained by the shedding of the blood of the wicked, all the more so for the blood of the righteous!"

The punishment suffered by Jewish sinners is most certainly not an occasion to celebrate. God Himself is pained, so-to-speak, by the tragedies suffered even by those who violate His Torah, and He Himself commanded us to preserve their dignity. There is thus absolutely no validity to the argument that we can celebrate, or even be apathetic to, the punishment of sinners, even if we were so brazen, arrogant and callous as to definitively determine that victims of an anti-Semitic assault deserved this tragic fate.

תינוק שנשבה

Moreover, it has been all but universally accepted that Jews who were not raised and educated to observe *halacha* are to be regarded as אנוסים — Torah violators who bear no responsibility whatsoever for their disregard of Torah law, for which their upbringing is to blame. A person who was raised by non-observant parents is assigned the status of תינוק שנשבה — a young child who was taken captive by gentiles who then

---

1. *Devarim* 21:23.
2. The Gemara in several places infers this requirement from the verses in *Sefer Bamidbar* (35:24-25): ושפטו את העדה...והצילו העדה. (See, for example, *Rosh Hashanah* 26a.)

raised him, and who thus did not receive a proper religious upbringing, and is therefore not held responsible for his non-observant lifestyle, even in adulthood.

This ruling, famously articulated by the *Chazon Ish*,[3] is rooted in the Rambam's comments in *Hilchos Mamrim*.[4] After defining the status of אפיקורוס (heretic), the Rambam writes:

> במה דברים אמורים, באיש שכפר בתורה שבעל פה במחשבתו ובדברים שנראו לו
> והלך אחר דעתו הקלה ואחר שרירות לבו וכופר בתורה שבעל פה תחילה... אבל
> בני התועים האלה ובני בניהם שהדיחו אותם אבותם ונולדו בין הקראים וגדלו
> אותם על דעתם הרי הוא כתינוק שנשבה ביניהם וגדלוהו, ואינו זריז לאחוז בדרכי
> המצות שהרי הוא כאנוס... כך אלו שאמרנו האוחזים בדרכי אבותם הקראים
> שטעו. לפיכך ראוי להחזירן בתשובה ולמשכם בדברי שלום...

> Regarding what is this said — a person who rejected the oral law in his thoughts, because of that which he felt correct, following his own lowly mind and the wishes of his heart, and initiating rejection of the oral law... But the children of these wayward people, and their grandchildren, whose parents misled them, and were born among the Karaites who raised them according to their views — such a person is like a child taken captive among them whom they raised, and is not quick to embrace the paths of *mitzvos*, because he is like coerced [to live in violation of the *mitzvos*]... This is true of those who, as we said, adhere to the ways of their forefathers, the mistaken Karaites. It is therefore appropriate to bring them to repent and to draw them with peaceful words...

Today, the vast majority of Jews who do not observe *halacha* — whether they belong to non-Orthodox movements, or are entirely secular — fall under this category, as they were not given a proper religious education. As such, they are not held accountable for their neglect of the Torah's commands, and thus they certainly cannot be regarded as "sinners." And so even if one would argue that a sinner's death is not an occasion to mourn, this would not be true of contemporary non-observant Jews.[5]

There is also an additional reason why modern-day non-observant Jews are not to be regarded as "sinners." The Chafetz Chayim appended to his work *Ahavas Chesed* a

---

3. Y.D. 2:28.

4. 3:3.

5. The classification of modern-day non-observant Jews as תינוק שנשבה has been discussed at length by many *poskim*. One of the earliest discussions appears in Rav Yaakov Ettlinger's *Binyan Tziyon* (*Chadashos*, 23), where he raises the possibility of permitting the wine of the assimilated Jews of his time. See Rav Eliezer Waldenberg's extensive treatment of this topic in his treatise *Meshivas Nefesh* (chapter 5), published in the eighth volume of *Tzitz Eliezer* (15).

treatise entitled *Marganisa Tova* written by Rabbi Yehonasan of Wohlin, which consists of a series of brief instructions. In one passage in this treatise,[6] Rabbi Yehonasan of Wohlin notes the ruling of the Maharam Lublin[7] that the prohibition of לא תשנא את אחיך בלבבך ("Do not hate your brother in your heart"[8]) forbids despising even evildoers, unless they had heard and rejected proper תוכחה (reproof).[9] Rabbi Yehonasan then writes: אין בדור הזה מי שיודע להוכיח, שמא אם היה לו מוכיח היה מקבל — nowadays, people are generally incapable of reproving effectively,[10] and so all sinners are considered as not having received proper תוכחה. He then adds the Mishna's famous admonition in *Pirkei Avos* (2:4), אל תדין את חברך עד שתגיע למקומו — "Do not judge your fellow until you are in his place." We are not entitled to despise sinners until we can definitively eliminate the possibility of mitigating circumstances — such as never having been properly or effectively educated about the importance of religious observance. There can be no question that in modern-day conditions, when the vast majority of Jews are not raised with the beliefs of Torah Judaism, they cannot possibly be classified as "sinners" who may be despised, and whose murder should not be regarded as a terrible tragedy.

הרוגי מלכות

In truth, however, even without the factors of תינוק שנשבה and the lack of effective תוכחה, there is still reason to grieve the loss of Jews killed by anti-Semitic violence and to honor their memories. Even if one could argue that contemporary non-observant Jews are to be classified as "sinners," this cannot be said of Jews who are targeted because of their Jewish identity.

The Gemara in *Maseches Pesachim* (50a) famously comments, הרוגי מלכות, אין אדם יכול לעמוד במחיצתן — "Those killed by the government, no person can stand in their quarters [in the next world]." Jews who are executed by evil governments occupy a special place, and their memories are to be honored and cherished. The Gemara emphasizes that this refers not only to martyrs such as Rabbi Akiva, who surrendered their lives for the sake of Torah study or observance, and who in any event are guaranteed a special place in the afterlife, but even laymen who are targeted and killed by the government.

Elsewhere, in *Maseches Sanhedrin* (47a), the special category of הרוגי מלכות is

---

6.   17.

7.   Responsa, 13.

8.   *Vayikra* 19:17.

9.   This view appears already earlier, in *Hagahot Maimoniyos, Hilchos Dei'os* (6:1).

10.   This phrase is taken from *Maseches Arachin* (16b), where Rabbi Elazar ben Azarya is cited as lamenting, "I wonder if there is anybody in this generation who knows how to reprove."

addressed in the context of a debate among the *Amoraim* regarding the status of evil-doers who die without repenting. Rava asserts that a sinner who is killed, regardless of the circumstances, receives atonement for his wrongdoing even though he never repented. As a basis for his contention, Rava cites a verse in *Tehillim*[11] bemoaning the violent plundering of *Eretz Yisrael* by enemy nations, and describing how נתנו את נבלת עבדיך מאכל לעוף השמים — "They gave the corpses of Your servants as food to the birds of the heavens." Rava asserts that the victims spoken of in this verse were individuals who had committed capital offenses, but once they were killed, they became worthy of the title עבדיך — "servants" of the Almighty — thus proving that once a sinner is killed, his wrongful actions are atoned. Abayei qualifies this claim, arguing that this is true only of הרוגי מלכות — Jews killed by hostile gentiles — but not of those who were executed by *beis din* after being found guilty of capital offenses. It clearly emerges that according to all opinions, Jewish sinners who are killed by enemies of the Jewish Nation are forgiven for their misdeeds.

On the basis of the Gemara's discussion, the *Maharach Or Zarua*[12] rules that if a sinner is killed by hostile gentiles, his death is to be mourned. Falling at the hands of enemies of the Jewish People brings atonement, and therefore, victims of anti-Semitism are to be mourned regardless of their religious standing. The *Maharach Or Zarua* cites this ruling from both his father and his grandfather.

This view is cited by the Rama in the laws of mourning,[13] though he appears not to accept this opinion.[14] The *Shach* questions this conclusion, noting that in his *Darchei Moshe* commentary to the *Tur*, the Rama cited the *Maharach Or Zarua*'s ruling without bringing a differing opinion, and that this ruling seems to clearly emerge from the Gemara's discussion in *Maseches Sanhedrin*, as mentioned. The Vilna Gaon, in his notes to the *Shulchan Aruch*, likewise accepts the view of the *Maharach Or Zarua*, as does Rav Avraham Danzig, in *Chochmas Adam*,[15] where he writes: מומר שנהרג בידי לסטים מתאבלין עליו, דכיון שנהרג הוי ליה מיתתו כפרה — "An apostate who was killed by thieves is mourned, for once he was killed, his death brings him atonement." This was

---

11.   79:2.

12.   14.

13.   Y.D. 340:5.

14.   After bringing this ruling of the *Maharach Or Zarua*, the Rama proceeds to mention the ruling that one mourns for a person whose parents abandoned the faith when he was a child, and never embraced observance thereafter. The Rama then writes, "Some say that one does not mourn for him, and this is the accepted ruling." The *Shach* understood this conclusion as referring even to the previous discussion of a sinner who was killed by gentiles.

15.   *Sha'ar Ha-Simcha*, 152:4.

also the ruling issued by the *Chasam Sofer* in one of his published responsa,[16] where he cites the aforementioned discussion in the Gemara as proof that the moment a Jew is killed by a gentile, he immediately attains the status of עבדיך (a "servant" of God) and must be given the respect of a proper burial, irrespective of his spiritual standing. [17]

The different views on this subject are noted and discussed by Rav Menashe Klein, in his *Mishneh Halachos*,[18] where he establishes an important distinction between two different cases: a Jew who is killed by a lone gentile, and a Jew who is killed by an anti-Semitic regime. Rav Klein contends that in the latter case, all agree that the victim is to be mourned and his memory honored, as clearly indicated by the Gemara's discussion in *Maseches Sanhedrin*. The point of dispute among the later authorities relates to the former case, where a Jew was killed out of personal animus, or because of a crime he committed. Regarding such a case, some *poskim* maintain that the sinner's wrongdoing is atoned through the murder, whereas others maintain that his atonement is contingent upon his repentance. According to all views, however, a Jew who is targeted because of his Jewish identity must be mourned, regardless of his level of observance, because his sins are atoned.[19]

In fact, not only should these victims be granted the standard rites of burial and bereavement, but they are deserving of special honor and respect.

Earlier, we noted Rava's interpretation of the verse in *Tehillim* that describes a deadly assault by enemies of the Jewish Nation: נתנו את נבלת עבדיך מאכל לעוף השמיים, בשר חסידיך לחיתו ארץ — "They gave the corpses of Your servants as food to the birds of the heavens; the flesh of Your pious ones to the beasts of the earth." The *Midrash Shocher Tov* makes a different comment on this verse, explaining that the victims to which it refers had committed grievous religious offenses, and regularly engaged in sexual immorality.[20] However, כיון שנעשה בהן דין חסידים היו — once they received their punishment, they were considered "pious." Although they were habitual sinners, guilty

---

16. Y.D. 333.

17. The Meiri, commenting to the Gemara's discussion in *Maseches Sanhedrin*, claims that הרוגי מלכות receive atonement only if they had repented. This is also the view of Rabbeinu Yona, in *Sha'arei Teshuva* (4:20). However, this is not the implication of the Gemara's comments, and indeed, the *Or Zarua*, *Shach* and *Chasam Sofer* all clearly maintained that הרוגי מלכות earn atonement regardless of whether they had repented.

18. 16:121.

19. This distinction drawn by Rav Klein might perhaps be applied also to the view of the Meiri and Rabbeinu Yona referenced in note 17.

20. The Midrash points specifically to the verse in *Sefer Yirmiyahu* (5:8) which describes the people during the generation of the Temple's destruction as lusting after each other's wives like horses. According to the Midrash, these are the people described in this verse in *Tehillim* as having been killed and whose corpses were then defiled.

of the most severe Torah violations, they are worthy of the title חסידך — "God's pious ones" — once they fell victim to the cruelty and hostility of the enemies of the Jewish People.

Rashi follows the Midrash's interpretation of this verse in his commentary to *Tehillim*, explaining, משקבלו פורענותם הרי הם חסידים — "Once they received their punishment, they are pious." The Midrash's comments are cited also by the Maharil[21] in affirming that הני דנהרגו מתוך רשען...מיקרי קדוש וחסיד — evildoers who are killed by gentiles are considered "sacred and pious."[22]

Rav Menashe Klein, in a later responsum addressing the status of non-observant Jews killed by hostile enemies,[23] makes an important point regarding the practical implications of this atonement earned by Jews tragically killed by gentiles. The Gemara[24] establishes that it is forbidden to remind a *ba'al teshuva* — a Jew who was non-observant in the past but has since embraced religious observance — of the misdeeds he had once committed. Rav Klein writes that by the same token, it is forbidden to speak of the sins committed by those who were later killed. Like a sinner who has sincerely repented, their sins have since been forgiven, and so it is prohibited to bring to mind their past misdeeds, and their memories must instead be somberly and reverently respected.

And thus our reaction to tragedies such as the Tree of Life massacre must be grief and anguish, and the level of the victims' religious observance is not a subject that should receive any mention whatsoever in our response to this horrific loss of innocent life.

Are They *Kedoshim*?

A more difficult question arises concerning the common designation of victims of anti-Semitic attacks as קדושים. The Maharil, as mentioned, states that a Jew killed by gentiles is קדוש וחסיד, though it seems clear that he uses the term קדוש informally, as an expression of praise (like חסיד), pointing to the fact that such a person's sins have been atoned through his murder. But many people assume that those killed in anti-Semitic attacks should be formally regarded as קדושים — a term associated with קידוש ה', the obligation to surrender one's life to avoid transgressing the Torah under certain conditions. These conditions are famously outlined by the Rambam in the fifth chapter of *Hilchos Yesodei Ha-Torah*. The Rambam writes of one who surrenders his life for the sake of Torah observance when *halacha* demands martyrdom הרי זה קידש את השם —

---

21. Responsum 72.
22. See also *Shita Mekubetzes, Kesubos* 37b, citing the Ramah.
23. *Mishneh Halachos*, 19:122.
24. *Bava Metzia* 58b.

"he has thereby glorified the Name." And so martyrs who refused to renounce their faith or violate the Torah in the face of persecution have always been given the special title קדושים, expressing their having fulfilled the great *mitzva* of קידוש ה׳, glorifying the Name of God by making the ultimate sacrifice for His honor.

This title is commonly used also in reference to the victims of the Holocaust, despite the fact that they were not given the option of living. And, as cited earlier, Agudath Israel issued a statement after the Pittsburgh massacre referring to the victims as "the Pittsburgh *kedoshim*." It seems questionable, however, whether this term can be legitimately used in reference to the victims of these tragedies. A קדוש, seemingly, is one who created a קידוש ה׳, bringing glory to God by remaining steadfastly loyal to the divine will even at the expense of his life. It is difficult to say about helpless victims of anti-Semitism that they created a קידוש ה׳ by being killed solely because of their ethnicity, without having been given any alternative, as they were not offered the option of renouncing their belief or their Jewish identity. While we must certainly honor and revere their memory, speaking of them as קדושים seems unjustified.

This question was addressed by Rav Menashe Klein, in two of his published responsa,[25] where he takes the position that victims of the Holocaust, as well as victims of Arab terror in Israel, indeed deserve the title קדושים. He suggests drawing proof from the Rambam's comments in *Ma'amar Kiddush Hashem* (also known as *Iggeres Ha-She-mad*), the letter he wrote to the Jews of Spain and Morocco suffering under Moslem persecution, who were forced to renounce their faith and proclaim their acceptance of Islam. There the Rambam writes:

> איש שיזכהו הקל לעלות במעלה עליונה כזאת, כלומר שנהרג על קדושת השם,
> אפילו היו עונותיו כמו ירבעם בן נבט וחבריו, הוא מעולם הבא ואפילו לא היה
> תלמיד חכם.

> A man whom the Almighty grants the privilege of rising to this supreme level — that is to say, who is killed for the glorification of the Name — then even if his iniquities were like those of [the wicked king] Yeravam ben Nevat and his comrades, he has a share in the next world, even if he is not a Torah scholar.

The Rambam here speaks of a sinner comparable to Yeravam being killed על קדושת השם. Rav Klein understood the Rambam as saying that, in Rav Klein's words, כל איש ישראל...כיוון שנהרג על ידי הגויים בשביל שהוא ישראל הרי הוא קדוש גמור — "Any Jewish person...once he is killed by the gentiles because he is a Jew, he is thereby an outright 'martyr.'" His proof, seemingly, is from the Rambam's statement that this status can be earned even by a sinner like Yeravam, indicating that even if one has done nothing meritorious whatsoever, he is still a קדוש if he is killed for being a Jew.

---

25. *Mishneh Halachos*, 16:121 and 19:122.

This reading, however, is difficult to accept. In the previous sentence, the Rambam gives as examples those who made the decision to sacrifice their lives rather than bow to idols, mentioning Chananya, Mishael and Azarya, who refused to bow to the statue erected by Nevuchadnetzar; Daniel, who risked his life by defying the government's ban on prayer; the עשרה הרוגי מלכות — the ten Sages who were killed by the Romans for continuing to teach Torah; and the seven sons of Chana, who were killed for refusing to bow to an idol during the period of Greek persecution. The Rambam here does not speak of a person killed בשביל שהוא ישראל, but rather of those who made the choice to surrender their lives rather than abandon their faith. When he describes a martyr whose sins resemble those of Yeravam, he most likely refers to somebody who had committed sins in the past but now surrendered his life על קידוש ה׳, and is thus guaranteed a share in the next world and achieves the מעלה עליונה ("supreme level"). There is no reason to interpret the Rambam's remarks as referring to an individual who was killed because of his Jewish ethnicity without being given the option of saving himself by violating or renouncing the Torah.[26]

One possible source for applying the term קדוש to any victim of an anti-Semitic murder is the responsum of the *Chasam Sofer* noted earlier. The *Chasam Sofer* addresses the question that arose regarding the burial of a certain Jew named David Sacralam who was murdered by a non-Jew. The circumstances of his murder are not specified in the responsum. The people in charge of the burial asked whether the victim should be buried outside the Jewish cemetery, as perhaps his gruesome murder proved that he

---

26. Rabbi Aaron Rakeffet addressed the question regarding the use of the term "*kedoshim*" in reference to Holocaust victims, in his *Rakaffot Aharon* (vol. 2; available online at https://www.yutorah.org/lectures/lecture.cfm/852572/rabbi-dr-aaron-rakeffet-rothkoff/the-kedoshim-status-of-the-holocaust-victims/). He cites a passage from a volume secretly written in the Warsaw Ghetto by Rabbi Simon Huberband and recovered after the war, in which Rabbi Huberband discusses the definition of קידוש ה׳, and states, "Maimonides already declared that when a Jew is killed because of his Jewishness, he is called a *kadosh*. This status is attained even where religious persecution is not at issue." However, Rabbi Rakeffet adds that he is not aware of any source for this conclusion in the Rambam's writings.

Rav Klein also notes the passage in the *Avinu Malkeinu* prayer recited on fast days and during the High Holiday season: אבינו מלכנו עשה למען הרוגים על שם קדשך — "Our Father and King, act for the sake of those killed for Your sacred Name." This prayer speaks generically of הרוגים על שם קדשך, without specifying righteous people who were killed for their faith, and Rav Klein thus infers that anybody killed for being Jewish is included. It seems far more likely, however, that the expression הרוגים על שם קדשך indeed refers specifically to those who glorified the Name of God by surrendering their lives for the sake of His laws or the Jewish faith.

was guilty of a capital offense. The *Chasam Sofer* penned a responsum dismissing this consideration, and twice uses the term קדוש. He begins his discussion by saying that the remains of an איש קדוש הנהרג בידי עכו״ם רוצח — "a sacred man who was killed by a non-Jewish murderer" — were brought to his community. Later, after establishing that anybody who was killed by a gentile is forgiven for his sins, the *Chasam Sofer* writes, "הנהרג על ידי רוצח האורב לדם...אוקמיה ליה בחזקת צדקות וכשרות וקדוש יאמר לו — "One who is killed by a murderer who waits in ambush to kill…may be given the presumption of being righteous and upright, and he shall be called sacred."

As no information about the murder is given (other than the indication that the victim was "ambushed"), it is very possible, and even likely, that the victim was killed out of pure anti-Semitic hate, or robbed, and not for refusing to transgress the Torah or renounce his faith. The fact that the *Chasam Sofer* used the term קדוש in this context would then indicate that this term is, in his view, appropriate in reference to any Jew killed by a gentile, despite the circumstances, unless the *Chasam Sofer* used this term casually, and not in the formal sense.[27]

Rav Elchanan Wasserman's *Beracha*

Another relevant source is a famous account told by Rav Efrayim Oshry, a renowned *posek* in the Kovno Ghetto who survived World War II and later published his responses to the heartbreaking halachic questions he received during the Holocaust. In one of his responsa,[28] Rav Oshry writes that he heard that before Rav Elchanan Wasserman was killed by the Nazis, he instructed his son, Rav Naftali, to recite the *beracha* which the *Shelah Ha-Kadosh* required reciting before surrendering one's life in fulfillment of the *mitzva* of קידוש ה׳. The text of this *beracha*, as cited in the *Pis'chei Teshuva*,[29] is ברוך...אשר קדשנו במצוותיו וצוונו לקדש שמו ברבים. Rav Oshry adds that a grandson of the Chafetz Chayim reported that the Chafetz Chayim instructed Jews to recite this *beracha* during the deadly anti-Semitic riots in Russia during World War I. The Jewish victims of these atrocities were not given any alternative, and yet, according to these reports, they were nevertheless in fulfillment of the *mitzva* of קידוש ה׳, and were therefore to recite a *beracha* over this *mitzva*.

---

27. It should be noted that the expression קדוש יאמר לו is taken from a verse in *Sefer Yeshayahu* (4:3) (והיה הנשאר בציון, והנותר בירושלים, קדוש יאמר לו), and so the *Chasam Sofer* may have used this phrase poetically, borrowing from the Biblical text, and may not have meant to ascribe to any murder victim the formal title of קדוש. On the other hand, the *Chasam Sofer* begins his responsum, as mentioned, by describing the victim as an איש קדוש, suggesting that he indeed felt that the man was worthy of this appellation.

28. *Mi'ma'amakim*, 2:4.

29. Y.D. 157:6.

However, Rav Asher Weiss[30] questioned the validity of this account, noting that the *Shelah* himself requires reciting this *beracha* only in the particular circumstance where one publicly defies a command to transgress the Torah at the threat of death. After all, this *beracha* is formulated as a standard ברכת המצווה — a *beracha* recited before the performance of a *mitzva* — and one cannot be said to perform a *mitzva* by being killed with no possibility of escape. It is only when one actually surrenders his life for the sake of God that he fulfills the *mitzva* of קידוש שם שמיים such that a *beracha* is warranted.[31]

American Jewry's *Akeida*

The Rambam, in *Hilchos Beis Ha-Bechira*,[32] emphasizes the significance of the location chosen as the eternal site of the altar in the *Beis Ha-Mikdash*:

> המזבח מקומו מכוון ביותר, ואין משנין אותו ממקומו לעולם... ובמקדש נעקד
> יצחק אבינו...ומסורת ביד הכל שהמקום שבנה בו דוד ושלמה המזבח בגורן ארונה
> הוא המקום שבנה בו אברהם המזבח ועקד עליו יצחק, והוא המקום שבנה בו נח
> כשיצא מן התיבה, והוא המזבח שהקריב עליו קין והבל, ובו הקריב אדם הראשון
> קרבן כשנברא ומשם נברא, אמרו חכמים אדם ממקום כפרתו נברא.

> The location of the altar is especially precise, and it may not ever be moved from its [designated] location... It was at the [site of the] *Mikdash* that Yitzchak was bound [upon the altar]... There is a universal tradition that the place where David and Shlomo constructed the altar, in Aravna's granary, is the same place where Avraham constructed the altar and bound Yitzchak upon it, and this is the place where Noach built [an altar] when he left the ark, and this is the altar upon which Kayin and Hevel sacrificed, and Adam offered a sacrifice on it when he was created. And it was from there that he was created — as the Sages said: "He was created from the site of his atonement."

The site of the "*akeida*," of sacrifice, is the site of atonement. A place where painful sacrifices were made, such as the site where Avraham was prepared to sacrifice his

---

30. www.torahbase.org/מצות-קידוש-ה-תשעט/.

31. As Rav Weiss cites, the *Shelah* writes that the *beracha* is valid even if the gentile thereafter changes his mind and decides not to kill the Jew, because the *mitzva* is fulfilled not by being killed, but rather by surrendering one's life, and thus the moment the individual refuses to yield even at the threat of death, he fulfills the *mitzva*, regardless of whether the gentile follows through on his threat. Clearly, then, this *beracha* is warranted only when one makes the decision to give his life for God's honor, and not when he is killed because of his Jewish ethnicity without any opportunity to save his life.

32. 2:1–2.

beloved son, is a sacred site and a site especially suited for prayer. It would thus seem appropriate for those who find themselves at the site of the Tree of Life synagogue in Pittsburgh, where eleven precious Jewish souls were sacrificed, to pray. This was the "*akeida*" of American Jewy, and so this site serves as מקום כפרתו, a place where we can pray to earn God's compassion and atonement.

Conclusion

There is no question that the victims of the Pittsburgh massacre, and all other anti-Semitic attacks, must be mourned and their memories must be honored and cherished irrespective of their level of religious observance. As for the use of the formal term קדושים, however, while it is common to use this word to describe victims of anti-Semitism, it seems more correct to reserve this special term for those who made the choice to surrender their lives for God's honor, as opposed to those who were tragically killed without being given any choice.

According to Jewish tradition, the site of an "*akeida*," where painful sacrifices were made, is a site especially suited for prayer. It would thus seem appropriate for those who happen to be at the site of the Tree of Life tragedy to offer a prayer.

The making of an Orthodox woman rabbi

December 25, 2019
By Simon Rocker

Miriam Camerini is in the midst of a course that will earn her a slot in Jewish history.

When she graduates in two years, she aims to be the first female Orthodox rabbi in Italy.

Miriam Camerini at Limmud

She is currenty enrolled at Har-El, a pioneering yeshivah in Jerusalem for men and women founded by Rabbi Herzl Hefter (who has previously spoken at Limmud UK). It ordained its first women rabbis four years ago.

And although she has the rabbinate in her blood – her father's father was a rabbi in Italy – it took her some time before she embarked on the road to Har-el.

She was born in Jerusalem on Purim 1983 to Italian parents, who later moved back to Milan.

Although she attended the Jewish school, her knowledge was based more on practical observance than a desire to know the sources in depth. Girls of her generation were not taught Talmud then (and are still not at her school).

It was only after graduating from university in theatre and linguistics that she sought more in-depth learning and returned to Jerusalem to spend four years at the co-educational Pardes Institute.

Back in Italy, she founded a theatre company specialising in Jewish-themed productions and concerts, although she has also directed some opera including The Magic Flute.

But it was a couple of years ago that a series of incidents led her to want to become a rabbi.

She had started a bat mitzvah class which had grown from two to 11 girls. "I wanted to teach them something they don't teach at Jewish school – how to learn Gemara," she told Limmud.

Then, a friend sought her guidance. "She wanted to give a dvar Torah because her son was reading the haftarah but she had no idea how to prepare for it".

Before she could reach the required level to start the rabbinic course, she was told she needed to brush up her Talmud – which meant her finding a chavruta, a study partner, who was more advanced than her. In Milan that was not so easy. "The people who knew more than me were more frum and wouldn't learn one to one with a woman."

But she was able to persuade the city's chief rabbi, whom she had known from schooldays, to learn with her – he discreetly avoided asking her to what end.

Now she travels back and forth between Italy and Israel, combining her studies with her theatrical work. It is not a choice without cost: one community in Italy turned down a performance from her company because, as she later learned, the local rabbi objected to her rabbinical training.

She took the plunge because "I see it as a way to bring about something that will come anyway", she explained. "Now it will come earlier." In a decade or so, women rabbis will be commonplace she believes, and "there won't even be a session on it [at Limmud], it will be normal".

For her, the primary role of a rabbi is as an educator. "I don't imagine leading a community or being a pulpit rabbi. I'd like to continue my work in interfaith dialogue, in writing and theatre."

It may take a little while for Italy to get used to a woman rabbis, where a rabbi is seen "as a Jewish priest" and priests are male in the predominantly Catholic country.

The Orthodox establishment feels fearful of the prospect because they see the recognition of women rabbis as a "Trojan horse" for Reform.

But from her Limmud audience came only encouragement. "I think you are enormously courageous," one man told her. "You will never be accepted by them but don't stop that you going ahead. The Jewish community will be richer and better for it."

Women in Positions of Leadership

The subject of women holding positions of religious leadership is among the most charged issues facing modern Jewry. We live in a society that regards as anathema any role distinction between genders, and impulsively assails any such distinction as an attempt to oppress or subjugate women. Indeed, one of the most important orthodoxies of contemporary society is that men and women must be given all the same opportunities, that any door open to one gender must be equally open to the other.

Orthodox Judaism, of course, differentiates between men and women in many different areas, most notably with regard to the obligation of Torah study and certain other *mitzvos*, and in regard to תפילה בצבור (public prayer), which is defined as prayer with ten adult male participants. Additionally, in Jewish communities, as in the rest of the world, women did not commonly hold leadership positions, and generally lived private lives focused on their homes and families. Orthodox Judaism's response to the drastically different realities of women in the modern era has highlighted the complexity of applying an ancient sacred tradition to a rapidly changing world. And among the most heated and controversial aspects of this response has been in regard to ordaining women and allowing them to fill leadership positions.

Let us, then, briefly review the basic source material relevant to this question, and examine which halachic restrictions may or may not be at play in determining the permissibility of women serving as leaders.

It goes without saying that the considerations addressed here do not represent the only relevant factors. The relentless assaults on Orthodox belief and tradition, many of which include charges of primitive misogyny, demand a firm, unwavering stance upholding our fealty to the clear halachic distinctions between men and women. How precisely we balance this firm position with the undeniable, seismic shift in women's role in society is one of the great challenges facing Torah Jewry today. Some might argue that women should be excluded from even technically permissible roles for the sake of resisting modern feminist trends, whereas others might maintain that to the contrary, traditional roles must be adjusted to accommodate our new realities to the extent that *halacha* allows.[1] This essay steers clear of this very difficult

---

1. This topic also, of course, hinges on the issue of *tzniyus*, the propriety of women making themselves public, a subject dealt with as a separate chapter in this volume ("כל כבודה בת

and delicate question of policy, and focuses instead on the specific halachic issues at stake.

מלך ולא מלכה

The most explicit source for forbidding women from serving as leaders is the Rambam's ruling in *Hilchos Melachim*,[2] — כל משימות שבישראל, אין ממנים בהם אלא איש "…any appointments in Israel, only men are to be appointed." The Rambam makes this comment in the context of the Torah's command to appoint a king — שום תשים עליך מלך (*Devarim* 17:15) — from which the *Sifrei* infers, מלך ולא מלכה — that a female may not be named monarch.[3] According to the Rambam, this restriction applies not only to the kingship, but also to all משימות שבישראל — formal appointments.

The Mabit, in his *Kiryas Sefer*, explains that the Rambam reached this conclusion — that this law is relevant to all formal appointments — on the basis of *Chazal's* inference from this verse that one who was not born to a Jewish mother may not serve as a leader. The Torah here requires appointing a king מקרב אחיך — somebody born a Jew, to the exclusion of converts — and the *Sifrei* and Gemara[4] extended this restriction to all leadership positions. Accordingly, the Mabit writes, the Rambam assumed that the rule of מלך ולא מלכה — that only males may be appointed monarch — likewise applies to all leadership posts. This explanation for the source of the Rambam's ruling is proposed also by Rav Moshe Feinstein.[5]

        מלך פנימה: Do Women Need to Hide?").

2.   1:5.

3.   The Vilna Gaon, in his commentary to *Megillas Esther* (4:17), writes that Mordechai obeyed Esther's instruction to declare a three-day fast (as the *Megilla* states, ויעש ככל אשר צוותה עליו אסתר) because she was a queen, and he was therefore bound to obey her wish. Similarly, the Gaon writes later in his commentary (9:32) that the sages of the generation fulfilled Esther's wish that Purim be instituted as a festive holiday because of her status as queen. It seems difficult to understand why the Gaon felt that a queen's commands must be obeyed, in light of the *Sifrei's* explicit ruling that only a man can achieve the status of a monarch. Some have suggested that a queen who is married to a king enjoys the formal status of monarch by virtue of her relationship to the king, and thus Esther's commands needed to be obeyed because she was married to Achashveirosh. (See Rav Uriel Berman's *Ner Chava, Bereishis*, pp. 226–7.) However, the Gaon's remarks are difficult also for a different reason — Esther did not rule over the Jewish kingdom, but was rather a queen appointed by gentiles over a gentile kingdom, and her edicts were thus, seemingly, not binding upon the Jews. (This question is asked and left unanswered by Rav Asher Weiss, *She'eilos U-Teshuvos Minchas Asher*, 2:122.)

4.   *Yevamos* 45b.

5.   *Iggeros Moshe*, Y.D. 2:44. The *Aruch Ha-Shulchan* (C.M. 7:4) offers a different explanation,

In the commentary to the *Sifrei* attributed to the Ra'avad, the *Sifrei* itself states in this context, האיש ממנין פרנס על הצבור ולא האשה — that all leadership positions are restricted to males, in which case the source of the Rambam's ruling is an explicit comment in the *Sifrei*.

This view is expressed also by the Ritva (*Shavuos* 30a), in addressing the question of how Devora was permitted to serve as judge over *Bnei Yisrael* (היא שופטה את ישראל בעת ההיא, *Shoftim* 4:4). The Ritva explains that Devora did not receive any formal appointment, but was rather looked to as a source of guidance, for an appointment would have been impermissible due to the rule of מלך ולא מלכה, which, the Ritva says, applies to all formal leadership posts.[6]

The *Aruch Ha-Shulchan*[7] brings the Rambam's ruling as a universally accepted position, without noting any dissenting opinions. Likewise, Rav Aharon Levine of Reisha, in *Avnei Cheifetz* (1:6), applies the Rambam's ruling to forbid appointing women to positions of communal leadership. And it is told[8] that Rav Yosef Dov Soloveitchik explained the practice that women do not perform *shechita*[9] based on the fact that the role of *shocheit* has become in modern times a formal public post, which may not be filled by a woman, according to the Rambam. Rav Soloveitchik applied this rule to forbid women from serving in other leadership capacities, as well, such as clergy and synagogue presidents.

A Halachic Debate?

However, while the Rambam and Ritva explicitly apply the restriction of מלך ולא מלכה to all leadership posts, other *Rishonim* appear to have disagreed, as Rav Moshe Feinstein notes.[10]

The *Sefer Ha-Chinuch*[11] cites the rule of מלך ולא מלכה in his discussion of the laws

---

suggesting that the phrase מקרב אחיך (literally, "from among your brothers") implies that only אחיך — males — may be appointed, as opposed to אחיותיך ("sisters"), and that this refers to all leadership positions.

6. Rav Moshe Feinstein (*Iggeros Moshe*, Y.D. 2:45) asserts that the Ritva did not need to add this point — that the rule of מלך ולא מלכה applies to all formal appointments of leadership — to prove his contention that Devora did not fill a formal post, because all the שופטים who led *Bnei Yisrael* before the monarchy was established had the status of a king. As such, it would have been forbidden for Devora to receive the appointment as שופטת even if the rule of מלך ולא מלכה were restricted to the kingship.

7. Referenced above, note 5.

8. שעורי הרב על ענייני שחיטה מליחה בשר וחלב ותערובות, *Mesorah*, 2005.

9. Rama, Y.D. 1:1.

10. In the responsa referenced above, notes 5 and 6.

11. 497.

relevant to the monarchy, without mentioning its extension to other leadership roles. Later, in discussing the law that the kingship is inherited by a deceased monarch's son, the *Chinuch* notes the *Sifrei*'s comment that this applies to all positions of authority. The fact that this extension is noted in regard to the law of inheritance, but not in regard to the rule of מלך ולא מלכה, suggests that in the *Chinuch*'s view, it is only the monarchy which is restricted to males, and not other leadership posts.

Rav Moshe observes that this also appears to have been the position of Rashi and the Ran, in their respective commentaries to *Maseches Kiddushin* (76b). The Gemara there establishes the rule that just as the Torah requires appointing a king מקרב אחיך — "from among your brethren," referring to born Jews — all other leadership posts, too, are restricted to born Jews. Rashi and the Ran explain that the Gemara infers this extension from the multiple times the Torah mentions the word "appoint" in commanding that only members of the nation be named king: שום תשים עליך מלך... מקרב אחיך תשים עליך מלך (*Devarim* 17:15). This repetition is intended to expand the rule established in this verse beyond the specific context of the monarchy, to all leadership positions. If so, Rav Moshe reasons, then this expansion is limited to this particular rule, in reference to which the Torah alludes to other leadership positions, and not to other rules relevant to kingship, such as the exclusion of women.

Rav Moshe notes also *Tosfos'* comments in *Maseches Sota* (41b) establishing that even when it comes to the rule of מקרב אחיך, which bars foreigners from serving as leaders, the extension from the monarchy to other leadership posts is not absolute. *Tosfos* contend that when it comes to the kingship, only those born to two Jewish parents are eligible, whereas for other leadership posts, it suffices to have been born to a Jewish mother. Rav Moshe understood from *Tosfos* that the extension of the laws regarding a king's appointment to other leadership roles is very limited, and certainly does not go so far as to exclude women from positions of leadership.

Additionally, Rav Moshe references the discussions of the Ramban and Rashba (in their respective commentaries to *Shavuos* 30a) concerning the permissibility of Devora's role as judge. As we cited earlier, the Ritva presented this question by stating that all appointments — and not just the kingship — are restricted to males. However, Rav Moshe notes, the Ramban and Rashba formulated this question by simply citing the Gemara's inference of מלך ולא מלכה, without mentioning the application of this rule to other leadership posts. Rav Moshe contends that in the view of the Ramban and Rashba, only the kingship is restricted to males, and the שופטים who ruled over Israel before the establishment of the monarchy had the status of kings.[12] We might also add

---

12. This explanation of the Ramban and Rashba's comments was also offered by Rav Yitzchak Herzog (*Techuka Le-Yisrael Al Pi Ha-Torah*, p. 103). Rav Herzog proceeds to support at length the contention that the *Shoftim* had the halachic status of king.

that *Tosfos*, in several contexts,[13] raise the question of how to reconcile Devora's role as שופטת with the *halacha* disqualifying women from serving as judges. In none of these discussions do *Tosfos* ask how Devora was permitted to receive an appointment to a leadership post — perhaps suggesting that according to *Tosfos*, although women may not serve as judges, they are not restricted from holding other leadership positions.[14]

Another relevant source is a passage in Rabbeinu Avraham ben Ha-Rambam's Torah commentary (*Shemos* 18:22), where he discusses the different meanings of the verb שפט. He asserts that this term can denote judgment as well as general leadership, and he adds that when Devora is described as שופטה את ישראל, this means not that she judged — a role which may not be filled by a woman — but rather that she led the people. Interestingly enough, whereas the Rambam explicitly disqualifies women from official positions of leadership, the Rambam's son seems to have maintained that although women may not serve as judges, they may serve in other leadership capacities.

Rav Yitzchak Herzog[15] posits that this also appears to have been the position of the Talmud Yerushalmi. In *Maseches Yoma* (6:1), the Yerushalmi establishes the law disqualifying women from serving as judges on the basis of an association between witnesses and judges. Since women do not serve as witnesses, they are likewise ineligible to serve as judges. Seemingly, if women were disqualified from any leadership post, there would be no need for the Yerushalmi to resort to the association between judgement and testimony, as women in any event would be ineligible to be appointed as judges. Necessarily, then, the Yerushalmi worked off the assumption that *halacha* does not bar women from assuming leadership positions.

As for the final *halacha*, Rav Moshe Feinstein rules that although generally we should follow the stringent view of the Rambam in this regard, the fact that several — if not most — other *Rishonim* felt otherwise allows for leniency under extenuating circumstances. The case he addresses is that of a *kashrus* supervisor who died, leaving behind a family, and whose widow wished to assume his role as *mashgiach* (supervisor) in order to support the family. Rav Moshe ruled that although the position of *mashgiach* likely meets the criteria of שררה — a position of authority, nevertheless, in light of the family's dire financial situation, she may be hired for this job on the basis of those *Rishonim* who disputed the Rambam's position.

---

13. *Yevamos* 45b, *Gittin* 88b, *Bava Kama* 15a, *Nidda* 50a.

14. Rav Bentzion Meir Chai Uziel (*Mishpetei Uziel*, vol. 4, C.M. 6) notes that in *Maseches Nidda*, *Tosfos* actually raise the possibility that a woman is, in fact, permitted to serve as judge, clearly indicating that *Tosfos* did not follow the view forbidding women from assuming formal leadership positions.

15. In the essay referenced above, note 12, p. 108.

Defining שררה

The question then becomes what defines a leadership position that is restricted to males according to the Rambam's view.

Rav Moshe cites the Gemara's comment in *Maseches Kiddushin* (76b) that a convert may not be appointed even as a ריש כורי — which Rashi interprets to mean an overseer of weights and measures. Such an official is regarded as an authority figure, and this position is thus subject to the restriction of מקרב אחיך, requiring that it be filled only by a born Jew. According to the Rambam, then, such a job may not be filled by a woman, either.

On this basis, Rav Moshe concludes that the role of *mashgiach* — which is very similar to that of an overseer of weights and measures — is restricted to men according to the Rambam. Although this job is not generally regarded as a distinguished post, it nevertheless qualifies as שררה because, in Rav Moshe's words, a *mashgiach* is נשכר לעשות נגד רצון בעה"ב — "hired to oppose the wish of the employer." Whereas an employee is bound to fulfill the employer's wishes, an authority figure is appointed specifically for the purpose of restraining and exercising a degree of control over the one who appointed him.[16]

In light of this definition, Rav Moshe proposes a solution for allowing a woman to serve as *mashgiach* — by having her hired by the rabbi or certifying agency. If the woman is hired by, and thus accountable to, somebody other than the owner of the supervised facility, then her status is that of an employee, and not an authority figure. Under such an arrangement, the woman has no authority whatsoever over the facility's owner. She simply performs the work assigned to her by her employer — the certifying rabbi or organization, who is the one hired to exercise control.[17]

Elsewhere,[18] Rav Moshe applies this definition of שררה to permit hiring a convert as a Rosh Yeshiva or lecturer in a yeshiva. He writes that those who fill such positions are simply paid employees, without the power to exert any control over those who hire them. In Rav Moshe's view, the power invested in an administrator to refuse to accept an applicant to his institution, or to expel a student, resembles the authority of an employer to hire and fire employees, and does not qualify as שררה. As such, a convert may be hired for such a position.[19]

---

16. Rav Moshe formulates this definition of שררה also in a different responsum (C.M. 1:75), in reference to the question of whether a *mashgiach* can be dismissed from his job, stating that this would be forbidden due to the prohibition against deposing somebody from a position of שררה (without just cause).

17. Rav Moshe explains that when the Gemara speaks of the overseer of weights and measures as a position of שררה, it refers to a public official hired by the community, who indeed exercised a degree of control over the local merchants, as he was invested with the power to invalidate their scales and yardsticks.

18. *Iggeros Moshe*, Y.D. 4:26.

19. Significantly, Rav Moshe introduces this responsum by stating that the Biblical command

Indeed, the Maharshal, in one of his responsa,[20] cites the tradition he received from his grandfather, Rav Yochanan Luria, that Rabbi Yochanan's wife, Miriam, led a yeshiva for several years, delivering lectures on *halacha* to advanced students from behind a curtain.

Amidst his discussion of this topic, Rav Moshe briefly touches upon the topic of women serving as presidents of synagogues,[21] and he makes it clear that such an appointment would be forbidden. The reason, apparently, is because the congregants elect a president to govern them, empowering the president to make executive decisions which may not be to their liking. As such, this position qualifies as שררה and may not be assigned to a woman.

Rav Shlomo Zalman Auerbach[22] formulated a different definition of שררה, maintaining that any position of honor and distinction falls under the category of שררה. In addressing the permissibility of dismissing teachers in a yeshiva in favor of others who accept lower salaries, Rav Shlomo Zalman cites the *Sefer Ha-Chinuch*[23] as stating that כל השררות שהן במעשה או בשם כבוד — "all leadership appointments which involve practice or a title of distinction" — are passed through inheritance.[24] Similarly, the Mabit[25] writes that the positions of *chazan*, *mohel* and *shochet* are posts which are passed down through inheritance, as they are positions of distinction. As such, even titles of honor may not be taken away from a person unless he was found guilty of some wrongdoing. Rav Shlomo Zalman maintained that the position of a teacher of Torah qualifies as a שם כבוד which may not be taken away from somebody without a justifiable reason.

Later in his discussion, Rav Shlomo Zalman concedes that Torah education may

---

to deal kindly with converts requires *poskim* to find bases for leniency when it comes to a convert's employment opportunities and the like. Therefore, his lenient ruling in this context cannot necessarily be applied to other situations, such as questions involving a woman's hiring for an administrative position.

20.　29.

21.　This issue arose because after Rav Moshe issued his ruling permitting a woman to work as a *kashrus* supervisor under the auspices of a rabbi or agency, there were those who objected, arguing (among other things) that this practice could open the door for women being appointed to other positions which are impermissible.

22.　*Minchas Shlomo*, 1:87.

23.　497.

24.　Although, as noted earlier, the *Sefer Ha-Chinuch* appears not to follow the Rambam's ruling that women may not be appointed to leadership roles, such that the *Sefer Ha-Chinuch*'s broad definition of שררה may not necessarily impact our discussion, which to begin with presumes the Rambam's stringent view.

25.　3:200.

not qualify as a שם כבוד[26], and he cites the *Chikrei Lev*[26] as disputing the Mabit's ruling regarding the positions of *chazan, mohel* and *shochet*.[27]

Interestingly, Rav Moshe Feinstein agrees with this ruling, distinguishing between the status of שררה in regard to demotion, and the status of שררה in regard to the restrictions on whom may be appointed. He writes[28] that a rabbi hired to lead a congregation or just to teach may not be demoted without a justifiable reason, both because of his rights as an employee, and because of the שררה status of his position. In his aforementioned responsum regarding the hiring of a convert as a Rosh Yeshiva, Rav Moshe explains that the prohibition against demoting a person of distinction applies to a שררה של כבוד, whereas the prohibition against appointing a convert applies to what he calls שררה דכפייה — a position that authorizes one to determine policy against the people's wishes.[29]

In any event, according to Rav Moshe, a position of שררה from which women are barred is one which empowers the appointee to go against the wishes of those who appointed him. According to Rav Shlomo Zalman, any honorable position might qualify as שררה with respect to this prohibition.

An entirely different approach is advanced by Rav Shaul Yisraeli, in his *Amud Ha-Yemini*.[30] In addressing the permissibility of electing gentiles to government positions in the State of Israel, Rav Yisraeli posits that modern-day, democratically elected positions do not qualify as שררה. Government officials are elected not to rule over the citizens, but rather to act on their behalf in choosing, implementing and overseeing the policies which they feel best serve the country's interests. An elected official acts as the voters' agent, not as their ruler, and thus such positions do not qualify as שררה.

Rav Yisraeli draws proof to this conclusion from the simple fact that modern-day elected officials serve for limited terms and do not bequeath their posts to their children, even if their children are qualified. The Rambam clearly writes — just several passages after establishing the rule of מלך ולא מלכה and extending it to all leadership positions[31] — that like the monarchy, appointments to all leadership posts are bequeathed to one's

---

26. O.C. 15.

27. As Rav Shlomo Zalman notes, the *Chikrei Lev* nevertheless acknowledged the accepted practice not to depose people serving in these capacities.

28. *Iggeros Moshe*, C.M. 2:34.

29. Rav Moshe does not cite a source for this important distinction. Seemingly, the fact that both *halachos* — the restrictions on eligible candidates for leadership positions, and the prohibition against demoting an appointed official — are derived from the laws governing the appointment of kings would suggest that they apply to the precisely same kinds of leadership positions.

30. 12:8.

31. *Hilchos Melachim* 1:7.

inheritors.[32] By definition, then, any position which is not bequeathed to inheritors is not bound by the restrictions that apply to the appointment of a king.

This final point would, seemingly, appear to call into question the entire premise that women should be barred from modern-day leadership positions by force of the Rambam's view excluding them from positions of שררה. As we saw, the entire basis for this conclusion is the Rambam's opinion, applying the restrictions relevant to kingship to all leadership appointments. It would thus seem inherently inconsistent to exclude women from leadership positions that are not inherited. If we classify the position of synagogue president, for example, under the category of שררה, then we must also require congregations to confer this position upon the president's child after his passing, which nobody suggests doing. It is thus difficult to understand how a position which is not bequeathed to one's children is forbidden to be filled by a woman.

One may, however, easily refute this argument. Even if, due either to state laws or to accepted protocol, a position is not passed through inheritance, this does not negate the fact that it is subject to halachic inheritance. If a position is included in the Torah's inheritance laws, then we may assume that it is off-limits to women even if, in practice, this position is not generally inherited.

We should add that Rav Moshe Sternbuch[33] ruled that the position of a modern-day synagogue rabbi does not qualify as שררה with respect to inheritance rights. Synagogue rabbis today act as the membership's employees, and do not exert actual authority over the members. As such, this position is not bequeathed to the rabbi's son after his passing.[34] By extension, we should assume that modern-day leadership positions which do not lend the official actual authority and rule should not be denied to women on the grounds of שררה.[35]

Women Leading Women

Even if we conclude that women should not serve in leadership roles, whether due to the prohibition of שררה or due to *tzniyus* concerns, it seems clear that women may serve as leaders over other women. Rav Yitzchak Herzog,[36] among others, noted the widespread

---

32. ‏ולא המלכות בלבד, אלא כל השררות וכל המינויין שבישראל ירושה לבנו ולבן בנו עד עולם.

33. *Teshuvos Ve-Hanhagos*, 3:460.

34. This point is the subject of a different chapter in this volume ("Legal Inheritance or Nepotism? Sons Succeeding Fathers in the Rabbinate").

35. Rav Bentzion Meir Chai Uziel (see note 14) likewise asserted that a group of people voluntarily choosing a woman to lead them does not violate the rule of ‏מלך ולא מלכה, which refers only to the imposition of a woman as leader upon the public. This was also the position of Rav Eliyahu Bakshi-Doron, *Binyan Av*, 1:65.

36. In the essay referenced above, note 12, p. 113.

custom that women's organizations are led by women, and these positions certainly do not fall under the restrictions of שררה, even according to the most stringent approach.

Additionally, a number of *poskim*, including Rav Eliyahu Bakshi-Doron,[37] cite the comment of the Riva[38] that the great sages Shemaya and Avtalyon were permitted to serve as religious leaders, despite their being converts, because they were uniquely qualified for the position. The premise underlying this remark is that the general restrictions of שררה are waived to allow the candidate with the best credentials to assume the position in question. In principle, then, if a woman is generally considered the most suitable and qualified for a position, then, at least according to this opinion, the prohibition of שררה — even if we assume it to be otherwise applicable — is overridden.

A compelling argument could be made that especially in modern times, when girls and women are daily exposed to female celebrities and public figures, there is an urgent need for charismatic and influential female religious personalities. In previous generations, when hardly any women served in public positions, a girl's female role models were her mother and close family members and friends. In today's world, however, unfortunately, girls are exposed to female fashion models, entertainers and politicians, whose values and lifestyles, quite obviously, stand in direct contrast to those championed by the Torah. Without a doubt, our generation's women require impressive and inspiring female representatives of Torah they can admire and emulate, if for no other reason than to offset the influence of female celebrities. This need would appear to not only justify, but demand, having women serving as leadership figures for other women.

The same can perhaps be said about the contemporary "*yoatzot*" movement, whereby learned, devout women undergo extensive training in the field of family purity in order to advise women who might, understandably, be uncomfortable consulting with a rabbi about matters relating to menstruation and intimacy. As the title "*yoatzot*" suggests, these women are named not as authority figures, but rather as advisors, and complex questions requiring a *psak* are brought to proficient rabbis. But even were we to regard these female scholars as authority figures, such a position might likely be considered one for which women are uniquely suited, given the natural hesitation many women have towards consulting with rabbis about such matters. This itself might provide legitimate halachic grounds for this role.

Women in the Synagogue

It must be emphasized that even if one acknowledges the permissibility of women holding leadership positions, a distinction must be made between religious institutions and other settings.

---

37. Referenced above, note 35.

38. *Shemos* 21:1.

Synagogues have always been subject to heightened sensitivity to *tzniyus* and strict separation between the genders. The Gemara[39] famously describes the synagogue as מקדש מעט — a "miniature" *Beis Ha-Mikdash*, a place designated for an encounter with the Divine Presence. And the Torah warns in *Sefer Devarim* (23:15), ולא יראה בך ערות דבר ושב מאחריך — strict standards of purity are required in order to experience the Almighty's presence. Rav Hershel Schachter[40] suggested that this might be Rashi's intent in noting[41] that the curtain hanging over the entrance to the *Mishkan* resembles a כלה צנועה — "modest bride" — who covers her face with a veil. The site of the Divine Presence is associated with *tzniyus* because especially high standards of modesty are required in order to be worthy of encountering God in the manner facilitated by the *Mishkan* — and, by extension, the synagogue.[42]

This is true of *yeshivos*, as well. The Gemara applies the term מקדש מעט also to בתי מדרשות — places of Torah study — because, presumably, study, like prayer, is an experience of encountering the Almighty. The Mishna in *Maseches Avos* (3:6) teaches that when people sit and learn Torah, שכינה שרויה ביניהם — the Divine Presence rests among them. When we pray, we encounter God by speaking to Him, and when we study Torah, we encounter God by hearing Him speak to us, as it were. And thus when it comes to houses of prayer and study, we must be especially vigilant in striving to avoid ערות דבר — impropriety of any kind, which includes maintaining separation of the genders.

This requirement suffices to preclude the possibility of a woman serving in a clerical role that involves frequent public appearances in a synagogue (or yeshiva). Publicly officiating during the service in the synagogue would compromise the standards of *tzniyus* that are warranted in a מקדש מעט, and is thus inappropriate.

Semicha

Until now, we have addressed the question of appointing a woman to serve in a leadership capacity. A separate question arises concerning the mere conferral of the title "rabbi" upon a woman who satisfactorily masters selected portions of Torah. The issue of ordaining women has long set Orthodoxy apart from the other streams of Judaism,

---

39. *Megilla* 29a.

40. *Eretz Ha-Tzvi*, p. 96.

41. *Shemos* 26:9.

42. Rav Schachter suggested explaining on this basis also the famous story of Kimchis (*Yoma* 47a) who was rewarded for her strict standards of modesty by having sons who served as *kohanim gedolim*. As encountering the Divine Presence is contingent upon *tzniyus*, Kimchis was rewarded for her modesty by begetting sons worthy of serving God in the *Mikdash*.

and even the Jewish Theological Seminary, the flagship institution of the Conservative movement, did not ordain a woman until 1985 — two years after the passing of Rabbi Saul Lieberman, arguably the movement's most influential figure, who staunchly opposed granting *semicha* to women.

In a letter dated Rosh Chodesh Adar 5739 (1979),[43] Rabbi Lieberman expressed the view that the title "rabbi" means more than simply a confirmation of the student's mastery of material. He writes that this title "reflects on the fitness to issue legal decisions and to judge." Warning that "we should not empty the title '*rav*' of its meaning from the way it has been understood by the Jewish people throughout the generations," Rabbi Lieberman concludes, "Since a woman is not fit to judge, and she cannot become qualified for this, she cannot be ordained by this title."

More recently, in early 2017, this view was upheld by a panel of distinguished rabbis commissioned by the Orthodox Union to formulate a position on the matter of ordination for women.[44] The panel stated:

> While contemporary semikhah differs from classic *semikhah* (as described in the Talmud) in many regards, it must, nevertheless, be viewed as an extension of the original institution of *semikhah*. Parallels between the current and original forms of *semikhah* therefore, are relevant and valid. Various sources indicate that the classic *semikhah* involved, and in fact may have centered on, designating individuals to serve as court judges. Since the majority halakhic view is that only men are eligible to be ordained as judges, even contemporary ordination would be restricted to men.

Seemingly, this conclusion requires us to avoid conferring *semicha* also upon converts, who, like women, are disqualified from serving as judges. Rav Hershel Schachter,[45] however, distinguished between converts and women in this regard, noting that converts are permitted to preside over cases involving other converts, and therefore, the title "rabbi" is suitable for converts. Women, however, who under no circumstances are eligible to serve as judges, should not be granted such a title.

This restriction, however, does not preclude the possibility of conferring some other title of distinction upon women who have achieved mastery over portions of Torah. Even if we insist on reserving the formal title "rabbi" for those who are eligible to serve as judges, this does not prevent us — at least from a strictly halachic stand-

---

43. Available online at http://hirhurim.blogspot.com/2010/02/prof-saul-lieberman-on-womens.html.

44. The full text of the panel's conclusion is available at https://www.ou.org/assets/Responses-of-Rabbinic-Panel.pdf.

45. *Hakirah*, volume 11, p. 23.

point — from choosing some other way to certify a woman's scholarly achievements, just as, for example, nobody would object to women be awarded academic degrees from universities. Whether or not this is advisable as a matter of policy can be debated, but halachically, there does not appear to be any reason not to confer other titles upon learned women. One well-known example is the title of "*yoetzet halacha*," given by the Nishmat school in Jerusalem to women who have completed the intensive study of the laws of family purity.[46]

Conclusion

1. Women as synagogue rabbis: Such a role is forbidden, due to the strict standards of modesty and gender separation required in houses of worship and Torah study.

2. Women as synagogue presidents: Rav Moshe Feinstein and Rav Yosef Dov Solovetichik explicitly forbade women from serving in such a capacity, whereas others maintained that any democratically elected position does not constitute a leadership post from which women should be barred.

3. *Yoatzot* (halachic advisors on matters of family purity): These women are appointed to advise, not to govern or exert any sort of authority, and, moreover, they provide a valuable service for which they are likely more qualified than men, given the reluctance of many women to consult with men on issues involving their menstrual cycles and marital lives. For both these reasons, this role should be permissible.

4. *Semicha*: As the term "rabbi" is associated with the eligibility to serve as judge, its use as a title for learned women has always been deemed improper by Orthodox Jewry. In principle, other titles may be used to recognize women for their scholarly achievements and affirm their credentials as Torah teachers and guides.

---

46. See interview with Rebbetzin Chana Henkin, below.

   The panel commissioned by the Orthodox Union, in its statement, noted the lack of unanimity among its members regarding the advisability of the *yoatzot* movement as a practical matter.

INTERVIEWS

Rebbetzin Chana Henkin

Interviewed on *Headlines with Dovid Lichtenstein*, May 6, 2017

Many years ago, I began trying to educate women in *taharas ha-mishpacha*. I worked very hard on this. I discovered that in any community with which I had contact, women were not asking enough questions. Generally, they weren't asking questions because matters of *taharas ha-mishpacha* are intimate, and they were uncomfortable to go to a rav. Many were *meikel* [lenient] when there weren't supposed to be, and many were *machmir* [stringent] when they weren't supposed to be, at a very high cost to *shalom bayis* [domestic harmony]. They felt more comfortable that way than by exposing themselves in discussing intimate things with a rav. So I spent decades trying to get women to bring their questions to *rabbanim*, speaking to them about how sensitive *rabbanim* are. But I realized I was beating my head against a brick wall. Women weren't going to *rabbanim* with their questions, and the costs were terrible — these included violations of *halacha*, and these included, as I said before, costs to *shalom bayis*, as well as a lot of personal suffering.

So I created a program in which women are being instructed at a very high level in *taharas ha-mishpacha* as well as in women's health — areas such as gynecological issues, fertility, and women's cancers, and how all these interface with *taharas ha-mishpacha*. We set up a telephone hotline so questions could be asked. The women who graduate our program are called *yoatzot halacha*. When a question requires *pesika* [an expert halachic ruling], then they consult with a rav. The telephone hotline is accessible from the U.S., with the wonderful number 1-877-YOETZET. It's a toll-free number. Our hotline works every day of the week, including Erev Shabbos and Motza'ei Shabbos. We also have a wonderful website about women's health and halacha — www.yoatzot.org — with hundreds of FAQs and hundreds of articles. Questions can be sent via the website, and the answers are written by *yoatzot halacha* and reviewed by a *posek*. In the course of around 15 years, we've received over 300,000 questions on the hotline and the website.

The more people know about *yoatzot halacha*, the more they recognize the tremendous benefit this program provides for women who just do not feel *tzanua* going to *rabbanim* with these questions.

Recently, there was a statement issued by the OU, by a panel of seven *rabbanim*, addressing women's roles. We were the only program to be singled out in this statement, and I was extremely pleased by what the panel said. They said that *yoatzot* are motivated by *yiras Shamayim* and a desire to improve women's lives, and that women in many communities are addressing their questions to *yoatzot halacha* because of reasons of *tzniyus* and comfort. The panel said it was divided in its opinion, and in the final analysis, it said that if a *yoetzet halacha* was going to be employed in a particular community, then it should be under the aegis of the local rav — which is exactly what we want — and the decision should be left up to the community. I was extremely pleased by that, because it meant that this wasn't being confused with other initiatives which are coming from a very different place, a political place, a gender place. This is about improving women's lives and enhancing the observance of mitzvos.

"*Paskening*" in halachic jargon refers to לדמות מילתא למילתא — extrapolating from one situation and applying it to another. We don't do that. We give straightforward answers to a questioner who does not know the answer.

The *yoatzot* are tested over the course of two years — each time they finish a *siman* in the *Shulchan Aruch*, they take a written exam, and after two years, they go through four hours of testing by *poskei halacha*. One of our first women to be tested is a physician, and she said that her medical boards were "a piece of cake" compared to the rigorous tests in our program. And yet, despite the women's background, they don't go to the place of לדמות מילתא למילתא, answering questions which are not clear-cut and written down, and which require שיקול הדעת (halachic judgment).

There are women out there who are really suffering. They need to be able to bring their questions to another woman, and that woman will know whether or not she can answer it. The *yoetzet* has learned enough to know whether she can answer the question, or if she needs to call up a *posek*, because she will understand what is being asked.

A woman once called me up, and said, very emotionally, "Thank you for helping my daughter. Where were you all these years when I needed you?"

The mother and daughter had a hereditary problem that caused their bodies to function in a particular way. This problem caused the mother untold anguish over the years in the area of *taharas ha-mishpacha*.

"You solved this problem for my daughter," she said to me, referring to the help she received from a *yoetzet*. "Now she won't need to suffer the way I did."

We have situations like this all the time.

There are situations where a woman isn't getting to the *mikveh* on time in order to conceive, and if she would ask her question, she could get to the *mikveh* on time. Not always is there a halachic solution, but in many situations, there are. And if she's not comfortable asking the question, because of what I regard as a wonderful sense of modesty and propriety, then the question is not going to be asked.

Women in enormous numbers are expressing that this is a *mitzva* which they wish to observe, but we should make it comfortable for them and dignified for them to observe this *mitzva*.

⊗ HAARETZ

Opinion | To the Rabbis Who Banned Jews From Owning Dogs: You Must Be Barking

July 29, 2019
By Jonathan Wittenberg

The Israeli city of Elad is clearly not the place for me. As a dog-lover, I have zero inclination to live where the local chief rabbi, Mordechai Malka, and several of his colleagues, signed an edict declaring "all dogs bad" and their owners accursed.

I wonder what they would make of my hound's regular attendance at Shacharit, or my habit of saying the Shema with him before bed, because, like all communion with nature, this deepens my kavvanah in the awareness that God's sacred gift of life flows through us both.

Rabbi Malka and his colleagues are correct in noting that dogs have a bad press in the classic sources. In Talmudic times, dogs were often carriers of rabies. They frequently served as guard dogs, both of flocks and borders, and were liable to be fierce. Their barking frightened beggars, preventing tzedakah, and risked making pregnant women abort.

People interact with a dog as they dine near a portrait spray-painted on a metal shutter of a closed storefront in Mahane Yehuda, one of Jerusalem's most popular outdoor markets. (Reuters)

In the outstanding book on the subject, A Jew's Best Friend, which he co-edited, Philip Ackerman devotes a chapter to analysing rabbinic references to dogs in the context of medieval Islam. While frank that Maimonides manifests "an environmental disdain towards dogs and canine husbandry" (supported by clear Talmudic precedent), he also observes of "the rabbinic elite" that its "bark seems to have been worse than its bite."

For neither the Tanakh nor subsequent Jewish teaching is as totally negative as the present-day rabbinical edict of Elad suggests.

The Torah rewards dogs for not barking on the night of the Exodus, instructing that treif meat be thrown to them, thus engendering the rabbinic saying that "God does not constrict the reward of any creature." The hero of the apocryphal book of Tobit is followed on his long journey by his faithful dog.

The Mishnah rules that shepherds who bake bread solely for their dogs are exempt from the obligation of taking challah, the portion of dough given to the Cohanim, whereas if they plan to share the meal with their canine companion, the mitzvah remains mandatory (Mishnah Challah 1:8). This implies that dogs were, at least sometimes, treated by their owners with attention and affection.

The Talmud notes that in Rav Hisda's home there was sufficient high-quality bread for the dogs, indicating that they formed an integral part of the household (Mo'ed Katan 28a).

In the early medieval Perek Shirah, dogs praise God with the verse, "Come let us bow down and kneel before God who made us." For God "is merciful to all his works," (Psalm 145) a verse which may have inspired the late Chief Rabbi of Haifa, She'ar-Yeshuv Cohen to say, some years ago, contra Rabbi Malka, that having pets teaches children loving-kindness. There is no suggestion that dogs were excluded from this recommendation.

Uziel Elyahu, the chief Orthodox rabbi of the northern municipality of Misgav, in 2002 ruled that keeping guard dogs is allowed, as well as guide dogs and those kept "to develop a person's emotions."

No doubt, though, more recent history has contributed to negative views about dogs among Jews. Nazi camp guards famously used dogs, especially German shepherds, as tools of their own sadism. Especially notorious were Amon Goeth's two beasts, Rolf and Ralf, who tore their victims apart. But it is the SS and their partners who must be held responsible for abusing animals in this manner, and not the dogs themselves.

For dogs were not to be found only among the oppressors. Emmanuel Levinas, a prisoner of war, remembered the stray dog Bobby who spent weeks among the prisoners, treating them with affection. He later wrote that, contrary to Nazi rhetoric, to Bobby the prisoners definitely were human beings.

More significantly, in German-occupied territory during WWII, pets in Jewish households were killed, both as an independent act of cruelty and to make their owners suffer. In Berlin and Prague, they had to be delivered to the Nazi authorities. In Kovno, Jews had to take them to the small synagogue, where the animals were shot. Such fellow suffering deserves a measure of compassionate recognition.

But dogs can't only be judged only by the past. They are a significant part of the lives of many Jews today, offering faithfulness, love and healing.

Israel's training centre for guide dogs, established at Bet Oved in 1991, was recently extended to include a new kalbiyya, a puppy-rearing building. Dogs are also trained there as companions for people, especially soldiers, suffering from post-traumatic stress disorder. Other dogs, no

Members of the IDF's elite canine unit, Oketz. Credit: Ilan Assayag

doubt with stresses of their own, have served, and sometimes died, in the IDF's elite Oketz unit, where they save human lives from concealed explosives.

It is therefore scarcely surprising that, despite the cano-phobic edicts of a number of Israel's municipal rabbis, the country as a whole is becoming increasingly dog-friendly. In 2016, Tel Aviv declared itself the most welcoming place in the world for canines, claiming, not necessarily accurately, that it has more dogs per (human) capita than any other city in the world.

According to Israel's National Dog Registration Center, there were 477,000 registered dogs in Israel in 2018, a rise of 12.5 percent in the last two years. German Shepherds now account for the third highest number of puppies born in the country, evidently a sign of reconciliation.

Yet the edicts evidently express the consensus in ultra-Orthodox localities. Thus in the entire town of Modiin Illit, with a population of 73,000, there are just four registered dogs.

There clearly need to be more sermons noting that the word kelev [dog] can be broken down into ke-lev, "like the heart," and, as the Hasidic masters liked to remind us, "The Merciful One desires the heart."

Like Britain, no doubt Israel already is or soon will be training Canine Assistance and Medical Detection Dogs, the latter capable of scenting cancers as a very early stage, or warning parents when a diabetic child is having a dangerous blood-sugar low. None of this, of course, contradicts the requirement that owners take due responsibility for their animals' behavior.

Such realities challenge Rabbi Abraham Yosef of Holon's inability to find "any grounds for permitting any dog whatsoever in any manner," though he concedes that medical reasons for owning dogs may be considered by the Bet Din, each case on its merits. One wonders what specialized rabbinical qualifications are needed for this task.

What is saddest about the Elad edict, especially when the acute global environment crisis requires us to rethink our relationship to the natural world and question our hitherto anthropocentric dominance of it, is the lack of awareness of the profound value that the presence of animals brings, not least that of dogs.

Dogs offer companionship, kinship, comfort, love and the feeling of belonging together to both creation and Creator.

Pets — Is It a Jewish Thing?

In the summer of 2019, the Sephardic rabbis of the Israeli city of Elad — including the city's Chief Rabbi, Rabbi Mordechai Malka — signed a strongly worded letter establishing in no uncertain terms that owning dogs is strictly forbidden according to *halacha*. It went so far as to pronounce, כל מי שמגדל כלב הוא ארור — "Anyone who raises a dog is accursed!" The letter warned the people of Elad not to own dogs, and urged those who had a specific medical need that required owning a dog to obtain special permission, in writing, from a local *beis din*.

Not surprisingly, the reaction from liberal and non-Orthodox streams of Judaism was fast and furious. A reporter for the Jewish Telegraphic Agency cynically introduced his coverage by quipping, "In the latest reminder that man's best friends are not Orthodox rabbis, more than a dozen rabbis from the city of Elad near Tel Aviv issued an edict declaring that a dog's bark is as bad as its bite…"[1] A Masorti rabbi in England proudly announced to the readers of Haaretz, "I have zero inclination to live where the local chief rabbi, Mordechai Malka, and several of his colleagues, signed an edict declaring 'all dogs bad' and their owners accursed.."[2]

Outside the world of knee-jerk, gut reactions that characterizes so much of today's journalism and social media, this topic deserves to be treated like any other question of *halacha* or Jewish values, with a serious study and consideration of the relevant texts and their commentaries.

What, then, do our texts say about owning dogs, or pets in general? Is the natural aversion that many Orthodox Jews feel towards dogs an outgrowth of the long, tragic history of dogs being used by our nation's tormentors as part of their campaign of persecution — most notably, by SS guards in Nazi Germany? Or, is this discomfort simply a function of the novelty of the concept of pets, a relatively new phenomenon which became popular only in the modern era, when people have the time and resources to raise animals for enjoyment and company?

---

1.   Cnaan Liphshiz, "Israeli Rabbis Ban Dogs," https://jewishstandard.timesofisrael.com/israeli-rabbis-ban-dogs/.

2.   Rabbi Jonathan Wittenberg, "To the Rabbis Who Banned Jews From Owning Dogs: You Must Be Barking," https://www.haaretz.com/israel-news/.premium-to-the-rabbis-who-ban-dogs-and-call-their-owners-accursed-you-must-be-barking-1.7580902.

כלב רע

The Mishna in *Maseches Bava Kama (79b)* establishes that one may not raise a dog unless it is "tied with iron chains" such that it cannot run loose. Rashi explains that having an unchained dog is forbidden because it might bite people, or bark and frighten a pregnant woman, which could result in a miscarriage. This interpretation is based on the Gemara, which brings Rav Dustai's remark that God's presence resides among the Jewish Nation only if their population reaches a certain number,[3] and so if a dog's barking frightens a pregnant woman and causes her to miscarry, the dog's owner is blamed for keeping God's presence away from the nation. The Gemara proceeds to relate the tragic story of a woman who indeed miscarried as a result of a dog barking at her. The owner's assurances that the dog had no fangs and was thus harmless came only after the fetus was dislodged from its place. This story is, presumably, told to demonstrate that even a harmless dog poses danger if it is not chained.

Later, the Gemara makes certain exceptions to this prohibition. Rabbi Yishmael is cited as permitting raising כלבים כופרין, a type of harmless dog which serves the useful purpose of eliminating rodents from the home (80a). And the Gemara later (83a) cites a *beraysa* establishing that in border towns, where heightened security measures are necessary, one may leave a dog unleashed overnight for protection.

A more significant qualification of this prohibition appears much earlier in Maseches *Bava Kama* (15b), where a *beraysa* teaches, לא יגדל אדם **כלב רע** בתוך ביתו — one may not raise a violent dog in his home. The *beraysa* presents this prohibition together with the prohibition against having a סולם רעוע — an unsteady ladder — in one's home, both of which are inferred from the Torah's command in *Sefer Devarim*[4] ולא תשים דמים בביתך — "you shall not place bloodguilt in your homes." (This command appears in the context of the *mitzva of* מעקה, which requires erecting a parapet around one's flat roof to prevent accidents.) This prohibition is clearly understood as part of the broader requirement to maintain appropriate safety standards in one's home, and is therefore limited to a כלב רע — a dog that could cause harm.

One could have claimed that the *beraysa*'s ruling, which is cited in the name of Rabbi Nasan, represents a minority view among the *Tannaim*, which takes a more lenient position and prohibits raising only a כלב רע — a violent dog which could cause harm. This appears to be the view of the Rambam, who writes in *Hilchos Nizkei Mammon* (5:9) that it is forbidden to raise את הכלב אלא אם כן היה קשור בשלשלת — "a dog unless it is tied with a chain," without specifying a כלב רע. However, the *Shulchan Aruch*[5] clearly understood that Rabbi Nasan does not dispute the Mishna's ruling, but rather interprets it. The *Shulchan Aruch* writes:

---

3.   22,000.

4.   22:8.

5.   C.M. 409:3.

אסור לגדל כלב רע, אלא אם כן הוא אסור בשלשלאות של ברזל וקשור בהם.
ובעיר הסמוכה לספר, מותר לגדלו; וקושרו ביום ומתירו בלילה.

It is forbidden to raise a violent dog unless it is bound by iron chains and
tied with them. In a city near the border, it is permissible to raise it, and
one ties it by day and lets it free by night.

The Rama adds that in his time, when Jews lived among hostile gentiles, there was
room to allow raising dogs and letting them loose. He emphasizes, however, that if
there is any concern that a dangerous dog might cause harm to innocent people, then
it must be tied with metal chains.

It emerges, then, that dogs which can cause harm — either by biting or even just by
barking and frightening people — may be owned as long as they are securely chained,
and dogs which do not bite or frighten people do not even need to be chained.

Another relevant source is the Gemara's ruling elsewhere[6] that a widow should not
raise a dog, either because she might be tempted to use it for sexual purposes (Rashi),
or because people might cast such aspersions (*Tosfos*). This ruling is codified in the
Shulchan Aruch.[7] The clear implication is that for all other people, raising a dog is
permissible, as noted by the *Sefer Ha-Yerei'im*.[8]

This is, indeed, the conclusion of several *poskim*, including the Maharshal[9] and the
Shulchan Aruch Ha-Rav.[10] In their view, a hostile dog may be owned if it is securely
chained, and a dog that neither bites nor barks may be owned and does not have to be
chained.

Rav Yaakov Emden's Stringent Ruling

A different view, however, was advanced by Rav Yaakov Emden, in one of his published
responsa,[11] where he strictly forbids raising a dog.

Surprisingly, Rav Emden asserts that the view permitting raising harmless dogs
represents a minority position that is not accepted as *halacha*. He contends, לא חילקו
הפוסקים בין כלב לכלב — that the *poskim* draw no distinction between different kinds

---

6. *Bava Metzia 71a, Avoda Zara 22a.*

7. E.H. 22:18. There is some discussion as to whether the Gemara's statement was intended
    as an outright prohibition, or as a non-binding measure of stringency, but the *Shulchan
    Aruch*'s formulation — אלמנה אסורה לגדל כלב — certainly implies that this is strictly
    forbidden. See Rav Shmuel Wosner, *Shevet Ha-Levi*, vol. 5, 205:7.

8. 210.

9. *Yam Shel Shlomo, Bava Kama,* 7:45.

10. C.M., *Hilchos Shemiras Guf Va-Nefesh, 3.*

11. *She'eilas Yabetz, 1:17.*

of dogs.[12] This claim seems to completely ignore the *Shulchan Aruch's* ruling, which forbids raising only a כלב רע — a dog that can cause harm.

Equally startling is Rav Emden's second contention, that even one who owns a dog which he keeps chained is "accursed." Rav Emden notes Rabbi Eliezer's comment cited by the Gemara[13] that one who raises dogs — like one who raises pigs — is "accursed," and he understood this to mean that although the Mishna permits raising a dog if it is kept chained, one who does so is nevertheless "accursed." Indeed, the Rambam, after establishing the prohibition against raising a dog that is not chained, adds, אמרו חכמים ארור מגדל כלבים וחזירים מפני שהזיקן מרובה ומצוי — "The Sages said: Accursed is one who raises dogs or pigs, because their damage is extensive and common." This could be understood to mean that despite the technical permissibility of raising dogs that are chained, those who do so are accursed. It seems more likely, however, that this "curse" is placed upon those who do not comply with the requirement to chain their dogs, and allow them to walk about freely. Another possibility emerges from the Rambam's sudden shift from the singular form (לא יגדל...את **הכלב**) to the plural form (ארור מגדל **כלבים**). The Rambam perhaps meant that although *halacha* permits having one dog, as long as it is properly chained, the Sages sharply condemned those who raise dogs on a large scale, due to the damage they can cause.

Regardless, the *Shulchan Aruch* makes no mention whatsoever of this "curse," and evidently understood that Rabbi Eliezer's remark represents a minority view which is not accepted,[14] or that this "curse" refers only to those who own dangerous dogs and fail to keep them chained.

As for the special law forbidding a widow from owning a dog — which would imply that for everyone else this is allowed — Rav Emden refutes this argument, explaining that one might have assumed that a special dispensation is given to unmarried women living alone, who require additional protection. In truth, he claims, it is forbidden for all people to own a dog, but the Gemara emphasized that this prohibition applies even to vulnerable individuals whom we might have thought to allow having a dog for security purposes. Clearly, this is a strained reading of the Gemara, and is contradicted by the *Sefer Ha-Yerei'im*, which, as mentioned above, drew proof from this ruling that others are allowed to own dogs.

מושב לצים

Towards the end of his discussion, Rav Emden argues that owning dogs for fun and

---

12.   Rav Emden further posits that even the lenient view allows raising a single harmless dog, but not multiple dogs.

13.   *Bava Kama 83a.*

14.   Indeed, Rabbi Eliezer very often took minority positions that were rejected by the consensus of *Tannaim.*

play[15] falls under the category of מושב לצים — inappropriate frivolity and silliness.

The source for the prohibition of מושב לצים is a passage in *Maseches Avoda Zara* (18b), where the Gemara forbids attending "stadiums" (איצטדינין)[16] and "circuses" (כרקום), as well as events where various forms of magic are practiced. The Gemara cites as the source for this prohibition the opening verse of *Sefer Tehillim* which praises the person who במושב לצים לא ישב — avoids "the company of jokers." The events listed there by the Gemara — such as "stadiums" and "circuses" — are regarded as מושב לצים, which we are to avoid. The Gemara concludes, שדברים הללו מביאין את האדם לידי ביטול תורה — these activities lead a person to waste time that can be used for Torah study.

The *Mishna Berura*,[17] citing the *Bach*, applies this prohibition to attending the gentiles' competitions and dances, as well as שום דבר שמחתם — any form of entertainment. Later,[18] the *Mishna Berura* includes theaters and circuses, and laments the fact that these forms of entertainment have become כהפקר אצל איזה אנשים — an accepted practice among some people. He cites the Gemara's warning there in *Maseches Avoda Zara*, כל המתלוצץ נופל בגיהנם — "Whoever engages in frivolity falls into *Gehinnom*." The *Bach*'s comments are cited also by the *Chayei Adam*,[19] who elaborates on the practical applications of the מושב לצים prohibition, and he defines מושב לצים as כל דבריהם כשהן נאספים לשחוק וללצון — "any of their [the gentiles'] activities where they gather for laughter and frivolity." The *Chayei Adam* strongly condemns those Jews who attend בתי שחוק והיתול — "houses of laughter and silliness," such as circuses and the like. He also laments those otherwise observant and learned Jews who engage in דברי ליצנות — frivolous speech. The *Chayei Adam* admonishes, אין לו לאדם רק לדבר בדברי תורה או משא ומתן שהוא חייו — "A person should speak only words of Torah or business, which is his livelihood."

More recently, Rav Moshe Feinstein[20] ruled that attending theaters and sports events in the United States falls under the category of מושב לצים, and is therefore forbidden.

The common denominator between all the examples mentioned in these sources is that they involve a public event where people assemble for the sole purpose of levity and amusement. This is, indeed, the plain meaning of the term מושב לצים — a gathering of people who have come to engage in inappropriately puerile entertainment. Playing with a dog in the privacy of one's home — and perhaps even in one's yard, or in a park — would not appear to constitute a מושב לצים.

---

15. In Rav Emden's words: באותן כלבים...וקונים אותם בדמים יקרים לשחק ולהשתעשע בהן ולגעגע עמהן.

16. Rashi explains that this term refers to stadiums used for bullfighting.

17. 224:3.

18. 307:59.

19. 63:17.

20. *Iggeros Moshe*, Y.D. 4:11:1.

What's more, Rav Chaim Pinchas Scheinberg is cited[21] as ruling that the prohibition of מושב לצים is limited to activities aimed at ridiculing or otherwise undermining the Jewish faith, such that attending sports activities nowadays is permissible. According to this view, playing with pets would certainly not fall under this prohibition.

It is worth noting that Rav Eliezer Deutsch of Bonyhad, in his *Peri Ha-Sadeh*,[22] rules that visiting a zoo is forbidden, as this constitutes מושב לצים. Clearly, however, common practice does not follow this opinion, and Torah-observant Jews frequently visit zoos. In fact, there are explicit accounts of great Torah sages who went to see animals. The work *Leket Yosher*[23] writes that the *Terumas Ha-Deshen* once took a walk on Shabbos especially to see lions, because he had never before seen a lion and wanted to know what it looked like. And the Chida, in his *Midbar Kedeimos*,[24] describes the fascinating animals he observed when he visited the Tower of London Menagerie. And in his *Ma'agal Tov* (13a), the Chida tells of his visit to a taxidermy exhibit in Holland featuring a vast array of animals and insects.

Kabbalistic Sources

These accounts of sages who intentionally went to observe animals would appear to refute another argument that has been advanced to forbid owning pets — namely, the warnings in Kabbalistic sources about the harmful spiritual effects of seeing non-kosher animals.

For example, Rabbi Tzvi Hirsch Kaidanover, in his *Kav Ha-Yashar*,[25] warns that regularly looking upon non-kosher animals leads a person to look upon inappropriate sights which could arouse temptation and thus lead to sin. Although the *Shulchan Aruch*[26] rules that one who sees an elephant or monkey recites a special *beracha* (...ברוך משנה הבריות), which would certainly imply that *halacha* permits looking upon these animals, Rav Kaidanover insists that this is allowed only דרך ארעי — incidentally — but one should not gaze upon such creatures, as this could yield harmful spiritual effects.

In a somewhat similar vein, the Lubavitcher Rebbe famously warned against exposing children to even pictures of non-kosher animals.[27]

It is questionable, however, whether these esoteric teachings suffice to override the explicit accounts of the *Terumas Ha-Deshen* and the Chida going out of their way

21. *Divrei Chachamim*, Y.D., *Hilchos Avoda Zara*, chapter 5.
22. 3:173.
23. *Melachos Shabbos*, 57.
24. *Ma'areches Beis*, 22.
25. Chapter 2.
26. O.C. 225:8.
27. *Sha'arei Halacha U-Minhag*, p. 223.

to see and marvel at animals. And, the halachic requirement to recite a *beracha* over seeing certain non-kosher animals plainly suggests that there is nothing wrong with beholding such a sight, as the *Kav Ha-Yashar* noted.[28]

Another relevant source is a passage in *Divrei Torah*[29] by Rav Chaim Elazar Spira of Munkatch stating that dogs are associated with the impurity of the evil nation of Amalek, and for this reason, he explained, the corrupt gentiles of his time found companionship and enjoyment mainly in the company of dogs. Rav Spira explained the association between dogs and the impurity of Amalek based on the fact that dogs are עזי נפש[30] — especially brazen. Interestingly, however, the Maharsha[30] expressed a far more favorable attitude towards dogs, asserting that they are called כלב because כולו לב נאמן לאדוניו — a dog's heart is loyal and devoted to its master. And so the view that we must dissociate from dogs due to their inherently evil nature does not appear to be accepted by all.[31]

Some have pointed to the Rama's ruling[32] that after a woman immerses in a *mikveh*, she should ensure that she first encounters a fellow Jew, and not a non-kosher creature or a gentile — perhaps suggesting that one should not own non-kosher animals. However, for one thing, virtually every observant woman today immerses in a *mikveh* with an attendant who ensures to be the first living creature the woman sees upon emerging from the water. And, the fact that women are encouraged to avoid such sights immediately after immersion does not imply that these sights ought to be entirely avoided, but simply reflects a heightened standard that is encouraged as the woman regains her status of purity and prepares to reunite with her husband. The same can be said about the comment of the *Rokei'ach*[33] that the day young schoolchildren begin learning the letters of the Hebrew alphabet, they should be shielded from the sight of

---

28. Rav Eliezer Papo, in *Pele Yoetz* (ערך כלב), admonishes against having dogs, citing the Gemara's aforementioned statement that one who raises dogs is "accursed," though he omits the Gemara's broader discussion and the ruling in the *Shulchan Aruch*, cited earlier.

29. *Mahadura Tinyana*, 45.

30. *Sanhedrin* 97a.

31. We should perhaps add that one of the animals mentioned by the Chida as having been on display in the London Menagerie was a lion that was the product of crossbreeding a cat and a lion. It is difficult to imagine such a creature being any less spiritually harmful than a typical pet dog, and yet the Chida appeared to have no qualms about seeing this animal.

32. Y.D. 198:48.

33. *Hilchos Shavuos*, 296. Incidentally, as the Vilna Gaon references in his *Bei'ur Ha-Gra* notes to the *Shulchan Aruch*, the source of the practice mentioned by the Rama, that a woman ensures not to see a prohibited animal right after immersion, is the *Rokei'ach* (*Hilchos Nidda*, 317).

dogs. This does not necessarily indicate that we should dissociate ourselves from dogs, but rather that certain occasions warrant special spiritual focus and awareness, which includes avoiding the sight of a dog.[34]

Pets in the Midrash and Talmud

Additionally, these mystical sources are offset by numerous Midrashic and Talmudic passages that appear to prove that it is acceptable to own dogs or other non-kosher animals.

One passage in *Bereishis Rabba*[35] tells that God actually gave Kayin a dog for protection after he killed Hevel and was afraid that other people would kill him. Later in *Bereishis Rabba*,[36] the Midrash brings an argument as to whether Yaakov owned 600,000 dogs or twice that amount in order to protect his herds. And *Pesikta De-Rav Kahana*[37] tells the unusual story of a dog that died after drinking poisoned milk, and the people erected a tombstone at the dog's burial site out of respect for the dog.

The Mishna in *Maseches Shabbos* (126b) cites Rabban Shimon ben Gamliel as permitting moving a certain plant (לוף) on Shabbos, despite its being inedible for human beings (such that we would think to regard it as *muktzeh*), because it is used as fodder for ravens. Rashi explains that wealthy people used to own ravens — a non-kosher bird[38] — for luxury. The Gemara (128a) comments that Rabban Shimon ben Gamliel embraced the principle כל ישראל בני מלכים הם — all Jews are "royal" and thus worthy of conducting themselves in regal fashion. As such, he permitted all Jews to move the לוף plant, even though its practical use was limited to the aristocracy. The Gemara clearly works off the assumption that it is acceptable to raise ravens in the home as a sign of luxury, despite their non-kosher status.

---

34. In the first chapter of Rav Yaakov Emden's *Toras Ha-Kanaus*, a work he wrote to condemn the followers of the false messiah Shabtai Tzvi, he relates that when word of Shabtai Tzvi's self-proclaimed messiahship reached the community of Izmir, Turkey, the rabbis who believed his claims instructed the people to clean their homes and rid them of all non-kosher animals, including dogs and cats. They felt that Eliyahu would soon be arriving, and he would not enter homes with non-kosher animals. While this anecdote is certainly a source of great historical intrigue, it hardly provides a compelling basis for forbidding or even discouraging owning dogs. If anything, it demonstrates that it was customary to own pets, and it was only in anticipation of Eliyahu's imminent arrival that the rabbis urged their followers to send their pets away.

35. 22:12.

36. 73:13.

37. 11.

38. *Vayikra* 11:15.

Interestingly enough, the Netziv, in his *Ha'amek Davar* commentary to the Torah,[39] suggests that the raven and dove which Noach sent out from the ark were not the birds which he brought into the ark in fulfillment of God's command to preserve every species, but were rather his pets. Citing the aforementioned discussion in the Gemara, the Netziv notes that noblemen would keep ravens as pets, and thus Noach brought a raven and dove with him onto the ark in addition to the birds he needed to bring for the preservation of their species. (The Netziv answers on this basis the question of how Noach was allowed to send the raven and dove out of the ark before God granted permission to leave the ark. The answer, according to the Netziv, is that Noach sent away his pet birds, and not those which God commanded him to bring onto the ark.)

In his *Herchev Davar*, the Netziv suggests explaining on this basis the story told in *Maseches Bava Basra* (8a) of Rabbi Yonasan ben Amram who came before Rabbi Yehuda Ha-Nasi and asked, "Support me like a dog and a raven." Whereas Rashi understands this request as an allegorical reference to Torah wisdom, the Netziv explains that Rabbi Yonasan asked for a job cleaning Rabbi Yehuda Ha-Nasi's property along with the dog and ravens which Rabbi Yehuda owned to keep the premises clean of rodents and the like. The Netziv explicitly states that one of the greatest and most righteous Sages in Jewish history — Rabbi Yehuda Ha-Nasi — owned a dog.

Another example is Rabbi Yehuda's ruling later in *Maseches Shabbos* (90b) that carrying a non-kosher grasshopper of any size through a public domain on Shabbos constitutes an act of Shabbos desecration "because they are put away for the child to play with." Even if a grasshopper is smaller than the minimum size normally required for carrying to be considered a Torah violation of Shabbos, its value as a toy for a child renders it significant enough to qualify for Shabbos desecration. This clearly indicates that non-kosher creatures were commonly kept as pets.

Further proof may be drawn from the discussion among the *poskim* as to whether a pet should be treated as *muktzeh*, and thus forbidden to be handled on Shabbos. Rav Moshe Feinstein, in one responsum,[40] forbade handling a pet on Shabbos, though there is considerable controversy surrounding his view, with some claiming that if the animal is owned exclusively for playing, then it may be held.[41] This was also the posi-

---

39. *Bereishis* 8:7.

40. O.C. 4:16.

41. See the editors' note to *Iggeros Moshe*, O.C. 5:22:21, and *Pesichos Ha-Iggeros*, p. 314. Below we present the transcription of an interview with Rabbi Eliezer Eisenberg, who noted that his esteemed father-in-law, Rav Reuven Feinstein, cited his father (Rav Moshe) as permitting handling pets on Shabbos, claiming that their status resembles that of a ball which is designated for play, and is thus allowed to be played with on Shabbos according to the Rama's ruling (O.C. 308:45).

   Rav Shlomo Zalman Auerbach's view on this issue is also subject to some controversy.

tion of Rav Binyamin Zilber, in *Az Nidberu*.[42] The *poskim* who addressed this question implicitly accepted the phenomenon of pets, and discussed merely the status of pets vis-à-vis the *muktzeh* prohibition.

The Historical Context of Rav Yaakov Emden's Ruling

As the halachic sources quite clearly suggest that there is no reason to forbid owning dogs (with the exception of Kabbalistic sources, which discourage looking at non-kosher creatures), we might speculate as to what prompted Rav Yaakov Emden to so forcefully and vehemently condemn the practice.

There may be evidence that owning dogs was a characteristic feature of some leading *Maskilim* of the time, against whom Rav Yaakov Emden struggled in championing traditional Jewish values and practice, and from whom he suffered not a small amount of grief. In his autobiography[43] he speaks of a certain secular leader named Aaron Gakish, who had a dog which he named Yaakov Emden — specifically to deride and ridicule the rabbi. Rav Emden returns to this later in book,[44] as well. He also[45] speaks with derision of a certain person who paid an exorbitant sum of money for a poodle. It seems possible that owning dogs in Rav Yaakov Emden's time was specifically associated with gentile conduct, and was characteristic of the lifestyle of the secularized Jews in his society. Indeed, in his condemnation of raising dogs, Rav Emden writes that this constitutes not only מושב לצים, but also מעשה ערלים — the conduct of gentiles. Quite possibly, these designations need to be placed in historical context, and understood on the basis of the cultural norms of the time, when owning dogs was very closely associated with the rejection of Jewish tradition.

Ethical Concerns

It goes without saying that, although there appears to be no basis for forbidding pets, extreme care must be taken — as with all areas of conduct — to ensure that one's pet does not cause any harm or discomfort to neighbors. When the dog is taken out of the home, it must be securely tied to a leash and never allowed to roam free, which could potentially frighten people, particularly children. And, of course, a dog that

---

See *Shemiras Shabbos Ke-Hilchasah*, 27:101; and *Shulchan Shlomo*, 308:74.

42. 8:38.
43. *Megillas Sefer*, chapter 4.
44. Chapter 8.
45. In chapter 15.

barks may never be allowed outside the home in the nighttime hours when it could disturb neighbors who are trying to sleep.[46]

Another concern which is often overlooked, but should be strongly emphasized, emerges from the Gemara's remark in *Maseches Shabbos* (63a), כל המגדל כלב רע בתוך ביתו מונע חסד מתוך ביתו — "Whoever raises an evil dog in his house bars kindness from his house." As Rashi explains, needy individuals seeking assistance will be deterred from coming to the home to ask for the help they need, out of fear of the dog. It appears that even if a person satisfies the halachic requirement to keep the dog securely chained, nevertheless, this is discouraged, because it could deny the family numerous opportunities to assist people in need. Interestingly, the Maharsha's version of the text of this passage omitted the word רע ("evil"), such that the Gemara discourages owning any dog, even a dog that is not hostile, as solicitors might nevertheless be frightened by the dog, not knowing that it is harmless.

Putting the Gemara's exhortation into a broader context, the Torah's ideal is for the home to be an inviting place, where relatives, neighbors, friends, and all who need assistance or just companionship feel comfortable and welcome. While the primary purpose of the home is to serve as a warm, happy place of residence for the family, in addition, *Pirkei Avos*[47] teaches, יהי ביתך פתוח לרווחה ויהיו עניים בני ביתך — "Your home shall be open wide, and the poor shall be members of your household." We are to encourage other people to visit our home and seek our assistance.

Those who wish to have a pet must consider very carefully whether their pet helps to realize the ideal of יהי ביתך פתוח לרווחה, or undermines it. A dog that is loud and aggressive could have the unintended effect of discouraging visitors, in which case owning such an animal would certainly be inconsonant with the spirit of Torah Judaism.[48]

---

46. See *Pischei Choshen, Nezikin*, 5:43:98.

47. 1:5.

48. It must also be noted that owning pets gives rise to numerous halachic questions of which the owner must be aware. These include:
    - The requirement to feed one's animal before eating;
    - The permissibility of feeding one's animal non-kosher food, milk with meat, or *chametz* during Pesach;
    - Walking a dog in an area without an *eiruv*;
    - Feeding animals on Shabbos and Yom Tov;
    - Reciting *berachos, davening,* or learning Torah near an animal's bodily waste;
    - Castrating or neutering animals.

Rabbi Eliezer Eisenberg

Interviewed on *Headlines with Dovid Lichtenstein*, 17 Tammuz, 5779 (July 20, 2019)

The idea that people aren't afraid of chained dogs might not be true in all circumstances, such as in places where they're not used to dogs. The *halachos* are place- and time-sensitive (especially given that the Rambam omitted the words כלב רע and writes simply, אסור לגדל כלב). This is besides the *hashkafic* aspect, which isn't supported in the *Shulchan Aruch*, but based more on Kabbalah, that a pregnant woman shouldn't look at a non-kosher animal, as this could be spiritually damaging to the child, or that really any person shouldn't. There are many who abide by this concept and don't take their children to zoos. Certainly, they won't make an animal part of the family.

I have a friend whose grandmother grew up in Russia, and she was petrified of dogs. She grew up in an environment where the non-Jews' sport was to have their dogs chase the Jews and bite them. Even though that might have been just in that culture, and also with big dogs, nevertheless, if a barking dog frightens somebody, then this is what they call a כלב רע. This is considered הזיקן מצוי [likely to cause harm] because the dog frightens people.

The Gemara in *Bava Basra* (7b) tells the story of a certain righteous individual whom Eliyahu Ha-Navi used to visit, until he made a doorway in front of his house, whereupon Eliyahu stopped visiting. The reason Eliyahu stopped visiting at that point was because the doorway prevented the pious man from hearing poor people knocking on the door to ask for help. The same is true of owning a dog. When you come to a house and hear a dog barking, it's not welcoming. The purpose of a dog is to bark at strangers. It causes people to move back. You hesitate to approach the house. The dog might also bite strangers. It diminishes from the עדינות [warm, welcoming atmosphere] of a Jewish family.

A famous story is told of a person who made a "bark mitzvah" for his dog. He made an enormously extravagant celebration for his Kaddishel, his dog. He and his dog were inseparable. It was his faithful companion, so he threw a party for his dog.

Unfortunately, many people transfer the love that a person naturally should have for children or for other people, to dogs. They do so because dogs don't compete with them, they're not threatening. It's not a good sign. True, there are people who love human beings and animals, but for some people, the love of animals is a symptom of a lack of sympathy for fellow humans.

Additionally, we should be busy learning Torah and doing *chesed*, not playing catch with dogs. *Klal Yisrael* has the Torah, and other people have dogs. Dogs don't help one's *ruchniyus* [spirituality].

Rabbi Chaim Jachter

Interviewed on *Headlines with Dovid Lichtenstein*, 17 Tammuz, 5779 (July 20, 2019)

Different opinions exist as to whether it is forbidden to own a dog. According to the Rambam, it's categorically forbidden. According to the other *Rishonim*, only owning a כלב רע is forbidden, and there is a discussion how to define כלב רע, whether this refers even to a dog with an annoying bark, or only to a dog that bites. I can understand why the *rabbanim* say it's forbidden, but on the other hand, many very religious Jews own pets. Sometimes it's important for therapeutic reasons, or for people who are older and lonely, and need support service animals. It really depends on the situation. I think the *rabbanim* are coming from places where people are not used to dogs and they get scared from their bark.

Hashkafically, it could be argued that it's a waste of time and resources. Hashem put us in the world to accomplish positive things — to grow spiritually in Torah and *yiras Shamayim*, and to contribute to *Am Yisrael*. How does owning a pet further any of these noble goals? On the other hand, it teaches children responsibility. For many families, it can be therapeutic, and for older people, it can be good for companionship. So it depends — for some families it doesn't work, for other families it does.

A family that is going to get a pet should first learn the *halachos* to stay on the right side of the *Shulchan Aruch*.

Rabbi Dr. Natan Slifkin

Interviewed on *Headlines with Dovid Lichtenstein*, 17 Tammuz, 5779 (July 20, 2019)

In general, pet keeping for both Jews and non-Jews is a modern phenomenon. Long ago, people didn't have the resources to have pets as a leisure item. Having pets was a thing of royalty. Regular people couldn't afford them. Dogs were work dogs. More recently, before the Holocaust, dogs were used by non-Jews against Jews. That's why culturally, you'll find in the Jewish community a very negative attitude toward dogs.

In *Chazal*, we find many negative references to dogs. But we also find some positive references. The question is how you balance them out halachically. There's been much halachic discussion about it over the centuries.

The fear that Jews have of dogs stems from the lack of familiarity, as dogs were used against Jews. It became something foreign and that causes fear. But there has been a change. In Israel, in *dati leumi* communities, it's very common. Even in Anglo yeshivish crowds, it's not uncommon to have dogs. You can see people with black hats and dogs. Eventually, that will seep into the Israeli *chareidi* world.

The *kol koreh* [placard] in Elad is interesting. There are a lot of places where people have dogs and such a *kol koreh* never came out. If you're not familiar with them, they can be very frightening. It's possible that in Elad they have a problem with stray dogs that are scary. It's possible the *kol koreh* is a social policy.

The *Nevi'im* and *Chazal* were much more in touch with nature and animals. They drew upon the animal kingdom to teach us lessons. We're very removed from that. We live in a world of cars and computers and are very removed from animals. It's a valuable thing to be more connected to the animal kingdom and to draw from the lessons that the *Nevi'im* and *Chazal* said they teach us.

Physical discipline of children: When does punishment become abuse?

July 17, 2018
By Justin Ong

SINGAPORE: When her two sons - aged four and six - misbehave, Therese Tay either smacks them on the bum or palm, or chooses to send them to a "naughty corner" to reflect on themselves.

But just like all but one out of 10 parents interviewed by Channel NewsAsia, the 38-year-old is unaware of the point where physical discipline becomes illegal and potentially a criminal act.

"Lawfully and technically, no," said Ms Tay. "But personally, I think it would be where it is repeated, causes or is likely to cause grave injury, and is not really done to teach the child anything but rather to relieve anger or gain a feeling of power."

Any act that causes injury to a child - including deliberately causing bruises, cuts and others by actions such as beating, shaking and "excessive discipline" - constitutes physical abuse, according to the Ministry of Social and Family Development (MSF).

And under the Children and Young Persons Act, physical abuse - and the causing of "unnecessary" physical pain, suffering or injury - amounts to ill-treatment. This was the charge levelled at a 35-year-old man for beating his son, nine, last year.

The father had held the boy upside down by one leg, hit him with a hanger and kicked him among other acts. A neighbour called the police when he heard a child crying out, thinking it was child abuse.

Some lawyers, however, acknowledged the legislation as "quite broad" and potentially confusing for the average parent.

"There is no clear demarcation when punishment crosses the line," said Shashi Nathan, the regional head of dispute resolution and partner at law firm Withers KhattarWong. "What is looked at is whether the punishment is appropriate and reasonable. Obviously when real and long-term harm and physical injury is caused, then the line is clearly crossed."

Lin Xiaoling, the deputy director of advocacy and public education at the Singapore Children's Society, said: "There is often a very thin line between discipline and child abuse.

"Rather than debate on where to fix the line before punishment becomes illegal, our focus can instead be on helping families become safer and stronger ... The simple rule to remember is: 'Every child has the right to feel safe all the time.'"

"A SOFTER APPROACH" THESE DAYS?

When he first heard of the case of the father imprisoned for ill-treating his son, veteran family lawyer Rajan Chettiar said he was "a little taken aback".

"Such behaviour was very common during the days when I was a kid - which is about 40 years ago," he said. "Now, this is seen as child abuse and illegal."

All the parents Channel NewsAsia spoke to were physically punished by their own parents too - whether by hand, cane, ruler or belt - and one said: "In those days, it was quite normal for my sister and I to be beaten into submission."

"My siblings and I grew up perfectly fine," said Michelle Ang, editor of The New Age Parents online magazine and community. "Now we are older, we understand it was my mother's way of teaching us right from wrong. We don't blame her for the 'hurt' she inflicted, because we know it comes from good intentions.

"Of course, not everyone who grew up being caned by their parents might feel the same way as me and my siblings, because we all receive and internalise these experiences differently."

Yet what was once a strictly private family affair can easily spill into the open today, when filmed and uploaded to social media.

Last month, a child was videoed kneeling and being slapped in a car park - prompting outrage online as well as MSF and police investigations. And earlier this year, a Facebook clip of a man caning and kicking a boy also sparked polarising debate over whether it was plain abuse.

"I do see today's parents taking a softer approach when it comes to disciplining children," said Ms Ang. "This could be why, when such cases of corporal punishments get leaked on social media, they generate a stronger reaction from the public."

Asked for their thoughts on potentially being filmed punishing their children, one parent said: "If this saves a kid from abusive parents, then it's not a bad thing at all. And if you're not unreasonable, then you should have nothing to fear."

But another slammed the practice, saying there are "too many keyboard warriors sharing incidents where there is usually more than meets the eye".

Ms Tay commented: "People need to do less of the showing - on social media - and more of the doing, for example approaching the family and asking if they can help (or) asking what's wrong."

CROSSING THE LINE

Parents also revealed their internal safeguards for ensuring they do not cross the line while punishing their kids, with some choosing to restrict the volume or intensity of caning while others make it a point to remind themselves of the purpose - to discipline rather than express anger.

"I try to keep my emotions in check and be rational," said a mother of two daughters. "And verbal warnings are given before any caning, to make sure the child understands the next course of action will be the cane if she doesn't behave."

Said Ms Lin of the Children's Society: "Many parents' intention may be to discipline their child, but asserting power using brute force means one can easily cross the line, simply because the child is much smaller and weaker than the adult.

"There are alternatives to physical punishment when it comes to discipline," she added. "We urge parents to explore and try other methods and logical consequences, including withdrawal of privilege, reasoning and explaining."

Speaking in her personal capacity, Ms Ang said: "I don't think corporal punishment is totally wrong or should be banished or totally frowned upon. How a parent chooses to discipline their child is their choice – and not for me to judge or intervene, unless it crosses the line of unlawful territory."

Should a member of the public be worried about a child's safety, there is a range of reporting options (see below) - but MSF noted that in the event a life is in danger, people should immediately call the police.

"The urgent question to ask ourselves is: 'Could this child be in danger, whether now or later?'" Ms Lin advised. "And the next is: 'Should I be worried that the child could possibly be harmed, in any way?'

"Injuries could both be seen and unseen. So if we are unsure, it is always safer to tell or ask someone who can help."

She said: "Informing the authorities of a case does not mean an immediate report. It can be to voice out your concern and seek advice on what to do next … Don't wait until it becomes too late.

"Families, neighbours, schools, agencies, the public. We all make up the village that keeps our children safe."

The Abusive Parent in Halacha

Harsh parenting is not just a bad idea, but a clear halachic violation.

The Gemara in *Maseches Mo'ed Katan* (17a) tells that Rabbi Yehuda Ha-Na-si's housekeeper witnessed a man striking his grown child, and she announced that the man must be placed in excommunication for violating the Torah prohibition of לפני עור לא תתן מכשול ("Do not place a stumbling block before a blind man"),[1] which forbids causing people to sin. As Rashi explains, an older child who is provoked by his father might likely respond violently, transgressing the prohibition against striking a parent.[2] Accordingly, the Rambam[3] rules that one who strikes a grown child deserves excommunication.

Moreover, *Maseches Semachos* (2) tells two stories of children whose fathers threatened to punish them for misconduct — one ran away from school, and the other broke a dish — and the children were so frightened that they committed suicide. In both instances, it was ruled that the case constituted one of מאבד עצמו שלא לדעת — involuntary suicide, such that the procedures for honoring the dead were to be followed as usual.[4]

The Rambam[5] writes that notwithstanding the far-reaching scope of the Torah obligation to respect parents, אסור לאדם להכביד עולו על בניו ולדקדק בכבודו עמהם — "It is forbidden for a person to place a heavy yoke upon his children, or to be strict with them about his honor." Instead, the Rambam writes, ימחול ויתעלם — a parent should be forgiving and overlook the child's disrespect. The Rambam's comments are cited by the *Shulchan Aruch*.[6]

---

1. *Vayikra* 19:14.
2. ומכה אביו ואמו מות יומת (*Shemos* 21:15).
3. *Hilchos Mamrim* 6:9.
4. In principle, those who voluntarily commit suicide are not eulogized and mourned, though in practice, nowadays, it is assumed that anyone who commits suicide suffers from mental illness, such that the suicide may be classified, in some sense, as involuntary.
5. *Hilchos Mamrim* 6:8.
6. Y.D. 240:19.

287

הקרוב קרוב קודם

Rav Pinchas Eliyahu of Vilna, in his *Sefer Ha-Bris*,[7] issues a scathing condemnation of parents who show kindness and sensitivity to people outside the family, but mistreat their children:

> יש אנשים ששומרים עצמם מלהרע לשום אדם ואוהבים את הבריות כולם אבל
> שונאים את בניהם ומכוונים לצער אותם ולהקניטם, ואומרים אין בזה עוון כי
> יאמרו בלבותם הבנים בני והבנות בנותי וכבר אני יוצא ידי חובת אהבת הבריות
> כולם כי אין אני מצער לשום אדם אלא נתח מנתחי אשר נתנם הבורא יתברך בידי
> והכריחם לסור למשמעתי, והמה אסורים וקשורים על פי התורה תחת כפות רגלי
> וכל אשר יחפוץ לבבי הרשות נתונה מאל עליון בידי לעשות עמהם כטוב בעיני...
> ואני מכווין עם זה לייסרם ולהוכיחם בדרכי אלוקים חיים לפי מחשבתי, ובאמת
> דבריו לא בהשכל ולא על פי התורה, שלמה יגרעו הבנים מלהיות בכלל לא תשנא
> את אחיך ובכלל ואהבת לרעך כמוך. ואמנם כמו שבעניין ההטבה והצדקה כל
> הקרוב קרוב קודם, כך בעניין השנאה והרעות יש יותר עונש על המצער את קרובו
> מאדם אחר, והמצער את בניו על חנם עתיד ליתן את הדין ביותר...

There are people who guard themselves from mistreating anybody and love all people, but they despise their children and intentionally cause them distress and mock them. They say this is not a sin, because they tell themselves, "These boys are my sons, and these girls are my daughters, and I already fulfill the obligation to love all people, because I do not cause harm to anybody except my own kin whom the Creator, may He be blessed, entrusted to me and required to obey me, and so according to the Torah, they are bound and chained under my feet, and I have been authorized by the Supreme God to deal with them however I see fit... and my intention is to punish them and reprimand them to follow the ways of the living God as I see it." But in truth, his words are not wise and not in accordance with the Torah. For why should the children not be worthy of inclusion in [the Torah prohibition of] "Do not despise your brother"[8] or [the command of] "You shall love your fellow as yourself"?[9] And, in fact, just as with regard to benefitting and giving charity, those who are closest take precedence, the same is true with regard to hatred and evildoing — there is greater punishment for one who causes pain to his relative than to somebody else. And one who baselessly causes his children pain will be especially called to account in the future...

---

7.   Vol. 2, 13:16.

8.   לא תשנא את אחיך, *Vayikra* 19:17.

9.   ואהבת לרעך כמוך, *Vayikra* 19:18.

Indeed, Rav Chaim Vital is famously cited as teaching, in the name of his mentor, the Arizal, that no matter how much kindness one performs, he forfeits all the merit of his kindness if he does not act kindly to his wife and children.

Rav Pinchas Eliyahu proceeds to cite a fascinating remark of the *Sefer Chassidim* (565) in his discussion of the Torah's command, איש אמו ואביו תיראו ("Each of you shall fear his father and mother").[10] The *Sefer Chassidim* asserts that the Torah uses here the plural form of תיראו to include the parents in this command — meaning, just as the child is required to treat them reverently, they are commanded שלא יכעיסו את הבן כל-כך עד שלא יוכל להתאפק להמרוד וימרוד בהם — not to anger the child to the point where he cannot be reasonably expected to restrain himself and avoid rebelling. Later (567), as Rav Pinchas Eliyahu notes, the *Sefer Chassidim* urges parents to follow the example set by God Himself, who did not overburden His children — the Jewish Nation — in His expectations of us. For instance, He commanded us to offer easily accessible domesticated animals as sacrifices, rather than requiring us to hunt wild beasts. By the same token, the *Sefer Chassidim* instructs, לא יצווה האב את בנו דברים קשים וכבדים עליו לעשות — one should not impose difficult demands upon his children, as this will, almost inevitably, result in disrespect and disobedience.

The Gemara already warns in *Maseches Gittin* (6b), לעולם אל יטיל אדם אימה יתירה בתוך ביתו — one should not impose "excessive fear" upon his family members, adding that doing so can result in the most grievous violations. As an example of the dangers of excessively harsh treatment of one's family members, the Gemara points to the tragic story of the פילגש בגבעה (*Shoftim* 19), the woman whose husband became angry and threw her out of the home, after which he went to bring her back. Along the trip home, the couple stayed overnight in a certain town, and the townspeople violently raped the wife, triggering a bloody civil war in which tens of thousands of people perished. This dreadful catastrophe began with a husband growing angry at his wife — thus showing the devastating effects of anger and hostility in the home. The point being made is that an overly harsh, strict environment in the home causes considerable long-term damage and harm.[11]

A grandson of the *Chasam Sofer*[12] relates that when the *Chasam Sofer* was ten years

---

10. *Vayikra* 19:3.

11. Rav Yechiel Michel Lefkowitz, in one of his published letters (*Darchei Chayim*, vol. 1, p. 80), addressed the case of a boy who was especially disrespectful to his father. He wrote that while there is no justification for the child's conduct, nevertheless, it seems clear that the boy had legitimate complaints against the father. After citing the Rambam's ruling forbidding imposing excessive demands upon one's children, Rav Lefkowitz urged the father to initiate a process of reconciliation, which would likely have a positive impact upon the young man's behavior.

12. Rav Shlomo Sofer, in his *Chut Ha-Meshulash* (a collection of biographical sketches of

old, he was delivering a *shiur* one Shabbos and mentioned a question posed by his great-grandfather, the Maharshashach (Rav Shmuel Schotten). He then said that with all due respect, the question was mistaken, because it can easily be answered. The *Chasam Sofer's* father was incensed over what he regarded as an expression of disrespect to the great-grandfather, and in full view of the audience, he smacked his son on the face. The *Chasam Sofer* was terribly ashamed, and he ran away and hid. Rav Nasan Adler, under whom the *Chasam Sofer* was learning at the time, heard about the incident, and instructed the *Chasam Sofer* not to speak with his father again. He was afraid that his father's strict approach would discourage the *Chasam Sofer* and cause him to lose interest in Torah learning. Rav Nasan Adler took the *Chasam Sofer* as his own son, caring for him and teaching him. He understood that dealing harshly with youngsters can easily backfire and discourage them from Torah learning and observance.

Protecting Oneself from an Abusive Parent

If a parent does treat his child abusively, does this affect the child's obligation of כיבוד אב ואם — to respect parents? As we know, the Torah commands children both to show their parents respect — כבד את אביך ואת אמך (*Shemos* 20:12, *Devarim* 5:16), and to treat them with reverence — איש אמו ואביו תיראו (*Vayikra* 19:3). Do these obligations apply when the parent mistreats the child?

This question should be addressed on two levels. First, does the obligation of כיבוד אב ואם require the child to passively endure abusive treatment, or is he allowed to escape the abuse, even if this entails disrespecting the parent, such as by severing his ties with him or her? The second question arises after the child no longer suffers abuse — either because he has moved in with a different family, he is grown and lives on his own, or the parent discontinued the abusive treatment. Must he respect the parent who abused him, or does the painful experiences of the past absolve him forever more of the obligation of כיבוד אב ואם?

Let us begin with the first question — whether כיבוד אב ואם requires a child to accept the abusive treatment without protest and without trying to avoid it.

At first glance, the answer to this question appears explicitly in the Gemara, in one of the famous stories told in *Maseches Kiddushin* (31a) of Dama ben Nesina, a gentile who lived in Ashkelon whom the Sages extolled for his boundless respect for his parents. On one occasion, the Gemara tells, he was wearing special gold clothing and sitting with the Roman noblemen, when his mother suddenly came and embarrassed him. She tore his robe off his body, smacked him on the head, and spat on him. Dama did not respond, committed to show his mother respect despite the abuse he had just suffered at her hands.

Rabbi Akiva Eiger, the *Chasam Sofer*, and the *Kesav Sofer*).

Seemingly, this story, which the Gemara tells as part of its praise for Dama's extraordinary devotion to his parents, proves that a child must tolerate a parent's abusive behavior, due to the obligation of כיבוד אב ואם. Indeed, the *Shulchan Aruch*[13] rules on the basis of this account that if one's parent acts this way towards him, "he should remain silent and fear from the King of kings who commanded him such."

Tosfos, however, commenting on this story, cite a Midrashic source which tells that Dama's mother suffered from mental illness (היתה מטורפת מדעתה).[14] The clear implication is that Dama did not respond only because his mother was mentally unstable and thus could not be held responsible for her abhorrent conduct, but otherwise, a child is not expected to tolerate a parent's abuse. Accordingly, the Maharshal writes in *Yam Shel Shlomo*[15] that ordinarily, unless the parent suffers mental illness, a child may stop the parent from inflicting financial or physical harm, and after the fact, the child may bring a lawsuit against the parent to claim compensation. The Maharshal proceeds to note that, as mentioned, the *Tur* and *Shulchan Aruch* disagree, stating plainly that one may not humiliate a parent who acts this way, without limiting this ruling to the particular circumstance of a psychiatrically impaired parent. However, the Maharshal asserts that this ruling applies only after the fact, once the parent has perpetrated the abusive act. At that point, the child may not humiliate the parent (though, if the parent caused financial harm, the child can claim the damages in *beis din*). But if the child is able to avoid the parent's abuse, he is certainly entitled to do so, and is not required to subject himself to the parent's abusive treatment.

כבוד הבריות

A similar conclusion seems to emerge from the comments of the *Shita Mekubetzes*,[16] which, citing *Tosfos*, presents three reasons why one is not required to endure humiliation for the sake of the *mitzva* of honoring parents. The first is based on the rule of זקן

---

13. Y.D. 240:3.

14. Interestingly, Rav Moshe Feinstein (*Dibros Moshe, Kiddushin* 50:17; *Iggeros Moshe*, Y.D. 5:26:2) speculates that Dama's father may have likewise suffered from mental illness. A more famous story of Dama ben Nesina is told about the time he turned down an exceptionally lucrative offer because the key to the safe containing the merchandise was hidden under his father's pillow, and his father was sleeping at the time. Rav Moshe notes that any normal father would happily be awakened by his son if an enormous profit was at stake. If Dama is applauded for sacrificing this lucrative opportunity to avoid waking his father, Rav Moshe suggests, we might assume that the father was mentally ill and would thus not have received any satisfaction from his son's earning a large fortune.

15. *Kiddushin* 1:64.

16. *Bava Metzia* 32a.

ואינו לפי כבודו, which exempts one from the obligation of השבת אבידה (returning a lost object) if returning the object would compromise כבוד הבריות — a person's dignity — by causing him embarrassment. The classic example is a distinguished rabbi who sees somebody's chicken, and in order to return the chicken to its owner, he would have to degrade himself by walking in public carrying the bird. The Gemara in *Maseches Berachos* (19b) derives this exemption from a textual inference, and suggests the possibility of viewing it as a precedent establishing a blanket exemption from all Biblical commands when one's personal dignity is at stake. This theory is dismissed, but only because איסורא מממונא לא ילפינן — we cannot extrapolate from the realm of civil law to ritual law. The Gemara's implication is that indeed, when it comes to interpersonal conduct, Torah obligations are waived in situations where they would cause embarrassment. Quite possibly, the *Shita Mekubetzes* writes, the obligation of honoring parents falls under the category of civil law, and is thus suspended for the sake of preserving one's dignity.

Secondly, the Gemara in *Maseches Yevamos* (6a) establishes that one is not obligated to obey his parent's wish that involves transgressing the Torah, and it gives the example of a parent who instructs his child not to return a lost object to its owner as the Torah requires. In such a case, the child must ignore his parent's command and return the lost object. The *Shita Mekubetzes* reasons that if the *mitzva* of returning lost objects overrides the *mitzva* of honoring parents, and the concern for כבוד הבריות overrides the *mitzva* of returning lost objects (as discussed above), then *a fortiori*, the concern for כבוד הבריות overrides the *mitzva* of honoring parents.

Finally, the *Shita Mekubetzes* notes, this conclusion flows directly from the fact that the obligation to honor parents does not override Torah law. The Gemara[17] explains this provision by noting, כולכם חייבים בכבודי — meaning, although a child must respect his parents, the parents themselves must respect the Almighty, and thus respect for God supersedes respect for one's parents. Therefore, as the Torah requires maintaining people's dignity and forbids causing people embarrassment, a child has no obligation to allow a parent to violate Torah law by embarrassing the child.

Rav Yitzchak Zilberstein[18] applied the *Shita Mekubetzes*'s ruling to the case of a man who would always bring his elderly father to the synagogue for prayers, but the father then became mentally ill and began shouting at the son in public. Rav Zilberstein determined that in light of the *Shita Mekubetzes*'s discussion, the son was exempt from escorting his father to the synagogue, which would expose him to embarrassment.[19]

---

17. Ibid.
18. *Chashukei Chemed*, Yevamos 5b.
19. Rav Zilberstein noted, however, that the third consideration presented by the *Shita Mekubetzes* did not apply in this case, as the elderly father had the status of a שוטה (mentally disturbed individual) and was thus not held accountable for his behavior. As such, embarrassing his son did not, technically, constitute a prohibited act.

Certainly, then, a child has no obligation to endure a parent's abusive treatment which causes him shame and humiliation. A child of abusive parents is fully entitled, expected and encouraged to do anything necessary to protect himself from their abusive treatment, even if this means cutting ties with them.

לא חייב להקריב את חייו

Another relevant source is the Rambam's explicit ruling in *Hilchos Ishus*[20] that a spouse has the right to bar his or her in-laws from the home if they cause him or her distress. The Rambam explains, אין כופין את האדם שיכנסו אחרים ברשותו — a person cannot be forced to allow people into his property without his consent. Quite obviously, barring a parent from one's home infringes upon their honor — but this is nevertheless allowed if the parent's presence brings displeasure to one's spouse, thus disrupting marital harmony. Accordingly, Rav Moshe Shapiro[21] writes that if one's mother meddles in his and his wife's personal affairs, he must prevent her from intervening. Rav Shapiro explains:

> פשוט לגמרי שאין כאן שום עניין של כיבוד אם. הוא לא חייב להקריב את חייו
> בשביל כבודה.

> It is plainly obvious that there is no issue of honoring one's mother. He is not required to sacrifice his life for her honor.

The obligation to respect one's parents does not extend so far as to require a child to "sacrifice his life," to make himself miserable, such as by compromising marital harmony, for the sake of his parents. Undoubtedly, then, a child bears no obligation to subject himself to a parent's abusive treatment, and is perfectly entitled to do anything necessary to protect himself from the abuse, even if this means severing ties with the parent.

---

20. 13:14.

21. *Binas Ha-Middos*, p. 86.

The extent of one's responsibility to respect a mentally ill parent is subject to a dispute among the *Rishonim*. The Rambam (*Hilchos Mamrim* 6:9) writes that one should do what he can to help the parent, but if the parent's mental condition becomes so severe that he simply cannot care for the parent anymore, then he may leave the parent and put the parent under somebody else's care. The source of this ruling, as noted by the Ran (to *Kiddushin* 31b) and *Beis Yosef* (Y.D. 240), is the story told in the Gemara of Rav Assi, who tended to his mentally ill mother until he felt no longer capable of handling the challenge, whereupon he left her. The Ra'avad disputes the Rambam's position, but the Rambam's view is accepted by the *Shulchan Aruch* (Y.D. 240:10).

Refusing a Parent's Demands

One form of abusive parenting is the imposition of oppressive demands upon the child purely for the sake of upsetting the child, without yielding any benefit for the parent. Must a child obey a parent's requests that have no benefit for the parent, other than the satisfaction of his authority being respected?

The Gemara in *Maseches Kiddushin* (31b) defines the obligation to respect parents as requiring a child to care for a parent's physical needs, such as feeding and dressing the parent, when such assistance is needed. The Rashba, commenting to *Maseches Yevamos* (6a), infers from this definition that a child has no obligation to obey a parent's wishes that do not involve the parent's own wellbeing:

אמר לו לעשות דבר שאין לו בה הנאה של כלום, אין זה כבוד שנצטווה עליה.

If he told him to do something from which he derives no benefit at all —
this is not the "respect" regarding which he was commanded.

Likewise, the Maharik, in a famous responsum[22] cited approvingly by the Rama,[23] rules that one may marry the person he wishes to marry even against his parent's protests. The Maharik gives several reasons for this ruling, the second of which is that במילתא דלא שייך בגוויה...פשיטא דאין כח לאב למחות ביד בנו — "regarding that which is not relevant to him...the father clearly has no authority to object to his son." According to the Maharik, one is obligated to help the parent with the parent's own needs, but is not obligated to obey a parent's wishes which do not directly involve the parent. The Maharik emphasizes that wishes which do not involve the parent fall neither under the obligation of כיבוד אב ואם, nor under the obligation of מורא אב — showing reverence to one's parent.

Rav Pinchas Horowitz, in his *Ha-Makneh* commentary to *Maseches Kiddushin*,[24] advances a different view, claiming that disobeying any wish by a parent, even one which yields no benefit to the parent, violates the command of מורא. The Gemara there lists the various requirements included under this command, one of which is לא סותר את דבריו — not to dispute a parent's words. The *Makneh* asserts that disobeying a parent's wish, regardless of whether the wish has to do with the parent's personal needs, amounts to disputing a parent's words, and is thus forbidden. As for the Rama's ruling allowing one to marry the woman of his choice against his parent's wishes, the *Makneh* points to this ruling as the exception that proves the rule, demonstrating that regarding all other matters, including those which do not involve the parent's own needs, a child must obey the parent.[25]

------

22. 166:3.

23. Y.D. 240:25.

24. 31b.

25. The *Makneh* proves his position from the Gemara's comment earlier (30b) regarding the

However, Rav Yosef Shalom Elyashiv[26] asserts that even according to the *Makneh*, the child is not required to obey such a wish if doing so causes him harm. After all, Rav Elyashiv explains, if the request has nothing at all to do with the parent's personal interests, then the requirement to obey stems solely from the fact that the disobedience itself expresses disrespect. But if it is clear that the child disobeys not out of disrespect, but rather to avoid the harm he would suffer by fulfilling the wish, then his disobedience does not amount to disrespect for the parent. We might reasonably assume, then, that if the parent imposes unreasonable demands upon a child, he is permitted to disobey to save himself the extreme inconvenience or psychological damage that this kind of subservience could potentially cause.

Moreover, Rav Yisrael Yaakov Fisher, in *Even Yisrael*,[27] writes that the *Makneh* forbids expressly refusing the parent's request from which the parent receives no benefit, but does not require the child to obey in such a case. According to Rav Fisher's understanding of the *Makneh*, even the *Makneh* permits the child to ignore a parent's wish in such a case, and forbids only explicitly opposing the parent.

Thus, certainly according to the Maharik, and quite likely even according to the *Makneh*, a child whose parent imposes unreasonable demands that do not benefit the parent is permitted to disobey.

Respecting a Formerly Abusive Parent

Let us now turn our attention to the second question — whether a history of abusive treatment affects a child's obligation of כיבוד ואם in the present, when he no longer suffers abuse.

The Rambam writes explicitly in *Hilchos Mamrim*[28] that the obligation of honoring

---

command of איש אמו ואביו תיראו. Although this *mitzva* applies to both men and women, the Torah directs the command specifically to men (איש), because, the Gemara explains, the woman is not always available to fulfill her parents' wishes, due to her responsibilities to her husband. The *Makneh* finds it significant that this point is expressed specifically in regard to מורא, which is fulfilled not through active favors to one's parent (as the obligation of כבוד is), but rather by refraining from sitting in one's parent's seat and other forms of disrespect — requirements which are hardly incompatible with a wife's responsibilities to her husband. Apparently, the *Makneh* contends, even the command of מורא includes proactive measures — which the *Makneh* identifies as the obligation to obey a parent's wishes that do not fall under the rubric of כבוד, namely, wishes that do not benefit the parent.

26.   *Kovetz Teshuvos, 1:12.*

27.   Vol. 9, p. 147.

28.   6:11.

parents applies even if one's parent is a habitual sinner: אפילו היה אביו רשע ובעל עבירות מכבדו ומתיירא ממנו — "Even if his father was evil and a sinner, he must respect him and have reverence for him."[29] The *Tur*,[30] however, disagrees, and rules that a child must respect a sinful father only after the father repents, drawing proof from the Gemara's discussion in *Maseches Bava Kama* (94b) regarding a thief who dies before returning the stolen goods. The Gemara establishes that if the thief repented before his death, then the children must return the stolen item to its owner, out of respect for their deceased father. But if the father never repented before his death, there is no obligation to respect him — proving that the obligation of respecting parents does not apply if the parent is an evildoer.

Several different approaches have been offered to defend the Rambam's ruling. Rav Yosef Karo, in his *Kessef Mishneh*, asserts based on the Gemara's discussion of this topic in *Maseches Bava Metzia* (62a) that the case being addressed involves not stolen goods, but goods taken as forbidden interest on a loan. *Halacha* requires the lender to return interest taken in violation of Torah, but it does not require the inheritors to return forbidden interest received by the deceased before his death. Therefore, the children in this case are not strictly required to return this object to the borrower, once they had received it as part of their father's estate. This is required as a special measure of respect for their father, if he had repented. If he had not repented, then this special measure would not be required, but the children would still be obligated to show basic respect to their father, despite his sinfulness.

Rav Avraham de Boton, in his *Lechem Mishneh* commentary, suggests a distinction between respecting a parent during the parent's lifetime, and respect after the parent's passing. The Rambam requires respecting a sinful parent when the parent is alive, whereas the Gemara speaks of the respect owed to a parent who is no longer alive — but not if the parent was an evildoer. This distinction was made also by the Chida, in his *Pesach Einayim*,[31] in reference to the *Zohar*'s stern condemnation of Rachel for causing anguish to her wicked father, Lavan, by stealing his statues,[32] attributing her premature death to the disrespect she showed to her wicked father. The Chida notes the seeming contradiction between the *Zohar*'s clear implication that one must respect a sinful parent, and the Mishna's description of how King Chizkiyahu publicly dishonored his evil father, Achaz, after his passing, with the rabbis' approval.[33] These sources are easily

---

29. The *Bach* (Y.D. 240:13) asserts that even according to the Rambam, the Torah obligation to respect parents does not apply in such a case, and the requirement to respect a sinful parent applies only by force of rabbinic enactment. This position was taken also by Rav Yehonasan Eibushitz, cited below.

30. Y.D. 240.

31. *Bava Kama.*

32. *Bereishis* 31:19.

33. *Pesachim* 56a.

reconciled by distinguishing between a living sinner, whose children must respect him despite his iniquitous conduct, and a deceased sinner, who no longer deserves respect from his children. Rachel was punished because she disrespected his father during his lifetime, whereas Chizkiyahu's dishonoring his wicked deceased father was acceptable.[34]

Another distinction is suggested by Rav Yehonasan Eibushitz, in his *Ya'aros Devash*,[35] applying the concept of מראית העין — giving the appearance of violating the Torah. Rav Eibushitz postulates that the Rambam requires honoring a sinful father only because otherwise, people who are unaware of the father's improper conduct will presume that the child is neglecting the vitally important *mitzva* of respecting parents. Fundamentally, no respect is owed to a sinful parent, before or after his death, but in practice, this is necessary to avoid giving the mistaken impression of violating this command. This explains why Chizkiyahu was permitted to publicly dishonor his father, who was a king known throughout the country for his cruelty and idol-worship. (This might also refute the proof against the Rambam's ruling from the Gemara's discussion of the deceased thief, as the Gemara might refer to a case where the victims know the thief's identity, and are thus well aware of his criminal behavior, such that respect is not required unless the father repented.)

Another possibility, proposed by the *Aruch Ha-Shulchan*,[36] is to distinguish between actual disrespect, and proactive measures to show respect. The Rambam perhaps requires one to avoid denigrating and humiliating his wicked parent, but concedes that one is not required to show honor to such a parent. And thus the Gemara does not require children to go out of their way to return goods stolen by their deceased father unless he had repented. However, the *Aruch Ha-Shulchan* concedes that the Rambam's formulation implies that all requirements of the כיבוד אב ואם obligation apply even to iniquitous parents.

The *Aruch Ha-Shulchan* proceeds to suggest yet another distinction, between the case of a רשע לתיאבון — a parent who sins to fulfill his desires for comfort, convenience, luxury or pleasure — and the case of a רשע להכעיס — a parent who sins for the sake of theological rebellion, knowingly rejecting the Torah's authority. When the Rambam requires respecting a sinful parent, the *Aruch Ha-Shulchan* posits, he perhaps refers only to a father in the first category, who sins out of desire. But if a parent rejects *mitzva* obligation as a matter of theological objection, his children do not need to respect him. It should be noted that this distinction does not suffice to refute the proof from the Gemara's discussion of the deceased thief, who, in all likelihood, falls under

---

34. This distinction is suggested also by the Radbaz, in his commentary to *Hilchos Mamrim*, and he explains that the Rambam requires the children of an evildoer to respect him because of the possibility that he might repent in the future, and thus after his passing, when he can no longer repent, they are not obliged to honor his memory.

35. Vol. 2, 18.

36. Y.D. 240:39.

the category of רשע לתיאבון, and whose children are nevertheless exempt from respecting him unless he had repented.[37]

Regardless, this matter is subject to dispute between the *Shulchan Aruch*,[38] who cites the Rambam's ruling, and the Rama, who brings the view of the *Tur*. The *Aruch Ha-Shulchan* accepts the Rama's ruling, as does Rav Yaakov Ettlinger, who, in his *Binyan Tziyon Ha-Chadashos*,[39] infers from the comments of the *Shach* and the *Taz* that they sided with the Rama's view.

Certainly, a careful distinction must be drawn between a parent who employs unduly harsh disciplinary measures and an outright abuser.[40] But when dealing with a cruel, abusive parent, who regularly strikes or insults a child, there is little question that such a parent qualifies as a רשע, whom, according to the Rama's view, a child has no obligation to respect. After the parent's death, it is possible that even according to the *Shulchan Aruch*, the child is not required to respect the parent's memory.

If, however, the parent shows genuine remorse, sincerely apologizing to his children, and he seeks to correct his behavior such as by receiving counseling or therapy, then he is considered a רשע who has repented, such that the children must, at least in principle, respect him — though this will depend on additional factors, as we will now proceed to discuss.

Preserving the Child's Psychological Wellbeing

Rav David Cohen[41] noted that in many cases of abuse, tragically, the victim suffers psychological harm well into the future, for years after he suffered the maltreatment, and the process of recovery often requires the child's dissociation from the abuser. A child's continued contact with his abusive parent can, very often, maintain or even exacerbate the emotional pain. This concern for the child's psychological wellbeing, Rav Cohen ruled, suffices to excuse the child from the requirement to respect his parents. The Rama[42] writes that one is not required to spend more than one-fifth of

---

37. This distinction between a רשע לתיאבון and a רשע להכעיס in regard to the Rambam's ruling was advanced also by Rav Chaim Ben-Attar, both in his *Or Ha-Chayim* commentary to the Torah (*Vayikra* 19:3) and his *Rishon Le-Tziyon* (Y.D. 241:4).

38. Y.D. 240:18.

39. 112.

40. Rav Eliezer Melamed writes: אמנם צריכים להבחין בין הורים שמפריזים בכעס וחינוכם קפדני יתר על המידה, אבל כוונתם הבסיסית היא חיובית, שאותם צריך לכבד ולדון לכף זכות, לבין הורה שמתאכזר באופן סדיסטי כלפי ילדיו (*Peninei Halacha, Likutim*, vol. 3, p. 31).

41. Cited by Dr. Bentzion Sorotzkin in his essay, "Honoring Abusive Parents" (available at https://drsorotzkin.com/honoring-abusive-parents/), p. 6.

42. O.C. 656.

his assets for the sake of a *mitzva*, and Rav Cohen writes that one's physical or mental health is certainly worth more than this value. Indeed, Rav Moshe Feinstein ruled in *Iggeros Moshe*[43] that a mental patient need not be released from his facility against the advice of his psychiatrists for the sake of fulfilling *mitzvos*, because one's mental health is worth far more than one-fifth of his possessions.[44]

Moreover, the *Shulchan Aruch*[45] rules explicitly that the obligation of כיבוד אב ואם does not require one to spend money for the sake of honoring his parents. We can reasonably assume that *a fortiori*, one is absolved from respecting parents when this would cause psychological harm.

Therefore, even if, in principle, the כיבוד אב ואם obligation applies to a penitent abuser, the child would be exempt if respecting the parent would interfere with his psychological treatment.

Another factor to consider is that the very definition of the *mitzva* to respect parents might make it impractical — and hence inapplicable — in the case of a child who suffered abusive parenting. Rav Avraham Danzig, in his *Chayei Adam*,[46] cites the *Sefer Chareidim* as establishing that the command of כיבוד אב ואם includes respecting one's parents in his mind, holding them in high esteem.[47] According to the *Sefer Chareidim*, one is required not only to treat his parents with honor, but also to look upon them with honor. Rav Chaim Shmuelevitz[48] recalled how his father, Rav Raphael Alter Shmuelevitz, always made a concerted effort to find in his father qualities that set him apart from other people, so that he could view him as special and unique in that regard, greater than anyone else on earth. The reason, Rav Chaim explained, is because the *mitzva* requires truly and genuinely respecting the parent, and this requires finding the parent's special qualities that deserve admiration and esteem.

If, indeed, the mitzva of כיבוד אב ואם requires one to genuinely hold his parent in high esteem, it would stand to reason that a victim of parental abuse is exempt from this command. After all, one who suffered severe physical or emotional pain at the hands

---

43. O.C. 1:172.

44. See *Headlines* 2, pp. 312–313, where we cited Rav Asher Weiss as applying this line of reasoning to exempt patients afflicted with obsessive-compulsive disorder from certain *mitzvos* when this is necessary for their treatment and recovery.

45. Y.D. 240:5.

46. 1:67.

47. The *Sefer Chareidim* proves this theory from the verse in *Tehillim* (15:4), נבזה בעיניו ימאס ואת יראי ה' יכבד — which lauds one who looks with disdain upon wrongdoing, and shows respect (יכבד) to those who live with fear of God. The term יכבד is thus used as a point of contrast to silent disdain, such that the command of כבד את אביך ואת אמך, too, must refer to one's overall view of his parents, and not just the way he speaks and acts towards them.

48. *Sichos Mussar*, p. 357.

of a parent who mistreated him cannot be expected to honestly admire the parent. At most, he could go through the motions, formally displaying honor without any true feelings of respect. If, as the *Sefer Chareidim* and Rav Chaim Shmuelevitz indicate, insincere demonstrations of honor do not fulfill the כיבוד אב ואם obligation, then we might assume that a victim of parental abuse cannot, as a practical matter, fulfill this *mitzva*.

Honoring Foster Parents

If an abused child is adopted by foster parents, does the כיבוד אב ואם obligation require him to respect the foster parents as though they were his biological parents?

A number of Aggadic passages appear to equate the relationship between parents and their adopted children with the relationship between parents and their biological children. The Gemara teaches in *Maseches Sanhedrin (19b)*, כל המגדל יתום בתוך ביתו מעלה עליו הכתוב כאילו ילדו — "Whoever raises an orphan in his home, is considered by the verse as though he gave birth to him." The Midrash[49] goes so far as to say, כל הפותח פתחו לחבירו חייב בכבודו יותר משל אביו ומאמו — somebody who is brought into another person's home and cared for owes that individual even greater respect than he owes his parents. And the *Sefer Ha-Chinuch*,[50] in explaining the rationale behind the obligation to respect parents, writes:

> באמת ראוי לו לעשות להם כל כבוד וכל תועלת שיוכל, כי הם הביאוהו לעולם, גם
> יגעו בו כמה יגיעות בקטנותו.

> It is truly proper to grant them [parents] every type of honor and every benefit one can, because they brought him into the world, and also exerted themselves in several ways on his behalf when he was young.

The obligation of כיבוד אב ואם is rooted not only in the parents' having created the child, but also in the enormous efforts they expended and expend caring for him. If so, then we might expect the obligation to apply even to foster parents who work or worked tirelessly to care for the child.

The Gemara, however, suggests otherwise. In *Maseches Sota* (49a), we read that Rav Acha bar Yaakov once asked his grandson, Rav Yaakov, whom he had adopted, for water, and the grandson replied, "I am not your son." Rashi explains that since he was his grandson, and not his son, he was not obligated to honor him. The *Chasam Sofer*[51] cites this story as proof that the obligation of כיבוד אב ואם does not apply to foster parents, though he adds that there is a requirement of מקצת כבוד — "a little respect," and thus an adopted child should recite *kaddish* for the foster parent. This is likely

---

49. *Shemos Rabba* 4:2.
50. 33.
51. O.C. 164.

inferred from Rashi's comments explaining Rav Yaakov's response to his grandfather: **כבן** אין עלי לכבדך — "I do not need to respect you **like a son**." As a number of *Achar-onim*[52] noted, Rashi implies that Rav Yaakov was not required to honor his grandfather to the same extent that a child must honor a parent, but nevertheless owed him some degree of respect. Rav Chaim Chizkiyahu Medini, in *Sedei Chemed*,[53] suggests that the מקצת כבוד mentioned by the *Chasam Sofer* is required not by force of the formal obligation of כיבוד אב ואם, but rather as a matter of basic decency (in the *Sedei Chemed's* words: דרך אנושיות). He adds that this is likely the intent of the Midrash, cited above, requiring one to accord greater respect to a foster parent than to a biological parent — that basic decency mandates that a child show gratitude and appreciation for those who brought him into their family and cared for him.[54]

Already the Rama, in one of his published responsa,[55] writes that one should recite *kaddish* for his foster parent, citing the Gemara's teaching that raising an orphan is akin to fathering a child.

Conclusion

Abusive parenting is clearly forbidden, and a parent's obligation to discipline the child does not authorize the parent to inflict severe physical or emotional pain. Victims of parental abuse are clearly allowed to do what needs to be done to protect themselves from their parent's mistreatment, even if this means disobeying them or dissociating themselves from them. If a child moved out of the home and is no longer subject to the parent's abuse, or if the parent discontinued his abusive treatment, according to some views, the child must, in principle, respect the parent, whereas others maintain this is

---

52. See, for example, *Shevus Yaakov* 2:94, *Teshuva Mei-Ahava* 1:178.

53. *Ma'areches Aveilus, 156.*

54. We might add that the term מקצת כבוד used by the *Chasam Sofer* might hearken to the Rambam's comments in *Hilchos Mamrim* (5:11) stating that although a convert to Judaism is, technically, no longer required to respect his parents, to whom he is no longer halachically related, he must nevertheless treat them with מקצת כבוד. Otherwise, the Rambam explains, the convert would end up acting less ethical after converting than before converting, suddenly stopping to respect the parents who brought him into the world and cared for him. (See *Iggeros Moshe*, Y.D. 2:130, where Rav Moshe Feinstein explains the Rambam as referring to not merely the concern that people will disrespect Jews upon seeing the convert stopping to respect his parents, but rather to the basic moral obligation of gratitude.) In the case of foster parents, too, it appears that the technical obligation of כיבוד אב ואם does not apply, but basic decency demands that the child respect those who expended great efforts on his behalf.

55. 118.

not required until the parent sincerely repents. In practice, however, if the child is incapable of holding the abusive parent in esteem due to the mistreatment he suffered, or if continued contact with the parent causes emotional harm, then the child is exempt from respecting the parent.

The formal, technical obligation of כיבוד אב ואם does not apply to foster parents, though the child is certainly required to respect them as a matter of decency and gratitude.

INTERVIEWS

Dr. Bentzion Sorotzkin

Interviewed on *Headlines with Dovid Lichtenstein*, 2 Av, 5778 (July 14, 2018)

I try to give my patients a broader perspective of what the possibilities are so they could discuss the matter with their *rav* and their *posek*. Many patients come to therapy believing — in part based on the story in the Gemara of Dama ben Nesina [who is applauded for remaining respectful to his mother even after she publicly humiliated him] — that the Torah requires them to have absolute *kavod* and *yira*, regardless of the cost, even if the parents drive them insane, even if the parents are overly abusive, without any flexibility. This is what they believe, and this is simply not true. Exactly where you can be lenient, and where there is room for flexibility — this is something for a *rav* to *pasken*, and this is not what I want to do. But I do want to open for them the possibility that things aren't as simple as they perhaps think.

All kids learn about the story of Dama ben Nesina. But *Tosfos* there say that the mother was מטורפת בדעתה — she was insane. It wasn't just a mother being mean to her child and embarrassing him in front of everybody. *Nebach*, she had Alzheimer's. She didn't know what she was doing. Anyone who, unfortunately, has had to deal with a parent with Alzheimer's, knows how testing this is on one's patience, and how difficult it is. So it's to Dama's credit that he did not react. But usually, kids do not learn that she was מטורפת בדעתה. And so they grow up thinking that even if a parent acts with רשעות, the child must have unlimited *kavod* regardless…

The *Yam Shel Shlomo* discusses this at length. He says that the mother must have been מטורפת בדעתה, because otherwise, he would not have had to let her treat him this way.

I once posed the following question to one of the prominent *poskim* in *Eretz Yisrael*, and I have his answer in writing. The *halacha* is that if you see your father about to commit a forbidden act, you are obligated to tell him respectfully, "Father, does not it not say in the Torah that you're not allowed to do that?" So, if a father is mistreating his child, in a way that the *halachos* of *chinuch* clearly consider wrong, and which is thus an *aveira*, isn't there an obligation to respectfully tell the father that this is not the way a child is supposed to be treated? This *posek* told me that this is correct, that there is an obligation to tell the father, just as there would be if he was doing any other *issur*.

Aside from the halachic perspective, which is obviously the most significant thing, it's not beneficial to the parent to intimidate his child such that he respects him even though he is angry about it. It undermines the whole relationship. The Rambam, after bringing all the *halachos* of *kibbud av va'eim*, writes, אסור לאדם להכביד עולו על בניו ולדקדק בכבודו עמהם שלא יביאם לידי מכשול, אלא ימחול ויתעלם. And this is brought down by the *Shulchan Aruch*. Technically, the child has to respect you in all which ways, but if you're going to be too heavy-handed about it, this will backfire. You might intimidate them so that they overtly have to respect you, but you won't see much *nachas*. Waving the "*kibbud av va'eim* flag" is not a substitute for developing a loving, caring relationship, and is of no benefit to either the child or the parent.

I think I saw it written that somebody once asked Rav Michel Yehuda Lefkowitz about a child who was *chutzpadik*, and he said that there was probably a reason why the child was being *chutzpadik*, he was probably upset, and it's up to the father to repair the relationship. If you take the initiative to repair the relationship, then it's a favor not only for the child, but also for you, the parent, because he won't act this way anymore. Using *kibbud av va'eim* as a way of controlling the child backfires.

If a child is in therapy, the goal of the therapy is to talk about the anger that the child already has that he is hiding, and is causing all kinds of symptoms that are worrying the parents. The parents love the child, and they are very disturbed that the child suffers anxiety and depression. They want him to get better. It might be hard for them when they realize that the child's problem is partially due to the way they've treated him, and this will be painful for them, but most parents, at the end of the day, will give their lives for their children. So when the child is finally able to express what he is angry about, you help the child learn how to speak to his parents. Either you meet together with the parents, or you just talk to the child and explain, "It's very understandable that your father doesn't realize how critical he is of you, and that this is why you don't want to talk to him, and then he gets angry when you don't want to talk to him. But you can tell him." And you have the child practice how to say it in a respectful way: "Tatty, I know you want me to have an open relationship with you, and you many times have asked me why I don't tell you more about what's going on in my life. Is it ok if I tell you why, without you getting angry at me?" The father will probably say yes. And the child will then say, "Usually when I tell you, you end up getting angry at me, so I hesitate. If you won't get angry with me, I'd be happy to tell you." The end goal is to improve the relationship.

Somebody once came to the Steipler Gaon and said, "My son talks to me with chutzpah, and so I'm very worried about his *olam ha-ba*. What's going to be with him?"

The Steipler answered, "As far as your son's *olam ha-ba* is concerned, there's a very simple solution — you can be *mochel*. The problem is that you probably provoke him to speak that way, and he is not able to be *mochel* [because he's a minor]. So I'm worried about your *olam ha-ba*, not his."

It's an interesting thing — when children are in conflict with their parents, people are very worried about the kids' *olam ha-ba*, what's going to be with these kids who don't fulfill *kibud av va'eim*. They don't seem to be worried about the parent's *olam ha-ba*. That's really not fair. When a father speaks in a demeaning way to the child, provokes him, gets very angry at him for not very good reasons, he violates many, many *issurim*. There's really no *heter* to embarrass a child. This is mentioned in *sefarim*. A certain educator who gave parenting classes once asked Rav Chaim Kanievsky what he should emphasize to the parents, and Rav Chaim said, "Tell them that the *halachos* of בין אדם לחבירו apply also to their children. What's more, children aren't able to be *mochel*." There's no *heter* to shame or insult a child. The notion that a parent "owns" a child and is therefore allowed to harm him is incorrect. This is so obvious that it shouldn't need to be said.

Many parents look at *kibbud av va'eim* as a "perk" — if you take care of your children, feed them and give them clothing and shelter, then you get a perk. Just like an employee who reaches a certain level in the company gets a car, as a parent you get a perk that your children respect you. This is not true. This is not something that they owe you. They are obligated in *kibbud av va'eim* the same way they're obligated to put on *tefillin*. And you, as a parent, have to teach them how to do *kibbud av va'eim* the same way you have to teach them to put on *tefillin*. It's not something that they owe you; it's something they are obligated to do for the *Ribono Shel Olam*. You happen to be the recipient. It's not a perk.

There's a *sefer* called *Sefer Ha-Bris*. I think it was written around 250 years ago by a distinguished *rav* in Vilna. Rav Shach wrote that when he couldn't sleep at night, he looked at this *sefer*. In this *sefer* there is a very lengthy discussion which Rabbi Litwack brings in his *sefer*, *Kibbud Av Va'eim*. He writes that many parents think that because of the obligation of *kibbud av va'eim*, they are not bound by all the obligations of ואהבת לרעך כמוך and אונאת דברים. Not only is this not true — they are bound by all the obligations בין אדם לחבירו — but they're actually more obligated. When it comes to *tzedaka*, if somebody has a poor brother who needs *tzedaka* but does not give him, his *aveira* is much greater than if he does not give to a stranger. One's obligation is greater towards the people who are closest to him. And so the obligation of ואהבת לרעך כמוך is much bigger for family members than for others. It's well known what Rav Chaim Vital said in the name of the Arizal — that if somebody does *chesed* to everybody except his family members, he receives no reward for what he did for others, because obviously he did not do it לשם שמיים. The *Sefer Ha-Bris* says explicitly — and Rav Chaim Kanievsky and others say this, as well — that it is a דבר פשוט that all the obligations בין אדם לחבירו apply also to a parent's relationship with his children.

Of course, there is an obligation of *chinuch*. But just like there is an obligation of *tocheicha* for other fellow Jews, this is not a *heter* to embarrass them, and this must be done within the proper parameters, the same is true when a person has to give *mussar* to his child. Everyone knows that a great *rebbe* is one whom you continue loving even after he gives *mussar* because he gives it in a sincere way, in a certain tone and with a certain attitude. The same is true of parents. Of course they need to give *mussar* and *tocheicha*, but it has to be done in a way which doesn't cause hatred or distance.

Like everything in life, there's a balance. People usually get into trouble when they know only one side of the equation. I deal with some parents who are aware only of the dangers of too much discipline, so they don't discipline at all, and I deal with some parents who are aware only of the dangers of not disciplining their child. Both are really dangerous. You have to find the middle road. Of course, finding the exact "sweet spot" is always a challenge. I tell people that this is like going to a doctor who thinks that the cure for every medical problem is surgery, and to another doctor who's afraid to ever perform surgery. Neither is going to give sound medical advice. You need somebody who understands the dangers of both, and thus knows how to find the right balance…

Every attempt should be made to try to reconcile the child with the parents, and to work out a relationship that's tolerable and that won't undermine the child's mental health. That's always the number-one rule. Sometimes, the parents are incredibly hurtful, but sometimes they're just mildly unreasonable, and the child can learn to live with that in a tolerable way that does not undermine his mental health. If it is extreme, this has to be discussed with a *posek* who has a lot of experience dealing with this. Sometimes I need to get permission from the patient to speak to the *rav* to present a clear picture. And sometimes the *rav* will say that the child should have no association with them, there's no solution. But that's very rare…

A big part of my job is to prepare the patient to speak to the *posek*, because they tend to totally underreport the problem. They're sometimes embarrassed to admit, to themselves or to the *rav*, just how unreasonable the parents are, and so they don't report the situation accurately. I remember one situation where somebody I know — a married adult — told me that he would go visit his father once a month, and it was a horrible experience each time. His father would yell at him, embarrass him and insult him. But he told me that he felt he had to go. I told him this isn't so simple, and he should ask a *rav*. He spoke to a certain *posek*, whom I have dealt with, and he came back and told me that the *posek* told him, "*Mitzvos* don't always have to be so easy. You have to go anyway."

"Really?!" I said. "He told you that?! This doesn't fit with anything he ever told me in the past."

I went to meet with this *rav* and I asked him about his conversation with that fellow. He said that this man had told him that his visits with his father aren't so pleasant. He had totally underreported. I explained to the *rav* the whole picture, and he said, "Well, that's a whole different story! Tell him to come back to me and tell me the truth."

So part of my job is to role-play, to sit down and ask the patient what he is going to tell the *rav*. Sometimes I need to speak to the *rav* myself to make sure that he gets the complete picture, and realizes how serious the situation is so he could *pasken* what the person needs to do…

I was once treating a young lady who was sexually molested by her stepfather. It went on for a number of years until she was old enough to leave the house. She did not talk to her stepfather or to her mother, who never really protected her. The siblings were hounding the girl because she stopped talking to her parents, asking her, "Where's the *kibbud av va'eim*?" I thought this was insane, and I told her she was not obligated to respect her parents. But she was very nervous about violating the *aveira*. So I wrote to one of the major *poskim* in *Eretz Yisrael* who I know has dealt with these issues. He wrote me back — and I have this in writing — that the family members are מטורפות בדעתם, out of their minds, for asking her to respect her parents. When I showed this to her, it settled her mind a little.

I then realized how many people in these extreme cases are tortured, while nobody in their right mind could expect the child to have *kibbud av va'eim*, and it was totally undermining the child's emotional sanity, because adding onto all their problems was the torture of the fear of not fulfilling *kibbud av va'eim*. So I wrote an article about this. In response, I received a tremendous amount of emails from tortured people. It was heartbreaking reading about people who not only have to deal with parents who were terribly abusive — though I must emphasize that these are, *baruch Hashem*, a small minority of cases — but also have the burden of feeling guilty that they're not fulfilling *kibbud av va'eim*...

I find that if you speak to *rabbanim*, if they're not so familiar with these things, they'll become familiar. The problem is more that the patients are not open enough with the *rabbanim* to tell them exactly what's going on. They underplay. The *rabbanim* who have more experience know to elicit the full information.

Unfortunately, most people are not aware that there's no obligation to respect a parent who is a *rasha*. That's one of the reasons why I wrote my article. And even in less extreme cases, people should know that it's a *she'ila*. Don't assume anything before you speak to a *rav* and give him the complete story.

In my article, I quote from the *sefer Binas Ha-Middos*, which tells that Rav Moshe Shapiro was once asked about a situation where a mother-in-law was interfering in the family's life, causing problems with *shalom bayis*. He said that they should tell the mother-in-law that she is not welcome into the house. This is stated explicitly in the *sefer*. The author adds that of course, one needs to ask a *she'ila* in such a case, saying, "It is advisable to first consult with an impartial Torah scholar." He emphasizes that the *rav* must be impartial, because sometimes you have a *rav* who is very involved and close with the parents, and there is a concern that he might not be impartial. But if you first speak to an impartial *rav* and *posek*, and explain to him the whole situation, how it is undermining *shalom bayis*, you'll sometimes be surprised by what he'll tell you. But you have to tell him the full extent of the problem. If you tell him that the mother-in-law comes in and demands lukshen kugel and his wife likes to make potato kugel, he'll tell you to get over it, you have to learn how to accommodate your parents and in-laws in a reasonable fashion, even if it is a little difficult. But if it is "over the top," and extreme, then you have to know at least there is a good possibility that you shouldn't do it, and you shouldn't harm your *shalom bayis*. You need to ask a knowledgeable *rav*.

HACKNEY CITIZEN

Orthodox Jewish school that bans women from driving seeks state funding

June 2, 2015
By Hackney Citizen

One of the Jewish schools in Stamford Hill which has come under fire for banning women from driving their children to school has applied for 'voluntary aided' status, the Hackney Citizen can reveal.

Beis Malka Girls Primary, an Independent Orthodox Jewish day school with around 400 pupils, has put in a proposal to set up as a voluntary aided (VA) school from September 2015.

VA schools are state-funded with a foundation or trust (usually a religious organisation) contributing to building costs and holding substantial influence over the running of the school.

The school is one of two primaries run by the Belz sect, part of the Orthodox branch of Hassidic Judaism, which recently sent letters to parents asking women to stop driving to the school gates, or risk having their children withdrawn.

A Hackney Council spokesperson confirmed the school has been asked to provide a copy of the letter issued to parents and to confirm the school's position.

In the letter, seen by the Jewish Chronicle the Belz rabbis said that having female drivers goes against "the traditional rules of modesty in our camp."

One Stamford Hill Rabbi said it has "always been regarded in Chasidic circles as not the done thing for a lady to drive".

But the order was met with anger by many leading Jewish figures including Chief Rabbi Ephraim Mirvis and UK Ambassador of the Jewish Orthodox Feminist Alliance Dina Brawer.

Education Secretary Nicky Morgan criticised the order as "completely unacceptable in modern Britain".

Community Cohesion

Ahron Klein, the chief executive of the Beis Malka Trust which runs both schools told the Evening Standard: "We fully accept that despite being private schools we have responsibilities to our members and to the wider public. However, as private schools we have the freedom to set our own high standards by which we seek to live and bring up our children."

But the school has now applied to join three Jewish primaries and two secondaries as a Voluntary Aided school.

Hackney Council must decide the proposal within two months of the end of the representation period or the decision defaults to the Schools Adjudicator.

A Council spokesperson said that in reaching a decision on the proposal the Local Authority is required to have "regard to a number of factors such as equal opportunity issues and community cohesion".

Both the Talmud Torah Machzikei Hadass school for boys and Beis Malka school for girls, which are run by the Belz sect, were rated 'good' by Ofsted in 2010 and 2013.

The 2013 Ofsted report for Beis Malka Girls states: "Provision for [the pupils] spiritual, moral, social and cultural development is also outstanding."

The Hackney Citizen contacted Beis Malka Girls School to ask about its application for VA status but has not received a reply.

כל כבודה בת מלך פנימה
Do Women Need to Hide?

The Gemara, in a number of places, cites the verse in *Tehillim* (45:14), כל כבודה בת מלך פנימה — "All the honor of a princess is inward" — as establishing that it is honorable for Jewish women to remain inside their homes, rather than appear in public.

For example, in *Maseches Yevamos* (77a), the Gemara enlists this concept to explain why women from the nations of Amon and Moav are permitted to marry Jews after converting, despite the Torah's prohibition against marrying male converts from these nations. The Torah[1] writes that members of these nations are barred from joining the Jewish People because they did not greet *Bnei Yisrael* with provisions after the Exodus. As women do not normally go out in public, the Gemara explains, it was not expected that the women of these nations would go out to bring food to *Bnei Yisrael*, and so they are welcome to join the Jewish People in marriage.[2]

Mahari Brona[3] boldly suggested that this principle represents a minority position. His contention is based on the Gemara's discussion in *Maseches Gittin* (12a) establishing that if a wife is capable of financial independence, then her husband can forfeit his right to her earnings and thereby release himself of his obligation to support her. The Gemara states that one might have thought otherwise, due to the concept of כל כבודה בת מלך פנימה, which would make it disrespectful for a woman to have to find work to support herself. As this line of reasoning is not accepted in the Gemara's conclusion, Mahari Brona suggests, it seems that the principle of כל כבודה is not viewed as normative. To further support this argument, Mahari Brona notes that the expectation that Jewish women remain in the home stems from the fact that all Jews are, in a sense, considered בני מלכים — members of royalty — such that a Jewish woman, as a בת מלך, should uphold the standard of כל כבודה בת מלך פנימה. Indeed, Rashi, commenting on the Gemara's discussion in *Maseches Gittin*, writes that the principle of כל כבודה

---

1. *Devarim* 23:5.
2. The Maharshal (*Yam Shel Shlomo, Yevamos*) explains that the women of *Bnei Yisrael* would not have left their tents to receive gifts of food of water from the women of Amon and Moav, and so these nations' women were not expected to bring provisions and are therefore not barred from joining the Jewish Nation.
3. 242.

בת מלך as establishing the impropriety of a woman leaving her home is based upon the notion of כל ישראל בני מלכים — all Jews have regal status. Mahari Brona shows from the Gemara in *Maseches Bava Metzia* (113a) that the rule of כל ישראל בני מלכים represents a minority position which is not accepted. By extension, then, the rule of כל כבודה בת מלך פנימה is likewise held by a minority view which does not represent normative *halacha*.

By contrast, the *Chasam Sofer*[4] writes that the principle of כל כבודה בת מלך פנימה is indeed accepted as *halacha*, noting the Gemara's invocation of this rule to explain the distinction between the men and women of Amon and Moav, as discussed.

Indeed, the rule of כל כבודה is cited in numerous different sources as authoritative. Most notably, the Rambam, in *Hilchos Ishus,*[5] references this principle in discussing a wife's right to occasionally leave her home. The Rambam writes that a husband owes it to his wife to give her money for respectable attire with which to appear in public. He explains:

> לפי שכל אשה יש לה לצאת ולילך לבית אביה לבקרו ולבית האבל ולבית המשתה לגמול חסד לרעותיה או לקרובותיה כדי שיבואו הם לה, שאינה בבית הסוהר עד שלא תצא ולא תבוא.

> For every woman is entitled to leave and go to her father's home to visit him, and to a house of mourning and house of celebration to perform kindness for her peers or relatives, in order that they come to her, because she is not in a prison such that she may not come or go.

However, the Rambam immediately qualifies this statement, stating that women should limit their trips out of the home:

> אבל גנאי הוא לאשה שתהיה יוצאה תמיד פעם בחוץ פעם ברחובות ויש לבעל למנוע אשתו מזה ולא יניחנה לצאת, אלא כמו פעם אחת בחודש או כמו פעמים בחודש לפי הצורך, שאין יופי לאשה אלא לישב בזוית ביתה שכך כתוב כל כבודה בת מלך פנימה.

> But it is dishonorable for a woman to always go out, sometimes outside, sometime in the streets, and a husband may prevent his wife from doing so, and not allow her to leave, except for once or twice a month, as needed, for there is no greater beauty for a woman than staying inside her home, for such is it written: כל כבודה בת מלך פנימה.

Accordingly, the Rama[6] writes, citing the *Tur*:

> אשה לא תרגיל עצמה לצאת הרבה, שאין יופי לאשה אלא לישב בזויות ביתה.

---

4. E.H. 2:99.

5. 13:11.

6. E.H. 73:1.

A woman should not accustom herself to leave often, for there is no greater beauty for a woman than to remain inside her home.

This seemingly clear-cut halachic ruling should have far-reaching implications, and require women to leave home as infrequently as possible. Certainly, if taken at face value, the rule of כל כבודה בת מלך פנימה should make it strictly forbidden for women to take jobs outside the home — a policy followed by, at most, a very small minority of observant communities in our time.

Avoiding the Front Yard

Indeed, a brief survey of some applications of this rule over the ages, even into the 20th century, forces us to conclude either that it is no longer binding, or that its precise parameters are flexible and subject to societal norms.

The *Chasam Sofer*[7] famously enlisted the principle of כל כבודה בת מלך פנימה to explain why it is customary for women not to light Chanukah candles. Although Ashkenazic practice is that each member of the household lights Chanukah candles, wives commonly do not. The *Chasam Sofer* explained that since the Chanukah candle lighting is, ideally, to be done outside the home, in public view, women do not light, as they do not normally go outdoors. It is clear that in the view of the *Chasam Sofer*, the rule of כל כבודה בת מלך פנימה prevents women even from going right outside their homes for the few moments it takes to light Chanukah candles. Needless to say, nowadays, even in communities that follow the most stringent standards of female modesty, women do not confine themselves to their homes to such an extent.[8]

Rav Moshe Sternbuch[9] references the *Chasam Sofer's* comments in discussing the question of whether women should recite *birkas ha-ilanos* (the *beracha* recited over the sighting of blossoming trees during the month of Nissan). He writes that because of the rule of כל כבודה בת מלך פנימה, women need not specifically make a point of looking for blossoming trees to recite this *beracha*, as men customarily do. Once again, we find כל כבודה בת מלך applied to something which modern-day observant women would not think twice about doing — in this instance, taking a springtime walk around the neighborhood.

Rav Shmuel Wosner[10] writes that women should not drive vehicles, because driving

---

7. *Shabbos* 21b.
8. The *Chasam Sofer's* strict approach to כל כבודה can be seen also in the aforementioned responsum (referenced in note 4) where he writes that if a woman left home and was subsequently raped, then although she is not guilty of infidelity, she nevertheless forfeits her rights to her *kesuba* payment because she violated the law of כל כבודה בת מלך פנימה.
9. *Teshuvos Ve-Hanhagos*, 1:190.
10. *Shevet Ha-Levi*, 4:1.

constitutes, in his words, "the polar opposite" of כל כבודה בת מלך פנימה. This application, too, is accepted nowadays by, at most, a negligible fringe minority of observant Jews.

Rav Eliezer Waldenberg[11] writes that it is preferable for women not to teach in schools because of כל כבודה בת מלך פנימה, as this requires them to be out of their homes. Nowadays, of course, observant women who are qualified to teach are strongly encouraged to pursue a career in education.

In the early 20th century, a number of *poskim* referenced the notion of כל כבודה בת מלך פנימה as a reason to forbid women from participating in the political process, including voting. Rav Avraham Yitzchak Kook, in a letter dated 11 Tishrei, 5680 (October 5, 1919),[12] expressed his opinion that women should not vote in democratic elections, and amidst his discussion, he wrote:

חובת עבודת הצבור הקבועה מוטלת היא על הגברים...ו...תפקידים של משרה, של משפט ושל עדות, אינם שייכים לה, וכל כבודה היא פנימה.

The obligation of permanent public service is cast upon the men... and...jobs of governance, of justice and of testimony do not belong to her, and all her honor is inward.

He elaborated further in a different letter, dated 10 Nissan, 5680 (March 29, 1920), positing that Judaism, unlike other value systems, accords great religious importance and sanctity to the home and family. And therefore, whereas other people consider it degrading for a woman to remain at home tending to her family, Torah Judaism sees this as a source of great honor. Rav Kook explicitly applied this guiding principle to forbid women from going to the polls to cast their vote for a political candidate or party.

Others expressed this viewpoint, as well, including Rav Yechiel Yaakov Weinberg, in *Seridei Eish*.[13]

Once again, in virtually no Orthodox community today are women discouraged — let alone prohibited — from voting, and to the contrary, voting for the candidates supporting causes that are important to Orthodox Jewry is considered by many a *mitzva* for both men and women alike.

An Obsolete *Halacha*?

A number of *poskim* observed that indeed, for better or for worse, this *halacha* is simply no longer practiced in today's day and age.

The *Aruch Ha-Shulchan*[14] makes this observation in endeavoring to explain why

---

11.   *Tzitz Eliezer* 14:97:6.

12.   *Ma'amarei Ha-Re'aya*, pp. 189–194.

13.   1:156.

14.   O.C. 303:22.

women in his day regularly wore all their jewelry outside in the public domain on Shabbos. *Chazal* introduced various restrictions on jewelry due to the concern that women might remove it to show their friends, and will then carry the pieces through the public domain, in violation of Shabbos.[15] The *Aruch Ha-Shulchan* proposes a number of theories in order to justify the widespread disregard of these restrictions, and concludes that there is no longer any reason to fear that women would remove their jewelry in the street to show their peers. He explains:

הנה ידוע דבימיהם היו הנשים יושבות בביתן ולא היו יוצאות תדיר לרחוב, וכשיוצאות לפרקים היו יוצאות עטופות בסדיניהן, וגם לא היה להם בתי כנסיות של נשים. אם כן לא ראו זו את זו רק לפרקים ומעט שנכנסו אחת לבית חברתה, והיה החשש גדול שבפגען זו את זו בשבת בהלוכן ברחוב שלפי ומחוי. אבל עכשיו הנשים הולכות הרבה תדיר ברחובות ובשווקים, ונכנסות זו לזו בבתיהן ורואות זו את זו בבית הכנסת של נשים, אם כן ממילא שיכולה להראות לה תכשיטיה בבתיהן ובבתי כנסיות. ובודאי שאין מדרכן לפשוט ברחוב תכשיט ולהראות לחברותיהן, והרי אנו רואין בחוש שגם בחול וביום טוב אין עושות כן ולמה נחוש בשבת, וזהו היתר נכון וברור.

Now it is known that in those days, the women would remain in their homes and would not go out into the street frequently. When they would, on occasion, go out, they would go out wrapped in their sheets. They also did not have synagogues for women. Therefore, they saw one another on only rare occasions, infrequently going into each other's homes. There was a real concern that when they would encounter one another on Shabbos as they walked in the street, they would remove [their jewelry] and show it [to one another]. But now, the women frequently walk a lot through the streets and markets, go into each other's homes and see each other in the women's synagogues. Therefore, they in any event can show one another their jewelry in their homes and in the synagogues. Certainly, it is not customary for them to remove a piece of jewelry in the street and show it to their friend. We see with our own eyes that they don't do this even on weekdays or Yom Tov, so why would we be concerned [that they would do this] on Shabbos? This is a correct and clear basis for leniency.

The *Aruch Ha-Shulchan* makes this observation in a matter-of-fact manner, accepting the reality that women in modern times no longer remain confined to their homes.

Rav Eliyahu Klatzkin[16] applies this change in women's conduct to justify the widespread practice to permit unmarried men to work as schoolteachers. The *Shulchan*

---

15.   See *Shulchan Aruch*, O.C. 303.

16.   *Devar Halacha*, 26.

Aruch[17] forbids this practice, because the mothers bring their children to and from the teacher each day, leading to inappropriately frequent interaction between the unmarried teacher and these women. Rav Klatzkin writes that this *halacha* was relevant in the times when women rarely left their homes, such that men would not normally encounter women. Under such conditions, it was inappropriate for an unmarried man to teach young students, putting himself in a position of encountering numerous women twice each day. In modern times, however, women spend a good deal of time outside the home, and so to the contrary, an unmarried man who works in a different job, requiring him to go about in the town, encounters women far more frequently than one who makes a living as a teacher. Therefore, Rav Klatzkin writes, in our day and age, teaching is actually a preferable profession for unmarried men as far as the interest in avoiding excessive interaction with women is concerned.

Once again, it was acknowledged and accepted that women no longer spend most of their time at home.

Another example is a responsum by Rav Waldenberg[18] addressing the prohibition against walking behind a woman, which is mentioned explicitly by the *Shuchan Aruch*.[19] Rav Waldenberg concludes that this law does not apply nowadays, and he presents the following explanation:

בזמן הקדום לא היתה האשה רגילה ללכת ברחובות קריה והיתה יושבת בירכתי
ביתה, וכדברי הרמב"ם...וכן נפסק ברמ"א...דאשה לא תרגיל עצמה לצאת
הרבה...ולכן הפגישה וההילוך אחריה ברחוב היה מביא ביותר לידי הרהור, אבל
משא"כ בזמן הזה שהמציאות לא כן, אלא האשה אינה יושבת בירכתי ביתה
כבזמן הקדום ורגילין יותר בראיית אשה ברחוב, לכן קלקלתם תקנתם אין כ"כ
עתה חשש הרהור בהליכה אחריה כפי אז...

In ancient times, a woman would not regularly walk in the city streets, and would remain inside her home, as the Rambam says...and such did the Rama rule...that a woman should not accustom herself to frequently go out... Therefore, meeting [a woman] and walking behind her in the street was especially prone to cause [improper] thoughts. Such is not the case nowadays, when the reality is different, and a woman does not remain inside her home as in ancient times, and we are more accustomed to seeing a woman in the street. Therefore, their ruin is their repair; there is not as much of a concern of [improper] thoughts when walking behind her as there was then.[20]

---

17. E.H. 22:20.

18. *Tzitz Eliezer*, 9:50.

19. E.H. 21:1.

20. Others disagreed, and maintained that walking behind a woman is forbidden even in modern times. This was the position of the Klausenberger Rebbe in *Divrei Yatziv* (E.H.

Rav Waldenberg references a comment by the *Levush*[21] regarding weddings where men and women are seated in a manner such that they are visible to one another. The *Sefer Chassidim* (393) writes that the *beracha* of השמחה במעונו which is generally recited at a wedding is omitted in such a case, because, in his words, "there is no joy before the Almighty where there are sinful thoughts." The *Levush* observes that this policy is not followed, and proposes a possible explanation:

> אפשר משום דעכשיו מורגלות הנשים הרבה בין האנשים ואין כאן הרהורי עבירה
> כל-כך...

> Perhaps, this is because women are commonly accustomed to be among men, and so there aren't sinful thoughts to such an extent.

By the same token, Rav Waldenberg writes, the prohibition against walking behind a woman does not apply nowadays, when women do not avoid public spaces.

Rav Waldenberg certainly does not celebrate the new realities of the modern era, stating קלקלתם תקנתם — the regrettable abandonment of traditional modesty standards yields the leniency permitting walking behind women. He clearly regarded this development as unfortunate. At the same time, Rav Waldenberg made no attempt — at least in this responsum — to oppose this trend and call for a return to the standards articulated by the Rambam and the Rama.

Rav Waldenberg proceeds to cite a letter written to him by Rav Shlomo Zalman Auerbach agreeing with his conclusion, and noting:

> From the formulation of the *Shulchan Aruch*…it appears that it was not common for women to be in the streets… And, as it is known, it was customary in the past that modest women would be at home, as it is written, כל כבודה בת מלך פנימה, and it is famously brought from the *Chasam Sofer* that the reason why women do not light Chanukah candles for themselves is so that they do not stand by the entrance to the home near the public domain…

Rav Shlomo Zalman, too, simply observed this reality without protesting it, accepting the fact that the rule of כל כבודה בת מלך פנימה is no longer practiced, or at least not in its original form.

Rav Ovadia Yosef[22] makes this observation in discussing the Mishna's famous exhortation,[23] אל תרבה שיחה עם האשה — "Do not indulge in conversation with a

---

39), and of Rav Shmuel Wosner, in *Shevet Ha-Levi* (11:285:7).

21. O.C., *Minhagim*, 30.
22. *Yabia Omer*, vol. 6, O.C. 13.
23. *Avos* 1:5.

woman", which the Gemara[24] indicates requires using as few words as possible even when posing a simple question to a woman.[25] He writes:

> ודוקא בזמנם שלא היו רואים אשה בחוץ שכל כבודה בת מלך פנימה, ובראיית אשה מיד באים לידי הרהור במחשבה שבלב, משא"כ עתה שהנשים עוסקות במשא ומתן, ומורגלות בינינו, ואין האדם מתפעל בראייתן ובשיחתן לבוא לידי הרהור.

[This applied] only in their times, when they did not see women outside, because כל כבודה בת מלך פנימה, and seeing a woman immediately brought [improper] thoughts into the heart. This is not the case now, when women engage in commerce and are commonly among us, and a person is not affected by seeing them and speaking to them such that he would come to have [improper] thoughts.[26]

Rav Yosef acknowledges the reality that כל כבודה is no longer practiced nowadays, without protesting this phenomenon.

Similarly, Rav Menashe Klein[27] writes:

> בזמן הזה הא דינה דכל כבודה בת מלך בעוני"ה כמעט ליכא...

These days, as a result of our many sins, this rule of כל כבודה בת מלך hardly exists.

He explains that whereas in previous generations, האשה לא יצאה מביתה — women simply remained home, nowadays, this is no longer possible.

In an earlier responsum,[28] Rav Klein addresses the propriety of sending girls to solicit charitable donations. He concludes that women who adhere to the rule of כל כבודה בת מלך פנימה should be encouraged to continue doing so, but the majority, who in any event do not follow this practice, should be encouraged to involve themselves

---

24. *Eiruvin* 53b.
25. The Gemara tells that Rabbi Yossi Ha-Galili was reprimanded by Bruria (Rabbi Meir's wife) for asking her, "Which road do I take to get to Lod?" instead of asking more succinctly, "Which is to Lod?"
26. Rav Bentzion Meir Chai Uziel (*Mishpetei Uziel*, vol. 4, C.M. 6) makes a similar point in rejecting the claim that it is immodest for women to vote:

    > איזו פריצות יכולה להיות בדבר הזה, שכל אחד הולך אל הקלפי ומוסר את כרטיס בחירתו, ואם באנו לחוש לכך לא שבקת חיי לכל בריה, ואסור יהיה ללכת ברחוב, או להכנס לחנות אחת אנשים ונשים יחד, או שאסור יהיה לישא ולתת עם אשה משום שעל ידי כך יבואו לידי קרוב דעת, וממילא גם לידי פריצות, וזה לא אמרו אדם מעולם.

27. *Mishneh Halachos*, 9:250.
28. 4:125.

in *mitzvos* — such as collecting charity — if for no other reason than to lower their chances of getting involved in inappropriate activities.

While clearly lamenting the current state of affairs, and saluting those women who resist the modern trend and indeed remain in the home, Rav Klein acknowledges that this rule is simply not practiced in our time.

Rav Klein's lament of this reality, as well as his encouraging those girls who remain at home to continue doing so, suggests that in his view, the principle of כל כבודה is, essentially, no less binding today than in the past, and its widespread neglect is an unfortunate condition which we are powerless to reverse. Ideally, women should remain at home, but alas, this is not done.

Certainly, this is an uncomfortable conclusion — that the overwhelming majority of observant women today, who are otherwise pious and scrupulous in their compliance with *halacha*, flagrantly violate an explicit ruling of the Rama each and every day, without any halachic justification. We would, undoubtedly, prefer finding some explanation for why meticulously observant women today freely leave their homes and even build for themselves successful careers, a basis on which to redefine כל כבודה in such a way that allows us to conclude that this precept does not apply nowadays the way it did in the past.

Protecting Women

Several Midrashic sources establish that a woman should not appear in public in order to reduce the risk of falling victim to sexual assault. The Torah in *Sefer Devarim* (22:23) addresses the punishment for a man who assaults a woman in a city, and the *Sifrei* comments, אילו לא יצאת בעיר לא היה מסתקף לה — this tragedy would not have befallen the woman if she had not ventured out into the public. Likewise, *Bereishis Rabba*[29] comments, האיש כובש אשתו שלא תצא לשוק שכל אשה שיוצאה לשוק סופה להכשל — "A man should restrain his wife from going outside to the market, for any woman who goes out into the market ends up stumbling." The Midrash points to the example of Dina, Yaakov's daughter, who was abducted and raped after she "went out" to socialize among the women of the city of Shechem.[30] The *Kessef Mishneh* cites this Midrashic passage as the source of the Rambam's aforementioned ruling that a husband should not allow his wife to frequently venture out of the home.

If, indeed, this is the reason why women are to remain at home, one could argue that in modern times, when public spaces are safer for women than in the past, this rule no longer applies. While the situation today is, of course, very far from perfect, nevertheless, assaulting or harassing a woman today is a prosecutable crime, which was not the case in ancient times. Women's rights are fully protected by the law, and so

---

29. 8:12.

30. ותצא דינה...לראות בבנות הארץ, *Bereishis* 34:1.

they feel safe leaving the home to engage in all kinds of activities without fear. Today, it is simply not true that כל אשה שיוצאה לשוק סופה להכשל, as the Midrash said about women's experiences in the ancient world.

It goes without saying that common sense and discretion is needed to avoid situations where one's safety is compromised. But in most conventional public settings today, women are not at risk of assault, and thus the warning of לא תצא לרחוב שלא תיכשל simply does not apply.

By contrast, the *Midrash Tanchuma*[31] states that a married woman should not venture outside because she should not be seen by men, which could lead to sinful conduct:

> צריכה אשה להיות יושבת בתוך הבית ולא תצא לרחוב שלא תיכשל עצמה ולא
> תביא מכשול לבני אדם ונמצאו מסתכלין באשת איש.

> A woman must remain inside the home and not go out into the street, lest she stumble, and lest she present a stumbling block before people, as they will end up gazing at a married woman.

This Midrashic passage seems to point not to the danger of sexual assault, but rather to the risk of voluntary relationships developing. If so, then we might assume, at least at first glance, that women should be urged to remain home nowadays no less than in ancient times, and perhaps even more so, given the low moral standards that plague modern society.

The Privilege of כל כבודה

Alternatively, it is possible that in contrast to the viewpoint expressed in these Midrashic sources, which speak of the need for women to be protected, כל כבודה might be rooted in an entirely different concept.

The Gemara in *Maseches Shavuos* (30a) seeks to establish that when the Torah speaks of two "men" appearing in court,[32] it refers to the witnesses, and not the litigants. Initially, the Gemara reasons that since the Torah implies that this is something relevant only to men, and not women, it cannot refer to litigants, because women indeed come to court as plaintiffs or defendants. Necessarily, then, the Torah speaks of testimony, for which only men are eligible. The Gemara refutes this proof, suggesting that the Torah perhaps excuses women from personally coming to court because of כל כבודה בת מלך פנימה.

The *Rishonim*'s reaction to this brief Talmudic passage is revealing. Rav Yosef ibn Migash, as cited by the Ritva, established on the basis of the Gemara's comments that

---

31. *Vayishlach*, 5.

32. ועמדו שני האנשים אשר להם הריב לפני ה׳, *Devarim* 19:17.

certain women cannot be coerced to personally come to *beis din*, and may have their claims recorded and brought by a bailiff:

נשים יקרות דתבעי להו לדינא לא מזלזלינן בהו למיתי לבי דינא.

Distinguished women who are summoned to court — we do not disrespect them by bringing them to court.

The Gemara's refutation, according to Ibn Migash, shows that it is disrespectful for a woman to leave her home to appear in court, and so a woman of stature has the option of refusing a summons and delivering her testimony to the court's scribes in her home.

Ibn Migash acknowledged that the Gemara later (30b) tells of a distinguished woman — the wife of the famous *Amora* Rav Huna — who came before *beis din* as a litigant. However, it is likely that she chose to do so, and so this does not prove that a prominent woman may be coerced to appear in court. Ibn Migash writes that the Rif would not force distinguished women to appear in his court, and the *Shulchan Aruch*[33] rules accordingly.

This discussion highlights the notion of כבוד — "honor" — around which the principle of כל כבודה בת מלך פנימה revolves. This principle respects the right of women to remain in their homes rather than disrespect themselves by getting involved in affairs outside the home. It is a privilege, not a requirement. And therefore, Rav Huna's wife had the option of waiving this privilege and appearing in court, and women who are not יקרות ("distinguished"), and do not conduct themselves in an especially noble, aristocratic fashion, are not entitled to excuse themselves from a court summons.

This perspective on כל כבודה בת מלך emerges also from the Ritva's response to Ibn Migash's inference from the Gemara, refuting his proof. The Ritva writes that the Gemara does not necessarily indicate that a court may not force women to appear, but rather indicates simply that it was customary not to. In the Ritva's words, העולם נוהגים בהם כבוד בכך — "everyone treats them respectfully in this way."

It is clear according to these *Rishonim* that כל כבודה בת מלך is a privilege allowing women to avoid the disrespect they would suffer outside the home. In ancient times, apparently, it was belittling for women to appear in public. We can speculate as to why this was the case, but the aforementioned *Rishonim* make it clear that the rule of כל כבודה establishes the requirement to respect women's wishes to conceal themselves, and not to force them to appear in public.

We should perhaps understand the Rambam and Rama's ruling along similar lines. A wife's obligations to her husband include maintaining her attractiveness — what the Rambam and Rama call יופי ("beauty"). A wife owes it to her husband to avoid compromising her dignity by acting in a self-degrading manner — such as by frequently going out, which, in earlier generations, was undignified for women. And thus the Rambam

---

33. C.M. 124:1.

and Rama authorize a husband to limit his wife's outings, in order that she retain her attractiveness in his eyes.

If so, then we understand why this policy is not followed in our times, when to the contrary, remaining isolated at home is considered, by some, degrading. In today's world, there is nothing disrespectful about spending time out of the house, and so the notion of כל כבודה בת מלך, which is aimed at protecting women from the indignity of public appearance, does not apply as it once did.

One might, at first glance, challenge this perspective based on a passage in *Maseches Eiruvin* (100b) which lists the ten "curses" which befell women as a result of Chava's sin in the Garden of Eden. One "curse" listed is חבושה בבית האסורין — a woman is "locked in prison," and Rashi explains, כל כבודה בת מלך פנימה. According to Rashi, it appears, the principle of כל כבודה is a "curse" that effectively "imprisons" a woman, forcing her to remain in her home and forbidding her from leaving. Seemingly, this disproves the contention that כל כבודה בת מלך פנימה expresses a woman's privilege, as opposed to a restriction.

Truth be told, Rashi's comments in any event are difficult to understand, as the very expression כל **כבודה** בת מלך פנימה describes a woman's home-based life as a source of honor and royal distinction, not "imprisonment." Moreover, the Gemara brings different opinions in listing the ten "curses," and חבושה בבית האסורין appears in only one of the two lists cited. It is certainly conceivable that the other opinion argued that women remain at home as their preference, as a source of honor, and not as a state of confinement imposed upon them. Additionally, the Gemara's comment could be understood to mean that Chava's sin created a new, dark reality in the world, which became less innocent, resulting in a public sphere that was less safe and inviting for women. As a result of the fall caused by Chava's partaking of the forbidden fruit, women no longer felt comfortable in public around men, and found it necessary to remain home to preserve their purity and their honor.

More importantly, the Gemara's list of "curses" also includes blessings such as pregnancy, labor and childrearing— all of which women happily embrace despite the hardships involved. Women in ancient times preferred staying home just as women have always desired bearing children, notwithstanding the pain of labor and the challenges of parenting. They found a home-based life a source of joy and honor, despite being denied the opportunities that present themselves outside the home, no less than women find bearing and raising children a source of profound gratification despite the discomfort and demands they entail.

Regardless, the Rambam, in the passage cited earlier, writes explicitly שאינה בבית הסוהר עד שלא תצא ולא תבוא — a woman is not "imprisoned" in her home, in clear contradistinction to the Gemara's negative depiction of a woman's home-based life.

Limiting the Parameters of כל כבודה

Even if כל כבודה בת מלך פנימה indeed imposes an obligation upon women to remain at home, it is likely that this obligation is limited in scope, and does not prohibit women from going out to work or to involve themselves in other productive pursuits.

Rav Avraham Yaakov Horowitz of Probuzna[34] advances a novel approach to explain the Gemara's discussion in *Gittin* addressed earlier concerning a husband's right to relieve himself of the responsibility to support his self-sufficient wife. As we saw, the Gemara noted that we might have intuitively disallowed such an arrangement, due to the consideration of כל כבודה בת מלך פנימה, which discourages women from venturing outside the home. But in truth, the Gemara concludes, this arrangement is acceptable — a conclusion which might lead us to believe that the principle of כל כבודה is not accepted as a binding rule. On the other hand, as discussed earlier, the Gemara elsewhere applies the principle of כל כבודה to explain why female converts from Amon and Moav are permitted to marry into the Jewish Nation, as these nations' women were not expected to bring provisions to *Bnei Yisrael* in the desert.

To reconcile these seemingly conflicting passages, Rav Horowitz distinguishes between two different models of כל כבודה בת מלך פנימה. The first model is one of nobility and aristocracy, whereby a woman has the luxury of comfortably remaining at home and has everything she needs brought to her. The Gemara proposed that perhaps all Jewish women, by virtue of the Jewish People's special status, are entitled to this privilege, such that a husband must support his wife even if she is capable of earning a living on her own, but the Gemara dismissed this possibility. We are thus left with a second model of כל כבודה בת מלך פנימה, whereby a woman leaves home only for her needs. This model is shared by Jewish and non-Jewish women alike, which is why the Gemara applied this rule even to the women of Amon and Moav.[35]

According to Rav Horowitz, כל כבודה בת מלך פנימה does not mean that women must remain at home. Rather, it means that they should not frequently venture out of their homes unnecessarily, for no productive purpose.[36]

A similar point is made by Rav Bentzion Meir Chai Uziel[37] in his responsum allowing women to serve in positions of leadership. Addressing the question of whether this would compromise appropriate standards of modesty, he writes:

---

34. *Tzur Yaakov*, 75.

35. This reading of the Gemara's discussion in *Yevamos* is in contrast to that suggested by the *Maharshal*, mentioned earlier, note 2.

36. The flaw in Rav Horowitz's approach is the Gemara's application of כל כבודה to explain why the women of Amon and Moav were not expected to bring provisions to *Bnei Yisrael* in the desert. Seemingly, this gesture would certainly qualify as a worthwhile, constructive purpose that justified a trip outside. Perhaps, Rav Horowitz understood that since the men of Amon and Moav were available to fulfill this role, there would have been no reason for the women to participate in this charitable endeavor.

37. Referenced above, note 26.

הסברא נותנת לומר דכל כנסיה רצינית ושיחה מועילה אין בה משום פריצות, וכל
יום ויום האנשים נפגשים עם הנשים במשא ומתן מסחרי, ונושאים ונותנים, ובכל
זאת אין שום פרץ ושום צוחה... ולא אמרו רבותינו אל תרבה שיחה עם האשה
(אבות א' ה') אלא בשיחה בטלה שלא לצורך, ושיחה כזאת היא הגוררת עון, אבל
לא שיחה של וכוח בענינים חשובים וצבוריים; ואין הישיבה במחיצה וכפיפה
אחת לשם עבודת הצבור, שהיא עבודת הקדש, מרגילה לעבירה, ומביאה לידי
קלות ראש, וכל ישראל האנשים והנשים קדושים הם, ואינם חשודים בפריצת גדר
הצניעות והמוסר.

Logic dictates that any serious gathering and constructive conversation
does not constitute immodesty. Every single day, men encounter women
in commercial exchanges, and engage with one another, and yet there is
no breach and no outcry... Our Sages said, "Do not indulge in conversation with a woman" (*Avos* 1:5) only with regard to idle, unnecessary talk,
and such conversation leads to sin — but not when engaging in arguments over important, public matters. Sitting together in the same area
and space for the sake of public service, which is holy work, does not
lend itself to sin or lead to frivolity. All Israel — men and women — are
sacred, and are not suspected of breaching the boundaries of modesty
and ethics.[38]

The Torah ideal of *tzniyus* does not require women to hide and avoid being seen by
men. It instead requires men and women to conduct themselves in a responsible
manner, recognizing the fierce nature of the sexual urge, such as by avoiding provoc-
ative dress and overly casual friendships with members of the opposite gender. It does
not, however, require a woman to stay at home rather than using her skills and talents
for the benefit of society.

Indeed, Rav Wosner concludes his discussion of כל כבודה בת מלך פנימה by noting
the example of Rus, who was praised for spending full days during the harvest in Boaz's
fields collecting gleanings in order to support herself and her mother-in-law, who

---

38. Rav Shimshon Raphael Hirsch, in his commentary to *Avos*, notes that the Mishna specifically instructed אל תרבה **שיחה** עם האשה — that one avoid excessive שיחה, as opposed to
excessive דברים ("words"). The word שיחה, Rav Hirsch writes, has the specific connotation
of idle, unproductive chatter. For example, the Mishna later in *Avos* (3:14) warns against
engaging in שיחת ילדים — childish chatting, and מיעוט שיחה (minimizing שיחה) is listed
among the prerequisites for acquiring Torah knowledge (*Avos* 6:6), implying that שיחה
refers to meaningless talk. אל תרבה שיחה עם האשה, Rav Hirsch explains, means that even
with one's wife, one should limit nonconstructive chatter, and try to engage in meaningful
conversation.

suffered destitution.[39] The Gemara[40] comments, הלכה ובאת הלכה ובאת עד שמצאה בני אדם
המהוגנין לילך עמהם — Rus made every effort to ensure that she would be with upstanding people in the fields as she collected. And for this reason, Rav Wosner writes, it was
permissible for Rus to spend her days out in the fields. The rule of כל כבודה בת מלך
פנימה does not prevent women from going out in an appropriate manner and with
appropriate company. It is entirely permissible for a woman to leave home — and even
to spend most of the day outside the home, as in Rus' case — in order to involve herself
in meaningful, constructive activities, together with upstanding people.

We should also emphasize the Gemara's comment[41] that Rus made a point of collecting the gleanings in an especially modest, non-provocative manner.[42] It goes without
saying that when a woman is in public, she must ensure not to display herself in a potentially arousing manner, and this, too, is something to be learned from Rus' example. But
the fact that Rus was specifically praised for spending entire days out in Boaz's fields
demonstrates that the principle of כל כבודה was never intended to prevent women from
leaving the home to engage in meaningful activities in an appropriate manner.

This is implied also by the Rambam's comments cited earlier. He writes explicitly
that a woman is entitled to leave to visit her parents, to comfort mourners, to celebrate
at her friends' happy occasions, and to perform acts of kindness. It is inappropriate,
the Rambam says, for a woman "to always go out, sometimes outside, sometime in
the streets…" The principle of כל כבודה requires a woman to limit her recreational
excursions, not to refrain from constructive and valuable pursuits outside the home.
Even where the Rambam establishes the impropriety of a woman's frequent excursions,
he clearly approves of her leaving for worthwhile purposes.[43]

With this in mind, we can easily understand why כל כבודה is not practiced today,
even if we assume that this principle is to be understood as a halachic prohibition.
In earlier generations, when women did not receive an education and did not pursue
careers, there were few constructive activities in which women could engage outside
the home. Frequently venturing out of the home would be a "red flag" and a legitimate
cause for concern of improper behavior, because there weren't many other reasons for
a woman to leave the house. This is simply not the case today, when women are fully
integrated into every area of society and no less capable of producing and contributing than men. Under modern-day conditions, the principle of כל כבודה — which to
begin with discourages frequent trips from the home for non-constructive purposes
— simply does not apply.

---

39. ותבוא ותעמוד מאז הבוקר ועד עתה זה שבתה הבית מעט (*Rus* 2:7).

40. *Shabbos* 113b.

41. There in *Maseches Shabbos*.

42. Specifically, when she needed to collect grain that was lying on the ground, she would sit,
    instead of bending down.

43. See Rav Yehuda Henkin's *Bnei Banim*, vol. 1, 40.

Another relevant source to this discussion is a brief comment by Rav Binyamin Zilber[44] regarding the Vilna Gaon's famous letter to his wife, in which he advised her not to attend the synagogue, where she would be all but certain to experience jealousy and hear improper speech.[45] Rav Zilber (after observing that this recommendation does not appear in other versions of the Gaon's letter) asserts that this advice is not applicable in our times, when synagogue attendance, in Rav Zilber's words, "strengthens *Yiddishkeit*." It is quite possible that in 18th-century Lithuania, the spiritual pitfalls of the social aspects of synagogue attendance (such as petty competition and gossip) outweighed its spiritual benefits. In modern times, however, in Rav Zilber's view, the spiritual benefits of participating in public prayer outweigh the spiritual risks.

More generally, we might explain that כל כבודה בת מלך פנימה establishes the value of a woman remaining out of the public view to avoid the real, undeniable spiritual dangers posed by interaction with men. However, this value is not absolute, and may be superseded by opportunities for spiritual growth and fulfillment, and for making important contributions to society. In the modern era, such opportunities abound for both men and women alike, and the value of what women are capable of achieving outside the home outweighs the benefits of remaining in their homes.

Conclusion

Several *poskim* applied the principle of כל כבודה בת מלך פנימה to arrive at restrictions to which no observant women adhere nowadays, and indeed, several recent *poskim* observed that this rule is simply not practiced in our time. To justify this modern-day reality, it could be argued that the requirement for women to remain indoors was rooted in the danger of sexual assault, a risk which is far lower today than it was in ancient times. Alternatively, it is possible that כל כבודה בת מלך פנימה was not established as a halachic restriction, but rather reflected the reality in ancient times that women found it disrespectful and degrading to leave their homes. Women preferred staying at home, rather than compromising their dignity by frequently leaving.

Additionally, even if כל כבודה should indeed be understood as a halachic requirement, it could be argued that it refers only to frequent non-constructive trips outside the home, and does not at all forbid women from going out and making meaningful contributions to society, as the vast majority of observant women do today. Unlike in the ancient world, women today have countless opportunities for growth, self-fulfillment and achievement outside the home, and the value of these achievements overrides the spiritual dangers that lurk, dangers which, needless to say, they must seek to avoid through proper attire, proper conduct, and ensuring to be in the company of upstanding people.

---

44.   *Az Nidberu*, 7:89.

45.   עיקר הגדר בבדידות שלא תצא חס ושלום מפתח ביתך חוצה, ואף בבית הכנסת תקצר מאד ותצא, ויותר טוב להתפלל בבית, כי בבית הכנסת אי-אפשר להינצל מקנאה ולשמוע דברים בטלים ולשון הרע.

Newsweek

Rabbi Urges Congregation to Bring Guns to Synagogue Amid Rise in Hate Crimes

June 27, 2019
By Daniel Avery

As hate crimes and incidents of mass shootings continue to rise, one Massachusetts rabbi is telling his congregation to come armed to synagogue on the Sabbath.

"We can't think, 'I'm just praying, and God will save me,' " Rabbi Dan Rodkin of Shaloh House, a synagogue and Jewish day school in Boston, told WBUR. "We need to take care of situations ourselves."

Rodkin cited the massacre at a Pittsburgh synagogue in October, as well as other attacks on houses of worship: "I know it sounds horrible, but I think it's a very logical approach for the situation we're in," he said. "I don't want people to have guns. But I think to protect our families, it's a necessity now."

Shooting suspect Robert Bowers reportedly shouted "all Jews must die" before bursting into the Tree of Life Congregation on October 27 and opening fire, killing 11 worshippers.

In April, one person died at a shooting at a synagogue in San Diego.

During the Sabbath, observant Jews are prohibited from strenuous activity, using electricity or otherwise violating "the day of rest." That woulds seem to extend to carrying weapons, according to the Talmud, the primary source for Jewish religious law: "One must not go out [on Shabbat] with a sword, nor with a bow, nor with a triangular shield, nor with a round one, nor with a spear; if he does so he is liable for a sin-offering... The sages say they are nothing but a stigma."

According to Chabad, one of the largest Hassidic movements in America, "Weapons and their possession are a reproach to mankind–and not anything desirable."

"We can't think, 'I'm just praying, and God will save me,' " Rabbi Dan Rodkin of Shaloh House. (DAN RODKIN/FACEBOOK)

But other congregations are also considering asking members to arm themselves.

"We're talking about the worst situation that anyone could imagine," Jeremy Yamin, director of security and operations at Combined Jewish Philanthropies, told the New York Post. "Federal agents and police officers spend an entire career training for something like this."

After the San Diego shooting, one member of an Orthodox shul in New York told the Post in May that he always brings a Glock to services: "I'm not trying to be a tough guy or a cowboy. My top priority is protecting my family plus the hundreds of congregants at my synagogue, many of whom are friends"

For his part, Rodkin says he wants to obey the tenets of his faith, but keeping his community safe is paramount.

"In Judaism, life is the most sacred thing," he told WBUR. "Political correctness is important, too, but not as important as a life. So I think whatever it takes to save a life, it is the most important task."

Guns in Shul: Halachic Considerations

The unfortunate and tragic spate of attacks on houses of worship in the United States in the late 2010s — including the deadly shooting in a Pittsburgh congregation in 2018, and a machete attack during a Chanukah gathering a Monsey rabbi's home in 2019 — has aroused considerable discussion about synagogue security. Many questions were raised, including the need for armed security guards at the entrance to every synagogue, and the possibility of avoiding heavy security costs by enlisting synagogue members to train in the use of firearms and then bring a concealed weapon with them to the synagogue.

These questions revolve mainly around the concerns that arise from the presence of guns in public places. Some fear that a cadre of armed citizens poses more risk than the danger it is intended to protect against, as a proliferation of firearms could result in guns ending up in the wrong hands, or in accidental shootings. Others raise the educational effects of having firearms visible in the presence of children.

But assuming that armed security at synagogues is a prudent safety measure to protect against violent attacks, the idea to arm congregants also raises a number of interesting halachic questions:

1. Is it permissible to carry a gun in its holster in one's belt on Shabbos through a public domain where there is no *eiruv*?
2. Is a firearm considered *muktzeh* on Shabbos?
3. Is it permissible for women to carry firearms?
4. Would bringing a firearm into a synagogue fall under the prohibition mentioned by the *Shulchan Aruch*[1] against bringing a "large knife" into a synagogue, because such knives are used as weapons?

Defining פקוח נפש

Before examining each of these halachic concerns, it is worth noting a broader question, one with which many *poskim* grappled, as to the definition of פיקוח נפש — the famous provision which suspends virtually all the Torah's laws for the sake of protecting human life. It is clear that in situations of danger, all prohibitions — the only excep-

---

1. O.C. 151:6.

tions being murder, idol-worship and illicit sexual relations — may be transgressed for the sake of ensuring safety. Far less clear, however, is when a situation qualifies as a dangerous circumstance that warrants Torah violation. It goes without saying that a patient who suffers a heart attack may be rushed to the hospital and treated on Shabbos, and that one who stubs his toe may not. In between these two extremes, however, is a very large grey area, and many *poskim* attempted to determine how serious a risk is needed to apply the rule of פיקוח נפש and suspend Torah violations for the sake of ensuring health and safety.

One of the earliest and most important sources relevant to this discussion is a responsum penned by the *Noda Be-Yehuda*[2] regarding the permissibility of dissecting human cadavers for medical research. The specific question brought to the *Noda Be-Yehuda* involved an ill patient who died, and scientists wished to study his remains in order to learn how to treat this condition in the future. The *Noda Be-Yehuda* strongly forbade dissecting the cadaver, which would violate the prohibition against desecrating a human corpse, establishing that the possible life-saving benefit of the dissection did not suffice to suspend the prohibition. Although the Torah's laws are suspended even for the sake of ספק פיקוח נפש — possibly saving human life — the *Noda Be-Yehuda* averred that this applies only ביש ספק סכנת נפשות לפנינו כגון חולה או נפילת גל — "when there is a possible risk to life in front of us, such as an ill patient or a fallen avalanche." Only if a particular situation of potential danger arises, do we suspend Torah law to protect against the threat to human life. However, the *Noda Be-Yehuda* establishes, we cannot suspend Torah law in order to address a potentially threatening situation that may arise in the future. Therefore, if there was a dangerously ill patient whose life could possibly be saved by dissecting and studying the body of a patient who died from the same illness, then this would be allowed, but this cannot be permitted for the sake of having the necessary medical information available when we are confronted in the future by a patient in need of treatment.

This ruling was similarly issued by the *Chasam Sofer*[3] in addressing the case of one who during his lifetime donated his body for medical research. The *Chasam Sofer* ruled that the body may not be dissected unless there was presently a dangerously ill patient who might be saved by the information gleaned from studying the cadaver.

Applying this principle to the question of violating *halacha* for the sake of arming synagogues, it would appear that the according to the *Noda Be-Yehuda* and *Chasam Sofer*, Torah law could be suspended only if there is a clear, direct threat to synagogues. As long as no particular individual or group has threatened an attack, violating Torah law to protect against somebody who might launch an assault would be unjustified. Accordingly, we might distinguish between the situation in Israel, which is, unfortu-

---

2.   *Mahadura Tinyana*. Y.D. 201.

3.   Y.D. 336.

nately, in an ongoing state of war against the Palestinian Arabs, and the situation in the United States. In Israel, there is a specific enemy that openly seeks to murder Jews, and thus prudent security measures would override Torah law. In the United States, however, even with the concerning increase in anti-Semitic attacks, it is difficult to claim that American Jews face a clear, present threat that warrants suspending Torah law for the sake of synagogue security.

However, the *Chazon Ish*,[4] after referencing these responsa of the *Noda Be-Yehuda* and *Chasam Sofer*, asserts that the determining factor is not whether or not there is a particular patient who could possibly be helped, but rather the likelihood of a forbidden act yielding life-saving benefits. He thus rules that during an outbreak, or when dealing with a common fatal illness, it would be permissible to dissect a cadaver if this could possibly result in the discovery of a cure, since there is a high likelihood of the prohibited act resulting in the rescue of human life. The *Chazon Ish* notes the Gemara's ruling in *Maseches Eiruvin* (45a) that if a foreign nation invades a border town, then even if their immediate goal is to seize resources, and seem to have no intention to kill, nevertheless, war may be waged even on Shabbos against the invaders. Since the invaders might seek to occupy this territory and then launch additional military assaults, this constitutes a potential risk to life. Even though this concern relates to the future, and not to a present danger, nevertheless, it suffices to override the Shabbos prohibitions. Necessarily, the *Chazon Ish* concludes, future threats are not discounted if they are likely to unfold.

According to the *Chazon Ish*, then, the question in regard to synagogue protection becomes whether the threat of an anti-Semitic attack on a synagogue crosses the threshold of likelihood that justifies suspending the Shabbos restrictions. In his view, any threat within the realm of likelihood — even if no specific dangerous situation currently exists — suffices for applying the principle of פיקוח נפש and suspending the Torah's prohibition. We must then ask whether the current risk facing synagogues given the rise of anti-Semitism — which is still, thankfully, quite low — qualifies as a level of likelihood that constitutes פיקוח נפש.

A different definition of פיקוח נפש is presented by Rav Shlomo Zalman Auerbach, in a letter to Rav Eliezer Waldenberg which Rav Waldenberg cites and critiques in the ninth volume of his *Tzitz Eliezer*.[5] Rav Auerbach asserted that פיקוח נפש is defined as כל שאנשים מפחדים או נבהלים מזה — any situation that generally causes people fear. Rav Auerbach noted that earlier *poskim* forbade violating Shabbos for the sake of studying medicine, even though this knowledge will enable them to save lives, because during the week, aspiring medics and physicians do not tend to their studies with a sense

---

4.   Y.D. 208:7.

5.   17:2:9. See also *Minchas Shlomo, Mahadura Tinyana*, 37, and Rav Waldenberg's lengthy discussion of פיקוח נפש in *Tzitz Eliezer*, 8:15:7.

of fear and urgency, and so their study cannot qualify as פיקוח נפש. But if there is a situation that generates fear and concern among most people because of the danger entailed, then even if the statistical likelihood of death is very small, this suffices to permit suspending Torah law. If so, then the question for us becomes whether or not the level of danger has risen to the point where Jews are fearful of attending the synagogue without armed security guards.

The question of allowing carrying arms on Shabbos as a matter of פיקוח נפש was addressed already by the *Or Zaru'a*,[6] who writes:

> עתה שאנו דרים ביניהם...כשהקול יוצא שרוצים לבוא לשלול, אע"פ שלא באו
> עדיין, מותר ללבוש כלי זיין ולשמור ולעשות קול בעיר כדי שלא יבואו, דאין
> מדקדקין בפיקוח נפש.

> Now that we live among them...when it becomes known that they [hostile gentiles] wish to come and plunder, then even though they had not come yet, it is permissible [even on Shabbos] to wear weapons, guard and create a stir in the city so they will not come, for we are not so precise when it comes to threat to life.

The *Or Zaru'a* rules that when Jews live among hostile gentiles, then the moment there is word of violent enemies planning to launch any sort of attack, it is permissible for the Jews to arm themselves on Shabbos even in violation of the Shabbos prohibitions, given the potential risk to life. Conceivably, this could be applied to our current condition, as well, when we live among non-Jews and are all too aware of hostile elements who seek to shed Jewish blood. On the other hand, one could argue that there is no comparison between the conditions in which Jews lived in 13th-century Europe and those of 21st-century America, where Jews enjoy full civil rights, and the threat comes from isolated, fringe elements, and not from the mainstream of society. Under such conditions, it is far from certain that the *Or Zaru'a* would permit violating Shabbos for the sake of armed protection, notwithstanding the principle of אין מדקדקין בפיקוח נפש.

In truth, this discussion might be immaterial, given the possibility of hiring non-Jewish security guards. As long as this option is available, there would appear to be no justification for allowing a Jew to carry a weapon if this entails an act of Shabbos desecration on the level of Torah law. There is no question that one who has the possibility of avoiding a Torah violation by paying money is required to do so. Therefore, even if one could argue that the threat of ant-Semitism has reached the point where armed protection in synagogues must be viewed as a matter of פיקוח נפש, no Torah laws could be suspended for this purpose if there is the option of engaging non-Jewish security personnel, even if this entails considerable expense.

_____

6.   Vol. 2, *Hilchos Shabbos*, 84:13.

הוצאה — Carrying a Firearm through a Public Domain

The issue of carrying a weapon through a public domain on Shabbos without an *eiruv*, from a practical standpoint, is the easiest to avoid, by securely locking the gun in a concealed location in the synagogue, such that it does not have to be carried. But where this is not possible, is there a halachic basis to permit carrying a gun, despite the prohibition against carrying into or through a public domain on Shabbos?

The *Shulchan Aruch*,[7] following the majority opinion in the Mishna (*Shabbos* 63a), rules explicitly that one may not walk outside on Shabbos with a sword, bow, shield or dagger, and that doing so constitutes a Torah violation. Although Rabbi Eliezer permitted walking about on Shabbos with weapons, because they are considered like תכשיטין ("jewelry," or accessories, which have the status of garments), the majority of *Tannaim* disagreed, and ruled that weapons are no different from other objects, which may not be carried in a public domain on Shabbos.

The *Aruch Ha-Shulchan*,[8] however, writes that going about with weapons is forbidden — מפני שדברים אלו אינם תכשיטין בעצם אלא לבעלי מלחמה הרי הם כבגדיו — "because these items are not inherently accessories, except for men of war, for whom they are like his garments." According to the *Aruch Ha-Shulchan*, soldiers or security professionals, who carry firearms as part of their uniforms, would be permitted to walk outside on Shabbos with a gun, since the gun is considered part of their attire. Thus, while it would still be forbidden for ordinary congregants to carry a firearm to the synagogue on Shabbos, uniformed security guards, who "wear" a gun as part of their garb, such as in a holster attached to their belts, would be allowed to do so.[9]

However, a number of later *poskim*, including Rav Yosef Shalom Elyashiv,[10] disputed the *Aruch Ha-Shulchan*'s position.[11]

---

7. O.C. 301:7.

8. O.C. 301:51.

9. The *Aruch Ha-Shulchan* reached this conclusion on the basis of Rabbeinu Ovadia Me-Bartenura's comments to the Mishna, where he writes that military garb may not be worn outside on Shabbos "because they are worn only during times of war." Apparently, the *Aruch Ha-Shulchan* understood this to mean that military garb is worn only by soldiers, and so they cannot be considered "garments" for others — implying that soldiers are allowed to walk through the public domain with military garb on Shabbos. The Klausenberger Rebbe, in *Divrei Yatziv* (O.C. 148), notes that this also seems to have been the understanding of the *Levush*.

10. *Kovetz Teshuvos*, 3:51.

11. Rav Elyashiv noted that Rashi, and others, understood that the Mishna forbids going out in military boots and the like because of מראית העין — this would give the appearance of going out to war in violation of Shabbos. Accordingly, it would certainly be forbidden for anyone, and certainly a soldier, to carry a gun outdoors on Shabbos.

Accordingly, it seems difficult to permit carrying a gun on Shabbos in an area without an *eiruv*. This would certainly be forbidden for ordinary congregants, and it is likely forbidden even for uniformed security guards.

Muktzeh

If the neighborhood is encircled by a valid *eiruv*, or if the firearm is kept inside the synagogue, the question becomes whether the gun might be considered *muktzeh* and thus forbidden to be handled on Shabbos. Since its primary use is for causing injury or death, both of which would constitute a desecration of Shabbos, a gun would seemingly fall under the category of כלי שמלאכתו לאיסור — a utensil used mainly for an action that is forbidden on Shabbos — and thus subject to the restrictions that apply to such a utensil.

This is, indeed, the view of Rav Yosef Shalom Elyashiv,[12] who ruled that precisely for this reason, it is permissible to carry a weapon on Shabbos for protection (indoors, or in an area with a valid *eiruv*). A כלי שמלאכתו לאיסור may be handled if it is needed for a permissible purpose (לצורך גופו), or if one needs the space it occupies (לצורך מקומו). Handling such a utensil is forbidden only for its own protection (מחמה לצל), such as if it was left outdoors and is thus exposed to the elements or to the risk of theft. Therefore, Rav Elyashiv writes, it is entirely permissible to carry around a weapon on Shabbos for the purpose of deterring potential criminals.

---

12.   In the essay referenced above, note 10. Rav Elyashiv actually uses the expression מוקצה מחמת איסור — the term referring to something which may not be handled on Shabbos because it was forbidden to be handled when Shabbos began. It is reasonable to assume that he meant כלי שמלאכתו לאיסור, because an object designated as מוקצה מחמת איסור may not be handled on Shabbos even לצורך גופו. Indeed, in a different manuscript (*Kisvei Ha-Gaon Rav Yosef Shalom — Shabbos*, p. 171), Rav Elyashiv writes explicitly that a firearm is a כלי שמלאכתו לאיסור. Likewise, Rav Elyashiv's closest disciple, Rav Yosef Efrati, understood the passage from *Kovetz Teshuvos* to mean that a weapon falls under the category of כלי שמלאכתו לאיסור (*Yisa Yosef*, O.C. 2:81).

Rav Yaakov Emden (*Lechem Shamayim*, *Shabbos* 6:4), suggests classifying weapons under the category of מוקצה מחמת חסרון כיס — items which are designated for a forbidden purpose, and which are valuable or fragile such that their users would never use them for any other purpose. The Klausenberger Rebbe dismisses this contention, arguing that the rule of מוקצה מחמת חסרון כיס applies to something which people are careful not to use for anything other than its intended purpose out of concern of ruining it, which is not the case with a gun, which is not easily broken. This question is discussed also by Rav Efrati, who notes that a gun-owner would be willing to use the gun as a hammer, for example, and this suffices to exclude guns from the category of מוקצה מחמת חסרון כיס.

According to this view, it would be forbidden, in principle, to move a gun for its own protection, such as if it was accidentally dropped, or it was forgotten somewhere, before one returned it to its place after it is no longer needed. (For example, after the prayer service, the gun's owner realized that he had left it on his seat in the sanctuary.) If a weapon falls under the category of כלי שמלאכתו לאיסור, then seemingly, it would be forbidden to return it to its place once the services have ended and the crowd has dispersed, such that there is no longer any fear of attack, given the prohibition against moving a כלי שמלאכתו לאיסור for its own protection.

Clearly, however, leaving a gun exposed and unattended poses considerable danger, and thus it would certainly be permissible to move the gun back to its place. The *Shulchan Aruch*[13] rules explicitly that a sharp *muktzeh* object may be moved on Shabbos if it could potentially hurt people. This would apply all the more so to a firearm.

In any event, Rav Shlomo Zalman Auerbach[14] disagreed with Rav Elyashiv, and ruled that a gun falls under the category of כלי שמלאכתו להיתר — utensils designated for a permissible purpose. Except on the battlefield, Rav Shlomo Zalman argued, a gun's primary function is not to inflict harm, but to instill fear. A policeman or security guard carries a gun not because he intends to shoot a bullet at somebody, but in order to deter prospective criminals. Deterring potential delinquents is, of course, permissible on Shabbos, and thus we may classify a gun as a כלי שמלאכתו להיתר.[15] Rav Auerbach notes the Chafetz Chaim's ruling in *Bei'ur Halacha*[16] that if a utensil is generally used for both an action which is permissible on Shabbos, and an action that is forbidden, it still constitutes a כלי שמלאכתו היתר — even if it is more commonly used for a purpose which is forbidden on Shabbos. Hence, even though a gun is used both to inflict injury and as a deterrent, it is treated as a כלי שמלאכתו להיתר and may be handled on Shabbos without any restriction.[17]

---

13. O.C. 308:18.

14. *Shulchan Shlomo*, 308:3:16.

15. Rav Auerbach notes that one could, at first glance, challenge his claim based on the view cited by the *Magen Avraham* (308:18) forbidding the practice observed in some communities to hold a candle when bringing one's child to the synagogue on Shabbos for the first time. According to this view, the candle may not be handled because it does not serve any function, even though it is held as a sign of respect — perhaps proving that if an object is not used for any specific action, but merely displayed for some emotional impact, it may not be handled on Shabbos. Rav Auerbach refutes this proof, noting that holding a gun itself instills fear, whereas holding a candle, in and of itself, does not necessarily display respect. He further notes that although this view is cited and briefly discussed by the *Magen Avraham*, the *Magen Avraham* did not necessarily concur.

16. 308:3, ד״ה קורדום.

17. This is also the conclusion of the Klausenberger Rebbe, in the responsum referenced

לא יהיה כלי גבר על אשה — May a Woman Carry a Weapon?

The Torah in *Sefer Devarim*[18] commands, לא יהיה כלי גבר על אשה ולא ילבש גבר שמלת אשה, forbidding cross-dressing. *Targum Onkelos* translates the first half of this clause to mean לא יהי תקון זין דגבר על אתתא — that a woman may not wear military gear like a man. This translation appears also in the Gemara in *Maseches Nazir* (59a), which cites Rabbi Eliezer ben Yaakov as inferring from this verse that לא תצא אשה בכלי זיין למלחמה — "a woman may not go out to war with weapons." Similarly, the Midrash[19] comments that Yael killed the enemy general Sisera with a peg, because she was not permitted to have a weapon, given the prohibition of לא יהיה כלי גבר על אשה.

Accordingly, the Rambam,[20] in formulating the prohibition forbidding a woman to wear men's attire, writes that a woman may not wear armor (שריון). The Rambam's comments are brought by the *Shulchan Aruch*.[21]

Significantly, however, after listing the garments that a man or woman may not wear because they are customarily worn by the opposite gender, the Rambam adds, הכל כמנהג המדינה — a given garment's status is determined based on societal convention. A garment normally worn by one gender in a particular time and place is forbidden in that time and place to be worn by members of the opposite gender. And thus the Rama, in his glosses to the *Shulchan Aruch*, writes, citing the *Tur*, לפי מנהג המקום ההוא — "according to the practice of that place." Accordingly, we might conclude that nowadays, when many women serve in the military and police force, and as security guards, weapons are no longer considered כלי גבר, and may thus be worn by women.

Secondly, the *Bach*, cited by the *Taz*,[22] rules that cross-dressing is forbidden only if one wears the garment for purely cosmetic purposes. If, however, one wears the garment to serve a practical need — such as for protection from the rain, or for warmth — then this is allowed.[23] The Maharsham[24] notes that this view, seemingly, is contradicted by the Midrash's remark about Yael, who needed to protect herself from Sisera with a peg due to the prohibition against a woman using weapons. The answer, the Maharsham explains, is that since Yael had the option of using something other than a weapon, she was not permitted to use a weapon to kill the general. Otherwise, if no other option were available, Yael would have been permitted to protect herself with

---

above, note 9.

18. 22:5.

19. *Yalkut Shimoni, Shoftim*, 56.

20. *Hilchos Avoda Zara* 12:10.

21. Y.D. 182:5.

22. Y.D. 182:4.

23. The *Shach* (182:7) writes that the *Bach's* remarks "are not very compelling," though he stops short of dismissing this ruling.

24. 2:243.

a weapon, in accordance with the *Bach*'s position, limiting the prohibition of כלי גבר to clothing worn for cosmetic purposes.

If so, then the prohibition against women carrying weapons is very limited in scope, applicable only if the woman wears the gear to appear like a man, but not if she needs to use the weapons.

Rav Shabtai Rappaport presented this line of reasoning (though without citing the Maharsham) to his grandfather, Rav Moshe Feinstein, who wrote a lengthy response which was later published.[25] Rav Moshe dismissed this argument, stating that the prohibition of wearing weapons differs from the prohibition of wearing garments. The *Bach*'s qualification, Rav Moshe averred, pertains only to clothing, whereas weapons are forbidden to be worn by women even for a purely military purpose. To the contrary, Rav Moshe contended, if a woman wishes to wear a certain weapon as part of her garb for strictly aesthetic purposes, then this is permissible, because the prohibition against wearing weapons is distinct from the prohibition against wearing men's attire, and forbids wearing military gear for its usual purpose.

Nevertheless, Rav Moshe permitted women to carry guns in dangerous areas[26] for other reasons. Besides the concern of life-threatening danger, Rav Moshe asserted that small pistols, which, unlike rifles, are not normally brought to war, do not fall under the prohibition of כלי גבר. Additionally, Rav Moshe wrote that when dealing with the threat of terrorism, as opposed to conventional warfare, all citizens are targeted and thus require protection, such that there is no distinction between men and women with respect to the need for firearms. Under such circumstances, a gun is not a uniquely male accessory, and so it would be permitted for a woman to carry a gun.[27]

According to Rav Moshe, then, we would, seemingly, permit women to carry handguns with them in synagogues for protection, for two reasons: 1) handguns are not included in the prohibition to begin with; 2) when dealing with the threat of attacks on civilians, weapons of self-defense are not considered a male garment.[28]

---

25.   *Iggeros Moshe*, O.C. 4:74.

26.   The specific question posed to him related to the permissibility of women living in West Bank settlements carrying guns for protection from Palestinian terrorists.

27.   In Rav Moshe's words: במלחמות קטנות אלו הא נמצאות הנשים כאנשים בהכרח שלכן לא שייך חילוק בין גברי לנשי במה שצריכין ליקח להנצל...וכל ענייני נשק יש להחשיב דרכן, דתרוייהו בין גברי בין נשי בזה.

28.   Rav Moshe concludes his discussion by stating, רק לצאת למלחמה...אסורות וכן בסתם מקומות שבחזקת שלום אסורות — "Only going out to war...is forbidden for them, and also in ordinary situations, where there is a state of peace, they are forbidden [to wear weapons]." He thus allows women to carry weapons only if there is no חזקת שלום — "state of peace" such that weapons are not necessary. It seems likely that in a time of increased anti-Semitism, after several houses of worship have been targeted, there is no longer a

Another basis for permitting women to carry a weapon emerges from a responsum by Rav Yitzchak Isaac Herzog[29] addressing the issue of women enlisting in the Israel Defense Forces, in which he analyzes the Rambam's aforementioned ruling forbidding women to wear armor. The *Kessef Mishneh* commentary writes that the Rambam follows Rabbi Eliezer ben Yaakov's statement brought by the Gemara, לא תצא אשה בכלי זיין למלחמה — that a woman may not go out to war with weapons. However, Rav Herzog notes, the Rambam formulated this prohibition much differently, simply including military gear in his examples of male clothing which a woman is forbidden to wear. Rav Herzog thus proposes that the Rambam did not accept Rabbi Eliezer ben Yaakov's position,[30] and followed instead the view in the Gemara that לא יהיה כלי גבר על אשה forbids a woman from wearing clothing that gives her a male appearance. This prohibition would include military garb, but would not include carrying a weapon, which is not actually worn as a garment. According to Rav Herzog's understanding of the Rambam, then, although women are forbidden from wearing military garb, there is no prohibition against women carrying weapons.

Rav Herzog concludes that although he would not encourage the inclusion of women in the Israel Defense Forces as a practical matter, he sees no reason to forbid women to carry weapons for self-defense or to serve as security guards.

Bringing a Weapon into a Synagogue

The *Shulchan Aruch*[31] writes, יש אוסרים ליכנס בסכין ארוך — "there are those who forbid entering a synagogue with a 'long knife.'" The source of this view is a ruling cited by the *Orchos Chayim* in the name of the Maharam Mei-Rotenberg. The reason, as explained by the *Beis Yosef*, is that "prayer extends a person's life and a knife shortens it" — meaning, it is inappropriate to bring a weapon, which cuts life short, into a synagogue, where we beg the Almighty for longevity.

A possible Talmudic source for this prohibition is the Gemara's comment in *Maseches Sanhedrin* (82a), אין נכנסין בכלי זיין לבית המדרש — "One may not enter a study hall with weapons." The Gemara infers this rule from the story of Pinchas, who, after leaving the *Sanhedrin* which deliberated the punishment for those who partici-

---

חזקת שלום, and thus arming women would be permissible.

29. *Pesakim U-Kesavim*, vol. 1, 52:6.

30. Although there is a general rule that Rabbi Eliezer ben Yaakov's positions are accepted as authoritative (משנת רבי אליעזר קב ונקי), Rav Herzog notes that this rule is relevant only to Rabbi Eliezer ben Yaakov's rulings that appear in the Mishna, as the *Kessef Mishneh* establishes in a different context (*Hilchos Beis Ha-Bechira* 2:18), and Rabbi Eliezer ben Yaakov's ruling regarding women carrying weapons is cited in a *beraysa*, not a Mishna.

31. O.C. 151:6.

pated in the sins with Moavite women, picked up a spear[32] and proceeded to kill Zimri and Kozbi. Pinchas did not have his weapon with him in the *beis midrash*, as evidenced by his having to take hold of it only after leaving, thus indicating that a weapon may not be brought into a study hall.[33]

Seemingly, then, it is forbidden to bring firearms into a synagogue, at any time, even on weekdays.

However, the *Mishna Berura*[34] notes the *Elya Rabba*'s ruling that a weapon may be brought to the synagogue if it is covered. Similarly, Rav Eliezer Waldenberg[35] cites the *Yad Aharon* as explaining on this basis why the Maharam Mei-Rotenberg forbade only a "long knife," but not small knives. Since small knives are generally concealed, they may be brought into a synagogue, and the prohibition is thus limited to large knives which cannot be fully covered. If so, then, seemingly, there is room to permit bringing a concealed firearm into a synagogue.

However, as Rav Waldeberg notes, Rav Yaakov Emden (in *Mor U-Ketzia*), who likewise permits bringing a concealed weapon into a synagogue, adds that a long knife may not be brought משום דאי-אפשר לכסותו שלא יהא נרגש לעין — "because it is impossible to cover it such that it will not be discernible." According to Rav Yaakov Emden, then, concealing a weapon suffices to permit bringing it to the synagogue only if it cannot be noticed at all, even under one's clothing. Generally speaking, those who carry firearms keep the gun in a holster in the belt, where it is visible. In fact, when firearms are carried for security, the intention is for the gun to be noticed and thus deter prospective assailants.

Additionally, the *Taz*[36] writes explicitly that covering the knife does not suffice to allow bringing it into a synagogue. He explains that for this reason the prohibition was stated only in regard to large knives — since the knife needs to be brought out of the synagogue, and not merely covered — the Sages did not apply this prohibition to small knives, as they are far more common, and it would be very inconvenient to have to bring them somewhere else each time one enters the synagogue. According to this position, even a concealed weapon may not be brought into the synagogue. On the

---

32. ויקח רומח בידו, *Bamidbar* 25:7.

33. Already the *Maharitz Chayos*, in his notes to *Maseches Sanhedrin*, raises the question of why the *poskim* did not reference this passage as the source for the prohibition against entering a synagogue with a weapon. Numerous *Acharonim* answered that the sanctity of a *beis midrash* exceeds that of a synagogue (as ruled by the *Shulchan Aruch*, O.C. 153:1). See Rav David Yosef's *Halacha Berura*, vol. 7, *Sha'ar Ha-Tziyun* 151:62.

34. 151:22.

35. *Tzitz Eliezer*, 10:18.

36. 151:2.

other hand, as noted by Rav Ovadia Yosef,[37] the *Taz's* comments may provide a basis for bringing small pistols into the synagogue, which, like small knives, would be inconvenient to put away, and might thus have the same status as small knives in this regard. More generally, the *Taz* might permit bringing any gun into the synagogue if it would be very inconvenient to store it somewhere else. If so, then the *Taz* would certainly permit bringing a gun into the synagogue if this is necessary for security purposes.

In practice, Rav Waldenberg ruled that one who carries a weapon and has no option to leave it somewhere else during prayers may bring it to the synagogue, but should conceal it. Rav Ovadia Yosef concurred, adding that if one is unable to conceal the gun, then he may nevertheless bring it to the synagogue. This conclusion is based on the combination of numerous considerations, including the fact that Rabbeinu Peretz, as cited by the *Beis Yosef*, disputed the Maharam Mei-Rotenberg's position, and allowed bringing a weapon into a synagogue, and his lenient view can be given consideration in situations of need.

In the case of a weapon used for security, there may an additional basis for permitting bringing the weapon into the synagogue. If, as we have seen, the reason for forbidding weapons in the synagogue is because they "shorten" lives, then we may presume that weapons used for protection and self-defense, and thus have the effect of prolonging life, are permitted. Weapons carried for safety do not, in any way, undermine the sanctity of the synagogue, or contrast with the values represented by our houses of worship, and it thus stands to reason that they are not included in the prohibition against bringing weapons into a synagogue.[38]

A possible proof to this conclusion is the story told in *Sefer Nechemia* (4) about the rebuilding of Jerusalem when Jews returned from Babylonian exile. We read there (4:15) of guards who were stationed in the area to protect the workmen from the Jews' adversaries. A number of sources indicate that the construction described in these

---

37.   *Yechaveh Da'as* 5:18.

38.   This argument is advanced by Rav Yaakov Epstein in *Chevel Nachalaso*, 11:4. Rav Epstein adds that the sword of Goliyas, the Philistine warrior who was killed by David, was kept inside the *Mishkan* in Nov as a commemoration of David's miraculous victory (*Shmuel I* 21:10; see the commentaries of the Radak and Ralbag). And a verse in *Sefer Melachim II* (11:10) mentions את החנית ואת השלטים אשר למלך דוד אשר בבית ה׳ — David's weapons that were kept in the *Beis Ha-Mikdash*. The *Metzudos David* commentary indicates that David had made these weapons specifically to have them displayed in the *Beis Ha-Mikdash*. This would seem to prove that weapons that are not used to kill may be brought into a place of sanctity. (Significantly, however, Goliyas' sword is described as having been wrapped in a garment, perhaps lending support to the view of the *Elya Rabba* permitting bringing concealed weapons to the synagogue.)

verses included not only the city walls, but also the *Beis Ha-Mikdash* itself.[39] As such, we have a clear precedent for having armed guards on the sacred ground of the Temple Mount, such that we should likewise permit armed guards in synagogues.

Summary

1. While the precise definition of פיקוח נפש is unclear, the risk of anti-Semitic attacks on synagogues in generally safe neighborhoods, such as the majority of Jewish communities in the United States, does not appear to qualify as a life-threatening situation that would justify suspending Torah law for the sake of heightened security. As such, it is forbidden to carry a weapon through a public domain on Shabbos without an *eiruv*. If armed security is determined to be a matter of vital importance, and there is no *eiruv* and no possibility of safely storing a weapon in the synagogue, then every effort must be made to engage non-Jewish security guards, even if this entails a considerable expense.
2. If the weapon is stored in the synagogue, it may be handled and carried on Shabbos, and it is not considered *muktzeh*.
3. If possible, a gun should be concealed if it is brought into the sanctuary, ideally, in a manner such that it is completely indiscernible.
4. Women are permitted to train in the use firearms, and to serve as armed security guards.

INTERVIEWS

Rav Shimon Silver

Interviewed on *Headlines with Dovid Lichtenstein*, 25 Marcheshvan, 5779 (November 3, 2018)

At first glance, a gun is a כלי שמלאכתו לאיסור... But it is probably מוקצה מחמת חסרון כיס, because you're מייחד לו מקום; you have to set aside a specific place for a gun. It needs to be kept in a very secure place, because of לא תשים דמים בביתך. And, you wouldn't use it for anything else.

---

39. The Rambam (*Hilchos Beis Ha-Bechira* 1:12) rules that the building of the *Beis Ha-Mikdash* takes place from daybreak until nightfall, and the commentators (*Kesef Mishneh*, Mahari Kurkus) explain that the source of this ruling is the verses in *Nechemia* which speak of these builders working from daybreak until nightfall. *Tosfos* in *Maseches Bava Metzia* (83b) likewise assume that this verse speaks of the construction of the *Beis Ha-Mikdash* itself, and not just the walls around Jerusalem.

...It's a *chiddush* to say that a gun is a כלי שמלאכתו להיתר because it's used to frighten and intimidate. For that purpose, you don't need to carry it. You can have it sitting in front of you. You don't need to move it to have this intimidation value...

I would rather go with צער. There are situations where there is no actual danger, but there is צער, because a person is worried. There are certain *heteirim* for an איסור דרבנן in situations of צער. Assuming we're not talking about פקוח נפש — in which case we allow everything — but about a situation where you're trying to give some sort of מנוחת הנפש to the congregants, feeling that there is someone in the building to protect them, so you're allowing something like *muktzeh* to take away this צער and discomfort — maybe I can hear this a little bit.

As for carrying a gun to shul [through a place without an *eiruv*] — if a person is walking through a dangerous place, then maybe it's different, but if he's going in a place where you let children walk by themselves, this is not a dangerous place...

The *poskim* use the term שעת חירום — referring to a time when things are *hefker*, and people have no fear of the law. Here, in our situation, sure, there are crazy people all the time, you hear about it on the news, but when was the last time you saw it? I was a few blocks away from this [the shooting at the Tree of Life Synagogue in Pittsburgh], but for the vast majority of people, it's not a שעת חירום.

...If somebody asks me if he can wear a gun in a holster in a place with no *eiruv*, through a רשות הרבים דרבנן for his peace of mind — I would have to be very careful. People could get the wrong idea. If this is someone who will take דרבנן's lightly as a result, then I would not want to give him this kind of *heter*. It's not a real danger, and he's doing it to placate his nerves — which is a valid consideration, but you can't violate הוצאה for this. But, it's not a real רשות הרבים according to Rabbi Yehuda, and you have the *Aruch Ha-Shulchan* [who says that carrying a gun is allowed on Shabbos as part of a uniform] — we have to decide whether or not we accept the *Aruch Ha-Shulchan* [as many later *poskim* disagreed]. It might depend on the person, whether he is a ירא שמים. If he is very careful about these *halachos*, then maybe we would allow it.

As for having a gun in shul — there's a nice *teshuva* of the *Tzitz Eliezer*... He goes through the different sources. He does not bring the Mishna in *Middos*, which says that iron is not used for the *Mizbeiach* in any way because iron shortens a person's life, whereas the *Mizbeiach* prolongs a person's life. The same is true of *tefilla* and a shul. (There is a *machlokes* among the Acharonim as to whether this applies to *tefilla*, or to a *beis ha-knesses*. According to those who hold that it applies to *tefilla*, even when you're *davening* outside you should not have a long knife.) The *Tzitz Eliezer* has an interesting conclusion. He writes that if you take out the bullets, then it's ok, because the gun itself doesn't do anything. This is an interesting *chiddush*, if you think about it, because a gun is something that was created to shorten people's lives. There is nothing that shortens people's lives more than guns. But then he says that if it's covered, then there's a *heter*, like if it is inside a pocket, or hidden away. If there's no other way, then he says you can rely on those *poskim* who say it would be ok. You need שיקול הדעת in every particular situation. If you're in a place where there have been incidents, or the incidents have been increasing, and waiting for the police isn't necessarily an option, and you want to have protection right there and then, you can rely on the lenient opinion when it comes to this kind of thing, at least to have the gun covered. If somebody is in the hallway — this would be the best. In the *beis midrash* or *beis ha-knesses*, it should be covered, or in a shoulder holster or something like that.

...Regarding a woman carrying a gun, anywhere, there is a question of כלי גבר. If we can establish that there is a *heter* for her to have a gun in general, then the *heter* in the *ezras nashim* is much easier... It would definitely be inappropriate to send a male armed guard to stand in the *ezras nashim*. It's easier to have a female armed guard.

Rav Moshe has a *teshuva* on this topic, regarding an in-between situation — where it's not actual פקוח נפש (in which case there would be no question), but on the other hand, there's a reason the gun is needed, to placate nerves. I wrote an article about a husband who wore a gun because he was under threat by people at work, and he was afraid that the people threatening him might threaten his wife. The question was whether the wife should learn how to use a gun and train and get one. The *issur* of לא יהיה כלי גבר על אשה is understood by the *Targumim* and also in the Gemara as כלי זיין, and the reason is debated by the *poskim*. Some *poskim* explain that this is because כלי זיין are worn not every day, but only when going out to war, and women do not go out to war. According to these *poskim*, it could be that if a woman is not going out to war, but is rather using the gun as a deterrent, or something like that, then this might be ok. There are other *heteirim*, as well. She's not wearing it as an article of clothing, and there is a debate among the *poskim* whether it's forbidden only when worn as clothing, or even if it is in her purse or somewhere else. Then there are those who say that there's such a thing as a "woman's gun." If we say that there are occasions when a woman has to protect herself, and especially in the example of the *ezras nashim*, then this would be another *heter*.

There is a *machlokes* about the story of Yael, who used a יתד האהל, a peg of a tent, to kill Sisra. Why did she use a יתד האוהל? Some people say she did not want to use a regular weapon [because of לא תלבש], and so she drugged Sisra so she could kill him without taking out a regular weapon. Some people say that no, the יתד is considered a regular weapon. She happened to use a יתד, because this was the best weapon she could come up with.

There are arguments for permitting a woman to carry a gun. My conclusion was that if there's a real danger, then you have to take the best measures to protect yourself, but even if there's no real danger, but you feel safer being protected, then women may train for using these weapons, but in a modest manner. This is another issue — who is going to train her? If she's going to do training with men, what kind of people are going to be doing the training? She has to find a way to train without violating the גדרי צניעות. In fact, one of the reasons given for the prohibition of לא יהיה כלי גבר is because it will lead to *ta'arovos* [inappropriate mingling]. So if a woman is going to be trained, she needs to do so in a way that won't lead to *ta'arovos*. Maybe another woman can train her. Then she can carry the weapon, concealed. She can carry it openly only if there is a woman's model which is acceptable for women to carry in her society.

Anytime a person arms himself, he's touching upon the issue of לא תשים דמים בביתך. He needs to be very sure that he knows what he's doing 100 percent, and it won't lead to more problems than there would be without it. Professionals are highly trained, and they learn how to react in ways that people who are not professionals would not know how to. They go through training how to react in critical situations. This is a reason to hire professionals. It's safer. The reason to take people from within, is like in *hilchos Shabbos*, there's a *halacha* that in a situation of פקוח נפש, if a Jew can be מחלל שבת, then you don't let a non-Jew do so. One of the reasons is because he might be מתעצל a little bit, because they don't have the same value for life that we have. (Look at the medical establishment — we have all these end-of-life issues. With *Am Yisrael*, it's different.) Being מתעצל for a second could be the difference between life and death. So there is an argument to say — send people of our own to get highly professional training, and they'll be the people we'll rely on to be there…

Rabbi Tzvi Ortner

Interviewed on *Headlines with Dovid Lichtenstein*, 13 Iyar, 5779 (May 18, 2019)

I received a call from a rabbi in Lakewood who got an offer for a free security training service. I said we should definitely think about it, and every *rav* should choose specific people who would be responsible to do it. I feel that if we're doing it in a responsible way, and the *rabbanim* or people in charge of the communities will control it, then it should be done. We have to discuss if the need is there. There should be a conversation about whether the need is there or not.

There is a discussion in the *Shulchan Aruch* (O.C. 151) about bringing arms into shul, even during the week. This comes up already in the early *Rishonim*… The shul is a place to continue a person's life, and the gun does just the opposite. This is a clear *halacha* in the *Shulchan Aruch*.

This is discussed by the *Tzitz Eliezer* and other *poskim*, most directly, regarding soldiers who have guns and need to go to shul. They recommend covering the gun or having it emptied of its bullets. Of course, if we decide the situation is one of פקוח נפש, where a person needs to have a gun to protect the shul, then this conversation is not necessary. I think it's very difficult to say that today's situation is one of פקוח נפש… I feel that at this point we are not at the level of פקוח נפש.

As far as carrying a gun to shul on Shabbos, there is a famous *machlokes* between

Rabbi Eliezer and the *Chachamim* as to whether a weapon is considered a תכשיט [part of one's attire, such that it may be worn through a public domain on Shabbos]. The conclusion of the *sugya* in *Maseches Shabbos* is that there is an איסור דרבנן to carry a gun [through a public domain] on Shabbos. Now, there are two major issues in the *poskim* that we can consider to see if maybe there is room for a *kula*. First, the *poskim* quote the famous Maharik that if a person is forced to do something because of the law, or some situation, it might be considered a מלאכה שאינה צריכה לגופה. This gets you down to two דרבנן's... Then we have the famous *chiddush* of the *Aruch Ha-Shulchan* — and I think it's already in the *Magen Avraham* — that certain articles can be considered a תכשיט for certain people. This means that if the situation changes because of the times or because of some other reason, carrying certain things is considered a person's garment or תכשיט. And thus the *Aruch Ha-Shulchan* says that for an איש מלחמה ["man of war"] a gun would be considered part of his attire. The question then becomes, what is an איש מלחמה? I would say that in general, a soldier is obviously an איש מלחמה, and when a security guard is hired by a shul, maybe we can also consider him an איש מלחמה, because he has his uniform. But if a member of the shul is being trained, and he comes to shul with his regular Shabbos clothes together with everyone, I don't think we can say he is an איש מלחמה. So in his case, if he's not wearing a uniform, I think we have to make sure the gun is getting to shul before Shabbos. I can't really call him an איש מלחמה, so the gun is not a garment. We should point out that if we're dealing with a כרמלית, then since it might be a מלאכה שאינה צריכה לגופה, and the *sugya* concludes that this entire *issur* is דרבנן, we might have some basis for considering allowing it. But still, I would suggest having the gun in shul before Shabbos.

As for the issue of *muktzeh* — a gun is considered a כלי, which means we're not getting into problems of מוקצה מחמת גופו, and I don't feel this is getting into the issue of מוקצה מחמת חסרון כיס, because it's not something that you really deal with such care. For example, the *Shulchan Aruch* (O.C. 308) talks about סכין של מילה, a knife that you're using for something which you're not allowed to do on Shabbos, but in certain situations — מילה בזמנה — you are allowed to do it on Shabbos. The *Shulchan Aruch*'s conclusion is that it's מוקצה מחמת חסרון כיס once you finish with the *mila*, since this is something you really care about, and you are very careful about it. A gun is not going to fall under the category of חסרון כיס, I don't think, because it is not something you care about like a סכין של מילה. A gun is a כלי, and usually it's מלאכתו לאיסור — used to kill people. So my first thinking would be that it's a כלי שמלאכתו לאיסור, which may be carried לצורך מקומו and לצורך גופו... The question is then what is גופו and מקומו... If you're carrying it because of a [security] need, this would seem to be considered צורך גופו...

We can also go to the next level. There's an interesting *sevara* given by both the *Divrei Yatziv* (the Klausenberger Rebbe) and Rav Shlomo Zalman Auerbach. Rav Shlomo Zalman is more uncertain about it, but it seems like he accepts it. He feels that besides the actual purpose of shooting in a case where you have to shoot, the gun itself has a purpose — the fact that we know someone is carrying a gun, especially if it's done all over, and the crazy people around us know that there are people with guns in shul — this is already להטיל אימה, to instill fear. This itself is the purpose. Rav Shlomo Zalman feels, very interestingly, that the gun becomes a כלי שמלאכתו להיתר, because the purpose is not just shooting, but the fact that you carry it and people see it. (He had the same *sevara* about a candle in one's home. He felt that the beautiful silver candles, besides being a כלי שמלאכתו לאיסור, are also a כלי שמלאכתו להיתר, as they adorn the house.) This is a big *chiddush*.

I want to point out here that our conclusion with regard to having guns in shul generally would seem to be in conflict with this argument for allowing handling guns on Shabbos. We said that the only *heter* to carry a gun in shul generally, is covering it, it's being hidden. But if we consider it a כלי שמלאכתו להיתר because its purpose is to be seen, להטיל אימה, this is a kind of conflict that we have, whether to cover the gun or have it exposed.

Whether women should have guns to protect women's places — we're getting into the conversation of לא תלבש. The Rambam in *Hilchos Avoda Zara paskens* like Rabbi Eliezer ben Yaakov, and one of the examples he gives of לא תלבש is שריון וכיוצא בו. However, there's a famous Rashi that לא תלבש applies only if the garment is being worn for the purpose of mingling with the other gender. The other discussion we find in the *poskim* — Rav Moshe Feinstein has a *teshuva* about this — is that this *issur* might apply only to women going out to war. But if she's wearing it just to protect herself, then, Rav Moshe writes, she can carry a gun, though he makes a distinction between an assault rifle and a pistol, because the military doesn't use pistols.

In general, we know that the world has changed, and many women today take part in wars, and women carrying guns has become a normal thing. We have to consider whether לא תלבש still applies, because the Rambam there in *Hilchos Avoda Zara* says הכל כמנהג המדינה. So it could be that things will change. But we need bigger *poskim* to determine this.

I would suggest hiring a guard, but if the situation would be like a women's gathering and the like, I would recommend based on Rav Moshe, that a woman should carry a pistol.

Rabbi Yoel Asher Labin

Interviewed on *Headlines with Dovid Lichtenstein*, 13 Iyar, 5779 (May 18, 2019)

There is a *halacha* that a person should not go into a shul with a long knife, and the reason is based on the *pasuk* of לא תניף עליהם ברזל, as Rashi brings from the *Mechilta* — the *Mizbei'ach* is meant to prolong life, and the knife is מקצר ימיו של אדם. The *Avudraham* and *Shibolei Ha-Leket*, and others, apply this also to *batei midrash*, that you should not go into a *beis midrash* with a knife…

This *shei'la* is coming up more often, as more observant people have weapons, and the question is whether they can enter a מקום קדוש. The *Tzitz Elizer* and, I think, Rav Ovadia Yosef, write about it, and discuss that you should take out the bullets, or cover it. If you have a suit and the gun is in the pocket, then the gun is covered, but some say you should take out the bullets…

I agree that if we would be able to have a very sophisticated system of security, like Hatzalah, a responsible group that would be on top of it, then probably it would be ok. The question is whether this is possible. If it's just about people having weapons — this is already very dangerous. Should we bring up this discussion, put it on the table, in the hope that the right people will do the right thing, or will we then have a dangerous situation by making guns more available?

Our community has its problems, but our problems are less severe because of the fact that we don't have weapons. We have problems of domestic violence…of kids falling away, and suicide… We need to think what effect it will have on the community if it will be easier to have guns around. This is a very important point.

Also, sometimes guns have the opposite effect, by giving you a false sense of security. This is something that we [*rabbanim* in Toms River] discussed with the police. We need awareness of what to do [during an emergency]… This is what the police chief told us. There are many studies that show that when people have their weapons, their reaction is "let me get my weapon," and this is the very wrong approach when there's an active shooter… Sometimes you're in shul on Shabbos and you don't know if there's someone with a cell phone…

We should realize how dangerous this is and how easily it could go wrong. If we want to have lots of guns in every shul, this raises the risk of friendly fire. Every day, there are stories of kids who shoot a gun by mistake. There are more suicides in places where there are a lot of guns. The big question is whether having guns in the community is no less of a threat than the threat of a killer coming to shul. We might be running from one problem to another which is even worse… Weapons in the community means weapons in the hands of people with emotional issues, with domestic violence, and so on. Guns make all these things much more dangerous. Unfortunately, we have recently had suicide cases in the community. Guns will make this so much worse… Also, it is not so certain than this will help in the case of a shooting. Many studies show that even people with training were not effective against a shooter, because a shooter is catching you by surprise. The chances that having more guns will save lives is not high enough.

Having a guard by the door, a greater police presence —these things have no negative [consequence], no concern…

We should focus on security matters. Many shuls do not have enough doors, and do not pay enough attention to security. They should make sure there are active telephones on the wall in case something's happening on Shabbos. Having people with weapons will create a culture that will bring more weapons. So we should focus on other security measures. I don't see a way how it could be kept a total secret, and it can be assured that his child will not one day take the weapon and play with it. We can't control it. I know we can't control it. It will bring in competition and have very negative effects…

Seichel ha-yashar says that guns in the community would be terrible. More weapons mean more trouble.

Don't Set New Year's Resolutions, Do This Instead!

January 9, 2020
By Corey Poirier

Some studies estimate that 90% of all New Year's Resolutions fail within the first two weeks of the New Year.

The message?

New Year's Resolutions don't work.

You know what does?

Goal-setting. Rewarding yourself for achieving small (and big) goals. Creating a new desired habit to replace a habit you're trying to get rid of.

I've personally interviewed over 5,000 influencers, including everyone from Jack Canfield to Les Brown to Lisa Nichols to Bob Proctor to JJ Virgin to the late Zig Ziglar. One thing I have discovered is that most influencers don't set resolutions. For a reason.

The takeaway?

So, don't set New Year's Resolutions.

Instead, write your goals (including habits you want to create, things you want to 'resolve' to start or stop), and decide on the rewards you will give yourself to carry you through until your new actions become a true habit.

Oh, and don't wait until New Year's Day to start. Do it instead on any other day of the year. And don't wait until the first of the month or the first of the week.

Start now, or start 10 minutes from now.

This is why. When you start on the first day of the year, or week or month, you are building up way too much anticipation and pressure around this. You are making it a THING.

It's okay to start on Tuesday at 9:30am, or Saturday at 7pm. Just start. That's the most important thing.

Also, it's okay if you have a set-back. It's okay if you mess up while trying to eat healthy. It's okay if you miss an exercise day.

It's more important that you get back on the horse after falling than that you stay on the horse perfectly forever.

Hopefully you're seeing a trend here?

What I'm saying is to do what has enjoyed more success. New Year's Resolutions are typically failed from the start.

I mean, trying to eat healthy the day after partying until after midnight? Good luck. What has a better track record? Well, anything else really.

But let's focus on what I've shared here as this has a much better track record than New Year's Resolutions.

1. Set (written) big and small goals.
2. Decide on the rewards you will give yourself when you achieve each goal. This is super important when you get near the stage where most people quit (before it becomes a true habit)
3. Push yourself past the point where it becomes a habit by delivering on the rewards you have decided upon. Little known fact, it isn't 21 days to create a habit – it's 66. Source: The One Thing. So make sure you have rewards in place to keep you moving forward for more than a couple of months, not just a few weeks.
4. Don't worry about starting at a certain time or on a certain day.
5. Be okay when you have a set back. The long game is way more important than the short game, but many people use the small mis-step as a reason to give up. Don't be most people.
6. Celebrate…

Is Our Teshuva Worth Anything?

Year after year, we go through the process of the *Yamim Noraim* (High Holidays), confessing our sins, beseeching God for forgiveness, and promising to be better. Many of us, understandably, wonder whether there is really any value to this annual procedure. We look at ourselves during the *Yamim Noraim* and realize that we are not all that different from the way we were the year before. We have the same bad habits we had last year, we still struggle with the same vices that plagued us last year, and we still engage in the same improper activities as we engaged in last year. Hopefully, we mature to some extent each year, and perhaps make some slow improvement. But still, many of our sins and character flaws continue to dog us just as they had in the past. Realistically, there seems little reason to believe that anything will change during the coming year.

This is not to say we are not sincere in our desire to change. All conscientious Jews are troubled by their faults, their bad habits, and their inadequacies in their Torah observance. They want to be better spouses, better parents, better friends, and better servants of the Almighty. But after years of unfulfilled High Holiday commitments, they find it difficult to take their repentance seriously, and so they find it difficult to take the High Holidays seriously.

How do we approach this phenomenon? Is there value to our sincere regret, feelings of guilt and efforts to effect change, if the change does not happen? Are we considered to have repented if our conduct more or less remains the same?

ויעיד עליו יודע תעלומות שלא ישוב

One famous passage in the Rambam's *Hilchos Teshuva* appears to suggest — depressingly — that such *teshuva* is utterly worthless, because *teshuva* by definition requires permanent change.

In the second chapter of *Hilchos Teshuva* (*halacha* 2), the Rambam presents his definition of *teshuva*:

> מה היא התשובה? הוא שיעזוב החוטא חטאו ויסירו ממחשבתו ויגמור בלבו
> שלא יעשהו עוד... וכן יתנחם על שעבר...**ויעיד עליו יודע תעלומות שלא ישוב לזה**
> **החטא לעולם**... וצריך להתודות בשפתיו ולומר עניינות אלו שגמר בלבו.

What is repentance? It is that the sinner abandons his sin, removes it

349

from his thoughts, and resolves in his heart not to commit it again… And he also regrets the past…**and the Knower of hidden things shall testify about him that he will never again return to this sin…** And he must verbally confess and say these matters which he resolved in his heart.

Part of the Rambam's definition of *teshuva* is committing to change in such a way that God, who knows the future, can testify that the sinner will never again repeat the forbidden act. The Rambam cites as the source of this aspect of *teshuva* the verse in *Hosheia* (14:4) in which the prophet calls upon the people to repent for their idol-worship, and tells them to proclaim as part of their repentance ולא נאמר עוד אלוקינו למעשה ידינו — "we will not call our handiwork our god," indicating that repentance is defined as a real commitment to never repeat the offense.[1]

Seemingly, then, whenever we end up repeating a sin for which we've repented, our relapse retroactively voids our repentance, rendering it worthless. After all, if repentance by definition requires permanent change, that God foresees at the time of repentance that the act will never recur, then any recurrence reveals a fatal flaw in the repentance process, that it did not meet the definition of *teshuva* and is thus entirely invalid and futile.

Could this really be true?

And if it is true, does this mean we should not bother? Should we just stay at home during *Selichos* and Yom Kippur? According to the Rambam's definition of *teshuva*, aren't we wasting our time by making commitments to change which we know with near certainty will go unfulfilled?

Moreover, does this mean that few — if any — of us fulfill the *mitzva* of repentance? The Rambam[2] explicitly lists repentance as a Biblical command, and mentions as well

---

1.   The *Kessef Mishneh* explains that the phrase ולא נאמר עוד אלוקינו למעשה ידינו is what the prophet exhorts the people to say to God as they repent (קחו עמכם דברים ושובו אל ה', אמרו אליו…ולא נאמר עוד אלוקינו למעשה ידינו), and the Rambam understood that the prophet here urges the people to summon God as their "witness" to the fact that they will never repeat their sin of idolatry.

It should be mentioned that there is no clear source, neither in the Gemara nor in the Midrash, to this concept of summoning God to testify that one will never repeat the sin. A number of *Acharonim* (e.g. *Bnei Binyamin*) suggest that the Rambam's remarks are rooted in the *Yalkut Shimoni* (*Hosheia* 532) which tells of *Bnei Yisrael* expressing their concern to God, "If we perform repentance, who will testify about us?" to which God then responds that He will testify to their repentance, just as He testifies to their wrongdoing. However, this passage describes God as testifying only about the sincerity of our repentance, not to the fact that we will never repeat the sin again.

2.   *Sefer Ha-Mitzvos, asei* 73; *Hilchos Teshuva* 1:1.

a particular obligation to repent on Yom Kippur.[3] (Rabbeinu Yona, in his *Sha'arei Teshuva*,[4] writes that the special requirement to repent on Yom Kippur is introduced by the Torah in the famous verse, כי ביום הזה...מכל חטאתיכם לפני ה' תטהרו — "For on this day...you shall be cleansed from all your sins before God."[5]) According to the Rambam, is it at all possible to fulfill this *mitzva*?

לא מצאנו ידינו ורגלינו בתשובה

Even more sobering is a Talmudic passage which seems to provide proof to this notion, that an unfulfilled commitment never to repeat a sin retroactively invalidates one's repentance.

The Gemara in *Maseches Yoma* (86b) establishes that after one confessed a sin on Yom Kippur, he does not need to repeat his confession on Yom Kippur in subsequent years. We must confess on Yom Kippur only sins committed since the previous Yom Kippur, or earlier sins which, for whatever reason, we had not confessed on Yom Kippur in previous years. However, the Gemara adds, ואם שנה בהן, צריך להתוודות יום הכיפורים אחר — if we repeated a sin for which we had confessed on a previous Yom Kippur, then we must confess that sin again this Yom Kippur.

As noted by several writers, including Rav Raphael Cohen of Hamburg, in *Marpei Lashon*[6] and *Da'as Kedoshim*,[7] this remark seems to prove that repeating a sin for which one had repented invalidates the repentance. After all, if the Gemara makes a point of requiring confession for sins committed after having confessed them the previous Yom Kippur, it must be referring to repentance for the initial sin. There would obviously be no reason for the Gemara to instruct that one must confess for the most recent instance of sin, which is no different than any other sin which was committed during the year. Undoubtedly, the ruling ואם שנה בהן, צריך להתוודות יום הכיפורים אחר must mean that after repeating a sin, one must repent anew for the first instance of this violation, as the repentance he performed has been retroactively undermined by the relapse.

The Gemara's ruling, then, appears to provide strong support for the Rambam's definition of *teshuva*, that repentance is worthless without permanent change. Does this mean that our repentance has no value?

Among those who addressed this question was Rav Yechezkel Sarna, in *Daliyos Yechezkel*,[8] where he writes that according to the plain meaning of the Rambam's

---

3.   חייבים הכל לעשות תשובה ולהתוודות ביום הכיפורים (*Hilchos Teshuva* 2:7).

4.   2:14.

5.   *Vayikra* 16:30.

6.   *Amud Le-Yom Ha-Din*, p. 328.

7.   *Derush* 3, p. 34.

8.   *Yemei Ha-Rachamim Ve-Ha'din*, p 154.

comments, לא מצאנו ידינו ורגלינו בתשובה — we have no possibility of repenting. Rav Sarna somberly observes:

מי הוא זה שיוכל להונות עצמו ולחשוב בדעתו שהסכמתו וקבלתו לחזור מדרכו
ולשוב מחטאו היא חזקה כל כך עד שיעיד עליו היודע תעלומות שלא ישוב לזה
החטא לעולם, ולא עוד אלא שכל אדם הנאמן ברוחו לא רק שלא יעיד עליו את
היודע תעלומות, אלא אדרבה יעיד על עצמו שאינו בטוח בעצמו כלל וכלל שלא
ישוב לחטאיו ששב מהם והתודה עליהם.

Who is the person who can delude himself and think in his mind that his decision and acceptance to change his ways and repent from his sin is so strong to the point where "the Knower of hidden things shall testify about him that he will never again return to this sin?" Moreover, any person who is honest with himself — not only will the Knower of hidden things not testify about him, but to the contrary, he will testify about himself that he is not sure about himself at all that he will not return to his sins from which he repented and which he confessed.

Calling upon God as a Witness

Rav Avraham de Boton, in his *Lechem Mishneh* commentary to the Rambam's *Mishneh Torah*, addresses a different question regarding the Rambam's comments,[9] and arrives at a slightly different reading of this passage. He explains the Rambam to mean that one must be so sincere in his resolve never to repeat the sin, that he could call God as witness to his sincerity. The Rambam's intent is not that a future relapse retroactively shows that the repentance was inadequate, but rather that the person must truly

---

9.   The *Lechem Mishneh* questions how this requirement can be reconciled with the doctrine of free will. Since all people have the free choice at any moment to act properly or improperly, there is never the possibility of God testifying that a penitent sinner will never repeat the sin.

This question, however, appears to be simply one manifestation of the broader issue of the much-debated paradox of בחירה and ידיעה, that God knows all future events and yet human beings have the freedom to choose how to act. Elsewhere in *Hilchos Teshuva* (5:5), the Rambam famously writes that as God's knowledge exceeds the limits of human comprehension, we are entirely incapable of understanding anything about this knowledge, and so this question cannot even be asked. Indeed, Rav Sarna, in his treatment of this topic, asserts that the Rambam addressed the general question of בחירה and ידיעה in *Hilchos Teshuva* precisely because *teshuva* must be performed in such a way that God can testify that the sinner will never repeat the wrongful act, which touches upon the paradox of ידיעה and בחירה.

commit to never repeat the offense, and must be confident enough to summon God —
the only being in existence that knows the unspoken thoughts in a person's mind — to
bear witness to his sincerity.[10]

Rav Sarna cites the *Lechem Mishneh*'s interpretation, and observes, לא הוקל לנו בזה
הרבה — this reading offers us little solace as we wonder whether there is any value to
our repentance. He writes:

> מי זה אשר יאמר זכיתי לבי לבוא לידי הסכמה וקבלה חזקה כל כך, והלא
> יודעים ומכירים אנו את עצמנו, כי לבנו הקשה כאבן ביצר הרע הוא גם רך ודונג
> ביצר הטוב, ומחשבתנו הטובה כאצבע בקירא, ואיך נעיד עלינו השי״ת על שעת
> תשובתנו שאינה לשעה...וספק גדול אם יש בדור הזה מי שהכין את לבו עד שבא
> לידי מצב זה.

Who is the one who can say, "My heart is pure enough to reach such a
firm decision and commitment?" We know and are quite familiar with
ourselves, that our heart which is hard like stone with our evil inclination
is also soft like wax with our positive inclination, and our noble inten-
sions are like a finger in hard wax. How can we summon God to testify
about us, about our moment of repentance, that it is not just temporary?
...It is highly doubtful whether there is anybody in this generation who
has set his heart straight to the point where he reaches this condition.

We might add that this reading does not appear to account for the Gemara's indication
that a subsequent relapse undermines the initial repentance. As we saw, the Gemara
seems to require repenting anew for a sin for which one had repented if he later
repeated the act — suggesting that regardless of how sincere the initial repentance was,
repeating the sin after repentance undermines the validity of the repentance, seemingly rendering it worthless.

תקנת השבין

In Chassidic thought, this quandary has been resolved through an analogy comparing
a sinner's temporary change to a temporary change undergone by a stolen object.

As the Gemara discusses in *Maseches Bava Kama*,[11] *halacha* allows a thief to keep

---

10. Rav Sarna notes that support for the *Lechem Mishneh*'s position may perhaps be drawn
from the fact that the Rambam in this passage speaks of God not as יודע עתידות — "Knower
of future events" — but rather as יודע תעלומות — "Knower of hidden things." The point
being emphasized is that only God knows a person's unspoken thoughts and intentions,
and can thus testify to a penitent sinner's sincerity, not that God knows the future and can
thus testify that the sinner will never repeat the forbidden act.

11. 93b–94b.

a stolen object which has since been transformed, and to instead pay the victim the amount the object was worth. The Torah (*Vayikra* 5:23) requires a thief to return הגזילה אשר גזל — the item which he had stolen, suggesting that if the object had undergone a fundamental transformation, such that the thief can no longer return what he stole, he may keep the object and pay money, instead. The Mishna gives several examples, such as wood which was stolen and then made into a utensil, or wool that was stolen and then made into clothing. In such cases, the thief keeps the utensil or the garment, and instead pays the victim the value of the goods he stole.

The Gemara clarifies that according to Torah law, this provision applies only in cases of a permanent transformation, such as those enumerated in the Mishna. But if the stolen article was only temporarily transformed — such as if the thief had stolen wool and laundered it — then, on the level of Torah law, he does not acquire ownership over the wool, and must return it to the victim. Since the change is only temporary, the object retains its initial identity, and the thief is therefore obliged to return it. However, in the interest of תקנת השבין — encouraging thieves to confess their wrongdoing and repent — the Sages enacted that the thief may keep the stolen item even if it has undergone only a temporary transformation. The Sages felt that thieves would be more likely to come forward, confess their crime and make amends if they were permitted to keep the stolen goods which they had begun using. They therefore relaxed to some extent the rules governing when a thief is permitted to keep the stolen goods, extending the Torah's provision to include even a שינוי החוזר לברייתו — an impermanent change.

The *Chiddushei Ha-Rim*[12] cleverly suggested that this תקנת השבין is relevant also to all בעלי תשובה — sinners contemplating repentance. *Teshuva* is about changing who we are, and strictly speaking, as in the case of stolen goods, only a permanent transformation qualifies as "change." However, like a thief who would be reluctant to return stolen goods in which he had already invested time and effort, we likewise naturally feel hesitant to repent. And so for the purpose of תקנת השבין, in order to encourage us to take this bold step, the Sages established that even a שינוי החוזר לברייתו, a temporary change, constitutes a significant change that meets the requirements of *teshuva*. And so although in principle, as the Rambam writes, a recurrence of sin reveals that the repentance was insufficient, nevertheless, even temporary *teshuva* is accepted by force of תקנת השבין.

The Mabit's Position

Regardless of how one chooses to understand the Rambam's remark, we can take comfort in the fact that at least one other scholar states explicitly that sincere *teshuva* is valuable even if one ultimately relapses into sin.

---

12.   Cited in *Siach Sarfei Kodesh*, 1:668.

Rav Moshe of Trani, one of the leading rabbis of Safed in the 16th century, composed a seminal work of Jewish thought entitled *Beis Elokim*, which includes a section devoted to the subject of repentance (*Shaar Ha-Teshuva*). In the sixth chapter of this section, he addresses the status of repentance when the sinner later relapses:

ראוי לבאר ענין התשובה ששב האדם בכל שנה ושנה, וחוזר אחר כך למה שחטא,
אם תועיל התשובה שעשה על העונות הקודמים גם כי חזר אח"כ לחטוא אותם
החטאים, או אם נאמר שכיון שחזר למה שחטא, יראה שלא היתה תשובתו נכונה
ושלימה ולא גמר בלבו לעזוב החטאים והעונות הואיל וחזר אליהן אחר כך.

ואומר כי נראה מדברי רבותינו ע"ה כי כיון שחזר האדם בתשובה מן החטאים
שעשה, וגמר בלבו שלא לעשותם עוד, השם יתברך מעביר חטאתו בתשובה זאת,
ואם אח"כ חזר לחטוא, יצר הרע הוא שפיתה אותו מחדש לחזור למה שחטא,
ולא יהיו החטאים הראשונים חוזרים וניעורים אחר שנתבטלו בתשובה הקודמת.

It is worth explaining the nature of repentance which a person performs each and every year, and then returns to the sin he had committed, whether the repentance he performed for the previous iniquities is effective despite his again committing those sins, or if we say that since he repeated the sin, it seems that his repentance was not honest and complete, and he did not resolve in his heart to abandon the sins and iniquities, for he repeated them afterward.

I say that it appears from the words of our rabbis, of blessed memory, that once a person repented for the sins he committed, and resolved in his heart not to commit them again, God eliminates his sin through this repentance, and if he sins again afterward, it is the evil inclination which lured him anew to return to his sin, and so the first sins are not now "reawakened" after they had been annulled through the previous repentance.

The Mabit writes explicitly that as long as a person is sincere in his repentance, and truly resolves not to repeat the offense, then his repentance is valid and accepted by the Almighty, regardless of what happens thereafter. The relapse is viewed as a new failure, unrelated to the previous instances of sin, and so the repentance remains perfectly valid, and the initial sinful act is still forgiven.

The Mabit proceeds to acknowledge that the Gemara cited earlier, requiring confession for sins of earlier years after repeating them, seems to indicate otherwise. To refute this proof, the Mabit explains that although the *teshuva* performed for the initial instance of sin remains intact, the Gemara nevertheless requires confessing anew for the purpose of reflecting upon the recurrence, and redoubling one's efforts to make the change permanent. The Mabit writes that the Gemara requires the sinner who repeats the offense after repenting to recall the first occasion when he sinned לסיבת קיום

התשובה והוידוי השני — to help ensure that his renewed commitment will endure. The Sages want the individual to reflect upon the fact that he had already unsuccessfully tried to change, so he can determine what he can do to increase the chances of success this time.

The Value of Partial Repentance

We might, however, still wonder, as Rav Sarna lamented, מי זה אשר יאמר זכיתי לבי לבוא לידי הסכמה וקבלה חזקה כל כך — if any of us can say that our commitments to change each year during the *Yamim Noraim* are made with such firm conviction, that subsequent failures can be seen as entirely new, unrelated to our previous sinful actions. Even if our sins' recurrence after Yom Kippur does not, in and of itself, undermine the validity of our repentance, perhaps the likelihood of recurrence, of which we are well aware as we stand in prayer on Yom Kippur, renders our *teshuva* meaningless.

We find our answer several chapters later (12), where the Mabit asserts unequivocally that *teshuva* is not an "all-or-nothing" undertaking, and that any efforts made to repent are valuable and a partial fulfillment of the *mitzva* of *teshuva*. He writes:

> אחר שנתבאר ענין התשובה כי היא החרטה ועזיבת החטא, נאמר כי אינם כשאר המצוות, שהעושה חלק המצווה אין לו חלק שכר המצווה, כמו שתאמר מצוות ציצית הוא בד׳ הכנפות והעושה ציצית בג׳ כנפות לבד אינו מקיים ג׳ חלקי המצווה...והרי הוא כאילו לא עשה שום דבר. ואולם התשובה גם כי אינה שלימה עד שתהיה בחרטה לשעבר ועזיבת החטא לעתיד, עם כל זה החרטה לבד בלי עזיבת החטא מועיל קצת...

> Now that the concept of repentance has been explained, that it constitutes remorse and abandoning the sin, we will say that they are unlike other *mitzvos*, that if one performs a part of a *mitzva*, he has no partial reward for the *mitzva* — for example, the *mitzva* of *tzitzis* is with four corners, and one who makes *tzitzis* on only three corners does not fulfill three parts of the *mitzva*... but is considered to have done nothing. Repentance, however, even if it is not complete to the point where there is regret over the past and abandoning the sin in the future, nevertheless, the remorse alone without abandoning the sin is somewhat beneficial...

The Mabit draws proof to this assertion from the Biblical story of Achav, king of the Northern Kingdom of Israel who institutionalized the worship of the pagan god *Baal* in his country. At one point during his reign, Achav's queen devised a scheme falsely accusing and then executing an innocent man who refused to sell his property to Achav. God sent the prophet Eliyahu to deliver to the king a blistering condemnation, and to warn of the devastation that would befall his family. Achav responded by rending his garments and fasting, on account of which God decided to delay the punishment until after the king's death.[13] Although Achav did not abandon his sinful conduct,[14] his remorse for his crimes was nevertheless deemed significant and valuable. The Mabit points also to the famous story told in *Sefer Yona* of the people of Nineveh, who responded to the prophet's warning of catastrophe by fasting and praying. And although they changed their conduct (וישובו איש מדרכו הרעה ומן החמס אשר בכפיהם),[15] the Mabit understands the text as implying that they returned stolen goods that were still intact, but did not repay the victims for stolen food which was already consumed. Moreover, according to one view in the Talmud Yerushalmi,[16] thieves in Nineveh returned only visible stolen goods, but not those which were already hidden in chests and closets. In any event, the townspeople's repentance was far from complete, yet it sufficed for God to rescind His decree of annihilation and spare the city.

Accordingly, the Mabit establishes that although a penitent sinner must, obviously, strive for complete repentance, to permanently eliminate his vices and character flaws, even partial repentance is valuable, and we are therefore bidden to try as best we can, even if the results fall far short of ideal *teshuva*.

Rereading the Rambam

Some writers suggested interpreting the Rambam's comments in this fashion, as well.

Rav Yirmiyahu Low, in his *Divrei Yirmiyahu* commentary to the Rambam's *Mishneh Torah*, writes that the Rambam speaks here of התשובה השלימה ביותר — perfect repentance, whereby one fundamentally transforms to the point where God foresees that he will never again commit the wrongful act. But even if a penitent sinner does not reach this level of complete transformation, his repentance is nevertheless valuable. Rav Low points to the Gemara's famous discussion in *Maseches Yoma* (86a) of the different categories of sins, where it establishes that more severe violations require more than just repentance for atonement. Some transgressions are not atoned without some degree of suffering, and others are not atoned until death, even if one repents. Rav Low boldly suggests that the Gemara refers here to incomplete repentance, which achieves incomplete atonement, whereas complete repentance — the kind spoken of by the Rambam — achieves complete atonement.

According to this reading of the Rambam's comments, there is certainly value to our confession, prayers and sincere efforts to change, even if they fail to bring about the permanent transformation that we would ideally want and to which we are to constantly strive.

---

13. ויהי דבר ה' אל אליהו התשבי לאמר: הראית כי נכנע אחאב מלפני, יען כי נכנע מפני לא אביא הרעה בימיו..., *Melachim I* 21:29.

14. In fact, there is no indication in the text that he returned the property to the inheritors.

15. *Yona* 3:8.

16. *Ta'anis* 2:1.

Rav Sarna likewise concludes his discussion by asserting that our efforts to repent have great value even according to the Rambam's definition, though for a different reason. He writes:

בכל זאת אנחנו לפי מצבנו מוצאים אנו את ידינו ורגלינו בקיום מצות התשובה כהלכתה, לאלה המתייצבים על דרך לא טוב, והיא להשתדל להתייצב על דרך טוב, ורק על זה להעיד את השי"ת, כי אמנם נכון לבנו בזה, ונהיה נאמנים בבריתנו גם לעתיד, והיינו בהשתדלות הטבת דרכנו...

> Nevertheless, [even] we, in our condition, are capable of properly fulfill-
> ing the *mitzva* of repentance, for those who are set on the wrong path,
> and that is by trying to set themselves on the right path, and calling God
> to testify just to that — for indeed, our hearts are truthful in this respect,
> and we will be true to our pledge even in the future, meaning, to try to
> improve our path.

Rav Sarna here seems to suggest that when the Rambam speaks of God "testifying" that the penitent sinner will never again repeat the act, he means that the sinner will make a sincere effort to never again repeat the act. The Rambam did not intend to say that repentance requires permanent change, but rather that it requires a commitment to try to make a permanent change, and as long as one is sincere in committing to try to improve, he has performed *teshuva* properly.

שמא הרהר תשובה

The value of partial, incomplete *teshuva* is indicated by a startling ruling of the Gemara in *Maseches Kiddushin* (49b) concerning the peculiar case of a person who betroths a woman on the condition שאני צדיק — "that I am a righteous person." The Gemara establishes that even if this man is known to be an unabashed evildoer, the woman is nevertheless presumed betrothed to him, because שמא הרהר תשובה בדעתו — he may have entertained thoughts of repentance in his mind. Even if no outwardly discernible changes in his conduct occur, it is nevertheless possible that the condition was met, that this man was a צדיק, by virtue of his thoughts of repentance.

Clearly, even if this individual had indeed entertained thoughts of repentance at those moments, he had not performed complete *teshuva*, as his conduct remained more or less the same. Nevertheless, sincere thoughts of *teshuva* are significant and valuable, to the point where the individual at that time can be legitimately described as a צדיק.

Elsewhere, in *Maseches Nidda* (70b), the Gemara notes a seeming contradiction between two verses, one of which states that God does not wish to kill the wicked, but rather wishes that they repent,[17] and another which tells that God wished to kill

---

17.   כי לא אחפוץ במות המת, *Yechezkel* 18:32.

the sons of Eli because of their evil conduct.[18] The Gemara reconciles these verses by distinguishing between evildoers who have repented — and who God thus does not wish to kill — and those who have not repented. Rav Yisrael Salanter[19] raised the question of why it would be necessary for the first verse to inform us that God has no interest in killing a penitent sinner. If he has repented, is it not obvious that God accepts his repentance, and does not wish to kill him?

Rav Yisrael answered that necessarily, the Gemara speaks of a sinner who merely entertained thoughts of repentance. Once his heart has been stirred, then even if the sinner is still very far from complete repentance and a permanent change in conduct, nevertheless, God embraces him and anticipates the completion of his process of *teshuva*.

Rav Yisrael Salanter's Prescription for *Teshuva*

In one of his published letters,[20] Rav Yisrael presents a more detailed prescription for repentance. He acknowledges that קבלת עזיבת החטא — committing to never repeat one's sins — constitutes הקשה מכל העבודות ביוה"כ — the most difficult obligation we have on Yom Kippur. And the way to approach this challenge, he explains, is by prioritizing our commitments: האדם צריך לחפש לעשות תשובה לכה"פ החלק היותר חמור — "A person must seek to perform repentance at least for the most grievous aspect" of every sin of which he is guilty.

Rav Yisrael proceeds to explain that "grievousness" is measured in terms of both inherent severity, and level of difficulty. And so even if we feel incapable of complete repentance, we must, at very least, commit ourselves with regard to that which is most severe, and that which is not exceedingly difficult. Rav Yisrael writes:

> האדם צריך לחפש דרכיו לעשות קבלה חזקה, כמעט בכל פרטי ענייניו, להשמר
> לכה"פ את אשר נקל לפניו בכל פרטי התורה והמצווה, ובזה יש דרך אשר יקיים
> מצות התשובה ברוב חלקי עונותיו...

> A person must examine his ways to make a firm commitment, in virtually every detail of his conduct, to avoid at least that which is easy for him [to refrain from] in all details of Torah and *mitzvos*, and this gives him a way to fulfill the *mitzva* of *teshuva* in part of the majority of his sins…

The point being made is that our *teshuva* commitments must be very carefully prioritized. We should not be making blanket commitments to refrain entirely from sins that we know we regularly commit, because such commitments are unrealistic and thus worthless. Instead, we should pinpoint specific forms of misconduct that we should

---

18. ולא ישמעו לקול אביהם כי חפץ ה' להמיתם, *Shmuel I* 2:25.

19. *Or Yisrael*, 30.

20. *Or Yisrael*, letter 15.

focus on changing, and this selection should be made based on the severity of our bad habits, and the level of difficulty we would have refraining from them. We must give priority to the especially grievous sins that we commit, and to the sins which we can stop committing with relative ease.

Rav Yisrael gives the example of theft, which is an especially grievous offense.[21] Given the unique severity of theft, one who knows he regularly deceives and cheats people must make repentance for this sin a priority. The other example mentioned by Rav Yisrael is *bittul Torah* (wasting time that could be used for Torah learning), which is relatively easy to avoid, as one needs only to pick up a book during his spare time. As we set out to make resolutions for the coming year, we must carefully determine priorities and set practical, realistic goals for us to achieve. According to Rav Yisrael Salanter, this is what קבלת עזיבת החטא requires — that we set for ourselves attainable goals, committing to make changes that we know we are fully capable of making.

Rav Yisrael here formulates for us a very practical, common-sense prescription of repentance, one which could make everybody's *Yamim Noraim* experience far more meaningful and productive. If we approach the High Holiday season with the simple reading of the Rambam's comments in mind, we are likely to go through this period without much motivation to try to change our lives, realizing that we cannot honestly commit to never repeat any of the sins we've committed. Rav Yisrael's definition of *teshuva*, however, challenges us to make a handful of specific, realistic commitments which we can meet, thereby making ourselves just a little better, one year at a time.

Repentance Is for Us All

Another important source for the value of even partial, incomplete repentance is the Midrash's depiction of Korach's sons as they were devoured by the ground.[22] The Midrash writes: לא יוכלו להתוודות בפיהם אלא כיוון שרחש לבם בתשובה, הקב״ה מקבלם — "They were incapable of confessing with their mouths, but since their hearts stirred with repentance, the Almighty accepted them." During those moments, as Korach's sons began descending into the underworld, they could not repent properly. But the stirring in their hearts sufficed, because that was all they were capable of doing at that time under the circumstances. And so their repentance was lovingly accepted by God.

Rav Yosef Shalom Elyashiv[23] suggested that this might be the reason why we customarily recite the 47th chapter of *Tehillim* — למנצח לבני קורח מזמור — before

---

21. Rav Yisrael cites the Midrash's comment (*Vaiyikra Rabba* 33:3) that no matter how many sins a person commits, the one that "prosecutes" against him before any of the others is theft.

22. *Midrash Shocher Tov*, 45.

23. *Divrei Aggada, Yamim Noraim*, p. 433.

shofar blowing on Rosh Hashanah. As we stand in judgment on Rosh Hashanah, we might feel that our situation is hopeless, that we are incapable of repenting, of making real change, and so our prayers are worthless. We therefore read the song of praise composed by Korach's sons to remind ourselves that their repentance began with a silent stirring of the heart — and even that stirring was deemed precious. No matter what condition we are in, we are expected to do the best we can, to make an effort, every ounce of which is warmly and compassionately accepted by the Almighty.

It is told that one year, on the night of Yom Kippur, Rav Chaim Shmuelevitz, the Mirrer Rosh Yeshiva, spoke to the yeshiva, and described his experiences during the day of Erev Yom Kippur. He first went to pray at the Western Wall, and he sensed that a voice was telling him that his prayers were ineffective. He then went to Rachel's Tomb, figuring that there his prayers would be accepted, but there, too, he heard a voice telling him that his prayers were not helping.

He then went to the tomb of Avshalom, the son of King David, and he prayed, citing David's lament for Avshalom after he was killed in his failed attempt to overthrow and murder his father: בני אבשלום, בני בני אבשלום, מי יתן מותי אני תחתיך אבשלום בני בני ("My son, Avshalom, my son, my son, Avshalom! If only I could die in your place, Avshalom, my son, my son").[24] Rashi, citing *Chazal*, writes that David cried the words "Avshalom" and בני ("my son") eight times in order to elevate his son's soul from the seven domains of the underworld and then lift it to the eternal world.

"No matter what evil a son commits against his father," Rav Chaim shouted, "the father still has compassion for his son! And so, Master of the world, You said, בנים אתם להי׳ אלוקיכם ('You are sons to Hashem your God').[25] A father always has compassion for his children!"

He then he heard a voice that exclaimed, "Mirrer Rosh Yeshiva! Very good. Have a good year!"

We are God's children, and a father desperately waits for his son to return. Even if his son is not perfect, and even if his son is far from perfect, he is ready to embrace his son when he comes. And so even if we cannot perform *teshuva* in accordance with the Rambam, and we perform *teshuva* only in accordance with the Mabit, will we not be accepted?

---

24.   *Shmuel II* 19:1.

25.   *Devarim* 14:1.

Rabbi Efrem Goldberg

Interviewed on *Headlines with Dovid Lichtenstein*, 6 Tishrei, 5780 (October 5, 2019)

One of the universal struggles that people have with *teshuva* is the failure to believe in their capacity to do *teshuva*. Fundamental to the entire *teshuva* process is the belief that we are capable of change, that we are able to transform ourselves, that we can shape and mold our own destiny. I think there are a lot of people who feel that they are stuck in a pattern and routine, that they're a victim of genetics, of circumstance, and so they relinquish ownership over their lives.

You see this in every which realm. When it comes to health, for example, there are people struggling with their health, with their diet, with exercise, with obesity — not because they can't change, but because they don't believe they can change. You see this with Torah, with *mitzva* observance, and with *middos*. One of the big challenges which is universal and crosses all sections of the community is instilling within people a sense of confidence, the fundamental belief that they are capable of change, that they are worthy of change, and that change can be transformational and enduring.

There's a great book *Extreme Ownership* written by two Navy SEALS, and I used it once as the theme of my *Shabbos Shuva drasha*, which I entitled, "Extreme *Achrayus*." It was about the notion that the prerequisite to *teshuva* is the capacity to take responsibility for one's life. Rav Chaim Shmuelevitz, in *Sichos Mussar*, has a beautiful piece describing how this is fundamental not only to *teshuva*, but to life. We are not objects that are acted upon by things outside ourselves; we are subjects, we contribute to, influence and shape our own destiny, and we need to take ownership over our lives. As long as we point fingers and blame others — whether it's our ancestors, genetics, other people, circumstances, our boss, our spouse, our children — we forfeit the ability to change. So *teshuva* begins with looking in the mirror and realizing אין הדבר תלוי אלא בי — I can do it, it's within me.

When people get past this hurdle, the change and the transformation is not immediate, overnight — that never lasts — but rather incremental. People eat well one day, or start going for walks, and then add a little — and we see people losing enormous amounts of weight, even 100 pounds, and they can even train and compete in marathons. You see it with Torah learning. There are people who were practically illiterate in Torah, but then they take on a *limud*, a *daf yomi*, and 2,711 days later they're making a *siyum* on Shas. It all begins with believing.

Pharaoh's strategy against the Jewish People was מקוצר רוח ומעבודה קשה. The *Or Ha-Chayim* explains קוצר רוח to mean not just that the people were out of breath because of the labor, but that they had shortness of vision. They failed to see a picture of a better version of their lives. They were stuck in the pattern of who they were.

"I'm an impatient husband." "I'm a father who isn't hands-on." "I'm an underachieving employee." It all begins with the belief, with the confidence of knowing that I can change and the change can be permanent, that I can really transform myself.

Too many people are spectators of their own lives, watching as though they're on the sidelines as their lives unfold. One of the most empowering insights I saw has to do with *Hakadosh Baruch Hu's* pronouncement when creating man, נעשה אדם. There are many different *pshatim* explaining to whom He is speaking, and why He spoke this way. The *Zohar Ha-Kadosh* says that Hashem here is talking to us. He is inviting each and every one of us, saying, "נעשה אדם — let's create you, you and I together. I'll get it started. I'll put you in this world, I'll give you a body, I'll endow it with a *neshama*, I'll give you a personality, potential and predispositions, and you'll be My partner, finishing what I started. Now go ahead and make yourself."

But many people are consumed by making excuses, instead of making themselves.

The *Zohar* continues that Hashem uses the word נעשה instead of נברא in order to reflect the way *Am Yisrael* would answer this invitation thousands of years later, announcing, נעשה ונשמע. They were saying, "We will take Your project to the next step. You got us started, and we will take it to the next step, through the holy Torah. We will write the next scene, the script of Torah."

We are not actors in somebody else's script. We're writing our own play, and the next scene, the best scene, is the one that is up to us.

We plead in *Selichos*, אל תשליכני לעת זקנה. Rav Waldenberg writes that this does not refer only to old age. We associate youth with vibrancy, with potential, with the future, with a sense that the best is yet to come, whereas we mistakenly assume that for older people, the best is already behind them. But there are even young people who act "old," who feel trapped, that they cannot change, that "this is who I am." We ask, אל תשליכני לעת זקנה — that we should not fail to believe in ourselves, that we never feel like we're stuck, that we never assume that it's too late.

The Gemara teaches, יש קונה עולמו בשעה אחת. A person can be 119 years old, and still achieve נעשה אדם, making himself, even at an advanced age. Herman Wouk published his last book when he was 100 years old. You're never too old to write that next scene, to make your next contribution, to answer the call of נעשה.

This is a fundamental obstacle that many people confront. They feel stuck, locked in place. They are spectators of their own lives, assuming, "This is who I am, this is what my life looks like, and it's too late for me to change." This is the biggest failure and the biggest obstacle. We have to overcome this hurdle and realize that נעשה אדם — we can make ourselves. We have to take "extreme ownership" and extreme responsibility.

Rav Aharon Lichtenstein explained that Esther [when she initially refused to approach Achashveirosh] was making excuses, saying, "I can't do it." Mordechai then said to her, רוח והצלה יעמוד ליהודים ממקום אחר — as if to say, "*Hakadosh Baruch Hu* will get this done. He doesn't need you. But you need this in order to be you." We are each here for a mission, for a reason, and *Hakadosh Baruch Hu* renews our contract for the coming year because we have something to contribute to His world. When we take "extreme ownership" over our personal mission, and we achieve it, that's how we make ourselves, and answer the call of נעשה אדם. During the *Yamim Noraim*, we challenge ourselves to show that we are taking "extreme ownership."

Rav Soloveitchik said that the concept of חפצא and גברא applies not only in *lomdus*, but also in the way we see ourselves. When we are acted upon by others, when we are mere spectators, then we're a חפצא, an object. This is why the Torah speaks of somebody who made a terrible mistake with the expression ירידה — "falling." Gravity applies to objects, whereas a subject can transcend gravity, can oppose gravity. If you let go of a cup, it falls to the ground. But you can lift your hand — because you have the power to go against gravity. We have to ask ourselves, "Am I an object or a subject? Am I living my life like a חפצא or like a גברא?"

The Rambam speaks of an enormously high level of *teshuva* — ויעיד עליו יודע תעלומות שלא ישוב לזה החטא לעולם. I don't think we should all measure ourselves against the highest level. I think you can aspire to the highest level without needing to measure yourself against it or to beat yourself up if you don't achieve it. What the Rambam's statement means to me is that a person's conviction becomes so strong that it wouldn't even enter his mind to commit this sin, that he is incapable of it, that it would violate his very being. This is what the Torah expects of us in a number of ways. For example, the Torah says that when you find a lost object, לא תוכל להתעלם — "you cannot ignore it." You have to turn yourself into a person that is incapable of ignoring it. Your conviction should be so strong that you will never walk past a lost object. It's not just that you go through the action of returning it to its owner, but that you transform your persona, you shape your personality such that you're incapable of just walking by it. It speaks to our conviction.

The way I relate to this is by thinking of an allergy. If a person has an allergy to something, then because his conviction to protect himself and preserve his health is so strong, he does not consider for a moment to violate the boundaries, to the point where people will testify about him that he will never violate them. If you know a family who has a child with a peanut allergy — they are so careful wherever they go to make sure there are no nuts anywhere. Our conviction must be so strong that *aveiros* are dangerous for us, that they compromise our spiritual health, that they threaten us — to the point where somebody can testify about us that we will stay away from them. I think this is what we're trying to aspire to — to get to that level where we have a strong, demonstrated conviction to the point where everybody knows about our "allergy" and will accommodate us because of it.

Of course, this a very high level. And the Rambam uses a very unusual term: ישתדל אדם לעשות תשובה — "A person must try to perform repentance." The Rambam does not tell us to "try" to take a *lulav* and *esrog*, to "try" to observe Shabbos, or to "try" to put on *tefillin*. The Rambam's understanding is that we're setting the barometer very high, and this is something to aspire to. It's a life journey, and maybe we'll never get there, but we never give up trying.

One thing which is overarching, reaching so many areas of life, but we don't think of it in the context of *teshuva* because it's not necessarily a particular *cheit*, is mindlessness. We're doing everything as מצות אנשים מלומדה, by rote, going through life as creatures of habit. Technology is robbing us of our being present in every experience. I think this really covers so many areas of our lives. Our relationships are suffering, and are compromised. Our *davening*, our *avodas Hashem*, is suffering, because we are not fully present. We are not experiencing anything entirely. Our minds are elsewhere. The *Ba'al Shem Tov* famously said that we are wherever our mind is. So in terms of *teshuva*, we should try to take measures to be mindful, to be present in all that we're doing, whether it's בין אדם למקום, בין אדם לחבירו, or even בין אדם לעצמו — setting aside time to hear ourselves in reflection and *hisbodedus*, to get back to a place where we can rise above all the noise and all the distraction, all the things that are pulling us in a million different directions, leaving us feeling so fractured.

The *Chovos Ha-Levavos* quotes somebody who would *daven* every day to be protected from פיזור הנפש — that he should not be fractured, fragmented, split and divided. I know I feel like this all the time. We're struggling to breathe. Research has shown that today we are not breathing properly, because we're always looking down at our devices, closing our airways. We're always rushing. We're running, we're going, we're doing — and we're not breathing deeply. We know that נשמה ("soul") and נשימה ("breath") have the same root — because we are in touch with our *neshama* when we take deep breaths and slow things down. We need to slow things down. I'm not saying we should ditch technology. I try to harness technology and benefit from the efficiency and productivity that it brings. But we need to do so judiciously and cautiously, using it to enhance our lives, not to take away our lives. We need to be more mindful and present, more conscious and more conscientious.

You cannot even begin the process of *teshuva* if you don't think. A prerequisite to *teshuva* is thinking, envisioning, aspiring. You can't even get started if you're running at such a rapid pace and you don't have space for thinking. *Teshuva* has to begin with carving out a place to think, to dream, to want to become the best version of ourselves.

ועתה ישראל מה ה' שואל ממך. The Chafetz Chayim writes that all Hashem wants of us is ועתה — to be present, to be there. *Hakadosh Baruch Hu* told Moshe, עלה אלי ההרה **והיה שם** — "Ascend the mountain to Me, **and be there.**" The Rebbes have explained this to mean, "Climb the mountain, and when you're there, turn off your phone. Disconnect. Be present. Be there."

This is the biggest *nisayon* (challenge) of our generation — to be there. Relationships are suffering. Children are suffering because they are not receiving enough time or attention. Our *davening* is suffering. And our own sense of self is suffering, because we have so much noise and we're so preoccupied.

Another challenge to *teshuva* is the ability to move forward, to not beat ourselves up or get stuck in the past. I think a lot of people look back at their lives with a sense of regret, and because of that, they think they cannot go forward. We need to realize that we cannot go backwards; we can only live forwards. There is an amazing Gemara in *Maseches Rosh Hashanah*: אין דנין לאדם אלא לפי מעשיו של אותה שעה — "a person is judged only in accordance with his actions at that moment." If you would ask anyone what the *Yamim Noraim* season is all about, he would tell you that we're being judged for how we acted over the last year, how my merits line up with what I did wrong. But that's not what the Gemara says. We're not being judged for last year, because last year is gone. It doesn't matter, because the only dimension I live in is the present. The past matters only if I'm holding onto it, if I'm proud of it, if it continues to inform today, and I want to repeat it. Then I'm accountable for the past. Otherwise, all that matters is the here and now.

The proof is the Gemara in *Maseches Kiddushin* which speaks of the case of somebody who betroths a woman על מנת שאני צדיק גמור — on the condition that he is a completely righteous person. The Gemara says that the woman needs a גט, because שמא הרהר תשובה באותה שעה — that man might have had thoughts of *teshuva* at that moment. We saw this fellow walk out of McDonald's eating a cheeseburger just a few minutes earlier, but we still consider the betrothal possibly valid — because the past doesn't matter if we've since moved on.

I think this is a very empowering message. We take stock of the past year because we want to learn from it. We don't take stock of our past year to be stuck in our past year. There's a fundamental difference between taking stock and getting stuck. All that really matters is the here and now, and where I'm going from here.

ואנחנו נברך י-ה מעתה ועד עולם. Rav Shlomo Hoffman says that the way we praise Hashem is when we live מעתה ועד עולם — from now and moving forward, when we ask, "What is my mission? What do I need to do? What's the next pressing *mitzva*? What's the next opportunity? How can I better myself going forward?" — without getting stuck in the past.

So many people beat themselves up for the past. In the *teshuva* season, we have to forgive others who genuinely ask for forgiveness, and we have to ask forgiveness from those whom we've wronged, but sometimes we have to make amends to ourselves, and forgive ourselves, and tell ourselves that we cannot change the past. All we can do is change who we are in the present, and I think a lot of people get stuck there. If we can overcome that, then we can make enormous changes.

The *Sefas Emes* says that the foundation of the *mitzva* of ואהבת לרעך כמוך is that we have to love ourselves. In order to love our fellow like ourselves, we need to first love ourselves. Some people love themselves a little too much, and their *avoda* is maybe to love themselves a little less. But there is a world of people who stopped loving themselves, who don't believe in themselves, who don't think they deserve happiness and success, and they end up subconsciously sabotaging themselves. A big part of the *teshuva* season is not only forgiving others, but also learning to forgive ourselves, to live in the here and now.

Jewish Action
THE MAGAZINE OF THE ORTHODOX UNION

Answering the Tough Questions: Parenting Experts Weigh In

Summer, 2013

By Aaron Katsman

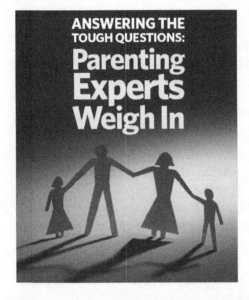

ANSWERING THE TOUGH QUESTIONS:
Parenting Experts Weigh In

How Do We Raise Confident, Happy Children?

By Simi Yellen, as told to Barbara Bensoussan

Many parents think that you can build a child's self-esteem simply by showering him with constant compliments. Others believe that a child will gain self-esteem by feeling successful all the time; hence, they bend over backwards to make sure that happens. For example, if the homework is too hard, they'll call the teacher to ask for an easier assignment.

These strategies only backfire in the end. They hinder rather than help a child develop real self-esteem. If a child never faces challenges, he'll never learn how to push himself or how to function in less-than-ideal situations. If you constantly set a child up to win, he will never learn to lose. But knowing how to lose is an important life skill.

This isn't called tough love; it's called real life. In the real world, nobody is going to smooth everything over for your children all the time. The biggest gift you can give your children is to allow them to work through less-than-ideal situations. Let them develop the psychological muscles they need to cope with hard challenges. Too many kids today grow up without having acquired the ability to work hard to accomplish a goal.

A fourth grade class was assigned a rebbe who had a reputation for being difficult. The students' parents handled the situation differently. One set of parents coddled their son. They righted any wrongs, brought their complaints to the administration and basically shielded their child from dealing with the situation. Another set of parents told their son, "Not every rebbe is easy to deal with, but in life, not every boss is easy either. Your job is to learn as best as you can despite the circumstances." They made it clear that whining and complaining his way through the year was not an option. They didn't coddle him, but when the year was over, they praised him for having gotten through it so well.

The lesson carried over into the months that followed. If his sister annoyed him, his parents would remind him, "Hey, you just got through ten months with a hard rebbe; this is nothing for you!" Having endured a difficult situation allowed their son to build character, and gave him the confidence that he could handle other bumps on the road of life.

Parental love is a necessary ingredient in instilling self-esteem—as essential as flour in a cake recipe. If a child doesn't receive enough time, attention and affection, and a sense that her parents believe in her, it will be hard for her to feel confident—even as an adult. It's not so much about the reality of the situation as it is about the child's perception of the situation. A person who felt emotionally deprived as a child may make bad decisions in life because she may misinterpret attention—including inappropriate forms of attention—as love. She may grow up seeing herself as unworthy or inferior, and will see every deficit as evidence of her unworthiness. For example, a child with a positive self-image who's not good at sports can still feel okay about himself knowing that he's good at other things; a child with low self-esteem will see his failure in sports as part of a larger picture of inadequacy.

Since our children spend most of their day in school, if a child isn't a strong student, it's incumbent upon his parents to find other areas in which he can excel. If there's no stage on which a child can shine, the parent has to build him one.

Identify your child's strengths and find an arena where they can be displayed, allowing him to feel worthwhile. For example, I know a few boys who are in charge of the local shul's seudah shelishis, a meal attended by hundreds of people. They know they have a responsibility; if they don't come, congregants won't have a seudah. There are other children who raise tzedakah for various causes or who work with younger children, helping them with homework, et cetera.

A young boy I know is dyslexic, which makes it difficult for him to read and process information. His father researched if any of the gedolim were dyslexic, but couldn't find such a role model for his son. When it became clear that his son probably wouldn't be a gadol hador, his father began pointing out the names of benefactors prominently displayed on the walls of neighborhood yeshivos. He would tell his son, "You see these men? They're businessmen. It's because they're so successful in business that we're able to have a kollel." He showed his son that there's more than one way to be a successful and influential Jew.

Another parent had a child with disabilities related to language processing. Whenever the child would make an insightful comment, the father would say, "You're smart as a whip!" The child internalized that he has the ability to understand things well and is very bright. He viewed his language-processing deficiencies as a problem to work on, but he didn't perceive himself as being dumb as a result of his learning difficulties.

Parents' attitudes toward grades also make a big difference. You can communicate to your child that effort matters much more than grades. You can say, "Your 75 means much more to us than another child's 95, because we know how much effort you put in. Hashem's in charge of the results, anyway." The truth is that bright kids sometimes don't learn to work hard, and it doesn't serve them well later on. As mentioned earlier, a child needs to learn about hard work and effort. Parents can also model the right way to deal with tough situations by openly discussing their own struggles with tasks or difficult people.

We want our kids to be happy. But what people often don't realize is that happiness is a by-product, not a goal. You can make a crying child happy by giving him a lollipop, but that's just a short-term fix. In the end, you do him a disservice by depriving him of the opportunity to learn how to deal with disappointment. You create a self-centered child with a sense of entitlement, who will be more unhappy in the long run when things don't go his way.

Real happiness is ultimately based on spiritual satisfaction, on doing the right thing and having simchah shel mitzvah. Mitzvos and good deeds produce intrinsic satisfaction that doesn't require rewards like lollipops or stars on a chart. One of my clients was recently on her way into the house laden with packages when one of her children surprised her by offering to help. When they finished, this boy—whose teacher is big on charts and stars—asked her, "Mommy, will you give me a star?" She answered, "No, but you've got something better than a star."

The child asked, "What's that?"

"You have good middos," the mother replied.

"Ah," the child said, nodding wisely. "Yes, that's much better."

Simi Yellen has been positively transforming homes for over a decade through her teleconference parenting classes and private consultations. Her new ten-week series entitled "Raise the Bar Parenting" empowers parents to raise respectful, responsible and cooperative children through curtailing arguing, chutzpah and other negative behaviors.

Why We Need to Talk to our Children about Sexuality
By Yocheved Debow

As Orthodox Jewish parents, we strive to convey our commitment to halachah to our children. Imparting these values requires time and thought, and we therefore send them to schools which offer a thorough Jewish education. However, in the area of sexuality and relationships, about which most children—and particularly adolescents—show curiosity and interest, and about which the halachah has clear opinions, we, and the schools we send our children to, often choose to be silent. This silence itself communicates an important message. Not talking about sexuality, especially when it is so much talked about in movies and the media, gives an implicit message that Judaism is at the very least uncomfortable about sexuality or, worse, has nothing positive to say on the subject. In addition, there is no avoiding the automatic association that when parents refuse to talk about these topics, children perforce conclude that sexuality is bad and shameful.

In order for our children to view a Torah lifestyle as being relevant to them, they must experience Torah as addressing issues that concern them. Talking about sexuality and relationships from a halachic perspective helps our children appreciate the wisdom and relevance of Judaism to these significant aspects of their lives, and by extension, to their lives in general.

Why Do We Hesitate?

We often fail to educate in these areas because we feel ill-equipped to approach them properly. The topics of sexuality and intimacy can be complex and awkward. However, if we do not provide a thoughtful, open, honest forum for discussion, our children will look for information and a value system elsewhere.

Is Your Child Ready to Discuss Sexuality?

When considering what to tell your children about sexuality, it is helpful to consider the following factors:
- Child's milieu
- Child's maturity
- Openness in the family
- Norms of the community

Child's Milieu

Who are your child's friends and what is the nature of the information these friends might have? Is it likely that they are more aware than your child? Does your child watch television? And if so, what shows does he or she watch, and how often? Are there filters on the computer he uses, or is your child able to watch and explore whatever he chooses? Is your child an avid reader? If so, what is she reading? All of these factors will impact on how much access they may already have to information and can factor into your decision about what you would like to share with your child.

Child's Maturity

Do you think your child is mature enough to be able to differentiate between private and public? Will your child be able to respond to your conversation maturely, or will he become embarrassed? If you consider your child not so mature but she has asked questions, it is especially important to answer thoughtfully, perhaps beginning with partial information and moving on to more detailed information only if the child continues to question. Remember to find out what your child already knows and what she is really asking.

Openness in the Family
Each family has its own rules about what can and cannot be discussed. If your family speaks openly and easily about personal matters, the question of how to initiate a conversation about sexuality will not be too difficult. In families in which there are rarely conversations about personal matters, parents might need to be more thoughtful as to how, and at what age, they will want to broach these topics. Remember that your comfort level is also important here; try to ensure your own comfort, if at all possible.

Norms of the Community
While you may choose to be really open about sexuality in your family, or quite the opposite, very hesitant to speak about sexuality, be aware that your children spend much of their lives outside of the home. Be cognizant of the norms in your community; recognize that they constantly change as norms in secular society become more permissive. Children often walk around with partial information pieced together from comments by friends, fragments of television shows or parts of conversations they have overheard. If that might be the case for your child, the sooner you start a conversation with him in these areas, the sooner he will come to understand that you are, in fact, a very good resource for honest, accurate information about sexuality.

Sometimes we invoke the idea of tzeniut, modesty, and use it as an excuse to avoid discussing such topics with our children. While tzeniut is a core value and certainly applies to the way in which we converse with our children about these topics, we cannot escape the fact that our children's environment is already quite heavily saturated with sexuality. Choosing not to talk to our children about these issues will not advance the cause of tzeniut but, to the contrary, will succeed in promoting the values of the general culture and its anti-tzeniut stance as the children's sole source of sexual values. Openness and honesty are not compromised by sensitivity to tzeniut, properly understood.

It is important that we not delude ourselves. While we all try to protect our children from inappropriate material, we cannot be naïve and think that they are not going to hear, see or know anything about sexuality. For anyone who lives in a community which allows some modernity, it will be difficult—if not impossible—to protect children from at least partial knowledge of sexuality. Whether through friends or the Internet, television shows or books, they will gradually develop ideas about sexuality. Therefore, the onus is on us to speak to our children in the manner and in the context of our choosing. We must employ age-appropriate, correct information in order to provide an alternative message to those they absorb from the world around them.

Support from the Talmud

The Talmud, too, recognizes the importance of teaching about sexuality. In a surprising passage in Berachot 62a, we are told that Rav Kahana hid under his teacher's bed in order to learn about sexual relations. While his teacher instructs him to leave because his behavior is not appropriate, the Talmud does not criticize Rav Kahana. Rather, it gives him the final word when he explains his behavior saying, "This is Torah and I must learn it." And so, in fact, the Gemara explicitly supports the idea that sexuality is an important part of life, that it is natural to be curious about it and that it is the responsibility of parents and educators to share knowledge with their children on these topics. Our children are curious by nature, and this curiosity includes sexuality. One way or another, they will find ways to access the information they seek. Rav Kahana chose a most inappropriate way of learning about sexual relations, by hiding in his teacher's bedroom. Our teenagers have their own ways of finding out answers to their questions. However, these sources, though easily available, tend to be highly problematic and inaccurate. Our children turn to them when they are curious and have nowhere else to turn. If we choose to engage them in conversation at the right time and in the right context for each child, they will continue to view us as a reliable source of information.

The message that sexuality has innate kedushah in the appropriate context is rarely transmitted to our children. By working to overcome our own personal difficulties with these topics for the sake of our children, we can provide an alternative voice—one that is positive and based in traditional Jewish values.

Dr. Yocheved Debow holds a doctorate from Bar-Ilan University's School of Education. Her research focuses on sexuality and intimacy education in the Modern Orthodox community. She is the author of Talking about Intimacy and Sexuality: A Guide for Orthodox Jewish Parents, published by Ktav and OU Press. Dr. Debow currently teaches at Midreshet Moriah and is the academic principal at Midreshet Emunah v'Omanut. She resides in Alon Shevut, Israel, with her husband, Rabbi David Debow, and their six children.

How Do We Instill Emunah In Our Children?
By Ilan Feldman

The best way to instill emunah in children is to pick them up when they cry.

There is a common misconception about emunah. People think of emunah as the result of philosophic inquiry. If that were the case, no real emunah is possible for children; all we can hope for is to get them to talk as if they have emunah and sing songs that assert that God is here and everywhere. Actually, while contemplation might result in emunah, emunah is far more commonly a natural expression of the human condition. When it is absent, it is because something has happened that damages the natural capacity a person has to appreciate and trust his or her Source and Essence.

Emunah is not a mimetic behavior or a skill—or even an attitude. It's not a thought a person draws upon when encountering tough times; it's a way of being. For those who live with emunah, emunah is like gravity. Awareness of God as one Who exists, Who knows and cares, Who responds to my existence, Who believes in me and expects things from me as much as I believe in Him—all this is so real that decisions are made and actions are performed much the same way that the laws of physics are taken into account before passing the butter. It is so much a part of reality that one need not think about it. Emunah is not so much a belief as it is a context or a prism through which the world is filtered.

Yet, to live with emunah is to be clear about, and profoundly related to, an ephemeral, non-physical, invisible, unprovable realm whose existence has non-immediate consequences. For emunah to be present, an individual has to be sensitive to the presence of something beside, and beyond, the physical world. This is the challenge of life, felt more acutely in our modern world than ever before, where physical pleasure, power and fame are the currency of value: to live lives in a physical world that are devoted to a mission that exists in a nonphysical world.

The mishnah in Avot (4:21) asserts that three things "chase a person from the world," meaning, put one out of touch with reality: jealousy, desire and pursuit of honor. Any one of these three obsessions blinds a person to anything spiritual. They are the result of a single-minded focus on material things. They make it impossible to develop the senses needed to perceive the spiritual dimension of life—the reason for life—or even to be aware that there is such a realm. When material things become the currency in which we deal, emunah becomes impossible.

For children to live with emunah awareness, we must reinforce their natural tendency to trust, to depend on their parents. When a child cries, it is not the bottle that makes the difference, but the context in which the bottle is delivered—with love, reliability, connection and nurturance. These are all abstracts, and they point to a domain that is not physical, yet is as real as the bottle. As the child grows, she learns that she is loved, is provided for and can afford to trust without fear of betrayal. The child learns to appreciate, and the child learns that she is loveable as well. These are the foundations of emunah.

The question of imparting emunah to young children and teens is only a concern to parents and a society for whom emunah is a reality. Parents, teachers and other role models who don't deal with God as a personal reality will have no questions about imparting this awareness to children, which points to the most effective way of imparting emunah to the next generation—living and demonstrating in our own discourse and relationships the opposite of jealousy, desire and longing for recognition. It means passing up opportunities for personal pleasure in favor of spiritual pleasure, which is all about connection to others, and to the Other. And it means living a life of humility, aware as we are that there is a God who put us here for a purpose. Opportunities to make these statements abound in daily family living: in how parents relate to each other, in how religious obligations are met, in what topics dominate casual conversation, in the style of parenting our children experience. Being a reliable and dependable parent, or a loving and loyal spouse, creates the context in which emunah in a God with similar characteristics can thrive.

After a blessing is recited, we respond with "Amen," a derivative of the word emunah. A blessing affirms awareness of the Source, and expresses appreciation for being the recipient of gifts. Responding with Amen takes the affirmation of the blessing and keeps it alive in the world for others. The most effective way of passing emunah on to the next generation is to lead lives that embody and express a resounding Amen in the presence of the gifts around us.

Rabbi Ilan Feldman has been the rabbi of Congregation Beth Jacob in Atlanta, Georgia, since 1991 and has been struggling with emunah since he was five years old.

Should Schools and Yeshivos Skip Adult-Oriented Topics?

Many segments of Torah literature address topics of a squarely adult nature. Entire *masechtos* — *Nidda* and *Zavim* — deal with emissions from a person's genitals and their status vis-à-vis *tum'a* (halachic impurity). The laws of *nidda*, in particular, are the subject of many important volumes of halachic texts, given their everyday practical relevance to married couples, and these laws include discussions of the female anatomy and various aspects of the phenomenon of menstruation. And the Talmud contains no small number of passages with explicit references to intercourse. One famous example is the Talmud's discussion[1] of the case of a groom who claims the morning after his wedding that his bride was not a virgin (פתח פתוח מצאתי), a vitally important text relevant to several fundamental halachic concepts (such as ספק ספיקא and שויה אנפשיה חתיכא דאיסורא).

It is customary in many chassidic yeshivos to skip these portions of the Talmud, deeming it inappropriate for unmarried men to discuss topics that relate to the female body or marital intimacy. Such discussions can easily lead to sexually arousing thoughts, and thus many chassidic institutions feel these subjects should be avoided by unmarried students, deeming it inappropriate for them to openly discuss sex and the female anatomy.

This practice has its roots in a number of early sources. The famous Kabbalist Rabbi Moshe Cordovero writes in his *Tomer Devora*,[2] אפילו דבור טהור המביא לידי הרהור ראוי להשמר ממנו — "it is proper to avoid even 'pure speech' that causes inappropriate thoughts." This could be understood to mean that even Torah subjects which could arouse lust are to be avoided.[3] More explicitly, Rav Eliezer Papo writes in his *Pele Yoetz* (ערך דבור):

> הצנועים מושכים את ידיהם מלדבר אפילו דברי תורה בפרטי דיני איש ואשה... ובפרט לשרוי בלא אשה.

---

1. *Kesubos* 9a.
2. Chapter 8.
3. Although, later in this passage, Rav Cordovero speaks of speech אפילו שיהיה מותר — "even that is permissible," suggesting that he might be referring here only to general, innocent topics of conversation, but not Torah topics, which should not be avoided even if they could potentially lead to improper thoughts.

> The exceedingly modest refrain from speaking even words of Torah related to the details of the laws of a husband and wife…especially for one who lives without a wife.[4]

Rav Shimon Greenfeld (the Maharshag) twice mentions that he followed the practice that was accepted in his time not to study the laws of *nidda* with unmarried students.[5] And Rav Yaakov Ketina, in his *mussar* work *Rachamei Ha'av,*[6] speaks in praise of "the custom in Poland" to disallow the study of sexually related matters by unmarried men until just before their wedding.

There is a similar practice observed in some communities to skip portions of the Chumash — specifically, those that speak openly of sexual relationships, such as the story of Lot and his daughters, and the story of Yehuda and Tamar — when teaching young schoolchildren. Some institutions have even gone so far as to prepare for their students Chumashim with these verses omitted.

Volozhin and the *Chasam Sofer*

By contrast, there is ample evidence of widely respected institutions that did not hesitate to allow young, unmarried students to study the sections of the Talmud that address subjects such as female anatomy and intercourse. Most famously, perhaps, the legendary Volozhin Yeshiva studied the entire Talmud in order, from the first page of *Maseches Berachos* through the final page of *Maseches Nidda*, without skipping any sections. Whereas other yeshivos studied only particular *masechtos* or topics in the Talmud, the policy in Volozhin was to study the entire Talmud in order, one page a day.[7]

It is clear also that the *Chasam Sofer* would study *Maseches Nidda* and the laws

---

4. It is startling that Rav Papo encourages refraining from these subjects even for married men — a practice which does not appear in any other source. We can only wonder how, according to this extreme position, the vitally important *halachos* related to menstruation and marital relations can be accurately preserved if everyone, including people who are married, are discouraged from studying these portions of Torah.

5. *Shu"t Maharshag*, Y.D. 10, 11.

6. ערך ההרהור.

7. See Rav Meir Bar-Ilan's account in his *Mi'Volozhin ad Yerushalayim* (vol. 1, p. 90):
    בכל שאר הישיבות היו מגידים "שיעור" רק בסוגיות ידועות...ורק במסכתות מסויימות של הש"ס...
    ואילו בוולוז'ין היה ה"שיעור" מעין "קרבן תמיד"... את ה"שיעור" היו לומדים כסדר הש"ס ממסכת
    ברכות ועד מסכת נדה.

    Rav Hershel Schachter (*Nefesh Ha'Rav*, p. 29, note 44) points to this practice in Volozhin as the likely reason why Rav Yosef Dov Soloveitchik taught *Maseches Nidda* to single students in Yeshiva University, against the protests of Rav Mendel Zaks (the Chafetz Chayim's son-in-law), a faculty member at the yeshiva.

pertaining to a menstruating woman with his students. In his commentary to the Talmud, the *Chasam Sofer* concludes his writings on *Maseches Nidda* by announcing his completion of the study of *Maseches Nidda* with his students in the yeshiva of Mattersdorf, for whom he proceeds to offer a poetic prayer. Furthermore, in one of his responsa,[8] the *Chasam Sofer* speaks of a system proposed by an earlier scholar[9] whereby a woman can definitively determine that intercourse does not cause her menstrual bleeding, involving a small contraption which she inserts into her body. The *Chasam Sofer* writes that he prepared such a device, and he showed it to his students as part of their study of the relevant *halachos*. It is clear from these sources that the *Chasam Sofer* studied the *halachos* relating to menstruation with his students.

What's more, the *Chasam Sofer's* grandson, Rav Shlomo Sofer, in his *Chut Ha-Meshulash,*[10] relates that the *Chasam Sofer* had two professionally designed figurines — one male and one female — which he would use as visual aids when teaching his students topics that required knowledge of the human anatomy, such as the laws of *nidda*. Rav Sofer emphasizes, however, that the *Chasam Sofer* would use these figurines only to תלמידים מובהקים אשר יראת ה' אוצרם — "his outstanding students who were steeped in fear of God." This might suggest that the use of visual aids was reserved specifically for special students, as for others this would be inappropriate.

The Klausenberger Rebbe[11] tells that during his first trip to Israel, he met with the *Chasam Sofer's* great-grandson, Rav Akiva Sofer, who showed him a diagram of the female reproductive system which the *Chasam Sofer* used when learning with his students matters related to the laws of *nidda*. The Klausenberger Rebbe relates that Rav Sofer asked him what he thought of such a practice, and he responded by citing a remark made by his great-uncle, Rav Yechezkel Shraga Halberstam of Shinova, to justify the practice among the *Chasam Sofer's* students to delay marriage. Rav Yechezkel remarked that the *Chasam Sofer* had a profound spiritual effect upon his disciples that prevented them from sin, so they could remain pure even before marrying. The Klausenberger Rebbe applied this also to the *Chasam Sofer's* visual aids, indicating that the *Chasam Sofer's* use of these materials in his yeshiva does not necessarily serve as a valid precedent for other Torah educational institutions. If so, then the *Chasam Sofer's* study of the laws of *nidda* with his disciples similarly does not set an example we should necessarily follow.

On the other hand, there is evidence that the *Chasam Sofer's* followers also embraced this practice. The *Chasam Sofer's* famous disciple, the Maharam Shick, authored an

---

8.   Y.D. 153.

9.   Rav Aharon Shmuel Kaidanover, in his *Emunas Shmuel.*

10.   P. 95 in the *Machon Daas Sofer* edition (5760).

11.   *Shefa Chayim, Parshas Shelach,* p. 409.

entire responsum[12] to a student on the subject of הרגשת נדה — the physical sensations that confer upon a woman the status of *nidda* — and he addressed the letter to אהובי תלמידי הבחור — "my beloved, my student, the young man." The word בחור is normally used in reference specifically to unmarried men, and it thus appears that the Maharam Shick discussed the experience of menstruation as it relates to *halacha* with an unmarried student.

Similarly, the *Chasam Sofer's* grandson, Rav Shmuel Ehrenfeld, writes in a responsum[13] that he received a question regarding the case of a woman with a bruise (giving rise to the question of whether her bleeding was caused by menstruation, thus rendering her a *nidda*, or by the bruise), and he instructed הבחורים הגדולים — his older students — to look into the topic. He adds that in one of his lectures he discussed with his students a question he received regarding a woman who neglected to perform the required examination at the time menstruation was expected. Rav Ehrenfeld explicitly speaks of learning the intricacies of the laws of *nidda* — including details related to the experience of menstruation — with בחורים, referring, presumably, to unmarried men.

Learning *Kesubos* before the Bar-Mitzva

Another relevant source is a passage in the *Eizer Mi-Kodesh* commentary to the *Even Ha-Ezer* section of the *Shulchan Aruch*[14] by Rav Avraham David of Buchach. In discussing the prohibition against intentionally thinking erotic thoughts, he writes that it is entirely permissible to study portions of Torah that speak of sexual matters, observing that it was not customary to avoid such topics:

אין שום בחור נמנע מללמוד בספרים הקדושים דברים שיש בהם צד גרם הרהורים בכמה הלכות שבסדר נשים...וכל שהוא בסגנון שכתוב בספרים הקדושים אין בזה שום פתחון פה חשש דררא דניבול פה או גרם הרהורים.

> There is no young man who refrains from studying in the sacred books matters that have the possibility of causing [improper] thoughts, in several laws in the order of *Nashim*… Anything in the style written in the sacred books — there is no room for questioning, [and] no concern of violations of improper speech or causing [improper] thoughts.

It is told[15] that Rav Aharon Kotler learned the entire *Maseches Kesubos*, from beginning to end, under Rav Zalman Sender Shapiro, already before his bar-mitzva. This necessarily included topics related to marital relations. Similarly, Rav Chaim Kanievsky

---

12. *Teshuvos Maharam Shick*, Y.D. 184.
13. *Chasan Sofer*, 56.
14. 23:3.
15. *Eish Ha-Torah*, vol. 1, p. 27.

reportedly said that he studied *Maseches Nidda* as a teenager, before he got married.[16]

It is reported[17] that Rav Dov Berish Weidenfeld, the Gaon of Tchebin, could not understand why *Maseches Nidda* is not commonly studied in yeshivos, and that Rav Shmuel Wosner studied *Maseches Nidda* as a sixteen-year-old student.

Talmudic Sources

In 5662 (1902), an anonymous booklet was published in Vilna under the title, *Darkah shel Torah*, with the support of several leading European rabbis of that time.[18] The author[19] strongly condemned the practice of skipping portions of the Chumash when teaching schoolchildren, noting that מעולם לא חששו אבותינו ורבותינו לשמא יבוא הילדים הרכים לידי מכשול לב מפרשיות שבתורה הקדושה — "our fathers and rabbis were never concerned that young children would end up stumbling with their hearts as a result of sections of the sacred Torah." He noted, among other sources, the Gemara's ruling in *Maseches Megilla* (25b) that the story of Lot's intimate encounters with his daughters may be read and translated in public. The Gemara comments that one may have thought that this shameful incident should not be made public out of respect for Avraham, Lot's uncle, but this is not the case, and the story should, in fact, be public-ly read in the synagogue. Similarly, the Gemara establishes that the story of Yehuda's unusual relationship with his daughter-in-law Tamar may be read and explained in public, and should not be avoided out of respect for Yehuda. Significantly, the Gemara did not even consider the possibility of skipping these stories because of their sexual nature, in order to prevent arousing thoughts, clearly indicating that this is not a consideration in regard to reading and studying Torah material.

The author of *Darkah shel Torah* added that the Gemara draws no distinctions in this regard between different audiences. The Gemara gives no indication that teaching these stories is appropriate for certain ages or populations but not for others, and so we, too, should not skip these sections when teaching children.

Moreover, the Rogatchover Gaon, in a letter included in that treatise,[20] noted the

---

16. *Derech Sicha*, vol. 1, *Parshas Vayeira*, p. 80.

17. *Rabbeinu Ha'gadol Amaro*, p. 366.

18. This booklet received the endorsement of Rav Elya Feinstein of Pruzhan, Rav Eliezer Gordon of Telz, Rav Yechiel Michel Epstein of Novardok (author of the *Aruch Ha-Shul-chan*), and Rav Yitzchak Blazer of St. Petersburg, among others. It also includes contri-butions by Rav Chaim Soloveitchik of Brisk, Rav Chaim Ozer Grodzinsky, and the Roga-tchover Gaon (Rav Yosef Rosen of Dvinsk).

19. P. 5.

20. P. 28.

Tosefta's ruling[21] that even sections which are not publicly read — such as the story of David and Batsheva, which is not read in public out of respect for King David — are taught as part of an educational curriculum (הסופר מלמד כדרכו). Meaning, even portions which the Sages felt were inappropriate for the congregational reading are to be taught to schoolchildren. Certainly, then, stories such as Lot's relationship with his daughters, which are read publicly in the synagogue, should be taught, and not excluded from school curricula.

At first glance, one might suggest drawing proof in support of the practice of skipping certain topics from the Mishna's ruling in *Maseches Chagiga* (11b), אין דורשין בעריות בשלשה — one may not teach matters involving עריות, forbidden sexual relationships, in the presence of three or more people. Seemingly, this means that subjects of a sexual nature should not be taught publicly.

In truth, however, this is not the Mishna's intent at all. The Gemara explains that the Mishna forbade publicly teaching the laws of עריות because while one student asks the teacher a question, the other students might be inattentive and converse among themselves, thus losing vitally important information. Due to the unique strength of the sexual urge, the Gemara comments, people are prone to incorrectly permit relationships which are halachically proscribed, and so it is especially important for these *halachos* to be taught clearly and effectively, in order to avoid misinformation and misconceptions. For this reason, the Mishna requires teaching these laws privately, to one or two students, but not to a group, where there is a risk of inattentiveness. This explanation of the Mishna's ruling is mentioned by the Rambam, in his codification of this prohibition.[22]

Clearly, the Mishna's statement has nothing at all to do with the concern of arousal, and thus cannot be enlisted as a source for skipping certain sections of Torah in yeshiva curricula. What's more, the Rama, in *Darchei Moshe*,[23] cites the Re'avya as stating that the Mishna's ruling applied only in Talmudic times, when all learning was done orally, whereas now, when the majority of learning is done through the study of written texts, the concern of misinformation does not apply. Indeed, this *halacha* is not brought anywhere in the *Shulchan Aruch*, as it is no longer practically applicable.[24]

---

21. *Megilla* 3:19.

22. *Hilchos Issurei Bi'a* 22:17:

אין דורשין בסתרי עריות בשלשה מפני שהאחד טרוד בשאלת הרב והשניים נושאין ונותנין זה עם זה,

ואין דעתם פנויה לשמוע, שדעתו של אדם קרובה אצל עריות, אם נסתפק לו דבר ששמע, מורה להקל,

לפיכך אין דורשין אלא לשניים כדי שיהיה השומע האחד מפנה דעתו ויודע מה שישמע מן הרב.

23. Y.D. 246.

24. The Rama adds that the *Zohar* advanced a much different reading of the phrase אין דורשין בעריות בשלשה, explaining that it refers to teaching the Kabbalistic concepts underlying the Torah's restrictions on sexual relations, which must not be taught publicly.

בלימוד התורה אין יוצא רע

Having established a clear precedent for the study of such subjects even by unmarried men, and that this practice appears to be sanctioned already by the Gemara, let us turn our attention to the question of why this is acceptable. Is there not a legitimate concern of unnecessarily arousing inappropriate thoughts and desires?

The answer is found in a passage written by the Netziv — the famed Rosh Yeshiva in Volozhin — in his *Haamek Davar*.[1] The Netziv observes God's unusual introduction in presenting to Moshe and Aharon the laws relevant to bodily emissions: דברו אל בני ישראל ואמרתם אליהם — "Speak to the Children of Israel, and say to them…" The seemingly superfluous phrase ואמרתם אליהם, the Netziv explained, was added to emphasize that the intensive, in-depth study of these topics is included under the *mitzva* of Torah learning. One might have assumed that once Moshe transmitted the basic information he received from God regarding bodily emissions, it is proper to limit our discussions about such matters as much as possible, speaking only the bare minimum necessary to preserve the vital halachic information. The Torah therefore emphasized, ואמרתם אליהם — that subjects such as *nidda* are to be studied, discussed and analyzed no less than any other Torah subject, as part of the *mitzva* to learn Torah.

The Netziv concludes by explaining, משום שבאמת בלימוד התורה אין יוצא רע, והיא איילת אהבים ויעלת חן — "because in truth, nothing harmful can come from Torah study, and it is beloved and beautiful." These subjects should not be avoided, the Netziv asserts, because the sanctity of Torah makes this study valuable and enriching, by definition. Any material that is included within the corpus of Torah is necessarily worth learning and important to learn. It cannot, by definition, be harmful (of course, as long as this is done properly, in a mature and appropriate manner).

This concept was expressed by many others, as well. The *Chazon Ish* is said to have instructed the principal of the high school run under his auspices to learn the entirety of *Maseches Kesubos* without skipping any sections, כי דברי תורה אינם מזיקים — "because words of Torah cause no harm."[2]

Similarly, Rav Moshe Feinstein[3] penned a responsum forbidding teaching sex education curricula prepared by the public educational system, adding, לא דמי כלל למה שלומדים בסוגיות הגמרא שתורה מגנא ומצלא — "this is not at all similar to studying topics in the Gemara, because Torah protects and saves." Rav Moshe maintained that studying matters of a sexual nature that are included in Torah texts is permissible, because, as the Gemara famously teaches in *Maseches Sota* (21a), Torah learning מגנא ומצלא — "has protective powers," and will therefore not arouse inappropriate thoughts and desires.

---

1. *Vayikra* 15:2.
2. *Orchos Rabbeinu*, vol. 4, p. 159.
3. *Iggeros Moshe*, Y.D. 5:34.

The Klausenberger Rebbe[4] recalled that his teacher in his *cheder* (elementary school) taught and explained each and every verse in the Chumash, without skipping even a single one, and later, in yeshiva, he was taught every passage in the Gemara, and every *Tosfos*. The Rebbe said, "They did not see any difference between *Parshas Tazria* and *Parshas Metzora*, or between one *Tosfos* and another," because התורה קדושה וטהורה ואין בה כל גשם, וכל כולו רוחניות — "the Torah is sacred and pure, and it has no physicality; it is entirely spiritual." There is no reason for concern of spiritual harm from Torah study, which is inherently pure and pristine. On a different occasion,[5] the Klausenberger Rebbe observed that it is possible for a man to spend years delving into topics relevant to intimacy and *nidda* without experiencing inappropriate thoughts, adding אדרבה, הלימוד מקדש ומטהר אותו — "to the contrary, learning sanctifies and purifies him."

Rav Shmuel Wosner likewise took the position that topics of a sexual nature should not be omitted משום דדברי חז"ל יש בהם קדושה ובכוחם שלא יזיקו ח"ו למי שלומדם — "because the words of our Sages, of blessed memory, have sanctity, and they have the power not to cause harm, Heaven forbid, to those who study them."[6] And it is told[7] that Rav Avraham Yitzchak Kook encouraged an unmarried student who was completing the first volume of *Yoreh Dei'a* to proceed to the second section, which deals with the laws of *nidda*, without concern, שהתורה מטהרת ומנקה את נפשו של האדם וגם מרוממת אותו — "because the Torah purifies and cleanses the person's soul, and also uplifts it."[8]

4.　*Shefa Chayim*, vol. 17, p. 408.

5.　*Shefa Chayim — Shiur Chumash Ve'Rashi, Parshas Chayei-Sara*, 5726.

6.　*Rav Rabbanan*, p. 107.

7.　*Otzros Ha-Re'aya*, vol. 2, p. 377.

8.　The Gemara famously comments in *Maseches Yoma* (72b), זכה, נעשית לו סם חיים, לא זכה, נעשית לו סם מיתה — "If one is worthy, it [the Torah] becomes for him a life-giving potion; if one is unworthy, it becomes for him a death potion." This implies that Torah learning is not guaranteed to be beneficial and uplifting, and can have the precise opposite effect. One might argue, then, that contrary to the sources cited here, we must be discerning in choosing which subjects to learn, as subjects which arouse improper thoughts could render the learning harmful and destructive. However, it is clear from the context of this statement that the Gemara refers here specifically to somebody who studies Torah without יראת שמים (fear of God), engaging in the intellectual exercise of learning without the requisite religious devotion, as the Gemara comments several lines earlier, אוי להם לשונאיהם של תלמידי חכמים שעוסקין בתורה ואין בהן יראת שמים — warning of the punishment that will befall scholars who engage in Torah study without fear of God. As long as one approaches learning sincerely, as part of a genuine desire to draw close to God and absorb the sacred wisdom of the Torah, his study is a סם חיים and will not cause any harm.

שמועה זו נאה ושמועה זו אינה נאה

There is also another reason not to skip portions of Torah, besides the guarantee that no spiritual harm could result from the sanctity of Torah. The Gemara in *Maseches Eiruvin* (64a) warns, כל האומר שמועה זו נאה וזו אינה נאה מאבד הונה של תורה — "Whoever says, 'This passage is nice' and, 'This [passage] is not nice,' loses the 'wealth' [reward] of Torah [study]." We are not to judge which sections of Torah are appropriate to study and which aren't. Instead, we must humbly acknowledge and trust the inherent value and importance of each and every segment of Torah.

This concept is expressed also by the Midrash,[9] in interpreting the phrase in *Shir Hashirim* (5:11), שחורות כעורב (literally, "black as a raven"). The Midrash understands this phrase as a description of Torah, explaining that it might at times seem "black" and unseemly, but it is, in truth, כעורב — beautiful and pleasing (ערב):

> אע"פ שנראות כאילו הן כעורות ושחורות לאומרן ברבים, כגון הלכות זיבה ונגעים, נדה ויולדת, אמר הקדוש ברוך הוא: הרי הן עריבות עלי.

> Even though they seem hideous and "black" such that they should not be discussed publicly — such as the laws of bodily emissions, skin infections, menstruation and childbirth — the Almighty said: "These are pleasing to Me!"[10]

These sources are referenced by the author of the aforementioned *Darkah shel Torah*, in establishing that we have no right to determine that some sections of the Torah are unworthy of study. He emphasizes that כולן יפות ומתוקות — "every section of the Torah is inherently valuable and precious," and we are not authorized to declare certain portions inappropriate for teaching.

Educational Concerns

There are also two other factors that must be considered in determining the proper policy regarding yeshiva curricula.

The author of *Darkah shel Torah* notes the grave educational danger of withholding portions of Torah from schoolchildren:

> מה רע הרושם שעושים המדלגים בלב הילדים שהביאו אותם להרהר כי אכן יש

---

9.   *Vayikra Rabba* 19:3.

10.   The Midrash proceeds to explain on this basis the famous verse in *Malachi* (3:4), וערבה לה' מנחת יהודה וירושלים — "The offering of Judea and Jerusalem shall be pleasing to G-d." According to the Midrash, this verse emphasizes that all Torah study is an "offering" to the Almighty which He finds pleasing, even the study of subjects which one might initially find "hideous."

בתורה הנתונה מסיני דברים מכוערים שבושים המלמדים ללמדם, וכי זו היא
תורת ה' תמימה מאירת עיניים משמחת לב ומשיבת נפש!?

> What a terrible impression is made by those who skip [certain portions of
> the Torah] upon the heart of the students, causing them to think that the
> Torah, which was given at Sinai, actually contains ugly matters which the
> teachers are ashamed to teach. Is this the "complete" Torah of God, which
> illuminates the eyes, brings joy to the heart, and restores the soul!?

This writer points to the fact that any benefit that might result from "hiding" from
students portions of the Torah that involve sex, is offset by the dangerous impression it
leaves — that parts of the Torah are "dirty." Educators must instill within their charges a
sense that, as the author cites from *Tehillim* (19:8), תורת ה' תמימה — the Torah is perfect
and complete, and every word is precious and to be approached with love, reverence and
enthusiasm. This message is undermined when students discover that portions of the
Torah have been withheld from them because these portions were deemed unsuitable
and unbecoming. The impression they are left with is that the Torah — like other fields
— have "good" and "bad" aspects. This danger far outweighs whatever value one might
find in protecting innocent youngsters from sexual references in Torah texts.

Secondly, especially in our day and age, it is critically important for educational
institutions to speak to youngsters directly about sexual matters. Today, unfortunately,
even children — let alone adolescents — are exposed to an endless ocean of information, and are naturally curious about sex. It would be beyond delusional to think that
by avoiding exposure to passages in Torah literature that speak of intimacy, we successfully preserve our youngsters' innocence until they are ready for marriage. If children
are not taught such matters appropriately in their educational institutions, they will
receive information from other sources, leaving them confused. They will also reach
the conclusion that the Torah does not have what to say about intimacy between men
and women — which is, of course, very far from the truth — and, given human nature,
this could easily lead to disinterest in Torah, and defection.

The sections in Chumash and the Talmud that deal with matters such as intimacy
and the anatomy offer educators a valuable opportunity to provide their charges with
a correct and healthy understanding of sexuality, to show them that the Torah, which
governs and enriches every aspect of our lives, governs and enriches also this crucial
area of the human experience. Not only should these subjects not be avoided, but to
the contrary, they should comprise a critically important part of the curriculum in
modern Torah education, as part of our effort to resist the negative influences of our
society and inspire our youngsters to live pure, sacred lives as the Torah demands.

THE JERUSALEM POST

'Gedolim' are human

June 10, 2016
By Seymour Hoffman

Several years ago, I sent to an ultra-Orthodox periodical an article that mentioned an incident that took place in Warsaw in 1877. Rabbi Joseph Dov Soloveitchik, an outstanding Talmud scholar, religious personality and leader was overcome by a deep depression because of the incarceration of his highly revered and beloved mentor, Rabbi Joshua Leib Diskin, on false charges by the anti-Semitic authorities.

Ultra-orthodox men in Mea She'arim carry the body of Rabbi Raphael Shmuelevich, head of the Mir Yeshiva, at his funeral in January. (REUTERS)

The editor informed me that he would be interested in publishing the paper if I changed the wording regarding Rabbi Soloveitchik's emotional state from being depressed to being distressed regarding his mentor's situation. He explained that it is disrespectful to describe a gadol (one of the most revered rabbis of the generation) as being depressed, even though the description of his behavior and emotional condition clearly pictured a man suffering from a deep clinical depression.

In 2010, Rabbi Simcha Feuerman, a psychotherapist, wrote in an article for Jewishideas.com that "Not every sage was successful in managing his emotions. Learning about this can be a great source of strength and comfort to young people and adults who struggle with this as well." To support his contention, he cited an excerpt from the Talmud Bava Metzia (84a) that discusses the great despondency felt by Rabbi Yohanan subsequent to the death of his star student and study partner, Resh Lakish, which caused him to lose his sanity. Rabbi Feuerman concluded, "a frum (religious) person suffering from depression and mental illness could find much comfort in knowing that even the greatest of sages struggled with his emotions, and dare we say it, ultimately failed."

Rabbi Shalom Dov-Ber Schneersohn, the fifth Lubavitcher rebbe, traveled from

Russia to Vienna in 1902-3, to consult with the famous Prof. Sigmund Freud regarding a bout of depression and was accompanied by his son, Rabbi Josef Yitzhak Schneersohn. His son recalls that Freud made the following diagnosis: "The head grasps what the heart is unable to contain, and the heart cannot tolerate."

Liubov Ben-Noun, in a 2008 scholarly article, "What Was the Mental Disease that Afflicted King Saul?," discusses the case of the biblical King Saul and concludes that evaluation of the passages referring to King Saul's disturbed behavior indicates that he was afflicted by a bipolar 1 mental disorder.

In a letter to a student who was depressed from his failures, Rav Yitzhak Hutner, head of Yeshiva of Mesivta Chaim Berlin from 1936 until his death in 1980, was highly critical of gedolim stories that only spoke of their great stature, without relating any of their personal struggles and missteps on their way to greatness.

Rabbi Nathan Kamenetsky, son of Rabbi Yaakov Kamenetsky, authored Making of a Godol: A Study of Episodes in the Lives of Great Torah Personalities, a two-volume book written and published in 2002, about the lives of his father and of various other Jewish sages of the 19th and 20th centuries, who are revered by Orthodox (especially haredi) Jews.

Shortly after it was published, a group of 10 leading haredi rabbis in Israel, among them Rabbi Yosef Shalom Elyashiv, issued an official letter banning the book, claiming that it was disrespectful to the rabbis whose lives it describes.

For example, the book records that Rabbi Aharon Kotler read Russian books in his youth. Due to the banning of publication (an updated version was released in 2005), not more than 1,000 sets of each edition are in existence.

Kamenetsky stated that, in writing the book, he "naively believed that everyone would appreciate getting a true, human glimpse [of] our spiritual leaders," and that this honest portrayal "is what bothered the zealots." Kamenetsky is of the opinion that there is no need to hide anything, because knowing the truth about the gedolim only increases one's respect for them (due to their vast accomplishments, despite facing life's trials and being human).

There seems to be a strong tendency and need, especially from members of the haredi and hassidic community, to view their religious and spiritual leaders as perfect and infallible. This enables them to place their complete reliance and trust in them and their decisions and increases their dependency on them, which to a great extent is facilitated and encouraged by the leaders.

It seems, as Kamenetsky pointed out, there are people who wish to rule and those that wish to be ruled.

I am reminded of a haredi woman I treated many years ago who was suffering from depression as a result of a recent divorce after one year of marriage. After initially meeting her ex-husband, the patient sent a letter to the Lubavitcher Rebbe and asked his advice regarding accepting his marriage proposal. The rebbe gave his approval and blessing.

After several months in therapy, the patient reported that she met another man who after a few meetings proposed marriage to her. The patient mentioned that she again sought the rebbe's advice regarding marrying her present suitor.

I naively asked the patient why she was again asking his advice after the poor previous outcome. She calmly explained that she must have not provided him with accurate or sufficient information the previous time.

The writer is a supervising psychologist at the Mental Health Center Marbeh Da'at, Mayenei Hayeshua Medical Center. He recently published Psychologist, Acquire a Teacher for Yourself, 2016 (Hebrew) and co-edited Psychotherapy and the Ultra- orthodox Community: Issues and Treatment, 2014.

Supermen or Super Men?
Acknowledging the Faults and Mistakes of Gedolim

A major controversy erupted in the Orthodox Jewish world in 2002, with the publication of Rav Nosson Kamenetsky's *Making of a Godol*, a collection of biographical sketches of several outstanding Torah figures. *Making of a Godol* differed from conventional biographies of *gedolim* in that it depicted the human, imperfect side of these sages. For example, the author describes one great Torah figure as having been a "sore loser" when playing chess as a young man. Not long after the publication, a letter banning the work was signed by numerous leading rabbis of the time, including Rav Yosef Shalom Elyashiv, Rav Aharon Leib Shteinman, Rav Chaim Kanievsky and Rav Moshe Shapiro.

A similar controversy roiled American Orthodoxy in 1988, when a Lakewood institution distributed as a fundraiser ArtScroll's *My Uncle the Netziv* — a translation of a portion of Rav Baruch Epstein's *Mekor Chayim*, portraying his uncle. The institution later apologized for distributing the book and urged its supporters not to read it, as it contained material that, in this institution's assessment, did not accurately represent the Netziv's character and outlook. It is believed that the "disturbing" portions of the book were its descriptions of the human side of the Netziv, and the fact that he read newspapers on Shabbos, the halachic propriety of which is subject to some controversy.

What do our Torah sources say about the way we should perceive and describe spiritual giants? Should they be depicted as flawless, or should we be cognizant of their faults and failings? Do we undermine the authority and stature of Torah sages by portraying them as flawed human beings? Does this run the risk of dismissing scholars as ordinary people, not all that different from ourselves, such that their rulings and teachings need not be taken seriously? Or, to the contrary, does this portrayal raise our level of esteem and reverence for these outstanding figures, who, like the rest of us, struggled with human vices, and ultimately succeeded in achieving greatness?

Any serious discussion of this subject must begin with an emphasis on the importance of respecting Torah scholars, which constitutes an outright Torah obligation.[1]

---

1. As the Rambam writes in *Hilchos Talmud Torah* (6:1), כל תלמיד חכם מצוה להדרו, ואף על פי שאינו רבו, שנאמר מפני שיבה תקום והדרת פני זקן.

Torah tradition develops through the process of *mesorah*, whereby the Torah scholars of every generation are authorized to apply their thorough knowledge and understanding of the Torah's principles to the realities of their age. This process depends upon the trust and respect accorded to scholars and to their stature by Torah-observant Jewry. There can be no argument as to the need to acknowledge and respect the authority of the scholars to interpret *halacha* (albeit with the caveat that other scholars might disagree).

This point is developed at length by the *Sefer Ha-Chinuch* (496),[2] in explaining the Torah prohibition of לא תסור, which forbids deviating from the rulings of the *Sanhedrin*.[3] He writes that if the Torah's command would be understood and interpreted by each individual according to his analysis, we would not have an organized religion, but rather a large group of different people observing different practices. The Torah therefore commands us to follow in every generation the scholars שקבלו דבריהםושתו מים מספריהם ויגעו כמה יגיעות בימים ובלילות להבין עומק מליהם — "who accepted their [the earlier sages'] words, drank water from their works, and exerted tireless efforts day and night to understand the depth of their words." We are to follow their guidance and rulings, the *Sefer Ha-Chinuch* explains, because otherwise, תעשה התורה ככמה תורות — "the Torah will become several Torahs." On this basis, the *Sefer Ha-Chinuch* understands the *Sifrei*'s famous comment that we must follow the Sages' rulings "even if they say about right that it is left, or about left that it is right":

> כלומר שאפילו יהיו הם טועים בדבר אחד מן הדברים, אין ראוי לנו לחלוק עליהם,
> אבל נעשה כטעותם, וטוב לסבול טעות אחד ויהיו הכל מסורים תחת דעתם הטוב
> תמיד, ולא שיעשה כל אחד ואחד כפי דעתו, שבזה יהיה חורבן הדת וחלוק לב העם
> והפסד האומה לגמרי.

> That is to say, even if they are mistaken in a certain matter, it is not proper for us to disagree with them, but we shall follow their mistake, and it is preferable to bear one mistake so that everyone is always loyal to their sound judgment, rather than have every individual follow his own opinion, which would result in the destruction of the religion, divisions among the people, and the complete loss of the nation.[4]

---

2.   496.

3.   לא תסור מן הדבר אשר יגידו לך ימין ושמאל, *Devarim* 17:11.

4.   See also *Derashos Ha'Ran*, 11.

The *Chazon Ish* (*Emuna U-Bitachon* 3:30) notes the particular danger of attributing נגיעות — ulterior motives — to the positions and rulings of Torah sages. Once we regard their decisions as the product of some personal, unholy agenda, there is no longer any Torah tradition, because we no longer place any trust in the authority of Torah scholars as the arbiters of Torah law.

There is no question that we must respect Torah scholars as the bearers and conveyors of our ancient tradition.

The question we address here is whether this includes denying or concealing their faults and mistakes. Should they be perceived and/or portrayed as perfect, or is it acceptable — or perhaps even vitally important — to recognize their imperfections and shortcomings?

Fallibility of the Righteous

The premise upon which this entire discussion rests is that Judaism, unlike other faiths, does not accept a doctrine of infallibility. The Torah explicitly conveys that even the greatest, most righteous figures are capable of error, and even of grievous errors.

Soon after Moshe's appointment as God's prophet charged with the mission of bringing *Bnei Yisrael* out of Egypt and then bringing them the Torah, he was nearly killed for the sin of failing to circumcise his son.[5] And near the end of his life, of course, Moshe disobeyed God's command at *Mei Meriva*, when he was told to announce that a stone would produce water for the people.[6] Leaving aside the question addressed at length by the commentators as to the precise nature of Moshe's disobedience, God condemned him and Aharon for failing to "believe" in Him (יען לא האמנתם בי),[7] for "disobeying" Him (אשר מריתם את פי),[8] and for "betraying" Him (אשר מעלתם בי).[9]

Great people are capable not only of improper conduct, but also of making errors in judgment, or forgetting information. The *Sifrei*[10] comments that on three occasions, בא משה לכלל כעס ובא לכלל טעות — Moshe became inappropriately angry, resulting in his forgetting important halachic material. Even Moshe Rabbeinu was fallible, and capable of making mistakes.[11]

---

5.   *Shemos* 4:24–26.
6.   *Bamidbar* 20:1–13.
7.   *Bamidbar* 20:12.
8.   *Bamidbar* 20:24.
9.   *Devarim* 32:51.
10. *Parshas Matos*, 157.
11. The *Meshech Chochma*, in his introduction to *Sefer Shemos*, makes an astounding remark that seems, at first glance, to indicate otherwise. Based on the Rambam's famous comments in *Hilchos Yesodei Ha-Torah* (7–8), the *Meshech Chochma* discusses the difference between Moshe Rabbeinu and other prophets, and notes God's pronouncement at Mount Sinai before the Revelation, וגם בך יאמינו לעולם (*Shemos* 19:9) — that after seeing God speak with Moshe at Mount Sinai, the people would trust his word, forever. The *Meshech Chochma* raises the question of why the people were expected to trust Moshe for the rest of his life after the Revelation, given that Moshe, like all human beings, had the power of free

The Gemara[12] cites a number of *Amoraim* who attribute to Avraham Avinu several different wrongs — inappropriately forcing scholars to go out to battle (עשה אנגריא בתלמידי חכמים), questioning God's promise of offspring (במה אדע כי אירשנה), and allowing the people of Sedom whom he had freed from captivity to return to the rule of their wicked king, instead of converting them to monotheism (הפריש בני אדם מלהכנס תחת כנפי השכינה). And in *Maseches Yoma* (22b), the Gemara charges that King David inappropriately accepted the slanderous report of Tziva about his master, Mefiboshes, that he supported Avshalom's revolt against the king. These are just several of countless examples of where *Chazal* attribute wrongdoing to righteous Biblical figures.

A halachic expression of rabbinic fallibility is the פר העלם דבר של צבור, the command requiring the *Sanhedrin* — the nation's highest body of halachic authority — to offer a special sacrifice when [13] נעלם דבר מעיני הקהל — they issue an erroneous ruling which led people to transgress a severe offense (one which carries the punishment of *kareis*[14]). The members of the *Sanhedrin*, as the Rambam[15] describes, were חכמים ונבונים מופלגין בחכמת התורה, בעלי דיעה מרובה — "Scholarly and wise, outstanding in Torah scholarship, with extensive knowledge." Later,[16] the Rambam writes that these rabbis must be

---

will, and was thus capable at any point of changing course and becoming sinful, such that he could present false prophecies as the authentic word of God. To answer this question, the *Meshech Chochma* proposes the drastic theory that השי"ת שלל ממנו הבחירה לגמרי, ונשאר מוכרח כמלאכים — "God completely denied him [the power of] free will, and he was left compelled [to do the right thing] like angels." According to the *Meshech Chochma*, it seems, Moshe was, indeed, infallible like angels, incapable of error.

However, we must distinguish between Moshe's role as lawgiver — the faithful communicator of God's laws — and all other aspects of his character and existence. The *Meshech Chochma* establishes that in the capacity as conveyor of the divine word, Moshe could not have been granted the free will to distort or fabricate, as otherwise we would be unable to trust that he accurately transmitted God's laws. Indeed, the *Sifrei* (beginning of *Parshas Va'eschanan*) tells that Moshe begged God to record the sin of *Mei Meriva* for posterity, to make it clear that this was the sole instance where he disobeyed God's command, so that people would not question the authenticity of the Torah which he conveyed. In Moshe's role as lawgiver, he may have indeed been incapable of error, but this is not to say that in general he was a perfect, angelic being — as evidenced by the *Sifrei*'s assertion that בא לכלל טעות.

12. *Nedarim* 32a.
13. *Vayikra* 4:13.
14. See Rashi, citing *Toras Kohanim*.
15. *Hilchos Sanhedrin* 2:1.
16. 2:6.

מנוקין בצדק — men of perfect morality. The Rambam then adds[17] that even the judges of the lower courts, who were not expected to meet the credentials required of the *Sanhedrin*, must be men of "wisdom, humility, fear [of God], contempt for money, love of truth, love of people," and people with an upstanding reputation. The members of the *Sanhedrin* were the most accomplished scholars and most righteous men in the nation, and yet, even they were prone to issue mistaken rulings on matters of grave halachic importance. The *Sefer Ha-Chinuch*[18] writes that a special sacrifice is required in such a case because an erroneous ruling is the result of חולשת השכל ("flawed reasoning"), and offering a sacrifice would have the effect of reminding the judges of גריעות הנפש הבהמית הטועה וחשיבות השכלית המיושרת והזכה — "the deficiency of the animalistic spirit, and the importance of straight, pristine reasoning." Even the most outstanding rabbis are capable of mistakes, and might occasionally require motivation to improve and sharpen their analytical skills.

The Rambam writes explicitly in his *Shemona Perakim*,[19] אין מתנאי היותר שלם שבבני אדם השלמות הגמורה בלי חסרון — "Perfection completion, without fault, is not a condition of the most complete human beings."

The question then becomes, given this premise, that even the greatest scholars and spiritual giants make mistakes, should their mistakes be concealed as much as possible, in order to maximize the respect and reverence shown to them? Or should their failings be made known for the sake of showing their ability to achieve greatness despite the challenges of natural human vices?

התורה כיסתו ואתה מגלה אותו

This question appears to underlie a controversy recorded in the Gemara (*Shabbos* 96b–97a) surrounding the character of Tzelofchad, the man whose daughters approached Moshe after his passing to request rights to his allocated portion in the Land of Israel. In presenting their case, the women emphasized to Moshe that Tzelofchad had not participated in Korach's uprising against his authority, and that rather בחטאו מת — "he died as a result of his sin."[20] The Torah does not specify what this "sin" was, but Rabbi Akiva identified Tzelofchad as the מקושש עצים — the man who was found publicly desecrating Shabbos for which he was subsequently executed.[21] The

---

17. 2:7.

18. 120.

19. Chapter 7.

20. *Bamidbar* 27:3.

21. *Bamidbar* 15:32–36. Rabbi Akiva reached this conclusion based on Tzelofchad's daughters' account of their father perishing במדבר ("in the wilderness"), which parallels the Torah's introduction to the story of the public Shabbos desecrator: ויהיו בני ישראל **במדבר**.

Gemara relates that Rabbi Yehuda ben Beseira reacted angrily to Rabbi Akiva's remark, saying:

עקיבא בין כך ובין כך אתה עתיד ליתן את הדין —אם כדבריך, התורה כיסתו
ואתה מגלה אותו, ואם לאו, אתה מוציא לעז על אותו צדיק.

> Akiva, either way you are going to be called to account! If your words are correct — the Torah concealed it, and you are exposing it! And if not, then you are slandering that righteous man!

Rabbi Yehuda ben Beseira reacted similarly to a different assertion by Rabbi Akiva, claiming that at the time when Miriam was stricken with leprosy for speaking disparagingly about Moshe, Aharon was also stricken with this illness, for he, too, was guilty of improper speech about his righteous brother.[22] Once again, Rabbi Yehuda ben Beseira criticized Rabbi Akiva, charging that he was either making an inaccurate accusation, or disclosing an accurate accusation that the Torah wished to conceal.

Rabbi Yehuda ben Beseira appears to take the position that the failings of righteous individuals should not be exposed, that unflattering information about them — even if accurate — should not be shared. Perhaps, then, just as Rabbi Yehuda ben Beseira opposed the disclosure of sins committed by Tzelofchad and Aharon, we should likewise oppose the disclosing of uncomplimentary information about other righteous figures.

However, besides the fact that Rabbi Akiva clearly disagreed, and felt it appropriate to expose the failings of Tzelofchad and Aharon, even Rabbi Yehuda ben Beseira's position is quite limited in scope. The Gemara states that Rabbi Yehuda ben Beseira identified Tzelofchad as one of the מעפילים — the group that sought to proceed into the Land of Israel following the sin of the spies, in direct violation of God's strict command, and were promptly killed in battle.[23] Rashi explains that the sin of the מעפילים was less grievous than that of the מקושש עצים, and so Rabbi Yehuda ben Beseira did not object to disclosing Tzelofchad's guilt in participating in this iniquitous endeavor. And as for Aharon, the Gemara comments, Rabbi Yehuda ben Beseira conceded that Aharon received a נזיפה — "censure" — from God. Quite clearly, then, even Rabbi Yehuda ben Beseira accepted the validity of disclosing the mistakes of righteous men, and he objected only to Rabbi Akiva's exposing their severe transgressions.

Moreover, we might distinguish between the Gemara's discussion of righteous figures who were punished for their wrongdoing, and the publicizing of religious struggles which righteous figures successfully waged. Even if, in the view of Rabbi Yehuda ben Beseira, we should avoid disclosing the failings of outstanding figures, he might

---

22. This is indicated by the Torah's account of God's anger being aroused against both Miriam and Aharon: ויחר אף ה' **בם** (*Bamidbar* 12:9).
23. *Bamidbar* 14:40–45.

very well agree that there is value in noting the faults and mistakes made by people who later overcame their vices and grew to become Torah giants.

This point is made by Rav Baruch Epstein, in his *Torah Temima*,[24] in reference to the debate among the *Amoraim* (*Sota* 36b) as to whether or not Yosef had planned to commit an adulterous act with Potifar's wife. The Torah tells that Yosef entered Potifar's home at a time when only Potifar's wife was present לעשות מלאכתו — which, simply understood, means "to perform his work." According to one view, however, this actually means that Yosef entered the home in order to finally accede to Potifar's wife's advances. Rav Epstein wonders why the Gemara does not raise the objection of התורה כיסתו ואתה מגלה אותו, that this view exposes unflattering information about Yosef that the Torah had concealed. The answer, Rav Epstein explains, is that Yosef ultimately restrained himself and even fled from Potifar's home, such that his illicit intentions serve to magnify his greatness in resisting temptation. And thus even according to Rabbi Yehuda ben Beseira, disclosing this unflattering information about Yosef — that he was planning to sleep with a married woman — is permissible and even valuable, insofar as it makes the ending even more inspiring.[25]

By the same token, then, we might argue that exposing the struggles and shortcomings of Torah giants in their younger years serves the valuable educational purpose of providing examples of overcoming mistakes and challenges and achieving greatness even after experiencing failure.

The Chafetz Chayim's Struggles

Indeed, Rav Yitzchok Hutner, in one of his published letters,[26] lamented what he described as a רעה חולה (serious malady) — the phenomenon of assessing *gedolim* only on the basis of the final product, the stature of greatness which they achieved in the later stages of their lives. When people speak about great Torah sages, Rav Hutner observed, they make no mention of המאבק הפנימי שהתחולל בנפשם — "the inner struggle that transpired in their soul." The impression that is too often given is that these great figures were born in a state of near-perfection, without having to work to get there. Rav Hutner writes:

> הכל משוחחים מתפעלים ומרימים על נס את טהרת הלשון של בעל החפץ חיים זצ״ל, אבל מי יודע מן כל המלחמות המאבקים המכשולים הנפילות והנסיגות לאחור שמצא החפץ חיים בדרך המלחמה שלו עם יצרו הרע.

> Everybody speaks about, marvels at, and puts on a pedestal the pure speech of the Chafetz Chayim *zt"l*. But who knows about all the wars,

---

24. *Bereishis* 39:11.

25. See also *Teshuvos Maharlbach*, 126.

26. *Iggeros U-Ksavim*, 128.

struggles, pitfalls, failures and relapses that the Chafetz Chayim experienced over the course of his battle against his evil inclination?

If we perceive Torah giants as perfectly pure, pristine beings who never failed and never erred, then our own failings and struggles will lead us to depression and despair. Rather than motivating us to work harder, our mistakes will drive us to hopelessness. But once we realize that even the Chafetz Chayim was not perfect and needed to struggle, we will feel encouraged and inspired to work harder. There is thus immense benefit to portraying *gedolim* as flawed human beings who achieved greatness by struggling to overcome their flaws — as this portrayal motivates us to aspire to greatness by struggling to overcome ours. As Rav Hutner writes:

> החכם מכל אדם אמר שבע יפול צדיק וקם והטפשים חושבים כי כונתו בדרך
> רבותא אעי״פ ששבע יפול צדיק מ״מ הוא קם, אבל החכמים יודעים היטב שהכוונה
> היא שמהות הקימה של הצדיק היא דרך השבע נפילות שלו.

> The wisest of all men [King Shlomo] said: "Seven times a righteous man falls and then stands."[27] The fools think this means it is a novelty — that even if a righteous man falls seven times, he still rises. But the wise know very well that it means that the essence of a righteous man's rising is by way of his seven falls.

Indeed, the prophet *Micha* (7:8) proclaims, אל תשמחי אויבתי לי כי נפלתי קמתי, כי אשב בחושך ה׳ אור לי — "Do not laugh at me, my foe, for I have fallen and risen; when I reside in darkness, G-d is my light." The Midrash[28] explains this to mean:

> אלולא שנפלתי לא קמתי...אלולא שישבתי בחושך לא היה אור לי.

> If I had not fallen, I would not have risen... If I had not resided in darkness, I would not have had light.

Great people become great not despite their failures, but rather because of their failures, which they then utilize as catalysts for growth.[29]

---

27. *Mishlei* 24:16.
28. *Yalkut Shimoni, Tehillim* 628.
29. This concept lies at the heart of a famous, controversial passage in the *Tiferes Yisrael* commentary to the Mishna (*Kiddushin* 4:14) telling the story of a king during the time of the Exodos who, upon hearing of the miraculous events, set out to determine the nature of *Bnei Yisrael*'s leader. He sent artists to travel to the Israelite camp and paint an accurate portrait of Moshe, and when they returned, he summoned physiognomists to study the portrait and identify the nature of the Israelites' leader. To his amazement, the physiognomists described Moshe as a man of greed, arrogance, selfishness and all other possible negative qualities. Certain that this could not be true, the king personally journeyed to

This is indicated already in the Gemara's famous teaching (*Avoda Zara* 4b), לא דוד ראוי לאותו מעשה — a man of King David's stature of piety would not normally commit a grievous sin like that which he committed with Batsheva, but this was allowed to happen to serve as a model of repentance for other sinners to follow. We are told of King David's spiritual failure so we can follow his example of *teshuva*, which shows us that God accepts sincere, heartfelt repentance even for grave wrongdoing. It is clear from the Gemara that there is immense value in hearing of the mistakes and recovery of great spiritual figures, as they serve as a vital source of encouragement to work towards improving ourselves.

This point is expressed in the Rambam's depiction of the method that was used by the *Sanhedrin* in the case of a *sota* (wife suspected of infidelity) in an effort to convince her to confess if she was, in fact, guilty. The Rambam writes[30] that the judges would emphasize to the woman that even outstanding *tzadikim* have failed in the area of forbidden intimate relationships. They would tell her, בתי...אנשים גדולים ויקרים תקף יצרן עליהן ונכשלו — "My daughter...great, precious people were overpowered by their inclination and stumbled." The Rambam adds that the judges would tell her the stories of great Biblical figures who sinned — such as Yehuda's relationship with his daughter-in-law, Tamar, and Reuven's relationship with his stepmother, Bilha — כדי להקל עליה עד שתודה — to make it easier for her to confess. The stories of the failures of the righteous show us that we can be "great and precious" even though

---

the Israelite camp to ascertain whether his painters had produced an accurate portrait. Upon confirming the portrait's accuracy, the king approached Moshe himself and asked for an explanation. Moshe told the king that he indeed was, by nature, a terrible person, but through hard work and struggle he overcame his natural characteristics to achieve greatness.

Some later writers rejected this story, claiming that it originated from non-Jewish sources. The Maggid of Vilkomir (Rav Chaim Yitzchak Aharon Rappaport) published an essay entitled *Kelil Tiferes* to discredit this account, and this essay received a letter of approbation from Rav Eliyahu David Rabinowitz-Teomim (the Aderes), who said this story has no basis in *Chazal*. Nevertheless, the notion that Moshe Rabbeinu was naturally flawed and struggled to overcome his ingrained character traits was posited by a number of leading chassidic figures. The *Degel Machaneh Ephraim* (*Parshas Ki-Sisa*) cites his grandfather, the Ba'al Shem Tov, as teaching that משה רבנו נולד בבחינת שיהיה רשע גמור ויהיה לו כל המידות הרעות, אך שהוא היפך ושיבר כל המידות רעות והשתדל רק להכניס עצמו במידות טובות — "Moshe Rabbeinu was born such that he would be a completely evil man, and would have all the negative character traits, except that he reversed and shattered all the negative qualities and exerted effort to bring into himself only fine qualities." See also Rav Shimshon Raphael Hirsch's remark about Moshe Rabbeinu's humility in the passage cited below.

30. *Hilchos Sota* 3:2.

we occasionally fail, as long as we acknowledge and confess our wrongdoing, and we strive to improve.

A Warning to Us All

An additional benefit of knowing the faults of the righteous is to alert us of the constant need for vigilance in resisting human vices. The *Sefer Chassidim*[31] explains that the sins committed by great figures such as Shimshon, King David and King Shlomo involving women were written for posterity in the Bible כדי להודיע תוקף אהבת נשים שיותר מדאי — to warn us of the power of lust, that הגדיל יצר הרע על הטובים — it led even the most righteous figures to commit grave sinful acts. The *Sefer Chassidim* writes:

> הודיע מעשה דוד להודיע כי ראש החסידים שכל עסקו לשם שמים ואעפ״כ כשראה אשה נכשל ואף על פי שקרוב לזקנה, וכ״ש שבחור צריך להזהר מלהביט באשה ולהתרחק מאשה.

> [The Bible] informed us of the story of David [and Batsheva] to inform us that the greatest among the pious, whose interest was purely for the sake of Heaven, nevertheless, when he saw a woman, stumbled, even though he was near old age. All the more so, then, a young man must ensure not to glare at a woman and to keep a distance from a woman.

Knowing that even the righteous stumble serves as an important warning to all of us. Rather than lower our esteem for the righteous figure, it has the effect of alerting us to the power of negative human impulses, which threaten even the greatest people, requiring all of us to remain ever vigilant in our lifelong struggle to live in faithful obedience to God.

Finding Fault in Righteous Biblical Figures

A related question pertains to our perception of the righteous figures in the Bible, such as the patriarchs and matriarchs, Moshe Rabbeinu, the prophets, and righteous kings such as David and Shlomo. In our study and instruction of *Tanach*, is it appropriate to ascribe to these figures misdeeds that were not noted by *Chazal*? Or was it only our Sages, with the authority invested in them as bearers of the oral tradition, who had the right to identify the mistakes of ancient spiritual giants?

The Ramban, in a famous passage in his Torah commentary,[32] boldly asserts that Avraham Avinu committed a grave sin by deciding to move to Egypt when a famine struck Canaan, and posing as Sara's husband to avoid being killed by men who desired her. The Ramban writes:

31.　619.

32.　*Bereishis* 12:10.

ודע כי אברהם אבינו חטא חטא גדול בשגגה, שהביא אשתו הצדקת במכשול
עון מפני פחדו פן יהרגוהו. והיה לו לבטוח בהש״י שיציל אותו ואת אשתו ואת
כל אשר לו... גם יציאתו מן הארץ שנצטווה עליה בתחילה מפני הרעב עון אשר
חטא כי האלוקים ברעב יפדנו ממות. ועל המעשה הזה נגזר על זרעו הגלות בארץ
מצרים ביד פרעה.

> You should know that our patriarch Avraham inadvertently committed a
> grievous sin by leading his righteous wife to stumble onto iniquity out of
> fear that they might kill him. He should have trusted in God, may He be
> blessed, that He would save him, his wife, and everything he had... Also
> his departure from the land about which he was originally commanded
> due to famine was a sin which he committed — for God can redeem him
> from death during famine. And on account of this incident, exile in the
> land of Egypt at the hands of Pharaoh was decreed upon his offspring.

Later,[33] the Ramban writes that Sara sinned in oppressing her maidservant, Hagar,
after Hagar married Avraham and became pregnant. The Ramban adds that Avraham, too, sinned by allowing Sara to mistreat Hagar, and that God responded by
producing offspring from Hagar's son, Yishmael, who would oppress Avraham and
Sara's descendants.

Nowhere do we find *Chazal* pointing to these incidents as sins committed by Avraham and Sara, and yet the Ramban, based on his understanding of the text, explained
that these were mistakes committed by our saintly patriarch and matriarch. He clearly
found it acceptable to interpret the text of the Torah in a manner that is uncomplimentary to our righteous forebears, even if no such criticism of their actions appears
in the Midrash or Talmud.

The underlying premise of this approach is that spiritual giants are imperfect,
that nobody — not even the most pious and most spiritually accomplished individuals — are completely pure and entirely innocent of any wrongdoing. Once we've
established this basic principle, we understand that identifying mistakes committed
by people like Avraham and Sara does not in any way diminish from their greatness.
It rather reflects the simple fact that even the greatest people make mistakes from
which we can all learn.

Whitewashing Our Heroes

This point is eloquently and powerfully expressed by Rav Shimshon Raphael Hirsch,
in his Torah commentary. Addressing the story of Avraham's relocation in Egypt to

---

33. *Bereishis* 16:6.

escape the drought in Canaan,[34] Rav Hirsch cites the Ramban's theory, and although he disagrees with this view,[35] he seizes this opportunity to emphasize that our saintly ancestors are not to be regarded as flawless:[36]

> The Torah never presents our great men as being perfect, it deifies no man, says of none "here you have the ideal, in this man the Divine became human." Altogether it puts the life of no man before us as the pattern out of which we are to learn what is right and good, what we have to do, what to refrain from doing… We are never to say: This must be right for did not so-and-so do it! The Torah is no "collection of examples of saints." It relates what occurred, not because it was exemplary but because it did occur.
>
> The Torah never hides from us the faults, errors and weaknesses of our great men. Just by that it gives the stamp of veracity to what it relates. But in truth, by the knowledge which is given us of their faults and weaknesses, our great men are in no ways made lesser but actually greater and more instructive. If they stood before us as the purest models of perfection we should attribute them as having a different nature, which has been denied to us. Were they without passion, without internal struggles, their virtues would seem to us the outcome of some higher nature, hardly a merit and certainly no model that we could hope to emulate. Take, for instance, Moshe's ענוה [humility]. Did we not know that he could also fly into a passion, his meekness and modesty would seem to us to be his inborn natural disposition, and lost to us as an example. Just his [angry outburst] שמעו נא המורים gives his ענוה its true greatness, shows it to us as the result of a great work of self-control and self-ennoblement which we all should copy because we all could copy. The Torah also shows us no faults without at the same time letting us see the greater or lesser evil consequences. From our great teachers of the

---

34. *Bereishis* 12:10-13.
35. Rav Hirsch writes:

    …that God surrounds with special protection those that are fulfilling His commands… was an experience that Abraham and his descendants had still to have, no Abraham had preceded Abraham, and even having this experience does not preclude the duty of doing everything that is legally within one's own power first, and having confidence in God only for that which lies beyond. Abraham could well say to himself אין סומכין על הנס.

    This is also the implication of the Gemara in *Maseches Bava Kama* (60b), which derives from Avraham's relocation in Egypt, רעב בעיר פזר רגליך — "If there is famine in the city, scatter your legs" (meaning, one should live somewhere else).

36. The translation from German is taken from Isaac Levy, London, 1963.

Torah, and truly Ramban can be reckoned amongst the very greatest, we would accordingly learn that it may never be our task to whitewash the spiritual and moral heroes of our past, to appear as apologists for them. They do not require our apologies, nor do such attempts become them.

Rav Hirsch reiterates this point in the context of the story of Yaakov and Esav's child-hood,[37] elaborating at great length on the mistakes made by Yitzchak and Rivka in raising their children:

> Our sages, who never objected to draw attention to the small and great mistakes and weaknesses in the history of our great forefathers, and thereby make them just the most instructive for us, here, too…make a remark which is indeed a "signpost" for all of us. They point out that the striking contrast in the grandchildren of Abraham may have been due not so much to a difference in their temperaments as to the mistakes in the way they were brought up. As long as they were little, no atten-tion was paid to the slumbering differences in their natures, both had exactly the same teaching and educational treatment, and the great law of education חנוך לנער על פי דרכו — "bring up each child in accordance with its own way" was forgotten — that each child must be treated differently, with an eye to the slumbering tendencies of his nature, and out of them, be educated to develop his special characteristics for the one pure human and Jewish life…
>
> To try to bring up a Jacob and an Esau in the same college, make them have the same habits and hobbies, want to teach and educate them in the same way for some studious, sedate, meditative life is the surest way to court disaster. A Jacob will, with ever increasing zeal and zest, imbibe knowledge from the well of wisdom and truth, while an Esau can hardly wait for the time when he can throw the old books, but at the same time, a whole purpose of life, behind his back, a life of which he has only learnt to know from one angle, and in a manner for which he can find no disposition in his whole nature.
>
> Had Isaac and Rebecca studied Esau's nature and character early enough, and asked themselves how can even an Esau, how can all the strength and energy, agility and courage that lies slumbering in this child, be won over to be used in the service of God…then Jacob and Esau, with their totally different natures could still have remained twin-brothers in spirit and life; quite early in life Esau's "sword" and Jacob's "spirit" could have worked hand in hand, and who can say what a different aspect the whole

---

37. *Bereishis* 25:27.

history of the ages might have presented. But, as it was…only when the boys had grown into men, one was surprised to see that, out of one and the selfsame womb, having had exactly the same care, training and schooling, two such contrasting persons emerge.

Rav Hirsch later[38] introduces the story of Rivka's deception of Yitzchak by noting, "As repeatedly remarked, we follow the opinion of our sages, and do not consider it our task to be apologists for our great men and women, just as the Word of God, the Torah itself, never refrains from informing us of their errors and weaknesses." He cites the Midrash's comment[39] in reference to this episode, כל מי שאומר הקב"ה ותרן הוא יוותרון מעיו — anybody who believes that God does not hold pious individuals to account for their misdeeds "deserves to have his inwards torn out." The Midrash proceeds to assert that our nation has suffered bitterly at the hands of Esav's descendants because of the anguish caused to Esav by Rivka's ruse. Rav Hirsch writes that although some aspects of the ruse can be explained and justified, "enough will still remain which cannot be approved of, especially when measured with the yardstick of character of a nation whose name of honor is ישורן, which is only to achieve its purposes in the 'straight' (ישר) way, and is to oppose any crooked means for any purpose."

A Torah of Truth, a Torah of Life

This point is developed also by Rav Yosef Leib Bloch, in *Shiurei Da'as*:[40]

באותו שעה שהתורה מתארת לנו את גדולת האבות וקדושתם אינה עוברת בשתיקה על חסרונותיהם, אינה מחפה על מגרעותיהם. אינה מתארת אותם כאנשים אלוקיים בכל המעלות בלי מגרעות וחסרונות מופשטים מכל עניייי וכוחות החומר... תורתנו תורת האמת תורת חיים, היא היא מלמדת לנו כי האדם באשר הוא אדם אינו יכול להיות אלוקי, וכל זמן שנפשו מקושרת ומלובשת בחומר בהכרח יימצאו בו כל הכוחות והענייינים הטבעיים.

והנה בעד אנשי המעלה התועלת מסיפורי התורה האלה היא כי כשהם נכשלים לפעמים בדבר מה הידיעה הזאת מנחמת ומלמדת אותם שכּכה היא תכונת האדם כי באיזו מדרגה שיעמוד האדם ואיך שיהיה גודל הכרתו באמת בכל זאת מוכרח שימצאו בו כל הכוחות הטבעיים שמושכים אותו למטה ובכל זאת...אין לו להתרפות מלהמשיך עבודתו ויחזק את רוחו ולבו וישתדל בכל כוחותיו לפתח ולרומם את עצמו ולהתגבר על כוחותיי הטבעיים...

---

38. *Bereishis* 27:1.

39. *Bereishis Rabba* 67.

40. 2:13.

אולם לאנשים קטני הדעת גורם הדבר להקל ולהצטדק על מגרעותיהם ומעשיהם
הרעים באמרם הלא גם האבות הקדושים לא היו שלמים הלא חסרונותיו
ומגרעותיו הוא גם בהם נמצאו אבל באמת סכלות ושפלות רוח היא ושוטה גמור
צריך להיות האדם החושב כזאת כי מה גדול ורחוק הוא ההבדל בינינו לביניהם
ואין להביא שום דוגמא מחייהם הם לחיינו אנו הם חיו חיים נעלים קדושים
וטהורים והכוחות המעלים והמורידים היו כל כך דקים וטמירים וברגשות כל כך
נעלים ונעלמים דק מן הדק מה שאין אנו מסוגלים להרגיש בהם כלל.

Even as the Torah describes for us the greatness of the patriarchs and their sanctity, it does not pass quietly over their faults; it does not cover for their deficiencies. It does not describe them as divine men, with all the qualities, without any deficiencies or faults, detached from all physical qualities and forces… Our Torah is a Torah of truth and a Torah of life, and so it teaches us that a person, by virtue of his being a person, cannot be divine, and as long as his soul is bound to, and ensconced in, physical matter, he will necessarily have within him all natural forces and qualities.

Now for people of stature, the benefit of these Biblical narratives is that when they occasionally stumble in some manner, this knowledge consoles them and teaches them that this is human nature — that whatever level a person is on, and no matter how great his awareness truly is, nevertheless, he will necessarily have within him natural forces that pull him downward. But nevertheless, he should not let go from continuing his work, and he should strengthen his spirit and his heart, and try with all his strengths to develop and elevate himself, and to overcome his natural forces…

However, for small-minded people, this causes them to lighten [their burden of responsibility], to justify [themselves] on the basis of their [the righteous'] deficiencies and negative actions, saying, "Weren't even the sacred patriarchs imperfect? Weren't my faults and deficiencies found also within them?" But in truth, this is foolishness and lowliness of spirit. A person must be a fool to think this — for how great and vast is the difference between us and them! We cannot bring any example from their lives to our lives. They lived exalted, sacred, pure lives, and the forces that elevated and lowered [them] were so thin and invisible, and with feelings that were so exalted and hidden, ever so slight, that we cannot even sense at all.

Rav Bloch emphasizes that acknowledging the human forces that affect spiritual giants, and lead them to occasionally err, offers us an invaluable source of encouragement as we struggle with our own human vices, while warning that this recognition must not blind us to the greatness of our righteous forebears.

The Patriarchs as Flawless

By contrast, a number of 20th-century luminaries expressed a different view, strongly affirming that we cannot attribute ordinary human vices to the righteous figures in *Tanach*.

Rav Aharon Kotler, in an essay reproduced in *Mishnas Rabbi Aharon — Ma'amarim Ve-Sichos Mussar*,[41] writes that the actions of the patriarchs and matriarchs established יסודות לבניין עם ישראל והעולם כולו — "foundations for the building of the Jewish Nation and the entire world." And, as such, there is no possibility of attributing their actions to any human faults. Rav Kotler writes: אילו היה פגם כל שהוא באבות, ויהיה זה פגם דק מן הדק, הייתה כל מציאות עם ישראל אחרת — "If there were any defect in the patriarchs, even if this were the slightest defect, the entire reality of the Jewish Nation would be different."[42]

Similarly, Rav Eliyahu Dessler writes in *Michtav Mei-Eliyahu*[43] that the sins told by the Torah as having been committed by the righteous Biblical figures cannot be understood plainly as actual sins. They are considered sins only by the pristinely strict standards that are, in Rav Dessler's words, even smaller than microscopic. Rav Chaim Friedlander likewise comments in the introduction to *Sifsei Chayim al Ha-Torah* about the stories of our righteous ancestors' wrongdoing, אסור להבין את הדברים בהבנה שטחית וירודה בהתאם למבט שלנו על אותם מעשים — "It is forbidden to understand these matters with a superficial, shallow understanding, in accordance with our perspective on those matters."

In contradistinction to Rav Hirsch and Rav Bloch, these writers maintained that we cannot ascribe any human faults to the spiritual greats of the Bible, and even when the Torah speaks of their wrongdoing, it does not refer to anything remotely resembling the kinds of sins that we, ordinary people, commit.

Choosing a Rabbi and a *Gadol*

In conclusion, it is worth nothing a fascinating comment of the *Chazon Ish* in one of

---

41. Vol. 3, p. 175.

42. Rav Kotler goes so far as to say that even Yishmael, the product of Avraham's marriage to Hagar, Sara's maidservant, היה במדרגה גבוהה מאד בחכמה — "was on a very high level of wisdom," by virtue of being Avraham's son and of the outstanding education he undoubtedly received from Avraham. Sara's decision to banish Yishmael, Rav Kotler writes, stemmed from her awareness of the immense power and influence wielded by great people, such that Yishmael's influence would negatively affect Yitzchak, who was on an incalculably higher spiritual plane than Yishmael.

43. Vol. 1, p. 161.

his published letters,[44] instructing us לדעת את גדוליה באופייס האמיתי — "to know the giants of [Torah] in their true character," including their flaws. He writes that just as *halacha* permits sharing negative information about the inferior quality of a craftsman's work when necessary to warn prospective customers, it is certainly permissible — and all the more so — to inform people of the flaws of rabbis from whom they consider seeking guidance and inspiration. The *Chazon Ish* adds a warning that this must be done with extreme caution, as any imprecision or exaggeration would violate the grave Torah prohibition of slandering a Torah sage.[45]

If we wish to find Torah scholars from whom to learn, from whom to receive guidance, and to whom to look as role models — which we of course should — then it behooves us to know the truth about who they are and what and how they teach. If the Gemara[46] instructs us to learn only from a rabbi who is דומה למלאך ה' — "similar to an angel of God," then it is not just appropriate, but necessary, to know who rabbis really are, rather than blindly believing that they are perfect or near perfect. And therefore, just as parents naturally want to know about the principal and *rebbeim* of a school before enrolling their child, and just as a congregation naturally wants to know about a rabbi before hiring him as their *rav*, we should all want to know about Torah sages before choosing whom to follow and look to as our role model and guide. This necessarily requires knowing even the less flattering aspects of the rabbi's character, the faults and flaws that he has by virtue of his being human.

An Educational Perspective

Further insight into this topic might be gleaned from the comments of the Maharal of Prague[47] in explaining the Torah's command that the *Korban Pesach* be roasted whole, and may not be prepared through boiling in water.[48] When food is boiled, the Maharal writes, it typically dissolves, with various portions separating from one another. Boiling has the effect of extracting some of the food's "force" into the water, revealing its different components. When food is roasted over fire, however, the precise opposite occurs — it solidifies and contracts; it becomes stronger and more powerful. The Maharal explains that at the time of the Exodus, when *Am Yisrael* was taking its first steps as God's special nation, it was necessary to "roast" — to show their full spiritual force and power. They needed to be shown their extraordinary capabilities, the nation's unique greatness. This is represented by the process of roast-

---

44. *Kovetz Iggros*, vol. 2, 133.

45. צריך לזה זהירות יתירה, ופן משנה קוצו של יוד ונמצא מוציא שם רע על תלמיד חכם.

46. *Mo'ed Katan* 17a.

47. *Gevuros Hashem*, chapter 60. See also דרשה לשבת הגדול and הלכות פסח בקצרה.

48. אל תאכלו ממנו נא ובשל מבושל במים כי אם צלי אש ראשו על כרעיו ועל קרבו, *Shemos* 12:9.

ing, which has the effect of solidifying the meat's contents so it becomes stronger and more impressive.

Later, the Maharal observes, *Bnei Yisrael* were led into the wilderness and built *sukkos*.[49] The Gemara[50] comments with regard to the obligation of *sukka*, כל ישראל ראויים לישב בסוכה אחת — it is theoretically possible for all *Am Yisrael* to fulfill the *mitzva* by residing all together in a single *sukka*.[51] This means that on Sukkos, all members of the nation are encouraged to interact, the righteous sages together with the ignorant laymen. Whereas on Pesach, at the beginning of our nation's journey, the power and greatness of *Am Yisrael* must be brought to the fore, later, we can begin to see and take note of the many different elements, including the less impressive aspects.

Educationally, there is value during a child's early, formative years to present him a "roasted" *Korban Pesach* — to emphasize the greatness of *Am Yisrael*, the extraordinary achievements of our righteous luminaries. It is important to instill within youngers an appreciation and awe of Torah sages. To this end, it is appropriate in younger grades to depict great rabbis as flawless. However, once children grow older, they can only benefit from recognizing the imperfections of the *gedolim*, from understanding that nobody is or is meant to be perfect, so that they are not discouraged by their own struggles, failures and imperfections, and instead feel confident in their ability to achieve greatness despite their faults.

Conclusion

All people, including the greatest, most righteous figures, are flawed and imperfect. Recognizing the flaws of spiritual giants does not diminish from the respect we owe them, but to the contrary, raises our esteem for them, as we recognize that they achieved greatness despite their natural, human faults. This is also necessary in order for us to look to them as role models, for if we view them as perfect, we would despair from aspiring to, and working towards, achieving their exalted spiritual stature.

Of course, respecting the greatness and authority of Torah sages is vital for the successful transmission of Torah, and therefore, we must portray *gedolim* as they truly were or are, including their faults, while ensuring we maintain our high esteem for their knowledge and character, notwithstanding their shortcomings. While for younger children, it might be — and likely is — proper and worthwhile to portray *gedolim* as "supermen" for the sake of inspiring them, once children grow older, they should be taught that even *gedolim* struggle and have faults, so that they will not be discouraged by their own failings and struggles.

---

49. כי בסוכות הושבתי את בני ישראל בהוציאי אותם מארץ מצרים, *Vayikra* 23:43.

50. *Sukka* 27b.

51. This statement is made to explain the majority view among the *Tannaim* that one does not need to reside in his own *sukka* to fulfill this *mitzva*.

Rabbi Shimon Szimonowitz

Interviewed on *Headlines with Dovid Lichtenstein*, 24 Tammuz 5779 (July 27, 2019)

There were many issues with the *sefer* [*Making of a Godol*, by Rav Nosson Kamenetsky]. I would not want to say anything negative about Rav Nosson, because I liked him and I felt that our relationship was a good relationship… But I think Rav Nosson would appreciate if we critiqued his book and critique what he did, and so I don't think this would be an affront to him…

Look at the cover. There are pictures of some *gedolim* — some look very nice, distinguished and bearded, while others are clean-shaven, looking more modern. Everyone knows that back in the day not every *gadol* was born with a long white beard and rabbinical garb, but on the other hand, what do you highlight? What do you put on the cover? What are you stressing?

Tanach is full of negative things about our greatest figures. The Torah says things — but the *mefarshim* downplay what was done, even when the *Tanach* highlights it. There's a certain message that the Torah is teaching you and the Gemara is teaching you, and the question is whether we can apply it in our own lives… The *pasuk* says in *Mishlei* (28:12), בעלוץ צדיקים רבה תפארת ובקום רשעים יחופש אדם. Rabbeinu Yona explains this to mean that *tzadikim* always look to praise and glorify people, to emphasize anything good about them, while the *resha'im* מחפשים מומי בני אדם ושגיאותם להשפילם ואע"פ שכבר הזניחו המעשים ההם וחזרו בתשובה — "search for people's faults and mistakes in order to belittle them, even though they had already abandoned these behaviors and performed *teshuva*." If people are behaving in a different way today, you have no right to go back and say what they did back then…

[Many stories in] *Making of a Godol* don't serve to inspire people. Somewhere in your subconscious, you're thinking [after reading them] about the *gadol*'s faults today…

The question isn't whether the *gedolim* had struggles. I would say, from a Torah standpoint, what is the purpose in mentioning that someone had a *chisaron*?

I would not recommend the hagiographies. I'm not at all a fan of them. I can't even read them. If you want to read history, then I would recommend academic historical books, which give you the true version of history. But going back to inspiration — I don't believe that in the majority of cases, you draw inspiration from somebody because once he wasn't good and now he's better. The way to draw inspiration is by telling someone good things that somebody did.

Rav Yaakov Emden writes about himself that he had an incident similarly to Yosef Ha-Tzadik [when he was seduced by Potifar's wife], and a miracle happened [and he did not commit the act]. He wrote this about himself. Can you show me a precedent of a *gadol be'Yisrael* telling a story like this about a "Yosef Ha-Tzadik" two generations before him?

Hagiographies are false and it's perhaps not a good idea to read them or write them. They're lacking in *emes*. Books that are giving misinformation and telling people things that aren't true, are simply *sheker*. And if it's conveying a message which says that these people were perfect from the day they were born, it's sending the wrong message. It's perhaps telling people that if you weren't born like that, that if you didn't make a *beracha* on your mother's milk, you can't become a *gadol*. But for *chinuch* purposes, my position is that I don't see any great benefit in adding to the stories [of the faults of great people] in *Chazal* and *Tanach*. I see no precedent for it, and I see no benefit. It gives people the wrong message, to bring these figures down a notch. I don't see any benefit from a *chinuch* point of view. For the message of שבע יפול צדיק וקם (that the righteous fail and recover), we have that in the *Tanach* and Gemara. We don't have to go looking for more stories and digging up more negative things about people's past and publishing them, in order to give another proof that שבע יפול צדיק וקם. Rather, like Rabbeinu Yona says, a *tzadik* looks for people's good qualities and at the good things they did. I don't think people walk away from *Making of a Godol* saying, "Wow, if they can do it, then I can do it!"

…If you want to inspire people, send a positive message of great things that people can do. That's the most important message, and the strongest message. Everybody knows that people aren't born perfect…

Dr. Chaim Waxman

Interviewed on *Headlines with Dovid Lichtenstein*, 24 Tammuz 5779 (July 27, 2019)

What was "terrible" about the book (Rav Nosson Kamenetsky's *Making of a Godol*)? That he wrote about the *gedolim* and he portrayed the *gedolim* as they were.

One thing about the Kamenetskys is that they tell the truth. And the truth is that *gedolim* are human beings, not *malachim*. He portrayed them very positively, but as human beings, and there were those who were offended by the portrayal of some of the *gedolim* as human beings. And so they burned it, they called for a ban on it, they went to *rabbanim* and *gedolim*, and there were those who signed, putting a *cheirem* on it.

It ate him up. He had such aggravation from it, you can't imagine. He tried in every which way to meet with those who were calling for a ban so he could explain to them what was there. I don't know how many of them even read English to begin with. A number of the *rabbanim* who signed this ban — I am positive they do not read English, so I don't know how they signed it. He tried to meet with them so he could explain, but it was to no avail.

He told [in the book] about a fellow who interrupted Rav Aharon Kotler during a *shiur* he was giving to ask a question. It was unusual to interrupt the *shiur* with a question. He was a red-haired fellow, and Rav Aharon called him a "*para aduma*." It's a story that some in Rav Aharon's family took as an insult to Rav Aharon. And in the second, "improved" edition of the book, he took out that story. But the truth of the matter is, I know for a fact that he did not mean in any way to belittle Rav Aharon. He just told it over as it was. I know how people speak about Reb Yosef Ber Soloveitchik — if you would ask him a question, he could wipe the floor with you. If he felt it was a stupid question, he would tell you. That did not make him any less of a *gadol*. Did that minimize the respect for him? Anyone who knew his *shiur* knew that this was his temperament, and they accepted it. This was part of it. And I think that this was the case also with Rav Aharon Kotler.

I know his [Rav Nosson's] great admiration for Rav Aharon Kotler. He would not disrespect him. But this is what it was and he told what it was.

Look at the *Rishonim*, at how the Ra'avad talks about the Rambam. He really uses very strong language, much stronger than anything Rav Aharon ever said. And the Ra'avad is the Ra'avad and the Rambam is the Rambam. It doesn't diminish from their *gadlus*.

The book had a story that Rav Aharon wrote letters to his *kalla*, and Rav Isser Zalman made a snide comment about Rav Aharon. I can tell you about *gedolim* who wrote love letters to their *kallas*. Does this diminish from their greatness? In my mind, that he wrote love letters to his *kalla* is a positive thing. There are emotions that are appropriate before [the wedding] and emotions that are appropriate after, and I don't think anything he wrote was inappropriate. To say that he wrote them is taboo, and diminishes from his *gadlus* — I really don't understand.

A prominent doctor from California called me when he heard of the ban. He felt so terrible. "I'm a *ba'al teshuva*," he said, "and I get strength from finding out that *gedolim* are human beings, that they behave like human beings. If they're superhuman, then I have no models to work towards." I wrote to Rav Nosson at the time about that phone call. I told him that I don't understand the people who were criticizing him for portraying the *gedolim* as human beings, and that he was not portraying them negatively at all…

They believe that the *gedolim* are simply on a different level than we are, that we cannot understand them…

Rabbi Dovid Bashevkin

Interviewed on *Headlines with Dovid Lichtenstein*, 24 Tammuz 5779 (July 27, 2019)

The Gemara in *Mo'ed Katan* tells us to look for a *rav* הדומה למלאך — "who resembles an angel," and that only from such a person יבקשו תורה מפיהו — "we should seek Torah from his mouth." We should look for Torah from a *rav*, a leader, a role model, who is דומה למלאך.

One of the questions I deal with in my book is that this seems contradictory, because we have so many places in the Gemara where it says לא ניתנה תורה למלאכים

— "the Torah is not given to *malachim*." So there seems to be a contradiction of sorts about whether the *rav* should be pristine, pure, and free from all mistakes. On the one hand, we have this oft-quoted Gemara about רב דומה למלאך, and on the other hand, we have Gemaras right and left talking about how the Torah wasn't given to *malachim*, that our Torah has לא תחמוד and all sorts of *aveiros*, and is given to people with desires and a *yetzer ha-ra*. So does this apply to our leaders?

I heard from Rav Wolbe that when the Gemara says רב דומה למלאך, it isn't talking about a rabbi who is pristine, pure and perfect like an angel, but is rather talking about a מלאך in the sense of *shelichus*, as having been given a certain task. You want a role model who is loyal to his *talmidim*. Having a *rav* who is infallible — I don't think this is necessarily an ideal, because it doesn't exist. If somebody presents himself as perfect and infallible, he's either lying, or really is a מלאך and shouldn't be presenting Torah anyway. The people whom we want to hear Torah from are people who are human, who have all the difficulties of the human experience. That's what makes Torah so great and so valuable.

When it comes to leaders performing acts of outright abuse — whether it's sexual abuse or any sort of abuse of power — this needs to be spoken about in a very careful way, and not in a classroom necessarily. Let's put that in one category. In another category is stories of *tzadikim* that are meant to inspire. Within this category, there has been a debate throughout Jewish history about the role of mistakes that *rabbanim* make, what role they should play in the way we teach our children. On the one hand, you have people like Rav Schwab, who wrote very eloquently about how the history that we give over to our *talmidim* should be pristine, aspirational and inspirational, and that there's no reason to tell the mistakes, miscalculations and difficulties that our role models had. But not everybody agreed with Rav Schwab. Most notably, Rav Hutner wrote in a very famous letter, in his *Iggeros U-Ksavim* (128), that he lamented the fact that biographies of the Chafetz Chayim did not talk about how much the Chafetz Chayim must have struggled with *lashon ha-ra*. And the biographies of other *talmidei chachamim* don't talk about how they have struggled to get where they are. This plays out a lot in publishing.

I find a lot of memoirs of *gedolim* to be extraordinarily moving, because it shows their humanity. There was some debate over the memoirs of the Aderes, the father-in-law of Rav Kook. In that memoir, he talks about how he struggled, how he was so embarrassed over jobs and *shtelers* that he wasn't able to get. He talks very openly about prominent *rabbanim* who, he felt, wronged him. I look at that and I'm actually inspired. Because it shows you that they had emotions and struggles with disappointment and failure, and all the day-to-day things, like not getting a promotion, and we never think of our *gedolim* on those terms. To me, that is so inspiring. To hear somebody write about that is very moving.

I hear both sides, and I think there needs to be a balance. I don't put my kids to sleep every night telling them about every mistake that the Chafetz Chayim, the Aderes, and other *rabbanim* made. I tell them stories of inspiration. But I mix in there the humanity of the *gedolim*, because I think that this is the praise of *talmidei chachamim* — showing their humanity and how despite the normal human experience that everybody has, they were able to achieve what they achieved. This is the ultimate praise. In a way, it reminds me of the Gemara which says that the *nevi'im* stopped praising *Hakadosh Baruch Hu* because they said they didn't see greatness. Hashem's greatness wasn't explicit — the *Beis Ha-Mikdash* and all the miracles were gone. But the *Anshei Kenesses Ha-Gedola* were מחזיר עטרה ליושנה. They said that the fact that *Klal Yisrael* is here despite all their failures, and despite all the people who tried to take them down, זו היא גבורת גבורתו...ואלו הן נוראותיו. That's how I look at the human stories of *gedolim*, the people and the struggles behind all the *sefarim*, all the דרכי הלימוד, all the personal stories that we have — all those role models. There were very human paths that needed to be charted to get where they were, and those paths are filled with mistakes and failures and difficulties. I look at that, and I see אלו הן נוראותיו. That makes them more awesome, more astounding, and more inspiring.

I concede that what I'm saying is not necessarily agreed upon. As I mentioned, Rav Schwab didn't agree with it.

I would make a distinction between the way we give over *gedolim* stories and the way we approach and learn Chumash. I think there is an important distinction to be made here. There is an academic article, a brilliant piece, written by my dear friend Dr. Zev Eleff, where he talks about the history of applying psychobabble —psychoanalytic terminology — to Biblical characters, such as Avraham, Yitzchak and Yaakov. We have examples of people who took modern Freudian concepts and applied them to the *Avos*. I find that problematic. I don't find it problematic to talk about the *Avos* having sinned — Rav Hirsch talks about it, and the Ramban ascribes sins to the *Avos* and to other figures in Tanach which are not explicit. But I would caution that when it comes to applying contemporary readings of psychoanalytic terminology to personalities in *Tanach* — this could be dangerous. The danger, to me, isn't that you are diminishing the personalities of *Tanach*. I think that the greater danger — and this is something I remember reading from Rabbi Shalom Carmy — is diminishing your own self-conception. Somebody who's willing to apply very neat psychological terms to explain away all the actions of the *gedolim* — to me, he is diminishing his own sense of self and his own understanding of the complexities of human life and human emotion. To take Avraham, Yitzchak, Yaakov and the other personalities in *Tanach* and neatly put them in some psychological category, some Freudian complex — to me, this diminishes the human condition. It's not always so neat, it's not always so explainable. So where one can add complexity to the lives of the personalities in *Tanach*, I would caution people not to diminish them, because this could be a reflection of an overly simplistic view of your own life and your own motivation.

...In the memoirs of the *Aderes*, there are things said about *gedolim* that you would not want to hear. In later printing of the memoirs, they took out some of this. A similar issue came up regarding the printing of Rav Yaakov Emden's memoirs, in *Megillas Sefer*. Rav Yaakov Emden was very candid in self-disclosing some of his struggles. There are things written there that I don't even feel comfortable saying on our podcast. You can read it for yourself. There were people who openly said that the whole thing must be a forgery, because there's no way a *rav* could write that about himself.

I think an example in the *chassidishe* world is Rav Nachman. *Chayei Moharan*, which, I believe, was written by his *talmid*, Rav Nosson, has a whole chapter about Rav Nachman's struggles. And I think some of the oddity, complexity, and sweetness of Breslov *chassidus*, and why so many people find it so relevant, is because Rav Nachman was so comfortable writing about his struggles, about times when he felt bereft of *Hakadosh Baruch Hu*, when he couldn't find *Hakadosh Baruch Hu* in his life, when he had trouble *davening* — he felt comfortable writing about all this...

I think there were *rabbanim* who felt that there was an opportunity, and it was important, to connect with their *talmidim* specifically through their failures, to show their humanity, and there were others — and certainly publishers — who felt very strongly that there's no reason for it. I hear both sides, and I mix it up with my students and with my children. I tell them stories from both perspectives. I don't need to add in all the complexities which would diminish from the greatness of our *gedolim*. But there are times when I'll deliberately add in layers of the story that add to the richness and the complexity of the human experience...

I would not call it a *machlokes* — I would call it different emphases. I think there are people who emphasize the importance of a pristine look at our role models, and some people who look at them as human beings. And I think that both are true. When you raise young children, it is natural for young children to look at their parents as superhuman, perfect, infallible beings. As you grow up, you begin to see that your parents may have had financial troubles. They very likely had marital difficulties, like all couples. They probably fought when you didn't see, and they had strife and difficulties. You can only learn to appreciate that as you get older, but learning about your parents' struggles gives you more respect for them, and more respect for the human experience, not less. I think there's an element of maturity in the way you learn and the way you find out, and I would apply the same to our *gedolim*.

I heard directly from Rav Berel Gershenfeld, a rebbe in the *kiruv* movement in *Eretz Yisrael*...that Rav Wolbe struggled with his own children. He had a child whom he struggled with for a very long time, who struggled with his Yiddishkeit. He said that Rav Wolbe told him once that it was important for him to have a child who struggled with his Yiddishkeit so that when parents come to him to talk about their own children, he would not be judgmental of them. I think this is part of the story — learning the complexities of religious life, and learning that achieving spiritual and religious success is not a clearly paved road...

I think that the way we approach *gedolim* should reflect the way we approach our own lives. If you want a life that is filled with complexity, with nuance, with sophistication, then that's the way you should approach our role models, and that's the type of teacher you should seek out, and that's the way you should learn Chumash — with complexity. Diminishing somebody to me is a reflection of one's superficiality in his own life, making someone too pristine, whether it's your rebbi, your teacher or your parent, may lose some of the opportunity to appreciate and enjoy the unbelievable *chizuk* that you could get from life's complexities, and the inspiration we could receive from life's failures.

AG Mandelblit Combating Nepotism In The Chief Rabbinate Of Israel

September 12, 2018
By YWN Israel desk - Jeruslaem

Attorney General Avichai Mandelblit has intervened, stopping appointments of persons
close to Israel's Chief Rabbis, Rishon L'Tzion
HaRav Yitzchak Yosef and HaRav Dovid Lau.

Mandelblit has intervened and stopped
the appointment of Rabbi Mordechai Ralbag,
a brother-in-law of Rabbi Lau, as the new
Ravaad Yerushalayim. He also acted on the
appointment of Rabbi Mordechai Toledano, a brother-in-law of Rav Yosef, to the post of
Av Beis Din Yerushalayim.

According to the Yediot Achronot report, the attorney general decided to freeze
the two appointments following the approval of the appointments by the special
committee that was assigned the task. The committee is comprised of HaGaon HaRav
Zabadya Cohen, HaGaon HaRav Binyamin Atias and HaGaon HaRav Michael Amos, with
the latter serving on the Chief Rabbinate Supreme Beis Din.

Mandelblit instructed the Chief Rabbis to appoint retired dayanim to the committee, but the Chief Rabbinate ignored the request, explaining they were unable to find
retired dayanim to serve on the committee. The problem with the current committee
is the rabbonim were appointed by the Chief Rabbis and here too, there is a conflict of
interests as they were appointed by the serving Chief Rabbis.

According to Yediot's report, persons in the know explain the committee is nothing
more than a "rubber stamp" which will approve any appointments made by the Chief
Rabbis. The Justice Ministry was only informed of the members of the committee after
the appointments were approved. This has prompted Mandelblit to intervene, freezing
the appointments.

Yediot quotes officials in the Justice Ministry saying, "Following a request by the
Chief Rabbinate's legal advisor several months ago regarding the appointment of a
court president and the head of the courts, it was agreed that candidates who had

relatives with one of the chief rabbis would be examined by a committee of retired dayanim. The court administration announced that it had failed to appoint relevant retired dayanim, and therefore the committee was composed of dayanim currently serving.

"Following the committee's decision in its current makeup, the Ministry of Justice received arguments regarding its conduct, which were referred to the Rabbinical Court's administration, and the court administration was asked that the candidate who was elected would not take office until the completion of the investigation. The rabbis have repeatedly called for the appointment of a committee composed of retired dayanim, and in this context, the Beit Din's administration has repeatedly clarified that this is not possible for several reasons."

When asked to respond to the report, the administration of the Batei Din is quoted telling Yediot, "The matter is being probed by the Justice Ministry".

Legal Inheritance or Nepotism?
Sons Succeeding Fathers in the Rabbinate

Does a son have halachic rights to his retired or deceased father's rabbinical post? In chassidic circles, Rebbes are succeeded almost exclusively by sons or grandsons, and this system is quite common also with regard to the positions of congregational rabbi and Rosh Yeshiva. At first glance, this arrangement seems unreasonable. Intuitively, we would assume that people should be appointed to positions of influence strictly based on merit, and not because of any family connections. Is there a halachic basis for a nepotistic system of succession of religious leadership positions? Is there a difference between different positions? And from a halachic standpoint, which is the best policy for determining who should succeed a religious leader?

The King and the *Kohen Gadol*

The succession-through-inheritance model is found already in the Torah, which establishes that the two primary positions of national religious leadership — the *kehuna gedola* (high priesthood) and kingship — are passed from father to son. The Gemara in *Maseches Horiyos*[1] establishes that there is no need to formally anoint a king's son as his successor to the throne, because such succession occurs automatically, as indicated by the verse which promises a king who faithfully obeys the Torah יאריך ימים **הוא ובניו** בקרב ישראל — "he will have long days in kingship, **he and his children**, among Israel."[2] As for the *kehuna gedola*, the Torah states explicitly in *Sefer Shemos*,[3] שבעת ימים ילבשם הכהן תחתיו מבניו ("For seven days, the *kohen* among his sons who takes his place shall wear [the priestly vestments]") — meaning, when a *kohen gadol*'s son succeeds him, he must undergo a seven-day consecration process, just like the first *kohen gadol*, Aharon, did. The Gemara in *Maseches Yoma* (72b) infers from this verse that the post of *kohen gadol* passes through inheritance, noting that the verse concludes, אשר יבא אל אוהל מועד לשרת בקודש ("...who comes into the Tent

---

1. 11b.
2. *Devarim* 17:20.
3. 29:30.

of Meeting to serve in the Sanctuary"), indicating that this applies only to the *kohen gadol*, who performs the service inside the sacred chamber on Yom Kippur, but not to the כהן משוח מלחמה — the *kohen* who accompanies the soldiers to war.

The *Sifrei*,[4] commenting on the aforementioned verse that speaks of a king's succession (הוא ובניו בקרב ישראל), writes that this rule applies to כל פרנסי ישראל — all public figures in the Jewish Nation, whose positions are passed to their children. The phrase בקרב ישראל ("among Israel"), the *Sifrei* explains, implies that כל שהוא בקרב ישראל בנו עומד תחתיו — "anyone who is 'among Israel,' his son stands in his place."

The Rambam, in *Hilchos Kelei Ha-Mikdash*,[5] rules accordingly:

> כשימות המלך או כהן גדול או אחד משאר הממונים מעמידין תחתיו בנו או
> הראוי ליורשו, וכל הקודם לנחלה קודם לשררות המת, והוא שיהיה ממלא מקומו
> בחכמה, או ביראה אף על פי שאינו כמותו בחכמה שנאמר במלך הוא ובניו בקרב
> ישראל, מלמד שהמלכות ירושה, והוא הדין לכל שררה שבקרב ישראל שהזוכה
> לה זוכה לעצמו ולזרעו.

When a king, *kohen gadol*, or one of the other appointed figures dies, his son or someone eligible to inherit him is appointed in his place, and whoever has precedence to the estate has precedence to the deceased's leadership post,[6] as long as he fills his place in wisdom, or in fear [of

---

4.   *Shoftim*, 162.

5.   4:20.

6.   The Rambam here establishes that the kingship is passed not only to the son, but to the closest inheritor, just like standard inheritance. Meaning, if the leader had no children, then the position is given to his brother, who is the closest inheritor. And in *Hilchos Melachim* (1:7), the Rambam writes that an older brother takes precedence over a younger brother, which differs from standard inheritance, regarding which there is no distinction between brothers of different ages, unless the firstborn is male, in which case he receives a double portion of the estate. The basis of the Rambam's ruling is the Tosefta, *Shekalim* 2:15.

    Seemingly, there should be no basis for a son-in-law to inherit a father-in-law's post, as sons-in-law do not inherit fathers-in-law. Indeed, the Rama, in the passage cited below, speaks of a rabbi's בנו ובן-בנו — son and grandson — being granted precedence, making no mention of sons-in-law. Nevertheless, a number of *poskim* assumed that a leader's son-in-law enjoys succession rights. The Rama, in one of his responsa (133), cites this ruling from Rav Shaul ben Rav Heschel. By contrast, Rav Gershon Ashkenazi, in *Avodas Ha-Gershuni* (49), writes that since a woman does not inherit her father's position of leadership, it cannot be transferred to her husband. Rav Moshe Sternbuch (*Teshuvos Ve-Hanhagos*, 3:460) writes that this issue hinges on the question noted below, as to whether the concept of inheriting a leadership post is rooted in formal inheritance, or is a privilege

God], even if he is not like him in wisdom, as it says regarding the king, "he and his children, among Israel." This teaches that kingship is an inheritance, and this applies to every leadership post among Israel — the one who receives it receives it for himself and for his offspring.

Similarly, in *Hilchos Melachim,*[7] after establishing that a king is succeeded by his son, the Rambam writes:

ולא המלכות בלבד, אלא כל השררות וכל המינויין שבישראל ירושה לבנו ולבן בנו עד עולם, והוא שיהיה הבן ממלא מקום אבותיו בחכמה ביראה. היה ממלא ביראה, אף על פי שאינו ממלא בחכמה, מעמידין אותו במקום אביו ומלמדין אותו. וכל מי שאין בו יראת שמים אף על פי שחכמתו מרובה אין ממנין אותו למינוי מן המינויין שבישראל.

And not just the kingship — but all leadership positions and all appointments in Israel are an inheritance for one's son and grandson, forever, as long as the son fills his forefathers' place in wisdom and fear [of God]. If he filled [their place] in fear [of God], then even if he does not fill [their place] in wisdom, he is appointed in his father's place and is taught. But anyone who does not have fear of Heaven — even if he has great wisdom, he does not receive any appointment in Israel.

The Rambam's qualification of this rule — that the son must equal the father at least in fear of God, and preferably also in wisdom — is based on the Gemara's discussion in *Maseches Kesubos* (103b) regarding the succession of Rabbi Yehuda Ha-Nasi. The Gemara relates that before his death, Rabbi Yehuda Ha-Nasi announced that his son Rabban Gamliel would succeed him as *Nasi* — the head of the *Sanhedrin.* Even though Rabban Gamliel did not equal his father in scholarship, the Gemara explains, he nevertheless equaled his father in fear of God, and was therefore deemed worthy of succeeding his father.

---

owed to a leader, that his position remains in his family. If we view succession as part of the process of formal inheritance, then there is no reason for a son-in-law to succeed his father-in-law, as discussed. If, however, succession is a privilege granted to a leader by his constituency, then we might reasonably conclude that even a son-in-law would be given the right of succession in order to keep the position in the family. Rav Sternbuch expresses the latter view, that succession stands separate and apart from formal inheritance, and it thus would, in principle, apply even to a son-in-law. Indeed, we will later demonstrate that this perspective emerges from the Rashba's ruling authorizing an elderly cantor to appoint his son to fill in for him already during his lifetime.

7.   1:7.

This ruling is mentioned by the Rama,[8] who, after establishing that a rabbi that has been accepted by his city may not be deposed, writes, אפילו בנו ובן בנו לעולם קודמים לאחרים כל זמן שממלאים מקום אבותיהם ביראה והם חכמים קצת — "Even his son and grandson are always given precedence over others, as long as they fill their forefathers' place in fear [of G-d], and they are somewhat scholarly." This ruling appears to be based on the aforementioned comments of the Rambam, though the Rama seems to go even further, granting the son precedence even if he is just "somewhat scholarly." Also noteworthy is that whereas the Rambam required that a son of inferior scholarship "is taught" so that he becomes qualified for the role, the Rama does not add this condition, seemingly accepting an inferior level of scholarship as long as the successor possesses the required level of fear of God.

The Rama addresses the issue of succession elsewhere, as well, in the context of an elderly *chazan* who wants his son to occasionally replace him, when he feels frail.[9] Based on a responsum of the Rashba,[10] the Rama rules that as long as the son is qualified, even if his vocal talent is inferior to the father's, the congregation must honor the *chazan*'s wishes. This ruling is significant in that it establishes succession rights even during the appointee's lifetime. The fact that the Rama recognizes the son's right to serve in his father's place during his father's lifetime seemingly demonstrates that this right is not a function of the formal laws of inheritance, which, quite obviously, apply only once a person departs from this world. Rather, a son's succession is a privilege earned by the father by virtue of his position, the right he is given to be assured that his prestigious post would be filled by his son when he can no longer serve. Accordingly, this principle is relevant not only upon one's passing, but also upon his retirement. In both instances, according to the Rama, the appointed official is succeeded by his son.

כל הרוצה ליקח יבא ויקח

However, the *Magen Avraham*[11] cites those who dispute the Rama's ruling, distinguishing in this regard between positions of authority, and the role of Torah guidance or instruction. Rav Shmuel de Medina ("Maharashdam"), in one of his responsa,[12] asserts that when it comes to Torah scholarship, succession is not determined through inheritance. He cites the Gemara's famous teaching in *Maseches Yoma* (72b) that whereas the roles of kingship and the priesthood are reserved, respectively, for the Davidic dynasty and the *kohanim*, when it comes to the mantle of Torah scholarship, כל הרוצה ליקח יבא

---

8.   Y.D. 245:22.

9.   O.C. 53:25.

10. 9.

11. O.C. 53:33.

12. Y.D. 85.

ויקח — "whoever wishes to take it may come and take it." The Rambam similarly writes in *Hilchos Talmud Torah*,[13] "The crown of Torah — it is there standing and ready for anybody; whoever wishes may come and take it." The position of Torah teacher and guide is available to one and all, and therefore, a rabbinical post does not pass through inheritance from father to son.[14]

The *Magen Avraham* cites this view also from Rav Menachem Azarya de Fano's *Asara Ma'amaros*.[15] Rav Menachem Azarya notes that the position of *Nasi* was not passed through inheritance until the time of Hillel, who was succeeded by his son, Rabban Shimon, who was then succeeded by his son, and so on.[16] The reason for this transition in the system of succession, Rav Menachem Azarya speculates, was the sorry state of the monarchy during the later years of the Second Commonwealth. Once the kingship fell into the hands of Herod and his family, the *Sanhedrin* decided that its rabbinic leadership should assume a monarchical stature, and so the position of leadership began to be passed through inheritance, just like kingship. This system thus does not represent the normal manner of succession of rabbinic leadership, which should not, under usual circumstances, pass from father to son.[17]

The position of the Maharashdam and Rav Menachem Azarya de Fano is accepted by Rav Shneur Zalman of Liadi, in *Shulchan Aruch Ha-Rav*.[18]

This point is made also by Rav Elchanan Wasserman[19] in explaining the Gemara's account[20] of the appointment of Rav Acha bar Difti to replace Rav Ashi as Rosh

---

13. 3:1.
14. Rav Malkiel Tzvi Tannenbaum, in *Divrei Malkiel* (4:82), refutes this argument, noting that when the Gemara says, כל הרוצה ליקח יבא ויקח, it refers to Torah scholarship, which is available to one and all, as opposed to formal positions of Torah leadership, which could perhaps be passed down from father to son. Indeed, as Rav Tannenbaum cites, the Meiri comments on this Gemara, כל הרוצה **להתחכם** בתורה יבא ויטול.
15. *Chikur Din*, 2:19.
16. The Rambam, in his famous introduction to *Yad Ha-Chazaka*, traces the transmission of the oral tradition from Moshe Rabbeinu through Rav Ashi, and indeed, the only period in which the leading scholar was succeeded by his son was from the period of Hillel through the time of Rabbi Yehuda Ha-Nasi.
17. This also seems to have been the view of the *Sefer Chassidim* (757), who tells of an elderly cantor who specifically asked towards the end of his life that somebody else lead the services in his stead, so that his son would not demand the right of succession — to which he was not rightfully entitled. The *Sefer Chassidim* writes that whereas the *kehuna* and the kingship are passed from father to son, מצוות אינן ירושה — *mitzva* roles are not governed by the process of inheritance.
18. O.C. 53:33.
19. *Kovetz Shiurim*, Bava Basra 12b.
20. *Bava Basra* 12b.

Yeshiva in Sura. Significantly, Rav Ashi's son, Mar bar Rav Ashi, was not chosen for this position.[21] Rav Elchanan notes an exchange between Rav Ashi and his son recorded in *Maseches Chullin* (78a) which indicates that his son was a capable and accomplished scholar already during Rav Ashi's lifetime. Mar bar Rav Ashi was, seemingly, a qualified candidate for Rosh Yeshiva, but the position was nevertheless given to Rav Acha. Rav Elchanan comments:

> מוכח מזה דדוקא במינוי של שררות ושלטון ילפינן ממלך דבנו קם תחתיו, אבל לא במינוי של תורה להיות ריש מתיבתא.

> This proves that specifically with regard to an appointed position of authority and rule we learn from the king that his son succeeds him, but not with regard to an appointed Torah position, to be the head of an academy.

The *Chasam Sofer*,[22] too, advances the view that Torah leadership is not passed through inheritance, drawing proof from the fact that the Gemara, as noted earlier, inferred from a verse that a *kohen gadol* is succeeded by his son. Seemingly, once the Torah states, הוא ובניו בקרב ישראל, teaching that all official appointments are passed through inheritance, there is no need for a Scriptural source establishing succession through inheritance for the high priesthood. Evidently, the *Chasam Sofer* writes, the rule that children succeed fathers does not apply to religious functionaries, and so the Torah needed to instruct that the position of *kohen gadol* marks an exception, and is bequeathed to one's son.

The *Chasam Sofer* explains on this basis Rabbi Yehuda Ha-Nasi's proclamation before his death, cited earlier. Rabbi Yehuda declared that although his son Shimon was a more accomplished scholar than his son Gamliel, he should nevertheless be succeeded by Gamliel, because of his exemplary fear of God. The underlying rationale, the *Chasam Sofer* explained, is that Rabbi Yehuda was transferring to his son only his position of authority, and not his role as scholar, which is not passed through inheritance. Had the "crown of Torah" been passed through inheritance, it would have been granted to the more scholarly son. But since this aspect of the role of *Nasi* is not inherited, Rabbi Yehuda was bequeathing only the "political" aspect of this role, which would be better executed by the person with the greatest level of fear of God.

The *Chasam Sofer* suggests drawing proof to this view from God's appointment of Yehoshua — Moshe's closest disciple — as Moshe's successor. The Midrash[23] famously relates that Moshe assumed he would be succeeded by his sons, an assumption which, the *Chasam Sofer* notes, seemingly proves that they were qualified to serve as leaders.

---

21.   Although, Mar bar Rav Ashi was eventually named Rosh Yeshiva over twenty years later.

22.   Responsa, O.C. 12-13.

23.   *Yalkut Shimoni*, 776.

After all, Moshe himself demanded that God appoint a worthy successor, who would capably lead the nation to battle,[24] and who would understand and fill the unique needs of each individual.[25] Necessarily, then, if he assumed his sons would succeed him, they must have had these credentials. Nevertheless, God commanded Moshe to name Yehoshua his successor, because of Yehoshua's special devotion to Moshe and hard work tending to Moshe's study hall. The *Chasam Sofer* thus proves that the mantle of Torah leadership does not pass from father to son through inheritance, and a Torah leader's son has no greater claim to succession than any other qualified candidate.

A number of later writers[26] refuted this proof, noting the Midrash's comment elsewhere[27] that God informed Moshe that his sons were unworthy of succeeding him because they did not devote themselves to Torah study. Yehoshua's appointment thus does not prove that Torah leadership is not bequeathed to one's sons, because Moshe's sons were not qualified for the position.[28]

Moreover, proof to the Rama's position may be brought from *Tosfos'* comment in *Maseches Berachos* (4a) concerning the status of Benayahu ben Yehoyada, a leading figure in King David's army whom the Gemara identifies as a member of the *Sanhedrin*. According to Rabbeinu Tam's text of the Gemara, the Gemara presumed that since Benayahu served on the *Sanhedrin*, his son, Yehoyada, likewise served on the *Sanhedrin*. *Tosfos* explain that it stands to reason that Benayahu's son was capable of filling his father's role, and so the Gemara assumed that he succeeded him. This would certainly indicate that, in *Tosfos'* view, even positions of Torah authority are bequeathed through inheritance.[29]

Rabbis as Public Servants

In any event, at the end of his discussion, the *Chasam Sofer* proposes that notwithstanding this distinction between Torah leadership and positions of authority, the Rama's ruling regarding succession in the rabbinate might very well be correct. He writes that rabbis in modern times, who are assigned to lead the community and oversee all communal affairs, might likely qualify as authority figures, similar to the post of

---

24. Rashi, *Bamidbar* 27:17.

25. Rashi, *Bamidbar* 27:16.

26. Maharam Shick, Y.D. 228; *Avnei Neizer*, Y.D. 312:41.

27. *Tanchuma, Pinchas* 11.

28. Rav Shmuel Wosner (*Shevet Ha-Levi*, 4:128) adds that the appointment of Yehoshua, who was charged with the task of leading *Bnei Yisrael* into the Land of Israel, and of beginning the process of transmitting the Torah given through Moshe, was exceptional, and cannot serve as a model that is binding upon future appointments to positions of leadership.

29. This point is made by Rav Ephraim Weinberger, "*Yerusha Be-Rabbanus*," *Techumin*, vol. 1.

Nasi after the period of Hillel. Indeed, as mentioned earlier, the Rama cites the Rashba's ruling that if a formally appointed cantor needs a replacement, and he wants his son to lead the service in his place, then as long as the son is qualified, the synagogue cannot protest. The *Chasam Sofer* avers that the modern-day rabbinate should certainly be treated as no less a position of communal service than the cantorate, such that a rabbi's post should be bequeathed to his son just as a cantor's post is.[30]

In concluding his discussion, the *Chasam Sofer* writes, ב"ה שזכיתי להפך בזכותיהם דת"ח ובניהם אחריהם — celebrating his success in finding a justification for the practice of sons succeeding their fathers in positions of rabbinic leadership. This conclusion would seem to indicate that the *Chasam Sofer* did not fully accept this theory, but he proposed it in order to justify the widespread practice of sons inheriting rabbinical posts. However, his son Rav Shimon Sofer wrote a letter[31] affirming that at the end of his life, the *Chasam Sofer* established that this succession policy should be followed throughout Hungary.[32] Rav Sofer adds, וכן נוהגין עד היום הזה מצד הדין ומצד הטוב והישר בעיני אלקים ואדם — "And this is the practice to this day, both by force of the law and for the purpose of doing what is right and just in the eyes of God and man."

Thus, even the *Chasam Sofer*, who accepted the distinction drawn by the Maharash-dam and Rav Menachem Azarya de Fano between Torah leadership and other leadership positions, accepted as a matter of practice the policy of succession by inheritance.

Likewise, Rav Aryeh Frommer, in his *Eretz Tzvi*,[33] asserts that this debate does not pertain to modern-day rabbis who seek leadership posts mainly as a means of earning a livelihood. It is only in regard to Torah figures who did not receive payment for teaching and issuing rulings that some *poskim* excluded such positions from the standard policy of succession. However, the paid position of rabbi resembles that of cantor, which is passed from father to son.[34]

---

30. Rav Wosner (in the responsum referenced above, note 28) writes that according to the *Chasam Sofer*, the succession policy would depend upon the nature of the father's rabbinical post. The *Chasam Sofer* describes how in his time, rabbis were not merely scholars and teachers, but administrators assigned to oversee virtually all communal matters, and thus he felt that this position does not qualify as a Torah post, and would pass from father to son. However, Rav Wosner writes, in many communities nowadays, this is not the case, and the rabbi's role is largely restricted to matters involving Torah guidance and instruction, in which case the *Chasam Sofer*'s argument would not apply.

31. Published in *Michtav Sofer*, Y.D. 23.

32. Indeed, the *Chasam Sofer* himself was succeeded by his son, Rav Avraham Shmuel Binyamin Sofer (the *Kesav Sofer*), as rabbi of Pressburg and head of its illustrious yeshiva.

33. 103.

34. Later, we will see others who suggest that to the contrary, under the current system of rabbinical appointments, all would agree that a rabbinical post is not bequeathed to one's

Regardless, as mentioned, the Rama clearly ruled that a son succeeds his father's rabbinical post, and although the *Mishna Berura*[35] cites both views, without taking a definitive stance,[36] the consensus among the *poskim* appears to follow the Rama's position.[37]

Additionally, it stands to reason that even according to the view of the Maharashdam and Rav Menachem Azarya de Fano, if a community's custom is to name a rabbi's son as his successor, then this custom is binding. Thus, even if, in principle, a son does not have a halachic right to succeed his father, he is entitled to the post if this is the community's longstanding custom. This point is made by Rav Alter Yechiel Nebenzahl of Stanislav, in *Minchas Yechiel*.[38]

מנהג and Communal Consent

The factor of accepted מנהג (custom) is relevant also in the converse, such that even according to the conventional view, a son may not necessarily earn his father's post if there is an established custom not to automatically name sons as their fathers' successors.

As mentioned, the Rama, in *Yoreh Dei'a*,[39] applies the Rambam's ruling to the rabbinate, establishing that a rabbi's son takes precedence over all others to his father's post. However, immediately thereafter, the Rama seems to qualify this principle, citing the following ruling from the *Kolbo*:

ובמקום שיש מנהג לקבל רב על זמן קצוב,או שמנהג לבחור במי שירצו, הרשות
בידם.

But in a place where there is a custom to accept a rabbi for a fixed period,
or a custom to choose whomever they wish, they may do so.

The Rama establishes that the standard rules of succession are overridden by accepted local custom, and thus if a congregation follows the practice of choosing a rabbi of their liking whenever the position needs to be filled, they are entitled to do so, and they are not bound by the formal laws of succession. This is a crucial qualification, authorizing communities to abide by their own traditional

---

son.

35. 53:83.
36. Later, we will see the Chafetz Chayim's unique position regarding succession in the rabbinate in modern-day circumstances.
37. See the responsum of Rav Yitzchak Aripol printed in *Ginas Veradim*, Y.D. 3:8, and Rav Aharon Valkin's responsum in *Zekan Aharon*, vol. 2, Y.D. 64.
38. 2:100.
39. 245:22.

protocols for succession, even if, in principle, the post is to be passed on to the rabbi's son.[40]

Another significant qualification is mentioned by Rav Malkiel Tzvi Tannenbaum, in his *Divrei Malkiel*.[41] He notes the Gemara's remark in *Maseches Horiyos* (11b) that although a king's son automatically assumes the throne upon his father's passing, and does not require formal anointing, this applies only if there is a general consensus among the people accepting the son as the successor. But if there is disagreement, then even if ultimately the son is named successor, he must be formally anointed, as his succession did not occur automatically by virtue of his status as inheritor. The Gemara reaches this conclusion on the basis of the verse which establishes the rule that kings are inherited by their sons: הוא ובניו בקרב ישראל ("...he and his sons, among Israel"). The policy of הוא ובניו — whereby a son inherits his father's kingship — applies only בקרב ישראל, when there is general agreement among the populace.

Rav Tannenbaum raises the question of what significance there is to the procedure of inheritance if in any event the son's succession depends on the nation's consent. Once the Torah requires that the king's son be accepted by the people for him to succeed his father, then this no longer becomes a matter of inheritance, as the succession in any event is determined solely by the will of the nation.

To answer this question, Rav Tannenbaum establishes that undoubtedly, the policy of succession through inheritance assumes that the son has the necessary credentials. It is inconceivable, he writes, that the Torah would require bequeathing the monarchy, or any other leadership position, to somebody who does not have the knowledge or skills demanded by the given profession. In the case of the rabbinate, Rav Tanenbaum writes, this means proficiency in halachic literature to the point where the candidate can provide halachic guidance and instruction.[42] The sine qua non of any appointment is the credentials to capably fill the position in question, and thus the entire discussion concerning a son's inheritance of his father's post does not even begin unless the son is recognized as having the skills needed for the role. Rav Tannenbaum thus suggests that when the Gemara requires agreement among the nation for a son to automatically succeed his father to the throne, this refers to their agreement of the son's credentials.

---

40. Rav Alter Yechiel Nebenzahl, in the aforementioned responsum, explains that if the community's custom is not to bequeath the rabbinate to the rabbi's son, then every rabbi who assumes the position is presumed to waive this privilege, and so his son is not automatically entitled to the post. (See Rav Zalman Graus' interview transcribed below, in which he offered a different explanation of the Rama's position.)

41. Referenced above, note 14..

42. Of course, with the evolving nature of the rabbinate, the credentials will depend upon the expectations of rabbis in every time and place. Nowadays, it is expected — at least in most circles — that the rabbi also possesses rhetorical talent and strong interpersonal skills.

If it is generally assumed that the son can capably govern, then he inherits the throne even if there are other worthy candidates who enjoy popularity. The son's inheritance of the throne is not automatic when there is disagreement regarding his credentials, when large segments of the population deem the son incapable of properly governing.[43]

According to Rav Tannenbaum, then, even according to the generally accepted view, that rabbinical posts are bequeathed through inheritance, this applies only if the inheritor's credentials are generally acknowledged. But when there is disagreement as to whether the son possesses the necessary skills and proficiency, he does not automatically succeed his father, and outside, impartial arbitrators should be consulted.

Truth be told, the Rama's formulation does not appear to support this theory. As cited earlier, the Rama writes that sons inherit their fathers' posts as long as they are God-fearing like their fathers והם חכמים קצת — "and are somewhat scholarly." The Rama does not require the community to acknowledge the son's credentials as a worthy successor. For Rav Tannenbaum, however, this requirement is self-understood, and thus did not need to be explicated.

In any event, a number of *poskim* similarly asserted that if a community does not want the son to serve as their rabbi, they cannot be compelled to do so. Rav Chaim of Sanz, in *Divrei Chayim*,[44] writes that in such a case — where a deceased rabbi's son demands the rights of succession, against the will of the community — we may apply the rule of קים לי, granting a defendant the right to invoke a halachic position according to which he is not required to pay the plaintiff. If a halachic debate has not been conclusively resolved one way or the other, and one position results in the defendant's exemption, he may rely on that view. Hence, as the son demands that the community pay him a salary, and the community is thus considered the "defendant," they may invoke the position of the Maharashdam, according to which they have no obligation to hire the son.

Additionally, Rav Nebenzahl, in the aforementioned responsum, cites several earlier *poskim*[45] stating that even assuming that a son indeed inherits his father's rabbinical post, this right differs from standard inheritance. Unlike property, which automatically transfers to the inheritor's possession, the right to the father's position is a privilege

---

43. Rav Tannenbaum explains on this basis the story told in *Maseches Horiyos* (13b) of Rabban Shimon ben Gamliel, who served as *Nasi*, but there were those who sought to have him deposed by revealing that he lacked proficiency in *Maseches Uktzin*. The role of *Nasi* at that time, Rav Tannenbaum writes, required complete mastery of the entire Mishna, and thus ignorance of even a single *maseches* disqualified an otherwise accomplished scholar from holding this position.

44. Y.D. 52.

45. See Maharam Shick, Y.D. 228; Rav Yitzchak Shmelkes, *Beis Yitzchak*, Y.D. 1:34; Rav Shalom Mordechai Schwadron, *Da'as Torah*, responsa, 7.

which the community bears an obligation to grant to the son, but they cannot be compelled to do so if they do not want the son to serve as their rabbi. Indeed, the Gemara states explicitly in *Maseches Berachos* (55a), אין מעמידין פרנס על הציבור, אלא אם נמלכין בציבור — "A leader is not appointed over the community without consulting the community." This teaching is cited as authoritative *halacha* by both the Rif[46] and the Rosh.[47]

It should also by noted that Rav Yechiel Michel Epstein, in his *Aruch Ha-Shulchan*,[48] writes that nowadays, when rabbinical posts are, essentially, contractual agreements of employment, they pertain only between the community and the rabbi whom they hired. The *Aruch Ha-Shulchan* contends that when a community hires a rabbi, they hire only him, and have no intention to make any sort of commitment to his heirs, and thus after the rabbi's retirement or passing, his son has no rights whatsoever to his position.

In a generally similar vein, Rav Moshe Sternbuch[49] writes that if a rabbi is hired as an employee by the congregation's committee, then this position does not qualify as a leadership post which is bequeathed to one's sons. Such a rabbi is an employee, not an authority figure, and thus he does not resemble a king, whose status forms the basis for the entire notion of bequeathing a leadership position.

Of course, this argument runs in direct contrast to the theory advanced by the *Chasam Sofer*, who, as mentioned earlier, stated that there is greater reason for the modern-day rabbinical position to pass through inheritance, as modern-day rabbis oversee their communities, and do not just teach Torah and issue halachic rulings. Regardless, the view presented by the *Aruch Ha-Shuchan* and Rav Sternbuch provides yet another basis for allowing communities the right to refuse to hire their rabbi's son to succeed him.

Contemporary Rabbis and *Roshei Yeshiva*

There might also be an additional reason why sons should not be named presumptive successors to their fathers' positions of religious leadership.

Rav Moshe Sternbuch (in the aforementioned responsum) relates that the Chafetz Chayim was once brought a question regarding a rabbi who sought to exercise his right to succeed his father's post, and the Chafetz Chayim replied that in his time, there was no such privilege. He noted the Gemara's ruling in *Maseches Horiyos* (11b) that the role of the כהן משוח מלחמה — the *kohen* appointed to accompany the soldiers out to battle

---

46. *Berachos* 43a.
47. *Berachos* 9:4.
48. Y.D. 245:29.
49. In the responsum referenced in note 6.

— is not bequeathed from father to son. The כהן משוח מלחמה serves as a "general" of sorts, charged with the vitally important job of encouraging the soldiers and boosting their morale as they wage battle against the enemies of the Jewish People. This role cannot be entrusted to anyone other than the most qualified candidate, and so the son of a כהן משוח מלחמה has no more claim to succession rights than anybody else.

In modern times, the Chafetz Chayim felt, rabbis serve in the capacity of the כהן משוח מלחמה. They are leading the "battle" against the powerful forces of secularization sweeping the world, standing at the front lines to repel foreign influence and protect authentic Torah tradition and values. Nowadays, the rabbinate involves "warfare," resisting spiritually harmful trends. As such, the modern rabbi has the status of a כהן משוח מלחמה — who is succeeded by the most capable and skilled candidate, and not necessarily by his son.

This argument seems applicable not only to the rabbinate, but also to the position of Rosh Yeshiva. Whereas in earlier generations the yeshivas served mainly as institutions of scholarship, today they serve also as a means of protection, a critically important line of defense against the pervasive secular culture around us.[50] In the modern era, rabbinic leadership is needed not simply to guide communities or to teach students, but also to valiantly lead the difficult battle that Torah Jewry has found itself forced to wage. As such, it could be argued that every religious leader in today's day and age could be legitimately considered a כהן משוח מלחמה, the appointment of whom must be made exclusively on the basis of skills and credentials, and not based on familial connections.

A possible exception is the case of an individual who establishes and then leads a new institution. The Steipler Gaon, in *Kehillos Yaakov*,[51] based on a pair of responsa by the Maharam Shick,[52] asserts that although, at least according to some opinions, a person who decides on his own to accept a certain communal task does not earn rights to this job, one who devotes himself to a *mitzva* that would have otherwise been neglected indeed earns exclusive rights to this privilege. The Maharam Shick noted the precedent of the Jewish families in the beginning of the Second Commonwealth who took it upon themselves to donate wood for the altar in the *Beis Ha-Mikdash*, seeing that no wood was otherwise available. The prophets at that time enacted that these families, and their descendants for all time, would be granted the privilege of donating wood for the altar, even if the warehouses of the *Beis Ha-Mikdash* were well stocked with wood. If, indeed, these families serve as a binding precedent for a person's lifelong right to a *mitzva* which he had taken upon himself, then it stands to reason that his offspring, too, enjoy this privilege, just as in the case of those families. Accordingly, we

---

50. See Rav Yitzchak Hutner's comments regarding the dual function of modern-day yeshivos in *Pachad Yitzchak — Iggeros U-Muchtavim*, 75.

51. *Bava Kama* 44:6.

52. C.M. 18–19.

might conclude that if a rabbi opens a synagogue or a yeshiva, devoting a great deal of time and effort to building a community or a student body, he perhaps earns the right to bequeath his position to his children.

Chassidic Dynasties

In chassidic circles, inheritance has evolved as virtually the exclusive system of succession as far as the position of *Admor* is concerned. All chassidic rebbes, with hardly any exceptions, are succeeded by a son or grandson (or son-in-law, if there is no eligible son or grandson).

Interestingly, this system was challenged by the founder of one of the legendary chassidic dynasties — Rav Chaim of Sanz. In the responsum noted earlier, Rav Chaim expresses his astonishment over the assumption that the position of *Admor* should pass from father to son. He writes that the early *Admorim* received their positions naturally, by throngs of people recognizing their wisdom and greatness and flocking to hear their teachings and receive their blessings. Furthermore, he observes, neither the Ba'al Shem Tov nor the Maggid of Mezritch, the early leaders of *Chassidus*, were succeeded by their sons; instead, they were succeeded by their devoted students, who disseminated their ideas and teachings. When it comes to chassidic leadership, Rav Chaim writes, אין בזה שום ירושה ורק מעשיו יקרבוהו ומעשיו ירחקהו — "no inheritance applies; only one's actions bring him close [to leadership], and his actions distance him [from leadership]."

Ironically, however, inheritance of leadership has become the norm in chassidic circles, including among Rav Chaim of Sanz's own descendants. This was practiced even in Lubavitch, despite the explicit ruling of the movement's founder, Rav Shneur Zalman of Liadi, who, as cited earlier, followed the position of Maharashdam and Rav Menachem Azarya de Fano that Torah leadership is not bequeathed as an inheritance.

Conclusion

While some *poskim* maintained that Torah leadership is not bequeathed to a leader's son, the consensus among the *poskim*, following the straightforward reading of the Rambam, appears to be that a son indeed inherits his father's leadership post. In practice, however, it would appear that a community or institution reserves the right to refuse granting the position to the son, for several possible reasons:

1. The community or institution can absolve itself of any obligation towards the son by relying on the view that such positions are not bequeathed to one's offspring (קים לי).
2. Even if a community owes a rabbi the privilege of naming his son as successor, they cannot, as a practical matter, be compelled to do so against their will.
3. According to several *poskim*, the modern-day rabbinate is not a leadership

position that is passed through inheritance, either because the job is arranged as a contractual agreement directly with the rabbi, or because the rabbi is an employee and does not enjoy real authority.

4. The Chafetz Chayim was of the opinion that in today's day and age, the rabbi's vital role in protecting against hostile cultural influences necessitates appointing the most qualified candidate, such that a son should not be given preference.

INTERVIEWS

Rav Hershel Schachter

Interviewed on *Headlines with Dovid Lichtenstein*, 20 Shevat, 5780 (Feb 15, 2020)

I think this is going to be the utter destruction of those yeshivos, when they insist on having only family. The outsiders feel, "We're outsiders. Why should we donate to the yeshiva? Why should we enrich that family?" And you're cheating the *talmidim*. It's not right.

I don't think in *Shulchan Aruch* they're talking about a yeshiva where the *talmidim* are twenty years old. They're talking about *talmidim* before bar-mitzva. So how much do you have to know? You have to know some Torah to teach younger children. But if you're teaching older boys, you have to know a large amount, and the older son a lot of times is not qualified. He's not ראוי לכך. The ראוי לכך is the best one. Otherwise, the *talmidim* will go to a different yeshiva, and the yeshiva will lose out in the end. If you're going to insist on having only family, everyone from the same family, it's not going to happen. That will be the destruction of the yeshiva.

Rav Zalman Graus

Interviewed on *Headlines with Dovid Lichtenstein*, 20 Shevat, 5780 (Feb 15, 2020)

Whatever I will say is not the consensus. Everything is subject to *machlokes*.

In the Bavli and Yerushalmi, there is no mention anywhere that *rabbanus* is passed through *yerusha* [inheritance]. It is not mentioned anywhere. More than that — historically, we don't find that the one who took over for a *rav* or Rosh Yeshiva was the son. To the contrary, we almost do not find that the son took over. We find it only in the case of *Nesi'im*. And even in regard to the *Nesi'im*, most *poskim* say that it was not automatic that a son took over the father's position...

But the *Toras Kohanim* mentioned that all *seraros* — like the position of king — goes from son to son... However, in the language of the *Toras Kohanim*, it's not necessarily that *serara* goes through *yerusha*. It's only a דין קדימה [rule of precedence]. Like with regard to *tzedaka*, you have to give first to your relative. But this isn't a matter of *yerusha*, a monetary claim that can be made…

It's very hard to understand this contrast — that we don't find it at all in the Bavli or the Yerushalmi. Most interesting is that there's a whole story in the Gemara about Rav Ashi, that the townspeople wanted to hire somebody, and in the end [his son] Mar bar Rav Ashi got the position, but this was a whole story, and he did not get it automatically as a *yerusha*…

I see it as a דין קדימה — you want to appoint a king, then try, if possible, to give it to the son of the previous king. He has already learned under his father, he already probably knows the customs and protocols of kingship, how to handle it… Even though the Rambam said *yerusha*, the Rama understood that it's a דין קדימה. He therefore wrote that if the מנהג is not to abide by this order of precedence, and you prioritize other qualities, this is acceptable. This is the Rama's *psak*…

If you look in the *Darchei Moshe*, [you will see that the Rama] talks about a case of a *rav* who dies, and his son is twenty-five or thirty, just finished *kollel*, and doesn't have so much experience. The father didn't give him much training. But the potential is there. This is חכם קצת. He's not fully ready to integrate into the *rabbanus*. The Rambam says, מלמדים אותו — he has the potential to learn. It does not mean that someone who is just a חכם קצת [without potential to become a great scholar] can be a *rav*.

On the one hand, there is a positive side [to succession through inheritance], in our time. It gives incentive to a Rosh Yeshiva who builds a yeshiva, knowing that his son will take over. On the other hand, it's very hard, because you don't know how good he will be, and there are probably other candidates who are more qualified. These are the two sides of the coin.

If you look at history, until, let's say, 200 or 300 years ago, this didn't exist, that sons took over. Even in the beginning of *Chassidus*, the *Divrei Chaim* says, this didn't exist — not the Ba'al Shem Tov, not Reb Elimelech, no one. Later, a different kind of culture began.

Here's a very interesting example. Contrary to what people think, the *Chasam Sofer* did not have children until the age of around forty, or even later. There was a generation gap. The *Kesav Sofer* [the *Chasam Sofer*'s son] was twenty-four or so when his father passed away, and he became the *rav*. Had he been born when the *Chasam Sofer* was twenty-five, he definitely would not have taken the *rabbanus* in Pressburg [the position held by his father], because he would have been a *rav* somewhere else. Why would he take his father's position once he was established somewhere else? But he was a young man, not established, and so he took over… But usually, not even the oldest son took over. Most of the time, the older son already had a position.

On the other hand, if somebody grew up as the *rav*'s son, he has knowledge about the town, he knows the people, he knows how to handle the people, he knows the customs of the city — then it's much easier for the townspeople to accept him as their *rav* than a greater *gadol* who is not familiar with the people, the *minhagim*, and the nuances and problems of the community…

I can bring many quotes from the Chafetz Chayim and others saying that today, we need "generals," and not just a *rav*. We need a "warrior," and this role is not passed through *yerusha*. They bring proofs. Rav Moshe Sternbuch brings this in *Teshuvos Ve-Hanhagos*. Halachically, this is very weak. And, on the other hand — in the case of big companies, the owners are getting millions of dollars for themselves and their kids every year, and even if his son does not receive this position after him, he has money for him and his kids. But when it comes to a yeshiva, even the big Roshei Yeshiva are not earning a very high salary, and his kids will be left with nothing. Some of them will be very poor if they do not receive the position. If you want to make incentives, you need to give something.

According to strict halacha, there is no law of *yerusha* [when it comes to positions of leadership], but it became like a מנהג. In some places, he was hired על דעת כן [with the presumption that his son will take over for him]. If this is the case, then it's understandable that the sons have the right [of succession]…

A son-in-law is not a son in halacha. If you go through *Shas*, you will not find a single halacha [regarding which a son-in-law is treated like a son]. What's more, if you look in the *pesukim*, you will find that the kingship was taken away from Shaul Ha-Melech — and yet his son-in-law took over. *Chazal* and the *pesukim* themselves say that נכרת המלכות מזרעו — the kingship was denied to his offspring. We find it again by Asalya, who is said to have killed כל זרע המלוכה [all the offspring of the king] — but she left the king's daughter and son-in-law. The *mefarshim* explain that they were not זרע המלוכה. In *Chazal*, there is no mention of this [a son-in-law having the status of son]. Having said that, in many places, elderly people wanted their daughter to cook and care for them in their home, so the son-in-law would live together with the father-in-law. If the father-in-law was a *rav*, and the son-in-law lived with him, he became the one best equipped with the knowledge and connections with the people in the city, so they naturally wanted him. Additionally, you can't choose your son, but you can choose a son-in-law. A *rav* or Rosh Yeshiva would take the very best, and so naturally the son-in-law took over. This is not because of *yerusha*, but people think this is anchored in *halacha*.

Rav Zalman Gifter

Interviewed on *Headlines with Dovid Lichtenstein*, 20 Shevat, 5780 (Feb 15, 2020)

The source of this *halacha*, that there is a law of *yerusha* for *rabbanus*, is the *Sifri* in *Parshas Shoftim*, where the *pasuk* speaks of the king. The *pasuk* says, למען יאריך ימים על ממלכתו הוא ובניו בקרב ישראל, and the *Sifri* says that if the king dies, his son takes over for him. The *Sifri* then says that this law applies not only to a king, but לכל פרנס שבישראל — everyone who has a shul, or a Rosh Yeshiva; their children take over for them. Any position which is בקרב ישראל, which pertains to a *tzibbur* of *Klal Yisrael*, one's son takes his place when he passes away. The Rama brings this *halacha* in *Yoreh Dei'a*.

We have to understand — the *halacha* is that a son inherits *rabbanus* and the position of Rosh Yeshiva, as we see in every yeshiva in the history of *Klal Yisrael*. Of course, if the son is אינו ראוי — not worthy of the position — then there is no law of inheritance. But not every individual, or even every *talmid chacham*, can *pasken* about someone that he is אינו ראוי, just because he doesn't like what he's doing. אינו ראוי means he's not acting like someone in that position should be acting, such as if he's a thief, or a *menuval* [despicable person]. Even if he can say a *derasha* or a piece of Torah, this does not mean he can take his father's place. But כל שהוא ממלא מקומו ביראתו, if he follows his father's path of *avoda* and *yir'as Shamayim*, then even if he does not reach his father's level of *chochma* [scholarship], he inherits his father's position. The Rama *paskens* this way in *Yoreh Dei'a* (245:22) — that sons inherit כל זמן שהם ממלאים מקום אבותיהם ביראה והם חכמים קצת.

In Telz, there was a controversy when Rav Yosef Leib Bloch brought in his son, Rav Meir Bloch, to say a *shiur*. The *bochrim* made a fuss because he was coming from business, and they said he was not worthy of this position. But Rav Yosef Leib said, "I'm the boss over here, and this is what's going to be."

There's a concept of גדול שמושה גדול מלימודה [tending to a Torah scholar is greater than learning]. It could be that somebody else is more accomplished in learning, but there is a lot to be said for someone running a *tzibbur* or a yeshiva knowing how the previous *rav* or Rosh Yeshiva did it. This is where גדול שמושה comes in, and this is one of the reasons why the son should inherit [the position]...

I would *pasken* [in a case where the deceased Rosh Yeshiva's son is not as accomplished as other candidates] that the son who is a חכם קצת has the title, but for the benefit of the yeshiva, he should bring in a *Ram* who would attract students. He'll get *shlishi*, but let the other *Ram* say the *shiur* that will attract people. It's a win-win situation.

Rabbi Pini Dunner

Interviewed on *Headlines with Dovid Lichtenstein*, 20 Shevat, 5780 (Feb 15, 2020)

Part of the revolution — I would even call it a rebellion — of the Chassidic movement, and this is something that was quickly echoed in the non-chassidic world, was opposing the system that had emerged whereby only people who were great *talmidei chachamim* or from their families, or people with enormous amounts of wealth, controlled the communities. Generally speaking, it was wealth, and not knowledge of *halacha* or Gemara, that dominated. The Chassidic world wanted to democratize Judaism, and the way to do that was to remove this requirement. If you study sociology and politics, you will discover that this is a consistent theme throughout history, that those who lead a rebellion tend to emulate and echo the "sins" of those whom they had rebelled against. And so in the Chassidic world, ironically, what happened was that those people who led the rebellion, which began with its very enigmatic, charismatic leader, the Ba'al Shem Tov, whom we know very little about, quickly evolved into a system of dynastic inheritance, where succession was very much determined by who your father was or who your Rebbe was. This is something which actually became the norm in the Chassidic world, almost to the exclusion of any other system of determining where leadership should come from.

Scholarship would say that this represents the deterioration, or end, of the Chassidic revolution. I would say something different. I think people look for stability. And a community that has subscribed to a particular way of thinking wants to make sure that this way of thinking will be preserved and maintained, particularly if that way of thinking is slightly different or very different from the previous way of thinking. The only way they can be assured of this is if they align themselves with, or devote themselves to, a family or group that is going to maintain and sustain the standards that they want to uphold. That's from the "ordinary man on the street" point of view.

I don't want to sound too critical, but as far as the Rebbes themselves were concerned, once they had created the environments which they thought was correct for their followers, for example, let's say you have a Rebbe in a particular place in the Ukraine or Poland who established a court — if the court was going to fall apart when he died, then what was going to happen to all his followers, and what's going to happen to his family? So you create a system where a child — obviously, one would hope, who was worthy — would inherit the mantle of the father or grandfather. That being the case, those people who had devoted themselves to a particular way of Jewish life over a period of time — one would assume, decades — would continue in that way, as would their children and grandchildren. So a dynasty ensures continuity. That's extremely important if you think that your particular way in Judaism is something that is worthy of being sustained.

Let me use a practical example. In Chabad, the main *talmid* of the Ba'al Ha-Tanya [the founder of Chabad] was Rav Aharon of Staroselye, who was a remarkable individual. I imagine that everyone within the circle of the Ba'al Ha-Tanya assumed he would inherit the mantle from his Rebbe. But the Ba'al Ha-Tanya's son, the "Mitteler Rebbe," whom people know very little about, became the Rebbe, and Rav Aharon was marginalized... The son of the Ba'al Ha-Tanya was not an equal to Rav Aharon, and yet he inherited the mantle. I must assume that within Chabad, the prevailing feeling at that time was that in order to maintain and sustain the message of Chabad, we need to keep a Schneerson — which means "son of Shneur," referring to Rav Shneur Zalman, the Ba'al Ha-Tanya — to keep the family in charge of the organization in order to maintain the identity of this particular branch of the Chassidic movement. So even though Rav Aharon was a much greater person, and even though Rav Aharon would have taken the revolution of *Chassidus* —at least within the Chabad movement — a stage further, they didn't want that revolution to continue. They wanted now to consolidate and make sure that whatever had been achieved until that time would be sustained through the child of the Rebbe. That's how the Schneerson clan began this movement that we know today as Chabad.

There is a lot more to say about Chabad, but this is just one example of why it was that they opted for a dynastic approach, as opposed to choosing the one best suited to take the revolution forward.

Everyone thinks that the reason why the Volozhin yeshiva closed was because the authorities insisted on secular studies being incorporated into the curriculum. But this had nothing whatsoever to do with it. On a number of occasions, the Netziv [the Rosh Yeshiva of Volozhin] was told by the authorities that he would have to close the yeshiva unless he incorporated secular studies, and at some level he always incorporated those secular studies. The real reason the yeshiva died was because Rav Chaim Berlin [the Netziv's son] was brought in. He was the rabbi of Moscow, and after his first wife died, he remarried a very wealthy woman. He was a bit at a loss as to what he should do, and his father said, "Come and take over the management of the yeshiva. I'm getting older." The *bochrim* were not interested. They wanted Rav Chaim Soloveitchik to take over the yeshiva. This was in the late 1880s. The yeshiva collapsed because nobody liked Rav Chaim Berlin, and the yeshiva was closed down. It all had to do with this dynastic approach. Had the Netziv been more circumspect about choosing his successor, had he suggested that Rav Chaim Soloveitchik should take over the yeshiva, then perhaps the story would have been different.

I'm going to inject a note of reality into this conversation. Many years ago, my father told me something he heard from his rebbe, Rav Shmelke Pinter of London. He said (in Yiddish): "Unfortunately, when you have a family business, you're not going to be so eager to give the business over to somebody who's not a member of your family." If you managed to establish a yeshiva which is the source of income for your family, how pure would your motive be when you think about succession? And I'm sorry to inject this note of reality to this discussion, but one has to imagine that this is not a topic which is immune to bias.

The original Liska Rebbe, Reb Hershel, had a *talmid* — Reb Shayala of Kerestir — and he also had a son. Nobody was interested in the son, and everyone opted for Reb Shayala of Kerestir. I'm not suggesting that they made the correct choice, but I can tell you that the *Liska Chassidus* literally disappeared without a trace, while followers of Reb Shayala of Kerestir continue to maintain themselves to this day. There's no *Kerestir Chassidus*, but he is certainly a much brighter light in terms of people who want to subscribe to that particular mode of thought, than Liska.

The idea that just because somebody is the son of somebody else, he is an appropriate leader for a group of people — I'm not sure it can sustain itself beyond the immediate group of people who know the original person...

Any of the yeshivos we are familiar with who have chosen Roshei Yeshiva because they happen to be the son of the previous Rosh Yeshiva suffered as a result, because they did not choose the best person. In any corporation, let's say a CEO comes in, and eventually he says, "I'm sixty-four, I want to retire." What will the corporation do? Would they ask the son to become the CEO? Or would they search for the best CEO? If there is a great yeshiva with 1,000 *bochrim*, and the "CEO" has reached the age where he is no longer at the height of his power, in terms of being able to attract *bochrim*, give the best *shiur* — whatever it requires to be a Rosh Yeshiva — who are we going to choose as the new Rosh Yeshiva? If the board of the yeshiva, or whoever controls the yeshiva, will say, "We can't have this discussion because obviously the next Rosh Yeshiva is the son of the previous Rosh Yeshiva," then essentially you are leaving things to chance, because the son of the previous Rosh Yeshiva, just because he happens to be the son, may not be the best person to take the yeshiva into the next era, the next generation, whatever it is that needs to be done. The problem is that many yeshivos and many *Chassidus* operate on the basis that because somebody is somebody else's son, he is the natural heir to run the organization, the institution, or group which the father had led, but this is not necessarily the case... If it's an unbiased, uninfluenced decision, and you passed that opinion through other people, that's wonderful... I'm always struck when you go into a Marriot hotel and you see the picture of the person who founded the Marriot hotels with his son. I get that the child of a person who founded a business may be the best person to ensure the future of that business, but it's not always the case. If you go into a Hilton, you probably won't find that picture, because the children of the original Hilton owner were not appropriate to take over that business. And if you make that the rule, then you are basically confining your-self to people from within the family to run the family business, and they may not be the appropriate ones to do that. It might be tough to tell them that, because everyone wants to inherit the business from their father and grandfather and not have to worry about *parnasa*. But the universal issue is whether this is the best thing for the future of the institution, and it's not necessarily true that the child of the one who established the institution is the best person to take it forward. Maybe there are better people who have broader minds and broader shoulders, and better ideas as to how that institution should be taken forward. It doesn't mean you exclude the original family, but it means you are going to be able to maintain what this institution has achieved and take it forward to the next generation.

In Jerusalem, the world of Talmud study fetes its newest superstars — women

January 6, 2020

By Marissa Newman

If the plaza outside the Jerusalem Convention Center were a manuscript read from on high, the restless, long lines of people scoring the space on Sunday evening could be seen as uneven script, penned in a rush of inspiration. Over 3,000 people were eager to enter and they

The women's siyum HaShas in the Jerusalem Convention Center on January 5, 2020.

weren't hiding it. They were young, middle-aged, elderly. Most were Orthodox Jewish women. And for all, this was to be a first.

As the crowds filed into the sold-out hall, the anticipation steadily grew. Teenage students filled out the balcony. English and Hebrew mingled in the air. As the lights dimmed to reveal a video peopled by the speakers at the event, cheers and whoops and unabashed fandom rippled wildly through the crowd.

This was no pop concert or red carpet event; it was a celebration of a religious and intellectual achievement. And though standing ovations were plentiful, as per a Jewish tradition of reverence for scholars they preceded the performances as each speaker took the stage. The women who successively stepped into the limelight were teachers of the ancient Babylonian Talmud, the seminal, 2,711-page text of Jewish thought and law. They were celebrating the end of the 7.5-year cycle of a daily study of a double-sided page of the Talmud, known as daf yomi, instituted in 1923 by Rabbi Meir Shapiro of Lublin, Poland. The cycle is credited as a powerful democratizing force for the Talmud, bringing it to the masses, and hailed as a powerful unifier for Jews, as every day thousands from across the world linger over the same ancient words.

For centuries, the study of the complex, legalistic and mostly Aramaic-language Talmud was traditionally reserved for men and strongly discouraged if not prohibited by rabbinic edict for women. But in recent decades, the study of gemara in general, and the daf yomi in particular, has been also claimed by Orthodox women and educators. Almost universally accepted in modern Orthodox circles, the practice remains mostly taboo among ultra-Orthodox women, though Sunday's event spotlighted several from that community who have taken up the esoteric texts.

"It's no longer a locked book in front of us, but rather every single person can learn," said Michelle Cohen Farber, the US-born co-founder of the Hadran organization that arranged the mass event, who hosts a daily podcast on the daf.

Billed as the first-ever global event of its kind, the women's siyum hashas (completion) was also a culmination of a decades-long effort to spread intensive women's study, and was livestreamed to Jewish communities around the world.

"This is a formative moment for us all," added Farber, whose project began as a daily class in the central town of Ra'anana to a handful of women. "Shehihiyahu v'kiyemanu v'higiyanu lazman ha'ze," she said, using a classic blessing of thanksgiving.

Rabbi Benny Lau, founder of the six-year-old Israeli 929 initiative modeled on the daf yomi — which sees thousands read a chapter of the Bible per day in a four-year cycle — indirectly acknowledged in his remarks some of the criticism of the daily practice, namely that a daily review of the texts was too superficial to give it its due.

"This study of the daf hayomi doesn't presume to reach the heights of Jewish scholarship or the depths of inventiveness," said Lau. "It's... the adoption of a language. Of turning a foreign language into a mother tongue. The ability to open a page of gemara, to distinguish between its paragraphs, is a great gift that 100 years ago Rabbi Shapira gave the Jewish people."

After 13 7.5-year cycles, there are now "thousands of women, who come and say, we are coming to learn this intimate language, the deepest, most synchronized with the Jewish pulse," he added.

But another language permeated the hall on Sunday evening, between the murmurs of attendees and caught in the accents of many of the speakers: English. It was a testament to the American roots of the movement to bring Talmud study to Orthodox women, which began some 60 years ago by Modern Orthodox scion Rabbi Joseph B. Soloveitchik of Yeshiva University.

Esti Rosenberg, the founder of the Migdal Oz seminary, took a moment at the event to thank Soloveitchik, her grandfather, and her late father Rabbi Aharon Lichtenstein, also a pioneer of women's Torah study.

"I think it was not so much what they thought about women. It's what they thought about Torah study. I think they could not imagine that there could be people in the service of Hashem [God] who don't learn Torah," she mused.

Chaya Lampert, a teacher from Ma'alot in northern Israel and alumna of the Soloveitchik-founded Maimonides school in Boston, traveled some 2.5 hours on Sunday to accompany her teenage students to the event. Though the school where she teaches does not teach Talmud, the students were given the option to attend. Nine signed up. Ahead of the siyum, they signed up as part of the program to study a page of gemara, for the first time. When they opened it, she said, they discovered that much of the material was familiar from other religion classes.

"I wanted them to see women who learned gemara in a very serious way," she said.

As for whether she would take on the study of daf yomi, she said: "It still seems very ambitious to me, but maybe it will inspire me to do it."

The nine girls from northern Israel were among 3,091 who registered ahead of the event to study a daf, which added up to well over a full Babylonian Talmud, or 8.5 years of an individual daf yomi practice.

To the end, and back to the start

To thunderous applause, they got up on stage, nine representative women who completed the entire Babylonian Talmud in the past 7.5 years. Some had done it twice; one had completed her fourth round. Another woman had recently spent weeks ill and unconscious but after recovering made up for lost time in the hospital and stood there, miraculously, among her peers.

The hosts invited all women in the crowd who completed the Talmud to stand up and recite the traditional concluding prayer with them.

To astounded clapping, some 30 women, of different generations, quietly stood up in a crowd of 3,300.

They had done it: Every day. In sickness, health, good times and bad. For seven and a half years. Dipping into the minutia of Jewish thought even at the most inconvenient of times, finding comfort and inspiration in a convoluted legal conundrum, a perplexing story, or a searing debate.

Together, they said a prayer thanking God for the opportunity. They also thanked their relatives, husbands and children for giving them the time. The final text of the Niddah was read, and then back to the beginning — a lesson on the tractate of Brachot.

What was it, I wondered, that quality they all seemed to share? Not merely the intellectual infatuation and impossible work ethic, but the contentment and sincerity and apparent lack of pretense? What drove them, as many speakers underlined, to daily seek the embrace of the divine through the texts and funnel it into even the most mundane moments of day-to-day life?

Walking out of the hall, humming the song blasted over the speakers as each speaker took the stage, it crystallized: "Enlighten us in Your Torah, and let our hearts cling to Your commandments, unify our hearts to love and fear You, so that we should not be ashamed, and not be humiliated, and we should not stumble, ever," were its lyrics.

It was a song drawn from the morning liturgy, a prayer that begins "You have loved us with an eternal love," a plea to the divine for clarity and understanding of the Torah.

It was love.

Passing on the tradition

This was evident in the host of the evening, Rachelle Fraenkel, a Torah scholar at Nishmat, whose son Naftali was kidnapped and murdered along with two other teenagers in 2014 by Hamas terrorists in the West Bank.

"A small number of us were able to complete the Babylonian Talmud in the 7.5 years, but this joy and festivities and excitement belongs to all of us," she said, referring to all Jews, including the massive New Jersey gathering last week to celebrate the cycle, which drew some 90,000 people.

Invoking Ecclesiastes 12:13, which likens the words of the Jewish sages to spurs (kadorbanot) or well-fastened nails — underlining the texts' inherent sharpness and the role of Torah in keeping people in line — she cited a midrash on the phrase offering another, softer explanation for the word.

"It's like a ball that girls play with (kadur shel banot), that is passed, that is transmitted. It [paints] a picture of a group of girls, standing shoulder to shoulder, happy and excited and playful, passing the ball from hand to hand — not letting it fall. This is how it was passed: Moses received the Torah from Sinai and passed it Joshua and Joshua to the elders and the elders to the prophets and the prophets to the great assembly… and no word was lost," she said.

Urging the crowd to join the daily gemara study, she tilted her head almost conspiratorially.

"We started [the daf yomi cycle] today. But between us, so no one should hear, if daf hayomi is not suitable for you now, for now, there is a daily mishna, or a daily Rambam, or 929 [daily Bible study]… The important thing is that the [Torah] studies enter your veins, that it become part the pulse of your home, that we breathe it in deep, that we live it."

She paused and smiled widely at the crowd, excited and playful.

Catch!

Women's Torah Study:
Necessary, Permissible, or Sinful?

The 13th Siyum Ha-Shas in early January 2020, celebrating the completion of the Talmud by thousands upon thousands of Jews across the globe, saw numerous large, festive gatherings to honor this inspiring accomplishment. One event, which did not receive much attention in most circles within the Orthodox Jewish world, was the Siyum held in Jerusalem on January 5th by the Hadran organization, which seeks to promote and encourage Talmud study by women, and offers resources to assist women who wish to learn Talmud.

The phenomenon of advanced Torah learning by women is a relatively recent development, one which has been steadily progressing since the late 20th century, with a considerable number of high schools and seminaries offering Talmud study opportunities for women, and with a growing interest in *Daf Yomi* among women in certain circles. This development came on the heels of the revolutionary Beis Yaakov movement, founded by Sarah Schenirer, who opened the first school for girls in 1917 in Cracow.

לומדה תפלות

The notion of Torah education for women seems, at first glance, to stand in direct violation of an explicit *halacha*. The Mishna in *Maseches Sota* (20a) cites Rabbi Eliezer's ruling that כל המלמד בתו תורה לומדה תפלות — "Whoever teaches his daughter Torah, teaches her frivolity." (The Gemara [21b] clarifies that this means the parent is considered as though he teaches her "frivolity.") The reason, as the Gemara explains, is כיון שנכנסה חכמה באדם נכנסה עמו ערמומית — "Once wisdom enters a person, trickery enters him." The Meiri (20a) interprets this to mean that as women were not generally educated, a woman who was taught some Torah would not properly understand the material, and would thus end up foolishly presenting herself as a scholar.[1] Similarly, the Rambam[2] writes:

צוו חכמים שלא ילמד אדם את בתו תורה, מפני שרוב הנשים אין דעתם מכוונת

---

1. שמתוך הבנתה ביתר מגדרה היא קונה ערמומית מעט ואין שכלה מספיק להבנה הראויה, והיא סבורה שהשיגה ומקשקשת כפעמון להראות את חכמתה לכל.

2. *Hilchos Talmud Torah* 1:13.

להתלמד, אלא הן מוציאות דברי תורה לדברי הבאי לפי עניות דעתן.

The Sages commanded that a person should not teach his daughter Torah, because most women's minds are not suited for being taught, and they instead turn the words of Torah into words of nonsense, according to their inferior intellect.

Interestingly, however, the Rambam writes earlier in that same passage that although women are exempt from the *mitzva* of Torah study, a woman who learns Torah receives reward. It appears that, in the Rambam's view, a woman's Torah study is, in principle, valuable — and hence worthy of being rewarded — but the Sages nevertheless forbade teaching Torah to women because the potential dangers outweigh the benefits. The likelihood that women — who, in ancient times, were uneducated — would misunderstand and distort the Torah, and the risks this poses, supersede the theoretical value of a woman studying and understanding Torah properly.

The Rambam also draws a curious distinction between the study of *Tanach* and the study of תורה שבעל פה (the oral tradition — Mishna, Gemara, etc.). He writes that although one should not teach his daughter *Tanach*, if he does so, he is not considered to have taught her "frivolity." The *Taz*[3] qualifies the Rambam's ruling, asserting that teaching women the plain meaning of the Biblical text is entirely permissible, even according to the Rambam, and his ruling that one should not teach even *Tanach* to women refers to the in-depth analysis of the text.[4]

The Rambam's comments are cited by the *Shulchan Aruch*.[5] The Rama, based on the *Semag*, adds that a woman is required to learn practical *halacha* so that she knows how to live a proper Torah lifestyle. This follows the view of the *Sefer Chassidim*,[6] who writes that it is obligatory to teach women *halachos* which apply to them, "for if she does not know the laws of Shabbos, how will she observe Shabbos?" The *Sefer Chassidim* notes the tradition[7] that during the time of the Judean king Chizkiyahu, there was no boy, girl, man or woman who was not proficient in the intricate laws of ritual purity — clearly indicating that men and women are both required to master practical *halacha* (which, in the times of the *Beis Ha-Mikdash*, included the laws of purity). The Maharil,[8] interestingly enough, disagreed, and maintained that girls should learn *hala-*

---

3.   Y.D. 246:4.

4.   The *Taz* reaches this conclusion on the basis of the *mitzva* of *hakhel*, the septennial assembly of the entire nation who would stand and listen to the Torah reading. The Gemara in *Maseches Chagiga* (3a) comments that the women are required to attend *hakhel* לשמוע — "to listen," implying that women are allowed to learn the plain meaning of the Torah text.

5.   Y.D. 246:1.

6.   313.

7.   *Sanhedrin* 94b.

8.   Responsa, 199.

cha via tradition, and by asking questions when the need arises, without formal study. Regardless, the Rama rules that women must learn practical *halacha*.[9]

Self-Motivated Women

A number of later *poskim* distinguished between a general policy of teaching Torah to women, and teaching bright, self-motivated women. The *Perisha* commentary to the *Tur*[10] notes that the Rambam and *Shulchan Aruch* speak only of a prohibition against teaching Torah to women, due to the fact that most women will not understand the material properly, but אם למדה לעצמה, אנו רואין שיצאה מהרוב, ולכך...יש לה שכר — "if she teaches herself, then we see that she is not part of the majority, and therefore…she receives reward." Since, as mentioned, the Rambam sees Torah learning as valuable for women in principle, and forbids it as a practical matter due to the potential danger this poses, a woman who displays intelligence and sincerity may study Torah, and, in fact, will be rewarded for doing so.

Likewise, Rav Baruch Epstein, in his *Torah Temima*,[11] cites a responsum by the Italian scholar Rav Shmuel Akavalti, in his *Ma'ayan Ganim*,[12] positing that if a mature, motivated woman wishes to engage in Torah study, she should be encouraged to do so, and should be given such opportunities. Rav Akavalti writes:

הנשים אשר נדבה לבן אותנה לקרבה אל המלאכה...מלאכת ה', מצד בחירתן בטוב...הן הנה תעלינה בהר ה' תשכונה במקום קדשו, כי נשי מופת הנה, ועל חכמי דורן להדרן לאדרן לסדרן, לחזק ידיהן.

> Women whose hearts stir them to approach the work…the work of God, out of their free will…they shall absolutely ascend the mountain of God, reside in His sacred place, for they are wondrous women, and it behooves the sages of their generation to respect them, to glorify them, to make arrangements for them, and to support them.

According to this view, it appears, the prohibition is restricted to compulsory education, forcing girls to study when they are either disinterested in, or ill-suited for, study.

---

9. The *Beis Ha-Levi* (1:6) famously asserts that this requirement is purely pragmatic in nature, and does not apply by force of the *mitzva* of Torah learning. Meaning, according to the *Beis Ha-Levi*, the *mitzva* of *talmud Torah*, which requires daily Torah study, does not apply at all to women. As a practical matter, they must study *halacha* in order to enable them to fulfill the *mitzvos* they are required to observe, but not as a fulfillment of the obligation of *talmud Torah*.

10. Y.D. 246:15.

11. *Devarim*, chapter 11, #48.

12. 10.

But if a woman is sincerely driven to learn, this ought to be encouraged and facilitated.

Similarly, the Chida[13] writes that Bruria, Rabbi Meir's wife, who was famous for her scholarship, was taught Torah because הכירו בה שהייתה כוונתה ללמוד בכל לבה וגדל שכלה — "they discerned that she sought to learn with all her heart and the greatness of her intellect." Although, Rav Eliezer Waldenberg, in his *Tzitz Eliezer,*[14] cites the work *Meshareis Moshe* as refuting this argument, noting that the Sages would not allow making exceptions to this rule based on speculative presumptions of a woman's sincerity and talents. The *Meshareis Moshe* also points to Bruria's eventual spiritual failure as revealing that her scholarly endeavors were less than sincere.[15]

However, the Chida's view is found also in Rav Yerucham Ciechanowicz's *Toras Yerucham,*[16] where he notes *Tosfos'* discussion in *Maseches Bava Kama* (15a) concerning the permissibility of the prophetess Devora serving as a judge. *Tosfos'* treatment of the subject revolves around the disqualification of women as judges, without ever mentioning the prohibition against women studying Torah. Quite obviously, an ignoramus cannot serve as judge, and thus necessarily, Devora must have studied a great deal before serving a judge. *Tosfos* seem troubled not by Devora's scholarship, but by her position as judge, seemingly proving that a self-motivated, capable woman is allowed, and perhaps even to be encouraged, to study Torah.[17]

Changing Times

Thus far, we have seen that there is a clear halachic prohibition against teaching Torah to women, except practical *halacha* which they need to master for proper religious living, and that, according to some *poskim*, women who are bright and sincerely driven

---

13. *Tov Ayin,* 4.

14. 9:3.

15. This refers to the startling story brought by Rashi, in his commentary to *Maseches Avoda Zara* (18b), of how Bruria once ridiculed the Sages' reference to women's limited intellectual capacity, in response to which her husband, Rabbi Meir, sent a student to try to seduce her. The student succeeded in luring Bruria to agree to an adulterous relationship, whereupon she committed suicide. For a thorough discussion and analysis of this unusual passage in Rashi's commentary, see Rav Eitam Henkin's article, תעלומת מעשה דברוריא in *Akdamos,* Elul 5768.

16. O.C. 1.

17. Another relevant source is *Targum* in *Sefer Shoftim* (5:24), which says about Yael — the woman who killed the enemy general Sisera, and was praised for her heroism by Devora — כחדא מנשיא דמשמשין בבתי מדרשין (she is "as one of the women who attend in the study halls"). (This point is made by Rav Yehoshua Pfeffer, at tvunah.org/תלמוד-תורה-לנשים/.)

to learn are allowed to do so, and should even be encouraged and assisted in their pursuit of Torah knowledge.

The Chafetz Chayim, in two contexts, famously established that this prohibition is no longer practically applicable — at least not in its original form — in the modern age. In his *Likutei Halachos*[18] he writes:

ונראה דכל זה בזמנים שלפנינו שכל אחד היה דר במקום אבותיו וקבלת האבות
היה חזק מאד אצל כל אחד ואחד להתנהג בדרך שדרכו אבותיו... בזה היינו
יכולים לומר שלא תלמוד תורה ותסמוך בהנהגה על אבותיה הישרים, אבל כעת
בעוה"ר שקבלת האבות נתרופף מאד מאד וגם מצוי שאינו דר במקום אבותיו
כלל, ובפרט אותן שמרגילין עצמן ללמוד ולשון העמים בודאי מצוה רבה
ללמדם חומש וגם נביאים וכתובים ומוסרי חז"ל כגון מסכת אבות ומנורת המאור
וכדומה כדי שיתאמת אצלם ענין אומנותינו הקדושה, דאל"ה עלול שיסורו לגמרי
מדרך ה' ויעברו על כל יסודי הדת ח"ו.

> It appears that all this [applied] in earlier periods, when everyone resided in his forefathers' locale, and the tradition from the parents was very strong among everybody, following the path upon which one's forefathers treaded... Under such circumstances, we could say that she should not learn Torah, and should rely in her conduct on her upright forefathers. But now, when, in our abundant sins, the tradition of the forefathers is very frail, and it is common not to live at all in one's forefathers' locale, and especially for those who accustom themselves to learn the gentiles' writing and language — it is certainly a great *mitzva* to teach them Chumash, as well as *Nevi'im* and *Kesuvim*, and the religious teachings of *Chazal*, such as *Maseches Avos, Menoras Ha-Maor* and the like, so that the concept of our sacred faith will be affirmed for them. For otherwise, they are likely to stray entirely from the path of God and violate all the fundamentals of the religion, Heaven forbid.

More famously, the Chafetz Chayim penned a letter[19] towards the end of his life lending his support to the newly founded Beis Yaakov movement, affirming not only the permissibility, but the vital necessity, of providing formal education frameworks for girls in the modern era:

---

18. *Sota* 11a.

19. Printed in *Ha-Chafetz Chayim U-Fa'alav*, vol. 3, p. 1113; *Michtavim U-Ma'amarim*, vol. 2, 39. The letter is dated 23 Shevat, 5693 (Februaray 19, 1933) — just seven months before the Chafetz Chayim's passing. He wrote this letter to the community of Frysztak. As we will see later, the chief rabbi of Frysztak had penned a sharply worded condemnation of the Beis Yaakov movement.

כאשר שמעתי שהתנדבו אנשים יראים וחרדים לדבר ה' לייסד בעירם בית ספר
"בית יעקב" ללמוד בו תורה ויראת שמים, מדות ודרך ארץ זו תורה, לילדות
אחב"י, אמרתי לפעלם הטוב יישר ד' חילם ומעשה ידיהם יכונן, כי ענין גדול ונחוץ
הוא בימינו אלה אשר זרם הכפירה ר"ל שורר בכל תקפו והחפשים מכל המינים
אורבים וצודים לנפשות אחב"י. וכל מי שנגעה יראת ה' בלבבו המצוה ליתן את
בתו ללמוד בבית ספר זה, וכל החששות והפקפוקים מאיסור ללמד את בתו תורה
אין שום בית מיחוש לזה בימינו אלה, ואין כאן המקום לבאר באריכות, כי לא
כדורות הראשונים דורותינו, אשר בדורות הקודמים היה לכל בית ישראל מסורת
אבות ואמהות לילך בדרך התורה והדת לקרות בספר "צאנה וראינה" בכל שבת
קודש, משא"כ בעוה"ר בדורותינו אלה. וע"כ בכל עוז רוחנו ונפשנו עלינו להשתדל
להרבות בתי ספר כאלו ולהציל כל מה שבידינו ואפשרותינו להציל.

When I heard that God-fearing people, who have reverence for the word
of God, volunteered to establish in their city a "Beis Yaakov" school in
which to teach Torah, fear of God, character traits and Torah-based
lifestyle to the girls of our brethren, the people of Israel, I said about
their noble work, "May God make their work succeed and their efforts
materialize." For it is a great, urgent matter in these times of ours, when
the current of heresy, Heaven forbid, prevails in all its might, and the
"emancipated ones" of all types lie in ambush to hunt the souls of our
brethren, the people of Israel. Everyone whose heart feels fear of God
has the *mitzva* to have his daughter study in this school. All the appre-
hensions and hesitations about the prohibition against teaching one's
daughter Torah are of no concern at all in these times. This is not the
place to explain at length. For our generation is not like earlier generations. In earlier generations, every Jewish home had a tradition from
the father and mother to follow the path of Torah and religion, to read
the book *Tze'ena U-Re'ena* every Shabbos. This is not the case in these
generations of ours, in our abundant sins. Therefore, we must try, with
all the power of our spirit and soul, to have many such schools and to
[thereby] save all that we are able and is possible for us [to save].

The Chafetz Chayim firmly asserted that teaching Torah to girls was forbidden only
in times when girls were all but certain to receive proper training and education in
religious observance at home. In the modern era, however, this is no longer the case,
and so it is not only permissible, but vitally important, to provide girls with a formal
Torah education.[20]

---

20. Rav Zalman Sorotzkin, in his *Moznayim La-Mishpat* (42), develops this point at length,
and cites as proof the Talmud's description (noted earlier) of the widespread proficiency
in Torah during the time of King Chizkiyahu. Rav Sorotzkin explained that Chizkiyahu

The Modern-Day Threat of תפלות

The rationale likely underlying this ruling is expressed in an account of the Steipler Gaon's authorization of teaching Torah to girls nowadays:

אם לא ילמדוה תורה בזמנינו הוי תפלות טפי, כי תקרא ספרים חיצוניים שבזמנינו
לדאבוננו הדבר פרוץ. לכן מוטב להעסיקה בקריאת ספרי קודש וללמדה...

> If they do not teach her Torah in our times, this will be greater "frivolity," because she will read books of outsiders which in our times, to our dismay, has become common. Therefore, it is better to keep her occupied with reading sacred books and teaching her..."[21]

The prohibition against teaching girls Torah was enacted to safeguard against distortions of Torah which could lead to deviance. But at a time of rampant secularization, when the choice is not between the study of Torah and loyalty to the training received by one's parents, but rather between the study of Torah and the exposure to foreign influence, there is no question that the former is not only preferred, but a necessity.

The Beis Yaakov movement did not, initially, earn universal acceptance, and met with considerable opposition. Rav Chaim Elazar Shapiro of Munkatch, in one of his published letters condemning the Agudath Israel organization,[22] wrote approvingly of those who derisively called the "Beis Yaakov" schools "Beis Esav" as an expression of their contempt. Likewise, Rav Menachem Mendel Halberstam, Chief Rabbi of the Polish town of Frysztak, wrote a letter[23] excoriating Agudath Israel, and included the establishment of girls' schools in his condemnation, viewing the network of schools as a trap ensnaring otherwise innocent, devout young women. Later, the Klausenberger Rebbe[24] wrote — after emphasizing the great reverence he felt towards the Chafetz Chayim — that "the view of our rabbis and forefathers" was to strictly follow the *Shulchan Aruch*'s explicit ruling forbidding teaching Torah to women. The Klausenberger Rebbe noted the severity with which *Chazal* forbade teaching Torah to women, insisting that we cannot deem that which *Chazal* designated as תפלות a vitally necessary

---

succeeded his father, the wicked king Achaz, who had discontinued the service in the *Beis Ha-Mikdash* and eliminated all Torah study in the kingdom. As Chizkiyahu set out to rebuild the nation's religious infrastructure, it became necessary to provide a strong Torah education both for men and for women. Rav Sorotzkin asserts that the rampant secularization of the modern era is comparable in this respect to the period of Achaz's reign, thus making Torah education for girls a matter of absolute necessity.

21. *Orchos Rabbeinu*, vol. 1, p. 193.
22. *Divrei Ha-Iggeres*, 11.
23. Printed in *Tikkun Olam*, p. 80.
24. *Divrei Yatziv*, Y.D. 140.

method for preserving Torah belief and practice.[25] He further raised the concern that dismissing an explicit ruling of the *Shulchan Aruch* with the claim that it no longer applies in modern times is fraught with danger, paving the way for others, of far lower scholarly stature than that of the Chafetz Chayim, to deny the relevance of other rulings at whim.

With time, of course, the Beis Yaakov movement gained acceptance and popularity, and today, it is all but universally accepted to enroll girls in formal Torah education frameworks.

Rav Shlomo Gross, writing in the journal *Or Yisrael*,[26] explained at length the vital need for quality, high-level Torah education for young women in today's day and age, when sinful influences are so pervasive. He noted the Rambam's famous comments in concluding *Hilchos Issurei Bi'a* (22:21) that a man can help avoid inappropriate thoughts by delving into the in-depth study of Torah, because אין מחשבת עריות מתגברת אלא בלב פנוי מן החכמה — "thoughts of illicit relationships prevail only in a mind empty of wisdom." Rav Gross asserts that while the Rambam refers here to men's struggle with lust, nowadays, this admonition is just as pertinent to women, who are exposed to an alluring secular culture, and must be protected through the intellectual and emotional stimulation of advanced Torah study.

Ladies First

Rav Zalman Sorotzkin, in his *Ha-Dei'a Ve-Ha-Dibbur*,[27] develops the thesis that nowadays, the need for formal Torah instruction for girls is so urgent that it takes precedence over formal Torah instruction for boys.

He begins by noting two precedents to this sequence. First, the Midrash[28] comments that when Avraham Avinu arrived in Canaan, he pitched his wife's tent before his own. Rav Sorotzkin shows that this must refer not to an ordinary place of residence, but rather to the tent where people would gather to learn about God. Avraham taught men about monotheism, and Sara taught women.[29] Thus, when the Midrash speaks of Avraham pitching Sara's tent first, this means that he first established Sara's "school," the place where she would teach women, before setting up his own "school" for teaching men.

More famously, when *Bnei Yisrael* first arrived at Mount Sinai, God instructed

---

25. שלא לעשות גדר לאמונה וקדושה ממה שחז״ל קראו תפלות.
26. Monsey, Sivan 5757 (1997).
27. Chapter 17. Rav Sorotzkin also wrote a responsum on the subject, referenced above, note 20.
28. *Bereishis Rabba* 39.
29. See Rashi to *Bereishis* 12:5.

Moshe to communicate to the people the terms of the covenant, introducing His command by stating, כה תאמר לבית יעקב ותגיד לבני ישראל ("So shall you say to the house of Yaakov, and speak to the children of Israel"[30]). The Midrash[31] explains that the term בית יעקב refers to the nation's women,[32] and בני ישראל refers to the men. Moshe was to speak to the women before the men, and for this reason God commanded Moshe first תאמר לבית יעקב and only then תגיד לבני ישראל.

Rav Sorotzkin proceeds to explain that men are to experience the Torah intellectually, delving into the intricacies of Torah wisdom, whereas women are to experience the Torah emotionally, imbibing the Torah's broader messages and values. Therefore, in periods when faith is in decline, and there is widespread religious apathy, women's Torah education is to take precedence over men's Torah education. As the women are the vanguards of the emotional component of Torah tradition, the component which becomes more urgent in periods of general spiritual decay, their Torah education assumes priority over men's. And for this reason, Avraham, who launched a bold campaign to spread monotheism in a pagan world, prioritized women's learning over men's learning. Likewise, upon our ancestors' arrival at Sinai, just weeks after the Exodus, as the people were in the process of withdrawing from the pagan beliefs, values and culture in which they had been submerged for over two centuries in Egypt, the women needed to hear God's message before the men. Rav Sorotzkin implored his readership to make women's Torah education a top priority in the modern era, too, when Torah Judaism has experienced large-scale defection.

Similarly, Rav Moshe Sternbuch ruled[33] that if a community has limited funds, and cannot support both a yeshiva for older boys and a girls' school, priority should be given to the girls' school. He writes that without a religious girls' school, girls will end up studying either in non-Jewish schools, or non-Orthodox Jewish schools, and will thus be at risk of learning to reject Torah values and practice. Their Torah education, which helps ensure that they will grow up as committed Jewish women, takes precedence over advanced Torah education for young men.[34]

---

30. *Shemos* 19:3.

31. *Shemos Rabba* 28.

32. This Midrash, of course, is the reason why "*Beis Yaakov*" was selected as the name of the educational network for girls.

33. *Teshuvos Ve-Hanhagos*, 1:841.

34. Rav Sternbuch writes in this responsum that money donated to a religious girls' school counts towards מעשר כספים — the tithe of one's income for charity, given the importance of such an institution.

Interestingly, Rav Moshe Feinstein (*Iggeros Moshe*, Y.D. 2:113) rules that when it comes to paying tuition for one's daughter's religious education, since providing girls with a Torah education is an outright halachic obligation in the modern era, tuition payment for

What Should Girls Be Taught?

While it is all but universally accepted that girls must be given a strong Torah educa-tion, the curriculum differs from one institution to the next, and is a subject of some controversy. The question, to a large extent, revolves around the issue of how to under-stand the Chafetz Chayim's landmark ruling advocating for formal Torah education for women. On the one hand, one could argue that since his ruling amounts to the neces-sary suspension of a clear-cut *halacha* established by the Gemara and explicitly written in the *Shulchan Aruch*, it must be limited as much as possible. Meaning, although the Chafetz Chayim felt that modern realities call for overriding the prohibition against teaching Torah to women, we are allowed to teach them only the minimum amount necessary to prevent against the dangers which, as the Chafetz Chayim lamentedly observed, would otherwise present themselves. The question then becomes what this minimum amount is, which parts of Torah, and which level of depth, is needed to motivate and inspire young women to commit themselves to leading a Torah life. But however one answers this question, the general attitude, from this perspective, is to preserve the original prohibition and minimize the extent of its suspension that is necessitated by unfortunate modern realities.

More specifically, we might be inclined to limit the Chafetz Chayim's ruling to the study of *Tanach*, the prohibition regarding which, as the Rambam and *Shulchan Aruch* write, is less severe than the study of תורה שבעל פה. Earlier, we saw that the Rambam and *Shulchan Aruch* forbid teaching any Torah to girls (except practical *halacha*, and, according to the *Taz*, the straightforward meaning of *Tanach*), but they add that teach-ing *Tanach* does not amount to תפלות. Conceivably, then, we might limit the Chafetz Chayim's ruling to the study of *Tanach*, which to begin with is not forbidden on the same level of severity as the study of תורה שבעל פה. Indeed, the Klausenberger Rebbe, in the responsum referenced earlier, asserted that the Chafetz Chayim most certainly did not permit anything more than the study of *Tanach*, *mussar*, and practical *hala-cha*, and he warns against expanding the curriculum in girls' schools any further. Rav Shmuel Wosner, too, in *Shevet Ha-Levi*,[35] writes that girls may be taught only the plain meaning of the Chumash text, and practical *halacha*. He emphasizes that girls should not learn the commentaries to the Chumash — not even the commentary of Rashi, as it includes a great deal of interpretations from the Talmud and other sources in תורה שבעל פה, which is forbidden to teach to girls. Rav Wosner adds that it is question-able whether girls should even be taught from the text of the Chumash, as it might be permissible to teach them only orally.

Similarly, Rav Moshe Feinstein[36] ruled that Beis Yaakov schools may not teach

---

girls' education cannot count towards מעשר כספים, a requirement which one fulfills only through charitable payments which are not required as halachic obligations.

35. 6:150.
36. *Iggeros Moshe*, Y.D. 3:87.

Mishna (other than *Pirkei Avos*), noting that the Gemara designates the instruction of תורה שבעל פה to women as תפלות.

The premise underlying this approach, as Rav Wosner writes, is that the classification of Torah taught to women as תפלות remains in place even according to the Chafetz Chayim's ruling. Rav Wosner asserts that even if teaching girls תורה שבעל פה nowadays may seem educationally and spiritually appropriate in light of modern realities, we must accept *Chazal's* determination that such instruction constitutes תפלות, and trust that it will be proven destructive even if at the present time it appears beneficial. The Chafetz Chayim, according to this approach, permitted only the study of *Tanach*, which was never labeled as תפלות, and nothing beyond that.

Alternatively, however, one could interpret the Chafetz Chayim's ruling as establishing that the prohibition against teaching Torah to women, by definition, hinges on the educational needs arising from the unique realities of every era. The designation of such instruction as תפלות was never intended to be absolute, but rather expressed the dangers of teaching Torah to women in Talmudic times, when the preferred method of education was simple, hands-on halachic training in the home. When, however, circumstances are such that formal Torah study significantly increases the chances of a girl growing into a committed, spiritually driven adult, then the appropriate curriculum is the one which, based on our realistic estimation, maximizes the chances of this outcome. According to this understanding of the Chafetz Chayim's ruling, the prohibition against teaching Torah to women from the outset is dependent upon educational realities. As such, the curriculum should be chosen based on those realities, without distinguishing between *Tanach* and תורה שבעל פה unless the educational needs of the time warrant such a distinction.

This approach is taken by Rav Aharon Valkin of Pinsk, in his *Zekan Aharon*,[37] where he addresses the policy of a Beis Yaakov school to include the study of other subjects, besides practical *halacha*. This was done, he said, either לצורך שכלול והתפתחות — for the sake of intellectual sophistication — or שיהא להן כח המושך למשוך את לבות של האבות והבנות הרוצים גם בלימודים כאלו — to attract families who were interested in a broader curriculum. Rav Valkin strongly supports this policy, given the need to ensure that girls do not enroll in educational programs which are not based on Torah tradition. It is wholly insensible, he writes, to be concerned that such study might qualify as תפלות when the alternative is having young women study in institutions that are not run under Torah auspices. Rav Valkin argues that the entire prohibition against teaching Torah to women was because of the spiritual harm this could cause through their incomplete knowledge, but in modern times, the precise opposite is true — a rich, intensive Torah education is the way to protect against spiritual harm. He writes:

בעתות כאלה שהרחוב מלאה הוללות וסכלות בורות וקלות וגם רוח הכפירה
והמינות נזרקה בצעירים, ואנן סהדי כי רק אותן הבתולות הזוכות להסתופף

---

37. *Tinyana*, Y.D. 66.

בבתי ה' ובחצרות אלקינו יפריחו ואין להקב"ה בעולמו כעת אלא ד' אמות של
בית יעקב אשר שם רוח הקדושה שורר, ורק כל באיה לא ישובון עוד לתרבות
רעה חלילה, א"כ לו נניח שנמצא שם קצת למודים שאינן קדש כ"כ, ועיקרן הם
לצורך חולין, יפוי ושכלול, אבל כלום יוכל לצאת תקלה מחולין כאלו שנעשו רק
על טהרת הקדש?

In these times, the street is filled with merrymaking and silliness, ignorance and frivolity, and the spirit of heresy and apostasy has been inject-
ed in the youth, and we ourselves witness how only those young women
who are privileged to spend their time in the houses of Hashem, and who
blossom in the courtyards of our God — and nowadays, the Almighty
has in His world only the "four cubits" of Beis Yaakov,[38] where the spirit
of sanctity prevails, and only all those who enter do not then regress
to wayward conduct, Heaven forbid. Therefore, even if we acknowledge
that they have some studies which are not all that sacred, and they are
primarily for mundane purposes, for "beauty" and sophistication, can
any mishap result from such mundane matters, which are conducted in
the purity of sanctity?

Rav Valkin cites the ruling of the *Shiltei Ha-Gibborim*[39] that although it is forbidden
to teach Torah to gentiles,[40] it is permissible to teach them material from the *Nevi'im*
and *Kesuvim* to expose them to the prophecies and promises given to *Am Yisrael*, as
this might inspire them to join our nation. The prohibition against teaching Torah to
gentiles, Rav Valkin notes, constitutes a Biblical prohibition, and is thus far more stringent than the prohibition against teaching Torah to women, which was clearly enacted
by the Sages. And yet, the prohibition against teaching gentiles is waived when there is
a small chance of inspiring the gentile to convert to Judaism.[41] Certainly, then, when it
comes to Jewish girls, it would be permissible — and is critically important — to teach
them portions of Torah for the sake of attracting more students to religious schools and
thereby saving them from what Rav Valkin calls "the current of heresy which pervades
the streets." He asserts that the Beis Yaakov movement had already saved "several tens
of thousands of souls from eternal death," and so it behooves the movement to build
upon its success by establishing more institutions, even if this requires introducing
portions of Torah which might otherwise be forbidden to teach to women.

---

38.   A play on the Gemara's teaching in *Maseches Berachos* (8a): מיום שחרב בית המקדש אין לו
      להקב"ה בעולמו אלא ארבע אמות של הלכה בלבד.
39.   *Avoda Zara*, 6a in the Rif.
40.   *Sanhedrin* 59a.
41.   Rav Valkin adds that the goal of attracting converts itself is not necessarily one which we
      are generally encouraged to pursue.

According to this perspective, the question as to which material we should encourage women to study essentially depends on the unique circumstances of each era. The prohibition enacted by *Chazal* reflected the educational concerns of that time, which were very different from those of later generations. And therefore, according to Rav Valkin, the decision of what and how to teach girls must be made on the basis of how to best assure their religious growth.

We might add that in contemporary society, when both boys and girls receive an intensive formal education, it stands to reason that all girls and women, or at least most, should fall under the category of self-motivated women, who, according to some *poskim*, are allowed — and even to be encouraged — to study Torah. As we saw earlier, the *Perisha* and others asserted that *halacha* forbids teaching Torah to women because most women were not suited for serious intellectual engagement, but intelligent women who are sincerely driven to learn are to be supported in their quest for Torah knowledge. Nowadays, boys and girls, and men and women, are taught the same subjects on the same level of intensity. We may reasonably conclude, then, that according to the *poskim* noted earlier, women who wish to study Torah on an advanced level nowadays should be encouraged to do so.

Torah and the Competition

One final point which needs to be made is that today, in virtually all Orthodox communities, girls study subjects such as math, science, history and technology, and in many circles, they are encouraged to earn degrees that will grant them entry into the workforce and opportunities for gainful employment. This is particularly so in communities in which men are encouraged to devote themselves to full-time Torah learning or to pursue careers in Torah education and the like, which unquestionably require a second income, given today's cost of living, making it necessary for the wife to have a job.

It is senseless, in the view of this author, to open all intellectual doors for women except the door of advanced Torah learning. If girls are encouraged to study and work in fields such as healthcare, technology, law, accounting and finance, how can we possibly tell them that our sacred texts are off limits to them? What message are we sending if we give our daughters medical textbooks but keep them away from Torah literature? How can we possibly expect them to turn to our Torah tradition as their source of guidance, meaning, inspiration and fulfillment if we show them only the "competition," encouraging them to study all fields except Torah? If a woman is barred from advanced Torah study and urged to pursue the advanced study of other fields, from which she finds intellectual stimulation and satisfaction, she is unlikely to feel the kind of reverence towards, and connection with, Torah that Torah deserves.

But even more importantly, youngsters in today's day and age will, sooner or later, have access to technology that exposes them to all that mankind has to offer, both the good and the bad. How can we possibly expect to compete against the internet if we do not present Torah to them as an appealing alternative?

Any discussion of Torah learning for women must take into consideration what they would be doing if we do not permit them to study Torah. In ancient times, this was, presumably, housework and the like. But today, young women whose free time is not filled with Torah are, very likely, spending their free time on their devices. Can that possibly be a better alternative than the intensive study of Chumash, Gemara or *halacha*?

As we have seen, there is a halachic basis for expanding the Chafetz Chayim's ruling beyond the narrow confines of *Tanach*, *mussar* and practical *halacha*, notwithstanding the fact that many disagreed. If we are going to permit, and encourage, girls and women to be exposed to the world, then we have no choice but to expose them to the richness, depth and profundity of Torah wisdom. If we don't, we can hardly expect them to show loyalty to our sacred tradition instead of to the countless competing alternatives that are out there, and to which they are being regularly exposed.

Conclusion

The *Shulchan Aruch* explicitly forbids teaching Torah to women, besides practical halachic knowledge, but the Chafetz Chayim famously established that in modern times, when growing up in a Jewish household no longer suffices to set a youngster along the path of religious commitment, this prohibition no longer applies, and young women must be given a formal Torah education. The Chafetz Chayim thus lent his fervent support to the Beis Yaakov movement, and though there were some who strongly denounced the new phenomenon of Jewish schools for girls, the Chafetz Chayim's position has been all but universally accepted. Different opinions exist as to the scope and parameters of the Chafetz Chayim's ruling, whether this opens the door for women to study subjects other than *Tanach*, *mussar* and practical *halacha*. A convincing argument could be made that nowadays, when many women pursue higher education and challenging careers, and when technology exposes all of us to, quite literally, the entire world, we have no choice but to bring the profundity of advanced Torah learning to both boys and girls, as otherwise we cannot possibly expect them to develop respect and reverence for, and loyalty to, Torah.

INTERVIEWS

Dr. Leslie Klein

Interviewed on *Headlines with Dovid Lichtenstein*, 14 Elul, 5778 (August 25, 2018)

Sarah Schenirer started Beis Yaakov because she saw there was a whole generation of girls and young women who were very idealistic, and they were being attracted by the "isms" of the day — feminism, socialism, communism — all these movements, which were secular social movements in Poland. These girls were then going off the path. They were in state schools, because the government had compulsory education, much like our government today. They were learning high-level secular studies, and they had nothing Jewish to balance it. Judaism seemed to them like superstition. They had no intellectual connection to Judaism, or any emotional connection, for that matter. And the truth is, they often go hand-in-hand: if you learn, then you understand, and then you feel connected. These girls didn't. And so Sarah Schenirer started Beis Yaakov.

This was when there was compulsory education through high school. Now, today, our daughters are going out into secular workplaces, and some are going to secular college campuses for undergrad (though with so many frum college options, there really is no reason to do that), or secular programs for grad school. We are sending our daughters into those environments, and we're not going to give them that additional level of Torah learning? Girls' secular learning has grown exponentially. Their secular exposure is growing exponentially. You need to match that. Their *kodesh* learning has to be more inspiring than their secular learning.

A person who doesn't learn doesn't grow. If you're not learning, you're not growing. And if you're not growing, then you're going down.

If *chinuch* is about inspiration, about instilling within girls a love of learning and love of Torah, that's what's going to carry them through.

When I started working in a secular workplace, I starting learning "*Nach Yomi.*" I learned a perek of *Navi* every single day. Oftentimes I would learn during my commute. I was literally carrying Torah with me. I had a *Tanach* in my purse when I went to work. That's the kind of thing that keeps you grounded.

Rabbi Shmuel Yaakov Klein

Interviewed on *Headlines with Dovid Lichtenstein*, 14 Elul, 5778 (August 25, 2018)

Sarah Schenirer created a revolution, and she received the approval of *gedolim* such as the Imrei Emes, Rav Chaim Ozer, and others, including the Chafetz Chayim. This became the standard.

A woman makes the *beracha* לעסוק בדברי תורה every morning. The *Magen Avraham* and others explain that they make this *beracha* because they have a connection to the *halachos* which apply to them. So they do have a connection to *limud ha-Torah*, though it's not an intrinsic *mitzva* of *talmud Torah*.

Women today are so integral and so crucial in building the atmosphere of the home in which the children are being raised, and they have a great impact on the level of respect their children have for learning. It is therefore important that women get training in more than just *Tze'ena U-Re'ena*. This is today's reality.

The Kotzker Rebbe once said regarding the *pasuk*, בינו שנות דור ודור ("Understand the years of [prior] generations," *Devarim* 32:7) that the word שנות may be interpreted as "changes." We must understand what changes from one generation to the next. In our world, we cannot follow the standards that were in place once upon a time. It does not work, and it is dangerous to assume that it would work. If women learn to the point where they have respect for learning, and academics is a crucial feature of their lives, then I think it's beneficial for the children they will be raising. Whether it's a Ramban, *Pirkei Avos*, or even the *Kuzari* — each institution and each *kehilla* has to decide on a curriculum. But I would definitely lean towards the notion that there should be strong learning even among girls in our times.

Each *kehilla* should follow the *da'as Torah* that guides it. If you're learning in a Satmar kind of school, they won't even learn Rashi. In many other *chassidish* circles, such as Ger, they will learn Rashi. It depends on each community's *mesora*, though it's hard to speak about a *mesora* when it comes to girls' education, as it is not so old, just over a century. But nevertheless, each *kehilla* will have defined its own approach as to what to teach the girls.

In many *chassidish* communities, and in most — if not all — *Litvishe* communities, girls are taught Chumash and Rashi, without skipping Rashis that bring *Chazal*. This is considered part of תורה שבכתב, and so I suppose the Ramban and other *mefarshim* can also be taught. I wouldn't encourage teaching תורה שבעל פה — Mishna and Gemara. Even though there are those on the modern side of the spectrum who think that even this is acceptable, the conventional wisdom in *chareidishe* communities is that this is classically תורה שבעל פה [and should not be taught]. But even then, when we say that girls need to learn *halacha*, there might be a *machlokes* in a Mishna or a Gemara, or among the *poskim*, and when girls learn the *halachos*, it would be permissible, in my opinion, for them to know about the *machlokes*, how we *pasken*, and why. This is all within the range of permissibility when it comes to girls' education, according to most views. Of course, this does not account for everyone's view.

If the Ramban brings down a Gemara, this is not learning Gemara. This is being privy to a citation that somebody brings from a Gemara. Most of Rashi is quotations from *Chazal*, and to my knowledge, this is not viewed as beyond the pale of what girls' education should include, except in a few *kehillos*.

Mrs. Miriam Kosman

Interviewed on *Headlines with Dovid Lichtenstein*, 16 Adar II, 5779 (March 23, 2019)

If a particular woman wants to learn Gemara, and she finds *sipuk* [satisfaction] in it, and it inspires her, I don't think there's anything wrong with it, and I don't think anybody would say there's anything wrong with it. There have always been women throughout history who have done that. I know the Chida talks about the idea that *Chazal* praised Bruria for learning, which must mean that if a specific woman is open to it and capable of it, then it's a positive thing. There's a *Perisha* that says something similar. So there definitely is whom to rely on. But I think this is totally missing the point.

The real question is why it is that *Chazal* and the Torah world in general has always channeled men and women in different directions as far as learning is concerned. Why is that? What is that meant to accomplish?

I've heard people say that women's minds aren't equipped to learn Gemara. This is something that a lot of people said in the beginning of the feminist movement — that their intentions are good, but women can't be scientists, can't learn physics, can't be doctors and can't be lawyers, they just can't do it. Unless there is some mystical reason why women cannot learn Gemara, I think it would defeat our purpose to insist that they shouldn't if a woman really wants to. I think a lot of men are not suited for learning Gemara. I find it very difficult to say that "men are this" or "women are that." In my experience in life, it's very hard to make those kinds of statements — that men use their *seichel* [intelligence] and women use their *regesh* [emotions]; women are good at multitasking and men are focused. In real life, I don't see this. There are so many things that impact us besides gender — our culture, our nationality, our level of education, our personality types. I'm not comfortable saying that women are not able to learn Gemara — just like not all men are necessarily able to learn Gemara. Learning Gemara is very hard, and a lot of it has to do with level of intellect. So I don't think women can't learn Gemara or become excellent in Gemara. They can do everything else, so why can't they do that?

The Gemara says נשים דעתן קלות. Rashi, I believe, explains נוח להתפתות — women are more easily influenced, swayed and tempted. This is not necessarily a negative statement. Somebody who is more easily influenced is somebody who is more open to another person's opinion, more receptive, and more flexible…

The Rambam says, רוב נשים אין דעתן מכוונת להתלמד. This could be translated to mean that most women are not capable of being taught, but that's probably not what it means, because the Rambam himself says later on that anybody is capable of learning "the discussions of Abayei and Rava" — young and old, man and woman, those who are very bright and those who aren't. So maybe you can translate it to mean that their minds are not geared towards being taught; they're not directed toward being taught in that way, and because of that, they might distort the Torah. The classic way of understanding this is that since women are not obligated to learn, they will not likely give it the seriousness it deserves. You need to be tremendously dedicated to the process to take it through to the end. A person could be excused if, after listening to a whole discussion of Talmud, asking, "Okay, so what's the point of all this? What's the bottom line?" In truth, there might not be a bottom line. If you're not commanded, you'll wonder what the point of it is. And so because women are not commanded, this makes it trivial in their eyes.

My question, then, would be not can they or can't they, but rather should they or shouldn't they. As I said, I think for an individual woman, there are definitely precedents for individual women choosing that way of doing things. But we should ask, why haven't they been doing it until now?

My personal feeling is that it's very important that we have two different voices. I think men are encouraged to uphold a particular voice, and women are being encouraged to uphold a different voice. Either voice, without the other, would create a distorted world. שמע ישראל — כה תאמר לבית יעקב ותגיד לבני ישראל — this refers to two different voices. בני מוסר אביך ואל תטוש תורת אמך. There were always two different voices. Men were always channeled in the direction of learning in a particular way, and women were not channeled in that direction, because these two directions create two different ways of looking at the world. I think that the Gemara-type perspective is a mindset that's about discerning, dividing, grading, comparing — as opposed to bringing things together. It's either/or, making a *chiluk* [fine distinction], trying to figure out why this and not that. That really might not be the direction that a woman's mind should be directed toward.

I find it fascinating that the Maharal uses the word הבאי — the same word [used by the Rambam in describing the danger of teaching Torah to women] — to describe the mistake people make about Aggada. They don't understand that it's really a description of the world, and they think it's הבאי — something trivial. It could be that women have a more natural inclination toward Aggada than towards *halacha*. And it could be that when a mind is not directed towards a particular way of thinking, and then they're taught that particular thing, in their mind it is trivial. And it could be that the Torah wants to uphold this synthesis, so it is directing men and women toward different directions.

The Rambam says רוב נשים — not "all women," but "most women." One of the things we've seen through our observation of the world in recent years is that everything people thought women could never do, they actually could do. They developed all these skills which people were sure a woman could not do, and they excelled. So I don't think it's helpful to say that a woman cannot become a *talmid chacham*, or cannot excel in Gemara learning. If a woman puts her mind to it, she probably could. The question is, should she do it? What price would the world in general pay if that would be her particular mindset? Because then there would be only one voice. There wouldn't be a בית יעקב and בני ישראל. There would be just one voice, and this would have ramifications.

The Rambam says very clearly that a person cannot reach אהבת ה׳ [love of Hashem] without using the intellect. And even when the Rambam writes that women and *avadim* [servants] serve Hashem through *yir'a* [fear, instead of love], he says, מחנכין אותן לעבוד מיראה עד שתרבה דעתן ויעבדו מאהבה — "they are taught to serve out of fear until their knowledge increases and they can serve with love." This is a very clear statement — that the goal is to serve מאהבה, and this is only possible if you have דעת [knowledge]. I think it's exceedingly important that people should be able to connect to Hashem through their דעת, through understanding…

My feeling is that what men do when they're learning Gemara is one aspect of the relationship with Hashem. Traditionally, it has been the women who upheld the other voice. I think that Chassidus, generally, is upholding the feminine voice, the personal connection with Hashem, the *simcha* — this is a more feminine voice. It doesn't necessarily have to be just men and just women upholding these two different voices, but… in general, over history, it's been the women who have been holding up one voice and the men the other voice…

A man has the obligation to be קובע עתים — to set times for Torah learning, to be very structured. A woman needs to keep her fingers on the pulse of her relationship with Hashem, and to learn as much Torah as she needs to feel connected to Him. This is the ultimate goal, and this is going to be different, historically. Today — and this is something I always tell my students — they're getting an advanced degree, and so they need at least that same level of Torah knowledge in order for there to be balance in their lives.

Rabbi Ari Wasserman

Interviewed on *Headlines with Dovid Lichtenstein*, 16 Adar II, 5779 (March 23, 2019)

I think קביעת עתים [set times each day for learning] for women is a lovely idea, but I don't think every woman can do it. And I think that when it comes to women, they have other ways they connect. It's a very subjective thing — what a woman should learn, and how often… I spoke with a number of women who were inspired even if they did not have set times, if they were able to be inspired and stay connected in other ways… Some women were going to a *shiur* twice a week, but many found that kind of scheduling difficult, so what worked better for them was learning during their commute, or in their spare minutes. One woman told me she listened to Rabbi Akiva Tatz, Rabbi Avigdor Miller, or Shira Smiles. For shorter commutes, someone suggested torahalivein5.com, that has very short *shiurim*, or learning on the phone with a *rebbetzin* or with women in the same profession. One woman even recommended learning while nursing. Whatever works — do it. It's a subjective thing. The key is to stay connected. Find a way that works.

Most importantly, learn something that is relevant, and that you enjoy…

Rebbetzin Tzipporah Heller

Interviewed on *Headlines with Dovid Lichtenstein*, 16 Adar II, 5779 (March 23, 2019)

Women have always learned, as we remember from Chumash — Moshe taught the men, and Miriam taught the women. There was never a time when women didn't learn. The question is formal education for women. But nobody could possibly know without learning. People are here in the world to serve Hashem, to bring light to dark places, and people could have enormously good intentions but fail miserably if they don't know. That's why Torah is called "light" — because you cannot know if you do not learn. The question revolves around the formality of learning, and what to learn. Formal learning for women is not an ancient practice, but learning is. There was a time when women learned experientially, through osmosis. But now, the need to learn from a *sefer*, or from a teacher, is universally accepted in the Jewish world.

Women don't stop needing inspiration once they get married, or once they start working. The need to stay inspired is very deep, and people know this instinctively. That's why in virtually every *frum* area there are *shiurim* for women, and they are well attended. They don't give the women degrees, and sometimes they cost money, but they are well attended because of the basic recognition that staying inspired is important and something we have all come to realize.

A person should learn מה שלבו חפץ — what speaks to him. In women's *shiurim*, one basic topic will be *halacha*. Women attend *shiurim* in *hilchos Shabbos, shemiras ha-lashon*, whatever *halachos* they feel they wish to know more about. But there is also a need to stay inspired emotionally, spiritually, and intellectually. And for that, different women have different needs and different interests. But the *shiurim* to which women are drawn today are in *mussar*, Chassidus and *hashkafa*, which all reflect this need.

Learning תורה שבעל פה has historically been discouraged. I don't mean *Pirkei Avos, mussar, machshava* or Chassidus, but rather the give-and-take, the שקלא וטריא in the Gemara. In any event, this is not the learning that women on a basic level are drawn to.

Mrs. Penina Pfeiffer

Interviewed on *Headlines with Dovid Lichtenstein*, 16 Adar II, 5779 (March 23, 2019)

Women learning Gemara is becoming more common in the Modern Orthodox/Religious Zionist world, while in the *chareidi* world it is still an anomaly. I think it's an extension of that which already happened when Sarah Schenirer founded Beis Yaakov. When she went to the *rabbanim*, she showed them that this is what had to be done for that generation of women for them to acquire some kind of knowledge, rather than acquiring it through the home and tradition.

Look at today's generation of women. I have a Master's degree, and this is not unusual. Plenty of women are educated and know a lot about a lot of things. And then, all of a sudden, when it comes to Torah learning, they know very little. Beis Yaakov gives you some kind of education, but it doesn't teach you to read a text, definitely not a Gemara. Something about it seems unbalanced — that you're so knowledgeable in every type of subject, but not when it comes to Torah learning, which is something that guides our life, and something which a lot of women — at least in my world — sacrifice a lot to be a part of (even if their husbands don't learn forever, for those years he is in *kollel*, the women invest so much so their husbands can be more of a *talmid chacham*). To me, learning Gemara seems like a natural extension of that lifestyle.

EAST BAY TIMES

Would you pay $1,000 for this pastrami sandwich?

January 26, 2018
By Linda Zavoral

With old-school delis fading into history, most pastrami purists are willing to pay top dollar for a good stack of cured meat on rye.

But $1,000?

That's what a new restaurant in Cedarhurst on New York's Long Island is charging for its creation. Oscar Martinez, executive chef of DOMA Land & Sea, wanted to do something "extraordinary" for the Feb. 4 Super Bowl, and he certainly has. Get a load of these ingredients:

Prime-grade pastrami is only the start of this decadent sandwich. (PRNewsfoto/DOMA Land + Sea)

First, he starts with prime-grade beef short ribs that have been dry-aged for 28 days. Then he slathers on a rub made with Indonesian Luwak coffee and brines the meat for seven days in Glenlivet 25 Single Malt.

Here's the really extravagant part: The meat is piled onto "gold speck" Argentinean grilled rye whiskey flatbread along with (be still, my arteries) pan-roasted Hudson Valley foie gras; rare white truffles from Alba, Italy; crystal-infused French mustard; and a wasabi-infused roasted beet and cabbage horseradish made with Stoli elite. The sandwich is served with gold-dusted black truffle tater tots with saffron-tomato aioli and garnished with gold leaves and Mr. Pickle's kosher dills.

Plus you get a glass of ultra-swanky Cristal from Louis Roederer Champagne. (You're on your own if you want an egg cream.)

Ready to catch the next red-eye from the Bay Area to New York? If so, DOMA Land & Sea will be serving the sandwich from Monday, Jan. 29, through the day after the Super Bowl, Monday, Feb. 5.

A kosher New American steakhouse, DOMA is open for dinner from Mondays through Thursdays, after sundown Saturdays and on Sundays. The restaurant is closed Fridays.

Is the $1,000 Sandwich Kosher?

DOMA Land & Sea, an upscale kosher steakhouse in Cedarhurst, New York, made the headlines in early 2018 when it announced that it was offering for one week a special sandwich in honor of Superbowl Sunday, which could be purchased for the eyepopping price of $1,000. The beef ribs were dry-aged for 28 days, treated with Indonesian Luwak coffee, and brined for seven days in Glenlivet 25 Single Malt. Other features included grilled rye whiskey flatbread, together with pan-roasted Hudson Valley foie gras and other specialties. The dish was served with a glass of luxury champagne.

The prospect of a $1000 sandwich[1] made entirely from strictly kosher ingredients immediately brings to mind the famous comments of the Ramban in explaining the Torah's command of קדושים תהיו — "You shall be sacred."[2] The Ramban writes:

> והעניין כי התורה הזהירה בעריות ובמאכלים האסורים והתירה הביאה איש באשתו ואכילת הבשר והיין, א״כ ימצא בעל התאוה מקום להיות שטוף בזימת אשתו או נשיו הרבות, ולהיות בסובאי יין בזוללי בשר למו, וידבר כרצונו בכל הנבלות, שלא הוזכר איסור זה בתורה, והנה יהיה נבל ברשות התורה. לפיכך בא הכתוב, אחרי שפרט האיסורים שאסר אותם לגמרי, וציווה בדבר כללי שנהיה פרושים מן המותרות. ימעט במשגל, כעניין שאמרו שלא יהיו תלמידי חכמים מצויין אצל נשותיהן כתרנגולין, ויקדש עצמו מן היין במיעוטו, כמו שקרא הכתוב הנזיר קדוש, ויזכור הרעות הנזכרות ממנו בתורה בנח ובלוט... וגם ישמור פיו ולשונו מהתגאל בריבוי האכילה הגסה ומן הדבור הנמאס...

The concept is that the Torah forbade sexual immorality and prohib-

---

1. Our concern here relates solely to the issue of gluttony, and not to the other halachic questions that arise concerning this sandwich, including the controversy surrounding foie gras, regarding which there might be some concerns involving potential *tereifos* as well as צער בעלי חיים (causing suffering to animals). These issues were addressed at length by Rav Yair Hoffman in an article published on the Yeshiva World News website when the restaurant announced the sale of the $1000 sandwich ("The $1000 Sandwich and Halacha," https://www.theyeshivaworld.com/news/general/1464105/the-1000-dollar-sandwich-and-halacha.html).

2. *Vayikra* 19:2.

ited foods, and permitted relations between husband and wife and the consumption of meat and wine. Therefore, a person of lust can justify being addicted to intimacy with his wife or many wives and to be among those who indulge in wine and meat, and he will utter all obscenities, for this prohibition is not mentioned in the Torah, and this person will act disgracefully within the Torah's authority. The verse therefore comes after outlining the prohibitions which it has strictly forbidden, and commands in a general sense that we must withdraw from excesses — one should limit intimacy, as they said, "...so that Torah scholars will not be found with their wives like roosters,"[3] and one should sanctify himself by reducing his wine intake, just like the verse calls the nazirite "sacred,"[4] and one should remember the evils caused by it as mentioned in the Torah regarding Noach and Lot.... One should also guard his mouth and tongue from being soiled through excessive overeating and from objectionable speech...

According to the Ramban, the command of קדושים תהיו requires us to exercise moderation in our indulgence in physical pleasures. While we are certainly encouraged to enjoy the delights the world offers us,[5] excessive indulgence compromises our dignity and reduces us to not much more than animals. And so the Torah presented the command of קדושים תהיו, demanding that we lead "sacred" lives by putting limits on our indulgence in marital intimacy, food and wine, and thereby live as refined, dignified and noble servants of God. Gluttony and excessive preoccupation with food are "unholy," and thus, in the Ramban's view, violate the Biblical command of קדושים תהיו.

The בן סורר ומורה and Gluttony

Another relevant source is the Torah prohibition of לא תאכלו על הדם (literally, "Do not eat over blood"[6]), which has been interpreted in many ways, including as a prohibition against gluttony. The Gemara in *Maseches Sanhedrin* (63a) comments that a בן סורר ומורה — the child who rebels against his parents by stealing their money to consume large quantities of meat and wine — is guilty of violating this prohibition. Accordingly, the Rambam writes in *Sefer Ha-Mitzvos*[7] that the command of לא תאכלו

---

3. *Berachos* 22a.

4. *Bamidbar* 6:5.

5. The Talmud Yerushalmi (*Kiddushin* 4:12) teaches, עתיד אדם ליתן דין וחשבון על כל שראת עינו ולא אכל — "In the future, a person will be called to judgment for everything his eyes saw but he did not eat."

6. *Vayikra* 19:26.

7. *Lo ta'aseh* 195.

מהיות זולל וסובא במאכל ובמשתה introduces a Biblical prohibition forbidding us על הדם — בימי הנערות ובתנאים מתוארים בדין סורר ומורה — "from being gluttonous with food and drink during youth, in the conditions outlined in regard to the law of the wayward son." And although this prohibition applies specifically to a youngster at the age when he can become a בן סורר ומורה,[8] nevertheless, the *Sefer Ha-Chinuch*[9] explains that the broader message of this prohibition is relevant to all people. He writes: רוב חטאות בני אדם יעשו בסיבת ריבוי האכילה והשתיה — "most of people's sins are the result of excessive eating and drinking." Elaborating further, the *Sefer Ha-Chinuch* writes:

המזונות הם עיסת החומר, והתבוננות במשכל וביראת אלוקים ובמצוותיו היקרות,
הוא עיסת הנפש. והנפש והחומר הפכים גמורים הם כמו שכתבתי בראש הספר.
ועל כן בהתגבר עיסת החומר תחלש קצת עיסת הנפש.... ועל כן תמנענו תורתנו
השלמה לטובתנו מהרבות באכילה ושתיה יותר מדאי, פן יתגבר החומר על הנפש
הרבה עד שיחליאה ויאבד אותה לגמרי.

Food is the "dough" of the physical being, and contemplating wisdom and fear of God and His precious commands is the "dough" of the soul. And the soul and the physical being are polar opposites, as I have written at the beginning of this book. Therefore, when the "dough" of the physical being increases, the "dough" of the soul is weakened somewhat... For this reason, our perfect Torah prevents us for our benefit from excessive eating and drinking, lest the matter overtake the soul to the point where it becomes ill and is then completely lost.

Technically speaking, the *Sefer Ha-Chinuch* proceeds to explain, the prohibition pertains only at the beginning of halachic adulthood, so that מאותו הזמן יקח מוסר לכל ימיו — "one will take this lesson from that time throughout his life." It is clear that although the technical prohibition applies only for the brief period when a boy can become a בן סורר ומורה, the message is directly relevant to people of all ages. This point is made even more explicitly by the *Mishna Berura*:[10]

אף שלאחר שעבר ימי הנערות לא נתחייב בתורה מיתה על אכילה כזאת מ"מ נוכל
לראות כמה מגונה ומכוער הדבר ביותר...

Although one is not liable to execution by the Torah for eating of this nature after the days of youth have passed, nevertheless, we can see how exceedingly repulsive and loathsome this is...

---

8. The Gemara (*Sanhedrin* 69a) establishes that a boy can become a בן סורר ומורה only during the first three months after becoming a halachic adult.

9. 166.

10. 156:2.

The *Mishna Berura* also adds that irrespective of this prohibition, gluttony is certainly forbidden by force of the command of קדושים תהיו as understood by the Ramban.

Moreover, a number of *poskim* appear to indicate that this prohibition in fact applies throughout one's life, and not only during the period when a youth can become a בן סורר ומורה. The *Magen Avraham*, in his list of Biblical commands that apply each day,[11] includes the prohibition of gluttony, writing simply: שלא לאכול ולשתות דרך זולל וסובא — "not to eat and drink in a gluttonous manner." Likewise, the *Aruch Ha-Shulchan*[12] introduces his discussion of the *halachos* relevant to meals by stating: אסור — לאכול ולשתות דרך זולל וסובא...והרמב״ם חשיב לה בלא תעשה גמורה במניין המצוות "It is forbidden to eat and drink in a gluttonous manner...and the Rambam considers this an outright prohibition in his listing of the commands." Like the *Magen Avraham*, the *Aruch Ha-Shulchan* strongly implies that the prohibition of gluttony applies to all people of all ages.

This also seems to have been the view of Rav Moshe Feinstein, in his responsum on the subject of smoking marijuana.[13] Rav Moshe establishes that this is forbidden not only because of the danger posed to one's health, but also for a different reason:

ועוד, שהוא גורם תאווה גדולה אשר הוא יותר מתאוות אכילה וכדומה הצריכים
להאדם לחיותו, ויש שלא יוכלו לצמצם ולהעביר תאוותם, והוא איסור החמור
שנאמר בבן סורר ומורה על תאווה היותר גדולה שיש לו לאכילה אף שהוא
לאכילת כשרות, וכ״ש שאסור להביא עצמו לתאווה גדולה עוד יותר ולדבר שליכא
שום צורך להאדם בזה...

> Additionally, it causes a powerful craving that exceeds the craving for food and the like which a person needs for sustaining himself, and some will be unable to limit themselves and eliminate this craving. This is the strict prohibition stated in reference to the wayward son regarding the more powerful craving which he has for food, even though it is for kosher food. *A fortiori*, it is forbidden to bring oneself to an even more powerful craving, and for something which a person has no need for.

Rav Moshe clearly assumes that the prohibition derived from the בן סורר ומורה is applicable to all people. And, he defines this prohibition as forbidding one to engender cravings beyond the natural human craving for food and other basic necessities. Accustoming oneself to excessive eating has a certain addictive effect, as it results in a craving for unreasonably large quantities of food — and this is precisely, in Rav Moshe's view, what the prohibition of the בן סורר ומורה forbids.

It emerges, then, that gluttonous eating violates the command of קדושים תהיו as

---

11.   156:2.

12.   O.C. 157:2.

13.   *Iggeros Moshe*, Y.D. 3:35.

understood by the Ramban, and might also violate the prohibition of לא תאכלו על הדם according to the Rambam.

Moreover, the *Peri Megadim*[14] cites the *Shela* as remarking that האוכל אכילה מרובה — excessive eating — violates the Torah prohibition of השמר לך פן תשכח את ה׳ — "Take caution, lest you forget God,"[15] as well as the prohibition of בל תשקצו — engaging in revolting activities.[16] The Torah issues the warning of השמר לך פן תשכח את ה׳ after foreseeing the time when *Bnei Yisrael* would conquer the Land of Israel and then enjoy the homes, fields, vineyards and cisterns left by the vanquished Canaanites, and they would "eat and be satiated."[17] The Torah urges us to exercise caution when enjoying prosperity not to "forget God," and the *Shela* understood this warning as a prohibition against excessive indulgence in food, which leads us to forget the mission for which we were brought into this world — to serve our Creator.

In the view of this author, it is clear and obvious that spending $1,000 for a kosher sandwich falls under the category of נבל ברשות התורה, acting "disgracefully" within the technical halachic boundaries of permissible conduct. Irrespective of the size of the sandwich in question, simply paying such an exorbitant sum for a meal bespeaks a grossly excessive preoccupation with food. If, as the Ramban teaches, overindulgence constitutes "unholy" behavior that the command of קדושים תהיו proscribes, then it cannot be denied that spending $1,000 on a sandwich is likewise "unholy" and thus forbidden. And, the Mishna in *Maseches Sanhedrin* (71a) establishes as one of the defining characteristics of the בן סורר ומורה his stealing money from his parents to pay for his indulgence in food and wine. Part of the definition of זולל וסובא is an obsession with food that incurs unreasonable costs — a definition that would certainly seem to be met by the purchase of a sandwich for $1,000 because of its unique taste and quality. And, it can hardly be doubted that spending this outrageous sum on a sandwich constitutes "forgetting God" no less than consuming an outrageous quantity of food.[18]

---

14. *Mishbetzos Zahav*, 170:10.

15. *Devarim* 6:12. The *Shela* actually considers the command השמר לך פן תשכח את ה׳ as two separate prohibitions, following the principle that the words השמר and פן both introduce prohibitions (*Eiruvin* 96a), such that excessive eating violates a total of three Torah prohibitions.

16. *Vayikra* 11:43, as explained by the Gemara, *Makkos* 16b.

17. ואכלת ושבעת, *Devarim* 6:11.

18. Some might counter that a distinction exists between grotesquely wasteful spending, and gluttony. The Ramban's discussion of קדושים היו, and the sources cited here regarding זולל וסובא, speak about the quantity of food consumption, and not about the waste of money involved. It could be cogently argued, therefore, that these prohibitions relate to the volume one consumes, and not to the price one spends on his consumption, such that one violates these prohibitions by spending $5 on a box of donuts and proceeding to

Reciting a *Beracha* Over Gluttonous Feasting

Having established that purchasing and eating such a sandwich likely falls under one or several Torah prohibitions, we need to consider the question of whether one who chooses to nevertheless eat this product would recite a *beracha*. The Rambam rules in *Hilchos Berachos*[19] that one who eats food that is prohibited by *halacha* — regardless of whether the food is prohibited on the level of Torah law or by force of rabbinic enactment — does not recite a *beracha* over such food. Likewise, no blessing is recited after eating forbidden food. The Rambam emphasizes that this applies regardless of whether the person committed the violation intentionally or inadvertently. The *Shulchan Aruch*[20] rules accordingly:

> אכל דבר איסור אף על פי שאינו אסור אלא מדרבנן...אין מברכין עליו לא בתחלה ולא בסוף.

> If one ate a forbidden item, even if is forbidden only by the rabbis...a *beracha* is not recited, neither before nor after [eating].

The *Mishna Berura* (3), citing earlier sources, explains that since one violates God's will through this act of eating, he cannot possibly recite a blessing. The recitation of a blessing expresses gratitude for the opportunity to enjoy the world which God has created for us, and therefore, reciting a blessing over forbidden enjoyment is essentially blasphemy, thanking God for a forbidden pleasure. The source of this ruling is the Gemara's comment in *Maseches Sanhedrin* (6b) that if one steals grain and produces bread from it, if he then recites a *beracha* over the consumption of this food, אין זה מברך אלא מנאץ — this is not a blessing, but rather blasphemy.

Significantly, this adage — אין זה מברך אלא מנאץ — was said not with regard to intrinsically forbidden food, such as meat from a non-kosher animal, meat from a kosher animal that was not properly slaughtered, or produce which was not properly tithed, but rather regarding perfectly kosher food that was obtained illicitly. The impropriety of a *beracha* over prohibited eating stems not from the inherent status of the food, but rather from the forbidden nature of the act of eating it. This conclusion also emerges from the very concept expressed by the phrase אין זה מברך אלא מנאץ, which states that a blessing recited over an act that violates God's will is, by definition, blasphemy. Logic dictates that this is true regardless of the circumstances which make

---

eat the entire box in a single sitting, but not when spending $1,000 on a reasonably sized sandwich. In the view of this author, however, spending such an outrageous amount of money for food simply because of its high quality is truly gluttonous, in the sense that it bespeaks a repulsive obsession with, and prioritization of, physical enjoyment, at least as much as — and likely far more than — eating excessive quantities of food.

19. 1:19.
20. O.C. 196:1.

the act prohibited. If one's eating is in violation of *halacha*, for whatever reason, no *beracha* can be recited.[21]

Indeed, the *Mishna Berura*[22] writes that if a *nazir*, or someone else who vowed to abstain from wine, drinks wine in violation of his vow, no *beracha* is recited — even though the wine is perfectly kosher and permissible for everybody else — since the act of drinking violates *halacha*. On the basis of this ruling, Rav Shlomo Zalman Auerbach[23] determined that if one consumes food which causes him harm — such as somebody with a wine allergy who drinks wine — no *beracha* is recited, as this act of consumption violates the Torah's command to maintain one's physical wellbeing. Similarly, Rav Yitzchak Zilberstein,[24] citing his father-in-law, Rav Yosef Shalom Elyashiv, ruled that a diabetic who eats sugary food, such as cake, does not recite a *beracha acharona* after eating, since eating the cake endangers his health and thus violates the Torah. Interestingly, Rav Elyashiv ruled that the diabetic does recite a *beracha* before eating, because the first bit of cake which he ingests does not, presumably, seriously undermine his health, and it therefore warrants a *beracha*. A *beracha acharona*, however, is required only after the consumption of a *ke-zayis* (approximately thirty grams), and such a quantity of cake likely poses a threat to a diabetic. Therefore, eating this amount of cake is forbidden for the diabetic, and so, by extension, a *beracha acharona* cannot be recited.[25]

---

21. This premise can also be proven by the fact that the prohibition against reciting a *beracha* over forbidden food applies even to food prohibited only by force of rabbinic enactment. The *Nesivos* (234:3) famously asserted that by definition, violations of rabbinic enactments require willful intent to disobey the rabbis, because the action itself is not fundamentally wrong, and the problematic nature of the act relates only to the disobedience it expresses. We might thus conclude, at least according to the *Nesivos*, that the principle of אין זה מברך אלא מנאץ applies not only to intrinsically forbidden food, but anytime an act of eating transgresses halachic guidelines.

22. 196:1.

23. *Halichos Shlomo — Seder Leil Pesach*, p. 225.

24. *Chashukei Chemed, Berachos*, 36a.

25. Many *poskim* addressed the question that arises in various situations where one realized after reciting a *beracha* over food, before taking a bite, that he is not permitted to eat that food. For example, numerous *poskim* (see, for example, Rav Moshe Stern, *Be'er Moshe*, 4:24; Rav Ovadia Yosef, *Yabia Omer*, vol. 10, O.C. 6) ruled that if one recited a *beracha* over milk or dairy food within six hours of eating meat, he should take a sip of the milk or a bite of the food so that his *beracha* will not have been recited in vain. The rationale for this ruling is that the prohibition against consuming milk within six hours of eating meat is less severe than the prohibition of reciting a *beracha* in vain, and so the prohibition against consuming milk during this period is waived to protect against the recitation of a *beracha* in vain. Likewise, Rav Ovadia Yosef (in the aforementioned responsum) rules

Accordingly, we might conclude that in the case of gluttonous eating, too, a *beracha* should be recited before eating, since the initial quantities are permissible, and the

---

that if somebody recited a *beracha* over food in the morning and then realized he had not yet recited *Shacharis* — and thus eating is forbidden, due to the prohibition against eating before praying in the morning — he should take a bite of the food so his *beracha* will not have been recited in vain. And already the Rama (O.C. 275:5) ruled that if one recited a *beracha* over food after Shabbos and then realized he had not yet recited *havdala*, and thus eating is forbidden, he should take a bite of the food and then recite *havdala*.

Seemingly, according to what we have seen, the *beracha* in any event was recited in vain, given the rule of אין זה מברך אלא מנאץ, which forbids reciting a *beracha* over a prohibited act of eating. Therefore, even if the prohibition that forbids eating is less severe than the prohibition against reciting a *beracha* in vain, there is no purpose served in partaking of the food after reciting the *beracha*, since the *beracha* has already been recited over a halachically proscribed act of eating, and has thus been recited in vain. In the cases described, then, it would seem plainly obvious that one should not take a bite after reciting the *beracha*, and yet, as mentioned, numerous *poskim* ruled that one should, in fact, eat the food in violation of a prohibition to avoid being in violation of the more grievous prohibition of ברכה לבטלה (a *beracha* recited in vain). (This question was raised by Rav Shalom Schwadron, *Da'as Torah*, O.C. 271, in reference to the Rama's ruling regarding *havdala*. His answer is relevant only to that particular case, and does not explain the rulings mentioned earlier regarding eating dairy after meat and eating before *Shacharis*.)

One possible explanation is that although *halacha* forbids reciting a *beracha* over forbidden food, such a *beracha* is not considered a ברכה לבטלה. One who recites this *beracha* is not guilty of reciting a *beracha* in vain — because it was, after all, recited over food — but is in violation of the separate prohibition of אין זה מברך אלא מנאץ. Therefore, if, for example, one mistakenly recited a *beracha* over food intending to eat in the morning before praying, and realized his mistake before taking a bite, he cannot undo the violation of אין זה מברך אלא מנאץ, but he can avoid the prohibition of ברכה לבטלה, and so the *poskim* mentioned above rule that the individual in this case should take a bite.

Alternatively, one could argue that accidentally reciting a *beracha* over forbidden food does not violate the prohibition of אין זה מברך אלא מנאץ. By definition, ניאוץ — "blaspheming" — requires intent. And thus when the Gemara establishes that reciting a *beracha* over prohibited food constitutes ניאוץ, it means that one who ate in violation of *halacha* may not blaspheme God by knowingly including a blessing to Him in the framework of a sinful act (even if the sinful act was committed inadvertently). But if one recited a *beracha* in preparation for mistakenly eating in prohibited fashion, the *beracha* cannot possibly be regarded as "blasphemy," as there was no willful intent to include God in the context of a forbidden act. As such, the *poskim* addressed the question of whether one should then take a bite so that the blessing will not have been recited in vain.

prohibition against gluttony is violated only by eating unreasonably large amounts. And even after eating, perhaps, a *beracha acharona* is required, as no violation was committed through the consumption of the initial *ke-zayis*.

However, while this might likely be correct in the case of one who consumes grotesquely large quantities of food, it would seem that this would not be true of one who spends an outrageous sum for a sandwich. Even from the first bite, this eating can truly be considered "gluttonous" by virtue of the price paid, such that a *beracha* may not be recited before or after eating.[26]

Kosher Certification for Gluttony

The question then becomes whether the *kashrus* agency supervising the restaurant may certify the $1,000 sandwich as kosher, despite the likelihood that partaking of such a sandwich violates one or several Torah prohibitions.

Recent *poskim* debated the question of whether an establishment may be given a certificate of *kashrus* if the food is perfectly kosher but the establishment facilitates halachically proscribed activities. Rav Eliezer Waldenberg, for example, in *Tzitz Eliezer*,[27] addressed the situation of an Israeli hotel which served kosher food but offered its guests dairy products immediately after a meat meal, and insisted that the *mashgiach* overlook this overt breach of *halacha*. Rav Waldenberg adamantly forbade granting kosher certification to this hotel, asserting that this constituted נתינת יד רשמית לפושעים המלעיגים על דברי חכמים — "lending official support to violators who ridicule the words of the sages." And although ensuring the food's *kashrus* yields the benefit of saving guests from Torah violations, Rav Waldenberg writes that in his view, this benefit is outweighed by the damage caused by formally authorizing the outright violation of the rabbinic prohibition against eating dairy food after meat.

Rav Ovadia Yosef, in *Yabia Omer*,[28] disputed Rav Waldenberg's ruling. He conceded that were the rabbis to have the authority to enforce halachic observance, they would certainly enlist any measures necessary to stop hotels from offering dairy foods after a meat meal. However, under current conditions, such enforcement is not possible, and so it is far preferable to ensure the *kashrus* of Israeli hotels so that the large numbers

---

26. One could argue that prohibitions such as קדושים תהיו and זולל וסובא relate to one's general lifestyle and priority scale, and thus no particular act of eating, outrageously excessive as it might be, can be specifically labelled as a forbidden act of eating. Our assumption, however, is that there can be an act of eating so utterly abhorrent that it cannot be labelled as anything other than gluttony that is clearly in violation of the Torah.

27. 11:55.

28. Y.D. 8:12.

of guests — many of whom, as Rav Yosef points out, blindly assume that all Israeli hotels serve only kosher food — would not be in violation of the Torah's dietary laws. Protecting these guests from severe Torah violations is far more important, in Rav Yosef's opinion, than protesting the hotel's blatant disregard of the prohibition against consuming milk after a meat meal.

Rav Yosef proceeds to cite Rav Moshe Feinstein's response[29] to a rabbi in Mexico City who convinced the Jewish owner of a sports center to place the food served by the establishment under kosher supervision, but the owner insisted on allowing patrons to eat dairy products after the meat meal. Rav Moshe permitted the arrangement, explaining that *kashrus* certification "does not attest that they [the food sellers] are righteous...but rather that the rabbis watch and supervise the premises [to ensure] that the products sold there are kosher products." Certifying the food being served will not in any way be understood as authorizing all that transpires in the establishment, and so the *kashrus* agency is permitted to certify the food as kosher even if patrons will be eating dairy food after a meat meal. To the contrary, Rav Moshe credits the rabbi overseeing the *kashrus* of the foods with "saving thousands of souls from forbidden foods," adding, "even preventing evildoers as much as possible from violating prohibitions is a great *mitzva*."

Thus, whereas Rav Waldenberg forbids certifying an establishment as kosher if it allows forbidden activities, even if the food is kosher, Rav Ovadia Yosef and Rav Moshe Feinstein permit and even encourage ensuring the *kashrus* of such an establishment, arguing that the certification pertains only to the food's status and in no way expresses approval of everything that transpires in the facility.[30]

Returning to the $1,000 sandwich, it would seem that even according to the lenient position of Rav Yosef and Rav Moshe, a sandwich offered for this price should not be regarded as kosher by the supervising *kashrus* agency. Unlike in the cases addressed by the aforementioned *poskim*, in this instance, the sandwich itself is forbidden for consumption, for the reasons discussed. As such, in the view of this author, it is incumbent upon the *kashrus* agency certifying the establishment to publicly declare that the $1,000 sandwich is not certified, as it violates both the letter and, most certainly, the spirit, of *halacha*.

---

29. *Iggeros Moshe*, Y.D. 1:52.

30. Rav Waldenberg responded to Rav Yosef's argument in a later ruling, published in *Tzitz Eliezer*, vol. 12, תוספת לחלק יא, 55.

INTERVIEWS

Rabbi Aryeh Leibowitz

Interviewed on *Headlines with Dovid Lichtenstein* 25 Shevat, 5778 (Feb. 10, 2018):

I think that when you talk about זולל וסובא as an איסור דאורייתא, it is very, very difficult to define exactly what that includes. We have very high-end restaurants in Manhattan, and now, apparently, here in the Five Towns. Is somebody who orders a $60 steak in a restaurant in violation of the איסור דאורייתא of זולל וסובא?

I was once at a מכירת חמץ with Rav Willig *shlit'a* in Riverdale, together with about forty other *rabbanim*. One of the *rabbanim* sitting next to me showed me an inventory sheet which he had. A fellow selling *chametz* through him evaluated his Scotch collection at $150,000. There's a lot of that going on. In general, there is excess, and it is not spiritually healthy for us. But to say להלכה that one would not recite a *beracha* on something because we are so certain that it is an איסור דאורייתא — I think that's a little much...

Where do we draw the line in terms of giving *hashgacha* when it comes to things that do not pertain to the food's status vis-à-vis יורה דעה? This is a very, very challenging question. For example, you have a place that plays secular music which you find offensive. Do you not give a *hashgacha*? How *tzniyusdik* do the waitresses have to dress? There are all sorts of questions that come up.

It seems to me by observing the *kashrus* industry that they've decided, for the most part — with certain exceptions — to keep it to *kashrus*, that all they are certifying is the *kashrus*, and every person needs to use his common sense about what's right for him. There are sports restaurants with televisions all over, under very reputable *hashgachas*, and some people wonder how they do this, given that even the commercials shown during the games are undoubtedly a breach of *tzniyus*. This is true. But the *kashrus* agencies have made the decision that it would be impossible to police everything, every detail.

It is very difficult to make a judgment call on each case. If you have a restaurant with an especially aged bottle of Scotch that they sell for $100 or $50 a shot, this seems ridiculous, but it is very difficult to know where to draw the line.

In my opinion, what we can take from all of this, the message of it all, is not to look at the restaurant as the "bad guy" or to the *rabbanim* as the "bad guys," but for all of us to do an internal חשבון הנפש. If this is what a kosher restaurant decided would be a successful marketing strategy, to appeal to what is really a terrible *midda* of the community — a tremendous desire for higher and higher levels of *gashmiyus* — then as a community, and as individuals within the community, we have to really do a חשבון הנפש and think about what can be done to change this culture of *gashmiyus*. In our personal lives, if we are blessed with certain things, maybe we should be a little more *tzanua* about it. A communal חשבון הנפש is certainly in order, and maybe this [$1,000 sandwich] brings it to the forefront.

It's always healthier, rather than shooting the arrows at others, to take a look at ourselves. We should be asking, how do we enhance the value of what really matters in life, of things that are truly valuable? We don't have to be פרושים like Rav Aharon Leib Shteinman, but perhaps we should introduce a little more פרישות, some level, into our lives, and try to create a counterculture.

It's known in the *kashrus* industry that we are giving a *hechsher* on the *kashrus* of the meat, that the pastrami is kosher. We are not suggesting that you go there and spend your money there. *Baruch Hashem*, there are a lot of less expensive eateries where people can go… This is the way *hashgachas* in general have worked. Making decisions about issues that lie outside the area of *kashrus* is not a simple matter, unless there is a clear, blatant violation, such as Shabbos desecration. This is much easier because it is very clear to identify. But to identify excess, something that extends beyond what we consider acceptable levels of *gashmiyus*, is not easy. Similarly, there are *halachos* of *tzniyus*, but it is much more challenging to decide whether one should not be in a restaurant because of a commercial aired on the television.

It is the responsibility of the *rabbanim* — myself included — to try and inspire the community and ourselves to reach for higher levels in terms of valuing that which is truly valuable, and to make our decisions accordingly.

SCIENTIFIC
AMERICAN

I Hate to Break it to You, but You Already Eat Bugs

June 5, 2013
By Kyle Hill

I grabbed a box of cereal out of my cabinet. The flakes smelled stale, but I was hungry enough. I poured a cup or two into a bowl, followed by a splash of milk. Well into my third bite, I knew that stale cereal wasn't all I was eating. I saw what were likely grain beetles–small food pests capable of chewing through cardboard to get at your conflakes–swimming in the bottom of the bowl, extending their legs in hopes of finding a flake–like a desperate swimmer in a flood. I immediately discarded the cereal, repulsed by the other bugs I had surely already eaten. But while I didn't always see them, I had been eating bugs my whole life. So have you.

The UN's Food and Agricultural Organization recently released a report [PDF] touting the nutritional and environment benefits of eating our many-legged friends (or pests), which scuttled into all corners of the media. (You can read a very thorough write-up bug eating at io9 and here at Scientific American.) The gist is that insects may end up solving a real food crisis by giving up their lives for human consumption. To most of the world, this was old news–insects are considered staples and even delicacies in many cultures. But Western media still let out an audible cringe at the thought of crunching down on chitin.

Ignorance is bliss…

Out of Sight, Still In Your Mouth

You're deluding yourself if you think farming is as clean as making a microchip. We are always on insect territory. Try as we might with insecticides and other engineered poisons, bugs crawl all over our food to feed (and procreate) on it. When we harvest and package our crops, a lot of bugs come along for the ride. Be aware, all the hitch-hikers aren't removed. At least there are limits on how many bugs the Food and Drug Administration (FDA) lets you unknowingly eat.

The FDA's Defect Levels Handbook lays it all out. Staples like broccoli, canned toma-toes, and hops readily contain "insect fragments"–heads, thoraxes, and legs–and even whole insects. (I won't tell you about the rat hair limits…) Fig paste can harbor up to

13 insect heads in 100 grams; canned fruit juices can contain a maggot for every 250 milliliters; 10 grams of hops can be the home for 2,500 aphids.

All of these are merely aesthetic limits. It's seemingly for your mental well-being. Like a child moving a mountain of peas around on a plate until it looks like she's eaten more, the insect legs, bodies, and heads are less noticeable to us at the FDA's proposed concentrations. Your shredded wheat won't look like shredded thrips anytime soon. Anything over these limits would be aesthetically unpleasing, but it's doing you no harm. You obviously aren't keeling over from eating too much carapace.

The "action levels" sets by the FDA are for maximum insect contamination, so you ultimately ingest less than these limits. Nevertheless, bugs are making it into your gut whether you see them or not. Layla Eplett over at the Scientific American Guest Blog estimates that "an individual probably ingests about one to two pounds of flies, maggots and other bugs each year without even knowing it."

So, I hate to break it to you, but you already eat bugs. Not nearly enough for you to recognize it or to potentially harm you, but down the hatch they go. You don't really notice now, so just how much bug would have to be in your food for you to notice? If Westerners aren't ready to dive into katydid kabobs, we can at least calculate the equivalent amount of bug burgers in your food.

Bugs like thrips and aphids have to be tiny indeed to pepper our food with their parts without us noticing. By my estimation, 5,000 aphids weigh about the same as a paperclip (each aphid being 1/5 of a milligram). If you are feelings adventurous, that means you could mash and mold 567,000 of the little plant suckers into a leggy equivalent of a Mac Donald's quarter pounder.

You should be happy the bugs that call our food home aren't bigger. The largest insect with reliable data on its mass is New Zealand's Giant Weta, weighing about the same as a jumbo supermarket chicken egg. Just four of these bugs would be the same weight as a Big Mac. But you'll thankfully never find one of these insects in your food (you'd notice the crunch).

Following FDA guidelines, you don't have to order a bug burger to eat the same amount as one. If you are a fan of spinach, the action limit is 50 or more aphids, thrips and/or mites per 100 grams. That's spinach that is 0.01% bug by weight. By the time you eat 1,000 kilograms of spinach you have eaten a quarter pounder's worth of aphid. (Popeye has eaten a lot of bug burgers.)

Bug beer is even better. Many of the bugs and bug parts will be filtered out during brewing, but the FDA's limit on the hops that go into the tank is 2,500 aphids per 10 grams of hops. That's right, 5% of the total weight of the hops making your summer ale can be bug. ...

Dessert is the same. If we consider the "insect parts" that the FDA limits to be about the same weight as a tiny aphid–a conservative estimate–then once you eat around 100 kilograms of your favorite chocolate you've eaten a full kilogram of bug. That's a serious amount of cocoa, but nonetheless, bug you eat.

And if you fancy making bread from scratch, about one and a half kilograms of insect is sprinkled into every 100 kilograms you use.

Total up all the food you eat over the course of a lifetime, and I'd be surprised if we couldn't trace a cringe-worthy percentage back to bugs.

Despite all the potential knee-jerk revulsion, it's important to remember that like all the animals we eat, insects share the planet with us. They outnumber us by a wide margin. If anything, we share the Earth with them. To have insects spice up our food is unavoidable, but harmless. The op-ed pieces screaming about what "gross stuff" the FDA lets us eat are over-blown and under-informed. Think of how many pounds of food you have eaten in your lifetime. How many plates were infested, and how many times were you hospitalized with chitin-related injuries? The fact of the matter is that insects were here first. We do our best to minimize our contact with them, but the circle of life offers the little creepy crawlies up as a viable, nutritious food source, and we should embrace that.

After all, humans have eaten insects for millennia, and one day they will return the favor.

Do We Need to Worry About Insects in Our Fruits and Vegetables?

I. Introduction

One prominent *kashrus* agency states on its website that fresh blackberries and raspberries, among other products, should be avoided, because checking them for insects "requires specialized training or is not practical." It also outlines a complicated, seven-step procedure for cleaning common vegetables such as lettuce, cabbage, broccoli, cauliflower, parsley and kale using a "thrip cloth" to check for insects, in order to avoid violating the prohibition against eating insects.[1]

Many have wondered, legitimately, how to approach the widespread concern of infestation in vegetables among observant Jews today in light of the apparent disregard for these concerns by prior generations. Documented proof of berries being considered permissible for consumption is found in the discussions of the *poskim* regarding the proper *beracha* to recite over berries. Rav Mordechai Carmy, in *Maamar Mordechai* (203:3), addresses the question surrounding the *beracha* to be recited over the פריזי"ש, which is identified as a strawberry.[2] More recently, the *Mishna Berura* (203:1) rules that over מאלינע"ס — mulberries — as well as תותים הגדלים בסנה שקורין מוי"יל בעי"ר — raspberries — one recites the *beracha* of בורא פרי העץ. Later (203:3), he addresses יאגד"ש שחורים — blackberries — and notes that although a number of *poskim* ruled that they also require the *beracha* of בורא פרי העץ, common practice is to recite בורא פרי האדמה. The *Mishna Berura* also observes (203:5) the widespread practice to recite בורא פרי העץ over קאסטעה"ר בערי"ן — Chester blackberries.

The *Aruch Ha-Shulchan* (O.C. 203:2) similarly speaks of יאגידעי"ס — blackberries, describing them as "types of small fruits which grow in the fields and forests…

---

1. The Torah introduces the prohibition against eating insects in *Sefer Vayikra* (11:42): לכל השרץ השורץ על הארץ לא תאכלום. See Rambam, *Sefer Ha-Mitzvos*, lo saaseh 178.
2. Rav Meir Mazuz, in his letter of approbation to Rav Eitam Henkin's *Lachem Yiheyeh Leochla*, recalls that when he lived in Tunisia, strawberries were eaten after removing the top leaf and then rinsing the berry.

some black and some red, sweet and sour, which are not planted, but they grow by themselves on the grass like tiny branches, and every summer they are collected." He notes the different views that exist regarding the proper *beracha* over these berries, and concludes that one should recite בורא פרי האדמה. However, he adds that over וויינפערלא״ך — wine berries; סמאראדינע״ש — gooseberries; אגרעסיי״ן — Chester black-berries; and מאלינע״ס — raspberries, one recites בורא פרי העץ. The *Aruch Ha-Shul-chan* brings an opinion that the *beracha* over raspberries is בורא פרי האדמה, and strongly disputes this ruling.

Neither the *Mishna Berura* nor the *Aruch Ha-Shulchan* raises any questions concerning the permissibility of eating these berries due to presence of insects — in contrast to the guidelines of many modern-day *kashrus* agencies, which warn against the consumption of berries for this reason.[3] These guidelines are based on modern scientific research and studies which were not available until very recently, and thus appear nowhere in halachic literature. It is difficult to imagine that the great sages of yesteryear inadvertently violated the grave prohibition against eating insects because they did not have the knowledge of infestation that we have today, or the sophisticat-ed methods of inspection. Does it seem reasonable to require people today to avoid concerns that the pious Jews of generations past disregarded?

טמטום הלב

This question becomes especially troubling when we consider the Gemara's famous comment in *Maseches Yoma* (39a), עבירה מטמטמת לבו של אדם — sins "close a person's heart," meaning, they have a corrosive effect on a person's soul, citing a verse from the Torah's conclusion to its discussion of forbidden foods (ולא תטמאו בהם ונטמתם בם, *Vayikra* 11:43). The *Or Ha-Chayim*, commenting on this verse, emphasizes that the harmful spiritual effects of consuming insects occur even if one did so accidentally. This concept finds halachic expression in the Rama's famous ruling[4] advising against allowing a Jewish infant to nurse from a non-Jewish woman, even though this is technically permissible, because the gentile woman's milk is produced from the non-kosher food she eats, and this food will have a deleterious spiritual effect on the child. This proves that even if somebody cannot be blamed for his ingestion of forbidden foods — such as in the case of a person

---

3.   A granddaughter of Rav Yaakov Kamenetsky (speaking on *Headlines with Dovid Lichten-stein*, January 25, 2020; see transcription, below) recalled how, as child, she and other family members would go out into the forests in the summertime and collect berries. Her grandmother would soak the berries in water on Friday, and the family would enjoy them with sour cream at *se'uda shelishis* on Shabbos.

4.   Y.D. 81:7.

who was nursed by a non-Jewish woman as an infant — he can nevertheless be harmed by such foods.

In fact, a story is told in *Meʾoran Shel Yisrael*, a biography of Rabbi Akiva Eiger,[5] of a youngster who struggled mightily to understand Gemara, and Rabbi Akiva Eiger determined that his challenges were the result of his having consumed forbidden food as a youngster. It was discovered that once, as a child, he ate at a wedding where the food was kosher, but which — unbeknownst to him — the local rabbis had instructed people to avoid because the groom had not given a proper *get* to his first wife. This clearly shows that the ingestion of forbidden foods contaminates one's soul even if they are eaten by mistake (and even if the food is technically permissible, but served at an affair of which the rabbis disapproved).

Similarly, Rav Moshe Sternbuch asserts in his *Teshuvos Ve-Hanhagos*[6] that if a person ate a forbidden insect with his food, then even if the food was properly inspected or did not halachically require inspection, he experiences the effect of טמטום הלב (the "closing" of the heart). Rav Chaim Kanievsky likewise writes in *Orchos Yosher*[7]: אף באונס העבירה מטמטמת לבו אלא אם כן היה מחוייב כן מצד פיקוח נפש, שאז זכות המצווה תגן עליו שלא יזיק לו — even if one ingested a forbidden product due to circumstances entirely beyond his control, he suffers טמטום הלב. The only exception is where this was necessary for the sake of פיקוח נפש — avoiding risk to life — in which case the merit of the *mitzva* of preserving life protects one from the adverse spiritual effects of the forbidden food.[8]

Are we to conclude, then, that the great *tzadikim* of earlier generations were "contaminated" because they ate fruits and vegetables without realizing that they were infested? It certainly seems far more likely that there is halachic justification for eating fruits and vegetables that may likely contain insects which are not readily discernible.

---

5.   Vol. 2, 21:16.

6.   4:190.

7.   P. 46.

8.   The Netziv, in his *Meromei Sadeh* (*Chullin* 5b), appears to go even further, in explaining the view of the Raʾavad (cited by the Rosh, *Yoma* 8:14) regarding the case of a dangerously ill patient who must be fed on Shabbos. The Raʾavad ruled that if the choice needs to be made between cooking kosher food in violation of Shabbos, or feeding the patient readymade non-kosher food, kosher food should be prepared. Although Shabbos desecration is a graver violation than eating prohibited foods, the Netziv explains, the latter must be avoided, even at the expense of Shabbos observance, due to the long-term, harmful spiritual effects that the non-kosher food will have on the patient. The Netziv here clearly works off the assumption that ingesting forbidden food poses spiritual danger even when it is necessary for the sake of פיקוח נפש — extending the concept of טמטום הלב even further than Rav Kanievsky.

II. Historical Evidence

Rabbi Steven Adams, in a thorough article published in 2017, under the title "The Scientific Revolution and Modern Bedikat Tola'im Trends,"[9] traces the history of concern of insect infestation in produce as expressed in halachic literature. His thesis, which he compellingly supports, is that the concern to avoid hardly visible creatures such as aphids, thrips and mites arose with the advent of glass magnification devices — such as telescopes — in the early modern era, which made the world aware of tiny creatures which had never before been known to mankind. He notes, for example, that in the Gemara's discussion of forbidden insects in *Maseches Chullin* (67b), the Gemara speaks of creatures found in fruits and legumes, not in leafy vegetables — regarded nowadays as among the most infested products. The likely reason, Rabbi Adams avers, is that the insects in leafy greens are very small and notoriously difficult to identify, and were thus unknown to the Sages of the Talmud. Indeed, the creatures mentioned in this passage are relatively large — יבחושין and יתושין, which are gnats and mosquitos; דרני — warble fly; עקרב — scorpion; שילשול — translated by Rashi as a lizard-like creature as long as a snake; חפושית — beetle; and נדל — a centipede.

Likewise, in *Maseches Makkos* (16b), the Gemara speaks of the punishment for one who eats בינייתא דבי כרבא, which Rashi identifies as a caterpillar; פוטיתא — some sort of sea creature; נמלה — an ant; and a צרעה — wasp. The Gemara does not speak of one who eats aphids or mites, because these creatures were unknown until the early modern era.

Rabbi Adams draws our attention also to the Gemara's discussion in *Maseches Chullin* (6a) as to when one may rely on the *kashrus* standards of a halachically ignorant neighbor. The Gemara establishes that if one gives his dough or meat to an ignorant neighbor to prepare, then he need not be concerned that the herbs or yeast might not have been properly tithed, or have originated from *shemita* produce, whereas if he asked an ignorant neighbor to prepare a dish using the neighbor's own ingredients, then he must suspect that the herbs and yeast might not have undergone tithing or were from *shemita* produce. Revealingly, the Gemara does not require concerning oneself with the likelihood that the halachically ignorant neighbor failed to properly inspect the greens for insects.

Moreover, the Torah explicitly grants license to an employee in a vineyard to eat some of the employer's grapes as he harvests, provided that he does not save any for after work.[10] Neither the Chumash nor the Talmud gives any indication that the employee must thoroughly wash or inspect the grapes before eating them, nor do we have any reason to assume that agricultural workers of yesteryear had the means or

---

9.   *Hakirah*, vol. 22.

10.   *Devarim* 23:25.

expertise to clean and inspect produce according to modern standards. In fact, it is difficult to imagine employees having water available in the vineyards with which to even superficially rinse the produce.

Rabbi Adams further notes the time-honored tradition to eat lettuce in fulfillment of the *marror* obligation on Pesach, based on the Mishna's statement that one can fulfill this requirement with חזרת, which the Gemara identifies as חסא — lettuce. The *Chasam Sofer*[11] famously warned about the presence of insects on lettuce leaves, and urged people not to eat lettuce, and to use other options for *marror*, unless they have אנשים מיוחדים מסויימים בעלי יראה — special, God-fearing individuals — carefully inspecting the lettuce leaves for them. And this was, indeed, the *Chasam Sofer*'s own practice — to have a team of men inspect his lettuce with magnifying glasses before the *seder*.[12] But the silence of halachists in the centuries preceding the *Chasam Sofer* speaks much louder than his warnings in the late 18th or early 19th century. The absence of such a requirement in the Gemara's discussion of *marror*, and in the writings of the *Rishonim* and *poskim* before the time of the *Chasam Sofer*, would lead us to believe that this concern arose only in the modern era when awareness of microorganisms began to spread.

Also noteworthy, Rabbi Adams writes, is the fact that *Chazal* present several laborious methods of inspecting a *shechita* knife to ensure proper slaughtering of an animal,[13] but give us no techniques for inspecting produce for inspects. Of particular interest is the fact that one method of inspecting a *shechita* knife is holding it up to the sun (במערבא בדקי לה בשימשא) — a method proposed later by a number of *Acharonim* for inspecting produce.[14] It seems fair to ask why, according to these *Acharonim*, the Gemara did not instruct us to inspect produce the way it instructed inspecting *shechita* knives.

Rabbi Adams similarly questions the ruling of a number *Acharonim* cited by the *Darchei Teshuva*[15] requiring the inspection of vinegar in transparent glass vessels to assure the absence of vinegar eels. Transparent glass was not readily available until the modern era; in fact, the Gemara in *Maseches Chullin* (84b) speaks of זוגיתא חיורתא — relatively clear glass utensils — as a luxury item on which one is advised not to waste his money. It is hardly conceivable that *Chazal* expected the common person to avoid vinegar until it could be inspected in a clear glass utensil, a product which only the wealthiest of society owned.

When we add the consideration that people in generations past lived in homes with

---

11.   *Teshuvos*, O.C. 132.

12.   *Minhagei Ha-Chasam Sofer*, 10:18.

13.   *Chullin* 17b.

14.   See *Peri Chadash*, Y.D. 84:34; *She'eilas Yaabetz*, 2:124.

15.   Y.D. 84:45.

very poor lighting, did not have eyeglasses, and had very limited water rations, we have no alternative but to conclude that they had absolutely no possibility of identifying tiny aphids and mites in their produce, which modern *kashrus* agencies require taking great pains to avoid.

What, then, is the explanation? Were the Jews before the modern era daily in accidental violation of the Torah prohibition against eating insects, while we modern Jews have had the good fortune to access the knowledge needed to avoid this prohibition? Or are there halachic grounds for permitting the consumption of vegetables that may likely contain small creatures?

III. The Status of Invisible Creatures

לא ניתנה תורה למלאכים

Numerous *poskim* have established that insects which are not visible to the naked eye, and can be seen only through a microscope — or even a magnifying glass — are not prohibited for consumption.

The *Aruch Ha-Shulchan*[16] noted the scientific discovery of the presence of countless microorganisms in vinegar and in many natural water sources, and ruled that they nevertheless are permissible for consumption, because לא אסרה תורה במה שאין העין שולטת בו, דלא ניתנה תורה למלאכים — "the Torah did not proscribe that which the eye cannot discern, for the Torah was not given to angels." The Torah was given to human beings, not angels, and thus its prohibitions must be able to be avoided through ordinary human efforts, which, in the view of the *Aruch Ha-Shulchan*, do not include inspection with magnifying glasses or other devices. He proves this point from the scientists' discovery that the air we breathe is laden with innumerable microbes, which people ingest each time they inhale. Just as the Torah quite obviously could not prohibit breathing, it also does not prohibit the ingestion of organisms which cannot be seen with the naked eye.

This point is made also by Rav Moshe Feinstein, in a responsum[17] affirming that a comatose patient may not be determined halachically dead as long as the machines detect a heartbeat. Rav Moshe writes that generally speaking, *halacha* is determined based on readily discernible realities, and not on information which requires advanced technology, but the determination of the cessation of life marks an exception to this rule.[18] Amidst his discussion, he writes that it is plainly obvious that התורה לא אסרה

---

16. Y.D. 84:36.
17. *Iggeros Moshe*, Y.D. 2:146.
18. Rav Moshe writes that in the case of a comatose patient, the detection of a heartbeat by a machine prevents us from declaring the patient dead, because a patient may be

אלא תולעים ושקצים ורמשים שנראו לעיניים — the Torah forbade eating only readily visible creatures, noting the fact that we inhale air containing countless microbes. He cites Rav Simcha Zelig Riger, the famed *dayan* of Brisk, as similarly establishing that menstrual blood which can be seen only via a microscope is halachically inconsequential, and the square shape of a *tefillin* box does not need to be verified via scientifically precise measurements. Rav Moshe explains:

כי לא הוזכר זה בגמ' וכל הדורות הכשרים הגאונים והצדיקים והחסידים לא
השתמשו במיקראסקאפ, וברור שהם קיימו כל דיני התורה ולא נכשלו בשום דבר
אף באונס.

> …because this was not mentioned in the Gemara, and all the generations of upright [Jews], sages, and righteous and pious men did not use a microscope, and they clearly observed all the Torah's laws and did not stumble on anything, not even due to factors beyond their control.

Rav Moshe reiterates this principle in a later responsum,[19] where he rules that a person who was born deaf, but then gained the ability to hear through a hearing aid, retains the halachic status of חרש. According to Rav Moshe, this case differs from that of an individual with a hearing impairment who is able to hear loud voices without a device, because all people have different levels of hearing, and so as long as one is able to hear on his own, without an electric device, even if he requires a higher volume, he is not considered halachically deaf. By contrast, one who cannot hear at all without a device has the status of a חרש, because, in Rav Moshe's words, כל ענייני התורה נידונין כפי שרואין ושומעין בעצם לא ע"י מכונות וכדומה — "all Torah matters are determined based on the way people see and hear in essence, not through machines and the like." He then gives the example of small insects, noting that שרצים שלא נראו לעין אלא ע"י דבר המגדיל...אינו כלום — "insects that are visible to the eye only through a magnifying instrument…are nothing."[20] Rav Moshe points also to the example of a space in the ink that forms a letter in *tefillin* or a *mezuza*, which can be detected only

---

pronounced dead only if the chances that he is alive are negligible, which is obviously not the case when a machine detects a sign of life.

19. E.H., 3:33.

20. Rav Moshe's son, Rav Reuven Feinstein (on *Headlines with Dovid Lichtenstein*, Jan. 25, 2020; see transcription, below), suggested explaining on this basis the Gemara's references to spontaneous generation — the belief that certain organisms come into existence on their own, without being produced by other creatures, a theory that has been conclusively disproven by modern science. Rav Feinstein proposed that very small creatures "exist" from a halachic perspective only once they become visible, as before then they are not given any halachic consideration, and so halachically speaking, they come into existence on their own, when they become visible through the natural process of growth.

through a microscope. If the break in the letter is not visible to the naked eye, then the parchment is valid.

Rav Binyamin Aryeh Weiss of Tchernowitz, in a responsum published in *Even Yekara* (2:33), applies this principle to the case of a *Tanach* written in minuscule print which can be read only with a magnifying glass. Strictly speaking, Rav Weiss writes, such a *Tanach* does not have the status of sacred text, since it is not readable without a special device, and אנו אין לנו בכל מקום אלא מה שעינינו רואות במראה ולא בחידות — *halacha* takes into consideration only that which can be seen naturally, without sophisticated devices. Rav Weiss draws proof from the fact that microscopic inspection of animals' organs reveals pores that extend throughout the entirety of each organ. A perforation in one of an animal's vital organs renders it a *tereifa* (mortally ill) and thus forbidden for consumption. Necessarily, then, *halacha* disregards realities that are not discernible to the naked eye.

Poskim have applied this principle also in the opposite direction, to reach a stringent conclusion. For example, Rav Yisrael Liphshitz, in his *Tiferes Yisrael* commentary to the Mishna,[21] writes that a species of fish that has scales which can be seen only with a magnifying glass is forbidden for consumption. The Torah requires the presence of fins and scales for a species to be permissible,[22] and Rav Liphshitz asserts that these two features must be visible to the naked eye.

When Infestation Can Be Presumed

Rav Moshe Feinstein, in a responsum written towards the end of his life,[23] advances the view that this applies even when there is reason to suspect, or even assume, that small, invisible insects are present, given the statistical likelihood. Rav Moshe was asked about vegetables that are known to contain small insects (התולעים הקטנים שנודע שנמצאים בהרבה ממיני הירקות), and he writes that while he is unable to issue a definitive ruling on the matter (presumably, because of his declining health, which he noted at the beginning of his letter), he was inclined to rule leniently. In addition to the fact that such vegetables were eaten by prior generations without any concern, Rav Moshe writes, אפשר שדבר שלא נראה למעשה להדיא לעיניים אינו אסור — "it is possible that something which is not actually, clearly visible to the eyes is not prohibited." Rav Moshe expresses the view — albeit somewhat indecisively — that even products which are known to likely contain tiny insects are permissible for consumption, if the insects are not visible without magnification.

---

21.   *Avoda Zara* 2:6, *Boaz*, 3.
22.   *Vayikra* 11:9.
23.   *Iggeros Moshe*, Y.D. 4:2.

In fact, already one of the *Rishonim* — Rav Shalom of Neustadt[24] — ruled that water taken from a well that is known to have insects is permissible for drinking. The question brought to him involved a well in which small insects were visible only during the daytime, and he wrote that this water was permissible even at night, because the insects were visible only under certain conditions.

These sources run in contrast to the view of Rav Yaakov Emden, who, in one of his published responsa,[25] addresses the status of rice imported to Europe from the Southern Hemisphere, which was often infested. Rav Emden writes that the small insects are visible either by heating the rice, leaving it in the sun, or with a magnifying glass, and he rules that such an inspection must be made, and if insects are discovered, then the rice may not be eaten. This ruling is cited by the Chida, in his *Machazik Beracha*.[26] According to this opinion, if a product is known to have a high likelihood of infestation, even with insects that are not visible to the naked eye, then a magnifying glass or other means of inspection must be employed in order to assure that no insects are present.

As we have seen, however, other *poskim* disagreed, and maintained that *halacha* discounts that which cannot be seen with the naked eye.

What Is the "Naked Eye"?

The more difficult question is how to define "visible to the naked eye" with respect to this *halacha*.

Modern science and technology have made it possible for people to undergo specialized training in the field of infestation, and thus acquire the knowledge to recognize as an insect something which to ordinary people looks like an innocuous speck. Additionally, modern equipment such as magnification devices and "thrip cloths" can reveal insects which otherwise would not be discerned. One might argue that this knowledge, and modern equipment, impose upon us a strict halachic obligation to have all our produce professionally inspected — and thus purchase certified bug-free produce — or to receive detailed guidelines from experts in the field for how to clean or inspect our produce at home. Seemingly, if the basis for permitting the consumption of produce with tiny creatures is the concept of לא ניתנה תורה למלאכי השרת, then we are required to do everything humanly possible to assure the absence of forbidden insects, including buying only certified produce, or inspecting and cleaning our produce through modern methods. This stringent view is, indeed, accepted by a number of contemporary *poskim*.[27]

---

24. *Hilchos U-Minhagei Maharash*, 464 (Machon Yerushalayim edition, p. 141).
25. *She'eilas Yaabetz*, 2:124.
26. Y.D. 84:41.
27. Rav Moshe Vaye writes in *Bedikas Ha-Mazon Ke-Halacha* (2:4):

By contrast, Rav Shmuel Wosner, in *Shevet Ha-Levi*,[28] rules leniently on this matter:

אעפ״י ש...כאן נראה...כמין נקודת משהו, בעניותי אין זה גורם להחמיר דנקודות
כאלה נראים לאלפים על פרי וירק במים ובימים ואין בינם לנקודות בעלמא שאין
בהם חשש שרצים ולא כלום, וא״כ מראית העין לא גורם חומרא כלל רק הזכוכית
המגדלת וזה אינו בכלל האיסור של שרצים.

Even though...in this case, some sort of dot is visible, in my humble
opinion, this is not a factor for stringency, because these dots appear by
the thousands on fruits and vegetables, in water and in seas, and there is
no difference [in appearance] between these and general dots regarding
which there is no concern of insects. Therefore, the vision of the naked
eye does not give rise to any stringency at all, and only the magnifying
glass [reveals the grounds for stringency], and this is not included in the
prohibition of [consuming] insects.

In Rav Wosner's view, there is no difference at all between an insect that cannot be
seen at all without a magnification device, and an insect that can be seen but cannot
be identified as an insect without a magnification device. Even in the latter case, it is
the magnification, and not the naked eye, which would generate a prohibition, and the
Torah prohibits only that which can be detected normally.

This also appears to have been the view of Rav Moshe Feinstein, in the responsum
mentioned earlier.[29] After expressing his view that a creature שלא נראה למעשה להדיא
לעיניים — which is not readily discernible — is not forbidden, he adds that this consideration may provide justification for the widespread practice observed by the *Aruch
Ha-Shulchan*[30] to disregard מילבי״ן — mites that are often present in food products,
particularly in the summertime. The species of מילבי״ן, which is discussed by several
poskim, is clearly far more identifiable as an insect than an innocent-looking speck on
a leaf of lettuce, and yet Rav Moshe includes these creatures under the category of לא
נראה למעשה להדיא לעיניים.[31]

This lenient position is taken by former Sephardic Chief Rabbi Shlomo Amar, in

---

תולעת אשר ניתן לגלותה, אך אין אפשרות לזהות שהיא תולעת (כגון שהיא נראית כנקודה או כפס
שחור), ובהגדלה מזהים אותה כתולעת הרי היא בכלל התולעות האסורות.

    This view was expressed also by Rav Hershel Schachter, in an interview on *Headlines
with Dovid Lichtenstein*, Feb. 1, 2020.

28.   7:122.

29.   Y.D. 4:2.

30.   Y.D. 100:13. Later, we will discuss the *Aruch Ha-Shulchan*'s comments in greater detail.

31.   It must be emphasized, however, that Rav Moshe was intentionally tentative in making
    this assertion, using the word אפשר ("possible") and noting in this responsum that his
    declining health prevented him from issuing a definitive ruling.

a responsum regarding the consumption of strawberries,[32] adding that there is an argument to permit such specks even after it has been inspected with a magnification device and determined to be an insect, since it cannot be identified as an insect with the naked eye.

Similarly, Rav Asher Weiss[33] asserts that barely visible small organisms are permitted even if there are experts capable of identifying them. He explains that the principle of לא ניתנה תורה למלאכי השרת — the Torah is meant to be observed by human beings, and not by angels — should not be understood literally, as exempting us only from that which lies beyond the furthest limits of human capability. Rather, it means that Torah law does not impose unreasonable demands upon ordinary human beings — and thus if an ordinary person is unable to identify an insect in a piece of produce, that product is permissible, even if experts in the field can find the insect.

Rav Weiss draws proof from the Gemara's applications of the rule of לא ניתנה תורה למלאכי השרת to actions which are humanly possible, but unreasonably difficult. For example, in *Maseches Yoma* (30a), the Gemara states that although one may not read *Shema* in the presence of excrement, one may recite *Shema* if there is excrement on his body, as long as it cannot be seen (even if he were unclothed), due to the principle of לא ניתנה תורה למלאכי השרת. It is certainly possible for a person to thoroughly wash the area of the anus before reciting *Shema* to ascertain the complete absence of excrement, but this would be an unreasonable requirement, and thus would violate the rule of לא ניתנה תורה למלאכי השרת. Likewise, in *Maseches Kiddushin* (54a), the Gemara proves that *kohanim* are permitted to derive personal benefit from their special priestly garments with which they must perform the rituals in the *Beis Ha-Mikdash*, from the fact that otherwise, they would be required to immediately remove the garments the very moment they complete the service. Of course, Rav Weiss notes, this would not be impossible, but it would be an unreasonable demand, and so the rule of לא ניתנה תורה למלאכי השרת allows us to assume that this is not required by the Torah.

Rav Weiss points to numerous other sources, as well, including the comment of the *Tosfos Yeshanim* (*Yoma* 60a) explaining why the prohibition of *me'ila* (deriving personal benefit from hallowed property) does not apply to the *ketores* (the incense offered in the *Beis Ha-Mikdash*). The *Tosfos Yeshanim* applies the rule of לא ניתנה תורה למלאכי השרת, noting that it would be impossible for those involved in preparing and offering the incense not to derive enjoyment from its pleasant fragrance. Although it is possible to wear nose plugs to avoid smelling the fragrance, it was clear to *Chazal* (as understood by the *Tosfos Yeshanim*) that the Torah would not impose such a requirement, and so they concluded that the Torah does not forbid enjoying the scent of the *ketores*.

By the same token, Rav Weiss asserts, the Torah does not expect us to go to unreasonable lengths to avoid insects in food, and only those which can be seen by an ordinary

---

32. *Tenuvot Sadeh*, 85, pp. 9–21.

33. *She'eilos U-Teshuvos Minchas Asher*, 1:41.

person are forbidden, even if a trained expert in the field can find insects in the product.

Indeed, this standard of visibility is accepted also in other areas of *halacha*. For example, the *Mishna Berura*[34] makes the following remark concerning a discoloration in the upper segment of an *esrog*, which invalidates the *esrog* for use on Sukkos regardless of its size:[35]

> דווקא כשנראה לכל, אבל אם אין נראה לעין מחמת דקותו וצריך להסתכל, אין
> זה כל שהוא שפוסל.

> [This applies] specifically when it is seen to all, but if it is not visible to the eye because of its smallness, and one must look carefully, this is not a כל שהוא [slightest amount] that invalidates [the *esrog*].

The *Mishna Berura* makes a similar comment concerning broken letters in the text of *tefillin* scrolls,[36] ruling that if the letter looks complete to the naked eye, then the *tefillin* are valid even if a careful inspection reveals a disruption of the ink.[37]

IV. Inspections for Visible Creatures

Until now, we have discussed the status of insects which are either invisible or hardly visible to the naked eye. We have shown that creatures which cannot be seen at all

---

34.   648:46.

35.   כל שהוא בכל מראה שינוי כל חזית פוסל...ואילך מחוטמו , *Shulchan Aruch* O.C. 648:12.

36.   32:122.

37.   Rabbi Adams, in the aforementioned article, tells of his personal correspondence with Rav David Feinstein as a student in Mesivta Tifereth Jerusalem, in which Rav Feinstein related that in Russia, "whatever green vegetables available were checked by briefly looking at them at normal reading distance, with no sun or lightbox behind the leaf." Rav Feinstein also expressed the view that "an insect that is difficult to detect because it is the same color as the leaf it is resting upon is *battul* to the leaf." Rabbi Adams further recalls bringing Rav Feinstein fresh greens purchased in China Town, and he "held the herbs for a second, took a quick look, and pronounced it kosher." (By contrast, Rav Feinstein's close disciple, Rav Baruch Moskowitz, in *Ve-Dibarta Bam*, 1:206, cites Rav Feinstein as taking a far stricter stance vis-à-vis the requirement to inspect vegetables.)

Rabbi Adams cites the following testimony which was told to him by a "prominent Rosh Yeshiva at Yeshiva University" who asked to remain anonymous: "Rabbi Joseph Ber Soloveitchik stated that his mother only inspected greens cursorily. In the past, observant Jews were not inspecting their vegetables for tiny insects — only for the large clearly visible ones. Further inspection is unnecessary." This Rosh Yeshiva testified that he heard this statement directly from Rav Soloveitchik.

without magnification are certainly permissible, and that creatures which are visible but not identifiable without magnification are permissible according to some *poskim*.

We will now turn our attention to the requirement to inspect foods which might contain even readily visible insects. Clearly, according to all opinions, consuming these creatures constitutes a Torah violation, which must be avoided. The question, however, becomes, what level of likelihood requires us to be concerned about the presence of visible insects, and how far do we have to go to assure they are not present?

The *Shulchan Aruch*[38] rules that all products שדרכן להתליע — that normally are infested — require inspection before being permitted for eating. The Rama adds that even if one inspected the majority of the collection of fruits and did not find any insects, he must inspect the rest, because this falls under the category of מיעוט השכיח — also known as מיעוט המצוי, referring to a "common minority." Although generally *halacha* allows us to rely on a statistical majority to permit something that might be forbidden, this does not apply if the minority possibility is not uncommon, and must therefore be considered.

The precise definition of מיעוט המצוי is subject to dispute. The Rivash[39] defines this term as קרוב למחצה ורגיל להיות — "close to a half, and happens regularly." According to this view, then, inspecting produce would be required only if there is a near 50 percent chance that an insect is present. A far more stringent view is taken by Rav Yaakov of Karlin, in his *Mishkenos Yaakov*,[40] where he maintains that a probability of even 10 percent qualifies as a מיעוט המצוי.[41]

Significantly, several sources indicate that the requirement to concern oneself with a מיעוט המצוי applies only מדרבנן — by force of rabbinic enactment, whereas on the level of Torah law, one may rely on a statistical majority. Thus, for example, the *Shach*[42] asserts that the requirement to inspect an animal's lung after slaughtering, to assure the absence of lesions that would render the animal a *tereifa*, applies only מדרבנן. Since most animals are healthy, inspecting the lung is not required on the level of Torah law, despite the large minority of animals with lesions on the lungs. The *Shach* therefore writes that although the Rama forbids eating an animal if a lung was lost before being inspected, this practice is a measure of stringency, as according to the strict *halacha*,

---

38. Y.D. 84:8.

39. 191.

40. Y.D. 17.

41. Rav Shmuel Wosner, in *Shevet Ha-Levi* (4:81), defines מיעוט המצוי as a phenomenon which occurs in the minority of cases, even less than 10 percent of the time, but is a common and expected statistical minority: עניין מיעוט המצוי היינו שהופעת המיעוט ומציאותו הוא מצוי הרבה...והמועט מלווה את הרוב בכל עת ובכל מקום, והוא הוכחה שזה טבעית מציאותו.... Rav Meir Mazuz critiques this stringent definition of מיעוט המצוי in *Eit Ha-Zamir*, p. 296.

42. Y.D. 39:8.

the meat is permissible in such a case, given that the requirement to inspect the lung was enacted by the Sages.[43] The *Peri Megadim*[44] compares the requirement to inspect produce to the requirement to inspect lungs after slaughtering, and writes explicitly that this law applies only מדרבנן.

Once it is established that the requirement to inspect a product in cases of מיעוט המצוי applies only by force of rabbinic enactment, we have greater room for leniency in certain respects. For one thing, the דרבנן status of this requirement should, seemingly, affect the aforementioned debate between the Rivash and the *Mishkenos Yaakov*, and allow us to apply the famous rule of ספק דרבנן לקולא — that we may act leniently in situations of uncertainty when a rabbinic law, as opposed to Torah provision, is at stake. At least in principle, we may restrict the requirement to inspect produce to products which have a near 50 percent chance of infestation.[45]

But perhaps even more importantly, several *Acharonim* established that inspection in situations of מיעוט המצוי is not required if this entails a great deal of inconvenience, given that the requirement to begin with is rabbinic in origin. The Maharshal, in his *Amudei Shlomo* commentary to the *Sefer Mitzvos Gadol* (111),[46] questions why many avoid inspecting vinegar out of fear of finding insects, and writes, פשיטא אם הייתם מניחים הבדיקה מחמת טירחא יתירה או מחמת היזק אפשר מחמת ספק איסור אין צריך להחמיר ולבדוק — "It is obvious that if you avoid checking because of excessive inconvenience, or because of damage, then perhaps there is no need to be stringent and check due to the possibility of a prohibition."[47] Similarly, Rav Shimon Sofer of Erlau, in his *Hisorerus Teshuva* (4:35), writes that where there would be טירחא מרובה מאד לבדוק כל עלה ועלה — "a great deal of inconvenience to check each and every leaf" — then inspection is not required. Likewise, Rav Yaakov of Karlin, in the aforementioned responsum, writes:

כל שיכולים לתקן בקל, אין סומכין על הרוב...אבל לחפש לבדוק כל עלה ועלה
ולהוציא התולעת, הוא דבר של טורח, ולא חייבוהו חכמים .

---

43. This is also the implication of the Rashba, in his commentary to *Maseches Chullin* (9a), where he describes the requirement to inspect the lungs with the phrase חששו להן חכמים ואבותינו הראשונים ומנהג אבות קדושים קדמונים.

44. *Sifsei Da'as*, 84:28.

45. This is in contrast to most *kashrus* agencies today, which adopt the stringent position of the *Mishkenos Yaakov* and require inspection if there is even a 10 percent chance of the presence of insects.

46. Machon Yerushalayim edition, p. 76.

47. This passage is difficult to understand, as the Maharshal on the one hand says that this conclusion is "obvious" (פשיטא), but then says that "perhaps" (אפשר) the requirement is waived when it entails great inconvenience.

Whenever it can be easily resolved, one may not rely on the statistical majority [and must inspect to ensure permissibility]… But searching and inspecting each and every leaf to remove the insect is a matter of inconvenience, and so the Sages did not obligate one [to make such an inspection].

Rav Yaakov of Karlin draws a comparison to the Gemara's discussion in *Maseches Pesachim* (4a) concerning the case of one who rented a residence on Erev Pesach, and does not know whether the house had been checked for *chametz*. The Gemara raises the question of whether the new tenant may presume the residence had been checked, so that he does not need to go through the trouble of searching for *chametz*. Although there is a chance that the house had not been checked, nevertheless, the Gemara establishes that if the residence has a presumed status of בדוק (having been searched), the tenant would be absolved of the obligation to check for *chametz* to account for the possibility it had not been checked, given the great inconvenience entailed. Rav Yaakov of Karlin thus proves that although inspections are generally required in situations of מיעוט המצוי, this requirement is waived when this would involve considerable inconvenience.

Accordingly, as long as the majority of a given product does not contain insects, *halacha* does not require inspecting the product — even for readily visible insects — if this would involve a great deal of inconvenience. It goes without saying that when inspection is practically unfeasible, then one may eat the product without inspection, assuming that the possibility of an insect being present is less than 50 percent.[48]

מתעסק בחלבים

One might nevertheless insist that it is advisable to inspect potentially infested foods under all circumstances, even when this is technically not required, to avoid accidental violation of the prohibition against consuming insects. While there are limits, as we have seen, to the level of precaution required to avoid the possibility of an inadvertent violation, perhaps we should be encouraged to extend beyond the strict requirements in an effort to assure we do not inadvertently commit a forbidden act.

The basis for this conclusion, seemingly, is the Gemara's famous rule, המתעסק בחלבים ובעריות חייב שכן נהנה (*Kerisus* 19b). This principle establishes that Torah violations that involve physical enjoyment — namely, forbidden foods and forbidden sexual

---

48. This point is made by the *Chasam Sofer* (cited in *Pischei Teshuva*, Y.D. 84:5) regarding dried fruits, which often contain dead insects which cannot be discerned. He writes that since the obligation to concern oneself with a מיעוט המצוי applies only לכתחילה (optimally), a product that cannot be inspected is permissible for consumption if one can assume that the majority of such products do not contain insects.

relations — require atonement even if they were committed without any intention whatsoever. For example, if a person swallowed without realizing that a forbidden item was on his tongue, he must bring an atonement sacrifice. Generally, one who commits an offense in a manner of מתעסק — without any intention to perform the forbidden act[49] — does not require atonement, since the action was unintended. But if the unintended action resulted in physical gratification, then atonement is required. Applying this principle to insects in produce, we might conclude that if a person eats produce under permissible circumstances, and over the course of eating he ingests an insect, he has inadvertently committed a religious offense, such that he would require atonement. If so, then we might, indeed, encourage thoroughly cleaning and inspecting produce even when this is not halachically required, in order to ensure to avoid an accidental violation, even under excusable circumstances.

Several *Acharonim*, however, asserted that the rule of המתעסק בחלבים does not apply to the ingestion of creatures which people regard as revolting. After all, this rule is predicated on the fact that נהנה — one experienced enjoyment from the forbidden food, which makes him guilty of an inadvertent violation. In the case of the unintended ingestion of an insect, however, one receives no enjoyment, and so perhaps no guilt is incurred whatsoever.

This theory is advanced by Rav Shmuel Landau,[50] in his *Shivas Tziyon* (28), where he draws proof from a remark made by Rashi in his commentary to *Maseches Chullin* (67a). The Gemara there forbids filtering a beverage in the dark, given the concern that an insect might later fall from the filter into the glass, without the person seeing it. The simple explanation of this ruling, Rav Landau writes, is that the individual might then drink the cup in the dark, not seeing the insect, and will thus be in inadvertent violation of a Torah law. Rashi, however, explains this *halacha* differently, writing that the person might drink the beverage the next day, in the light, and although he sees the insect, he will wrongly assume that the creature had always been in the beverage, such that it is permissible for consumption.[51] He will not realize that the insect had first left the beverage during the filtering process, and later returned, and it is therefore forbidden. Rav Landau explains that Rashi did not accept the simple reading of this passage because there would be nothing wrong with unknowingly ingesting an insect

---

49. The case of מתעסק differs from that of שוגג — an accidental violation, where one knowingly committed a forbidden act thinking it was permissible, such as eating a piece of food which he did not realize was prohibited, or without realizing that it was Yom Kippur. An accidental violation of this nature requires atonement, whereas a מתעסק — one who did not even intend to perform the action — does not, unless physical enjoyment was experienced.

50. The son of Rav Yechezkel Landau, the *Noda Be-Yehuda*.

51. As the Gemara there discusses, insects that are born in natural water sources are permissible for consumption with the water unless they had left the water and then returned.

while drinking a beverage which one legitimately assumed was properly filtered. Since there was absolutely no intention to ingest the creature, and no enjoyment was experienced by consuming a repulsive insect, no wrong has been committed whatsoever. This explanation of Rashi's comments was offered also by the Rogatchover Gaon, in his *Tzofnas Pa'nei'ach* commentary to the Rambam's *Mishneh Torah*.[52]

However, after presenting this understanding of Rashi's comment, Rav Landau questions whether this conclusion can be applied as a matter of practical *halacha*. The Rama, both in his glosses to the *Shulchan Aruch*[53] and in *Toras Chatas*,[54] maintains that if food was cooked with insects, then since the flavor introduced by insects is considered a טעם פגום ("foul taste"), this flavor may be disregarded, as only the taste of forbidden food which enhances the mixture renders the mixture forbidden. The *Shach*, however, citing the Rashba and *Rokei'ach*, disagrees, and rules that the flavor of insects in food is not regarded as a טעם פגום, and therefore renders the food forbidden unless it comprises one-sixtieth or less of the mixture, such that its taste is not discerned. Rav Landau thus writes that he cannot definitively conclude that no violation is committed when one unknowingly ingests an insect, because according to some opinions, insects are not considered foul-tasting, and thus one can be said to derive some sort of enjoyment from the consumption of such creatures. Hence, we must apply the standard rule of מתעסק בחלבים, that unknowingly consuming a forbidden food product constitutes an accidental sinful act that requires atonement.

However, several *poskim* disputed the *Shach's* position, and upheld the Rama's ruling that insects have the status of פגום. This is the view of the *Aruch Ha-Shulchan*,[55] who, after referencing those who dispute the *Shach*, adds, והחוש מעיד כן שהתולעים פגומים למאד — we need to go no further than empirical evidence, which shows that the taste of insects is revolting.

Moreover, one could argue that even if an insect does not have the status of פגום with respect to its halachic impact on the food with which it is cooked, directly ingesting an insect — which people do not even regard as food — does not qualify as נהנה with regard to the principle of מתעסק בחלבים. Indeed, the Rogatchover Gaon writes that insects differ from other forbidden foods in that they provide no enjoyment or benefit whatsoever, such that ingesting such creatures does not even meet the definition of "eating." Consuming them is forbidden by a special גזירת הכתוב (Biblical decree), but this prohibition stands separate and apart from the prohibitions involving other forbidden foods. Therefore, insects are not subject to the rule of מתעסק בחלבים, and no wrong is committed if one unknowingly ingests an insect while eating food

---

52. *Hilchos Ma'achalos Asuros* 2:15.
53. Y.D. 104:3.
54. As cited and discussed by the *Shach*, Y.D. 84:30.
55. Y.D. 84:73.

permissibly. Similarly, Rav Shimon Sofer of Erlau[56] cites his uncle, Rav Shimon Sofer of Cracow, as positing that the principle of מתעסק בחלבים does not apply to one who unknowingly ingests an insect while eating if he did not have reason to suspect infestation.

It is told[57] that Rav Yisrael Salanter wondered, based on this line of reasoning, why there is ever a requirement to inspect produce. Since one in any event has no intention to eat the insects, eating them constitutes מתעסק, and as no enjoyment is experienced, one is not guilty of any wrongdoing. The story goes that Rav Yisrael sent this question to Rabbi Akiva Eiger, and never received a response. Years later, Rav Yisrael was told by Rabbi Akiva Eiger's son, Rav Shlomo Eiger, that Rabbi Akiva Eiger's famous, controversial essay on the topic of מתעסק, which is published in his work of responsa,[58] was written in response to Rav Yisrael's question.[59] In this essay, Rabbi Akiva Eiger advances the view that even a violation committed in a situation of מתעסק constitutes a מעשה איסור — a "forbidden act" — even though it does not require a sacrifice like other accidental violations do.[60] This answers Rav Yisrael's question, establishing that we must endeavor to avoid even situations of מתעסק, as violations which occur under such circumstances are considered sinful, notwithstanding the exemption from an atonement sacrifice.

It emerges, then, that Rabbi Akiva Eiger accepted the premise that the exemption of מתעסק applies to the case of unknowingly ingesting an insect, only in his view, such a situation must be avoided. The vast majority of *Acharonim*, however, disputed Rabbi Akiva Eiger's revolutionary theory that a violation in the case of מתעסק constitutes a מעשה איסור.[61] Accordingly, we are left with the conclusion that indeed, no guilt is incurred when one unknowingly ingests an insect while eating.

---

56. *Hisorerus Teshuva* 1:100.

57. This story is related by Rav Moshe Sternbuch, in *Teshuvos Ve-Hanhagos* 4:190. It appears also in Rav Yaakov Moshe Shurkin's *Achiza Ba'akeiv* commentary to Rabbi Akiva Eiger's responsa, *Mahadura Kama*, Y.D. 8 (p. 62). He writes that it was related by Rav Shmuel Auerbach, in the name of Rav Shmuel Yitzchak Hillman of London.

58. *Mahadura Kama*, Y.D. 8.

59. Rav Shlomo Eiger explained that out of respect to the rabbi of Salant, Rav Hersh, Rabbi Akiva Eiger did not want to address this essay to a member of Rav Hersh's community.

60. As Rabbi Akiva Eiger himself notes, this view is in contrast to that of Rav Yaakov Lorberbaum (author of the *Nesivos*), in *Mekor Chayim*, 430.

61. It is widely reported, for example, that Rav Chaim Soloveitchik of Brisk strongly dismissed Rabbi Akiva Eiger's theory, as mentioned by Rav Chaim's grandson, Rav Yosef Dov Soloveitchik (*Shiurim Le-Zecher Abba Mari z"l*, vol. 1, p. 43, note 58). Rav Soloveitchik noted that his father, Rav Moshe, brought compelling proof to Rav Chaim's view from the comments of the *Kessef Mishneh* to *Hilchos Issurei Bi'a* 1:12.

As for Rav Yisrael's question regarding the need for inspecting produce, the answer was given by Rav Shmuel Landau, in the aforementioned responsum. He explains that if one neglects to inspect a product that is known to often contain insects, then he cannot be considered as unknowingly consuming the insects, as he had reason to anticipate this outcome. It is only in situations where there is not a high likelihood of infestation that the law of מתעסק applies, and so inspection is required when eating products that are commonly infested.[62]

A different view is taken by Rav Meir Auerbach, in *Imrei Bina*,[63] where he rejects the premise that unknowingly ingesting an undesirable forbidden substance does not fall under the rule of מתעסק בחלבים. He argues that although the Gemara explains this rule based on the fact that נהנה — one has experienced enjoyment — in truth, this rule is not dependent upon enjoyment. If it were, then even other forms of unintended enjoyment, such as unwittingly placing one's hand through oil which is forbidden for personal benefit, would be subject to the rule of מתעסק בחלבים. Necessarily, then, the Gemara here designates prohibitions involving eating and sexual relations as exceptions to the general principle of מתעסק, such that anytime one ingests a forbidden food, under any circumstance, he is guilty of wrongdoing and requires atonement.

Even according to this stringent position of the *Imrei Bina*, we might consider applying here the rule of דבר שאינו מתכוין, which allows performing an action which might unwittingly result in a violation, as long as the violation is unintended and uncertain. The *Tur*[64] permits closing on Shabbos a chest which might contain flies, despite the possibility that this action will result in trapping flies, in violation of the prohibition against trapping on Shabbos. The *Taz*[65] explains that since the presence of flies is uncertain, and thus it is not definite that closing the chest will have the effect of trapping in violation of Shabbos, we may apply the rule of דבר שאינו מתכוין. Rabbi Akiva Eiger, in his notes to the *Yoreh Dei'a* section of the *Shulchan Aruch*,[66] infers from the *Taz*'s comments that the rule of דבר שאינו מתכוין applies even if the uncertainty relates to current circumstances, as opposed to the future outcome of the action. One might have assumed that *halacha* permits an action which could potentially result in an unintended violation only if the question is whether the act will indeed produce the prohibited result, but not if the question is whether current conditions render the act forbidden. The *Taz*'s explanation of the *Tur*'s ruling proves that even in a case where one is uncertain whether current conditions are such that an action will unwittingly yield a prohibited result, the rule of דבר שאינו מתכוין allows performing the action.

---

62. For a critique of Rav Landau's explanation, see Maharsham, *Da'as Torah*, Y.D. 41:16.

63. *Basar Ve-Chalav*, 4.

64. O.C. 316.

65. 316:3.

66. 87:6.

If so, then also in the case of a fruit or vegetable which could potentially contain an insect, *halacha* would permit eating the product, as it is uncertain whether eating would have the prohibited effect of ingesting an insect.

However, as Rabbi Akiva Eiger discusses, the Rama[67] cites a ruling which seems to imply otherwise. The Rama brings those who forbid stoking coals underneath a pot of food belonging to non-Jews, given the possibility that the pot might contain both meat and dairy foods, such that stoking the coals would have the effect of cooking meat and milk together. Rabbi Akiva Eiger notes that the act of stoking the coals should, seemingly, fall under the category of דבר שאינו מתכוין, as the individual has no intention to cook meat with milk, and it is not certain that his action yields such a result. Evidently, Rabbi Akiva Eiger writes, this view maintained that the rule of דבר שאינו מתכוין applies only when the future outcome of the action is unpredictable, but not when the uncertainty revolves around the current condition. And thus when current conditions might cause an action to produce a prohibited result, the action is forbidden. If so, then we might conclude that in the case of potentially infested food products, too, one who has reason to suspect the presence of insects in a product would be forbidden to eat it.

It should also be noted that according to this line of reasoning, even if a product does not halachically require inspection, it might very well be advisable to inspect it — for readily visible insects — in order to avoid the harmful effect of טמטום הלב. As discussed at length earlier, many sources indicate that the adverse spiritual effects of ingesting prohibited foods are not dependent upon guilt, and one can suffer these effects even if he consumes forbidden food under circumstances for which he bears no accountability. Therefore, it is perhaps recommended to take a reasonable amount of time to inspect potentially infested products to ensure the absence of readily discernible insects.[68]

Bugs and *Bittul*

However, there might also be a different reason for permitting the consumption of products that likely contain insects, without first inspecting them.

The halachic principle of *bittul* allows us to ignore a forbidden food item when it becomes mixed with permissible food. Even if the forbidden food item is large enough that, on its own, it could be identified as a forbidden product, nevertheless, if it mixes with permissible food to the point where it is indiscernible, and it constitutes 1/60th or less of the mixture, then the entire mixture may be eaten, as we may disregard the forbidden item.

---

67. Y.D. 87:6.

68. This point is made by Rav Avigdor Nebenzahl, in his letter of approbation to Rav Eitam Henkin's *Lachem Yiheyeh Le-Ochla*: אני מסתפק אם בכל המקרים שההלכה מתירה האכילה, אין גם טמטום הלב.

Conceivably, the law of *bittul* could be applied to fruits or vegetables containing very small insects. As they are embedded with the leaves of the vegetable, for example, and hence indiscernible, we should, seemingly, permit the vegetable by force of the principle of *bittul*.

It should be clarified that *bittul* is effective even if one has the possibility of going through the trouble of searching for and removing the morsel of forbidden food from the mixture. The *Issur Ve-Heter*[69] writes that the reason why *Chazal* required a proportion of 60:1 for *bittul* to take effect when dry products are mixed together is to encourage people to try to identify and remove the forbidden product from the mixture. In a proportion of 60:1, this is exceedingly difficult, and so the Sages permitted relying on *bittul*. This shows that even when it is possible to separate a forbidden item that is mixed with permissible items, this is not required if the forbidden item comprises 1/60th or less of the mixture, which is undoubtedly the case regarding small insects in fruits or vegetables. Indeed, Rav Menachem Mendel Schneersohn, the third Rebbe of Lubavitch, writes in his *Tzemach Tzedek*[70]:

> נראה כמה ראיות דהדבר מתבטל אפילו אם ניכר קצת כל שאי אפשר לברר או אפילו רק טורח גדול.

> There seem to be several proofs that the item is negated even if it is somewhat discernible, as long as it cannot be clearly identified, or even [if it can but only] with great trouble.[71]

However, before applying the concept of *bittul* to small insects in produce, we must reckon with the law of בריה — the unique status assigned to a whole entity. As the *Shulchan Aruch*[72] rules, based on the Gemara,[73] a בריה is not subject to the provision of *bittul*, and thus אפילו באלף לא בטלה — it is not "negated" by a majority even one-thousand times its size, and the entire mixture is forbidden for consumption. Examples given by the *Shulchan Aruch* include ants and flies. The *Shulchan Aruch* also mentions the case of cooked vegetables in which three worms have been found, such that the vegetables are presumed infested, and the vegetables are thus forbidden, because even a single worm constitutes a בריה that renders the mixture prohibited.

---

69. 23:8.

70. Y.D. 70:5.

71. This emerges also from the comments of the *Chazon Ish* cited later, regarding the mites found in flour, where he writes that since they are very difficult to identify, they are subject to *bittul*.

72. Y.D. 100:1.

73. *Chullin* 99b–100a.

Importantly, as noted by the *Taz*[74] and *Aruch Ha-Shulchan*,[75] the law of בריה applies מדרבנן — on the level of rabbinic enactment, as opposed to Torah law.[76] Therefore, when facing the likelihood of the presence of an insect in a food product, the issue at stake is a prohibition enacted by the Sages, not a Biblical violation.

This point becomes crucial when assessing the various halachic considerations at play in order to determine a product's status. The famous rule of ספק דרבנן להקל allows acting leniently in situations of uncertainty when a rabbinic law is at stake, and thus, as the *Taz* states explicitly, when there is some question as to whether a prohibited item falls under the category of בריה, we may assume the lenient possibility and view the item as negated by the majority.

With regard to small insects in produce, we find several possible reasons to exclude them from the law of בריה, such that the product in question should be permissible for consumption, in accordance with the principle established by the *Taz*.

These possibilities are noted by the *Aruch Ha-Shulchan*.[77] He addresses the phenomenon of bug-infested food which people customarily ate, and finds it inconceivable that otherwise pious, meticulously observant Jews are in flagrant violation of the prohibition against ingesting insects. He writes: חלילה לומר שכלל ישראל יכשלו באיסור גדול כזה — "Heaven forfend that we should say that all Israel stumbles upon such a great prohibition." In order to find a justification for what might at first appear as widespread negligence of a clear prohibition, the *Aruch Ha-Shulchan* proposes three possible reasons why small creatures in produce may be considered "negated," despite their seemingly falling under the category of בריה:

1. First, the *Aruch Ha-Shulchan* cites Rav Yehonasan Eibushitz[78] as raising the possibility of relying on the view among the *Rishonim* that a בריה may be ignored if it constitutes around one-thousandth of the mixture. Although the *Shulchan Aruch*, as we have seen, rules stringently in this regard, several *Rishonim* — including Rabbeinu Shimshon of Shantz, the Rashba and the Behag — maintained that while a בריה is not "negated" in a proportion of 60:1 like ordinary prohibited food, it is "negated" in a proportion of 1000:1, such as in the case of very small insects in produce. The *Aruch Ha-Shulchan* avers that this was also the position of the Rif, and may also have been the view of Rashi. He then writes: אפילו ביחיד במקום רבים סמכינן בשעת הדחק באיסור דרבנן — when dealing

---

74. Y.D. 100:1.

75. Y.D. 100:2.

76. The Maharil, in one of his responsa (72:3), maintained that the stringency of בריה applies on the level of Torah law, but this view is not accepted as mainstream.

77. Y.D. 100:13–18.

78. *Kreisi U-Pleisi*, Y.D. 100.

with a rabbinic prohibition, we may rely on even a minority lenient opinion in situations of dire need. Thus, given the great difficulty in avoiding barely discernible mites in food, and that we deal here with the rabbinic prohibition of בריה, we may rely on those *Rishonim* who permit a mixture with a בריה that comprises just one-thousandth of the mixture, even against the *Shulchan Aruch*'s stringent ruling.

2. The *Aruch Ha-Shulchan* then cites Rav Yaakov of Karlin, in *Mishkenos Yaakov*,[79] as suggesting that the rule of בריה does not apply to small insects that מעוצם קטנותן נאבד ממש והוא דבר המתערב ממש ונדבק בפת או שנתערב בתבשיל ואי-אפשר להפרידן כלל — are so small that they completely mix in with the food and cannot possibly be separated. The concept of בריה, Rav Yaakov of Karlin proposes, is that a whole entity retains its individual identity because of its importance, and it therefore cannot be ignored when it becomes mixed with other food. If so, then tiny insects, which can hardly be seen, do not fall under the category of בריה, as they cannot be regarded as significant enough to maintain their identity in a mixture.

The *Aruch Ha-Shulchan* questions this theory, contending that the Torah prohibition against ingesting a whole insect likely suffices to lend it halachic stature that prevents its negation in a mixture.

However, Rav Yaakov of Karlin's theory was espoused later by the *Chazon Ish*,[80] who asserted that mites להפלגת קטנותם ודאי אבדו הכרת עין — are certainly considered indiscernible, by virtue of their minuscule size, such that they cannot qualify as a בריה, a status which is rooted in an item's retaining its identity due to its discernible form that is preserved even in a mixture. As such, the *Chazon Ish* writes, יש כאן ביטול — such creatures are subject to *bittul*. He explains further, אפשר כל שאין העין שולט בו לאו בריה הוא — anything which is not readily visible to the naked eye might not qualify as a בריה. The law of בריה likely applies only to creatures large enough to be discerned in a mixture, on account of which they cannot be ignored, even if they comprise an infinitesimal percentage, because, in the *Chazon Ish*'s words, גופן מבחנת בינו לבין אחרים — "their body distinguishes between them and others," such that they retain their independent identity. Tiny creatures such as mites, however, cannot qualify as a בריה.

3. Thirdly, the *Aruch Ha-Shulchan* postulates that when the Sages enacted the special provision of בריה, they did not apply this law to דברים המאוסים כנמלים וזבובים — "repulsive things, such as ants and flies." He argues that, as mentioned, the law of בריה likely stems from the significance of a whole entity, which denies

---

79. Y.D. 36.
80. Y.D. 14:6.

us the possibility of ignoring it, even when it constitutes a small fraction of a mixture, and it is hard to imagine that *Chazal* regarded a whole worm or insect, which people naturally find revolting, as a significant entity which cannot be disregarded. Although the *Shulchan Aruch*, as mentioned, does not follow this view, as he applies the rule of בריה even to insects and worms, the *Aruch Ha-Shulchan* notes the Rama's ruling,[81] based on the anonymous *Issur Ve-Heter Ha-Aroch*, that a revolting בריה is subject to *bittul*, because the special law of בריה does not apply to something intrinsically foul-tasting. If so, the *Aruch Ha-Shulchan* contends, then the law of בריה certainly does not apply to insects, because אין לך פגום יותר מנמלה וזבוב ותולעת וכיוצא באלו שהרי הם מאוסים ונפשו של אדם קצה בהם — "there is nothing more foul-tasting than an ant, fly, worm and the like, which are revolting and people are naturally repulsed by them."[82]

    This was also the opinion of Rav Tzvi Hersh Kalischer, in his *Tzvi La-Tzadik* notes to the *Shulchan Aruch*.[83] He expresses his puzzlement over those *poskim* who voiced concern over the מילביי״ן found in many food products, noting that inherently revolting creatures do not fall under the category of בריה, and are therefore subject to *bittul*.

A similar argument was advanced by the *Kesav Sofer*,[84] who notes the two possible reasons underlying the stringency of בריה. One, as mentioned, is that the stature of a whole entity denies us the ability to regard it as "negated" by the majority of the mixture. If this is the case, the *Kesav Sofer* writes, then — just as the *Aruch Ha-Shulchan* asserted — a revolting creature would not be given the special status of a בריה. The second possible rationale is that the Sages suspended the rule of *bittul* in the case of a whole entity to impress upon us the unique status afforded by the Torah to whole entities. Normally, one is liable to punishment for eating prohibited food only if he consumes a *ke-zayis*, but the Torah made an exception in the case of whole forbidden creatures, the consumption of which renders one liable to punishment irrespective of its size. It was to highlight this distinction, perhaps, that the Sages decided to forbid eating a mixture containing a prohibited בריה, regardless of its proportion in the mixture. If this is the reason, the *Kesav Sofer* figures, then we should side with those *poskim* who permit a בריה if it comprises one-thousandth or less of the mixture, as the

---

81.   Y.D. 103:1.

82.   The *Aruch Ha-Shulchan* understood the Rama as establishing that inherently revolting creatures are excluded from the law of בריה, a reading of the Rama's comments advanced already by Rav Meir Eisenstadt, in *Panim Meiros* (2:67). Many others, however, understood the Rama as referring to a whole insect that has died and decayed. See Rav Asher Weiss' discussion in *She'eilos U-Teshuvos Minchas Asher*, 3:49.

83.   Y.D. 103:1.

84.   Y.D. 63.

fact that such creatures are not negated in a proportion of 60:1, like other prohibited foods, suffices to signify the unique stature of whole entities. And thus according to both explanations of the rule of בריה, we have reason to permit foods containing tiny insects which people naturally find loathsome.

Moreover, Rav Yehonasan Eibushitz,[85] in endeavoring to find a justification for those who do not avoid small insects in food products, notes that the status of בריה requires that the item has been forbidden since its inception.[86] Insects infesting fruits and vegetables become forbidden only once they leave the fruit or vegetable in which they came into existence,[87] and therefore they might not fall under the category of בריה. Although Rav Eibushitz himself did not recommend relying on this argument, and several later *poskim* disputed this claim,[88] it was actually presented as authoritative *halacha* by an earlier *posek* — Rav Eliyahu Landsofer, in his *Kanfei Yona*.[89] More recently, Rav Nosson Gestetner[90] discussed this theory at length, and concluded that it has a strong basis in earlier sources. Rav Ovadia Yosef[91] wrote that Rav Yehonosan Eibushitz's suggestion may be relied upon when there are also other considerations for a lenient ruling.

Another factor, noted by both the *Chazon Ish* (Y.D. 14:6)[92] and Rav Shlomo Zalman Auerbach,[93] is the likelihood that the insect is no longer whole by the time it is swallowed. The creature's disintegration as a result of chewing may suffice to divest it of its בריה status, such that *bittul* takes effect.[94]

---

85. *Pleisi*, 100:4.

86. וכן צריך שיהא דבר שאסור מתחילת ברייתו, *Shulchan Aruch*, Y.D. 100:1.

87. תולעים הגדלים בפירות בתלוש מותרים...במה דברים אמורים, שלא פירשו מן הפרי, אבל פירשו מן הפרי...אסור (*Shulchan Aruch*, Y.D. 84:4).

88. See, for example, *Peri Megadim – Sifsei Da'as* 84:31; *Dagul Mei-Revava, Mahadura Tinyana*, Y.D. 84; and sources cited by the *Darkei Teshuva*, 100:4.

89. Y.D. 84.

90. *She'eilos U-Teshuvos Le-Horos Noson*, vol. 6, Y.D. 62–67.

91. *Yabia Omer*, vol. 10, Y.D. 58.

92. Y.D. 14:6.

93. *Minchas Shlomo*, 2:61:2.

94. Rav Nachum Eliezer Rabinovitch, in his letter of approbation to Rav Eitam Henkin's *Lachem Yiheyeh Le-Ochla*, adds another consideration, namely, that when dealing with such tiny creatures, it is all but impossible to ascertain that an insect this size in a food product is whole. The Rambam (*Hilchos Ma'achalos Asuros* 2:21) writes that if a creature is missing even one leg, it does not qualify as a בריה. As it is impractical to determine that the thrips and aphids in food products are whole with all their organs intact, they might fall under the category of ספק בריה, which, as we cited earlier from the *Taz*, is subject to *bittul*.

While some, and perhaps all, of these claims are debated, the cumulative effect of these numerous possible grounds for leniency should suffice to permit eating foods with barely visible insects — particularly given that we deal with a rabbinic prohibition.

It should be emphasized that if we apply the rule of *bittul*, then these insects are entirely permissible for consumption. The Rosh[95] famously asserts that when *bittul* takes effect, the forbidden item becomes permissible; meaning, not only does *halacha* permit one to run the risk of mistakenly ingesting that item, but it is no longer prohibited at all, because it loses its identity as a result of its negation by the majority. Therefore, in the case of a hardly visible insect which is eaten as part of a fruit or vegetable, there is no concern even for טמטום הלב, as the insect is not prohibited at all.

V. The Arrogance of Newfangled Stringencies

In conclusion, we should briefly address the broader question as to the halachic significance of the fact that previous generations were not as concerned about bug infestation as modern-day *kashrus* agencies are. How much halachic weight should be given to this factor in determining the appropriate standards nowadays?

This question is not unique or new to our generation. Rav Hezekiah da Silva, writing in his *Peri Chadash*,[96] decries the fact that רבים וגדולים — many great people — including חכמים ויחידים, the scholarly and pious, were not vigilant in avoiding insects in food. Rabbi Adams, in the aforementioned article, demonstrates that Rav Hezekiah da Silva lived at the time when the discoveries by Antonie van Leeuwenhoek of microorganisms were drawing a great deal of attention. It could be speculated that these רבים וגדולים followed the tradition of showing no concern for the possibility of creatures which cannot be readily seen by the naked eye, whereas the *Peri Chadash*, attuned to the new discoveries, called upon his contemporaries to give this issue greater attention.

Rabbi Adams also documents the controversy that erupted in the 18th century when it was discovered that grape leaves were often infested. Rav Raphael Solomon Laniado of Aleppo, in his *Beis Dino Shel Shlomo*,[97] writes that in response to this discovery, some rabbis forbade the consumption of grape leaves, whereas other argued that כיון שכבר פשט המנהג בפני גדולי ישראל ולא מיחו, אין לבטל המנהג — "once the custom already spread in the presence of the leading sages of Israel, and they did not object, the custom should not be banned." Rav Laniado rejected the lenient attitude, insisting that since the custom was the result of a lack of knowledge, it holds no weight, and it may be

---

95. *Chullin* 7:37.
96. Y.D. 84:34.
97. Y.D. 19, cited in *Sdei Chemed*, vol. 4, p. 125.

assumed that the rabbis who permitted grape leaves in generations past would not have done so had they known of the small insects contained in the leaves.

By contrast, Rav Avraham Danzig of Vilna, in his *Binas Adam*,[98] points to tradition as a reason to allow ignoring the presence of tiny creatures in vinegar:

> מעולם לא שמענו פוצה פה, ואפילו חסידים ואנשי מעשה אוכלים מאכלם בחומץ
> ואין חוששין כלל לבדוק החומץ...ומנהג ישראל תורה היא.

> We never heard anybody open their mouth [in objection], and even pious people and men of distinction eat their food in vinegar and do not make a point of inspecting the vinegar… And the custom of Israel is like Torah.

Additionally, we find sources which go even further than simply relying on this lenient tradition as a basis for permitting potentially infested products, but warn against deviating from this tradition, which amounts to casting aspersions about the righteousness of our predecessors. Already in the 13th century, Rav Yaakov of Marvege, one of the Tosafists, who wrote a collection of halachic rulings taught to him in his quasi prophetic dreams, writes the following[99] regarding concerns of tiny insects in certain common food products:

> שאלתי אם יש לחוש לדברי האוסרים או הם מותרים. והשיבו : הטוב טוב אתה
> מאשר לפניך, ועמך כולם צדיקים...

> I asked if one should be concerned about the ruling of those who forbid [these products], or if they are permitted, and they responded: Are you better than those who came before you? "And your nation are all righteous…" (*Yeshayahu* 60:21)

Rav Moshe Feinstein, in a responsum noted earlier,[100] makes a similar comment regarding those calling for greater stringency with regard to vegetables:

> יש חשיבות גדולה בהלכה למנהג העולם ולהיכא עמא דבר, ואסור להוציא לעז על
> דורות הקדמונים שלא הקפידו בדברים אלה משום שלא ידעו מהם.

> There is great importance in *halacha* to common practice, and to the way people act, and it is forbidden to cast aspersions about the earlier generations who were not careful about these matters because they were unaware of them.

---

98. 35:38.

99. *Min Ha-Shamayim*, 66.

100. *Iggeros Moshe*, Y.D. 4:2.

Rav Shimon Schwab[101] expresses this position more forcefully:

> As far as our Jewish people are concerned, our fathers and mothers have
> for centuries used lettuce for *marror* on the *seder* night as well as parsley
> for *karpas* [greens], and in those days they were no less infested with
> vermin than they are today. So, we have no right to make new *issurim*
> and to forbid the eating of any vegetables per se to the general public.

In his view, stringency in regard to the possible presence of insects in produce should be
discouraged, as it implicitly shows disrespect to the righteous Jews of prior generations.

Conclusion

1. According to even the most stringent opinions, creatures which cannot be seen
   at all without a magnifying glass or other forms of magnification are entirely
   permissible for consumption.
2. Several prominent *poskim*, including Rav Shmuel Wosner, ruled that even creatures which can be seen by the naked eye, but cannot be identified as an insect
   without special training or magnification, are entirely permissible for consumption. And even according to the stringent view, that such creatures are, in principle, forbidden, several *poskim* maintain that these insects are subject to *bittul*.
   Therefore, even if a product can be presumed to contain such creatures, there
   are legitimate halachic grounds for permitting the product for consumption.
3. Insects which can be seen and identified with the naked eye are forbidden for
   consumption, and products with a 50-percent chance or more of containing
   such insects may not be eaten until after they are inspected. If the chances of
   infestation are less than 50 percent, then inspection is still required, though
   according to some *poskim*, this requirement applies only if the chances are not
   much lower than 50 percent. And, where inspection would entail considerable inconvenience, and purchasing certified insect-free produce would entail
   a considerable financial burden, there is room for leniency. Nevertheless, it is
   worthwhile, when reasonably possible, to try to assure the absence of readily
   visible insects even in situations where *halacha* does not strictly require inspection, to avoid the harmful spiritual effects of ingesting prohibited foods.
4. Historically, there is no doubt that generations of pious, meticulously observant
   Jews consumed produce without concern of the possible presence of hardly
   visible insects, which people did not even know existed until the early modern
   era. According to some *poskim*, stringency in this area is therefore inappropriate, as it implicitly calls into question the standards observed by our righteous

---

101. "Inspection of Vegetables," *Kashrus Magazine*, June, 1986.

predecessors. Others, however, encourage stringency and striving for stricter standards utilizing the capabilities afforded by modern science and technology to ensure to avoid the ingestion of all insects.

INTERVIEWS

Rabbi Reuven Feinstein

Interviewed on *Headlines with Dovid Lichtenstein*, 28 Teves, 5780 (January 25, 2020)

We definitely ate vegetables in the house. In those days, the problems didn't exist because the DDT was around. When they outlawed it, around five years before Reb Moshe passed away, that's when the problems began. When we notified Reb Moshe, he told us we shouldn't notify everyone, just the *kashrus* organizations, since there are *shittos* that are lenient, and it's only a דרבנן, [and] in order that people shouldn't lose their trust in the *rabbanim* who were not aware of it.

In Russia, they didn't have strawberries, though they ate blueberries. They had no lettuce; they only ate root vegetables. They ate cabbage — they checked the first three leaves, and if they were clean, they ate it. They didnt use a lightbox or microscope. You don't need to use a lightbox, but it makes the checking easier.

If you see a black spot, and you can't tell what it is, then it's not forbidden, but if you can see the lines on it, and under a microscope the lines are legs — I can't answer whether or not this is called נראה לעיניים [visible to the naked eye]. I would be inclined to say that it's not.

In my house, my wife washed the strawberries etc. according to the Star-K. The point of the cleaning methods these days is that if you do it, you don't have to check them afterwards.

Rabbi Dovid Goldstein

Interviewed on *Headlines with Dovid Lichtenstein*, 28 Teves, 5780 (January 25, 2020)

The *Shulchan Aruch* says to check, but it doesn't say how. You can use the sun, but it's easier with a lightbox. That's why we use lightboxes. People need to be taught what they are looking for, and once they learn, they can check themselves. Strawberries — you need to cut off the top and bottom, and peel them, and then they can be eaten without checking. Without peeling, it's not possible to clean. An average box of strawberries has in between 50–300 bugs, and a regular person won't be able to identify them. If you put strawberries in water…and remove the strawberries and sift the water through a 80-micron mesh, you'll see all the bugs on the mesh…

Anyone who says they didn't find a bug in triple-washed bags of lettuce has no clue what he's talking about. The restaurant that says they didn't find bugs in the triple washed bags? I'll go down and show them bugs. It's impossible that after three times washed it doesn't have bugs.

Rabbi Oren Duvdevani

Interviewed on *Headlines with Dovid Lichtenstein*, 28 Teves, 5780 (January 25, 2020)

When we talk about the obligation to check leaves of fruit, we have three different halachic situations. The first is מאכל הנגוע — food like lettuce, which in most cases has bugs in it, and so you cannot eat it without first checking. The second situation is מיעוט המצוי, which is the case with most vegetables and fruits, and those need to be checked לכתחילה, but if they were not checked, one may rely on the majority and eat them. The third situation is foods which are normally clean, such as white onion, which may be eaten without checking as long as there are no clear signs of bugs.

All *poskim* agree that if you have bugs which you cannot see with your own eyes, in a natural way, these are not the bugs which the Torah forbids. Rav Asher Weiss, who advises me a lot, wrote in his *teshuva* that we go according to the average housewife. If I see a piece of dirt or dust — it can't be forbidden. We can't define it as a בריה, because the definition of בריה is importance, and clearly, this bug has no importance. Most *poskim* say that *halacha* follows the ability of normal people, and this has been the custom in *Am Yisrael* for generations… This is the opinion of the *Iggeros Moshe* and the *Minchas Shlomo*, the *Avnei Neizer* says it, and also the *Chazon Ish, Chayei Adam* and *Yeshuos Yaakov*. In our generation, one of the biggest experts in *kashrus,* Rav Zev Vitman, the רב המכשיר of [the Israeli food company] Tnuva, follows this opinion. Just several weeks ago, one of the biggest *talmidei chachamim* here in Israel, Rav Eliezer Melamed, published a volume of *Peninei Halacha* on *kashrus*, and also held this way. We determine based on the vision of the average person. The same is true of an *esrog* — we follow the natural ability of a normal, average person.

I know there are opinions who rule stringently, but they should know two things. First, this [stringency] has not been the accepted *minhag* in *Am Yisrael* for generations. Secondly, if they chose to be very stringent, they must know that this is not the strict *halacha.*

As for strawberries — cut the green leaf on top with the white part of the fruit, because this is where most of the bugs are, then take the strawberries and place them for two to three minutes in cold water with cleaning material, such as soap, and then wash them. I assure you — and I've tested then in a laboratory, in Israel and in Europe — the strawberries will definitely be clean.

When it comes to other vegetables, such as cauliflower and broccoli, there are very good methods of cleaning at home, but in places such as restaurants and hotels, or public kitchens, I insist that they use only frozen products, not fresh products, because when you're dealing with very large quantities, it is very difficult to clean them properly.

Triple-washed lettuce — Rav Vitman and I checked a facility like that here in Israel — and the results were quite impressive. Also in Mexico, I supervised such a facility… With triple-washed lettuce, you'll find around three thrips in fifteen kilo [33 pounds] of lettuce, which is מיעוט שבמיעוט…

Frozen vegetables from any company are very clean…

Mrs. Etti Neustadt, granddaughter of Rav Yaakov Kamenetsky

Interviewed on *Headlines with Dovid Lichtenstein*, 28 Teves, 5780 (January 25, 2020)

Cabbage was checked — the core was taken out, it was cut into fours, and then soaked in a big bowl. They checked it leaf by leaf in the fluorescent light. If they had black specks that didn't come off, they threw it out. In Lithuania, they only had potatoes and radishes. In the bungalow, we used to pick strawberries and blueberries and they were soaked in a big bowl and looked through. Checking Romaine lettuce on Erev Pesach was a full day affair. They checked them in bowls and lights with Kosher salt.

Besides potatoes and radishes, he [Rav Yaakov] also ate beets, but those were peeled. We didn't grow up with lettuce, but we had later on, and it was checked the same way as cabbage. We washed off the grapes but didn't check them. He ate dates straight from the container, without opening them and checking them inside.

Rabbi Hershel Schachter

Interviewed on *Headlines with Dovid Lichtenstein*, 6 Shevat, 5780 (February 1, 2020)

When I was growing up, the American government allowed the farmers to spray pesticides, and there were no bugs. When they outlawed it, this became a problem. The government even advertises on a certain vegetable how much protein value it has from the bugs. The OU has pamphlets with instructions how to check everything. Most of these bugs are נראה לעיניים.

Blackberries were always a big problem. Blueberries are extremely infested, more than מיעוט המצוי — something like 50 percent of them have bugs.

In Europe, they checked, but in the early years in America, when they had the DDT, they didn't check.

Rabbi Moshe Vaye

Interviewed on *Headlines with Dovid Lichtenstein*, 6 Shevat, 5780 (February 1, 2020)

Something that is so small that you can't see is *mutar*. But if you can't see it only because it's mixed up with the food, then even if it's very small, it's *assur*. Something

512 HEADLINES 3: HALACHIC DEBATES OF CURRENT EVENTS

that you can see but you can't identify is *assur*. If a common person can't tell [that it is an insect], but an expert could, then it's *assur*.

A person is not used to seeing it — but when they show it to him, he sees it. So why is this considered unable to see? In the beginning he gets the rules of what is a problem and what is not a problem, and so he knows…

Rabbi Yitzchok Berkowitz

Interviewed on *Headlines with Dovid Lichtenstein*, 6 Shevat, 5780 (February 1, 2020)

There's no *heter* of מתעסק for eating bugs, because since *Chazal* said you need to check a מיעוט המצוי, it's *assur* until you check. However, if some process was performed that makes it less than a מיעוט המצוי, then even though the people who performed this process did not fulfill their obligation which *Chazal* required — nevertheless, if it reaches the consumer where there's no longer a מיעוט המצוי, then he is not obligated to check.

Rav Elyashiv wrote a *teshuva* about hotels, which have a hard time checking things thoroughly the way one is supposed to, and the way housewives do. Rav Elyashiv wrote that if by the time it reaches the consumer, it is a מיעוט שאינו מצוי, then there is no obligation to check.

This applies also if a company went ahead and cleaned the produce to the point where it is a מיעוט שאינו מצוי by the time you get it — when you buy it, you are allowed to eat it, and then, if you eat an insect, you're מתעסק or אנוס. It depends on the state of the food when it comes into your possession. If you're a guest at a restaurant, or you buy a package of lettuce, if we can determine that it's not a מיעוט המצוי at that point, then you are allowed to eat it.

Rabbi Eli Gerstein

Interviewed on *Headlines with Dovid Lichtenstein*, 6 Shevat, 5780 (February 1, 2020)

I've checked triple-washed lettuce and haven't found bugs, but I wouldn't eat it at home. If you can get something better, you shouldn't be eating these. Halachically, it's permissible, but you can do better…

As for the *gedolim* of yesteryear — for me, the question does not even begin. This is not a question, what they did. They were מוסר נפש for this matter. They were מלאכים. I don't know how a מלאך eats…

Hakadosh Baruch Hu gave us the *mitzva* of abstaining from דברים טמאים, and so we do the best we can with the methods we have in the generation we live in.